C++ for Engineers and Scientists

Gary J. Bronson

Contributing Editor:

G.J. Borse, Lehigh University

THOMSON
COURSE TECHNOLOGY

Australia • Canada • Mexico • Singapore • Spain • United Kingdom • United States

THOMSON
COURSE TECHNOLOGY

C++ for Engineers and Scientists, Second Edition

by Gary J. Bronson

Senior Product Manager:
Alyssa Pratt

Managing Editor:
Mary Franz

Production Editor:
GEX Publishing Services

Senior Marketing Manager:
Karen Seitz

Associate Product Manager:
Mirella Misiaszek

Editorial Assistant:
Jennifer Smith

Senior Manufacturing Coordinator:
Laura Astorino

Cover Designer:
Laura Rickenbach

Compositor:
GEX Publishing Services

Printer:
WebCom

Printed in Canada

3 4 5 6 7 8 9 WC 08 07

For more information, contact Course Technology, 25 Thomson Place, Boston, Massachusetts, 02210.

Or find us on the World Wide Web at: www.course.com

ISBN-13: 978-0-534-99380-1
ISBN-10: 0-534-99380-X

CONTENTS

PREFACE

The C++ programming language, which includes C as a proper sub-set, has become the preeminent programming language in the engineering and scientific fields. For most engineers and scientists, however, employing the full potential of C++, which is a hybrid language containing both structured and object-oriented features, involves a gradual refinement of programming skills from a structured approach to an object-oriented one. One of the reasons for this is that many engineering and scientific problems can be efficiently and conveniently solved using only C++'s structured elements.

The refinement approach, from structural to object-oriented programming, is the one taken by this text. Thus, like the first edition, this new edition initially provides a strong foundation in structured programming. This foundation is then expanded to a complete object orientation within the confines of a pedagogically sound and achievable progression. Additionally, to keep it current with the current ANSI/ISO C++ standard, this second edition has a number of significant changes and added features. These include the following:

- Use of the ANSI/ISO C++ iostream library and namespace mechanism in all programs
- The presentation of exception handling in a complete section, with practical applications of exception handling presented throughout the text
- Presentation of the new C++ string class
- A thorough discussion of input data validation and functions to both check the numerical data type of an input item and provide for re-entry of invalid numerical types
- A completely new section devoted to the Standard Template Library's (STL's) vector class

The basic requirements of this second edition, however, remain the same as the prior edition: that all topics be presented in a clear, unambiguous, and accessible manner to beginning students within the structure of a classroom setting. Toward this end, the central elements of the previous edition remain essentially unchanged in this second edition. Thus, the majority of topics, examples, explanations, and figures in the first edition, except for being updated to the current ANSI standards, will be found in this edition. Students should be familiar with fundamental algebra, but no other prerequisites are assumed.

In practical terms, this text has been written to support both a one- and two-semester technical C++ programming course. Additionally, it is constructed to be sufficiently flexible so that professors can mold the text to their individual preference of topic presentations. This is achieved in the following ways.

Excluding Chapter 1, which presents computer literacy material for those who require this background, Part I presents the basic structured syntax, flow control, and modularity topics that are needed for an effective understanding of C++'s structural features. When the topics of arrays (Chapter 11), files (Chapter 8), and classes (Chapter 9) are added to this material, a comprehensive one-semester course will have been completed. The presentation order of these last three topics is entirely up to the discretion of the professor, as each of these chapters has been specifically written to be dependent only on the material contained in Part I. Additionally, depending on time and inclination, the numerical techniques presented in Chapter 14 may also be presented at any point after Part I has been completed. Figure 1 illustrates this one-semester topic dependency.

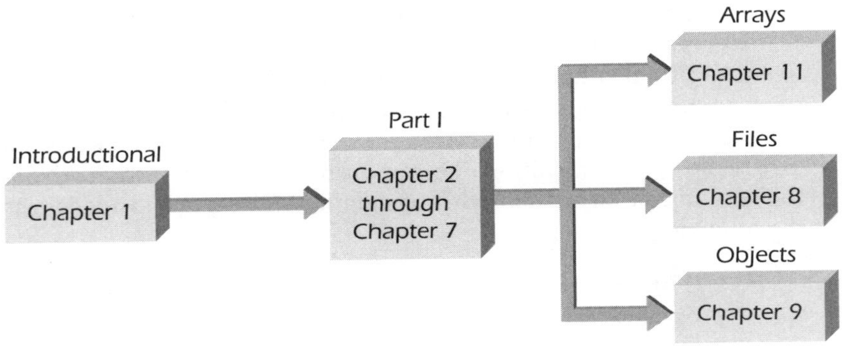

Figure 1. Topic dependency for a one-semester course.

A specific feature of this test is that Part II, on object-oriented programming, and Part III, on data structures, are interchangeable. Thus, if you want to present object-oriented programming early, you would follow a Part I – Part II – Part III progression. On the other hand, if you want to continue with additional strucutured programming reinforcement and present object-orientation either at the end of the course, or at the start of a second semester, you would use the sequence Part I – Part II – Part III. In either case, the material on files presented in Chapter 8, the material on arrays presented in Chapter 11, the material on classes presented in Chapter 9, and the material on numerical techniques presented in Chapter 14 can be introduced at any time after Part I. Figure 2 presents the topic dependency chart for the complete text, and illustrates the flexibility of introducing various topics within the overall umbrella of structured programming, object-oriented programming, and data structures.

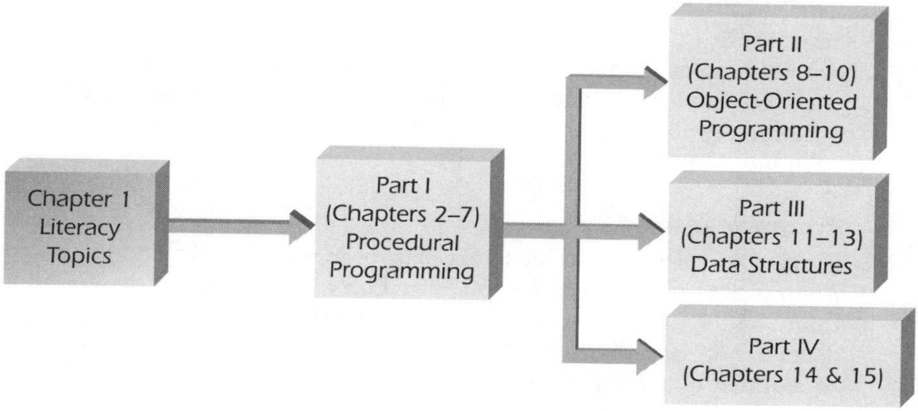

Figure 2. Topic dependency chart.

Distinctive Features of This Book

Writing Style

One of the things that I have found to be very important in my own classes is that once the professor sets the stage in class, the assigned textbook must continue to encourage, nurture, and assist the student in acquiring and "owning" the presented material. To do this the text must be written in a manner that makes sense to the student. My primary concern, and one of the distinctive features of this book, is that it has been written for the student. Thus, first and foremost, I feel the writing style used to convey the concepts presented is one of the most important aspects of this text.

Modularity

To produce readable and maintainable programs, modularity is essential. C++, by its nature, is a modular language. Thus, the connection between C++ functions and modules is made early in the text, in Section 2.1, and sustained throughout the book. The idea of parameter passing into modules also is made early, in Section 3.3, using C++'s mathematical library. This introduces students to function and argument passing as natural programming techniques. With the introduction of object-oriented programming techniques in Chapter 9, the basic concept of encapsulating both data and functions continues and strengthens this modular emphasis.

Software Engineering

Rather than simply introducing students to programming in C++, this text introduces students to the fundamentals of software engineering, from both a structured and object-oriented viewpoint. Section 2.1 introduces the software development cycle, presenting one of the main themes of the text, which is to emphasize problem-solving techniques. Thus, the importance of understanding and defining a problem, selecting and refining a solution, and understanding the relationship between analysis, design, coding, and testing is stated early and followed through with practical examples in all of the subsequent applications sections.

Applications

Starting with Chapter 2, each chapter contains an Applications Section with an average of two completed applications per chapter. Each application demonstrates and reinforces effective problem solving within the context of the software development cycle introduced in Section 1.2, and is extended to object-oriented development when classes are introduced in Chapter 9.

Program Testing

Every C++ program in this text has been successfully compiled, run, and Quality Assurance tested using Microsoft Visual C++ .NET. Source code for all programs can be found on the Course Technology Web site (*http://www.course.com*) This will permit students to both experiment and extend the existing programs and more easily modify them as required by a number of end-of-section exercises.

Pedagogical Features

To facilitate the goal of making C++ accessible as a first-level course, the following pedagogical features have been incorporated into the text:

End of Section Exercises Almost every section in the book contains numerous and diverse skill builder and programming exercises. Additionally, solutions to all exercises are provided in the Instructor Downloads section on *http://www.course.com*.

Common Programming Errors and Chapter Review

Each chapter ends with a section on common programming errors and a review of the main topics covered in the chapter.

Enrichment Sections

Given the many different emphases that can be applied in teaching C++, a number of enrichment sections have been included as chapter appendices. These allow you to provide different emphases with different students of different C++ classes.

Programming Notes

Programming notes are a separate set of shaded boxes that highlight alternative and advanced programming techniques, useful technical points, programming tips, and programming tricks used by professional programmers.

Point of Information Boxes

These are a set of shaded boxes that present additional brief clarification of commonly used and/or difficult concepts, such as abstraction, lvalues and rvalues, values versus identities, flags, and stream formatting.

Pseudocode Descriptions

Pseudocode is used throughout the text. Flowchart symbols are presented but are only used in visually presenting flow-of-control constructs.

Career Choices

A set of shaded boxes that describes various engineering career choices, such as electrical, chemical, mechanical, and aeronautical enigneers, are provided.

Appendices

An expanded set of appendices are provided. This includes appendices on Operator Precedence, ASCII codes, and Bit Operations. Additionally, Course Technology provides a number of tutorials for using various C++ compilers. These tutorials can be located on *http://www.course.com*.

Supplemental Materials

The following supplemental materials are available when this book is used in a classroom setting:

Electronic Instructor's Manual. The Instructor's Manual that accompanies this textbook includes:

- Additional instructional material to assist in class preparation, including suggestions for lecture topics
- Solutions to all the end-of-chapter materials, including the Programming Exercises

ExamView®. This textbook is accompanied by ExamView, a powerful testing software package that allows instructors to create and administer printed, computer (LAN-based), and Internet exams. ExamView includes hundreds of questions that correspond to the topics covered in this text, enabling students to generate detailed study guides that include page references for further review. These computer-based and Internet testing components allow students to take exams at their computers, and save the instructor time because each exam is graded automatically. The Test Bank is also available in WebCT and Blackboard formats.

PowerPoint Presentations. This book comes with Microsoft PowerPoint slides for each chapter. These are included as a teaching aid for classroom presentations, either to make available to students on the network for chapter review, or to be printed for classroom distribution. Instructors can add their own slides for additional topics that they introduce to the class.

Source Code. The source code for this text is available at *www.course.com* and is also available on the Teaching Tools CD-ROM.

Solution Files. The solution files for all programming exercises are available at *www.course.com*, and are also available on the Teaching Tools CD-ROM.

To Rochelle, Matthew, Jeremy, and David

ACKNOWLEDGMENTS

The writing of this second edition is a direct result of the success (and limitations) of the first edition. In this regard, my most heartfelt acknowledgment and appreciation is to the instructors and students who found this edition to be of service to them in their respective quests to teach and learn C++.

Next, I would like to thank Alyssa Pratt, my Product Manager at Course Technology. In addition to her continuous faith and encouragement, her ideas and partnership were instrumental in creating this text. Once the writing process was completed, the task of turning the final manuscript into a textbook depended on many people other than myself. For this I especially want to thank my copy editor at GEX Publishing Services, the interior designer, and Jennifer Roehrig of GEX Publishing Services. The dedication of this team of people was extremely important to me and I am very grateful to them. As always, any errors in the text rest solely on my shoulders.

As with the first edition, special acknowledgement goes to Dr. G. J. Borse of Lehigh University, who provided material that was adapted for this text. Specifically, his contribution includes almost all of Chapter 14, and the information contained within the Career Choice boxes, which Dr. Borse graciously permitted me to adapt from his FORTRAN 77 text (copyright held by PWS Publishing). Additionally, I want to thank Karen Langbert for providing specific insights and mathematical verification on a number of the engineering applications.

I would also like to acknowledge, with extreme gratitude, the direct encouragement and support of Fairleigh Dickinson University. Specifically, this includes the positive academic climate provided by the provost, Dr. Kenneth Greene, and the direct encouragement and support to make use of this environment by my Dean, Dr. David Steele, and my Chairperson, Dr. Paul Yoon. Without their support, this text could not have been written.

Finally, I deeply appreciate the patience, understanding, and love provided by my friend, wife, and partner, Rochelle.

Gary Bronson
2005

Chapter 1

Introduction

Topics

1.1 INTRODUCTION TO PROGRAMMING

A computer is a machine and like other machines, such as an automobile or lawn mower, it must be turned on and then driven, or controlled, to do the task it was meant to do. In an automobile, for example, control is provided by the driver, who sits inside of and directs the car. In a computer, the driver is a set of instructions called a program. More formally, a **computer program** is a self-contained set of instructions used to operate a computer to produce a specific result. Another term for a program or set of programs is **software**, and we will use both terms interchangeably throughout the text.[1]

The process of writing a program, or software, is called **programming**, while the set of instructions that can be used to construct a program is called a **programming language**. Available programming languages come in a variety of forms and types.

Machine Language

At its most fundamental level, the only programs that can actually be used to operate a computer are **machine language programs**. Such programs, which are also referred to as **executable programs**, or **executables** for short, consist of a sequence of instructions composed of binary numbers such as:[2]

```
11000000 000000000001 000000000010
11110000 000000000010 000000000011
```

Such machine language instructions consist of two parts: an instruction part and an address part. The instruction part, which is referred to as the **opcode** (short for operation code), is usually the leftmost set of bits in the instruction and tells the computer the operation to be performed, such as add, subtract, multiply, etc., while the rightmost bits specify the memory addresses of the data to be used. For example, assuming that the eight leftmost bits of the first instruction listed above contain the operation code to add, and the next two groups of twelve bits are the addresses of the two operands to be added, this instruction would be a command to "add the data in memory location 1 to the data in memory location 2." Similarly, assuming that the opcode 11110000 means multiply, the next instruction is a command to "multiply the data in memory location 2 by the data in location 3." (Section 1.6 explains how to convert from binary to decimal numbers.)

Assembly Languages

Because each class of computer—such as IBM, Apple, and Hewlett-Packard computers—has its own particular machine language, it is very tedious and time-consuming to write such machine language programs.[3] One of the first advances in programming was the substitution of word-like symbols, such as ADD, SUB, MUL, for the binary opcodes and both

---

[1] More inclusively, the term software is also used to denote both the programs and the data that the programs will operate on.

[2] Review Section 1.6 at the end of this chapter if you are unfamiliar with binary numbers.

[3] In actuality, the machine-level language is defined for the processor around which the computer is constructed.

decimal numbers and labels for memory addresses. For example, using these symbols and decimal values for memory addresses, the previous two machine language instructions can be written as:

ADD 1, 2

MUL 2, 3

Programming languages that use this type of symbolic notation are referred to as **assembly languages**. Because computers can only execute machine language programs, the set of instructions contained within an assembly language program must be translated into a machine language program before it can be executed on a computer. Translator programs that perform this function for assembly language programs are known as **assemblers** (see Figure 1.1).

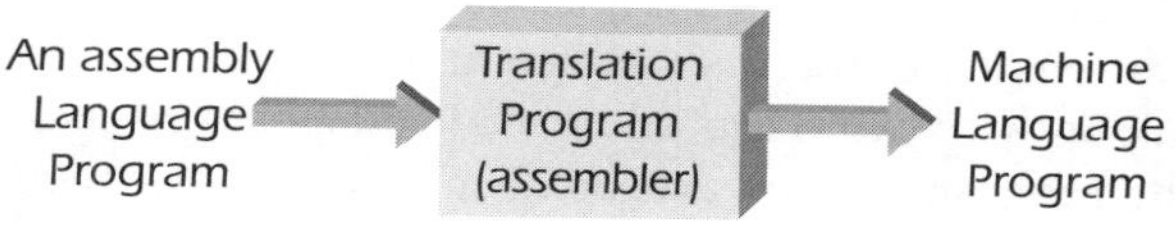

Figure 1.1 *Assembly programs must be translated.*

Low- and High-Level Languages

Both machine-level and assembly languages are classified as **low-level languages**. This is because both of these language types use instructions that are directly tied to one type of computer. As such, an assembly language program is limited in that it can only be used with the specific computer type for which the program is written. Such programs do, however, permit using special features of a particular computer type and generally execute at the fastest level possible.

In contrast to low-level languages are high-level languages. A **high-level language** uses instructions that resemble written languages, such as English, and can be run on a variety of computer types. Visual Basic, C, C++, and Java are all examples of high-level languages. Using C++, an instruction to add two numbers together and multiply by a third number can be written as:

```
result = (first + second) * third;
```

Programs written in a computer language (high or low level) are referred to as both **source programs** and **source code.** Once a program is written in a high-level language it must also, like a low-level assembly program, be translated into the machine language of the computer on which it will be run. This translation can be accomplished in two ways.

When each statement in a high-level source program is translated individually and executed immediately upon translation, the programming language used is called an **interpreted language**, and the program doing the translation is called an **interpreter.**

When all the statements in a high-level source program are translated as a complete unit before any one statement is executed, the programming language used is called a **compiled language**. In this case, the program doing the translation is called a **compiler.**

Both compiled and interpreted versions of a language can exist, although one typically predominates. C++ is predominantly a compiled language.

Figure 1.2 illustrates the relationship between a C++ source code program and its compilation into a machine language executable program. As shown, the source program is entered using an editor program. This is effectivley a word-processing program that is part of the development environment supplied by the compiler. It should be understood, however, that entering the code can begin only after an application has been thoroughly analyzed, understood, and the design of the program has been carefully planned. How this is accomplished is explained in the next section.

Translation of the C++ source program into a machine language program begins with the compiler. The output produced by the compiler is called an **object program**, which is a machine language version of the source code. In almost all instances, your source code will make use of existing preprogrammed code, with code you have written previously or code provided by the compiler. This could include mathematical code for finding a square root, for example, or code that is being reused from another application. Additionally, a large C++ program may be stored in two or more separate program files. In all of these cases, this additional code must be combined with the object program before the program can be executed. It is the task of the **linker** to accomplish this step. The result of the linking process is a completed machine language program, containing all the code required by your program, which is ready for execution. The last step in the process is to load this machine language program into the computer's main memory for actual execution.

Procedural and Object Orientations

In addition to classifying programming languages as high or low level, they are also classified by orientation as either procedural or object-oriented. In a **procedural language** the available instructions are used to create self-contained units, referred to as **procedures**. The purpose of a procedure is to accept data as input and transform the data in some manner to produce a specific result as an output. Until the 1990s the majority of high-level programming languages were procedural.

Currently, a second approach, object orientation, has taken center stage. One of the motivations for **object-oriented languages** was the development of graphical screens and support for graphical user interfaces (GUIs), capable of displaying multiple windows containing both graphical shapes and text. In such an environment, each window on the screen can be considered an object with associated characteristics, such as color, position, and size. Using an object-oriented approach, a program must first define the objects it will be manipulating, including a description of the general characteristics of the objects and specific units to manipulate them, such as changing size and position and transferring data between objects. Equally important is that object-oriented languages tend to support reusing existing code more easily, which removes the necessity for revalidating and retesting new or modified code. C++, which is classified as an object-oriented language, contains features found in procedural and object-oriented languages. In this text, we will design, develop, and present both types of code, which is how the majority of current C++ programs are written. Because object-oriented C++ code always contains some procedural code, and many simple C++ programs are written entirely using only procedural code, this type of code is presented first.

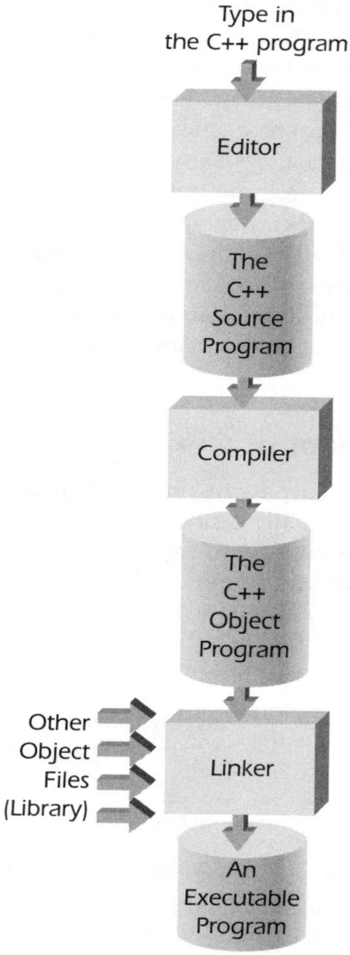

Figure 1.2 Creating an executable C++ program.

Application and System Software

Two logical categories of computer programs are application software and system software. **Application software** consists of those programs written to perform particular tasks required by the users. All the programs in this book are examples of application software.

System software is the collection of programs that must be readily available to any computer system in order for it to operate at all. In the early computer environments of the 1950s and 1960s, the user had to initially load the system software by hand to prepare the computer to do anything at all. This was done by using rows of switches on a front panel. Those initial, hand-entered commands were said to **boot** the computer, an expression derived from "pulling oneself up by the bootstraps." Today, the so-called **bootstrap loader** is a permanent, automatically executed component of the computer's system software.

Collectively, the set of system programs used to operate and control a computer is called the **operating system**. Tasks handled by modern operating systems include the following: memory management; allocation of CPU time; control of input and output units such as the keyboard, screen, and printers; and the management of all secondary storage devices. Many operating systems handle large programs, as well as multiple users concurrently, by dividing programs into segments that are moved between the disk and memory as needed. Such operating systems permit more than one user to run a program on the computer, which gives each user the impression that the computer and peripherals are his or hers alone. This is referred to as a **multi-user** system. Additionally, many operating systems, including most windowed environments, permit each user to run multiple programs. Such operating systems are referred to as **multiprogrammed** and **multitasking** systems.

The Development of C++

At a basic level, the purpose of almost all application programs is to process data to produce one or more specific results. In a procedural language, a program is constructed from sets of instructions, with each set referred to as a procedure, as noted previously. Effectively, each procedure moves the data one step closer to the final desired output along the path shown in Figure 1.3.

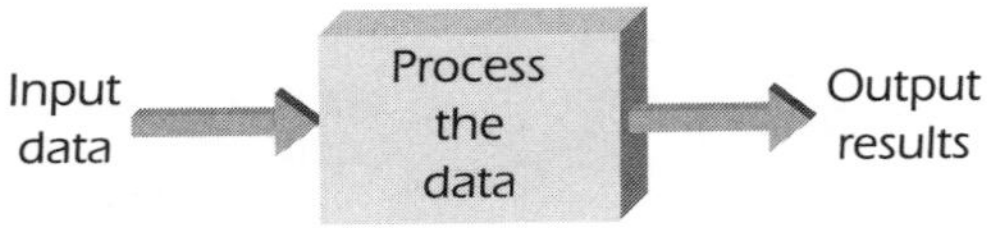

Figure 1.3 Basic procedural operations.

The programming process illustrated in Figure 1.3 directly mirrors the input, processing, and output hardware units used to construct a computer (see Section 1.6). This was not accidental because early programming languages were specifically designed to match and, as optimally as possible, directly control corresponding hardware units.

The first procedural language, named FORTRAN, whose name is derived from *FOR*mula *TRAN*slation, was introduced in 1957 and remained popular throughout the 1960s and early 1970s. (Another high-level programming language developed almost concurrently with FORTRAN, but that never achieved FORTRAN's overwhelming acceptance, was named ALGOL.) FORTRAN has algebra-like instructions that concentrate on the processing phase shown in Figure 1.3 and was developed for scientific and engineering applications that required high-precision numerical outputs, accurate to many decimal places. For example, calculating a rocket's trajectory or the bacterial concentration level in a polluted pond, as illustrated in Figure 1.4, requires evaluating a mathematical equation to a high degree of numerical accuracy and is typical of FORTRAN-based applications.

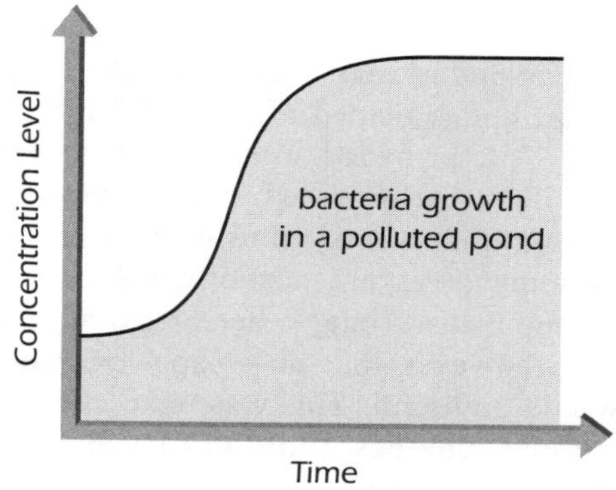

Figure 1.4 FORTRAN was developed for scientific and engineering applications.

The next significant high-level application language was COBOL, which was introduced in the 1960s and remained a major procedural language throughout the 1980s. COBOL is an acronym for COmmon Business-Oriented Language. This language had features geared toward business applications that required simpler mathematical calculations than those needed for engineering applications. One of COBOL's main benefits was that it provided extensive output formats that made it easy to create reports containing multiple columns of neatly formatted dollar and cents numbers and totals, as illustrated in Figure 1.5. It forced programmers to construct well-defined, structured procedures that followed a more consistent pattern than was required in FORTRAN.

Part No.	Description	Quantity	Price
12225	#4 Nails, Common	25 boxes	1.09
12226	#6 Nails, Common	30 boxes	1.09
12227	#8 Nails, Common	65 boxes	1.29
12228	#10 Nails, Common	57 boxes	1.35
12229	#12 Nails, Common	42 boxes	
12230	#16 Nails, Common		

Figure 1.5 COBOL was developed for business applications.

Another language, BASIC (or Beginners All-purpose Symbolic Instruction Code), was developed at Dartmouth College at about the same time as COBOL. BASIC was essentially a slightly scaled-down version of FORTRAN intended as an introductory language for college students. It was a relatively straightforward, easy-to-understand language that did not require detailed knowledge of a specific application. Its main drawback was that it neither required nor enforced a consistent or structured approach to creating programs. Frequently, a programmer could not easily figure out what her or his BASIC program did after a short lapse of time.

To remedy this and put programming on a more scientific and rational basis that made understanding and reusing code easier, the Pascal language was developed. (Pascal is not an acronym but is named after the 17th-century mathematician Blaise Pascal.) Introduced in 1971, it provided students with a firmer foundation in structured programming design than that provided by early versions of BASIC.

Structured programs are created using a set of well-defined structures organized into individual programming sections, each of which performs a specific task that can be tested and modified without disturbing other program sections. The Pascal language was so rigidly structured, however, that no escapes existed from the structured sections when such escapes would be useful. This was unacceptable for many real-world projects and is one of the reasons why Pascal did not become widely accepted in the scientific and engineering fields. Instead, the C language, which is a structured, procedural language developed in the 1970s at AT&T Bell Laboratories by Ken Thompson, Dennis Ritchie, and Brian Kernighan, became the dominant engineering applications language of the 1980s. This language has an extensive set of capabilities that permits it to be written as a high-level language while retaining the ability to directly access the machine-level features of a computer.

C++ was developed in the early 1980s, when Bjarne Stroustrup (also at AT&T) used his simulation language background to create an object-oriented programming language. A central feature of simulation languages is that they model real-life situations as objects. This object orientation, which was ideal for graphical screen objects such as rectangles and circles, was combined with existing C features to form the C++ language. Thus, C++ retained the extensive set of structured and procedural capabilities provided by C but added its own object orientation to become a true general-purpose programming language. As such, C++ can be used for everything from simple, interactive programs to sophisticated and complex engineering and scientific programs, within the context of a truly object-oriented structure.

Exercises 1.1

1. Define the following terms:
   a. computer program
   b. programming
   c. programming language
   d. high-level language
   e. low-level language
   f. machine language
   g. assembly language
   h. procedural language
   i. object-oriented language
   j. source program
   k. compiler
   l. interpreter
2. Describe the purpose and primary uses of application and system software.

3. a. Describe the difference between high- and low-level languages.
   b. Describe the difference between procedure- and object-oriented languages.

4. Describe the similarities and differences between assemblers, interpreters, and compilers.

5. a. Given the following operation codes,

```
11000000 means add the 1st operand to the 2nd operand
10100000 means subtract the 1st operand from the 2nd operand
11110000 means multiply the 2nd operand by the 1st operand
11010000 means divide the 2nd operation by the 1st operand
```

translate the following instructions into English:

opcode	Address of 1st operand	Address of 2nd operand
11000000	000000000001	0000000000010
11110000	000000000010	0000000000011
10100000	000000000100	0000000000011
11010000	000000000101	0000000000011

   b. Assuming the following locations contain the given data, determine the result produced by the instructions listed in Exercise 5a. For this exercise, assume each instruction is executed independently of any instruction.

Address	Initial value (in decimal) stored at this address
00000000001	5
00000000010	3
00000000011	6
00000000100	14
00000000101	4

6. Rewrite the machine-level instructions listed in Exercise 5a using assembly-language notation. Use the symbolic names ADD, SUB, MUL, and DIV for addition, subtraction, multiplication, and division operations, respectively. In writing the instructions use decimal values for the addresses.

1.2 Problem Solution and Software Development

No matter what field of work you choose or what your lifestyle may be, you will have to solve problems. Many of these, such as adding up the change in your pocket, can be solved quickly and easily. Others, such as riding a bicycle, require some practice but soon become automatic. Still others require considerable planning and forethought if the solution is to be appropriate and efficient. For example, constructing a cellular telephone network or creating an inventory management system for a department store are problems for which trial-and-error solutions could prove expensive and disastrous.

Creating a program is no different because a program is a solution developed to solve a particular problem. As such, writing a program is almost the last step in a process of first determining what the problem is and the method that will be used to solve the problem. Each field of study has its own name for the systematic method used to solve problems by designing suitable solutions. In science and engineering the approach is referred to as the **scientific method**, while in quantitative analysis the approach is referred to as the **systems approach.**

The method used by professional software developers for understanding the problem that is being solved and for creating an effective and appropriate software solution is called the **software development procedure**. This procedure, as illustrated in Figure 1.6, consists of three overlapping phases:

- Development and Design
- Documentation
- Maintenance

As a discipline, **software engineering** is concerned with creating readable, efficient, reliable, and maintainable programs and systems, and it uses the software development procedure to achieve this goal.

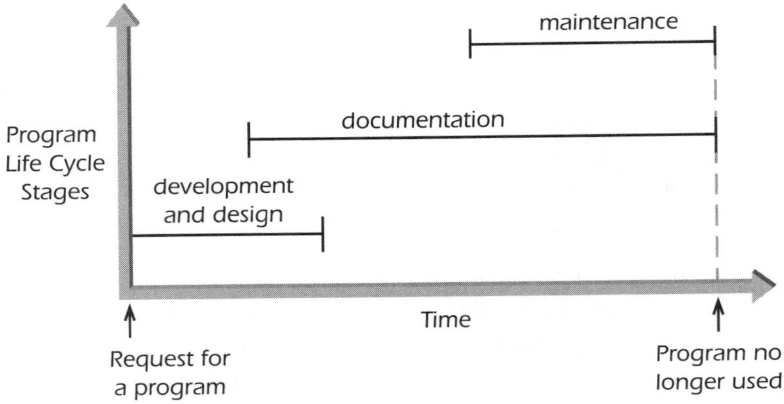

Figure 1.6 The three phases of program development.

Phase I. Development and Design

Phase I begins with either a statement of a problem or a specific request for a program, which is referred to as a **program requirement.** Once a problem has been stated or a specific request for a program solution has been made, the development and design phase begins. This phase consists of the four well-defined steps, as illustrated in Figure 1.7 and summarized next.

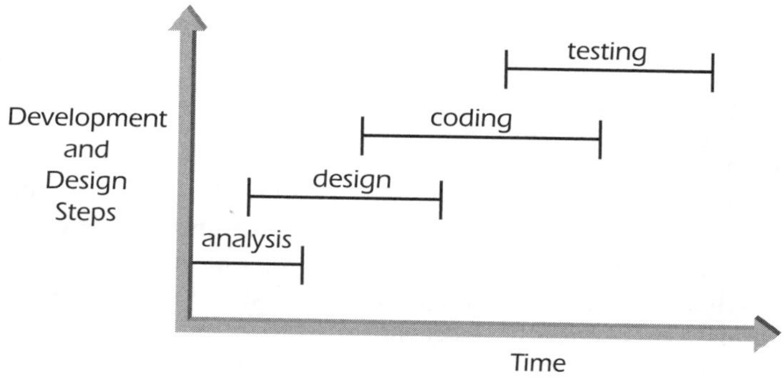

Figure 1.7 The development and design steps.

Step 1 Analyze the Problem

This step is required to ensure that the problem is clearly defined and understood. The determination that the problem is clearly defined is made only after the person doing the analysis understands what outputs are required and what inputs will be needed. To accomplish this the analyst must have an understanding of how the inputs can be used to produce the desired output. For example, assume that you receive the following assignment:

> ***Write a program that gives the information we need about circles.***
> ***Complete by tomorrow.***
>
> — ***Management***

A simple analysis of this program requirement reveals that it is not a well-defined problem at all because we do not know exactly what output information is required. As such, it would be a major mistake to begin immediately writing a program to solve it. To clarify and define the problem statement, your first step should be to contact "Management" to define exactly what the program is to produce (its outputs). Suppose you do this and you learn that what is really desired is a program to calculate and display the circumference of a circle when given the radius. Because a formula exists for converting the input to the output, you may proceed to the next step. If you are not sure of how to obtain the required output or exactly what inputs are needed, a more in-depth analysis is called for. This typically means obtaining more background information about the problem or application. It also frequently entails doing one or more hand calculations to ensure that you understand what inputs are needed and how they must be combined to achieve the desired output.

Countless hours have been spent writing computer programs that either have never been used or have caused considerable animosity between programmer and user because the programmer did not produce what the user needed or expected. Successful programmers understand and avoid this by ensuring that the problem's requirements are understood. This is the first step in creating a program and the most important because in it the specifications for the final program solution are determined. If the requirements are not fully and completely understood before programming begins, the results are almost always disastrous.

For example, imagine designing and building a house without fully understanding the owner's specifications. After the house is completed, the owner tells you that a bathroom is required on the first floor, where you have built a wall between the kitchen and the dining room. In addition, that particular wall is one of the main support walls for the house and contains numerous pipes and electrical cables. In this case, adding one bathroom requires a rather major modification to the basic structure of the house.

Experienced programmers understand the importance of analyzing and understanding a program's requirements before coding, especially if they also have constructed programs that later had to be entirely dismantled and redone. The key to success here, which ultimately determines the success of the final program, is to determine the main purpose of the system as seen by the person making the request. For large systems, the analysis is usually conducted by a systems analyst. For smaller systems or individual programs, the analysis is typically performed directly by the programmer.

Regardless of how the analysis is done, or by whom, at its conclusion there should be a clear understanding of:

- What the system or program must do
- What outputs must be produced
- What inputs are required to create the desired outputs

Step 2 Develop a Solution

In this step, we select the exact set of steps, called an algorithm, is selected that will be used to solve the problem. The solution is typically obtained by a series of refinements, starting with the initial algorithm found in the analysis step, until an acceptable and complete algorithm is obtained. This algorithm must be checked, if this was not already done in the analysis step, to ensure that it correctly produces the desired outputs. The check is typically done by doing one or more hand calculations not already done.

For small programs the selected algorithm may be extremely simple and consist of only one or more calculations that must be performed. More typically, the initial solution must be refined and organized into smaller subsystems, with specifications for how the subsystems will interface with each other. To achieve this goal, the description of the algorithm starts from the highest level (topmost) requirement and proceeds downward to the parts that must be constructed to achieve this requirement. To make this more meaningful, consider a computer program that is required to track the number of parts in inventory. The required output for this program is a description of all parts carried in inventory and the number of units of each item in stock; the given inputs are the initial inventory quantity of each part, the number of items sold, the number of items returned, and the number of items purchased.

For these specifications, a designer could initially organize the requirements for the program into the three sections illustrated in Figure 1.8. This is called a **top-level structure diagram** because it represents the first overall structure of the program selected by the designer.

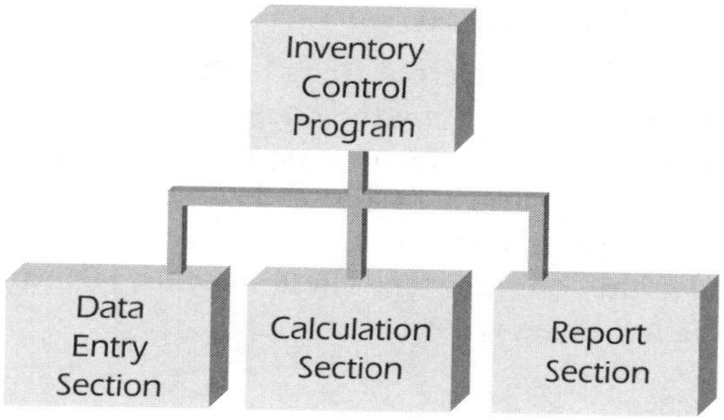

Figure 1.8 First-level structure diagram.

Once an initial structure is developed, it is refined until the tasks indicated in the boxes are completely defined. For example, both the data entry and report modules shown in Figure 1.8 would be further refined. The data-entry module certainly must include provisions for entering the data. Because it is the system designer's responsibility to plan for contingencies and human error, provisions must also be made for changing incorrect data after an entry has been made and for deleting a previously entered value altogether. Similar subdivisions for the report module can also be made. Figure 1.9 illustrates a second-level structure diagram for an inventory tracking system that includes these further refinements.

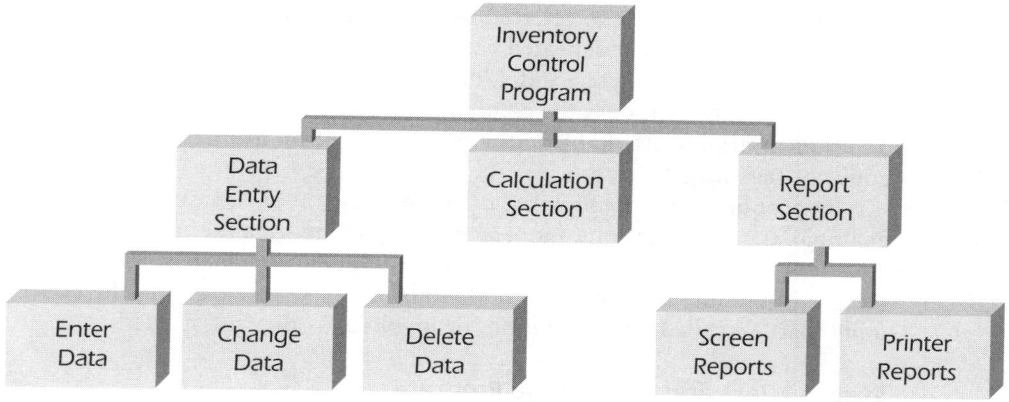

Figure 1.9 Second-level refinement structure diagram.

The process of refining a solution continues until the smallest requirement is included within the solution. Notice that the design produces a treelike structure where the levels branch out as we move from the top of the structure to the bottom. When the design is complete each task designated in a box is typically coded with separate sets of instructions that are executed as they are called on by tasks higher up in the structure.

Step 3 Code the Solution

This step, which is also referred to as both writing the program and implementing the solution, consists of translating the chosen design solution into a computer program. If the analysis and solution steps have been correctly performed, the coding step becomes rather mechanical in nature. In a well-designed program, the statements making up the program will, however, conform to certain well-defined patterns or structures that have been defined in the solution step. These structures control how the program executes and consist of the following types:

1. Sequence
2. Selection
3. Iteration
4. Invocation

Sequence defines the order in which instructions are executed by the program. The specification of which instruction comes first, which comes second, and so on, is essential if the program is to achieve a well-defined purpose.

Selection provides the capability to make a choice between different operations, depending on the result of some condition. For example, the value of a number can be checked before a division is performed. If the number is not zero, it can be used as the denominator of a division operation; otherwise, the division will not be performed and the user will be issued a warning message.

Iteration, which is also referred to as *looping* and *repetition*, provides the ability for the same operation to be repeated based on the value of a condition. For example, grades might be repeatedly entered and added until a negative grade is entered. In this case the entry of a negative grade is the condition that signifies the end of the repetitive input and addition of grades. At that point a calculation of an average for all the grades entered could be performed.

Invocation involves invoking, or summoning, a set of statements as it is needed. For example, the computation of a person's net pay involves the tasks of obtaining pay rates and hours worked, calculating the net pay, and providing a report or check for the required amount. Each of these individual tasks would typically be coded as separate units that are called into execution, or invoked, as they are needed.

Step 4 Test and Correct the Program

The purpose of testing is to verify that a program works correctly and actually fulfills its requirements. In theory, testing would reveal all existing program errors. (In computer terminology, a program error is called a **bug**.[4]) In practice, this would require checking all possible combinations of statement execution. Because of the time and effort required, this is usually an impossible goal, except for extremely simple programs. (We illustrate why this is generally an impossible goal in Section 4.8.)

---

[4]The derivation of this term is rather interesting. When a program stopped running on the Mark I, at Harvard University in September 1945, Grace Hopper traced the malfunction to a dead insect that had gotten into the electrical circuits. She recorded the incident in her logbook at 15:45 hours as "Relay #70. . . . (moth) in relay. First actual case of bug being found."

Because exhaustive testing is not feasible for most programs, different philosophies and methods of testing have evolved. At its most basic level, however, testing requires a conscious effort to ensure that a program works correctly and produces meaningful results. This means that careful thought must be given to what the test is meant to achieve and the data that will be used in the test. If testing reveals an error (bug), the process of debugging, which includes locating, correcting, and verifying the correction, can be initiated. It is important to realize that *although testing may reveal the presence of an error, it does not necessarily indicate the absence of one*. Thus, *the fact that a test revealed one bug does not indicate that another one is not lurking somewhere else in the program.*

To catch and correct errors in a program it is important to develop a set of test data by which to determine whether the program gives correct answers. In fact, an accepted step in formal software development many times is to plan the test procedures and create meaningful test data before writing the code. This tends to help the person be more objective about what the program must do because it essentially circumvents any subconscious temptation after coding to choose test data that will not work. The procedures for testing a program should examine every possible situation under which the program will be used. The program should be tested with data in a reasonable range as well as at the limits and in areas where the program should tell the user that the data are invalid. Developing good test procedures and data for sophisticated problems can be more difficult than writing the program code itself.

Table 1.1 lists the relative amount of effort that is typically expended on each of these four development and design steps in large commercial programming projects. As this listing demonstrated, coding is not the major effort in this phase. Many new programmers have trouble because they spend the majority of their time writing the program, without spending sufficient time understanding the problem or designing an appropriate solution. In this regard, it is worthwhile to remember the programming proverb, *"It is impossible to write a successful program for a problem or application that is not fully understood."* A somewhat equivalent and equally valuable proverb is *"The sooner you start coding a program the longer it usually takes to complete."*

Table 1.1 Effort Expended in Phase I

Step	Effort
Analyze the problem	10%
Develop a solution	20%
Code the solution	20%
Test the program	50%

Phase II. Documentation

So much work becomes useless or lost and so many tasks must be repeated because of inadequate documentation, that it could be argued that documenting your work is one of the most important steps in problem solving. Actually, many critical documents are created during the analysis, design, coding, and testing steps. Completing the documentation requires collecting these documents, adding user-operating material, and presenting it in a form that is most useful to you and your organization.

Although not everybody classifies them in the same way, there are essentially five documents for every problem solution:

1. Program description
2. Algorithm development and changes
3. Well-commented program listing
4. Sample test runs
5. Users' manual

"Putting yourself in the shoes" of a member of a large organization's team that might use your work—anyone from the secretary to the programmer/analysts and management—should help you to make the content of the important documentation clear. The documentation phase formally begins in the development and design phase and continues into the maintenance phase.

Phase III. Maintenance

This phase is concerned with the ongoing correction of problems, revisions to meet changing needs, and the addition of new features. Maintenance is often the major effort, the primary source of revenue, and the longest lasting of the engineering phases. While development may take days or months, maintenance may continue for years or decades. The better the documentation is, the more efficiently this maintenance can be performed and the happier the customer and user will be.

Backup

Although not part of the formal design process, it is critical to make and keep backup copies of the program at each step of the programming and debugging process. It is easy to delete or change the current working version of a program beyond recognition. Backup copies allow the recovery of the last stage of work with a minimum of effort. The final working version of a useful program should be backed up at least twice. In this regard, another useful programming proverb is *"Backup is unimportant if you don't mind starting all over again."*

Many organizations keep at least one backup on site, where it can be easily retrieved, and another backup copy either in a fireproof safe or at a remote location.

Exercises 1.2

1. a. List and describe the four steps required in the design and development stage of a program.

b. In addition to the design and development stage, what are the other two stages required in producing a program and why are they required?

2. A note from your supervisor, Mr. J. Bosworth, says:

   Solve our lighting problems.
   —J. Bosworth

   a. What should be your first task?
   b. How would you accomplish this task?
   c. How long would you expect this to take, assuming everyone cooperates?

3. Program development is only one phase in the overall software development procedure. Assuming that documentation and maintenance require 60% of the total software effort in designing a system, and using Table 1.1, determine the amount of effort required for initial program coding as a percentage of total software effort.

4. Many people requesting a program or system for the first time consider coding to be the most important aspect of program development. They feel that they know what they need and think that the programmer can begin coding with minimal time spent in analysis. As a programmer, what pitfalls can you envision in working with such people?

5. Many first-time computer users try to contract with programmers for a fixed fee (total amount to be paid is fixed in advance). What is the advantage to the user in having this arrangement? What is the advantage to the programmer in having this arrangement? What are some disadvantages to both user and programmer in this arrangement?

6. Many programmers prefer to work on an hourly rate basis. Why do you think this is so? Under what conditions would it be advantageous for a programmer to give a client a fixed price for the programming effort?

7. Experienced users generally want a clearly written statement of programming work to be done, including a complete description of what the program will do, delivery dates, payment schedules, and testing requirements. What is the advantage to the user in requiring this? What is the advantage to a programmer in working under this arrangement? What disadvantages does this arrangement have for both user and programmer?

1.3 ALGORITHMS

Before a program is written, the programmer must clearly understand what data are to be used, the desired result, and the procedure to be used to produce this result. The procedure, or solution, selected is referred to as an algorithm. More precisely, an **algorithm** is defined as a step-by-step sequence of instructions that must terminate and describes how the data is to be processed to produce the desired outputs. In essence, an algorithm answers the question, "What method will you use to solve this problem?"

Only after we clearly understand the data we will be using and select an algorithm (the specific steps required to produce the desired result) can we code the program. Seen in this light, programming is the translation of a selected algorithm into a language that the computer can use.

To illustrate an algorithm, we shall consider a simple problem. Assume that a program must calculate the sum of all whole numbers from 1 through 100. Figure 1.10 illustrates three methods we could use to find the required sum. Each method constitutes an algorithm.

Clearly, most people would not bother to list the possible alternatives in a detailed step-by-step manner, as we have done here, and then select one of the algorithms to solve the problem. But then, most people do not think algorithmically; they tend to think heuristically.

Method 1 - Columns: Arrange the numbers from 1 to 100 in a column and add them

```
   1
   2
   3
   4
   .
   .
   .
  98
  99
+100
----
5050
```

Method 2 - Groups: Arrange the numbers in groups that sum to 101 and multiply the number of groups by 101

```
1+100=101 ┐
 2+99=101 │
 3+98=101 │
 4+97=101 │ 50 groups
   .   .  │      ↓
   .   .  │   (50x101=5050)
49+52=101 │
50+51=101 ┘
```

Method 3 - Formula: Use the formula

$$\text{sum} = \frac{n(a+b)}{2}$$

where

n= number of terms to added (100)
a= first number to be added (1)
b= last number to be added (100)

$$\text{sum} = \frac{100(1+100)}{2} = 5050$$

Figure 1.10 Summing the numbers 1 through 100.

Symbol	**Name**	**Description**
	Terminal	Indicates the beginning or end of a program
	Input/Output	Indicates an input or output operation
	Process	Indicates computation or data manipulation
	Flow Lines	Used to connect the other flowchart symbols and indicate the logic flow
	Decision	Indicates a program branch point
	Loop	Indicates the initial, limit, and increment values of a loop
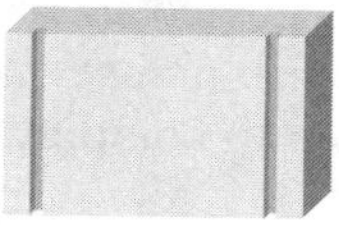	Predefined Process	Indicates a predefined process, as in calling a function
	Connector	Indicates an entry to, or exit from, another part of the flowchart or a connection point
	Report	Indicates a written output report

Figure 1.11 Flowchart symbols.

For example, if you had to change a flat tire on your car, you would not think of all the steps required—you would simply change the tire or call someone else to do the job. This is an example of heuristic thinking.

Unfortunately, computers do not respond to heuristic commands. A general statement such as "add the numbers from 1 to 100" means nothing to a computer because the computer can respond only to algorithmic commands written in an acceptable language such as C++. To program a computer successfully, you must clearly understand this difference between algorithmic and heuristic commands. A computer is an "algorithm-responding" machine; it is not an "heuristic-responding" machine. You cannot tell a computer to change a tire or to add the numbers from 1 through 100. Instead, you must give the computer a detailed, step-by-step set of instructions that, collectively, forms an algorithm. For example, the following set of instructions forms a detailed method, or algorithm, for determining the sum of the numbers from 1 through 100:

Set n equal to 100
Set $a = 1$
Set b equal to 100
Calculate $sum = \frac{n(a + b)}{2}$
Print the sum

Notice that these instructions are not a computer program. Unlike a program, which must be written in a language the computer can respond to, an algorithm can be written or described in various ways. When English-like phrases are used to describe the algorithm (the processing steps), as in this example, the description is called **pseudocode.** When mathematical equations are used, the description is called a **formula.** When diagrams that employ the symbols shown in Figure 1.11 are used, the description is referred to as a **flowchart.** Figure 1.12 illustrates the use of these symbols in depicting an algorithm for determining the average of three numbers.

Because flowcharts are cumbersome to revise and can easily support unstructured programming practices, they have fallen out of favor by professional programmers, while the use of pseudocode to express the logic of algorithms has gained increasing acceptance. In describing an algorithm using pseudocode, short English phrases are used. For example, acceptable pseudocode for describing the steps needed to compute the average of three numbers is:

Input the three numbers into the computer's memory
Calculate the average by adding the numbers and dividing the sum by three
Display the average

Only after an algorithm has been selected and the programmer understands the steps required can the algorithm be written using computer-language statements. The writing of an algorithm using computer-language statements is called coding the algorithm, which is the third step in our program development procedure (see Figure 1.13). Most of Part I of this text is devoted to showing you how to develop and code algorithms into C++.

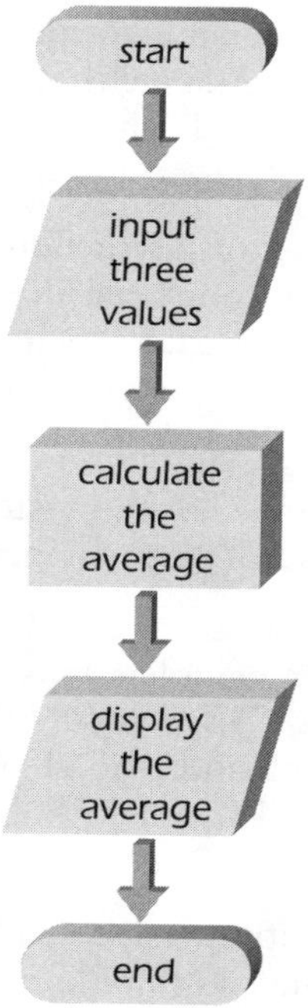

Figure 1.12 Flowchart for calculating the average of three numbers.

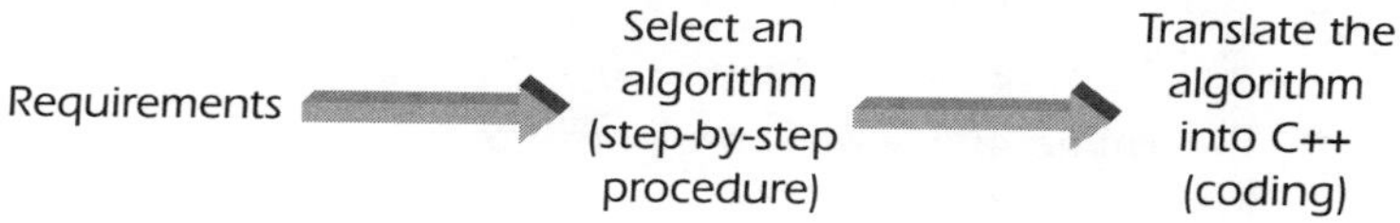

Figure 1.13 Coding an algorithm.

Exercises 1.3

1. Determine a step-by-step procedure (list the steps) to do the following tasks. (*Note: There is no one single correct answer for each of these tasks. The exercise is designed is to give you practice in converting heuristic-type commands into equivalent algorithms and making the shift between the thought processes involved in the two types of thinking.*)
   a. Fix a flat tire
   b. Make a telephone call
   c. Log in to a computer
   d. Roast a turkey
2. Are the procedures you developed for Exercise 1 algorithms? Discuss why or why not.

3. Determine and write an algorithm (list the steps) to interchange the contents of two cups of liquid. Assume that a third cup is available to hold the contents of either cup temporarily. Each cup should be rinsed before any new liquid is poured into it.

4. Write a detailed set of instructions, in English, to calculate the resistance of the following resistors connected in series: *n* resistors, each having a resistance of 56 ohms, *m* resistors, each having a resistance of 33 ohms, and *p* resistors, each having a resistance of 15 ohms. Note that the total resistance of resistors connected in series is the sum of all individual resistances.

5. Write a set of detailed, step-by-step instructions, in English, to find the smallest number in a group of three integer numbers.

6. a. Write a set of detailed, step-by-step instructions, in English, to calculate the fewest number of dollar bills needed to pay a bill of amount TOTAL. For example, if TOTAL were $97 the bills would consist of one $50 bill, two $20 bills, one $5 bill and two $1 bills. (For this exercise, assume that only $100, $50, $20, $10, $5, and $1 bills are available.)
   b. Repeat Exercise 6a, but assume the bill is to be paid only in $1 bills.

7. a. Write an algorithm to locate the first occurrence of the name JEANS in a list of names arranged in random order.
   b. Discuss how you could improve your algorithm for Exercise 7a if the list of names were arranged in alphabetical order.

8. Write an algorithm to determine the total occurrences of the letter *e* in any sentence.

9. Determine and write an algorithm to sort four numbers into ascending (from lowest to highest) order.

1.4 COMMON PROGRAMMING ERRORS

The most common errors associated with the material presented in this chapter are as follows:

1. A major programming error made by most beginning programmers is the rush to write and run a program before fully understanding what is required, including the algorithms that will be used to produce the desired result. A symptom of this haste to get a program entered into the computer is the lack of any documentation, or even a program outline or a written program itself. Many problems can be caught just by checking a copy of the program or even a description of the algorithm written in pseudocode.

2. A second major error is not backing up a program. Almost all new programmers make this mistake until they lose a program that has taken considerable time to code.

3. The third error made by many new programmers is the lack of understanding that computers respond only to explicitly defined algorithms. Telling a computer to add a group of numbers is quite different than telling a friend to add the numbers. The computer must be given the precise instructions for doing the addition in a programming language.

1.5 CHAPTER SUMMARY

1. The programs used to operate a computer are referred to as *software*.
2. Programming languages come in a variety of forms and types. *Machine language* programs, also known as *executable programs*, contain the binary codes that can be executed by a computer. *Assembly languages* permit the use of symbolic names for mathematical operations and memory addresses. Programs written in assembly languages must be converted to machine language, using translator programs called *assemblers*, before the programs can be executed. Assembly and machine languages are referred to as *low-level languages*.

   Compiler and *interpreter languages* are referred to as *high-level languages*. This means that they are written using instructions that resemble a written language, such as English, and can be run on a variety of computer types. Compiler languages require a *compiler* to translate the program into a binary language form, whereas interpreter languages require an *interpreter* to do the translation.
3. As a discipline, *software engineering* is concerned with creating readable, efficient, reliable, and maintainable programs and systems.
4. The software development procedure consists of three phases:
   - Program development and design
   - Documentation
   - Maintenance
5. The program development and design phase consists of four well-defined steps:
   - Analyze the problem
   - Develop a solution
   - Code the solution
   - Test and correct the solution
6. An *algorithm* is a step-by-step procedure that must terminate and describes how a computation or task is to be performed.

7. A *computer program* is a self-contained unit of instructions and data used to operate a computer to produce a specific result.
8. The four fundamental control structures used in coding an algorithm are
   - Sequence
   - Selection
   - Iteration
   - Invocation

1.6 CHAPTER APPENDIX: COMPUTER HARDWARE AND STORAGE CONCEPTS

All computers, from large super computers costing millions of dollars to smaller desktop personal computers, must perform a minimum set of functions and provide the capability to:

1. Accept input
2. Display output
3. Store information in a logically consistent format (traditionally binary)
4. Perform arithmetic and logic operations on either the input or stored data
5. Monitor, control, and direct the overall operation and sequencing of the system

Figure 1.14 illustrates the computer components that support these capabilities and collectively form a computer's **hardware**.

The **arithmetic and logic unit (ALU)** performs all the arithmetic and logic functions such as addition and subtraction and provided by the computer.

The **control unit** directs and monitors the overall operation of the computer. It keeps track of where in memory the next instruction resides, issues the signals needed to both read data from and write data to other units in the system, and controls execution of all instructions.

The **memory unit** stores information in a logically consistent format. Typically, both instructions and data are stored in memory, usually in separate and distinct areas.

The **input and output (I/O) unit** provides the interface to which peripheral devices such as keyboards, monitors, printers, and card readers are attached.

Secondary storage: Because main memory in very large quantities is still relatively expensive and volitale (which means that the information is lost when power is turned off), it is not practical as a permanent storage area for programs and data. Secondary or auxiliary storage devices are used for this purpose. Although data have been stored on punched cards, paper tape, and other media in the past, virtually all secondary storage is now done on magnetic tape, magnetic disks, and CD-ROMs.

In the first commercially available computers of the 1950s, all hardware units were built using relays and vacuum tubes, and secondary storage consisted of punched cards. The resulting computers were extremely large pieces of equipment capable of making thousands of calculations per second and costing millions of dollars.

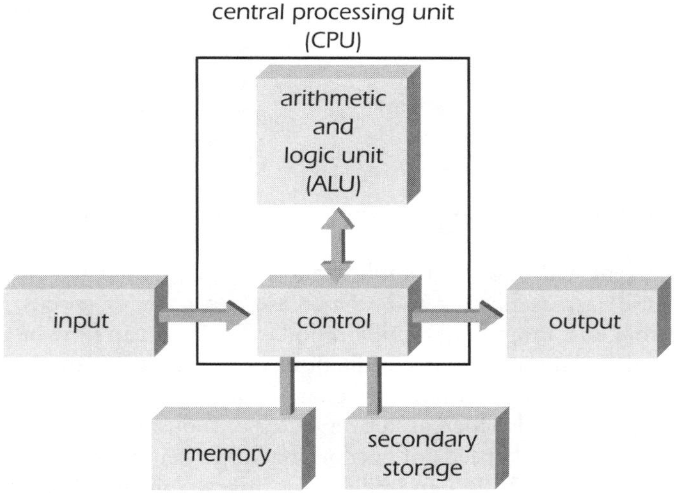

Figure 1.14 Basic hardware units of a computer.

With the introduction of transistors in the 1960s, both the size and cost of computer hardware were reduced. The transistor was approximately one-twentieth the size of its vacuum tube counterpart. The transistor's small size allowed manufacturers to combine the arithmetic and logic unit with the control unit into a single new unit. This combined unit is called the **central processing unit (CPU)**. The combination of the ALU and control unit into one CPU made sense because a majority of control signals generated by a program are directed to the ALU in response to arithmetic and logic instructions within the program. Combining the ALU with the control unit simplified the interface between these two units and provided improved processing speed.

The mid-1960s saw the introduction of integrated circuits (ICs), which resulted in still another significant reduction in the space required to produce a CPU. Initially, integrated circuits were manufactured with up to 100 transistors on a single 1 cm^2 chip of silicon. Such devices are referred to as small-scale integrated (SSI) circuits. Current versions of these chips contain hundreds of thousands to more than a million transistors and are referred to as very large-scale integrated (VLSI) chips.

VLSI chip technology has provided the means of transforming the giant computers of the 1950s into today's desktop and notebook personal computers. Each individual unit required to form a computer (CPU, memory, and I/O) is now manufactured on an individual VLSI chip, and the single-chip CPU is referred to as a **microprocessor**. Figure 1.15

illustrates how these chips are connected internally within current personal computers, such as the IBM-PCs.

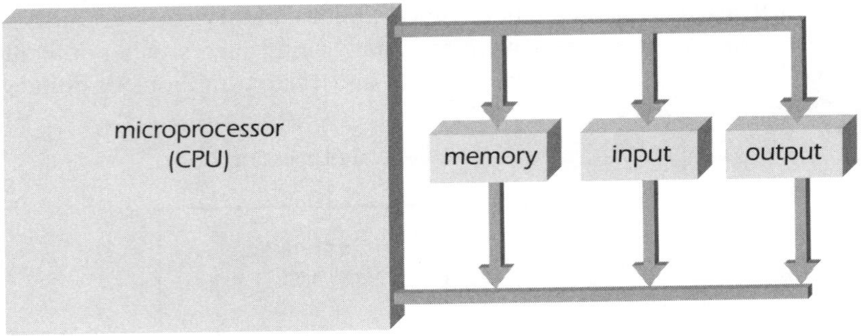

Figure 1.15 *VLSI chip connections for a desktop computer.*

Concurrent with the remarkable reduction in computer hardware size has been an equally dramatic decrease in cost and an increase in processing speeds. Equivalent computer hardware that cost more than a million dollars in 1950 can now be purchased for less than five hundred dollars. If the same reductions occurred in the automobile industry, for example, a Rolls Royce could now be purchased for ten dollars! The processing speeds of current computers have also increased by a factor of thousands over their 1950s predecessors, with the computational speeds of current machines being measured in both millions of instructions per second (MIPS) and billions of instructions per second (BIPS).

Computer Storage

The physical components used in manufacturing a computer require that the numbers and letters inside its memory unit are not stored using the same symbols that people use. The number 126, for example, is not stored using the symbols 1, 2, and 6. Nor is the letter that we recognize as *A* stored using this symbol. In this section we will see why this is so and how computers store numbers. In Chapter 2 we will see how letters are stored.

The smallest and most basic data item in a computer is called a **bit**. Physically, a bit is really a switch that can be either open or closed. The convention we will follow is that the open and closed positions of each switch are represented as a 0 and a 1, respectively.[5]

A single bit that can represent the values 0 and 1, by itself, has limited usefulness. All computers, therefore, group a set number of bits together, both for storage and transmission. The grouping of eight bits to form a larger unit is an almost universal computer standard. Such groups are referred to as **bytes**. A single byte consisting of eight bits, where each bit is either a 0 or 1, can represent any one of 256 distinct patterns. These consist of the pattern 00000000 (all eight switches open) to the pattern 11111111 (all eight switches closed), and all possible combinations of 0s and 1s in between. Each of these patterns can be used to represent either a letter of the alphabet, other single characters such as a dollar sign,

[5]This convention, unfortunately, is rather arbitrary, and you will frequently encounter the reverse correspondence where the open and closed positions are represented as 1 and 0, respectively.

comma, etc., a single digit, or numbers containing more than one digit. The collection of patterns consisting of 0s and 1s used to represent letters, single digits, and other single characters are called **character codes**. (Two such codes, called the ASCII and EBCDIC codes, are presented in Section 2.1.) The patterns used to store numbers are called **number codes**, one of which is presented below.

Two's Complement Numbers

The most common number code for storing integer values inside a computer is called the **two's complement** representation. Using this code, the integer equivalent of any bit pattern, such as 10001101, is easy to determine and can be found for either positive or negative integers with no change in the conversion method. For convenience we will assume byte-sized bit patterns consisting of a set of eight bits each, although the procedure carries over to larger-sized bit patterns.

The easiest way to determine the integer represented by each bit pattern is to first construct a simple device called a value box. Figure 1.16 illustrates such a box for a single byte. Mathematically, each value in the box illustrated in Figure 1.16 represents an increasing power of two. Since two's complement numbers must be capable of representing both positive and negative integers, the leftmost position, in addition to having the largest absolute magnitude, also has a negative sign.

```
-128| 64  | 32  | 16  |  8  |  4  |  2  |  1
----|-----|-----|-----|-----|-----|-----|---
    |     |     |     |     |     |     |
```

Figure 1.16 *An eight-bit value box.*

Conversion of any binary number, for example 10001101, simply requires inserting the bit pattern into the value box and adding the values having 1s under them. Thus, as illustrated in Figure 1.17, the bit pattern 10001101 represents the integer number –115.

```
-128 | 64  | 32  | 16  |  8  |  4  |  2  |  1
 ----|-----|-----|-----|-----|-----|-----|---
    1|  0  |  0  |  0  |  1  |  1  |  0  |  1
-128 +  0  +  0  +  0  +  8  +  4  +  0  +  1 = -115
```

Figure 1.17 Converting 10001101 to a base 10 number.

The value box can also be used in reverse to convert a base 10 integer number into its equivalent binary bit pattern. Some conversions, in fact, can be made by inspection. For example, the base 10 number –125 is obtained by adding 3 to –128. Thus, the binary representation of –125 is 10000011, which equals –128 + 2 + 1. Similarly, the two's complement representation of the number 40 is 00101000, which is 32 + 8.

Although the value box conversion method is deceptively simple, it is directly related to the underlying mathematical basis of two's complement binary numbers. The original name of the two's complement code was the weighted-sign code, which correlates directly to the value box. As the name **weighted sign** implies, each bit position has a weight, or value, of two raised to a power and a sign. The signs of all bits except the leftmost bit are positive and the sign of the leftmost bit is negative.

In reviewing the value box, it is evident that any two's complement binary number with a leading 1 represents a negative number, and any bit pattern with a leading 0 represents a positive number. Using the value box, it is easy to determine the most positive and negative values capable of being stored. The most negative value that can be stored in a single byte is the decimal number –128, which has the bit pattern 10000000. Any other non-zero bit will simply add a positive amount to the number. Additionally, it is clear that a positive number must have a 0 as its leftmost bit. From this you can see that the largest positive 8-bit two's complement number is 01111111 or 127.

Words and Addresses

One or more bytes may be grouped into larger units, called **words**, which facilitate faster and more extensive data access. For example, retrieving a word consisting of four bytes from a computer's memory results in more information than that obtained by retrieving a word consisting of a single byte. Such a retrieval is also considerably faster than four individual byte retrievals. This increase in speed and capacity, however, is achieved by an increase in the computer's cost and complexity.

Early personal computers, such as the Apple IIe and Commodore machines, internally stored and transmitted words consisting of single bytes. The first IBM-PCs used word sizes consisting of two bytes, while more current PCs store and process words consisting of four bytes each.

The number of bytes in a word determines the maximum and minimum values that can be represented by the word. Table 1.2 lists these values for 1, 2, and 4 byte words (each of the values listed can be derived using 8-, 16-, and 32-bit value boxes, respectively).

Table 1.2 Integer Values and Word Size

Word Size	Maximum Integer Value	Minimum Integer Value
1 Byte	127	–128
2 Bytes	32,767	–32,768
4 Bytes	2,147,483,647	–2,147,483,648

In addition to representing integer values, computers must also store and transmit numbers containing decimal points, which are mathematically referred to as real numbers. The codes used for real numbers, which are more complex than those used for integers, are presented in Appendix C.

Looking at Career Choices

Aeronautical/Aerospace Engineering

Among the youngest of the engineering disciplines, aeronautical/aerospace engineering is concerned with all aspects of the design, production, testing, and utilizing of vehicles or devices that fly in air (aeronautical) or in space (aerospace), from hang gliders to space shuttles. Because the science and engineering principles involved are so broad based, aeroengineers usually specialize in a subarea that may overlap with other engineering fields such as mechanical, metallurgical/materials, chemical, civil, or electrical engineering. Such subareas include the following:

1. Aerodynamics. The study of the flight characteristics of various structures or configurations. Typical considerations are the drag and lift associated with airplane design or the onset of turbulent flow. A knowledge of fluid dynamics is essential. The modeling and testing of all forms of aircraft is part of this discipline.
2. Structural design. The design, production, and testing of aircraft and spacecraft to withstand the wide range of in-flight demands on these vehicles, such as underwater vessels, are in the province of the structural engineer.
3. Propulsion systems. The design of internal combustion, jet, and liquid- and solid-fuel rocket engines and their coordination in the overall design of the vehicle. Rocket engines, especially, require innovative engineering to accommodate the extreme temperatures of storing, mixing, and burning fuels such as liquid oxygen.
4. Instrumentation and guidance. The aerospace industry has been a leader in developing and utilizing solid-state electronics in the form of microprocessors to monitor and adjust the operations of hundreds of air- and spacecraft functions. This field uses the expertise of both electrical engineers and aeroengineers.
5. Navigation. The computation of orbits within and outside the atmosphere, and the determination of the orientation of a vehicle with respect to points on the earth or in space.

Part One
Procedure-Oriented Programming in C++

CHAPTERS

Although C++ is an object-oriented language, it was developed as an extension to C, which is a procedural-oriented language. As such, C++ is a hybrid language having both procedural and object features. Because of this hybrid nature, it is not only possible to write a complete C++ program using only procedural code, it is impossible to write an object-oriented program in C++ that does not include procedural elements. Thus, a proper start to learning C++ requires familiarity with its procedural aspects.

CHAPTER 2
Problem Solving Using C++

TOPICS

2.1 INTRODUCTION TO C++

A well-designed program is constructed using a design philosophy similar to that used in constructing a well-designed building: It doesn't just happen; it depends on careful planning and execution if the final design is to accomplish its intended purpose. Just as an integral part of the design of a building is its structure, the same is true for a program.

Programs whose structures consist of interrelated segments, arranged in a logical and easily understandable order to form an integrated and complete unit, are referred to as **modular programs** (Figure 2.1). Modular programs are noticeably easier to develop, correct, and modify than programs constructed in some other manner. In programming terminology, the smaller segments used to construct a modular program are referred to as **modules.**

Each module is designed and developed to perform a specific task and is really a small subprogram all by itself. A complete C++ program is constructed by combining as many modules as necessary to produce the desired result. The advantage of modular construction is that the overall design of the program can be developed before any single module is written. Once the requirements for each module are finalized, the modules can be programmed and integrated within the overall program as they are completed.

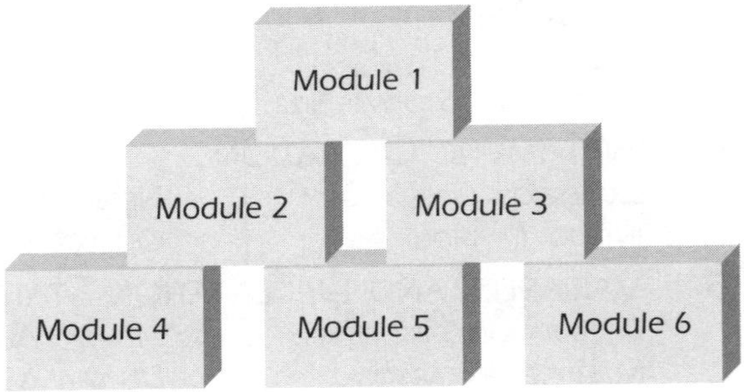

Figure 2.1 A well-designed program is built using modules.

In C++, modules can be either classes or functions. It helps to think of a **function** as a small machine that transforms the data it receives into a finished product. For example, Figure 2.2 illustrates a function that accepts two numbers as inputs and multiplies the two numbers to produce one output. As shown, the interface to the function is its inputs and results. The process of converting the inputs to results is both encapsulated and hidden within the function. In this regard, the function can be thought of as a single unit providing a special purpose operation. A similar analogy is appropriate for a **class.**

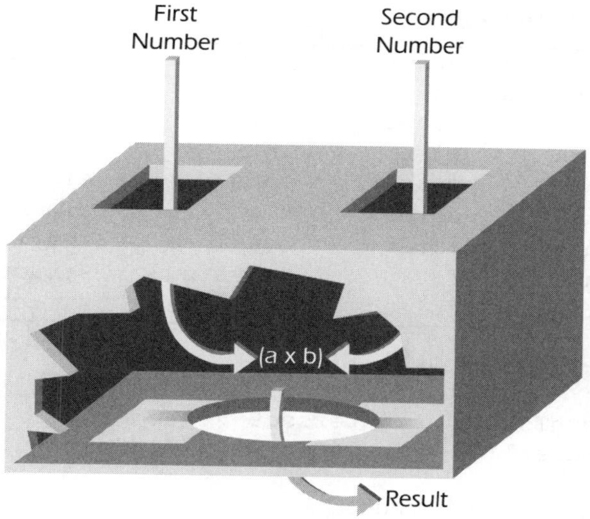

Figure 2.2 *A multiplying function.*

A **class** is a more complicated unit than a function because it contains both data and functions appropriate for manipulating the data. Thus, unlike a function, which is used to encapsulate a set of operations, a class encapsulates both data and one or more sets of operations. As such, each class contains all of the elements required for the input, output, and processing of its objects and can be thought of as a small factory containing raw material (the data) and machines (the functions). Initially, we will be predominantly concerned with the more basic function module.

One important requirement for designing a good function or class is to give it a name that conveys to the reader some idea of what the function or class does. The names permissible for functions and classes are also used to name other elements of the C++ language and are collectively referred to as **identifiers**. Identifiers can be made up of any combination of letters, digits, or underscores (_) selected according to the following rules:

1. The first character of the name must be a letter or underscore (_).
2. Only letters, digits, or underscores may follow the initial letter. Blank spaces are not allowed; either use the underscore to separate words in a name consisting of multiple words, or capitalize the first letter of one or more words.
3. A function name cannot be one of the keywords listed in Table 2.1. (A **keyword** is a word that is set aside by the language for a special purpose and can only be used in a specified manner.[1])
4. The maximum number of characters in a function name is 1024.[2]

---

[1]Keywords in C are also reserved words, which means they must be used only for their specified purpose. Attempting to use them for any other purpose will generate an error message.

[2] This is the minimum required by the ANSI standard.

Table 2.1 Keywords

auto	delete	goto	public	this
break	do	if	register	template
case	double	inline	return	typedef
catch	else	int	short	union
char	enum	long	signed	unsigned
class	extern	new	sizeof	virtual
const	float	overload	static	void
continue	for	private	struct	volatile
default	friend	protected	switch	while

Examples of valid C++ identifiers are:

```
degToRad     intersect     addNums     slope
bessel1      multTwo       findMax     density
```

Examples of invalid identifiers are:

1AB3 (Begins with a number, which violates rule 1.)

E*6 (Contains a special character, which violates rule 2.)

while (This is a keyword, which violates rule 3.)

In addition to conforming to C++'s identifier rules, a C++ function name must always be followed by parentheses. (The reason for this is explained shortly.) Also, a good function name should be a mnemonic. A **mnemonic** (pronounced knee-monic) is a word or name designed as a memory aid. For example, the function name `degToRad()` (note that we have included the required parentheses after the identifier, which clearly marks this as a function name) is a mnemonic if it is the name of a function that converts degrees to radians. Here, the name itself helps to identify what the function does.

Examples of valid function names that are not mnemonics are:

```
easy()     c3po()     r2d2()     theForce()     mike()
```

Function names that are not mnemonic should not be used because they convey no information about what the function does.

Additionally, function names can be typed in mixed upper- and lowercase letters. This is becoming increasingly common in C++, although it is not absolutely necessary. All uppercase identifiers are usually reserved for symbolic constants, a topic covered in Section 3.5.

Additionally, C++ is a **case-sensitive** language. This means that the compiler distinguishes between uppercase and lowercase letters. Thus, in C++, the names TOTAL, total, and TotaL represent three distinct names.

The `main()` Function

A distinct advantage of using functions and classes in C++ is that the overall structure of the program in general, and individual modules in particular, can be planned in advance, including provision for testing and verifying each module's operation. Each function and class can then be written to meet its intended objective.

To provide for the orderly placement and execution of modules, each C++ program must have one and only one function named `main()`. The `main()` function is referred to as a **driver function**, because it drives, or tells the other modules the sequence in which they are to execute (Figure 2.3).[3]

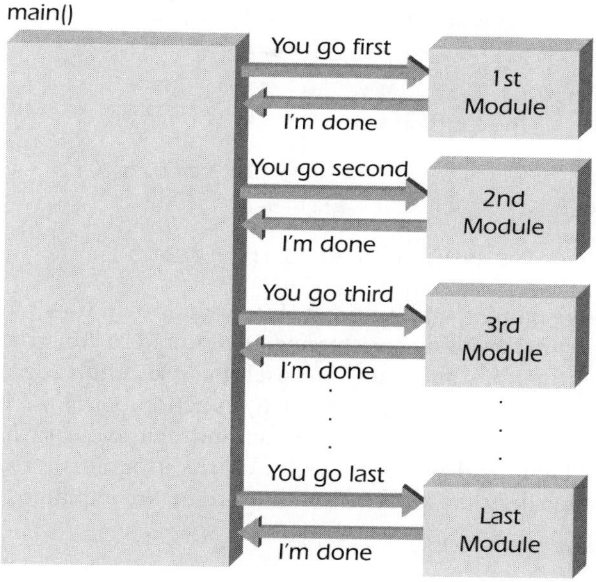

Figure 2.3 The `main()` function directs all other functions.

Figure 2.4 illustrates a structure for the `main()` function. The first line of the function, in this case `int main()`, is referred to as a **function header line**. A function header line, which is always the first line of a function, contains three pieces of information:[4]

1. What type of data, if any, is returned from the function.
2. The name of the function.
3. What type of data, if any, is sent into the function.

The keyword before the function name defines the type of value the function returns when it has completed operating. When placed before the function's name the keyword

[3] Modules executed from `main()` may, in turn, execute other modules. Each module, however, always returns to the module that initiated its execution. This is true even for `main()`, which returns control to the operating system in effect when `main()` was initiated.

[4] A class method must also begin with a header line that adheres to these same rules.

`int` (see Table 2.1) designates that the function will return an integer value. Similarly, when the parentheses following the function name are empty, it signifies that no data will be transmitted into the function when it is run. (Data transmitted into a function at run time are referred to as **arguments** of the function.) The braces, `{` and `}`, determine the beginning and end of the function body and enclose the statements making up the function. The statements inside the braces determine what the function does. Each statement inside the function must end with a semicolon (;).

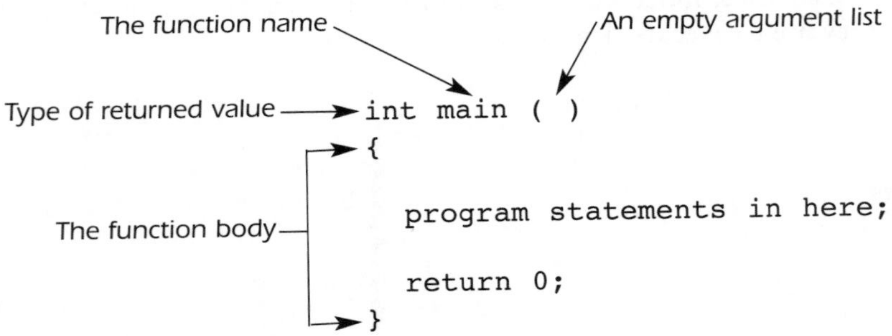

Figure 2.4 The structure of a `main()` function.

You will be naming and writing many of your own C++ functions. In fact, the rest of this book is primarily about the statements required to construct useful functions and how to combine functions and data into useful classes and programs. Each program, however, must have one and only one `main()` function. Until we learn how to pass data into a function and return data from a function (the topics of Chapter 6), the header line illustrated in Figure 2.4 will serve us for all the programs we need to write. For simple programs, consider that the first two lines (they are explained in detail in Chapter 6):

```
int main()
{
```

simply designate that "the program begins here," while the last two lines

```
  return 0;
}
```

designate the end of the program. Fortunately, many useful functions and classes have already been written for us. We will now see how to use an object created from one of these classes to create our first working C++ program.

The `cout` Object

One of the most versatile and commonly used objects provided in C++ is named `cout` (pronounced "see out"). This object, whose name was derived from Console OUTput, is an output object that sends data given to it to the standard output display device.[5] For

[5] The `cout` object is formally created from the `ostream` class, which is described in detail in Chapter 7.

most systems, this display device is a video screen. The `cout` object displays on the monitor whatever is passed to it. For example, if the data `Hello there world!` is passed to `cout`, this data is printed (or displayed) on your terminal screen. The data `Hello there world!` is passed to the `cout` object by enclosing the text within double quotation marks, `"string in here"`, and putting the insertion ("put to") symbol, <<, before the message and after the object's name, as shown in Figure 2.5.

```
cout << "Hello there world!";
```

Figure 2.5 Passing a message to `cout`.

Now let's put all this together into a working C++ program that can be run on your computer. Consider Program 2.1.

Program 2.1

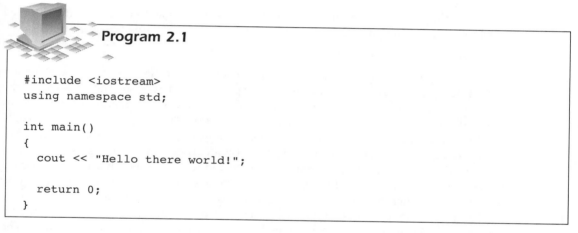

```
#include <iostream>
using namespace std;

int main()
{
  cout << "Hello there world!";

  return 0;
}
```

The first line of the program,

```
#include <iostream>
```

is a preprocessor command that uses the reserved word `include`. Preprocessor commands begin with a pound sign, (#), and perform some action before the compiler translates the source program into machine code. Specifically, the `#include` preprocessor command causes the contents of the named file, in this case the `iostream` file, to be inserted wherever the `#include` command appears in the program. The `iostream` is a part of the standard library that contains, among other code, two classes named `istream` and `ostream`. These two classes provide the data declarations and methods used for data input and output, respectively. The `iostream` file is referred to as a **header file** because a reference to it is always placed at the top, or head, of a C++ program using the `#include` command. You may be wondering what the `iostream` file has to do with this simple program. The answer is that the `cout` object is created from the `ostream` class. Thus, the `iostream` header file must be included in all programs that use `cout`. As indicated in Program 2.1, preprocessor commands do not end with a semicolon.

Point of Information

What Is Syntax?

A programming language's **syntax** is the set of rules for formulating grammatically correct language statements. In practice this means that a C++ statement with correct syntax has the proper form specified for the compiler. As such, the compiler will accept the statement and will not generate an error message.

It should be noted that an individual statement or program can be syntactically correct and yet logically incorrect. Such a statement or program would be correctly structured but would produce an incorrect result. This is similar to an English statement that is grammatically correct but makes no sense. For example, although the sentence "The tree is a ragged cat" is grammatically correct, it makes no sense.

Following the preprocessor `include` command is a statement containing the reserved word `using`. The statement,

```
using namespace std;
```

tells the compiler where to look to find the header files in the absence of any further explicit designation. You can think of a namespace as a source-code file accessed by the compiler when it is looking for prewritten classes or functions. Because the `iostream` header file is contained within a namespace named `std`, the compiler will automatically use the `iostream`'s `cout` object from this namespace whenever `cout` is referenced. Using namespaces permits you to create your own classes and functions with the same names as those provided by the standard library and to place them in differently named namespaces. You can then tell the program which class or function to use by indicating the namespace where we want the compiler to look for the class or function.

The `using` statement is followed by the start of the program's `main()` function. This function begins with the header line developed at the beginning of this section. The body of the function, enclosed in braces, consists of only two statements. The first statement in `main()` passes one message to the `cout` object. The message is the string `"Hello there world!"`.

Because `cout` is an object of a prewritten class, we do not have to write it; it is available for use just by activating it correctly. Like all C++ objects, `cout` can only perform certain, well-defined actions. For `cout`, the action is to assemble data for output display. When a string of characters is passed to `cout`, the object sees to it that the string is correctly displayed on your monitor, as shown in Figure 2.6.

```
Hello there world!
```

Figure 2.6 The output from Program 2.1.

Strings in C++ are any combination of letters, numbers, and special characters enclosed in double quotes ("string in here"). The double quotes are used to delimit (mark) the beginning and ending of the string and are not considered part of the string. Thus, the string of characters making up the message sent to `cout` must be enclosed in double quotes, as we have done in Program 2.1.

Let us write another program to illustrate `cout`'s versatility. Read Program 2.2 to determine what it does.

Program 2.2

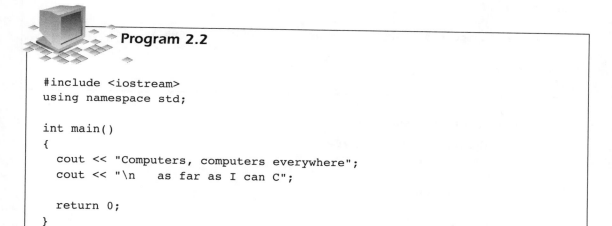

```
#include <iostream>
using namespace std;

int main()
{
  cout << "Computers, computers everywhere";
  cout << "\n   as far as I can C";

  return 0;
}
```

When Program 2.2 is run, the following is displayed:

```
Computers, computers everywhere
   as far as I can C
```

You might be wondering why the \n did not appear in the output. The two characters \ and n, when used together, are called a newline escape sequence. They tell `cout` to send instructions to the display device to move to a new line. In C++, the backslash (\) character provides an "escape" from the normal interpretation of the character following it by altering the meaning of the next character. If the backslash were omitted from the second `cout` statement in Program 2.2, the n would be printed as the letter n and the program would print out:

```
Computers, computers everywheren   as far as I can C
```

Newline escape sequences can be placed anywhere within the message passed to `cout`. See if you can determine the display produced by Program 2.3.

Program 2.3

```
#include <iostream>
using namespace std;

int main()
{
  cout << "Computers everywhere\n as far as\n\nI can see";

  return 0;
}
```

The output for Program 2.3 is:

```
Computers everywhere
 as far as

I can see
```

Exercises 2.1

1. State if the following are valid function names. If they are valid, state if they are mnemonic names. (Recall that a mnemonic function name conveys some idea about the function's purpose). If they are invalid names, state why.

power	density	m1234	newamp	1234	abcd
total	tangent	absval	computed	b34a	34ab
volts$	a2B3	while	minVal	sine	$sine
cosine	speed	netdistance	sum	return	stack

2. Assume that the following functions have been written:

   `getLength(),   getWidth(),   calcArea(),   displayArea()`

   a. From the functions' names, what do you think each function might do?
   b. In what order do you think a `main()` function might execute these functions (based on their names)?

3. Assume that the following functions have been written:

   `speed(),   distance(),   acceleration()`

   From the functions' names, what do you think each function might do?

4. Determine names for functions that do the following:
   a. Find the average of a set of numbers.
   b. Find the area of a rectangle.

c. Find the minimum value in a set of numbers.
d. Find the density of a steel door.
e. Sort a set of numbers from lowest to highest.

5. Just as the keyword `int` is used to signify that a function will return an integer, the keywords `void`, `char`, `float`, and `double` are used to signify that a function will return no value, a character, a single-precision number, and a double-precision number, respectively. Using this information, write header lines for a `main()` function that will receive no arguments but will return:

a. no value
b. a character
c. a single-precision number
d. a double-precision number

6. **a.** Using `cout`, write a C++ program that displays your name on one line, your street address on a second line, and your city, state, and zip code on a third line.

b. Run the program you have written for Exercise 6a on a computer. (*NOTE:* You must understand the procedures for entering and running a C++ program on the particular computer installation you are using.)

7. **a.** Write a C++ program to display the following:

```
The cosecant of an angle
   is equal to one over
     the sine of the angle.
```

b. Compile and run the program you have written for Exercise 7a on a computer.

8. **a.** How many `cout` statements would you use to display the following:

```
Degrees        Radians
0              0.0000
90             1.5708
180            3.1416
270            4.7124
360            6.2832
```

b. What is the minimum number of `cout` statements that could be used to print the table in Exercise 8a?

c. Write a complete C++ program to produce the output illustrated in Exercise 8a.

d. Run the program you have written for Exercise 8c on a computer.

9. In response to a newline escape sequence, `cout` positions the next displayed character at the beginning of a new line. This positioning of the next character actually represents two distinct operations. What are they?

10. a. Assuming a case-insensitive compiler, determine which of these program unit names are equivalent:

```
AVERAG    averag    MODE     BESSEL    Mode
Total     besseL    TeMp     Densty    TEMP
denSTY    MEAN      total    mean      moDE
```

b. Redo Exercise 10a assuming a case-sensitive compiler.

Project Structuring Exercises

Most projects, both programming and nonprogramming, can usually be structured into smaller subtasks or units of activity. These smaller subtasks can often be delegated to different people so that when all the tasks are finished and integrated, the project or program is completed. For Exercises 11 through 16, determine a set of subtasks that, taken together, complete the project. Be aware that there are many possible solutions for each exercise. The only requirement is that the set of subtasks selected, when taken together, complete the required task.

NOTE: The purpose of these exercises is to have you consider the different ways that complex tasks can be structured. Although there is no one correct solution to these exercises, there are incorrect solutions and solutions that are better than others. An incorrect solution is one that does not fully specify the task. One solution is better than another if it more clearly or easily identifies what must be done.

11. You are given the task of wiring and installing lights in the attic of your house. Determine a set of subtasks that, taken together, will accomplish this. (*Hint:* The first subtask would be to determine the placement of the light fixtures.)

12. You are given the job of preparing a complete meal for five people next weekend. Determine a set of subtasks that, taken together, accomplish this. (*Hint:* One subtask, not necessarily the first one, would be to buy the food.)

13. You are a sophomore in college and are planning to go to graduate school for a master's degree in electrical engineering after you graduate. List a set of major objectives that you must fulfill to meet this goal. (*Hint:* One subtask is "Determine the correct courses to take.")

14. You are given the job of planting a vegetable garden. Determine a set of subtasks that accomplish this. (*Hint:* One such subtask would be to plan the layout of the garden.)

15. You are responsible for planning and arranging the family camping trip this summer. List a set of subtasks that, taken together, accomplish this objective successfully. (*Hint:* One subtask would be to select the camp site.)

16. a. A national medical testing laboratory desires a new computer system to analyze its test results. The system must be capable of processing each day's results. Additionally, the laboratory wants the capability to retrieve and output a printed report of all results that meet certain criteria, for example, all results obtained for a particular doctor or all results obtained for hospitals in a particular state. Determine three or four major program units into which this system could be separated. (*Hint:* One possible program unit is "Prepare Daily Results" to create each day's reports.)

b. Suppose someone enters incorrect data for a particular test result, which is discovered after the data has been entered and stored by the system. What program unit is needed to take care of correcting this problem? Discuss why such a program unit might or might not be required by most systems.

c. Assume a program unit exists that allows a user to alter or change data that has been incorrectly entered and stored. Discuss the need for including an "audit trail" that would allow for a later reconstruction of the changes made, when they were made, and who made them.

2.2 Programming Style

C++ programs start execution at the beginning of the `main()` function. Because a program can have only one starting point, every C++ language program must contain one and only one `main()` function. As we have seen, all the statements that make up the `main()` function are then included within the braces `{}` following the function name. Although the `main()` function must be present in every C++ program, C++ does not require that the word main, the parentheses `()`, or the braces `{}` be placed in any particular form. The form used in the last section,

```
int main()
{
  program statements in here;

  return 0;
}
```

was chosen strictly for clarity and ease in reading the program. If one of the program statements uses the `cout` object, the `iostream` header file must be included, as well as the statement `using namespace std;`. For example, the following general form of a `main()` function would also work:

```
int main
 (
 ) { first statement;second statement;
          third statement;fourth
statement;
return 0;}
```

Notice that more than one statement can be put on a line, or one statement can be written across lines. Except for strings, double quotes, identifiers, and keywords, C++ ignores all white space. (White space refers to any combination of one or more blank spaces, tabs, or new lines.) For example, changing the white space in Program 2.1 and making sure not to split the string Hello there world! across two lines results in the following valid program:

```
#include <iostream>
using namespace std;

int main
(
){
cout <<
"Hello there world!";
 return 0;
}
```

Although this version of `main()` does work, it is an example of extremely poor programming style. It is difficult to read and understand. For readability, the `main()` function should always be written in standard form as:

```
int main()
{
  program statements in here;

  return 0;
}
```

In this standard form the function name starts in column 1 and is placed with the required parentheses on a line by itself. The opening brace of the function body follows on the next line and is placed under the first letter of the line containing the function name. Similarly, the closing function brace is placed by itself in column 1 as the last line of the function. This structure serves to highlight the function as a single unit.

Within the function itself, all program statements are indented at least two spaces. Indentation is another sign of good programming practice, especially if the same indentation is used for similar groups of statements. Review Program 1.2 to see that the same indentation was used for both `cout` object calls.

As you progress in your understanding and mastery of C++, you will develop your own indentation standards. Just keep in mind that the final form of your programs should be consistent and should always serve as an aid to the reading and understanding of your programs.

Comments

Comments are explanatory remarks made within a program. When used carefully, comments can be very helpful in clarifying what the complete program is about, what a specific group of statements is meant to accomplish, or what one line is intended to do. C++ supports two types of comments: line and block. Both types of comments can be placed anywhere within a program and have no effect on program execution. The compiler ignores all comments—they are there strictly for the convenience of anyone reading the program.

A **line comment** begins with two slashes (`//`) and continues to the end of the line. For example, the following lines are all line comments:

```
// this is a comment
// this program prints out a message
// this program calculates a square root
```

The symbols `//`, with no white space between them, designate the start of the line comment. The end of the line on which the comment is written designates the end of the comment.

A line comment can be written either on a line by itself or at the end of the same line containing a program statement. Program 2.4 illustrates the use of line comments within a program.

Program 2.4

```
// this program displays a message
#include <iostream>
using namespace std;

int main()
{
  cout << "Hello there world!"; // this produces the display

  return 0;
}
```

The first comment appears on a line by itself at the top of the program and describes what the program does. This is generally a good location to include a short comment describing the program's purpose. If more comments are required, they can be placed, one per line. Thus, when a comment is too long to be contained on one line, it can be separated into two or more line comments, with each separate comment preceded by the double slash symbol set `//`. The comment

```
// this comment is invalid because it
   extends over two lines
```

will result in a C++ error message on your computer. This comment is correct when written as

```
// this comment is used to illustrate a
// comment that extends across two lines
```

Comments that span across two or more lines are, however, more conveniently written as C-type block comments rather than as multiple line comments. **Block comments** begin with the symbols /* and end with the symbols */. For example,

```
/* This is a block comment that
   spans
   across three lines */
```

In C++, a program's structure is intended to make the program readable and understandable, making the use of extensive comments unnecessary. This is reinforced if function, class, and variable names, described in the next chapter, are carefully selected to convey their meaning to anyone reading the program. However, if the purpose of a function, class, or statement is still not clear from its structure, name, or context, include comments where clarification is needed. Obscure code with no comments is a sure sign of bad programming when the program must be maintained or read by others. Similarly, excessive comments are also a sign of bad programming, because they imply that insufficient thought was given to having the code itself be self-explanatory. Typically, any program that you write should begin with a set of initial program comments that include a short program description, your name, and the date that the program was last modified. For space considerations, and because all programs in this text were written by the author, initial comments will only be used for short program descriptions when they are not provided as part of the accompanying descriptive text.

Exercises 2.2

1. a. Will the following program work?

```
#include <iostream>
using namespace std;
int main() {cout << "Hello there world!"; return 0;}
```

   b. Why is the program given in Exercise 1a not a good program?

2. Rewrite the following programs to conform to good programming practice and correct syntax.

   a.
```
#include <iostream>
  int main(
  ){
  cout          <<
  "The time has come"
  ; return 0;}
```

   b.
```
#include <iostream>
using namespace std;
  int main
  (    ){cout << "Newark is a city\n";cout <<
  "In New Jersey\n"; cout <<
  "It is also a city\n"
  ; cout << "In Delaware\n"
  ; return 0;}
```

c.
```
#include <iostream>
using namespace std;
 int main() {cout << Reading a program\n";cout <<
 "is much easier\n"
 ; cout << "if a standard form for main is used\n")
 ; cout
 <<"and each statement is written\n";cout
 <<           "on a line by itself\n")
 ; return 0;}
```

d.
```
#include <iostream.h>
using namespace std;
 int main
 (     ){ cout << "Every C++ program"
 ; cout
 <<"\nmust have one and only one"
 ;
 cout << "main function"
 ;
 cout <<
 "\n the escape sequence of characters")
 ; cout <<
   "\nfor a newline can be placed anywhere"
 ; cout
 <<"\n within the message passed to cout"
 ; return 0;}
```

3. a. When used in a message, the backslash character alters the meaning of the character immediately following it. If we wanted to print the backslash character, we would have to tell `cout` to escape from the way it normally interprets the backslash. What character do you think is used to alter the way a single backslash character is interpreted?
   b. Using your answer to Exercise 3a, write the escape sequence for printing a backslash.

4. a. A **token** of a computer language is any sequence of characters that, as a unit, with no intervening characters or white space, has a unique meaning. Using this definition of a token, determine if escape sequences, function names, and the keywords listed in Table 1.2 are tokens of the C++ language.
   b. Discuss whether adding white space to a message alters the message. Discuss if messages can be considered tokens of C++.
   c. Using the definition of a token given in Exercise 4a, determine if the following statement is true: "Except for tokens of the language, C++ ignores all white space."

2.3 DATA TYPES

The objective of all programs is to process data, be it numerical, alphabetical, audio, or video. Central to this objective is the classification of data into specific types. For example, calculating a rocket's trajectory requires mathematical operations on numerical data, and alphabetizing a list of names requires comparison operations on character-based data. Additionally, some operations are not applicable to certain types of data. For example, it makes no sense to add names together. To prevent programmers from attempting to perform an inappropriate operation, C++ allows only certain operations to be performed on certain data types.

The types of data permitted and the appropriate operations defined for each type are referred to as a data type. Formally, a **data type** is defined as a set of values *and* a set of operations that can be applied to these values. For example, the set of all integer (whole) numbers constitutes a set of values, as does the set of all real numbers (numbers that contain a decimal point). These two sets of numbers, however, do not constitute a data type until a set of operations is included. These operations, of course, are the mathematical and comparison operations. The combination of a set of values plus operations becomes a true data type.

C++ categorizes data types into one of two fundamental groupings: class data types and built-in data types. A **class data type**, which is referred to as a class, for short, is a programmer-created data type. This means the set of acceptable values and operations is defined by a programmer, using C++ code.

A **built-in data type** is provided as an integral part of the C++ compiler and requires no external C++ code. Thus, a built-in data type can be used without recourse to supplementary language additions, such as that provided by the `iostream` header file needed for the `cout` object. Built-in data types, which are also referred to as **primitive** types, consist of the basic numerical types shown in Figure 2.7 and the operations listed in Table 2.2. As seen in this table, the majority of operations for built-in types are provided as symbols. This is in contrast to class types, where the majority of operations are provided as functions.

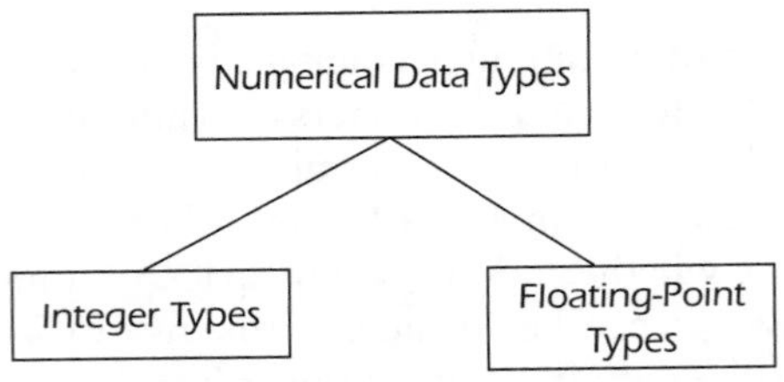

Figure 2.7 Built-in data types.

Table 2.2 Built-In Data Type Operations

Built-In Data Types	Operations

`Integer`	`+, -, *, /,`
	`%, =, ==, !=,`
	`<=, >=vsizeof(),`
	`and bit operations`
	(see Chapter 15)

`Floating Point`	`+, -, *, /,`
	`=, ==, !=,`
	`<=, >=, sizeof()`

In introducing C++'s built-in data types, we will use literals. A **literal** is an acceptable value for a data type. The term **literal** reflects that such a value explicitly identifies itself. (Another name for a literal is a **literal value** or **constant**.) For example, all numbers, such as 2, 3.6, and -8.2, are referred to as literal values because they literally display their values. Text, such as `"Hello World!"` is also referred to as a literal value because the text is displayed. You have been using literal values throughout your life and have commonly referred to them as numbers and words. In Section 2.5, you will see some examples of non-literal values, that is, values that do not display themselves but are stored and accessed using identifiers.

Integer Data Types

C++ provides nine built-in integer data types, as shown in Figure 2.8. The essential difference among the various integer data types is the amount of storage used for each type, which affects the range of values that each type is capable of representing. The three most important types used almost exclusively in the majority of applications are the `int`, `char`, and `bool` data types. The reason for the remaining types is historical, as they were provided to accommodate special situations (a small or a large range of numbers). This permitted a programmer to maximize memory usage by selecting a data type that used the smallest amount of memory consistent with an application's requirements. When computer memories were small relative to today's computers and expensive, this was a major concern. Although no longer a concern for most programs, these types still provide a programmer the ability to optimize memory usage when necessary. Typically, these situations occur in engineering applications, such as control systems used in home appliances and automobiles.

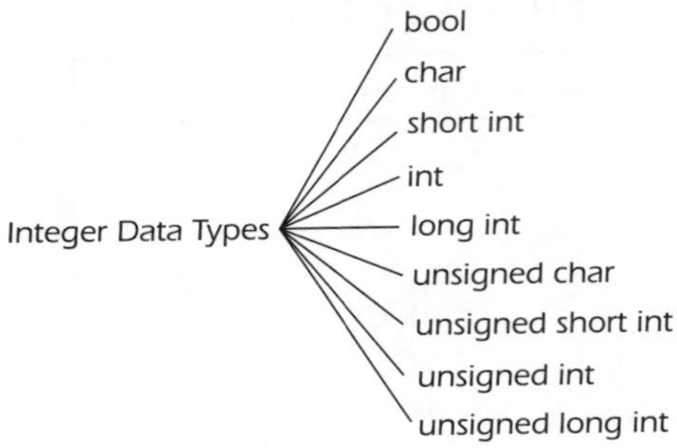

Figure 2.8 C++ integer data types.

The `int` Data Type

The set of values supported by the `int` data type are whole numbers, which are mathematically known as integers. An integer value consists of digits only and can optionally be preceded by a plus (+) or minus (–) sign. Thus, an integer value can be the number zero or any positive or negative numerical value without a decimal point. Examples of valid integers are:

0 5 –10 +25 1000 253 –26351 +36

As these examples illustrate, integers may contain an explicit sign. No commas, decimal points, or special symbols, such as the dollar sign, are allowed. Examples of invalid integers are:

$255.62 2,523 3. 6,243,892 1,492.89 +6.0

Different compilers have their own internal limit on the largest (most positive) and smallest (most negative) integer values that can be stored in each data type[6]. The most common storage allocation is four bytes for the `int` data type, which restricts the set of values permitted in this data type to represent integers in the range of `-2,147,483,648` to `2,147,483,647`.[7]

The `char` Data Type

The `char` data type is used to store individual characters. Characters include the letters of the alphabet (uppercase and lowercase), the ten digits 0 through 9, and special symbols such as the following: + $. , – and !. A single character value is any one letter, digit, or special symbol enclosed by single quotes. Examples of valid character values are the following:

`'A'` `'$'` `'b'` `'7'` `'y'` `'!'` `'M'` `'q'`

[6]The limits imposed by the compiler can be found in the `limits` header file and are defined as the hexadecimal constants `int_max` and `int_min`.

[7]In all cases, the magnitude of the most negative integer number is always one more than the magnitude of the most positive integer. This is due to the two's complement method of integer storage, which is described in Section 1.6.

Point of Information

Atomic Data

An **atomic data value** is a value considered a complete entity by itself and cannot be decomposed into a smaller data type. For example, although an integer can be decomposed into individual digits, C++ does not have a numerical digit type. Rather, each integer is regarded as a complete value by itself and, as such, is considered atomic data. Similarly, because the integer data type supports only atomic data values, it is said to be an **atomic data type**. As you might expect, all the built-in data types are atomic data types.

Character values are typically stored in a computer using the ASCII or Unicode codes. ASCII, pronounced AS-KEY, is an acronym for American Standard Code for Information Interchange. The ASCII code provides codes for an English language-based character set plus codes for printer and display control, such as new line and printer paper eject codes. Each character code is contained within a single byte, which provides for 256 distinct codes. Table 2.3 lists the ASCII byte codes for uppercase letters.

Additionally, C++ provides for the newer Unicode character set that uses two bytes per character and can represent 65,536 characters. This code is used for international applications by providing other language character sets in addition to English. As the first 256 Unicode codes have the same numerical value as the 256 ASCII codes (the additional byte is coded with all 0s), you need not concern yourself with which storage code is used when using English language characters.

Table 2.3 The ASCII Uppercase Letter Codes

Letter	ASCII Code	Letter	ASCII Code
A	01000001	N	01001110
B	01000010	O	01001111
C	01000011	P	01010000
D	01000100	Q	01010001
E	01000101	R	01010010
F	01000110	S	01010011
G	01000111	T	01010100
H	01001000	U	01010101
I	01001001	V	01010110
J	01001010	W	01010111
K	01001011	X	01011000
L	01001100	Y	01011001
M	01001101	Z	01011010

Using Table 2.3, we can determine how the characters 'B', 'A', 'R', 'T', 'E', and 'R', for example, are stored inside a computer using the ASCII character code. This sequence of six characters requires six bytes of storage (one byte for each letter) and would be stored as illustrated in Figure 2.9.

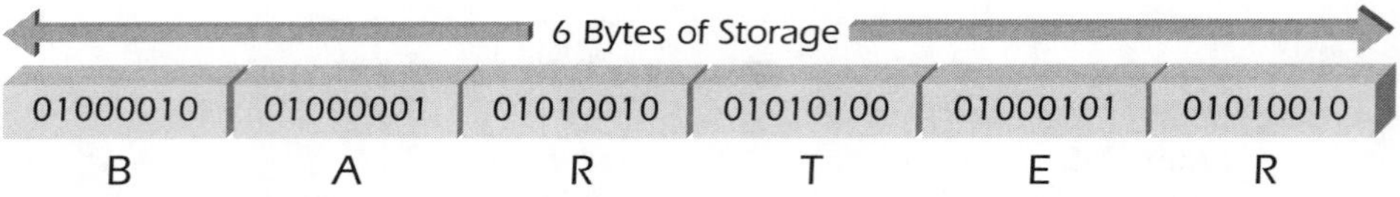

Figure 2.9 The letters BARTER stored inside a computer.

The Escape Character

One character that has a special meaning in C++ is the backslash, \, which is referred to as the **escape character**. When this character is placed directly in front of a select group of characters, it tells the compiler to escape from the way these characters would normally be interpreted. The combination of a backslash and these specific characters is called an **escape sequence**. We have encountered an example of this in the newline escape sequence, `'\n'`, in Chapter 1. Table 2.4 lists C++'s most common escape sequences.

Table 2.4 Escape Sequences

Escape Sequence	Character Represented	Meaning	ASCII Code
`\n`	Newline	Move to a new line	`00001010`
`\t`	Horizontal tab	Move to next horizontal tab setting	`00001001`
`\v`	Vertical tab	Move to next vertical tab setting	`00001011`
`\b`	Backspace	Move back one space	`00001000`
`\r`	Carriage return	Moves the cursor to the start of the current line; used for overprinting	`00001101`
`\f`	Form Feed	Issue a form feed	`00001100`
`\a`	Alert	Issue an alert (usually a bell sound)	`00000111`
`\\`	Backslash	Insert a backslash character (this is used to place an actual backslash character within a string)	`01011100`
`\?`	Question mark	Insert a question mark character	`00111111`
`\'`	Single quotation	Insert a single-quote character (this is used to place an inner single quote within a set of outer single quotes)	`00100111`
`\"`	Double quotation mark	Insert a double-quote character (this is used to place an inner double quote within a set of outer double quotes	`00100010`
`\nnn`	Octal number	The number `nnn` (`n` is a digit) is to be considered an octal number	—
`\xhhhh`	Hexadecimal number	The number `hhhh` (`h` is a digit) is to be considered a hexadecimal number	—
`\0`	Null character	Insert the Null character, which is defined as having the value 0	`00000000`

Although each escape sequence listed in Table 2.4 is made up of two distinct characters, the combination of the two characters, with no intervening white space, causes the compiler to create the single code listed in the ASCII code column of Table 2.4.

The `bool` Data Type

In C++, the `bool` data type is used to represent Boolean (logical) data. As such, this data type is restricted to one of two values: `true` or `false`. This data type is most useful when a program must examine a specific condition and, because of the condition being true or false, take a prescribed course of action. For example, in a sales application, the condition being examined might be "is the total purchase for $100 or more." Only when this condition is true is a discount applied. Because a Boolean data type uses an integer storage code, however, it has useful implications exploited by almost all professional C++ programmers. The practical uses of Boolean conditions are considered in Chapter 4, so we defer further discussion of Boolean data until then.

Determining Storage Size

A unique feature of C++ is that it permits you to see where and how values are stored. As an example, C++ provides an operator named `sizeof()` that provides the number of bytes used to store values for any data type name included within the operator's parentheses. (Review Section 1.6 if you are unfamiliar with the concept of a byte.) This is a built-in operator that does not use an arithmetic symbol to perform its operation. Program 2.5 uses this operator to determine the amount of storage reserved for the `int`, `char`, and `bool` data types.

Program 2.5

```
#include <iostream>
using namespace std;

int main()
{
  cout << "\nData Type  Bytes"
       << "\n---------  -----"
       << "\nint           " << sizeof(int)
       << "\nchar          " << sizeof(char)
       << "\nbool          " << sizeof(bool)
       << '\n';

    return 0;
}
```

Point of Information

The Character `'\n'` and the String `"\n"`

Both `'\n'` and `"\n"` are recognized by the compiler as containing the newline character. The difference is in the data types being used. Formally, `'\n'` is a character literal, while `"\n"` is a string literal. From a practical standpoint, both cause the same thing to happen: A new line is forced on the output display. In encountering the character value `'\n'`, however, the compiler translates it using the single byte code 00001010 (see Table 2.4). In encountering the string value `"\n"`, the compiler translates this string using the correct character code but also adds an extra, end-of-string character, which is `'\0'`.

Good programming practice requires that you end the last output display with a newline escape sequence. This ensures that the first line of output from one program does not end up on the last line displayed by the previously executed program

In reviewing Program 2.5, notice that a single character value is inserted into `cout` by enclosing it within single quotation marks, as is the escape sequence `'\n'` insertion at the end of the `cout` statement. Within the first five displayed lines, this character is included within each output string. Each time the compiler encounters the newline escape sequence, as a single character or as part of a string, it is translated as a single character that forces the display to start on a new line. Although double quotation marks can be used for the final newline insertion, as `"\n"`, this would designate a string. Because only a single character is being transmitted, and to emphasize that single characters are designated using single quotation marks, we have used `'\n'` in place of `"\n"`. From a practical standpoint, however, both notations will force a new line in the display.

The output of Program 2.5 is compiler dependent. That is to say, each compiler will correctly report the amount of storage that it provides for the data type under consideration. When run on the author's computer, which uses Microsoft's current Visual C++.net compiler, the following output was produced:

```
Data Type  Bytes
---------  -----
int          4
char         1
bool         1
```

For this output, which is the typical storage provided by almost all current C++ compilers, we can determine the range of values that can be stored in each of these `int` data types. To do so, however, requires understanding the difference between a signed and unsigned data type.

Point of Information

Object-Oriented and Procedural Programs

Except for the Boolean type, all of C++'s built-in data types are direct carryovers from the C procedural language. Not surprisingly, programs using only individual built-in types will not be object-oriented programs. Rather, as in Program 2.5, they become procedural programs, that is, a program primarily based on procedures, such as `main()`.

It is only when built-in types are bundled together to form a packet of data, which becomes an object, can an object-oriented program come into existence.

Signed and Unsigned Data Types

A **signed data type** is defined as one that permits storing negative values in addition to zero and positive values. As such, the `int` data type is a signed data type. An **unsigned data type** is one that provides only for non-negative (that is, zero and positive) values.

There are cases, however, where an application might only require unsigned numerical values. For example, many date applications store dates in the numerical form *yearmonthday* (thus, the date 12/25/2007 would be stored as 20071225) and are only concerned with dates after 0 CE. For such applications, which will never require a negative value, an unsigned data type can be used.

All unsigned integer types, such as `unsigned int`, provide a range of positive values that is, for all practical purposes, double the range provided for its signed counterpart. This extra positive range is made available by using the negative range of its signed version for additional positive numbers.

With the understanding of the difference between a signed and unsigned data type, Table 2.5 can be used to determine the range of integer values supported by current C++ compilers.

In Table 2.5, a `long int` uses the same amount of storage (four bytes) as an `int`. The only requirement of the ANSI C++ standard is that an `int` must provide at least as much storage as a `short int`, and a `long int` must provide at least as much storage as an `int`. On the first desktop computer systems (1980s), which were limited in their memory capacity to thousands of bytes, a `short int` typically used one byte of storage, an `int` two bytes, and a `long int` four bytes. This storage limited the range of `int` values from –32,768 to +32,767, while the use of an `unsigned int` provided a range of values from 0 to 65,535, thus doubling the number of possible positive values, which was significant. With the current range of `int` values in the –2 to +2 billion range, the doubling of positive values is rarely a consideration. Additionally, using a `long int` becomes unnecessary because it is uses the same storage capacity as an `int`.

Table 2.5 Integer Data Type Storage

Name of Data Type	Storage Size (in bytes)	Range of Values
`char`	1	256 characters
`bool`	1	true (which is considered as any positive value) and false (which is a zero)
`short int`	2	–32,768 to +32,767
`unsigned short int`	2	0 to 65,535
`int`	4	–2,147,483,648 to +2,147,483,647
`unsigned int`	4	0 to 4,294,967,295
`long int`	4	–2,147,483,648 to +2,147,483,647
`unsigned long int`	4	0 to 4,294,967,295

Floating-Point Types

A **floating-point number**, which is called a **real number**, can be the number zero or any positive or negative number that contains a decimal point. Examples of floating-point numbers are the following:

```
+10.625   5.   -6.2   3251.92   0.0   0.33   -6.67   +2.
```

The numbers 5., 0.0, and +2. are classified as floating-point values, but the same numbers written without a decimal point (5, 0, +2) would be integer values. As with integer values, special symbols such as the dollar sign and the comma are not permitted in real numbers. Examples of invalid real numbers are the following:

```
5,326.25   24   6,459   $10.29   7.007.645
```

C++ supports three floating-point data types: `float`, `double`, and `long double`. The difference between these data types is the amount of storage that a compiler uses for each type. Most compilers use twice the amount of storage for doubles than for floats, which allows a `double` to have approximately twice the precision of a `float.` For this reason, a `float` value is sometimes referred to as a **single-precision** number and a `double` value as a **double-precision** number. The actual storage allocation for each data type, however, depends on the particular compiler. The ANSI C++ standard only requires that a `double` has at least the same amount of precision as a `float` and a `long double` has at least the same amount of storage as a `double.` Currently, most C++ compilers allocate four bytes for the `float` data type and eight bytes for `double` and `long double` data types. This produces the range of numbers listed in Table 2.6.

Table 2.6 Floating-Point Data Types

Type	Storage	Absolute Range of Values (+ and –)

`float`	`4 bytes`	`1.40129846432481707e-45`
		`to`
		`3.40282346638528860e+38`

`double and`
`long double`
	`8 bytes`	`4.94065645841246544e-324`
		`to`
		`1.79769313486231570e+308`

In compilers that use the same amount of storage for `double` and `long double` numbers, these two data types become identical. (The `sizeof()` operator that was used in Program 2.5 can always be used to determine the amount of storage reserved by your compiler for these data types.) A `float` literal is indicated by appending an f or F after the number and a `long double` is created by appending an l or L to the number. In the absence of these suffixes, a floating-point number defaults to a `double`. For example, see the following:

9.234 indicates a double literal
9.234F indicates a float literal
9.234L indicates a long double literal

The only difference in these numbers is the amount of storage the computer may use to store them. Appendix C describes the binary storage format used for floating-point numbers and its impact on number precision.

Exponential Notation

Floating-point numbers can be written in exponential notation, which is similar to scientific notation and is commonly used to express large and small values in compact form. The following examples illustrate how numbers with decimals can be expressed in exponential and scientific notation:

Decimal Notation	Exponential Notation	Scientific Notation
1625.	1.625e3	1.625×10^3
63421.	6.3421e4	6.3421×10^4
.00731	7.31e-3	7.31 x 10-3
.000625	6.25e-4	6.25 x 10-4

In exponential notation, the letter e stands for exponent. The number following the e represents a power of 10 and indicates the number of places the decimal point should be moved to obtain the standard decimal value. The decimal point is moved to the right if the number after the e is positive or moved to the left if the number after the e is negative. For example, the e3 in 1.625e3 means move the decimal place three places to the right so the number becomes 1625. The e–3 in 7.31e–3 means move the decimal point three places to the left so that 7.31e–3 becomes .00731.

Point of Information

What Is Precision?

In numerical theory, the term **precision** typically refers to numerical accuracy. In this context, a statement such as "this computation is accurate, or precise, to the fifth decimal place" is used. This means that the fifth digit after the decimal point has been rounded, and the number is accurate to within ±0.00005.

In computer programming, precision can refer to the accuracy of a number or the amount of significant digits in the number, where significant digits are defined as the number of clearly correct digits plus 1. For example, if the number 12.6874 has been rounded to the fourth decimal place, it is correct to say that this number is precise (that is, accurate) to the fourth decimal place. In other words, all of the digits in the number are accurate except the fourth decimal digit, which has been rounded. Similarly, this same number has a precision of six digits, which means that the first five digits are correct and the sixth digit has been rounded. Another way of saying this is that the number 12.6874 has six significant digits.

The significant digits in a number need not have any relation to the number of displayed digits. For example, if the number 687.45678921 has five significant digits, it is only accurate to the value 687.46, where the last digit is assumed to be rounded. In a similar manner, dollar values in many large financial applications are frequently rounded to the nearest hundred thousand dollars. In such applications, a displayed dollar value of $12,400,000, for example, is not accurate to the closest dollar. If this value is specified as having three significant digits, it is only accurate to the hundred-thousand digit.

Exercises 2.3

1. Determine data types appropriate for the following data:
   a. the average of four grades
   b. the number of days in a month
   c. the length of the Golden Gate Bridge
   d. the numbers in a state lottery
   e. the distance from Brooklyn, N.Y., to Newark, N.J.
   f. the single-character prefix that specifies a component type
2. Convert the following numbers into standard decimal form:

   6.34e5 1.95162e2 8.395e1 2.95e–3 4.623e–4
3. Write the following decimal numbers using exponential notation:

   126. 656.23 3426.95 4893.2 .321 .0123 .006789
4. Compile and execute Program 2.5 on your computer.
5. Modify Program 2.5 to determine the storage used by your compiler for all of C++'s integer data types.

6. Using the system reference manuals for your computer, determine the character code used by your computer.

7. Show how the name KINGSLEY would be stored inside a computer that uses the ASCII code. That is, draw a figure similar to Figure 2.9 for the name KINGSLEY.

8. Repeat Exercise 7 using the letters of your own last name.

9. Modify Program 2.5 to determine how many bytes your compiler assigns to the `float`, `double`, and `long double` data types.

10. Because computers use different representations for storing integer, floating-point, double-precision, and character values, discuss how a program might alert the computer to the data types of the various values it will be using.

11. Although we have concentrated on operations involving integer and floating-point numbers, C++ allows characters and integers to be added or subtracted. This can be done because a character is stored using an integer code (it is an integer data type.) Thus, characters and integers can be freely mixed in arithmetic expressions. For example, if your computer uses the ASCII code, the expression 'a' + 1 equals 'b', and 'z' – 1 equals 'y'. Similarly, 'A' + 1 is 'B', and 'Z' – 1 is 'Y'. With this as background, determine the character results of the following expressions. (Assume that all characters are stored using the ASCII code.)
    a. 'm' – 5
    b. 'm' + 5
    c. 'G' + 6
    d. 'G' – 6
    e. 'b' – 'a'
    f. 'g' – 'a' + 1
    g. 'G' – 'A' + 1

NOTE: *To complete the following exercise, you need an understanding of basic computer storage concepts. Specifically, if you are unfamiliar with the concept of a byte, refer to Section 1.6 before doing the next exercise.*

12. Although the total number of bytes varies from computer to computer, memory sizes of 65,536 to more than several million bytes are common. In computer language, the letter K represents the number 1,024, which is 2 raised to the 10th power, and M represents the number 1,048,576, which is 2 raised to the 20th power. Thus, a memory size of 640K is really 640 times 1024, or 655,360 bytes, and a memory size of 4M is really 4 times 1,048,576, which is 4,194,304 bytes. Using this information, calculate the actual number of bytes in the following:
    a. a memory containing 128M bytes
    b. a memory containing 256M bytes
    c. a memory containing 512M bytes
    d. a memory consisting of 256M words, where each word consists of 2 bytes
    e. a memory consisting of 256M words, where each word consists of 4 bytes
    f. a disk that specifies 1.44M bytes
    g. a disk that specified 250MB

2.4 ARITHMETIC OPERATIONS

The previous section presented the data values corresponding to each of C++'s built-in data types. In this section, the set of arithmetic operations that can be applied to these values is provided.

Integers and real numbers can be added, subtracted, multiplied, and divided. Although it is usually better not to mix integers and real numbers when performing arithmetic operations, predictable results are obtained when using different data types in the same arithmetic expression. Surprisingly, you can add character data to, or subtract it from, character and integer data to produce useful results. (For example, 'A' + 1 results in the character 'B'.) This is possible because characters are stored using integer storage codes.

The operators used for arithmetic operations are called **arithmetic operators** and are as follows:

Operation	Operator
Addition	+
Subtraction	–
Multiplication	*
Division	/
Modulus Division	%

Do not be concerned at this stage if you do not understand the term "modulus division." You will learn more about this operator later in this section.

These operators are referred to as **binary operators**. This term reflects that the operator requires two operands to produce a result. An **operand** can be a literal value or an identifier that has a value associated with it. A **simple binary arithmetic expression** consists of a binary arithmetic operator connecting two literal values in the form:

`literalValue` *`operator`* `literalValue`

Examples of simple binary arithmetic expressions are the following:

```
3 + 7
18 - 3
12.62 + 9.8
.08 * 12.2
12.6 / 2.
```

The spaces around the arithmetic operators in these examples are inserted strictly for clarity and can be omitted without affecting the value of the expression. An expression in C++ must be entered in a straight-line form. Thus, for example, the C++ expression equivalent to 12.6 divided by 2 must be entered as 12.6 / 2 and not as the algebraic expression

$$\frac{12.6}{2}$$

You can use cout to display the value of any arithmetic expression on the console screen. To do this, the desired value must be passed to the object. For example, the statement yields the display 21:

```
cout << (6 + 15);
```

Strictly speaking, the parentheses surrounding the expression 6 + 15 are not required to indicate that the value of the expression (that is, 21) is being displayed.[8] In addition to displaying a numerical value, cout can display a string identifying the output, as was done in Section 1.3. For example, the statement causes two pieces of data, a string and a value, to be sent to cout:

```
cout << "The sum of 6 and 15 is " <<  (6 + 15);
```

Individually, each set of data sent to cout must be preceded by its own insertion operator symbol (<<). Here, the first data sent for display is the string "The sum of 6 and 15 is ", and the second item sent is the value of the expression 6 + 15. The display produced by this statement is the following:

```
The sum of 6 and 15 is 21
```

The space between the word "is" and the number 21 is caused by the space placed within the string passed to cout. As far as cout is concerned, its input is a set of characters that are sent on to be displayed in the order they are received. Characters from the input are queued, one behind the other, and sent to the console for display. Placing a space in the input causes this space to be part of the stream of characters that is displayed. For example, examine the following statement:

```
cout << "The sum of 12.2 and 15.754 is " <<  (12.2 + 15.754);
```

It yields the following display:

```
The sum of 12.2 and 15.754 is 27.954
```

When multiple insertions are made to cout, the code can be spread across multiple lines. Only one semicolon, however, must be used, which is placed after the last insertion and terminates the complete statement. Thus, the prior display is produced by the following statement:

```
cout << "The sum of 12.2 and 15.754 is "
     <<  (12.2 + 15.754);
```

However, when you allow such a statement to span multiple lines, two rules must be followed: A string contained within double quotation marks cannot be split across lines and the terminating semicolon should appear only on the last line. Multiple insertion symbols can always be placed within a line.

Floating-point numbers are displayed with sufficient decimal places to the right of the decimal place to accommodate the fractional part of the number. This is true if the number has six or fewer decimal digits. If the number has more than six decimal digits,

[8]This is because the + operator has a higher precedence than the << operator; thus, the addition is performed before the insertion.

the fractional part is rounded to six decimal digits, and if the number has no decimal digits, neither a decimal point nor any decimal digits will be displayed.[9]

Program 2.6 illustrates using `cout` to display the results of arithmetic expressions within the statements of a complete program.

Program 2.6

```
#include <iostream>
using namespace std;

int main()
{
  cout << "15.0 plus 2.0 equals "       << (15.0 + 2.0) << endl
       << "15.0 minus 2.0 equals "      << (15.0 - 2.0) << endl
       << "15.0 times 2.0 equals "      << (15.0 * 2.0) << endl
       << "15.0 divided by 2.0 equals " << (15.0 / 2.0) << endl;

  return 0;
}
```

The output of Program 2.6 is the following:

```
15.0 plus 2.0 equals 17
15.0 minus 2.0 equals 13
15.0 times 2.0 equals 30
15.0 divided by 2.0 equals 7.5
```

The only new item presented in Program 2.6 is the term `endl`, which is an example of a C++ manipulator. A **manipulator** is an item used to manipulate how the output stream of characters is displayed. In particular, the `endl` manipulator first causes a newline character (`'\n'`) to be inserted into the display and forces all of the current insertions to be displayed immediately, rather than waiting for more data. (Section 3.2 contains a list of the more commonly used manipulators.)

Expression Types

An **expression** is any combination of operators and operands that can be evaluated to yield a value. An expression that contains only integer values as operands is called an **integer expression**, and the result of the expression is an integer value. Similarly, an expression containing only floating-point values (single-precision and double-precision) as operands is called a **floating-point expression**, and the result of such an expression is

[9] None of this output is defined as part of the C++ language. Rather, it is defined by a set of classes and routines provided with each C++ compiler.

a floating-point value (the term **real expression** is also used). An expression containing integer and floating-point values is called a **mixed-mode expression.** Although it is usually better not to mix integer and floating-point values in an arithmetic operation, the data type of each operation is determined by the following rules:

1. If both operands are integers, the result of the operation is an integer.
2. If one operand is a real value, the result of the operation is a double-precision value.

The result of an arithmetic expression is never a single-precision (`float`) number. This is because, during execution, a C++ program temporarily converts all single-precision numbers to double-precision numbers when an arithmetic expression is being evaluated.

Integer Division

The division of two integer values can produce rather strange results for the unwary. For example, the expression 15/2 yields the integer result 7. Because integers cannot contain a fractional part, a value of 7.5 cannot be obtained. The fractional part obtained when two integers are divided, that is, the remainder, is always dropped (truncated). Thus, the value of 9/4 is 2, and 20/3 is 6.

Often, however, we may need to retain the remainder of an integer division. To do this, C++ provides an arithmetic operator having the symbol %. This operator, called the **modulus** (and also referred to as the **remainder operator**), captures the remainder when an integer number is divided by an integer (using a non-integer value with the modulus operator results in a compiler error):

```
 9 % 4 is 1  (that is, the remainder when 9 is divided by 4 is 1)
17 % 3 is 2  (that is, the remainder when 17 is divided by 3 is 2)
15 % 4 is 3  (that is, the remainder when 15 is divided by the 4 is 3)
14 % 2 is 0  (that is, the remainder when 14 is divided by 2 is 0)
```

More precisely, the modulus operator first determines the integer number of times that the dividend, which is the number following the % operator, can be divided into the divisor, which is the number before the % operator. It then returns the remainder.

Negation

In addition to the binary arithmetic operators, C++ provides unary operators. A **unary operator** operates on a single operand. One of these unary operators uses the same symbol as binary subtraction (–). The minus sign in front of a single numerical value negates (reverses the sign of) the number.

Table 2.7 summarizes the six arithmetic operations we have described so far and lists the data type for the result produced by each operator, based on the data type of the operands involved.

Point of Information

The `endl` Manipulator

On many systems, the `endl` manipulator and the `\n` escape sequence are processed in the same way and produce the same effect. The one exception is on those systems where the output is accumulated internally until sufficient characters collect to make it advantageous to display them all in one burst on the screen. In such systems, which are referred to as "buffered," the `endl` manipulator forces all accumulated output to be displayed immediately, without waiting for any additional characters to fill the buffer area before being printed. As a practical matter, you would not notice a difference in the final display. Thus, as a general rule, you should use the `\n` escape sequence whenever it can be included within an existing string and use the `endl` manipulator whenever a `\n` would appear by itself or to formally signify the end of a specific group of output display.

Table 2.7 Summary of Arithmetic Operators

Operation	Operator	Type	Operand	Result
Addition	+	Binary	Both are integers One operand is not an integer	Integer Double-precision
Subtraction	-	Binary	Both are integers One operand is not an integer	Integer Double-precision
Multiplication	*	Binary	Both are integers One operand is not an integer	Integer Double-precision
Division	/	Binary	Both are integers One operand is not an integer	Integer Double-precision
Modulus	%	Binary	Both are integers One operand is not an integer	Integer Double-precision
Negation	-	Unary	Integer or double	Same as operand

Operator Precedence and Associativity

In addition to such simple expressions as 5 + 12 and .08 * 26.2, more complex arithmetic expressions can be created. C++, like most other programming languages, requires you to follow certain rules when writing expressions containing more than one arithmetic operator. These rules are the following:

1. Two binary arithmetic operator symbols must never be placed side by side. For example, 5 * % 6 is invalid because the two operators, * and %, are placed next to each other.

2. Parentheses may be used to form groupings, and all expressions enclosed within parentheses are evaluated first. This permits parentheses to alter the evaluation to any desired order. For example, in the expression (6 + 4) / (2 + 3), the 6 + 4 and 2 + 3 are evaluated first to yield 10 / 5. The 10 / 5 is then evaluated to yield 2.

3. Sets of parentheses may be enclosed by other parentheses. For example, the expression (2 * (3 + 7)) / 5 is valid and evaluates to 4. When parentheses are included within parentheses, the expressions in the innermost parentheses are always evaluated first. The evaluation continues from innermost to outermost parentheses until the expressions in all parentheses have been evaluated. The number of closing parentheses,), must always equal the number of opening parentheses, (, so no unpaired sets exist.

4. Parentheses cannot be used to indicate multiplication; rather, the multiplication operator, *, must be used. For example, the expression (3 + 4) (5 + 1) is invalid. The correct expression is (3 + 4) * (5 + 1).

Parentheses should specify logical groupings of operands and indicate clearly, to the compiler and programmers, the intended order of arithmetic operations. Although expressions within parentheses are always evaluated first, expressions containing multiple operators, within and without parentheses, are evaluated by the priority, or **precedence**, of the operators. There are three levels of precedence:

- P1—All negations are done first.
- P2—Multiplication, division, and modulus operations are computed next. Expressions containing more than one multiplication, division, or modulus operator are evaluated from left to right as each operator is encountered. For example, in the expression 35 / 7 % 3 * 4, the operations are all of the same priority, so the operations will be performed from left to right as each operator is encountered. Thus, the division is done first, yielding the expression 5 % 3 * 4. The modulus operation is performed next, yielding a result of 2. Finally, the value of 2 * 4 is computed to yield 8.
- P3—Addition and subtraction are computed last. Expressions containing more than one addition or subtraction are evaluated from left to right as each operator is encountered.

In addition to precedence, operators have an **associativity**, which is the order in which operators of the same precedence are evaluated, as described in rule P2. For example, does the expression 6.0 * 6 / 4 yield 9.0, which is (6.0 * 6)/4: or 6.0, which is 6.0 * (6/4)? The answer is 9.0, because C++'s operators use the same associativity as in general mathematics, which evaluates multiplication from left to right, as rule P2 indicates. Table 2.8 lists the precedence and associativity of the operators considered in this section. As we have seen, the precedence of an operator establishes its priority relative to all other operators. Operators at the top of Table 2.8 have a higher priority than operators at the bottom of the table. In expressions with multiple operators of different precedence, the operator with the higher precedence is used before an operator with lower precedence. For example, in the expression 6 + 4 / 2 + 3, because the division operator has a higher precedence (P2) than addition, the division is done first, yielding an intermediate result of 6 + 2 + 3. The additions are then performed, left to right, to yield a final result of 11.

Table 2.8 Operator Precedence and Associativity

Operator	Associativity
unary -	right to left
* / %	left to right
+ -	left to right

Finally, let us use Table 2.8 or the precedence rules to evaluate an expression containing operators of different precedence, such as 8 + 5 * 7 % 2 * 4. Because the multiplication and modulus operators have a higher precedence than the addition operator, these two operations are evaluated first (P2), using their left-to-right associativity, before the addition is evaluated (P3). Thus, the complete expression is evaluated as the following:

```
8 + 5 * 7 % 2 * 4 =
   8 + 35 % 2 * 4 =
        8 + 1 * 4 =
            8 + 4 = 12
```

Exercises 2.4

1. Listed below are correct algebraic expressions and incorrect C++ expressions corresponding to them. Find the errors and write corrected C++ expressions.

	Algebra	*C++ Expression*
a.	(2)(3) + (4)(5)	(2)(3) + (4)(5)
b.	$\frac{6 + 18}{2}$	6 + 18 / 2
c.	$\frac{4.5}{12.2 - 3.1}$	4.5 / 12.2 - 3.1

d. `4.6(3.0 + 14.9)` `4.6(3.0 + 14.9)`

e. `(12.1 + 18.9)(15.3 - 3.8)` `(12.1 + 18.9)(15.3 - 3.8)`

2. Determine the value of the following integer expressions:
   a. 3 + 4 * 6
   b. 3 * 4 / 6 + 6
   c. 2 * 3 / 12 * 8 / 4
   d. 10 * (1 + 7 * 3)
   e. 20 – 2 / 6 + 3
   f. 20 – 2 / (6 + 3)
   g. (20 – 2) / 6 + 3
   h. (20 – 2) / (6 + 3)
   i. 50 % 20
   j. (10 + 3) % 4

3. Determine the value of the following floating-point expressions:
   a. 3.0 + 4.0 * 6.0
   b. 3.0 * 4.0 / 6.0 + 6.0
   c. 2.0 * 3.0 / 12.0 * 8.0 / 4.0
   d. 10.0 * (1.0 + 7.0 * 3.0)
   e. 20.0 – 2.0 / 6.0 + 3.0
   f. 20.0 – 2.0 / (6.0 + 3.0)
   g. (20.0 – 2.0) / 6.0 + 3.0
   h. (20.0 – 2.0) / (6.0 + 3.0)

4. Evaluate the following mixed-mode expressions and list the data type of the result. In evaluating the expressions, be aware of the data types of all intermediate calculations.
   a. 10.0 + 15 / 2 + 4.3
   b. 10.0 + 15.0 / 2 + 4.3
   c. 3.0 * 4 / 6 + 6
   d. 3 * 4.0 / 6 + 6
   e. 20.0 – 2 / 6 + 3
   f. 10 + 17 * 3 + 4
   g. 10 + 17 / 3. + 4
   h. 3.0 * 4 % 6 + 6
   i. 10 + 17 % 3 + 4.

5. Assume that `amount` stores the integer value 1, `m` stores the integer value 50, `n` stores the integer value 10, and `p` stores the integer value 5. Evaluate the following expressions:
   a. `n / p + 3`
   b. `m / p + n - 10 * amount`
   c. `m - 3 * n + 4 * amount`
   d. `amount / 5`
   e. `18 / p`
   f. `-p * n`
   g. `-m / 20`
   h. `(m + n) / (p + amount)`
   i. `m + n / p + amount`

6. Repeat Exercise 5, assuming that amount stores the value 1.0, m stores the value 50.0, n stores the value 10.0, and p stores the value 5.0.

7. Enter, compile, and run Program 2.2 on your computer system.

8. Determine the output of the following program:

```
#include <iostream>
using namespace std;

int main()  // a program illustrating integer truncation
{
  cout << "answer1 is the integer " << 9/4;
  cout << "\nanswer2 is the integer " << 17/3;

  return 0;
}
```

9. Determine the output of the following program:

```
#include <iostream>
using namespace std;

int main()  // a program illustrating the % operator
{
  cout << "The remainder of 9 divided by 4 is " << 9 % 4;
  cout << "\nThe remainder of 17 divided by 3 is " << 17 % 3;

  return 0;
}
```

10. Write a C++ program that displays the results of the expressions 3.0 * 5.0, 7.1 * 8.3 - 2.2, and 3.2 / (6.1 * 5). Calculate the value of these expressions manually to verify that the displayed values are correct.

11. Write a C++ program that displays the results of the expressions 15 / 4, 15 % 4, and 5 * 3 - (6 * 4). Calculate the value of these expressions manually to verify that the displayed values are correct.

2.5 VARIABLES AND DECLARATION STATEMENTS

All integer, floating-point, and other values used in a computer program are stored and retrieved from the computer's memory unit. Conceptually, individual memory locations in the memory unit are arranged like the rooms in a large hotel. Like hotel rooms, each memory location has a unique address ("room number"). Before high-level languages such as C++ existed, memory locations were referenced by their addresses. For example, to store the integer values 45 and 12 in the memory locations 1652 and 2548 (see Figure 2.10), respectively, required instructions equivalent to

Put a 45 in location 1652
Put a 12 in location 2548

To add the two numbers just stored and save the result in another memory location, for example at location 3000, we need a statement comparable to

Add the contents of location 1652
to the contents of location 2548
and store the result into location 3000

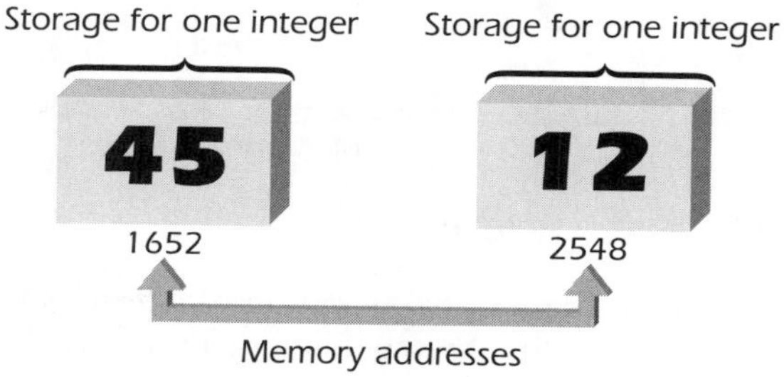

Figure 2.10 Enough storage for two integers.

Clearly this method of storage and retrieval is a cumbersome process. In high-level languages like C++, symbolic names are used in place of actual memory addresses. These symbolic names are called **variables**. A variable is simply a name given by the programmer that is used to refer to computer storage locations. The term variable is used because the value stored in the variable can change, or vary. For each name that the programmer uses, the computer keeps track of the actual memory address corresponding to that name. In our hotel room analogy, this is equivalent to putting a name on the door of a room and referring to the room by this name, such as the BLUE room, rather than using the actual room number.

In C++, the selection of variable names is left to the programmer as long as the rules for selecting identifier names are observed. These were presented on page 35 and summarized below.

1. The variable name must begin with a letter or underscore (_), and may contain only letters, underscores, or digits. It cannot contain any blanks, commas, or special symbols, such as ( ) & , $ # . ! \ ?
2. A variable name cannot be a keyword (see Table 2.1).
3. The variable name cannot consist of more than 1024 characters.

Additionally, variable names should be mnemonics that give some indication of the variable's use. For example, a good name for a variable used to store a value that is the total of some other values would be `sum` or `total`. Variable names that give no indication of the value stored, such as `r2d2`, `linda`, `bill`, and `getum` should not be selected. As with function names, variable names can be typed in uppercase and lowercase letters.

Now assume that the first memory location illustrated in Figure 2.11, which has the address 1652, is given the name `num1`. Also assume that memory location 2548 is given the variable name `num2`, and memory location 3000 is given the variable name `total`, as illustrated in Figure 2.11.

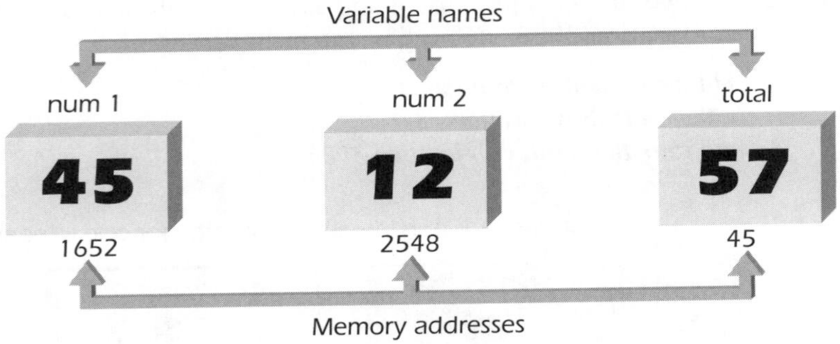

Figure 2.11 Naming storage locations.

Using these variable names, the operation of storing 45 in location 1652, storing 12 in location 2548, and adding the contents of these two locations is accomplished by the C++ statements

```
num1 = 45;
num2 = 12;
total = num1 + num2;
```

Each of these three statements is called an **assignment statement** because it tells the computer to assign (store) a value into a variable. Assignment statements always have an equal (=) sign and one variable name immediately to the left of this sign. The value on the right of the equal sign is determined first and this value is assigned to the variable on the left of the equal sign. The blank spaces in the assignment statements are inserted for readability. We will have much more to say about assignment statements in the next chapter, but for now we can use them to store values in variables.

A variable name is useful because it frees the programmer from concern over where data is physically stored inside the computer. We simply use the variable name and let the compiler worry about where in memory the data is actually stored. Before storing a value into a variable, however, C++ requires that we clearly declare the type of data that is to be stored in it. We must tell the compiler, in advance, the names of the variables that will be used for characters, the names that will be used for integers, and the names that will be used to store the other C++ data types.

Declaration Statements

Naming a variable and specifying the data type that can be stored in it is accomplished using **declaration statements**. A declaration statement has the general form

dataType variableName;

Point of Information

Atomic Data

The variables we have declared have all been used to store atomic data values. An atomic data value is a value that is considered a complete entity by itself and is not decomposable into a smaller data type supported by the language. For example, although an integer can be decomposed into individual digits, C++ does not have a numerical digit type. Rather, each integer is regarded as a complete value by itself and, as such, is considered atomic data. Similarly, since the integer data type only supports atomic data values, it is said to be an atomic data type. As you might expect, doubles, chars, and bools are atomic data types also.

where *dataType* designates a valid C++ data type and *variableName* is a user-selected variable name. For example, variables used to hold integer values are declared using the keyword `int` to specify the data type and have the form:

`int` *variableName;*

Thus, the declaration statement

```
int sum;
```

declares `sum` as the name of a variable capable of storing an integer value.

In addition to the reserved word `int` used to specify an integer, the reserved word **`long`** is used to specify a long integer.[10] For example, the statement

```
long datenum;
```

declares `datenum` as a variable that will be used to store a long integer. When using the `long` qualifier the keyword `int` can included. Thus, the previous declaration can also be written as

```
long int datenum;
```

Variables used to hold single-precision values are declared using the keyword **`float`**, whereas variables that will be used to hold double-precision values are declared using the keyword **`double`**. For example, the statement

```
float firstnum;
```

declares `firstnum` as a variable that will be used to store a single-precision number. Similarly, the statement

```
double secnum;
```

declares that the variable `secnum` will be used to store a double-precision number.

Although declaration statements may be placed anywhere within a function, declarations are typically grouped together and placed immediately after the function's opening brace. In all cases, however, a variable must be declared before it can be used, and

---

[10] Additionally, the reserved words `unsigned int` are used to specify an integer that can only store non-negative numbers and the reserved word `short` is used to specify a short integer.

like all C++ statements, declaration statements must end with a semicolon. If the declaration statements are placed after the opening function brace, a simple `main()` function containing declaration statements would have the general form

```
#include <iostream>
using namespace std;

int main()
{
  declaration statements;

  other statements;

  return 0;
}
```

Program 2.7 illustrates this form in declaring and using four double-precision variables, with the `cout` object used to display the contents of one of the variables.

Program 2.7

```
#include <iostream>
using namespace std;

int main()
{
  double grade1;  // declare grade1 as a double variable
  double grade2;  // declare grade2 as a double variable
  double total;   // declare total as a double variable
  double average; // declare average as a double variable

  grade1 = 85.5;
  grade2 = 97.0;
  total = grade1 + grade2;
  average = total/2.0;  // divide the total by 2.0
  cout << "The average grade is " << average << endl;

  return 0;
}
```

The placement of the declaration statements in Program 2.7 is straightforward, although we will shortly see that the four individual declarations can be combined into a single declaration. When Program 2.7 is run, the following output is displayed:

```
The average grade is 91.25
```

Notice that when a variable name is inserted into a `cout` object, the value stored in the variable is placed on the output stream and displayed.

Just as integer and real (single-precision, double-precision, and long-double) variables must be declared before they can be used, a variable used to store a single character must also be declared. Character variables are declared using the reserved word `char`. For example, the declaration

```
char ch;
```

declares `ch` to be a character variable. Program 2.8 illustrates this declaration and the use of `cout` to display the value stored in a character variable.

Program 2.8

```
#include <iostream>
using namespace std;

int main()
{
  char ch;      // this declares a character variable

  ch = 'a';     // store the letter a into ch
  cout << "The character stored in ch is " << ch << endl;
  ch = 'm';     // now store the letter m into ch
  cout << "The character now stored in ch is "<< ch << endl;

  return 0;
}
```

When Program 2.8 is run, the output produced is:

```
The character stored in ch is a
The character now stored in ch is m
```

Notice in Program 2.8 that the first letter stored in the variable `ch` is a and the second letter stored is m. Since a variable can only be used to store one value at a time, the assignment of m to the variable automatically causes a to be overwritten.

Multiple Declarations

Variables having the same data type can always be grouped together and declared using a single declaration statement. The common form of such a declaration is

dataType variableList;

For example, the four separate declarations used in Program 2.7,

```
double grade1;
double grade2;
double total;
double average;
```

can be replaced by the single declaration statement

```
double grade1, grade2, total, average;
```

Similarly, the two character declarations,

```
char ch;
char key;
```

can be replaced with the single declaration statement

```
char ch, key;
```

Note that declaring multiple variables in a single declaration requires that the data type of the variables be given only once, that all the variables names be separated by commas, and that only one semicolon be used to terminate the declaration. The space after each comma is inserted for readability and is not required.

Declaration statements can also be used to store a value into declared variables. For example, the declaration statement

```
int num1 = 15;
```

both declares the variable `num1` as an integer variable and sets the value of 15 into the variable. When a declaration statement is used to store a value into a variable, the variable is said to be **initialized**. Thus, in this example it is correct to say that the variable `num1` has been initialized to 15. Similarly, the declaration statements

```
double grade1 = 87.0;
double grade2 = 93.5;
double total;
```

declare three double-precision variables and initializes two of them. When initializations are used, good programming practice dictates that each initialized variable be declared on a line by itself. Constants, expressions using only constants (such as 87.0 + 12 – 2), and expressions using constants and previously initialized variables can all be used as initializers within a function. For example, Program 2.7 with declaration initialization becomes Program 2.7a.

Program 2.7a

```
#include <iostream>
using namespace std;

int main()
{
  double grade1 = 85.5;
  double grade2 = 97.0;
  double total, average;

  total = grade1 + grade2;
  average = total/2.0;  // divide the total by 2.0
  cout << "The average grade is " << average << endl;

  return 0;
}
```

Notice the blank line after the last declaration statement. Inserting a blank line after the variable declarations placed at the top of a function body is a good programming practice. It improves both a program's appearance and its readability.

An interesting feature of C++ is that variable declarations may be freely intermixed and even contained with other statements; the only requirement is that a variable must be declared prior to its use. For example, the variable `total` in Program 2.7a could have been declared when it is first used using the statement `double total = grade1 + grade2`. In very restricted situations (such as debugging, as described in Section 3.9, or in a for loop, described in Section 5.4), declaring a variable at its point of first use can be helpful. In general, however, it is preferable not to disperse declarations but rather to group them in as concise and clear manner as possible, at the top of each function.

Memory Allocation

The declaration statements we have introduced have performed both software and hardware tasks. From a software perspective, declaration statements always provide a list of all variables and their data types. In this software role, variable declarations also help to control an otherwise common and troublesome error caused by the misspelling of a variable's name within a program. For example, assume that a variable named `distance` is declared and initialized using the statement

```
int distance = 26;
```

Now assume that this variable is inadvertently misspelled in the statement

```
mpg = distnce / gallons;
```

In languages that do not require variable declarations, the program would treat `distnce` as a new variable and either assign an initial value of zero to the variable or use whatever value happened to be in the variable's storage area. In either case a value would be calculated and assigned to `mpg`, and finding the error or even knowing that an error occurred could be extremely troublesome. Such errors are impossible in C++ because the compiler will flag `distnce` as an undeclared variable. The compiler cannot, of course, detect when one declared variable is typed in place of another declared variable.

In addition to their software role, declaration statements can also perform a distinct hardware task. Because each data type has its own storage requirements, the computer can allocate sufficient storage for a variable only after knowing the variable's data type. Because variable declarations provide this information, they can be used to force the compiler to reserve sufficient physical memory storage for each variable. Declaration statements used for this hardware purpose are also called **definition statements** because they define or tell the compiler how much memory is needed for data storage.

All the declaration statements we have encountered so far have also been definition statements. Later, we will see cases of declaration statements that do not cause any new storage to be allocated and are used simply to declare or alert the program to the data types of variables that are created elsewhere in the program.

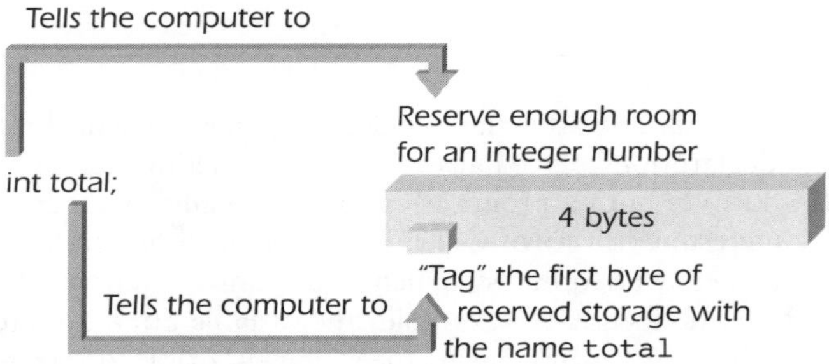

Figure 2.12a Defining the integer variable named `total`.

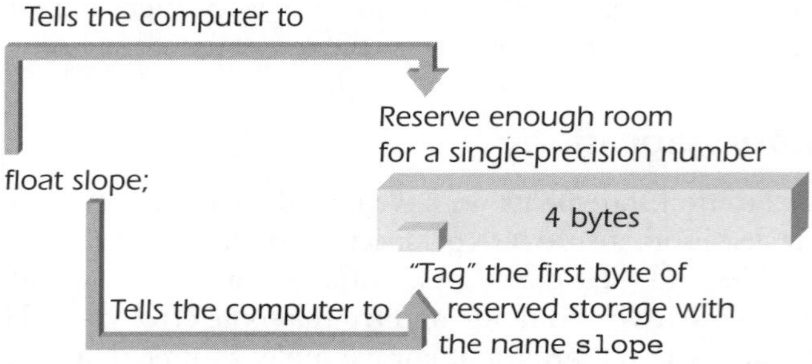

Figure 2.12b Defining the floating-point variable named `slope`.

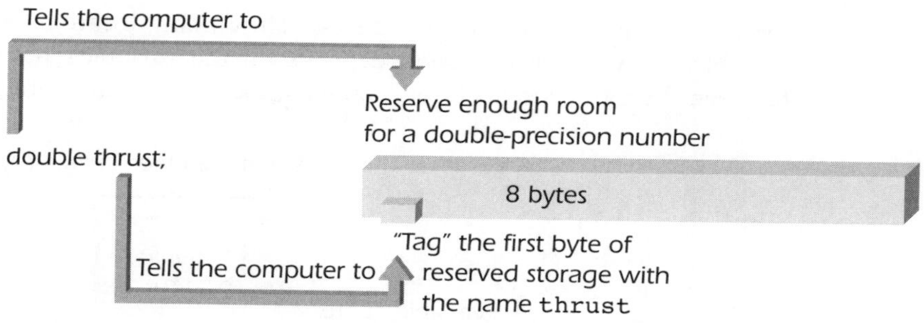

Figure 2.12c Defining the double-precision variable named `thrust`.

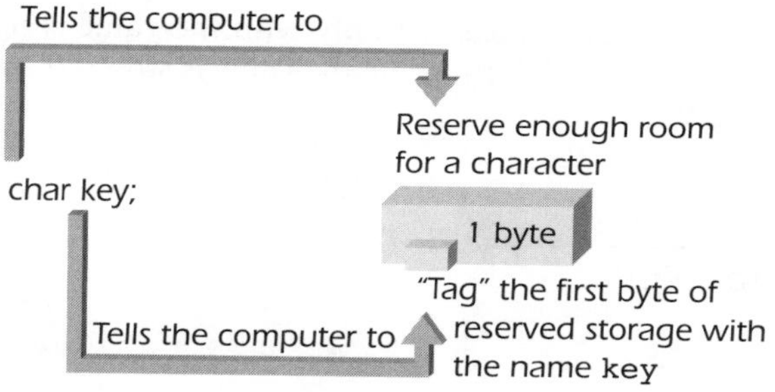

Figure 2.12d Defining the character variable named `key`.

Figure 2.12 (parts a–d) illustrates the series of operations set in motion by declaration statements that also perform a definition role. The figure shows that definition statements (or, if you prefer, declaration statements that also cause memory to be allocated) "tag" the first byte of each set of reserved bytes with a name. This name is, of course, the variable's name and is used by the computer to correctly locate the starting point of each variable's reserved memory area.

Within a program, after a variable has been declared, it is typically used by a programmer to refer to the contents of the variable (that is, the variable's value). Where in memory this value is stored is generally of little concern to the programmer. The compiler, however, must be concerned with where each value is stored and with correctly locating each variable. In this task the computer uses the variable name to locate the first byte of storage previously allocated to the variable. Knowing the variable's data type then allows the compiler to store or retrieve the correct number of bytes.

Displaying a Variable's Address[11]

Every variable has three major items associated with it: its data type, the actual value stored in the variable, and the address of the variable. The value stored in the variable is referred to as the variable's contents, while the address of the first memory location used

[11] This topic may be omitted on first reading without loss of subject continuity.

for the variable constitutes its address. How many locations are actually used for the variable, as we have just seen, depends on the variable's data type. The relationship between these three items (type, contents, location) is illustrated in Figure 2.13.

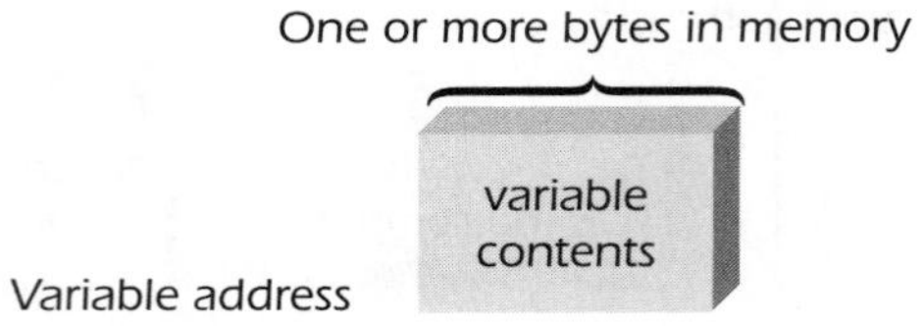

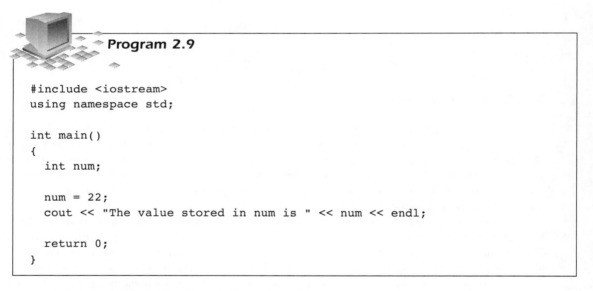

Figure 2.13 A typical variable.

Programmers are usually concerned only with the value assigned to a variable (its contents) and give little attention to where the value is stored (its address). For example, consider Program 2.9.

Program 2.9

```
#include <iostream>
using namespace std;

int main()
{
  int num;

  num = 22;
  cout << "The value stored in num is " << num << endl;

  return 0;
}
```

The output displayed when Program 2.9 is run is

```
The value stored in num is 22
```

Program 2.9 merely prints the value 22, which is the contents of the variable `num`. We can go further, however, and ask, "Where is the number 22 actually stored?" Although the answer is "in `num`," this is only half of the answer. The variable name `num` is simply a convenient symbol for real, physical locations in memory, as illustrated in Figure 2.14.

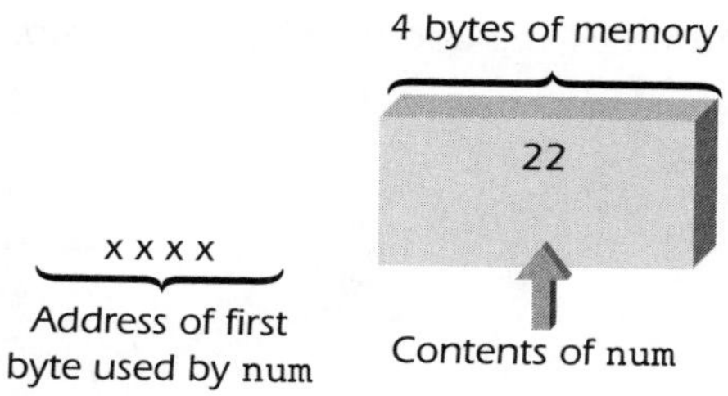

Figure 2.14 Somewhere in memory.

To determine the address of num, we can use C++'s address operator, &, which means "the address of." Except when used in an expression, the address operator placed in front of a variable's name refers to the address of the variable.[12] For example, `&num` means *the address of* num, `&total` means *the address of* `total`, and `&price` means *the address of* `price`. Program 2.10 uses the address operator to display the address of the variable num.

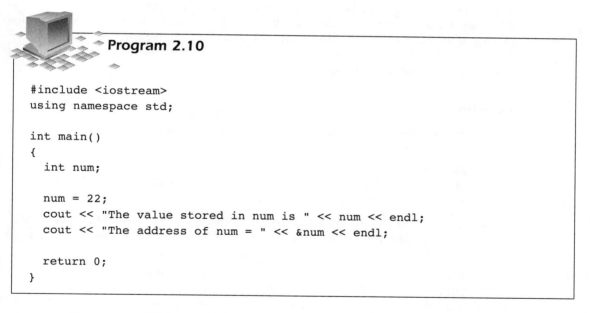

Program 2.10

```
#include <iostream>
using namespace std;

int main()
{
  int num;

  num = 22;
  cout << "The value stored in num is " << num << endl;
  cout << "The address of num = " << &num << endl;

  return 0;
}
```

The output of Program 2.10 is

```
The value stored in num is 22
The address of num = 0012FED4
```

[12] When used in declaring reference variables and arguments, which is presented in Chapter 7, the ampersand refers to the data type *preceding* it. Thus, the declaration `double &num` is read as "num is the address of a `double`", or more commonly as "num is a reference to a `double`."

Figure 2.15 illustrates the additional address information provided by the output of Program 2.9.

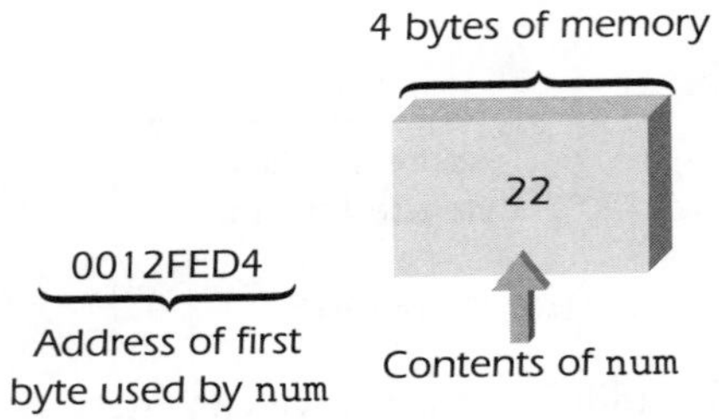

Figure 2.15 A more complete picture of the variable `num`.

Clearly, the address output by Program 2.10 depends on the computer used to run the program. Every time Program 2.10 is executed, however, it displays the address of the first memory location used to store the variable num. As illustrated by the output of Program 2.10, the display of addresses is in hexadecimal notation. This display has no effect on how addresses are used internal to the program; it merely provides us with a means of displaying addresses that is helpful in understanding them. As we shall see in Chapters 6 and 12, using addresses, as opposed to only displaying them, is an extremely important and powerful programming tool.

Exercises 2.5

1. State whether the following variable names are valid or not. If they are invalid, state the reason why.

```
prod_a      c1234      abcd       _c3       12345
newamp      watts      $total     new$al    a1b2c3d4
9ab6        sum.of     average    volts1    finvolt
```

2. State whether the following variable names are valid or not. If they are invalid, state the reason why. Also indicate which of the valid variable names should not be used because they convey no information about the variable.

```
current     a243      r2d2      firstNum    cc_a1
harry       sue       c3p0      total       sum
maximum     okay      a         awesome     goforit
3sum        for       tot.a1    c$five      netpower
```

3. a. Write a declaration statement to declare that the variable `count` will be used to store an integer.

b. Write a declaration statement to declare that the variable `volt` will be used to store a floating-point number.

c. Write a declaration statement to declare that the variable `power` will be used to store a double-precision number.
d. Write a declaration statement to declare that the variable `keychar` will be used to store a character.

4. Write declaration statements for the following variables:
   a. `num1`, `num2`, and `num3` used to store integer numbers
   b. `amps1`, `amps2`, `amps3`, and `amps4` used to store double-precision numbers
   c. `volts1`, `volts2`, and `volts3` used to store double-precision numbers
   d. `codeA`, `codeB`, `codeC`, `codeD`, and `codeE` used to store character types

5. Write declaration statements for the following variables:
   a. `firstnum` and `secnum` used to store integers
   b. `speed`, `acceleration`, and `distance` used to store double-precision numbers
   c. `thrust` used to store a double-precision number

6. Rewrite each of these declaration statements as three individual declarations.
   a. `int month, day = 30, year;`
   b. `double hours, volt, power = 15.62;`
   c. `double price, amount, taxes;`
   d. `char inKey, ch, choice = 'f';`

7. a. Determine what each statement causes to happen in the following program:

```
#include <iostream>
using namespace std;

int main()
{
  int num1, num2, total;
  num1 = 25;
  num2 = 30;
  total = num1 + num2;
  cout << "The total of" << num1 << " and "
       << num2 << " is " << total << endl;

  return 0;
}
```

   b. What is the output that will be printed when the program listed in Exercise 7a is run?

8. Every variable has three items associated with it. What are these three items?

NOTE FOR EXERCISES 9 THROUGH 11: *Assume that a character requires one byte of storage, an integer four bytes, a single-precision number four bytes, a double-precision number eight bytes, and that variables are assigned storage in the order they are declared. (Review Section 1.6 if you are unfamiliar with the concept of a byte.)*

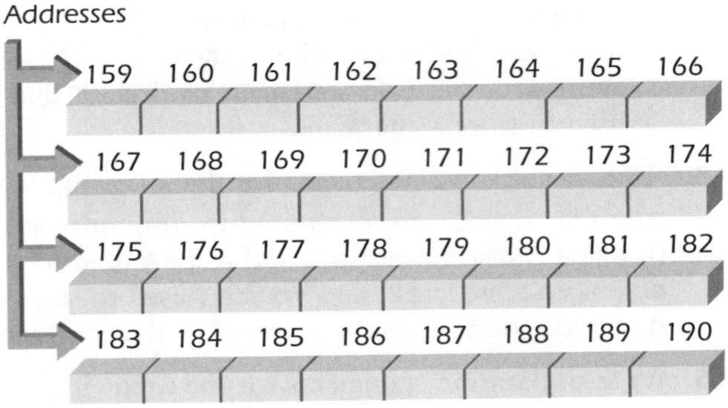

Figure 2.16 Memory bytes for exercises 9, 10, and 11.

9. a. Using Figure 2.16 and assuming that the variable name `rate` is assigned to the byte having memory address 159, determine the addresses corresponding to each variable declared in the following statements. Also fill in the appropriate bytes with the initialization data included in the declaration statements. (Use letters for the characters, not the computer codes that would actually be stored.)

```
float rate;
char ch1 = 'M', ch2 = 'E', ch3 = 'L', ch4 = 'T';
double taxes;
int num, count = 0;
```

b. Repeat Exercise 9a, but substitute the actual byte patterns that a computer using the ASCII code would use to store the characters in the variables `ch1`, `ch2`, `ch3`, and `ch4`. (*Hint:* Use Appendix B.)

10. a. Using Figure 2.16 and assuming that the variable named `cn1` is assigned to the byte at memory address 159, determine the addresses corresponding to each variable declared in the following statements. Also, fill in the appropriate bytes with the initialization data included in the declaration statements. (Use letters for the characters and not the computer codes that would actually be stored.)

```
char cn1 = 'P', cn2 = 'E', cn3 = 'R', cn4 = 'F', cn5 = 'E';
char cn6 = 'C', cn7 = 'T', key = '\\', sch = '\'', inc = 'A';
char inc1 = 'T';
```

b. Repeat Exercise 10a, but substitute the actual byte patterns that a computer using the ASCII code would use to store the characters in each of the declared variables. (*Hint:* Use Table 2.3.)

11. Using Figure 2.16 and assuming that the variable name `miles` is assigned to the byte at memory address 159, determine the addresses corresponding to each variable declared in the following statements.

```
float miles;
int count, num;
double dist, temp;
```

2.6 APPLYING THE SOFTWARE DEVELOPMENT PROCEDURE

Recall from Section 1.2 that writing a C++ program is essentially the third step in the programming process. The first two steps in the process are determining what is required and selecting the algorithm to be coded into C++. In this section we show how the steps presented in Section 1.2 are applied in practice when converting programming problems into working C++ programs. To review, once a program requirement or problem is stated, the software development procedure consists of the following steps:

◆ Step 1: Analyze the Problem

The analysis of a problem can consist of up to two parts. The first part is a **basic analysis** that must be performed on all problems and consists of extracting the complete input and output information supplied by the problems. That is, you must:

1. Determine and understand the desired output items that the program must produce
2. Determine the input items

Together, these two items are referred to as the problem's input/output, or I/O, for short. Only after a problem's I/O has been determined is it possible to select an algorithm for transforming the inputs into the desired outputs. At this point it is sometimes necessary and/or useful to perform a hand calculation to verify that the output can indeed be obtained from the inputs. Clearly, if a formula is given that relates the inputs to the output, this step can be omitted at this stage. If the required inputs are available and the desired output(s) can be produced, the problem is said to be clearly defined and can be solved.

For a variety of reasons it may not be possible to complete a basic analysis. If this is the case, an extended analysis may be necessary. An **extended analysis** simply means that you must obtain additional information about the problem so that you thoroughly understand what is being asked for and how to achieve the result. In this text any additional information required for an understanding of the problem will be supplied along with the problem statement.

◆ Step 2: Develop a Solution

This step is frequently referred to as the design step, and we will use the terms **design** and **development** interchangeably. In this step you must settle on an algorithm for transforming the input items into the desired outputs and refine it as necessary so that it adequately defines all of the features that you want your program to have. If you haven't performed a hand calculation using the algorithm in the analysis step, you should do so here, using specific input values.

In designing a solution, the specific approach we will take is often referred to as the **top-down approach**. This approach consists of starting with the most general solution and refining it in a manner such that the final program solution consists of clearly defined tasks that can be accomplished by individual program functions.

◆ Step 3: Code the Solution

At this point you actually write the C++ program that corresponds to the solution developed in Step 2.

◆ Step 4: Test and Correct the Program

This is done by means of selected test data and is used to make corrections to the program when errors are found. One set of test data that should always be used is the data used in your previous hand calculation.

To see how each of these steps can be implemented in practice, we now apply it to the following simple programming problem.

The electrical resistance, r, *of a metal wire, in ohms, is given by the formula* r = (ml)/a *where* m *is the resistivity of the metal;* l *is the length of the wire, in feet; and* a *is the cross-sectional area of the wire, in circular mils. Using this information, write a C++ program to calculate the resistance of a wire that is 125 feet long, has a cross-sectional area of 500 circular mils, and is copper. The resistivity of copper,* m, *is 10.4.*

Step 1 *Analyze the Problem*

The first step in developing a program for this problem statement is to perform a basic analysis. We begin by determining the required outputs. Frequently, the statement of the problem will use such words as *calculate, print, determine, find,* or *compare*, which can be used to determine the desired outputs.

For our sample problem statement, the key phrase is "to calculate the resistance of a wire." This clearly identifies an output item. Because there are no other such phrases in the problem, only one output item is required.

After we have clearly identified the desired output, the basic analysis step continues with the identification of all input items. It is essential at this stage to distinguish between input items and input values. An **input item** is the name of an input quantity, whereas an **input value** is a specific number or quantity that the input item can be. For example, in our sample problem statement, the input items are the resistivity, m, the length or the wire, l, and the cross-sectional area of the wire, a. Although these input item have specific numerical values, these input item values are generally not of importance at this stage.

The reason that input values are not needed at this point is that the selection of an algorithm is typically independent of specific input values. The algorithm depends on knowing what the output and input items are and if there are any special limits. Let us see why this is so.

From the problem statement it is clear that the algorithm for transforming the input items to the desired output is given by the formula $r = (ml)/a$. Notice that this formula can be used regardless of the specific values assigned to m, l, or a. Although we cannot produce an actual numerical value for the output item (resistance) unless we have actual numerical values for the input item, the correct relationship between inputs and outputs is expressed by the formula. Recall that this is precisely what an algorithm provides: a description of how the inputs are to be transformed into outputs that works for all inputs.

Step 2 Develop a Solution

The basic algorithm for transforming the inputs into the desired output is provided by the given formula. We must now refine it by listing, in detail, how the inputs, outputs, and algorithm are to be combined to produce a solution. This listing indicates the steps that will be taken by the program to solve the problem. As such it constitutes an outline of the final form that will be followed by the program code. Using pseudocode, the complete algorithm for solving this problems is

> *Assign values to m, l, and a*
> *Calculate the resistance using the formula r = (ml)/a*
> *Display the resistance*

Notice that the structure of this algorithm conforms to the sequential control structure presented in Section 1.2.

Having selected and refined the algorithm, the next step in the design (if it was not already done in the analysis step) is to check the algorithm by hand using specific data. Performing a manual calculation, either by hand or by using a calculator, helps to ensure that you really do understand the problem. An added advantage of doing a manual calculation is that the results can be used later to verify program operation in the testing phase. Then, when the final program is used with other data, you will have established a degree of confidence that a correct result is being calculated.

Doing a manual calculation requires that we have specific input values that can be assigned and used by the algorithm to produce the desired output. For this problem three input values are given: a resistivity of 10.4, a cross-sectional area of 500 circular mils, and a length of 125 feet. Substituting these values into the formula, we obtain a resistance = (10.4)(125)/500 = 2.60 ohms for the copper wire.

Step 3 Code the Solution

Because we have carefully developed a program solution, all that remains is to code the solution algorithm in C++. This means declaring appropriate input and output variables, initializing the input variables appropriately, computing the resistance, and printing the calculated resistance value. Program 2.11 performs these steps.

Program 2.11

```
#include <iostream>
using namespace std;
int main()
{
  double resistivity, area, length, resistance;

  resistivity = 10.4;
  area = 500;
  length = 125;
  resistance = (resistivity * length) / area;

  cout << "The resistance of the wire (in ohms) is "
          << resistance << endl;

  return 0;
}
```

When program 2.11 is executed, the following output is produced:

```
The resistance of the wire (in ohms) is 2.6
```

Now that we have a working program that produces a result, the final step in the development process, testing the program, can begin.

Step 4 Test and Debug the Program

The purpose of testing is to verify that a program works correctly and actually fulfills its requirements. Once testing has been completed the program can be used to calculate outputs for differing input data without the need for retesting. This is, of course, one of the real values in writing a program; the same program can be used over and over with new input data.

The simplest test method is to verify the program's operation for carefully selected sets of input data. One set of input data that should always be used is the data that was selected for the hand calculation made previously in Step 2 of the development procedure. In this case the program is relatively simple and performs only one calculation. Because the output produced by the test run agrees with our hand calculation we have a good degree of confidence that it can be used to correctly calculate the resistance for any input values.

Exercises 2.6

NOTE: *In each of these exercises a programming problem is given. Read the problem statement first and then answer the questions pertaining to the problem.* ***Do not*** *write a program to solve the problems, but simply answer the questions following the program specification.*

1. Assume that a C++ program is to be written to calculate the total resistance of a series circuit. In such a circuit the total resistance is the sum of all individual resistance values. Assume that the circuit consists of a number of 56 ohm, 33 ohm, and 15 ohm resistors.
   a. For this programming problem how many outputs are required?
   b. How many inputs does this problem have?
   c. Determine an algorithm for converting the input items into output items. Assume that the number of 56 ohm resistors is m, the number of 33 ohm resistors is n, the number of 15 ohm resistors is p.
   d. Test the algorithm written for part c using the following sample data: $m = 17$, $n = 24$, and $p = 12$.

2. Assume that a program is to be written to calculate the value of *distance*, in miles, given the relationship:

   distance = *rate* * *elapsed time*

   a. For this programming problem how many outputs are required?
   b. How many inputs does this problem have?
   c. Determine an algorithm for converting the input items into output items.
   d. Test the algorithm written for part c using the following sample data: *rate* is 55 miles per hour and *elapsed time* is 2.5 hours.
   e. How must the algorithm you determined in part c be modified if the elapsed time were given in minutes instead of hours?

3. Assume that a program is to be written to determine the value of *Ergies*, given the relationships:

   $$Ergies = Fergies * \sqrt{Lergies}$$
   $$Lergies = 2 * \pi * e^{\mu}$$

   a. For this programming problem how many outputs are required?
   b. How many inputs does this problem have?
   c. Determine an algorithm for converting the input items into output items.
   d. Test the algorithm written for part c using the following sample data: *Fergies* = 14.65, $\pi = 3.1416$, $\mu = 1.672$, and $e = 2.7818$.

4. Assume that a program is to be written to display the following specifications:

Voltage Amplification:	35
Power output:	2.5 watts
Bandwidth:	15KHz

   a. For this program problem how many lines of output are required?
   b. How many inputs does this problem have?
   c. Determine an algorithm for converting the input items into output items.

5. Write a C++ program to determine how far a car has traveled after 10 seconds, assuming the car is initially traveling at 60 miles per hour and the driver applies the brakes to uniformly decelerate at a rate of 12 miles/sec^2. Use the fact that *distance* = $s - (1/2)dt^2$, where *s* is the initial speed of the car, *d* is the deceleration, and *t* is the elapsed time.
   a. For this programming problem how many outputs are required?
   b. How many inputs does this problem have?
   c. Determine an algorithm for converting the input items into output items.
   d. Test the algorithm written for part c using the data given in the problem.

6. Consider the following programming problem: In 1627, Manhattan Island was sold to the Dutch settlers for approximately $24. If the proceeds of that sale had been deposited in a Dutch bank paying 5% interest, compounded annually, what would the principal balance be at the end of 2002? A display is required as follows: Balance as of December 31, 2002 is: xxxxxx, where xxxxxx is the amount calculated by your program.
   a. For this programming problem how many outputs are required?
   b. How many inputs does this problem have?
   c. Determine an algorithm for converting the input items into output items.
   d. Test the algorithm written for part c using the data given in the problem statement.

7. Write a program that calculates and displays the output voltages of two electrical circuits and the sum of the two voltages. The output voltage for the first circuit is given by the equation (150) $V / 0.38f$ and the output voltage for the second circuit is given by the equation

$$\frac{230V}{\sqrt{56^2 + (0.98f)^2}}$$

   where *V* is the input voltage to the circuit and *f* is the frequency in Hertz.
   a. For this programming problem how many outputs are required?
   b. How many inputs does this problem have?
   c. Determine an algorithm for converting the input items into output items.
   d. Test the algorithm written for part c using the following sample data: The first circuit is operated with an input voltage of 1.2 volts at a frequency of 144 Hertz and the second circuit is operated with an input voltage of 2.3 volts at 100 Hertz.

8. Consider the following programming problem: The formula for the standard normal deviate, *z*, used in statistical applications is

$$z = \frac{X - \mu}{\sigma}$$

   where μ refers to a mean value and σ to a standard deviation. Using this formula, write a program that calculates and displays the value of the standard normal deviate when $X = 85.3$, $\mu = 80$, and $\sigma = 4$.
   a. For this programming problem how many outputs are required?
   b. How many inputs does this problem have?

c. Determine an algorithm for converting the input items into output items.
d. Test the algorithm written for part c using the data given in the problem.

9. The equation of the normal (bell-shaped) curve used in statistical applications is

$$y = \frac{1}{\sigma\sqrt{2\pi}} e^{-(1/2)[(x-\mu)/\sigma]^2}$$

Using this equation, assume that a C++ program is to be written that calculates the value of y.
a. For this programming problem how many outputs are required?
b. How many inputs does this problem have?
c. Determine an algorithm for converting the input items into output items.
d. Test the algorithm written for part c assuming $\mu = 90$, $\sigma = 4$, $x = 80$, and $\pi = 3.1416$.

2.7 APPLICATIONS

In this section, the software development procedure presented in the previous section is applied to two specific programming problems. Although each problem is different, the development procedure works for both situations. This procedure can be applied to any programming problem to produce a completed program and forms the foundation for all programs developed in this text.

Application 1: Radar Speed Traps

A common highway-patrol speed detection radar emits a beam of microwaves at a frequency f_0. The beam is reflected off an approaching car, and the reflected beam is picked up and analyzed by the radar unit. The frequency of the reflected beam is shifted slightly from f_0 to f_1 due to the motion of the car. The relationship between the speed of the car, v, in miles per hour, and the two microwave frequencies is

$$v = (6.685 \times 10^8)(f_1 - f_0) / (f_1 + f_0)$$

where the emitted waves have a frequency of $f_0 = 2 \times 10^{10}$ sec^{-1}. Using the given formula, write a C++ program to calculate and display the speed corresponding to a received frequency of 2.000004×10^{10} sec^{-1}.

We now apply the software development procedure to this problem.

Step 1 Analyze the Problem

For this problem a single output is required by the program: the speed of the car. The input items required to solve for the speed are the emitted frequency, f_0 and the received frequency, f_1.

Step 2 Develop a Solution

The algorithm given for transforming the three input items into the desired output item is given by the formula $v = 6.685 \times 10^8(f_1 - f_0)/ (f_1 + f_0)$. Thus, the complete algorithm for our program solution is

> ***Assign values to f_1 and f_0***
> ***Calculate the speed using the formula $v = 6.685 \times 10^8(f_1 - f_0)/ (f_1 + f_0)$***
> ***Display the speed***

A hand calculation, using the data that $f_0 = 2 \times 10^{10}$ sec^{-1} and $f_1 = 2.000004 \times 10^{10}$ sec^{-1} yields a speed of 66.85 miles per hour.

Step 3 Code the Solution

Program 2.12 provides the necessary code.

Program 2.12

```
#include <iostream>
using namespace std;

int main()
{
  double speed, f0, f1;

  f0 = 2e-10;
  f1 = 2.0000004e-10;

  speed = 6.685e8 * (f1 - f0) / (f1 + f0);
  cout << "The speed is " << speed << " miles/hour " <<endl;

  return 0;
}
```

Program 2.12 begins with an `#include` preprocessor command followed by a `main()` function. This function starts with the keyword `main` and ends with the closing brace, `}`. Additionally, Program 2.12 contains one declaration statement, three assignment statements, and one output statement. The assignment statements `f0 = 2e-10` and `f1 = 2.0000004e-10` are used to initialize the `f0` and `f1` variables, respectively. The assignment statement

```
speed = 6.685e8 * (f1 - f0) / (f1 + f0);
```

calculates a value for the variable named `speed`. When Program 2.12 is compiled and executed the following output is produced.

```
The speed is 66.85 miles/hour
```

Step 4 Test and Correct the Program

The last step in the development procedure is to test the output. Because the single calculation and displayed value agrees with the previous hand calculation, we have verified the correct program operation. This permits us to use the program for different values of received frequencies. Note that if the parentheses were not correctly placed in the assignment statement that calculated a value for speed, the displayed value would not agree with our previous hand calculation. This would have alerted us to the fact there was an error in the program.

Application 2: Telephone Switching Networks

A directly connected telephone network is one in which all telephones in the network are directly connected and do not require a central switching station to establish calls between two telephones. For example, financial institutions on Wall Street use such a network to maintain direct and continuously open phone lines between firms.

The number of direct lines needed to maintain a directly connected network for n telephones is given by the formula:

$$lines = n(n - 1)/2$$

For example, directly connecting four telephones requires 6 individual lines (see Figure 2.17). Adding a fifth telephone to the network illustrated in Figure 2.17 would require an additional 4 lines for a total of 10 lines.

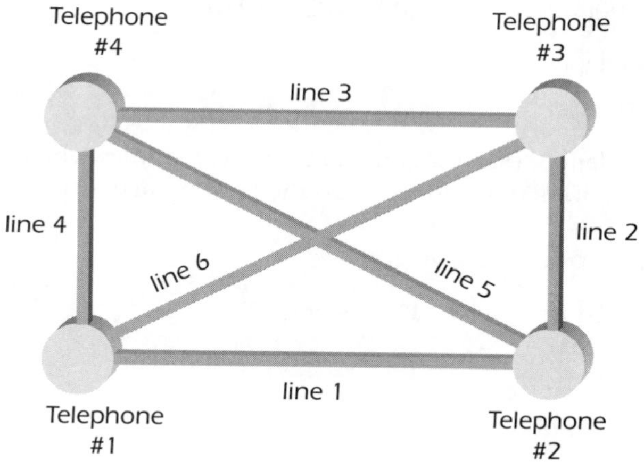

Figure 2.17 Directly connecting four telephones.

Using the given formula, write a C++ program that determines the number of direct lines required for 100 telephones, and the additional lines required if 10 new telephones were added to the network.

Step 1 Analyze the Problem

For this program two outputs are required: the number of direct lines for 100 telephones and the additional number of lines needed when 10 new telephones are added to the existing network. The input item required for this problem is the number of telephones, which is denoted as *n* in the formula.

Step 2 Develop a Solution

The first output is easily obtained using the formula:

$$lines = n(n - 1)/2$$

Although there is no formula given for additional lines, we can use the given formula to determine the total number of lines needed for 110 subscribers. Subtracting the number of lines for 100 subscribers from the number of lines needed for 110 subscribers will then yield the number of additional lines required. Thus, the complete algorithm for our program, in pseudocode, is

Calculate the number of direct lines for 100 subscribers
Calculate the number of direct lines for 110 subscribers
Calculate the additional lines needed, which is the difference between the second and first calculation
Display the number of lines for 100 subscribers
Display the additional lines needed

Checking this algorithm by hand, using the data given, yields the answer:

$$lines = 100(100 - 1)/2 = 100(99)/2 = 4950$$

for 100 telephones and

$$lines = 5995$$

for 110 telephones. Thus, an additional 1,045 lines would be needed to directly connect the ten additional telephones into the existing network.

Step 3 Code the Solution

Program 2.13 provides the necessary code.

Program 2.13

```
#include <iostream>
using namespace std;

int main()
{
  int numin1, numin2, lines1, lines2;

  numin1 = 100;
  numin2 = 110;
  lines1 = numin1 * (numin1 - 1)/2;
  lines2 = numin2 * (numin2 - 1)/2;
  cout << "The number of initial lines is " << lines1 << "." << endl;
  cout << "There are " << lines2 - lines1
       << " additional lines needed." << endl;

  return 0;
}
```

As before, the C++ program includes the `iostream` header file and consists of one `main()` function. The body of this function begins with the opening brace, `{`, and ends with the closing brace, `}`. Because the number of lines between subscribers must be an integer (a fractional line is not possible) the variables `lines1` and `lines2` are specified as integer variables. The first two assignment statements initialize the variables `numin1` and `numin2`. The next assignment statement calculates the number of lines needed for 100 subscribers and the last assignment statement calculates the number of lines for 110 subscribers. The first `cout` statement is used to display a message and the result of the first calculation. The next `cout` statement is used to display the difference between the two calculations. The following output is produced when Program 2.13 is compiled and executed:

```
The number of initial lines is 4950.
There are 1045 additional lines needed.
```

Step 4 Test and Correct the Program

As the two calculations and displayed values agree with the previous hand calculation, we have verified correct operation of the program.

Exercises 2.7

1. **a.** Modify Program 2.12 to calculate the speed of a car whose return radar frequency is $2.00000035 \times 10^{10}$ sec^{-1}.
   b. Compile and execute the program written for Exercise 1a on a computer.

2. a. Modify Program 2.12 to determine the frequency that will be returned by a car traveling at 55 miles per hour. Your program should produce the following display:

```
The returned frequency corresponding to 55 miles per hour is_____
```

where the underline is replaced by the actual value calculated by your program.

b. Compile and execute the program written for Exercise 2a on a computer. Make sure to do a hand calculation so that you can verify the results produced by your program.

c. After you have verified the results of the program written in Exercise 2a, modify the program to calculate the returned frequency of a car traveling at 75 miles per hour.

3. a. Modify Program 2.13 to calculate and display the total number of lines needed to connect 1,000 individual phones directly to each other.

b. Compile and execute the program written for Exercise 3a on a computer.

4. a. Modify Program 2.13 so that a new variable `numfin`, the additional number of subscribers to be connected to the existing network, is initialized to 10. Make any other changes in the program so that the program produces the same display as Program 2.13.

b. Compile and execute the program written for Exercise 4a on a computer. Check that the display produced by your program matches the display shown in the text.

5. a. Design, write, compile, and execute a C++ program to convert temperature in degrees Fahrenheit to degrees Celsius. The equation for this conversion is

Celsius = 5.0/9.0 (*Fahrenheit* - 32.0).

Have your program convert and display the Celsius temperature corresponding to 98.6 degrees Fahrenheit. Your program should produce the following display:

```
For a fahrenheit temperature of ______ degrees,
  the equivalent celsius temperature is______ degrees.
```

where appropriate values are inserted by your program in place of the underlines.

b. Check the values computed by your program by hand. After you have verified that your program is working correctly, modify it to convert 86.5 degrees Fahrenheit into its equivalent Celsius value.

6. a. Write, compile, and execute a C++ program to calculate the resistance of a series circuit consisting of twelve 56-ohm, twenty 39-ohm, thirty-two 27-ohm, and twenty-seven 15-ohm resistors. Use the fact that the resistance of a series circuit is the sum of the resistances of all individual resistances. Your program should produce the following display:

```
The total resistance, in ohms, is xxxx
```

where xxx is replaced by the actual resistance value calculated by your program.

b. Check the values computed by your program by hand. After you have verified that your program is working correctly, modify it to calculate the resistance of a series circuit consisting of no 56-ohm resistors, seventeen 39-ohm resistors, nineteen 27-ohm resistors, and forty-two 15-ohm resistors.

7. a. Design, write, compile, and execute a C++ program to calculate the elapsed time it took to make a 183.67 mile trip. The equation for computing elapsed time is

elapsed time = total distance / average speed

Assume that the average speed during the trip was 58 miles per hour.

b. Check the values computed by your program by hand. After you have verified that your program is working correctly, modify it to determine the elapsed time it takes to make a 372-mile trip at an average speed of 67 miles/hour.

8. a. Design, write, compile, and execute a C++ program to calculate the sum of the numbers from 1 to 100. The formula for calculating this sum is

$$sum = (n/2)\ (2^{*}a + (n - 1)d)$$

where n = number of terms to be added, a = the first number, and d = the difference between each number.

b. Check the values computed by your program by hand. After you have verified that your program is working correctly, modify it to determine the sum of the integers from 100 to 1000.

NOTE: *Exercises 9 through 13 require raising a number to a power. This can be accomplished using C++'s power function* `pow()`*. For example, the statement* `pow(2.0,5.0);` *raises the number 2.0 to the 5th power, and the statement* `pow(num1,num2);` *raises the variable* `num1` *to the* `num2` *power. To use the power function either place an* `#include <cmath>` *preprocessor command on a line by itself after the* `#include <iostream>` *command or include the declaration statement* `double pow();` *with the variable declaration statements used in your program. The power function is explained in more detail in Section 3.3.*

9. a. Newton's law of cooling states that when an object with an initial temperature T is placed in a surrounding substance of temperature A, it will reach a temperature $TFIN$ in t minutes according to the formula

$$TFIN = (T - A)\ e^{-kt} + A$$

In this formula e is the irrational number 2.71828 rounded to five decimal places, commonly known as Euler's number, and k is a thermal coefficient, which depends on the material being cooled. Using this formula write, compile, and execute a C++ program that determines the temperature reached by an object after 20 minutes when it is placed in a glass of water whose temperature is 60 degrees. Assume that the object initially has a temperature of 150 degrees and has a thermal constant of 0.0367.

b. Check the value computed by your program by hand. After you have verified that your program is working correctly, modify it to determine the temperature reached after 10 minutes when it is placed in a glass of water whose temperature is 50 degrees.

10. a. The voltage gain of an amplifier is given by the formula

$$voltage\ gain = [275 / (23^2 + (0.5f)^2)^{1/2}]^n$$

where f is the frequency, in Hertz, and n is the number of stages in the amplifier. Using this formula write, compile, and execute a C++ program that determines the value of the voltage gain for a 4-stage amplifier operating at a frequency of 120 Hertz. Your program should produce the following display:

```
At a frequency of xxxxx hertz, the voltage gain is yyyyy
```

where xxxxx is replaced by the frequency and yyyyy by the voltage gain.

b. Check the value computed by your program by hand. After you have verified that your program is working correctly, modify it to determine the voltage gain of a 12-stage amplifier operating at a frequency of 9500 Hertz.

11. a. The electrical current, i, in amps, that flows through the circuit illustrated in Figure 2.18 is given by the equation

$$i = \frac{E(1-e)^{-(R/L)t}}{R}$$

where E is the voltage of the battery in volts, R is the value of the resistor in ohms, L is the value of the inductor in henrys, t is the time in seconds after the switch is closed, and e is euler's number, which is 2.718 accurate to 3 decimal places. Using this formula, write, compile, and run a C++ program to determine the current flowing in the circuit illustrated in Figure 2.18 when t is 0.12 seconds.

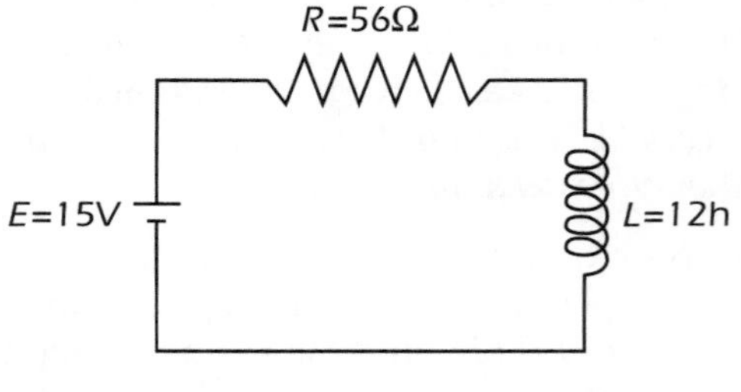

Figure 2.18 A series RL circuit.

b. Check the value computed by your program by hand. After you have verified that your program is working correctly, modify it to determine the current in 0.12 seconds if E is 25 volts, R is 33 ohms, and L is 15 henrys.

12. a. The electrical current, i, in amps, that flows through the circuit illustrated in Figure 2.19 is given by the following equation:

$$i = \frac{(E)e^{-t/RC}}{R}$$

where E is the voltage of the battery in volts, R is the value of the resistor in ohms, C is the value of the capacitor in farads, t is the time in seconds after the switch is closed, and e is euler's number, which is 2.718 accurate to 3 decimal places. Using this formula, write, compile, and run a C++ program to determine the voltage across the capacitor illustrated in Figure 2.19 when t is 0.31 seconds.

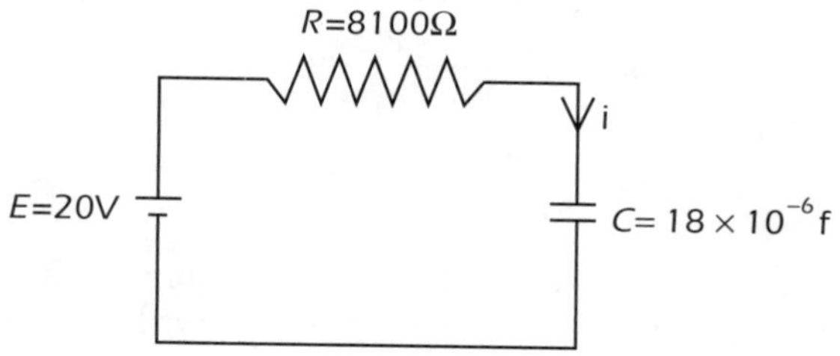

Figure 2.19 A series RC circuit.

b. Check the value computed by your program by hand. After you have verified that your program is working correctly, modify it to determine the current in 0.85 seconds if E is 25 volts, R is 220 ohms, and C is 0.00039 farads.

13. a. The electrical voltage, V, in volts, across the capacitor, C, illustrated in Figure 2.20 is given by the equation

$$V = \frac{E\left[1 - e^{-t/RC}\right]}{R}$$

where E is the voltage of the battery in volts, R is the value of the resistor in ohms, C is the value of the capacitor in farads, t is the time in seconds after the switch is closed, and e is euler's number, which is 2.718 accurate to 3 decimal places. Using this formula, write, compile, and run a C++ program to determine the voltage across the capacitor illustrated in Figure 2.20 when t is 0.42 seconds.

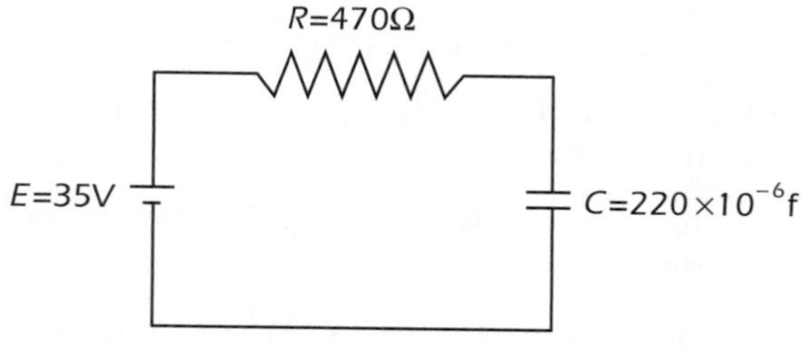

Figure 2.20 A series RC circuit.

b. Check the value computed by your program by hand. After you have verified that your program is working correctly, modify it to determine the current in 0.85 seconds if E is 25 volts, R is 220 ohms, and C is 0.00039 farads.

14. a. The set of linear equations

$$a_{11}X_1 + a_{12}X_2 = c_1$$

$$a_{21}X_1 + a_{22}X_2 = c_2$$

can be solved using Cramer's rule:

$$X_1 = \frac{c_1 a_{22} - c_2 a_{12}}{a_{11} a_{22} - a_{12} a_{21}}$$

$$X_2 = \frac{c_2 a_{11} - c_1 a_{21}}{a_{11} a_{22} - a_{12} a_{21}}$$

Using these equations, write, compile, and execute a C++ program to solve for the X_1 and X_2 values that satisfy the following equations:

$$3X_1 + 4X_2 = 40$$

$$5X_1 + 2X_2 = 34$$

b. Check the values computed by your program by hand. After you have verified that your program is working correctly, modify it to solve the following set of equations:

$$3X_1 + 12.5X_2 = 22.5$$

$$4.2X_1 - 6.3X_2 = 30$$

2.8 COMMON PROGRAMMING ERRORS

Part of learning any programming language is making the elementary mistakes commonly encountered as you begin to use the language. These mistakes tend to be quite frustrating because each language has its own set of common programming errors waiting for the unwary. The more common errors made when initially programming in C++ include the following.

1. Omitting the parentheses after `main`.
2. Omitting or incorrectly typing the opening brace `{` that signifies the start of a function body.
3. Omitting or incorrectly typing the closing brace `}` that signifies the end of a function.
4. Misspelling the name of an object or function; for example, typing `cot` instead of `cout`.
5. Forgetting to close a string sent to `cout` with a double quote symbol.
6. Forgetting to separate individual data streams passed to `cout` with an insertion ("put-to") symbol, <<.
7. Omitting the semicolon at the end of each C++ statement.

8. Adding a semicolon at the end of the `#include` preprocessor command.
9. Forgetting the `\n` to indicate a new line.
10. Incorrectly typing the letter O for the number zero (0), or vice versa. Incorrectly typing the letter l, for the number 1, or vice versa.
11. Forgetting to declare all the variables used in a program. This error is detected by the compiler and an error message is generated for all undeclared variables.
12. Storing an inappropriate data type in a declared variable. This error is detected by the compiler and the assigned value is converted to the data type of the variable it is assigned to.
13. Using a variable in an expression before a value has been assigned to the variable. Here, whatever value happens to be in the variable will be used when the expression is evaluated, and the result will be meaningless.
14. Dividing integer values incorrectly. This error is usually disguised within a larger expression and can be a very troublesome error to detect. For example, the expression

    3.425 + 2/3 + 7.9

    yields the same result as the expression

    3.425 + 7.9

    because the integer division of 2/3 is 0.
15. Mixing data types in the same expression without clearly understanding the effect produced. Since C++ allows expressions with "mixed" data types, it is important to understand the order of evaluation and the data type of all intermediate calculations. As a general rule, it is better never to mix data types in an expression unless a specific effect is desired.

The third, fifth, seventh, eighth, and ninth errors in this list are initially the most common, while even experienced programmers occasionally make the tenth error. It is worthwhile for you to write a program and specifically introduce each of these errors, one at a time, to see what error messages, if any, are produced by your compiler. Then when these error messages appear due to inadvertent errors, you will have had experience in understanding the messages and correcting the errors.

On a more fundamental level, a major programming error made by all beginning programmers is the rush to code and run a program before the programmer fully understands what is required and the algorithms and procedures that will be used to produce the desired result. A symptom of this haste to get a program entered into the computer is the lack of either an outline of the proposed program or a written program itself. Many problems can be caught just by checking a copy of the program, either handwritten or listed from the computer, before it is ever compiled.

2.9 CHAPTER SUMMARY

1. A C++ program consists of one or more modules called functions. One of these functions must be called `main()`. The `main()` function identifies the starting point of a C++ program.

2. The simplest C++ program consists of the single function `main()`.

3. Following the function name, the body of a function has the following general form:

```
{
   All C++ statements in here;
}
```

4. All C++ statements must be terminated by a semicolon.

5. Four types of data were introduced in this chapter: integer, floating-point, and Boolean. C++ recognizes each of these data types, in addition to other types yet to be presented.

6. The `cout` object can be used to display all of C++'s data types.

7. When the `cout` object is used within a program, the preprocessor command `#include <iostream>` must be placed at the top of the program. Preprocessor commands do not end with a semicolon.

8. Every variable in a C++ program must be declared as to the type of value it can store. Declarations within a function may be placed anywhere within a function, although a variable can only be used after it is declared. Variables may also be initialized when they are declared. Additionally, variables of the same type may be declared using a single declaration statement. Variable declaration statements have the general form:

   dataType variableName(s);

9. A simple C++ program containing declaration statements has the typical form

```
#include <iostream>
using namespace std;

int main()
{
  declaration statements;

  other statements;

  return 0;
}
```

Although declaration statements may be placed anywhere within the function's body, a variable may only be used after it is declared.

10. Declaration statements always play a software role of informing the compiler of a function's valid variable names. When a variable declaration also causes the computer to set aside memory locations for the variable, the declaration statement is also called a definition statement. (All the declarations we have used in this chapter have also been definition statements.)

11. The `sizeof()` operator can be used to determine the amount of storage reserved for variables.

Looking at Career Choices

Electrical Engineering

Electrical engineering deals with the application of the principles of electricity and electromagnetism to the manufacture of all forms of machines and devices that either use electricity or produce electrical energy. The field is the largest of all engineering fields. In its beginning, in the mid-1800s, it was concerned solely with generating electrical energy. It has evolved into a field with broad boundaries, encompassing communication, computers, robotics, solid-state devices, and integrated circuit design.

1. Power. This area involves generation of electrical energy in large fossil-fuel, nuclear, solar, or hydroelectric plants or the efficient utilization of electrical energy by means of motors or illumination devices. Also important are the transmission and distribution of electrical energy through overhead lines, microwaves, light pipes, and superconducting lines.
2. Solid-State Electronics. Through modern physics and materials science, exotic semiconducting materials are being developed and used to construct microcircuitry for monitoring and controlling the operations of all kinds of devices, from video games to assembly-line robots. The improved reliability, rapidly shrinking size, and reduced power requirements of modern miniaturized electrical components have created limitless opportunities for applications.
3. Communications. Communications involves the design and construction of equipment used in the transmission of information via electricity or electromagnetic waves (radio, light, microwaves, etc.) The use of the laser for communication is a topic of modern concern, whereas antenna characteristics and radar are somewhat older.
4. Computers and Robotics. While electronics deals with the principles associated with the functions of components, computer engineers are concerned with designing the complex circuitry that interweaves the components into a computer. Microprocessors, or small computers, are designed to constantly monitor and control the operations of a particular piece of equipment such as a lathe or an autopilot.

CHAPTER 3

Assignment, Formatting, and Interactive Input

TOPICS

In the last chapter we explored how results are displayed using C++'s `cout` *object and how numerical data is stored and processed using variables and assignment statements. In this chapter we complete our introduction to C++ by presenting additional processing and input capabilities.*

3.1 ASSIGNMENT OPERATIONS

We have already encountered simple assignment statements in Chapter 2. Assignment statements are the most basic C++ statements for both assigning values to variables and performing computations. This statement has the syntax:

variable = expression;

The simplest expression in C++ is a single constant. In each of the following assignment statements, the operand to the right of the equal sign is a constant:

```
length = 25;
width = 17.5;
```

In each of these assignment statements the value of the constant to the right of the equal sign is assigned to the variable on the left of the equal sign. It is important to note that the equal sign in C++ does not have the same meaning as an equal sign in algebra. The equal sign in an assignment statement tells the computer first to determine the value of the operand to the right of the equal sign and then to store (or assign) that value in the locations associated with the variable to the left of the equal sign. In this regard, the C++ statement `length = 25;` is read "length is assigned the value 25." The blank spaces in the assignment statement are inserted for readability only.

Recall that a variable can be initialized when it is declared. If an initialization is not done within the declaration statement, the variable should be assigned a value with an assignment statement or input operation before it is used in any computation. Subsequent assignment statements can, of course, be used to change the value assigned to a variable. For example, assume the following statements are executed one after another and that `slope` was not initialized when it was declared:

```
slope = 3.7;
slope = 6.28;
```

The first assignment statement assigns the value of 3.7 to the variable named `slope`.[1] The next assignment statement causes the computer to assign a value of 6.28 to `slope`. The 3.7 that was in `slope` is overwritten with the new value of 6.28 because a variable can store only one value at a time. It is sometimes useful to think of the variable to the left of the equal sign as a temporary parking spot in a huge parking lot. Just as an individual parking spot can be used only by one car at a time, each variable can store only one value at a time. The "parking" of a new value in a variable automatically causes the program to remove any value previously parked there.

---

[1]Since this is the first time a value is explicitly assigned to this variable it is frequently referred to as an initialization. This stems from historical usage that said a variable was initialized the first time a value was assigned to it. Under this usage it is correct to say that "total is initialized to 3.7." From an implementation viewpoint, however, this later statement is incorrect. This is because the assignment operation is handled differently by the C++ compiler than an initialization performed when a variable is created by a declaration statement. This difference is only important when using C++'s class features and is explained in detail in Section 9.1.

In addition to being a constant, the operand to the right of the equal sign in an assignment statement can be a variable or any other valid C++ expression. An **expression** is any combination of constants, variables, and function calls that can be evaluated to yield a result. Thus, the expression in an assignment statement can be used to perform calculations using the arithmetic operators introduced in Section 2.4. Examples of assignment statements using expressions containing these operators are

```
sum = 3 + 7;
diff = 15 - 6;
product = .05 * 14.6;
tally = count + 1;
newtotal = 18.3 + total;
taxes = .06 * amount;
totalWeight = factor * weight;
average = sum / items;
slope = (y2 - y1) / (x2 - x1);
```

As always in an assignment statement, the program first calculates the value of the expression to the right of the equal sign and then stores this value in the variable to the left of the equal sign. For example, in the assignment statement `totalWeight = factor * weight;` the arithmetic expression `factor * weight` is first evaluated to yield a result. This result, which is a number, is then stored in the variable `totalWeight`.

In writing assignment expressions, you must be aware of two important considerations. Since the expression to the right of the equal sign is evaluated first, all variables used in the expression must previously have been given valid values if the result is to make sense. For example, the assignment statement `totalWeight = factor * weight;` causes a valid number to be stored in `totalWeight` only if the programmer first takes care to assign valid numbers to `factor` and `weight`. Thus the sequence of statements

```
factor = 1.06;
weight = 155.0;
totalWeight = factor * weight;
```

tells us the values being used to obtain the result that will be stored in `totalWeight`. Figure 3.1 illustrates the values stored in the variables `factor`, `weight`, and `totalWeight`.

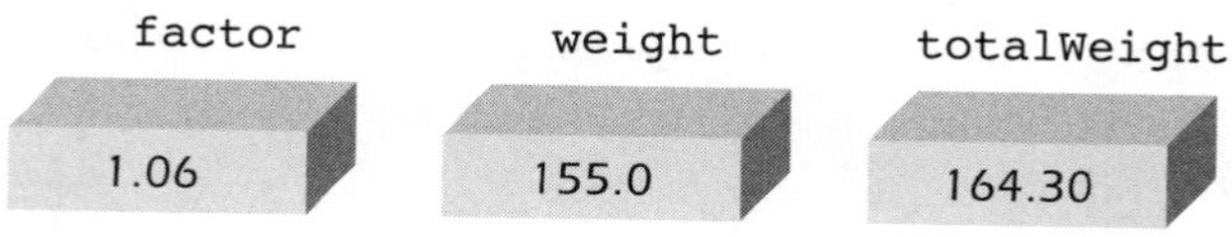

Figure 3.1 *Values stored in the variables.*

The second consideration to keep in mind is that since the value of an expression is stored in the variable to the left of the equal sign, only one variable can be listed in this position. For example, the assignment statement

```
amount + 1892 = 1000 + 10 * 5;
```

is invalid. The right-side expression evaluates to the integer 1050, which can only be stored in a variable. Because `amount + 1892` is not a valid variable name, the compiler does not know where to store the calculated value.

Program 3.1 illustrates the use of assignment statements to calculate the volume of a cylinder. As illustrated in Figure 3.2, the volume of a cylinder is determined by the formula, $volume = \pi r^2 h$, where r is the radius of the cylinder, h is the height, and π is the constant 3.1416 (accurate to four decimal places).

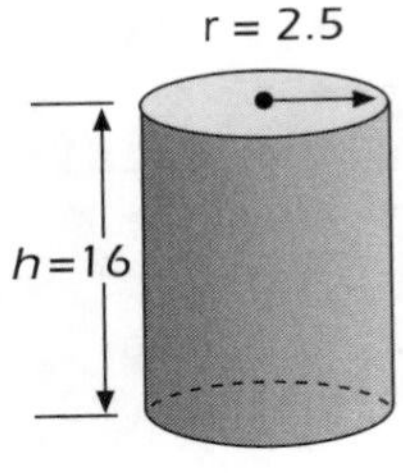

Figure 3.2 Determining the volume of a cylinder.

Program 3.1

```
//   this program calculates the volume of a cylinder,
//      given its radius and height
#include <iostream>
using namespace std;

int main()
{
  double radius, height, volume;

  radius = 2.5;
  height = 16.0;
  volume = 3.1416 * radius * radius * height;
  cout << "The volume of the cylinder is " << volume << endl;

  return 0;
}
```

When Program 3.1 is compiled and executed, the output is

```
The volume of the cylinder is 314.16
```

Consider the flow of control that the computer uses in executing Program 3.1. Program execution begins with the first statement within the body of the `main()` function and continues sequentially, statement by statement, until the closing brace of main is encountered.

This flow of control is true for all programs. The computer works on one statement at a time, executing that statement with no knowledge of what the next statement will be. This explains why all operands used in an expression must have values assigned to them before the expression is evaluated. When the computer executes the statement

```
volume = 3.1416 * radius * radius * height;
```

in Program 3.1, it uses whatever value is stored in the variables `radius` and `height` at the time the assignment statement is executed.[2] If no values have been specifically assigned to these variables before they are used in the assignment statement, the computer uses whatever values happen to occupy these variables when they are referenced. (On some systems all variables are automatically initialized to zero.) The computer does not "look ahead" to see if you assign values to these variables later in the program.

It is important to realize that in C++, the equal sign, =, used in assignment statements is itself an operator, which differs from the way most other high-level languages process this symbol. In C++ (as in C), the = symbol is called the **assignment operator**, and an expression using this operator, such as `interest = principal * rate`, is an **assignment expression**. Since the assignment operator has a lower precedence than any other arithmetic operator, the value of any expression to the right of the equal sign will be evaluated first, prior to assignment.

Like all expressions, assignment expressions themselves have a value. The value of the complete assignment expression is the value assigned to the variable on the left of the assignment operator. For example, the expression `a = 5` both assigns a value of 5 to the variable `a` and results in the expression itself having a value of 5. The value of the expression can always be verified using a statement such as

```
cout << "The value of the expression is " << (a = 5);
```

Here, the value of the expression itself is displayed and not the contents of the variable `a`. Although both the contents of the variable and the expression have the same value, it is worth realizing that we are dealing with two distinct entities.

From a programming perspective, it is the actual assignment of a value to a variable that is significant in an assignment expression; the final value of the assignment expression itself is of little consequence. However, the fact that assignment expressions have a value has implications that must be considered when C++'s relational operators are presented.

Any expression that is terminated by a semicolon becomes a C++ statement. The most common example of this is the assignment statement, which is simply an assignment expression terminated with a semicolon. For example, terminating the assignment expression `a = 33` with a semicolon results in the assignment statement `a = 33;` , which can be used in a program on a line by itself.

Since the equal sign is an operator in C++, multiple assignments are possible in the same expression or its equivalent statement. For example, in the expression `a = b = c = 25` all the assignment operators have the same precedence. Since the assignment operator has a

---

[2]Since C++ does not have an exponentiation operator, the square of the radius is obtained by the term radius * radius. In Section 3.3 we introduce C++'s power function `pow()`, which allows us to raise a number to a power.

right-to-left associativity, the final evaluation proceeds in the sequence

```
c = 25
b = c
a = b
```

In this case, this has the effect of assigning the number 25 to each of the variables individually and can be represented as

```
a = (b = (c = 25))
```

Appending a semicolon to the original expression results in the multiple assignment statement

```
a = b = c = 25;
```

This latter statement assigns the value 25 to the three individual variables equivalent to the following order:

```
c = 25;
b = 25;
a = 25;
```

Coercion

One thing to keep in mind when working with assignment statements is the data type assigned to the values on both sides of the expression, because data type conversions occur across assignment operators. In other words, the value of the expression on the right side of the assignment operator will be converted to the data type of the variable to the left of the assignment operator. This type of conversion is referred to as a **coercion** because the value assigned to the variable on the left side of the assignment operator is forced into the data type of the variable to which it is assigned. An example of a coercion occurs when an integer value is assigned to a real variable; this causes the integer to be converted to a real value. Thus, assigning an integer value to a real variable causes the integer to be converted to a real value. Similarly, assigning a real value to an integer variable forces conversion of the real value to an integer, which always results in the loss of the fractional part of the number due to truncation. For example, if `temp` is an integer variable, the assignment `temp = 25.89` causes the integer value 25 to be stored in the integer variable `temp`.[3]

A more complete example of data type conversions, which includes both mixed-mode and assignment conversion, is the evaluation of the expression

```
a = b * d
```

[3]The correct integer portion, clearly, is retained only when it is within the range of integers allowed by the compiler.

> **Point of Information**
>
> **lvalues and rvalues**
>
> The terms lvalue and rvalue are frequently used terms in programming technology. Both of these terms are language independent and mean the following: An lvalue can have a value assigned to it while an rvalue cannot.
>
> In both C and C++ this means that an lvalue can appear on both the left and right sides of an assignment operator while an rvalue can only appear on the right side of an assignment operator. For example, each variable we have encountered can be either an lvalue or rvalue, while a number can only be an rvalue. Not all variables, however, can be lvalues and rvalues. For example, an array type, which is introduced in Chapter 11, cannot be an lvalue or an rvalue, while individual array elements can be both.

where a and b are integer variables and d is a single-precision variable. When the mixed-mode expression b * d is evaluated[4], the value of d used in the expression is converted to a double-precision number for purposes of computation. (It is important to note that the value stored in d remains a single-precision number.) Since one of the operands is a double-precision variable, the value of the integer variable b is converted to a double-precision number for the computation (again, the value stored in b remains an integer) and the resulting value of the expression b * d is a double-precision number. Finally, data type conversion across the assignment operator comes into play. Since the left side of the assignment operator is an integer variable, the double-precision value of the expression (b * d) is truncated to an integer value and stored in the variable a.

Assignment Variations

Although only one variable is allowed immediately to the left of the equal sign in an assignment expression, the variable on the left of the equal sign can also be used on the right of the equal sign. For example, the assignment expression sum = sum + 10 is valid. Clearly, as an algebraic equation sum could never be equal to itself plus 10. But in C++, the expression sum = sum + 10 is not an equation—it is an expression that is evaluated in two major steps. The first step is to calculate the value of sum + 10. The second step is to store the computed value in sum. See if you can determine the output of Program 3.2.

[4]Review the rules in Section 2.4 for the evaluation of mixed-mode expressions, if necessary.

Program 3.2

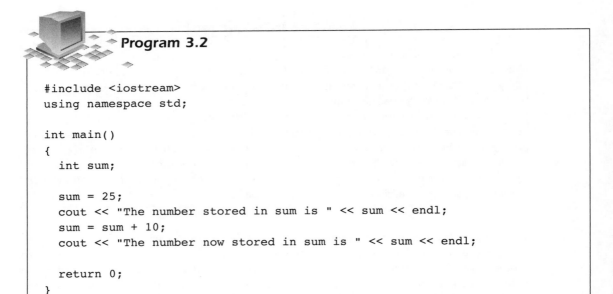

```
#include <iostream>
using namespace std;

int main()
{
  int sum;

  sum = 25;
  cout << "The number stored in sum is " << sum << endl;
  sum = sum + 10;
  cout << "The number now stored in sum is " << sum << endl;

  return 0;
}
```

The assignment statement `sum = 25;` tells the computer to store the number 25 in `sum`, as shown in Figure 3.3.

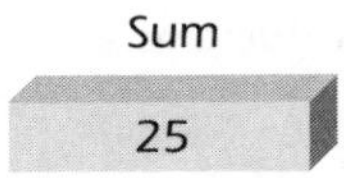

Figure 3.3 *The integer 25 is stored in* `sum`.

The first `cout` statement causes the value stored in `sum` to be displayed by the message `The number stored in sum is 25.` The second assignment statement in Program 3.2, `sum = sum + 10;` causes the program to retrieve the 25 stored in `sum` and add 10 to this number, yielding the number 35. The number 35 is then stored in the variable on the left side of the equal sign, which is the variable `sum`. The 25 that was in `sum` is simply overwritten with the new value of 35, as shown in Figure 3.4.

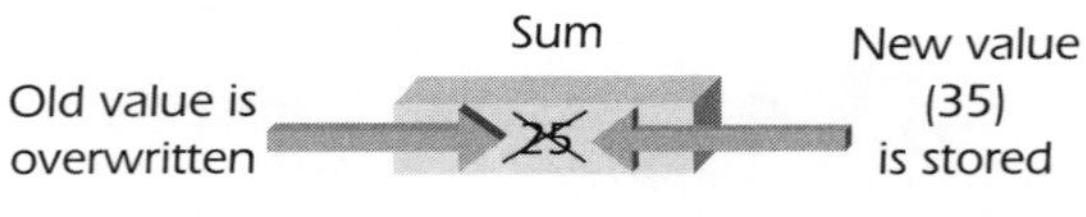

Figure 3.4 `sum = sum + 10;` *causes a new value to be stored in* `sum`.

Assignment expressions like `sum = sum + 25`, which use the same variable on both sides of the assignment operator, can be written using the following shortcut **assignment operators:**

```
+=   -=   *=   /=   %=
```

For example, the expression `sum = sum + 10` can be written as `sum += 10`. Similarly, the expression `price *= rate` is equivalent to the expression `price = price * rate.`

In using these new assignment operators it is important to note that the variable to the left of the assignment operator is applied to the complete expression on the right. For example, the expression `price *= rate + 1` is equivalent to the expression `price = price * (rate + 1)`, not `price = price * rate + 1.`

Accumulating

Assignment expressions like `sum += 10` or its equivalent, `sum = sum + 10`, are very common in programming. These expressions are required in accumulating subtotals when data is entered one number at a time. For example, if we want to add the numbers 96, 70, 85, and 60 in calculator fashion, the following statements could be used:

Statement	Value in sum
`sum = 0;`	0
`sum = sum + 96;`	96
`sum = sum + 70;`	166
`sum = sum + 85;`	251
`sum = sum + 60;`	311

The first statement initializes `sum` to 0. This removes any number ("garbage value") stored in `sum` that would invalidate the final total. As each number is added, the value stored in `sum` is increased accordingly. After completion of the last statement, `sum` contains the total of all the added numbers. Program 3.3 illustrates the effect of these statements by displaying `sum`'s contents after each addition is made.

Program 3.3

```
#include <iostream>
using namespace std;

int main()
{
  int sum;

  sum = 0;
  cout << "The value of sum is initially set to " << sum << endl;
  sum = sum + 96;
  cout << "  sum is now " << sum << endl;
  sum = sum + 70;
  cout << "  sum is now " << sum << endl;
  sum = sum + 85;
  cout << "  sum is now " << sum  << endl;
  sum = sum + 60;
  cout << "  The final sum is " << sum << endl;

  return 0;
}
```

The output displayed by Program 3.3 is:

```
The value of sum is initially set to 0
  sum is now 96
  sum is now 166
  sum is now 251
  The final sum is 311
```

Although Program 3.3 is not a practical program (it is easier to add the numbers by hand), it does illustrate the subtotaling effect of repeated use of statements having the form

variable = variable + newValue;

We will find many uses for this type of **accumulation statement** when we become more familiar with the repetition statements introduced in Chapter 5.

Counting

An assignment statement that is very similar to the accumulating statement is the counting statement. Counting statements have the form

variable = variable + fixedNumber;

Examples of counting statements are

```
i = i + 1;
n = n + 1;
count = count + 1;
j = j + 2;
m = m + 2;
kk = kk + 3;
```

In each of these examples the same variable is used on both sides of the equal sign. After the statement is executed the value of the respective variable is increased by a fixed amount. In the first three examples the variables `i`, `n`, and `count` have all been increased by one. In the next two examples the respective variables have been increased by two, and in the final example the variable `kk` has been increased by three.

For the special case in which a variable is either increased or decreased by one, C++ provides two unary operators. Using the increment operator,[5] ++, the expression `variable = variable + 1` can be replaced by either the expression `variable++` or `++variable`. Examples of the increment operator are

Expression	Alternative
`i = i + 1`	`i++ or ++i`
`n = n + 1`	`n++ or ++n`
`count = count + 1`	`count++ or ++count`

Program 3.4 illustrates the use of the increment operator.

[5]As a historical note, the ++ in C++ was inspired from the increment operator symbol. It was used to indicate that C++ was the next increment to the C language.

Program 3.4

```
#include <iostream>
using namespace std;

int main()
{
  int count;

  count = 0;
  cout << "The initial value of count is " << count << endl;
  count++;
  cout << "   count is now " << count << endl;
  count++;
  cout << "   count is now " << count << endl;
  count++;
  cout << "   count is now " << count << endl;
  count++;
  cout << "   count is now " << count << endl;

  return 0;
}
```

The output displayed by Program 3.4 is:

```
The initial value of count is 0
   count is now 1
   count is now 2
   count is now 3
   count is now 4
```

When the `++` operator appears before a variable it is called a **prefix increment operator**; when it appears after a variable it is called a **postfix increment operator**. The distinction between a prefix and postfix increment operator is important when the variable being incremented is used in an assignment expression. For example, the expression `k = ++n` does two things in one expression. Initially, the value of `n` is incremented by one and then the new value of `n` is assigned to the variable `k`. Thus, the statement `k = ++n;` is equivalent to the two statements

```
n = n + 1;    // increment n first
k = n;        // assign n's value to k
```

The assignment expression `k = n++`, which uses a postfix increment operator, reverses this procedure. A postfix increment operates after the assignment is completed. Thus, the statement `k = n++;` first assigns the current value of `n` to `k` and then increments the value of `n` by one. This is equivalent to the two statements

```
k = n;          // assign n's value to k
n = n + 1;      // and then increment n
```

In addition to the increment operator, C++ also provides a decrement operator, `--`. As you might expect, the expressions `variable--` and `--variable` are both equivalent to the expression `variable = variable - 1`.

Examples of the decrement operator are:

Expression	Alternative
`i = i - 1`	`i-- or --i`
`n = n - 1`	`n-- or --n`
`count = count - 1`	`count-- or --count`

When the `--` operator appears before a variable it is called a **prefix decrement operator**. When the decrement appears after a variable it is called a **postfix decrement operator**. For example, both of the expressions `n--` and `--n` reduce the value of `n` by one. These expressions are equivalent to the longer expression `n = n - 1`. As with the increment operators, however, the prefix and postfix decrement operators produce different results when used in assignment expressions. For example, the expression `k = --n` first decrements the value of `n` by one before assigning the value of `n` to `k`, while the expression `k = n--` first assigns the current value of `n` to `k` and then reduces the value of `n` by one.

Exercises 3.1

1. Write an assignment statement to calculate the circumference of a circle having a radius of 3.3 inches. The equation for determining the circumference, c, of a circle is $c = 2\pi r$, where r is the radius and π equals 3.1416.
2. Write an assignment statement to calculate the area of a circle. The equation for determining the area, a, of a circle is $a = \pi r^2$, where r is the radius and $\pi = 3.1416$.
3. Write an assignment statement to convert temperature in degrees Fahrenheit to degrees Celsius. The equation for this conversion is Celsius = 5/9 (Fahrenheit – 32).
4. Write an assignment statement to calculate the round-trip distance, d, in feet, of a trip that is s miles long, one way.
5. Write an assignment statement to calculate the elapsed time, in minutes, that it takes to make a trip. The equation for computing elapsed time is elapsed *time = total distance / average speed.* Assume that the distance is in miles and the average speed is in miles/hour.

6. Write an assignment statement to calculate the nth term in an arithmetic sequence. The formula for calculating the value, v, of the nth term is $v = a + (n - 1)d$, where a = the first number in the sequence and d = the difference between any two numbers in the sequence.

7. Write an assignment statement to calculate the linear expansion in a steel beam as a function of temperature increase. The formula for linear expansion, l, is $l = l_o[1+\propto(T_f-T_o)]$, where l_o is the length of the beam at temperature T_o, $\propto$ is the coefficient of linear expansion, and T_f is the final temperature of the beam.

8. Coulomb's law states that the force F, acting between two electrically charged spheres, is given by the formula $F = kq_1q_2/r^2$, where q_1 is the charge on the first sphere, q_2 is the charge on the second sphere, r is the distance between the centers of the two spheres, and k is a proportionality constant. Write an assignment statement to calculate the force, F.

9. Write an assignment statement to determine the maximum bending moment, M, of a beam. The formula for maximum bending moment is, $M = XW (L - X) / L$, where X is the distance from the end of the beam that a weight, W, is placed, and L is the length of the beam.

10. Determine the output of the following program:

```
#include <iostream>
using namespace std;

int main() // a program illustrating integer truncation
{
   int num1, num2;

   num1 = 9/2;
   num2 = 17/4;
   cout << "the first integer displayed is " << num1 << endl;
   cout << "the second integer displayed is " << num2 << endl;

  return 0;
}
```

11. Determine and correct the errors in the following programs.

a.
```
#include <iostream>
using namespace std;
int main()
{
  width = 15
  area = length * width;
  cout << "The area is " << area

}
```

b.
```
#include <iostream>
using namespace std;
int main()
{
  int length, width, area;
  area = length * width;
  length = 20;
  width = 15;
  cout << "The area is " << area;

  return 0;
```

c.
```
#include <iostream.h>

 int main()
 {
   int length = 20; width = 15, area;
   length * width = area;
   cout << "The area is " , area;

   return 0;
 }
```

12. By mistake a student reordered the statements in Program 3.3 as follows:

```
#include <iostream>
using namespace std;

int main()
{
  int sum;
  sum = 0;
  sum = sum + 96;
  sum = sum + 70;
  sum = sum + 85;
  sum = sum + 60;
  cout << "The value of sum is initially set to " << sum << endl;
  cout << "  sum is now " << sum << endl;
  cout << "  sum is now " << sum << endl;
  cout << "  sum is now " << sum << endl;
  cout << "  The final sum is " << sum << endl;

  return 0;
}
```

Determine the output that this program produces.

13. Using Program 3.1, determine the volume of cylinders having the following radii and heights.

Radius (in.)	Height (in.)
1.62	6.23
2.86	7.52
4.26	8.95
8.52	10.86
12.29	15.35

14. The area of an ellipse (see Figure 3.5) is given by the formula Area = πab.

Using this formula, write a C++ program to calculate the area of an ellipse having a minor axis, a, of 2.5 inches and a major axis, b, of 6.4 inches.

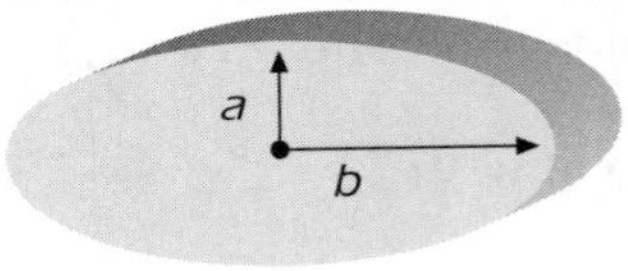

Figure 3.5 The minor axis *a* and the major axis *b* of an ellipse.

15. Modify Program 3.1 to calculate the weight, in pounds, of the steel cylinder whose volume was found by the program. The formula for determining the weight is weight = 0.28 $(\pi)(r^2)(h)$, where r is the radius (in inches) and h is the height (in inches) of the cylinder.

16. The circumference of an ellipse (see Figure 3.5) is given by the formula:

$$\text{Circumference} = \pi\sqrt{(a+b)^2}$$

Using this formula, write a C++ program to calculate the circumference of an ellipse having a minor radius of 2.5 inches and a major radius of 6.4 inches. (*Hint:* The square root can be taken by raising the quantity $2[a^2 + b^2]$ to the 0.5 power.)

17. a. The combined resistance of three resistors connected in parallel, as shown in Figure 3.6, is given by the equation

$$\text{Combined resistance} = \frac{1}{\frac{1}{R_1} + \frac{1}{R_2} + \frac{1}{R_3}}$$

Write a C++ program to calculate and display the combined resistance when the three resistors R_1 = 1000, R_2 = 1000, and R_3 = 1000 are connected in parallel. Your program should produce the display "The combined resistance, in ohms, is xxxxx", where the x's are replaced by the value of the combined resistance computed by your program.

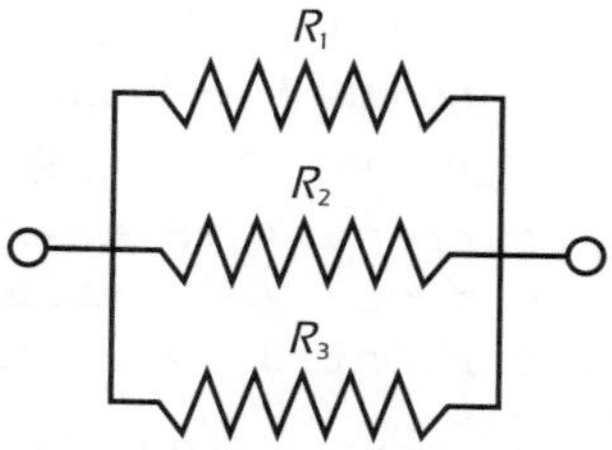

Figure 3.6 Three resistors connected in parallel.

b. How do you know that the value calculated by your program is correct?

c. Once you have verified the output produced by your program, modify it to determine the combined resistance when the resistors R_1 = 1500, R_2 = 1200, and R_3 = 2000 are connected in parallel.

18. a. Write a C++ program to calculate and display the value of the slope of the line connecting the two points whose coordinates are (3,7) and (8,12). Use the fact that the slope between two points having coordinates (x_1,y_1) and (x_2,y_2) is slope = $(y_2 - y_1) / (x_2 - x_1)$. Your program should produce the display "The slope is xxxx", where the x's are replaced by the value calculated by your program.

b. How do you know that the result produced by your program is correct?

c. Once you have verified the output produced by your program, modify it to determine the slope of the line connecting the points (2,10) and (12,6).

19. a. Write a C++ program to calculate and display the coordinates of the midpoint of the line connecting the two points given in Exercise 18a. Use the fact that the coordinates of the midpoint between two points having coordinates (x_1,y_1) and (x_2,y_2) are $[(x_1 + x_2)]/2$, $[(y_1 + y_2)]/2)$. Your program should produce the following display:

```
The x midpoint coordinate is xxx
The y midpoint coordinate is xxx
```

where the x's are replaced with the values calculated by your program.

b. How do you know that the midpoint values calculated by your program are correct?

c. Once you have verified the output produced by your program, modify it to determine the midpoint coordinates of the line connecting the points (2,10) and (12,6).

20. a. For the electrical circuit shown in Figure 3.7, the branch currents, i_1, i_2, and, i_3 can be determined using the formulas

$$i_1 = \frac{E_2R_3 + E_1(R_1 + R_3)}{(R_1 + R_3)(R_2 + R_3) - (R_3)^2}$$

$$i_2 = \frac{E_1R_3 + E_2(R_1 + R_3)}{(R_1 + R_3)(R_2 + R_3) - (R_3)^2}$$

$$i_3 = i_i - i_2$$

Using these formulas write a C++ program to compute the branch currents when R_1 = 10 ohms, R_2 = 4 ohms, R_3 = 6 ohms, E_1 = 12 volts, and E_2 = 9 volts. The display produced by your program should be

```
Branch current 1 is xxxx
Branch current 2 is xxxx
Branch Current 3 is xxxx
```

where the x's are replaced by the values determined in your program.

b. How do you know that the loop currents calculated by your program are correct?

c. Once you have verified the output produced by your program, modify it to determine the branch currents for the following values: R_1 = 1500, R_2 = 1200, R_3 = 2000, E_1 = 15, and E_2 = 12.

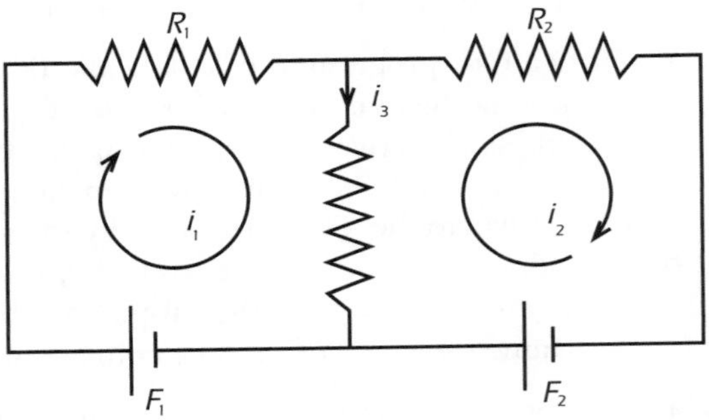

Figure 3.7 An electical circuit.

3.2 FORMATTING NUMBERS FOR PROGRAM OUTPUT

Besides displaying correct results, it is extremely important for a program to present its results attractively. Most programs are judged on the perceived ease of data entry and the style and presentation of their output. For example, displaying a monetary result as 1.897 is not in keeping with accepted report conventions. The display should be \$1.90 or \$1.89, depending on whether rounding or truncation is used.

The format of numbers displayed by `cout` can be controlled by field width manipulators included in each output stream. Table 3.1 lists the most commonly used manipulators available for this purpose.[6]

[6] As was noted in Chapter 2, the `endl` manipulator inserts a `newline` and then flushes the stream.

Table 3.1 Commonly Used Stream Manipulators

Manipulator	Action
`setw(`*n*`)`	Set the field width to *n*.
`setprecision(`*n*`)`	Set the floating-point precision to *n* places. If the `fixed` manipulator is designated, *n* specifies the total number of displayed digits after the decimal point; otherwise, *n* specifies the total number of significant digits displayed (integer plus fractional digits).
`setfill('`*x*`')`	Set the default leading fill character to *x*. (The default leading fill character is a space, which is output to fill the front of an output field whenever the width of the field is larger than the value being displayed.)
`setiosflags(`*flags*`)`	Set the format flags (see Table 3.3 for flag settings).
`scientific`	Set the output to display real numbers in scientific notation.
`showbase`	Display the base used for numbers. A leading `0` is displayed for octal numbers and a leading `0x` for hexadecimal numbers.
`showpoint`	Always display six digits in total (combination of integer and fractional parts). Fill with trailing zeros if necessary. For larger integer values, revert to scientific notation.
`showpos`	Display all positive numbers with a leading + sign.
`boolalpha`	Display Boolean values as true and false, rather than as 1 and 0.
`dec`	Set output for decimal display, which is the default.
`endl`	Output a newline character and display all characters in the buffer.
`fixed`	Always show a decimal point and use a default of six digits after the decimal point. Fill with trailing zeros if necessary.
`flush`	Display all the characters in the buffer.
`left`	Left-justify all numbers.
`hex`	Set output for hexadecimal display.
`oct`	Set output for octal display.
`uppercase`	Display hexadecimal digits and the exponent in scientific notation in uppercase.
`right`	Right-justify all numbers (this is the default).
`noboolalpha`	Display Boolean values as 1 and 0, rather than as true and false.
`noshowbase`	Do not display octal numbers with a leading 0 and hexadecimal numbers with a leading 0x.
`noshowpoint`	Do not use a decimal point for real numbers with no fractional parts, do not display trailing zeros in the fractional part of a number, and display a maximum of 6 decimal digits only.
`noshowpos`	Do not display leading + signs (this is the default).
`nouppercase`	Display hexadecimal digits and the exponent in scientific notation in lowercase.

For example, the statement `cout << "The sum of 6 and 15 is" << setw(3) << 21;` creates this printout:

```
The sum of 6 and 15 is 21
```

The `setw(3)` field width manipulator included in the stream of data passed to `cout` is used to set the displayed field width. The 3 in this manipulator sets the default field width for the next number in the stream to be three spaces wide. This field width setting causes the 21 to be printed in a field of three spaces, which includes one blank and the number 21. As illustrated, integers are right-justified within the specified field.

Field width manipulators are useful in printing columns of numbers so the numbers in each column align correctly. For example, Program 3.5 illustrates how a column of integers would align in the absence of field width manipulators.

Program 3.5

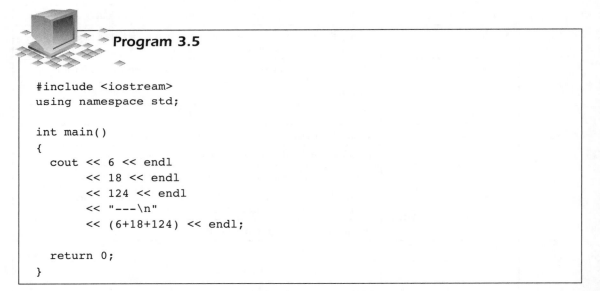

```
#include <iostream>
using namespace std;

int main()
{
  cout << 6 << endl
       << 18 << endl
       << 124 << endl
       << "---\n"
       << (6+18+124) << endl;

  return 0;
}
```

The output of Program 3.5 is the following:

```
6
18
124
---
148
```

Since no field width manipulators are included in Program 3.5, the `cout` object allocates enough space for each number as it is received. To force the numbers to align on the units digit requires a field width wide enough for the largest displayed number. For Program 3.5, a width of three would suffice. The use of this field width is illustrated in Program 3.6.

Program 3.6

```
#include <iostream>
#include <iomanip>
using namespace std;

int main()
{
  cout << setw(3) << 6 << endl
       << setw(3) << 18 << endl
       << setw(3) << 124 << endl
       << "---\n"
       << (6+18+124) << endl;

  return 0;
}
```

The output of Program 3.6 is

```
  6
 18
124
---
148
```

The field width manipulator must be included for each occurrence of a number inserted into the data stream sent to `cout;` this particular manipulator only applies to the next insertion of data immediately following it. The other manipulators remain in effect until they are changed.

When a manipulator requiring an argument is used, the `iomanip` header file must be included as part of the program. This is accomplished by the preprocessor command `#include <iomanip>`, which is listed as the second line in Program 3.6.

Completely formatting floating-point numbers requires the use of three field width manipulators. The first manipulator sets the total width of the display, the second manipulator forces the display of a decimal point, and the third manipulator determines how many significant digits will be displayed to the right of the decimal point. For example, examine the following statement:

```
cout << "|" << setw(10) << fixed << setprecision(3) << 25.67 << "|";
```

It causes the following printout:

```
|    25.670|
```

The bar symbol, |, in the example is used to delimit (mark) the beginning and end of the display field. The `setw` manipulator tells `cout` to display the number in a total field of 10, the fixed manipulator explicitly forces the display of a decimal point and designates that the `setprecision` manipulator is used to designate the number of digits to be displayed after the decimal point. In this case, a display of three digits after the decimal point is specified by `setprecision`. Without the explicit designation of a decimal point (which can also be designated as setiosflags(ios::fixed)), the `setprecision` manipulator specifies the total number of displayed digits, which includes the integer and fractional parts of the number..

For all numbers (integers, single-precision, and double-precision), `cout` ignores the `setw` manipulator specification if the total specified field width is too small, and it allocates enough space for the integer part of the number to be printed. The fractional part of single-precision and double-precision numbers is displayed up to the precision set with the `setprecision` manipulator. (In the absence of a `setprecision` manipulator, the default precision is set to six decimal places.) If the fractional part of the number to be displayed contains more digits than called for in the `setprecision` manipulator, the number is rounded to the indicated number of decimal places; if the fractional part contains fewer digits than specified, the number is displayed with the fewer digits. Table 3.2 illustrates the effect of various format manipulator combinations. Again, for clarity, the bar symbol, |, is used to delineate the beginning and end of the output fields.

Table 3.2 Effect of Format Manipulators

<table>
<tr><th>Manipulators</th><th>Number</th><th>Display</th><th>Comments</th></tr>
<tr><td><code>setw(2)</code></td><td><code>3</code></td><td><code>| 3|</code></td><td>Number fits in field</td></tr>
<tr><td><code>setw(2)</code></td><td><code>43</code></td><td><code>|43|</code></td><td>Number fits in field</td></tr>
<tr><td><code>setw(2)</code></td><td><code>143</code></td><td><code>|143|</code></td><td>Field width ignored</td></tr>
<tr><td><code>setw(2)</code></td><td><code>2.3</code></td><td><code>|2.3|</code></td><td>Field width ignored</td></tr>
<tr><td><code>setw(5)</code>
<code>fixed</code>
<code>setprecision(2)</code></td><td><code>2.366</code></td><td><code>| 2.37|</code></td><td>Field width of 5 with two decimal digits</td></tr>
<tr><td><code>setw(5)</code>
<code>fixed</code>
<code>setprecision(2)</code></td><td><code>42.3</code></td><td><code>|42.30|</code></td><td>Number fits in field with specified precision</td></tr>
<tr><td><code>setw(5)</code>
<code>setprecision(2)</code></td><td><code>142.364</code></td><td><code>|1.4e+002|</code></td><td>Field width ignored and scientific notation used with the <code>setprecision</code> manipulator specifying the total number of significant digits (integer plus fractional).</td></tr>
</table>

Point of Information

What is a Flag?

In current programming usage, the term **flag** refers to an item, such as a variable or argument, that sets a condition usually considered active or nonactive. Though the exact origin of this term in programming is unknown, it probably originated from the use of real flags to signal a condition, such as the Stop, Go, Caution, and Winner flags commonly used at car races.

In a similar manner, each flag argument for the `setiosflags()` manipulator function activates a specific condition. For example, the `ios::dec` flag sets the display format to decimal, and the flag `ios::oct` activates the octal display format. Since these conditions are mutually exclusive (only one condition can be active at a time), activating one such flag automatically deactivates the other flags.

Flags that are not mutually exclusive, such as `ios::dec`, `ios::showpoint`, and `ios::fixed` can all be set to on simultaneously. This can be done using three individual `setiosflag()` calls or combining all arguments into one call as follows:

```
cout << setiosflags(ios::dec | ios::fixed | ios::showpoint);
```

Table 3.2 Effect of Format Manipulators (continued)

Manipulators	Number	Display	Comments

`setw(5)`
`fixed`
`setprecision(2)`
	`142.364`	`|142.36|`	Field width ignored but precision specification used. Here the `setprecison` manipulator specifies the number of fractional digits

`setw(5)`
`fixed`
`setprecision(2)`
	`142.366`	`|142.37|`	Field width ignored but precision specification used. Here the `setprecison` manipulator specifies the number of fractional digits. (Note the rounding of the last decimal digit)

`setw(5)`
`fixed`
`setprecision(2)`
	`142`	`|  142|`	Field width used, fixed and `setprecision` manipulators irrelevant, because the number is an integer.

In addition to the `setw` and `setprecision` manipulators, a field justification manipulator is also available. As we have seen, numbers sent to `cout` are normally displayed right-justified in the display field, while strings are displayed left-justified. To alter the default justification for a stream of data, the `setiosflags` manipulator can be used. For example, examine the following statement:

```
cout << "|" << setw(10) << setiosflags(ios::left) << 142 << "|";
```

This causes the following left-justified display:

```
|142       |
```

As we have seen, since data passed to `cout` may be continued across multiple lines, the previous display would also be produced by the statement:

```
cout << "|" << setw(10)
        << setiosflags(ios::left)
        << 142 << "|";
```

As always, the field width manipulator is only in effect for the next single set of data displayed by `cout`. Right-justification for strings in a stream is obtained by the `setiosflags(ios::right)` manipulator. The symbol `ios` in the function name and the `ios::right` argument comes from the first letters of the words "input output stream."

In addition to the left and right flags that can be used with the `setiosflags()` manipulator, other flags may be used to affect the output. The most commonly used flags for this manipulator are listed in Table 3.3. The flags in this table effectively provide an alternate way of setting the equivalent manipulators previously listed in Table 3.1.

Table 3.3 Format Flags for Use with `setiosflags()`

Flag	Meaning
`ios::fixed`	Always show the decimal point with six digits after the decimal point. Fill with trailing zeros if necessary. This flag takes precedence if it is set with the `ios::showpoint` flag.
`ios::scientific`	Use exponential display on output.
`ios::showpoint`	Always display a decimal point and six significant digits in total (combination of integer and fractional parts). Fill with trailing zeros after the decimal point if necessary. For larger integer values, revert to scientific notation unless the `ios::fixed` flag is set.
`ios::showpos`	Display a leading + sign when the number is positive.
`ios::left`	Left-justify output.
`ios::right`	Right-justify output.

Point of Information

Formatting `cout` Stream Data

Floating-point data in a `cout` output stream can be formatted in precise ways. One of the most common format requirements is to display numbers in a monetary format with two digits after the decimal point, such as 123.45. This can be done with the following statement:

```
cout << setiosflags(ios::fixed)
     << setiosflags(ios::showpoint)
     << setprecision(2);
```

The first manipulator flag, `ios::fixed`, forces all floating-point numbers placed on the `cout` stream to be displayed in decimal notation. This flag also prevents the use of scientific notation. The next flag, `ios::showpoint`, tells the stream to always display a decimal point. Finally, the `setprecision` manipulator tells the stream to always display two decimal values after the decimal point. Instead of using manipulators, you can also use the `cout` stream methods `setf()` and `precision()`. For example, the previous formatting can also be accomplished using the code:

```
cout.setf(ios::fixed);
cout.setf(ios::showpoint);
cout.precision(2);
```

Note the syntax here: the name of the object, `cout`, is separated from the method with a period. This is the standard way of specifying a method and connecting it to a specific object. Which style you select is a matter of preference.

Addtionally, the flags used in both the `setf()` method and the `setiosflags()` manipulator can be combined using the bitwise Or operator, | (explained in Section 16.1). Using this operator, the following two statements are equivalent.

```
cout <<  setiosflags(ios::fixed | ios::showpoint);
cout.setf(ios::fixed | ios::showpoint);
```

The style you select is a matter of preference.

Because the flags in Table 3.3 are used as arguments to the `setiosflags()` manipulator method and because the terms "argument" and "parameter" are synonymous, another name for a manipulator method that uses arguments is a **parameterized manipulator.** The following is an example of parameterized manipulator methods:

```
cout << setiosflags(ios::showpoint) << setprecision(4);
```

This forces all subsequent floating-point numbers sent to the output stream to be displayed with a decimal point and four decimal digits. If the number has fewer than four decimal digits, it will be padded with trailing zeros.

In addition to outputting integers in decimal notation, the `oct` and `hex` manipulators permit conversions to octal and hexadecimal, respectively. Program 3.7 illustrates the use of these flags. Because decimal is the default display, the `dec` manipulator is not required in the first output stream.

Program 3.7

```
// a program that illustrates output conversions
#include <iostream>
#include <iomanip>
using namespace std;

int main()
{
  cout << "The decimal (base 10) value of 15 is " << 15 << endl;
  cout << "The octal (base 8) value of 15 is "
       << showbase << oct << 15 <<endl;
  cout << "The hexadecimal (base 16) value of 15 is "
         << showbase << hex << 15 << endl;

  return 0;
}
```

The output produced by Program 3.7 is the following:

```
The decimal (base 10) value of 15 is 15
The octal (base 8) value of 15 is 017
The hexadecimal (base 16) value of 15 is 0xf
```

The display of integer values in one of the three possible number systems (decimal, octal, and hexadecimal) does not affect how the number is stored inside a computer. All numbers are stored using the computer's own internal codes. The manipulators sent to `cout` tell the object how to convert the internal code for output display purposes.

Besides displaying integers in octal or hexadecimal form, integer constants can be written in a program in these forms. To designate an octal integer constant, the number must have a leading zero. The number 023, for example, is an octal number in C++. Hexadecimal numbers are denoted using a leading 0x. The use of octal and hexadecimal integer constants is illustrated in Program 3.8.

Program 3.8

```
#include <iostream>
using namespace std;

int main()
{
  cout << "The decimal value of 025 is " << 025 << endl
       << "The decimal value of 0x37 is "<< 0x37 << endl;

  return 0;
}
```

The output produced by Program 3.8 is the following:

```
The decimal value of 025 is 21
The decimal value of 0x37 is 55
```

The relationship between the input, storage, and display of integers is illustrated in Figure 3.8.

Finally, the manipulators specified in Tables 3.1 and 3.2 can be set using the `ostream` class methods listed in Table 3.4.

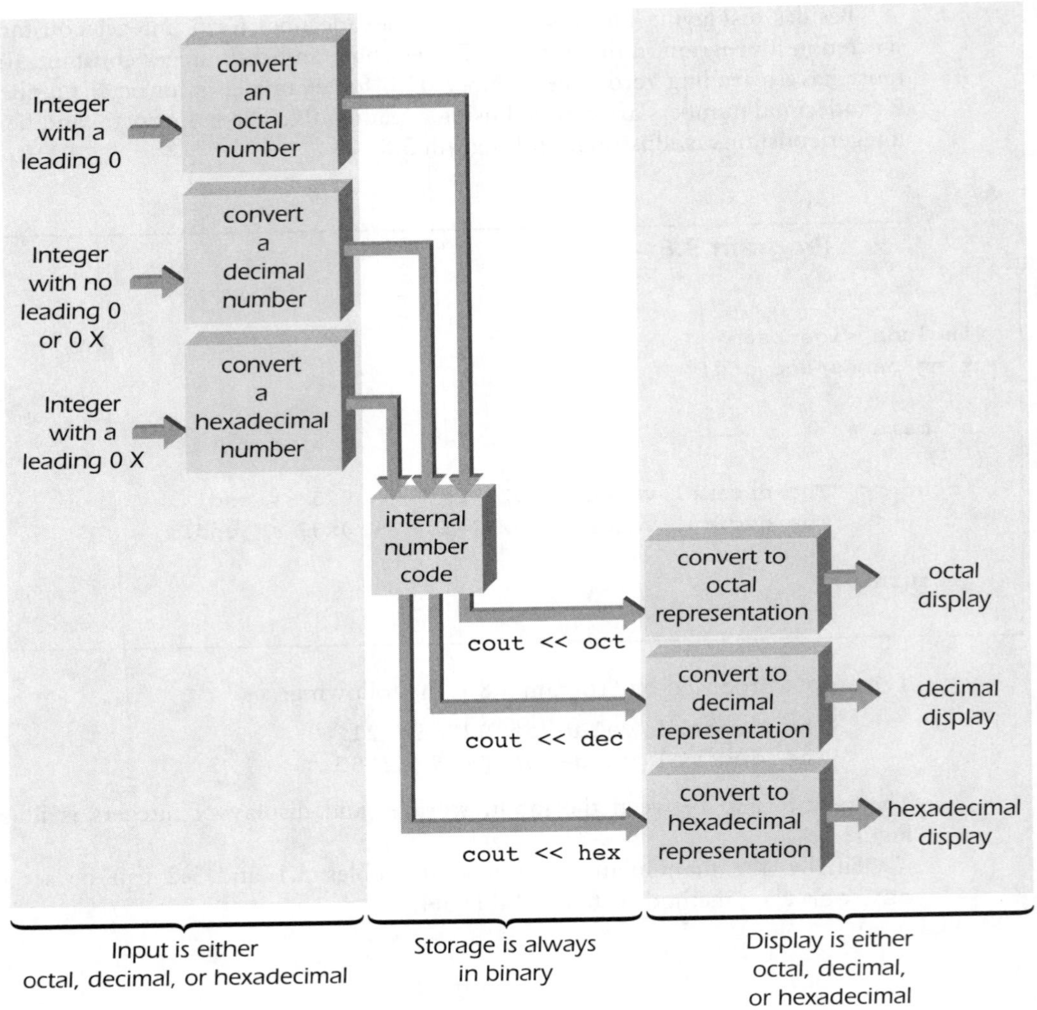

Figure 3.8 Input, storage, and display of integers.

Table 3.4 ostream Class Methods

Method	Comment	Example
`precision(n)`	Equivalent to `setprecision()`	`cout.precision(2)`
`fill('x')`	Equivalent to `setfill()`	`cout.fill('*')`
`setf(ios::fixed)`	Equivalent to `setiosflags(ios::fixed)`	`cout.setf(ios::fixed)`
`setf(ios::showpoint)`	Equivalent to `setiosflags(ios::showpoint)`	`cout.setf(ios::showpoint)`
`setf(iof::left)`	Equivalent to `left`	`cout.setf(ios::left)`
`setf(ios::right)`	Equivalent to `right`	`cout.setf(ios::right)`
`setf(ios::flush)`	Equivalent to `endl`	`cout.setf(ios::flush)`

In the Examples column of Table 3.4, the name of the object, cout, is separated from the method with a period. This is the standard way of calling a class method and providing it with the object it is to operate on.

Exercises 3.2

1. Determine the output of the following program:

```
#include <iostream>
using namespace std;

int main()  // a program illustrating integer truncation
{
  cout << "answer1 is the integer " <<  9/4
       << "\nanswer2 is the integer " <<  17/3 << endl;

  return 0;
}
```

2. Determine the output of the following program:

```
#include <iostream>
using namespace std;

int main()  // a program illustrating the % operator
{
  cout << "The remainder of 9 divided by 4 is " <<  9 % 4
       << "\nThe remainder of 17 divided by 3 is " <<  17 % 3 << endl;

  return 0;
}
```

3. Write a C++ program that displays the results of the expressions 3.0 * 5.0, 7.1 * 8.3 – 2.2, and 3.2 / (6.1 * 5). Calculate the value of these expressions manually to verify that the displayed values are correct.

4. Write a C++ program that displays the results of the expressions 15 / 4, 15 % 4, and 5 * 3 – (6 * 4). Calculate the value of these expressions manually to verify that the display produced by your program is correct.

5. Determine the errors in each of the following statements:

a. `cout << "\n << " 15)`
b. `cout << "setw(4)" <<  33;`
c. `cout << "setprecision(5)" <<  526.768;`
d. `"Hello World!" >> cout;`
e. `cout << 47 << setw(6);`
f. `cout << set(10) << 526.768 << setprecision(2);`

6. Determine and write out the display produced by the following statements:

a. `cout << "|" << 5 <<"|";`
b. `cout << "|" << setw(4) << 5 << "|";`
c. `cout << "|" << setw(4) << 56829 << "|";`
d.
```
cout << "|" << setw(5) << setiosflags(ios::fixed)
     << setprecision(2) << 5.26 << "|";
```
e.
```
cout << "|" << setw(5) << setiosflags(ios::fixed)
     << setprecision(2) << 5.267 << "|";
```
f.
```
cout << "|" << setw(5) << setiosflags(ios::fixed)
     << setprecision(2) << 53.264 << "|";
```
g.
```
cout << "|" << setw(5) << setiosflags(ios::fixed)
     << setprecision(2) << 534.264 << "|";
```
h.
```
cout << "|" << setw(5) << setiosflags(ios::fixed)
     << setprecision(2) << 534. << "|";
```

7. Write out the display produced by the following statements.

a.
```
cout << "The number is " << setw(6) << setiosflags(ios::fixed)
     << setprecision(2) << 26.27 << endl;
cout << "The number is " << setw(6) << setiosflags(ios::fixed)
     << setprecision(2) << 682.3 << endl;
cout << "The number is " << setw(6) << setiosflags(ios::fixed)
     << setprecision(2) << 1.968 << endl;
```
b.
```
cout << setw(6) << setiosflags(ios::fixed)
     << setprecision(2) << 26.27 << endl;
cout << setw(6) << setiosflags(ios::fixed)
     << setprecision(2) << 682.3 << endl;
cout << setw(6) << setiosflags(ios::fixed)
     << setprecision(2) << 1.968 << endl;
cout << "------\n";
cout << setw(6) << setiosflags(ios::fixed)
     << setprecision(2)
     << 26.27 + 682.3 + 1.968 << endl;
```

c.
```
cout << setw(5) << setiosflags(ios::fixed)
     << setprecision(2) << 26.27 << endl;
cout << setw(5) << setiosflags(ios::fixed)
     << setprecision(2) << 682.3 << endl;
cout << setw(5) << setiosflags(ios::fixed)
     << setprecision(2) << 1.968 << endl;
cout << "-----\n";
cout << setw(5) << setiosflags(ios::fixed)
     << setprecision(2)
     << 26.27 + 682.3 + 1.968 << endl;
```

d.
```
cout << setw(5) << setiosflags(ios::fixed)
     << setprecision(2) << 36.164 << endl;
cout << setw(5) << setiosflags(ios::fixed)
     << setprecision(2) << 10.003 << endl;
cout << "-----" << endl;
```

8. The following table lists the correspondence between the decimal numbers 1 through 15 and their octal and hexadecimal representation.

Decimal:	1	2	3	4	5	6	7	8	9	10	11	12	13	14	15
Octal:	1	2	3	4	5	6	7	10	11	12	13	14	15	16	17
Hexadecimal:	1	2	3	4	5	6	7	8	9	a	b	c	d	e	f

Using the above table, determine the output of the following program.

```
#include <iostream>
#include <iomanip>
using namespace std;

int main()
{
  cout << "\nThe value of 14 in octal is " << oct << 14
       << "\nThe value of 14 in hexadecimal is " << hex << 14
       << "\nThe value of 0xA in decimal is " << dec << 0xA
       << "\nThe value of 0xA in octal is " << oct << 0xA
       << endl;

  return 0;
}
```

9. The combined resistance of three resistors connected in parallel, as shown in Figure 3.9, is given by the equation

$$\text{Combined resistance} = \frac{1}{\dfrac{1}{R_1} + \dfrac{1}{R_2} + \dfrac{1}{R_3}}$$

Using this formula, write a C++ program to calculate and display the combined resistance when the three resistors $R_1 = 1000$, $R_2 = 1000$, and $R_3 = 1000$ are connected in parallel. The output should produce the display

```
The combined resistance is xxxx.xx ohms,
```

where xxxx.xx denotes that the calculated value should be placed in a field width of 7 columns, with two positions to the right of the decimal point.

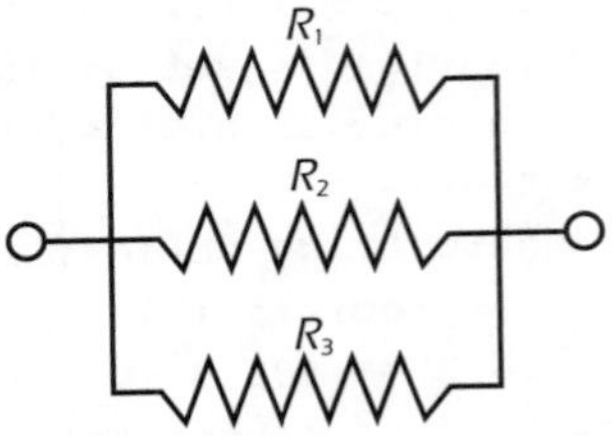

Figure 3.9 Three resistors connected in parallel.

10. Write a C++ program to calculate and display the value of the slope of the line connecting the two points whose coordinates are (3,7) and (8,12). Use the fact that the slope between two points having coordinates (x1,y1) and (x2,y2) is slope = (y2 – y1) / (x2 – x1). The display produced by your program should be: The value of the slope is xxx.xx, where xxx.xx denotes that the calculated value should be placed in a field wide enough for three places to the left of the decimal point, and two places to the right of it.

11. Write a C++ program to calculate and display the coordinates of the midpoint of the line connecting the two points whose coordinates are (3,7) and (8,12). Use the fact that the coordinates of the midpoint between two points having coordinates (x1,y1) and (x2,y2) are ((X1 + X2)/2, (Y1 + Y2)/2). The display produced by your program should be:

```
The x coordinate of the midpoint is xxx.xx
The y coordinate of the midpoint is xxx.xx
```

where xxx.xx denotes that the calculated value should be placed in a field wide enough for three places to the left of the decimal point, and two places to the right of it.

12. Write a C++ program to calculate and display the maximum bending moment, M, of a beam, which is supported on both ends (see Figure 3.10). The formula for maximum bending moment is, $M = XW(L - X) / L$, where X is the distance from the end of the beam that a weight, W, is placed, and L is the length of the beam. The display produced by your program should be

```
The maximum bending moment is xxxx.xxxx
```

where xxxx.xxxx denotes that the calculated value should be placed in a field wide enough for four places to the right and left of the decimal point.

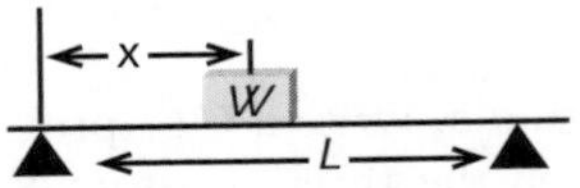

Figure 3.10 Calculating the maximum bending moment.

13. For the electrical circuit shown in Figure 3.11, the branch currents, i_1, i_2, and, i_3 can be determined using the formulas

$$i_1 = \frac{E_2R_3 + E_1(R_1 + R_3)}{(R_1 + R_3)(R_2 + R_3) - (R_3)^2}$$

$$i_2 = \frac{E_1R_3 + E_2(R_1 + R_3)}{(R_1 + R_3)(R_2 + R_3) - (R_3)^2}$$

$$i_3 = i_1 - i_2$$

Using these formulas write a C++ program to compute the branch currents when R_1 = 10 ohms, R_2 = 4 ohms, R_3 = 6 ohms, E_1 = 12 volts, and E_2 = 9 volts. The display produced by your program should be

```
Branch current 1 is xx.xxxxx
Branch current 2 is xx.xxxxx
Branch current 3 is xx.xxxxx
```

where xx.xxxxx denotes that the calculated value should be placed in a field wide enough for two places to the left of the decimal point and five places to the right of it.

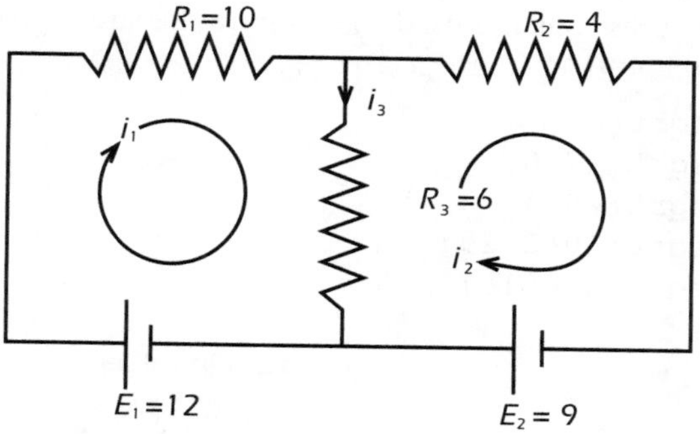

Figure 3.11 Calculating loop currents in an electrical circuit.

3.3 USING MATHEMATICAL LIBRARY FUNCTIONS

As we have seen, assignment statements can be used to perform arithmetic computations. For example, the assignment statement

```
volts = resistance * current;
```

multiplies the value in `current` times the value in `resistance` and assigns the resulting value to `volts`. Although addition, subtraction, multiplication, and division are easily accomplished using C++'s arithmetic operators, no such operators exist for raising a number to a power, finding the square root of a number, or determining trigonometric values. To facilitate such calculations, C++ provides standard preprogrammed functions that can be included in a program.

Before using one of C++'s mathematical functions, you need to know

- The name of the desired mathematical function
- What the mathematical function does
- The type of data required by the mathematical function
- The data type of the result returned by the mathematical function
- How to include the library

To illustrate the use of C++'s mathematical functions, consider the mathematical function named `sqrt`, which calculates the square root of a number. The square root of a number is computed using the expression

```
sqrt(number)
```

where the function's name, in this case `sqrt`, is followed by parentheses containing the number for which the square root is desired. The purpose of the parentheses following the function name is to provide a funnel through which data can be passed to the function (see Figure 3.12). The items that are passed to the function through the parentheses are called arguments of the function and constitute its input data. For example, the following expressions are used to compute the square root of the arguments 4., 17.0, 25., 1043.29, and 6.4516, respectively:

```
sqrt(4.)
sqrt(17.0)
sqrt(25.)
sqrt(1043.29)
sqrt(6.4516)
```

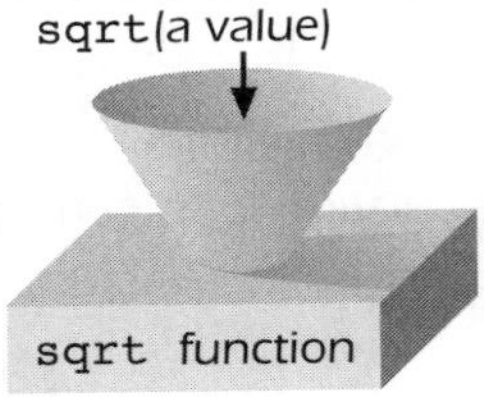

Figure 3.12 Passing data to the `sqrt()` function.

Notice that the argument to the `sqrt()` function must be a real value. This is an example of C++'s function overloading capabilities. Function overloading permits the same function name to be defined for different argument data types. In this case there are really three square root functions named `sqrt()`—one defined for float, double, and long double arguments. The correct `sqrt` function is called depending on the type of value given it. The `sqrt()` function determines the square root of its argument and returns the result as a double. The values returned by the previous expressions are

Expression	Value Returned
`sqrt(4.)`	2
`sqrt(17.0)`	4.12311
`sqrt(25.)`	5
`sqrt(1043.29)`	32.3
`sqrt(6.4516)`	2.54

In addition to the `sqrt` function, Table 3.5 lists the more commonly used mathematical functions provided in C++. To access these functions in a program requires that the mathematical header file named `cmath`, which contains appropriate declarations for the mathematical function, be included with the function. This is done by placing the following preprocessor statement at the top of any program using a mathematical function:

```
#include <cmath>   ◄——— no semicolon
```

Although some of the mathematical functions listed require more than one argument, all functions, by definition, can directly return at most one value. Additionally, all the functions listed are overloaded: this means the same function name can be used with integer and real arguments. Table 3.6 illustrates the value returned by selected functions using example arguments.

Table 3.5 Common C++ Functions

Function Name	Description	Returned Value
`abs(a)`	absolute value	same data type as argument
`pow(a1,a2)`	a1 raised to the a2 power	data type of argument a1
`sqrt(a)`	square root of a real number	double-precision
`sin(a)`	sine of a (a in radians)	double
`cos(a)`	cosine of a (d in radians)	double
`tan(a)`	tangent of a (d in radians)	double
`log(a)`	natural logarithm of a	double
`log10(a)`	common log (base 10) of a	double
`exp(a)`	e raised to the a power	double

Table 3.6 Selected Function Examples

Example	Returned Value
`abs(-7.362)`	7.362
`abs(-3)`	3
`pow(2.0,5.0)`	32
`pow(10,3)`	1000
`log(18.697)`	2.92836
`log10(18.697)`	1.27177
`exp(-3.2)`	0.040762

In each case that a mathematical function is used it is called into action by giving the name of the function and passing any data to it within the parentheses following the function's name (see Figure 3.13).

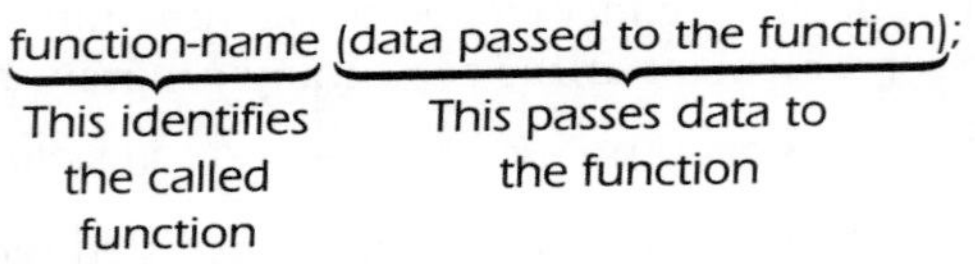

Figure 3.13 Using and passing data to a function.

The arguments that are passed to a function need not be single constants. Expressions can also be arguments provided that the expression can be computed to yield a value of the required data type. For example, the following arguments are valid for the given functions:

```
sqrt(4.0 + 5.3 * 4.0)          abs(2.3 * 4.6)
sqrt(16.0 * 2.0 - 6.7)         sin(theta - phi)
sqrt(x * y - z/3.2)            cos(2.0 * omega)
```

The expressions in parentheses are first evaluated to yield a specific value. Thus, values would have to be assigned to the variables theta, phi, *x*, *y*, *z*, and omega before their use in the above expressions. After the value of the argument is calculated, it is passed to the function.

Functions may also be included as part of larger expressions. For example,

```
    4 * sqrt(4.5 * 10.0 - 9.0) - 2.0
=   4 * sqrt(36.0) - 2.0
=   4 * 6.0 - 2.0
=   24.0 - 2.0
=   22.0
```

The step-by-step evaluation of an expression such as

```
3.0 * sqrt(5 * 33 - 13.71) / 5
```

is

Step	Result
1. Perform multiplication in argument	`3.0 * sqrt(165 - 13.71) / 5`
2. Complete argument calculation	`3.0 * sqrt(151.29) / 5`
3. Return a function value	`3.0 * 12.3 / 5`
4. Perform the multiplication	`36.9 / 5`
5. Perform the division	`7.38`

Program 3.9 illustrates the use of the `sqrt` function to determine the time it takes a ball to hit the ground after it has been dropped from an 800-foot tower. The mathematical formula used to calculate the time, in seconds, that it takes to fall a given distance, in feet, is

```
time = sqrt(2 * distance / g)
```

where *g* is the gravitational constant equal to 32.2 ft/sec^2.

Program 3.9

```
#include <iostream>  // this line may be placed second instead of first
#include <cmath>     // this line may be placed first instead of second
using namespace std;

int main()
{
  int height;
  double time;

  height = 800;
  time = sqrt(2 * height / 32.2);
  cout << "It will take " << time << " seconds to fall "
       << height << " feet.\n";

  return 0;
}
```

The output produced by Program 3.9 is

```
It will take 7.04907 seconds to fall 800 feet.
```

As used in Program 3.9, the value returned by the sqrt function is assigned to the variable time. In addition to assigning a function's returned value to a variable, the returned value may be included within a larger expression, or even used as an argument to another function. For example, the expression

```
sqrt( sin( abs(theta) ) )
```

is valid. Since parentheses are present, the computation proceeds from the inner to the outer pairs of parentheses. Thus, the absolute value of theta is computed first and used as an argument to the sin function. The value returned by the sin function is then used as an argument to the sqrt() function.

Note that the arguments of all trigonometric functions (sin, cos, etc.) must be in radians. Thus, to obtain the sine of an angle that is given in degrees the angle must first be converted to radian measure. This is easily accomplished by multiplying the angle by the term (3.1416/180.) For example, to obtain the sine of 30 degrees, the expression sin (30 * 3.1416/180.) may be used.

Casts

We have already seen the conversion of an operand's data type within mixed-mode arithmetic expressions (Section 2.4) and across assignment operators (Section 3.1). In addition to these implicit data type conversions that are automatically made within mixed-mode arithmetic and assignment expressions, C++ also provides for explicit user-specified type conversions. The operator used to force the conversion of a value to another type is the **cast operator.** C++ provides compile-time and run-time cast operators.

The compile-time cast is a unary operator having the syntax dataType (expression), where dataType is the desired data type that the expression within parentheses is converted to. For example, the following expression

```
int (a * b)
```

ensures the value of the expression a * b is converted to an integer value.[7]

With the introduction of the latest C++ standard, run-time casts were included. In this type of cast, the requested type conversion is checked at run time and is applied if the conversion results in a valid value. Though four types of run-time casts are available, the most commonly used cast and the one corresponding to the compile-time cast has the following syntax:

```
staticCast<data-type> (expression)
```

For example, the run-time cast staticCast<int>(a * b) is equivalent to the compile-time cast int (a* b).

[7]The C type cast syntax, in this case (int)(a * b), also works in C++.

Exercises 3.3

1. Write function calls to determine:
   a. The square root of 6.37.
   b. The square root of x – y.
   c. The sine of 30 degrees.
   d. The sine of 60 degrees.
   e. The absolute value of $a^2 - b^2$.
   f. The value of e raised to the third power.

2. For $a = 10.6$, $b = 13.9$, $c = -3.42$, determine the following values:
   a. `int (a)`
   b. `int (b)`
   c. `int (c)`
   d. `int (a + b)`
   e. `int (a) + b + c`
   f. `int (a + b) + c`
   g. `int (a + b + c)`
   h. `float (int (a)) + b`
   i. `float (int (a + b))`
   j. `abs(a) + abs(b)`
   k. `sqrt(abs(a - b))`

3. Write C++ statements for the following:
   a. $b = \sin x - \cos x$
   b. $b = \sin^2 x - \cos^2 x$
   c. $area = (c * b * \sin a)/2$
   d. $c = \sqrt{a^2 + b^2}$
   e. $p = \sqrt{|m - n|}$
   f. $sum = \dfrac{a(r^n - 1)}{r - 1}$

4. Write, compile, and execute a C++ program that calculates and returns the fourth root of the number 81.0, which is 3. When you have verified that your program works correctly, use it to determine the fourth root of 1,728.896400. Your program should make use of the `sqrt()` function.

5. Write, compile, and execute a C++ program that calculates the distance between two points whose coordinates are (7, 12) and (3, 9). Use the fact that the distance between two points having coordinates (x_1, y_1) and (x_2, y_2) is $distance = sqrt([x_1 - x_2]^2 + [y_1 - y_2]^2)$. When you have verified that your program works correctly, by calculating the distance between the two points manually, use your program to determine the distance between the points (–12, –15) and (22, 5).

6. If a 20-foot ladder is placed on the side of a building at a 85-degree angle, as illustrated on Figure 3.14, the height at which the ladder touches the building can be calculated as *height* = 20 * sin 85°. Calculate this height by hand and then write, compile, and execute a C++ program that determines and displays the value of the height. When you have verified that your program works correctly, use it to determine the height of a 25-foot ladder placed at an angle of 85 degrees.

Figure 3.14 Calculating the height of a ladder against a building.

7. The maximum height reached by a ball thrown with an initial velocity v, in meters/sec, at an angle of θ is given by the formula *height* = (.5 * v^2 * $\sin^2 \theta$) / 9.8. Using this formula, write, compile, and execute a C++ program that determines and displays the maximum height reached when the ball is thrown at 5 miles/hour at an angle of 60 degrees. (*Hint:* Make sure to convert the initial velocity into the correct units. There are 1609 meters in a mile.) Calculate the maximum height manually and verify the result produced by your program. After you have verified that your program works correctly, use it to determine the height reached by a ball thrown at 7 miles/hour at an angle of 45 degrees.

8. For small values of x, the value of sin(x) can be approximated by the power series:

$$x - \frac{x^3}{6} + \frac{x^5}{120} - \ldots$$

As with the sin function, the value of x must be in radians. Using this power series, write, compile, and execute a C++ program that approximates the sine of 180/3.1416 degrees, which equals one radian. Additionally, have your program use the sin function to calculate the sine and display both calculated values and the absolute difference of the two results. Verify the approximation produced by your program by hand. After you have verified your program is working correctly, use it to approximate the value of the sine of 62.2 degrees.

9. The polar coordinates of a point consist of the distance, r, from a specified origin and an angle, θ, with respect to the x axis. The x and y coordinates of the point are related to its polar coordinates by the formulas

$$x = r \cos \theta$$
$$y = r \sin \theta$$

Using these formulas, write a C++ program that calculates the x and y coordinates of the point whose polar coordinates are $r = 10$ and $\theta = 30$ degrees. Verify the results produced by your program by calculating the results manually. After you have verified your program is working correctly, use it to convert the polar coordinates $r = 12.5$ and $\theta = 67.8°$ into rectangular coordinates.

10. A model of worldwide population growth, in billions of people, since 2000 is given by the equation:

$$Population = 6.0\ e^{0.02[Year\ -\ 2000]}$$

Using this formula, write, compile, and execute a C++ program to estimate the worldwide population in the year 2005. Verify the result displayed by your program by calculating the answer manually. After you have verified your program is working correctly, use it to estimate the world's population in the year 2012.

11. A model to estimate the number of grams of a certain radioactive isotope left after N years is given by the formula

$$Remaining\ material = (Original\ material)\ e^{-0.00012N}$$

Using this formula, write, compile, and execute a C++ program to determine the amount of radioactive material remaining after 1000 years, assuming an initial amount of 100 grams. Verify the display produced by your program using a hand calculation. After you have verified your program is working correctly, use it to determine the amount of radioactive material remaining after 275 years, assuming an initial amount of 250 grams.

12. The number of years that it takes for a certain isotope of uranium to decay to one-half of an original amount is given by the formula

$$Half\text{-}life = \ln(2)/k$$

where k equals 0.00012. Using this formula, write, compile, and execute a C++ program that calculates and displays the half-life of this uranium isotope. Verify the result produced by your program using a hand calculation. After you have verified your program is working correctly, use it to determine the half-life of a uranium isotope having a $k = 0.00026$.

13. The amplification of electronic circuits is measured in units of decibels, which is calculated as

$$10\ \mathrm{LOG}\ (P_o/P_i)$$

where P_o is the power of the output signal and P_i is the power of the input signal. Using this formula, write, compile, and execute a C++ program that calculates and displays the decibel amplification in which the output power is 50 times the input power. Verify the result displayed by your program using a hand calculation. After you have verified your program is working correctly, use it to determine the amplification of a circuit whose output power is 4.639 watts and input power is 1 watt.

14. The loudness of a sound is measured in units of decibels, which is calculated as

```
10 LOG (SL/RL)
```

where *SL* is intensity of the sound being measured and *RL* is a reference sound intensity level. Using this formula, write a C++ program that calculates and displays the decibel loudness of a busy street having a sound intensity of 10,000,000 *RL*. Verify the result produced by your program using a hand calculation. After you have verified your program is working correctly, use it to determine the sound level, in decibels, of the following sounds:

a. A whisper of sound intensity 200 *RL*
b. A rock band playing at a sound intensity of 1,000,000,000,000 *RL*
c. An airplane taking off at a sound intensity of 100,000,000,000,000 *RL*

15. When a particular rubber ball is dropped from a given height (in meters) its impact speed (in meters/second) when it hits the ground is given by the formula *speed* = sqrt(2 * *g* * *height*). The ball then rebounds to 2/3 the height from which it last fell. Using this information write, test, and run a C++ program that calculates and displays the impact speed of the first three bounces and the rebound height of each bounce. Test your program using an initial height of 2.0 meters. Run the program twice and compare the results for dropping the ball on Earth (g = 9.81 meters/sec^2) and on the moon (g = 1.67 meters/sec^2).

16. a. A balance has the following size weights: 100 lb., 50 lb., 10 lb., 5 lb., and 1 lb. The number of 100 lb. and 50 lb. weights required to weigh an object whose weight is `WEIGHT` pounds can be calculated using the following C++ statements:

```
// Determine the number of 100 lb. Weights
     w100 = int(WEIGHT/100)
// Determine the number of 50 lb. Weights
     w50 = int((WEIGHT - w100 * 100)/50)
```

Using these statements as a starting point, write a C++ program that calculates the number of each type of weight necessary to weigh a 789 lb. object.

b. Without compiling or executing your program, check the effect, by hand, of each statement in the program and determine what is stored in each variable as each statement is encountered.

c. When you have verified that your algorithm works correctly, compile and execute your program. Verify that the results produced by your program are correct. After you have verified your program is working correctly, use it to determine the weights required to weigh a 626 lb. object.

3.4 PROGRAM INPUT USING THE `cin` OBJECT

Data for programs that are only going to be executed once may be included directly in the program. For example, if we wanted to multiply the numbers 30.0 and 0.05, we could use Program 3.10.

Program 3.10

```
#include <iostream>
using namespace std;

int main()
{
  double num1, num2, product;

  num1 = 30.0;
  num2 = 0.05;
  product = num1 * num2;
  cout << "30.0 times 0.05 is " << product << endl;

  return 0;
}
```

The output displayed by Program 3.10 is

```
30.0 times 0.05 is 1.5
```

Program 3.10 can be shortened, as illustrated in Program 3.11. Both programs, however, suffer from the same basic problem in that they must be rewritten in order to multiply different numbers. Both programs lack the facility for entering different numbers on which to operate.

Program 3.11

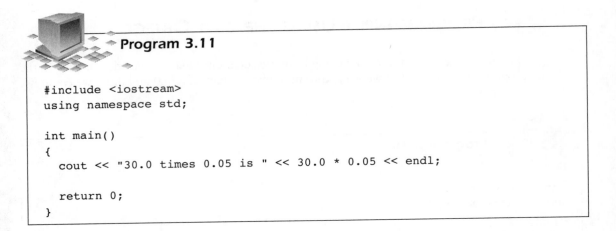

```
#include <iostream>
using namespace std;

int main()
{
  cout << "30.0 times 0.05 is " << 30.0 * 0.05 << endl;

  return 0;
}
```

Except for the practice provided to the programmer of writing, entering, and running the program, programs that do the same calculation only once, on the same set of numbers, are clearly not very useful. After all, it is simpler to use a calculator to multiply two numbers than to enter and run either Program 3.10 or 3.11.

This section presents the `cin` object, which is used to enter data into a program while it is executing. Just as the `cout` object displays a copy of the value stored inside a variable, the `cin` object allows the user to enter a value at the terminal (see Figure 3.15). The value is then stored directly in a variable.

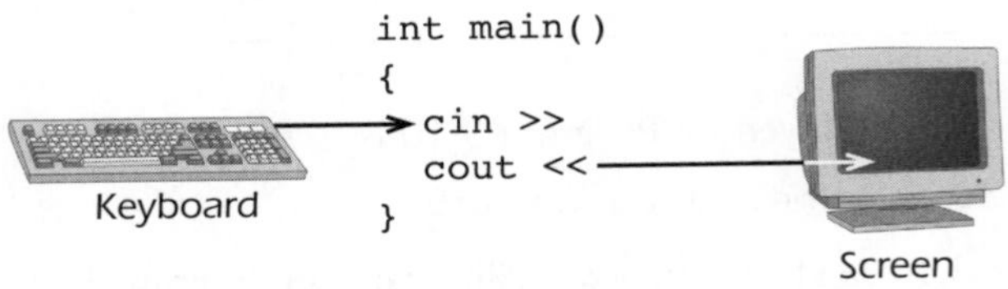

Figure 3.15 `cin` is used to enter data; `cout` is used to display data.

When a statement such as `cin >> num1;` is encountered, the computer stops program execution and accepts data from the keyboard. When a data item is typed, the `cin` object stores the item into the variable listed after the extraction ("get from") operator, >>. The program then continues execution with the next statement after the call to `cin`. To see this, consider Program 3.12.

Program 3.12

```
#include <iostream>
using namespace std;

int main()
{
  double num1, num2, product;

  cout << "Please type in a number: ";
  cin  >> num1;
  cout << "Please type in another number: ";
  cin  >> num2;
  product = num1 * num2;
  cout << num1 << " times " << num2 << " is " << product << endl;

  return 0;
}
```

The first `cout` statement in Program 3.12 prints a string that tells the person at the terminal what should be typed. When an output string is used in this manner it is called a **prompt**. In this case the prompt tells the user to type a number. The computer then executes the next statement, which uses a `cin` object. The `cin` object puts the computer into a temporary pause (or wait) state for as long as it takes the user to type a value. Then the user signals the `cin` object that the data entry is finished by pressing the return key after the value has been typed. The entered value is stored in the variable to the right of the extraction symbol, and the computer is taken out of its paused state. Program execution then proceeds with the next statement, which in Program 3.12 is another statement using `cout`. This statement causes the next message to be displayed. The following statement then uses `cin` to again put the computer into a temporary wait state while the user types a second value. This second number is stored in the variable `num2`.

The following sample run was made using Program 3.12.

```
Please type in a number: 30
Please type in another number: 0.05
30 times 0.05 is 1.5
```

In Program 3.12, each time `cin` is invoked it is used to store one value into a variable. The `cin` object, however, can be used to enter and store as many values as there are extraction symbols, >>, and variables to hold the entered data. For example, the statement

```
cin >> num1 >> num2;
```

results in two values being read from the terminal and assigned to the variables `num1` and `num2`. If the data entered at the terminal was

0.052 245.79

the variables `num1` and `num2` would contain the values 0.052 and 245.79, respectively. Notice that when actually entering numbers such as 0.052 and 245.79, there must be at least one space between the numbers. The space between the entered numbers clearly indicates where one number ends and the next begins. Inserting more than one space between numbers has no effect on `cin`.

The same spacing also is applicable to entering character data; that is, the extraction operator, >>, will skip blank spaces and store the next nonblank character in a character variable. For example, in response to the statements

```
char ch1, ch2, ch3;  // declare three character variables
cin >> ch1 >> ch2 >> ch3;  // accept three characters
```

The input

```
a  b  c
```

causes the letter `a` to be stored in the variable `ch1`, the letter `b` to be stored in the variable `ch2`, and the variable `c` to be stored in the variable `ch3`. Since a character variable can only be used to store one character, the input

```
abc
```

can also be used.

Any number of statements using the `cin` object may be made in a program, and any number of values may be input using a single `cin` statement. Program 3.13 illustrates using the `cin` object to input three numbers from the keyboard. The program then calculates and displays the average of the numbers entered.

Program 3.13

```
#include <iostream>
using namespace std;

int main()
{
  int num1, num2, num3;
  double average;

  cout << "Enter three integer numbers: ";
  cin >> num1 >> num2 >> num3;
  average =  (num1 + num2 + num3) / 3.0;
  cout << "The average of the numbers is " << average << endl;

  return 0;
}
```

The following sample run was made using Program 3.13:

```
Enter three integer numbers: 22 56 73
The average of the numbers is 50.3333
```

Note that the data typed at the keyboard for this sample run consists of the input

```
22 56 73
```

In response to this stream of input, Program 3.13 stores the value 22 in the variable `num1`, the value 56 in the variable `num2`, and the value 73 in the variable `num3` (see Figure 3.16). Since the average of three integer numbers can be a floating-point number, the variable average, which is used to store the average, is declared as a floating-point variable. Note also that the parentheses are needed in the assignment statement `average = (num1 + num2 + num3) / 3.0;`. Without these parentheses, the only value that would be divided by 3 would be the integer in `num3` (because division has a higher precedence than addition).

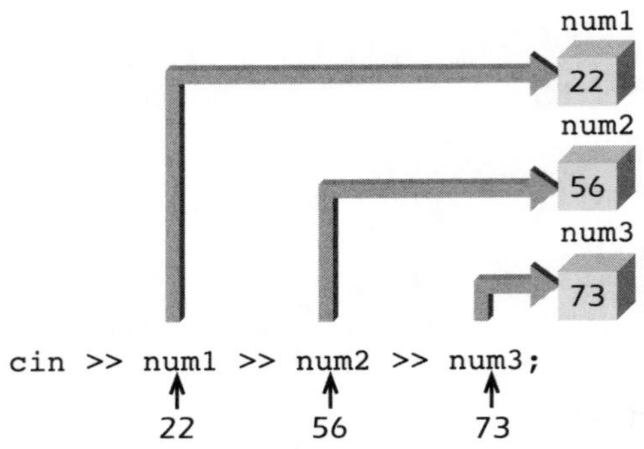

Figure 3.16 Inputting data into the variables `num1`, `num2`, and `num3`.

The `cin` extraction operation, like the `cout` insertion operation, is "clever" enough to make a few data-type conversions. For example, if an integer is entered in place of a double-precision number, the integer will be converted to the correct data type.[8] Similarly, if a double-precision number is entered when an integer is expected, only the integer part of the number will be used. For example, assume the following numbers are typed in response to the statement `cin >> num1 >> num2 >> num3;`, where `num1` and `num3` have been declared as double-precision variables and `num2` is an integer variable:

```
56  22.879  33.923
```

The 56 will be converted to 56.0 and stored in the variable `num1`. The extraction operation continues extracting data from the input stream sent to it, expecting an integer value. As far as `cin` is concerned, the decimal point after the 22 in the number 22.879 indicates the end of an integer and the start of a decimal number. Thus, the number 22 is assigned to `num2`. Continuing to process its input stream, `cin` takes the .879 as the next floating-point number and assigns it to in `num3`. As far as `cin` is concerned, 33.923 is extra input and is ignored. If, though, you do not initially type enough data, the `cin` object will continue to make the computer pause until sufficient data has been entered.

A First Look at User-Input Validation

A well-constructed program should validate user input and ensure a program does not crash or produce nonsensical output due to unexpected input. The term *validate* means checking that the entered value matches the data type of the variable that the value is assigned to within a `cin` statement and means that the value is within an acceptable range of values appropriate to the application. Programs that detect and respond effectively to unexpected user input are formally referred to as **robust programs** and informally as "bullet-proof" programs. One of your jobs as a programmer is to produce such programs. As written, Programs 3.12 and 3.13 are not robust programs. Let's see why.

---

[8]Strictly speaking, what comes in from the keyboard is not any data type, such as an `int` or `double`, but is simply a sequence of characters. The extraction operation handles the conversion from the character sequence to a defined data type.

The first problem with these programs becomes evident when a user enters a non-numerical value. For example, consider the following sample run using Program 3.13:

```
Enter three integer numbers: 10 20.68 20
The average of the numbers is -2.86331e+008
```

This output occurs because the conversion of the second input number results in the integer value 20 assigned to num2 and the value –858993460 assigned to num3.[9] This last value corresponds to an invalid character, the decimal point, being assigned to an expected integer value. The average of the numbers 10, 20, and –858993460 is computed correctly as –286331143.3, which is displayed in scientific notation with six significant digits as –2.86331e+08. As far as the average user is concerned, this will be reported as a program error. This same problem occurs whenever a non-integer value is entered for either of the first two inputs. (It does not occur for any numerical value entered as the third input because the integer part of the last input is accepted and the remaining input ignored.) As a programmer, your initial response may be "The program clearly asks you to enter integer values." This, however, is the response of an inexperienced programmer. Professional programmers understand that their responsibility is to ensure a program anticipates and appropriately handles all inputs a user will enter. This is accomplished by thinking about what can go wrong with your own program as you develop it and then having another person or group test the program.

The basic approach to handling invalid data input is referred to as **user-input validation**, which means validating the entered data during or immediately after the data have been entered and then providing the user with a way of re-entering any invalid data. User-input validation is an essential part of any commercially viable program; if done correctly, it will protect a program from attempting to process data that can cause computational problems. We will see how to provide this type of validation after C++'s selection and repetition statements have been presented in Chapters 4 and 5, respectively.

Exercises 3.4

1. For the following declaration statements, write a statement using the cin object that will cause the computer to pause while the appropriate data is typed by the user.

a. `int firstnum;`

b. `double grade;`

c. `double secnum;`

d. `char keyval;`

e.
```
int month years;
double average;
```

f.
```
char ch;
int num1,num2;
double grade1,grade2;
```

g.
```
double interest, principal, capital;
double price, yield;
```

[9] Some systems will accept the .68 as the third input. In all cases the last value of 20 is ignored.

h.
```
char ch,letter1,letter2;
int num1,num2,num3;
```
i.
```
double temp1,temp2,temp3;
double volts1,volts2;
```

2. a. Write a C++ program that first displays the following prompt:

```
Enter the temperature in degrees Celsius:
```

Have your program accept a value entered from the keyboard and convert the temperature entered to degrees Fahrenheit, using the formula *Fahrenheit* = (9.0 / 5.0) * *Celsius* + 32.0. Your program should then display the temperature in degrees Fahrenheit, using an appropriate output message.

b. Compile and execute the program written for Exercise 2a. Verify your program by calculating, by hand, and then using your program, the Fahrenheit equivalent of the following test data:

Test data set 1: 0 degrees Celsius
Test data set 2: 50 degrees Celsius
Test data set 3: 100 degrees Celsius

When you are sure your program is working correctly, use it to complete the following table:

Celsius	Fahrenheit
45	
50	
55	
60	
65	
70	

3. Write, compile, and execute a C++ program that displays the following prompt:

```
Enter the radius of a circle:
```

After accepting a value for the radius, your program should calculate and display the area of the circle. (*Hint: area* = *3.1416* * *radius*^{2}) For testing purposes, verify your program using a test input radius of 3 inches. After manually determining that the result produced by your program is correct, use your program to complete the following table:

Radius (in.)	Area (sq. in.)
1.0	
1.5	
2.0	
2.5	
3.0	
3.5	

4. a. Write, compile, and execute a C++ program that displays the following prompts:

```
Enter the miles driven:
Enter the gallons of gas used:
```

After each prompt is displayed, your program should use a `cin` statement to accept data from the keyboard for the displayed prompt. After the gallons of gas used number has been entered, your program should calculate and display miles per gallon obtained. This value should be included in an appropriate message and calculated using the equation *miles per gallon = miles / gallons used*. Verify your program using the following test data:

Test data set 1: Miles = 276, Gas = 10 gallons
Test data set 2: Miles = 200, Gas = 15.5 gallons

When you have completed your verification, use your program to complete the following table:

Miles driven	Gallons used	MPG
250	16.00	
275	18.00	
312	19.54	
296	17.39	

b. For the program written for Exercise 4a, determine how many verification runs are required to ensure the program is working correctly and give a reason supporting your answer.

5. a. Write, compile, and execute a C++ program that displays the following prompts:

```
Enter a number:
Enter a second number:
Enter a third number:
Enter a fourth number:
```

After each prompt is displayed, your program should use a `cin` statement to accept a number from the keyboard for the displayed prompt. After the fourth number has been entered, your program should calculate and display the average of the numbers. The average should be included in an appropriate message. Check the average displayed by your program using the following test data:

Test data set 1: 100, 100, 100, 100
Test data set 2: 100, 0, 100, 0

When you have completed your verification, use your program to complete the following table:

Numbers	Average
92, 98, 79, 85	
86, 84, 75, 86	
63, 85, 74, 82	

b. Repeat Exercise 5a, making sure that you use the same variable name, `number`, for each number input. Also use the variable `sum` for the sum of the numbers. (*Hint:* To do this, you may use the statement `sum = sum + number` after each number is accepted. Review the material on accumulating presented in Section 2.3.)

6. a. Write, compile, and execute a C++ program that computes and displays the value of the second-order polynomial $ax^2 + bx + c$ for any user input values of the coefficients a, b, c, and the variable x. Have your program first display a message informing the user as to what the program will do, and then display suitable prompts to alert the user to enter the desired data. (*Hint:* Use a prompt such as `Enter the coefficient of the x-squared term:`)

b. Check the result produced by the your program written for Exercise 6a using the following test data:

Test data set 1: $a = 0$, $b = 0$, $c = 22$, $x = 56$
Test data set 2: $a = 0$, $b = 22$, $c = 0$, $x = 2$
Test data set 3: $a = 22$, $b = 0$, $c = 0$, $x = 2$
Test data set 4: $a = 2$, $b = 4$, $c = 5$, $x = 2$
Test data set 5: $a = 5$, $b = -3$, $c = 2$, $x = 1$

When you have completed your verification, use your program to complete the following table:

a	b	c	x	polynomial value
2.0	17.0	−12.0	1.3	
3.2	2.0	15.0	2.5	
3.2	2.0	15.0	−2.5	
−2.0	10.0	0.0	2.0	
−2.0	10.0	0.0	4.0	
−2.0	10.0	0.0	5.0	
−2.0	10.0	0.0	6.0	
5.0	22.0	18.0	8.3	
4.2	−16	−20	−5.2	

7. The number of bacteria, B, in a certain culture that is subject to refrigeration can be approximated by the equation $B = 300000\ e^{-0.032t}$, where e is the irrational number 2.71828 (rounded to five decimal places), known as Euler's number, and t is the time, in hours, that the culture has been refrigerated. Using this equation, write, compile, and execute a single C++ program that prompts the user for a value of time, calculates the number of bacteria in the culture, and displays the result. For testing purposes, check your program using a test input of 10 hours. When you have verified the operation of your program, use it to determine the number of bacteria in the culture after 12, 18, 24, 36, 48, and 72 hours.

8. Write, compile, and execute a program that calculates and displays the square-root value of a user-entered real number. Verify your program by calculating the square roots of the following data: 25, 16, 0, and 2. When you completed your verification, use your program to determine the square root of 32.25, 42, 48, 55, 63, and 79.

9. Write, compile, and execute a program that calculates and displays the 4th root of a user-entered number. Recall from elementary algebra that the 4th root of a number can be found by raising the number to the ¼ power. (*Hint:* do not use integer division—can you see why?) Verify your program by calculating the fourth root of the following data: 81, 16, 1, and 0. When you have completed your verification, use your program to determine the fourth root of 42, 121, 256, 587, 1240, and 16,256.

10. For the series circuit shown in Figure 3.17, the voltage drop, V_2, across resistor, R_2, and the power, P_2, delivered to this resistor are given by the equations $V_2 = I\ R_2$ and $P_2 = I\ V_2$, where $I = E\ /(R_1 + R_2)$. Using these equations, write, compile, and execute a C++ program that prompts the user for values of E, R_1, and R_2, calculates the voltage drop and power delivered to R_2, and displays the results. Check your program using the test data: E = 10 volts, R_1 = 100 ohms, and R_2 = 200 ohms. When you have completed your verification, use your program to complete the following table:

E (volts)	R_1 (ohms)	R_2 (ohms)	Voltage drop (volts)	Power delivered (watts)
10	100	100		
10	100	200		
10	200	200		
20	100	100		
20	100	200		
20	200	200		

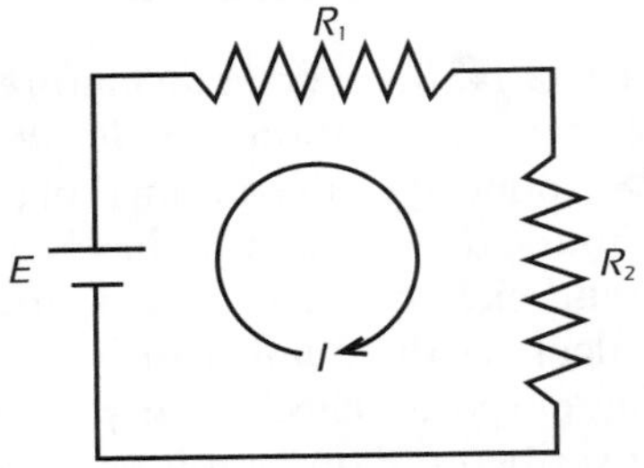

Figure 3.17 Calculating the voltage drop.

11. Write, compile, and execute a C++ program that computes the combined resistance of three parallel resistors. The values of each resistor should be accepted using a `cin` statement (use the formula for combined resistance given in Exercise 9 of Section 3.2). Verify the operation of your program by using the following test data:

Test data set 1: R_1 = 1000, R_2 = 1000, and R_3 = 1000.
Test data set 2: R_1 = 1000, R_2 = 1500, and R_3 = 500.

When you have completed your verification, use your program to complete the following table:

R1 (volts)	R2 (ohms)	R3 (ohms)	Combined Resistance (ohms)
3000	3000	3000	
6000	6000	6000	
2000	3000	1000	
2000	4000	5000	
4000	2000	1000	
10000	100	100	

12. Using `input` statements, write, compile, and execute a C++ program that accepts the x and y coordinates of two points. Have your program determine and display the midpoints of the two points (use the formula given in Exercise 11 of Section 3.2). Verify your program using the following test data:

Test data set 1: Point 1 = (0, 0) and Point 2 = (16, 0)
Test data set 2: Point 1 = (0, 0) and Point 2 = (0, 16)
Test data set 3: Point 1 = (0, 0) and Point 2 = (–16, 0)
Test data set 4: Point 1 = (0, 0) and Point 2 = (0, –16)
Test data set 5: Point 1 = (–5, –5) and Point 2 = (5, 5)

When you have completed your verification, use your program to complete the following table.

Point 1	Point 2	Midpoint
(4, 6)	(16, 18)	
(22, 3)	(8, 12)	
(–10, 8)	(14, 4)	
(–12, 2)	(14, 3.1)	
(3.1, –6)	(20, 16)	
(3.1, –6)	(–16, –18)	

13. Write, compile, and execute a C++ program that calculates and displays the value of the current flowing through an RC circuit. The circuit consists of a battery that is connected in series to a switch, resistor, and a capacitor. When the switch is closed the current, i, that flows through the circuit is given by the equation:

$$i = (E/R)\ e^{-t/\tau}$$

where E is the voltage of the battery (in volts), R is the resistance (in ohms), τ is termed the time constant, and t is the time (in seconds) since the switch was closed.

The program should prompt the user to enter appropriate values and use input statements to accept the data. In constructing the prompts, use statements such as `Enter the voltage of the battery.` Verify the operation of your program by calculating, by hand, the current for the following test data:

Test data set 1: Voltage = 20 volts, R = 10 ohms, τ = 0.044, t = 0.023 seconds.
Test data set 2: Voltage = 35, R = 10 ohms, τ = 0.16, t = 0.067 seconds.

When you have completed your verification, use your program to determine the value of the current for the following cases:

a. Voltage = 35, R = 10 ohms, τ = 0.16, t = 0.11 seconds.
b. Voltage = 35, R = 10 ohms, τ = 0.16, t = 0.44 seconds.
c. Voltage = 35, R = 10 ohms, τ = 0.16, t = 0.83 seconds.
d. Voltage = 15, R = 10 ohms, τ = 0.55, t = 0.11 seconds.
e. Voltage = 15, R = 10 ohms, τ = 0.55, t = 0.44 seconds.
f. Voltage = 15, R = 10 ohms, τ = 0.55, t = 0.067 seconds.
g. Voltage = 6, R = 1000 ohms, τ = 2.6, t = 12.4 seconds.

14. Program 3.12 prompts the user to input two numbers, where the first value entered is stored in `num1` and the second value is stored in `num2`. Using this program as a starting point, write a program that swaps the values stored in the two variables.

15. Write a C++ program that prompts the user to type in a number. Have your program accept the number as an integer and immediately display the integer using a `cout` object call. Run your program three times. The first time you run the program enter a valid integer number, the second time enter a double-precision number, and the third time enter a character. Using the output display, see what number your program actually accepted from the data you entered.

16. Repeat Exercise 16 but have your program declare the variable used to store the number as a double-precision variable. Run the program three times. The first time enter an integer, the second time enter a double-precision number and the third time enter a character. Using the output display, keep track of what number your program actually accepted from the data you typed in. What happened, if anything, and why?

17. **a.** Why do you think that successful application programs contain extensive data-input validity checks? (*Hint:* Review Exercises 16 and 17.)
b. What do you think is the difference between a data-type check and a data reasonableness check?
c. Assume that a program requests that a month, day, and year be entered by the user. What are some checks that could be made on the data entered?

3.5 Symbolic Constants

Certain constants used within a program have a more general meaning that is recognized outside the context of the program. Examples of these types of constants include the number 3.1416, which is π accurate to four decimal places; 32.2 ft/sec^2, which is the gravitational constant; and the number 2.71828, which is Euler's number accurate to five decimal places.

The meaning of certain other constants appearing in a program are defined strictly within the context of the application being programmed. For example, in determining the weight of various sized objects, the density of the material being used takes on a special significance. By themselves the density numbers are quite ordinary, but in the context of a particular application they have a special meaning. Numbers such as these are sometimes referred to by programmers as **magic numbers**. When the same magic number appears repeatedly within the same program it becomes a potential source of error, should the constant have to be changed. Multiple changes, however, are subject to error—if just one value is overlooked and not changed, the result obtained when the program is run will be incorrect and the source of the error difficult to locate.

To avoid the problem of having a magic number spread throughout a program in many places and to permit clear identification of more universal constants, such as π, C++ allows the programmer to give these constants their own symbolic name. Then, instead of using the number throughout the program, the symbolic name is used instead. If the number ever has to be changed, the change need only be made once at the point where the symbolic name is equated to the actual number value. Equating numbers to symbolic names is accomplished using the `const` declaration qualifier. The `const` qualifier specifies that the declared identifier can only be read after it is initialized; it cannot be changed. Three examples using this qualifier are

```
const double PI = 3.1416;
const double DENSITY = 0.238;
const int MAXNUM = 100;
```

The first declaration statement creates a double-precision constant named PI and initializes it with the value 3.1416, while the second declaration statement creates the double-precision constant named DENSITY and initializes it to 0.238. Finally, the third declaration creates an integer constant named MAXNUM and initializes it with the value 100.

Once a `const` identifer is created and initialized, the value stored in it cannot be changed. Thus, for all practical purposes the name of the constant and its value are linked together for the duration of the program that declares them.

Although we have typed the `const` identifiers in uppercase letters, lowercase letters could have been used. It is common in C++, however, to use uppercase letters for `const` identifiers to easily identify them as such. Then, whenever a programmer sees uppercase letters in a program, he or she will know the value of the constant cannot be changed within the program.

Once declared, a `const` identifier can be used in any C++ statement in place of the number it represents. For example, the assignment statements

```
circum = 2 * PI * radius;
weight = DENSITY * volume;
```

are both valid. These statements must, of course, appear after the declarations for all their variables. Since a `const` declaration effectively equates a constant value to an identifier, and the identifier can be used as a direct replacement for its initializing constant, such identifiers are commonly referred to as **symbolic constants** or **named constants**. We shall use these terms interchangeably.

Placement of Statements

At this stage we have introduced a variety of statement types. The general rule in C++ for statement placement is simply that a variable or symbolic constant must be declared before it can be used. Although this rule permits both preprocessor directives and declaration statements to be placed throughout a program, doing so results in a very poor program structure. As a matter of good programming form, the following statement ordering should be used:

```
preprocessor directives

int main()
{
  symbolic constants
  main function declarations

  other executable statements

  return value
}
```

As new statement types are introduced we will expand this placement structure to accommodate them. Notice that comment statements can be freely intermixed anywhere within this basic structure.

Program 3.14 illustrates this basic structure and uses of a symbolic constant to calculate the weight of a steel cylinder. The density of the steel is 0.284 lb/in^3.

Program 3.14

```
// This program determines the weight of a steel cylinder
//   by multiplying the volume of the cylinder times its density
// The volume of the cylinder is given by the formula PI * pow(radius,2) * height.
#include <iostream>
#include <iomanip>
#include <cmath>
using namespace std;

int main()
{
  const double PI = 3.1416;
  const double DENSITY = 0.284;
  double radius, height, weight;

  cout << "Enter the radius of the cylinder (in inches): ";
  cin  >> radius;
  cout << "Enter the height of the cylinder (in inches): ";
  cin  >> height;
  weight = DENSITY * PI * pow(radius,2) * height;
  cout << setiosflags(ios:: fixed)
       << setiosflags(ios::showpoint)
       << setprecision(4)
       << "The cylinder weighs " << weight << " pounds" << endl;

  return 0;
}
```

Notice in Program 3.14 that two symbolic constants have been defined: PI and DENSITY. The following run was made to determine the weight of a cylinder with a radius of 3 inches and a height of 12 inches.

```
Enter the radius of the cylinder (in inches): 3
Enter the height of the cylinder (in inches): 12
The cylinder weighs 96.3592 pounds
```

The advantage of using the named constant PI in Program 3.14 is that it clearly identifies the value of 3.1416 in terms recognizable to most people. The advantage of using the named constant DENSITY is that it permits a programmer to change the value of the density for another material without having to search through the program to see where the density is used. If, of course, many different materials are to be considered, the density should be changed from a symbolic constant to a variable. A natural question arises, then, as to the difference between symbolic constants and variables.

The value of a variable can be altered anywhere within a program. By its nature a named constant is a constant value that must not be altered after it is defined. Naming a constant rather than assigning the value to a variable ensures that the value in the constant can not be subsequently altered. Whenever a named constant appears in an instruction it has the same effect as the constant it represents. Thus, DENSITY in Program 3.14 is simply another way of representing the number 0.284. Since DENSITY and the number 0.284 are equivalent, the value of DENSITY may not be subsequently changed within the program. Once DENSITY has been defined as a constant, an assignment statement such as

```
DENSITY = 0.156;
```

is meaningless and will result in an error message, because DENSITY is not a variable. Since DENSITY is only a stand-in for the value 0.284, this statement is equivalent to writing the invalid expression 0.284 = 0.156. In addition to using a `const` statement to name constants, as in Program 3.14, this statement can also be used to equate the value of a constant expression to a symbolic name. A constant expression is an expression consisting of operators and constants only. For example, the statement

```
const double DEG_TO_RAD = 3.1416/180.0;
```

equates the value of the constant expression 3.1416/180.0 to the symbolic name `DEG_TO_RAD`. The symbolic name, as always, can be used in any statement following its definition. For example, since the expression 3.1416/180.0 is required for converting degrees to radians, the symbolic name selected for this conversion factor can be conveniently used whenever such a conversion is required. Thus, in the assignment statement

```
height = distance * sin(angle * DEG_TO_RAD);
```

the symbolic constant `DEG_TO_RAD` is used to convert the value in angle to radian measure.

A previously defined named constant can also be used in a subsequent `const` statement. For example, the following sequence of statements are valid:

```
const double PI = 3.1416;
const double  DEG_TO_RAD = PI / 180.0;
```

Since the constant 3.1416 has been equated to the symbolic name PI, it can be used legitimately in any subsequent definition, even within another `const` statement. Program 3.15 uses the named constant `DEG_TO_RAD` to convert a user entered angle, in degrees, into its equivalent radian measure for use by the `sin` function.

Program 3.15

```
#include <iostream>
#include <iomanip>
#include <cmath>
using namespace std;

int main()
{
  const double PI = 3.1416;
  const double DEG_TO_RAD = PI/180.0;
  double angle;

  cout << "Enter the angle (in degrees): ";
  cin >> angle;
  cout << setiosflags(ios:: fixed)
       << setiosflags(ios::showpoint)
       << setprecision(4)
       << "The sine of the angle is " << sin(angle * DEG_TO_RAD) << endl;

  return 0;
}
```

The following sample run was made using Program 3.15.

```
Enter the angle (in degrees): 30
The sine of the angle is 0.5000
```

Although we have used the `const` qualifier to construct symbolic constants, we will encounter this data type once again in Chapter 6, where we will show that they are useful as function arguments in ensuring that the argument is not modified within the function.

Exercises 3.5

1. Modify Program 3.9 to use the named constant GRAV in place of the value 32.2 used in the program. Compile and execute your program to verify it produces the same result as shown in the text.

2. Rewrite the following program to use the named constant FACTOR in place of the expression (5.0/9.0) contained within the program.

```
#include <iostream>
using namespace std;

int main()
```

```
{
  double fahren, celsius;
  cout << "Enter a temperature in degrees Fahrenheit: ";
  cin  >> fahren;
  celsius = (5.0/9.0) * (fahren - 32.0);
  cout << "The equivalent Celsius temperature is "
       << celsius << endl;

  return 0;
}
```

3. Rewrite the following program to use the symbolic constant PRIME in place of the value 0.04 contained within the program.

```
#include <iostream>
using namespace std;

int main()
{
  float prime, amount, interest;
  prime = 0.04;      // prime interest rate
  cout << <Enter the amount: ";
  cin  >> amount;
  interest = prime * amount;
  cout << "The interest earned is"
       << interest << " dollars" << endl;

  return 0;
}
```

4. Rewrite the following program so that the variable `volts` is changed to a symbolic constant.

```
#include <iostream>
using namespace std;

int main()
{
  double current, resistance, volts;

  volts = 12;
  cout << " Enter the resistance: ";
  cin >> resistance;
  current = volts / resistance;
  cout << "The current is " << current << endl;

  return 0;
}
```

3.6 APPLICATIONS

In this section we present two applications to further illustrate both the use of `cin` statements to accept user input data and the use of library functions for performing calculations.

Application 1: Acid Rain

The use of coal as the major source of steam power began with the Industrial Revolution. Currently coal is one of the principal sources of electrical power generation in many industrialized countries.

Since the middle of the 19th century it has been known that the oxygen used in the burning process combines with the carbon and sulfur in the coal to produce both carbon dioxide and sulfur dioxide. When these gases are released into the atmosphere the sulfur dioxide combines with the water and oxygen in the air to form sulfuric acid, which itself is transformed into separate hydronium ions and sulfates (see Figure 3.18). It is the hydronium ions in the atmosphere that fall to earth, as components of rain, that change the acidity levels of lakes and forests.

The acid level of rain and lakes is measured on a pH scale using the formula

$$\text{pH} = -\log_{10}(\text{Concentration of hydronium ions})$$

where the concentration of hydronium ions is measured in units of moles/liter. A pH value of 7 indicates a neutral value (neither acid nor alkaline), whereas levels below 7 indicate the presence of an acid, and levels above 7 indicate the presence of an alkaline substance. For example, sulfuric acid has a pH value of approximately 1, lye has a pH value of approximately 13, and water typically has a pH value of 7. Marine life usually cannot survive in water with a pH level below 4.

Using the formula for pH, we will write a C++ program that calculates the pH level of a substance based on a user input value for the concentration of hydronium ions. Using the development procedure described in Section 2.6 we have the following steps.

Step 1 Analyze the Problem

Although the statement of the problem provides technical information on the composition of acid rain, from a programming viewpoint this is a rather simple problem. Here there is only one required output (a pH level) and one input (the concentration of hydronium ions).

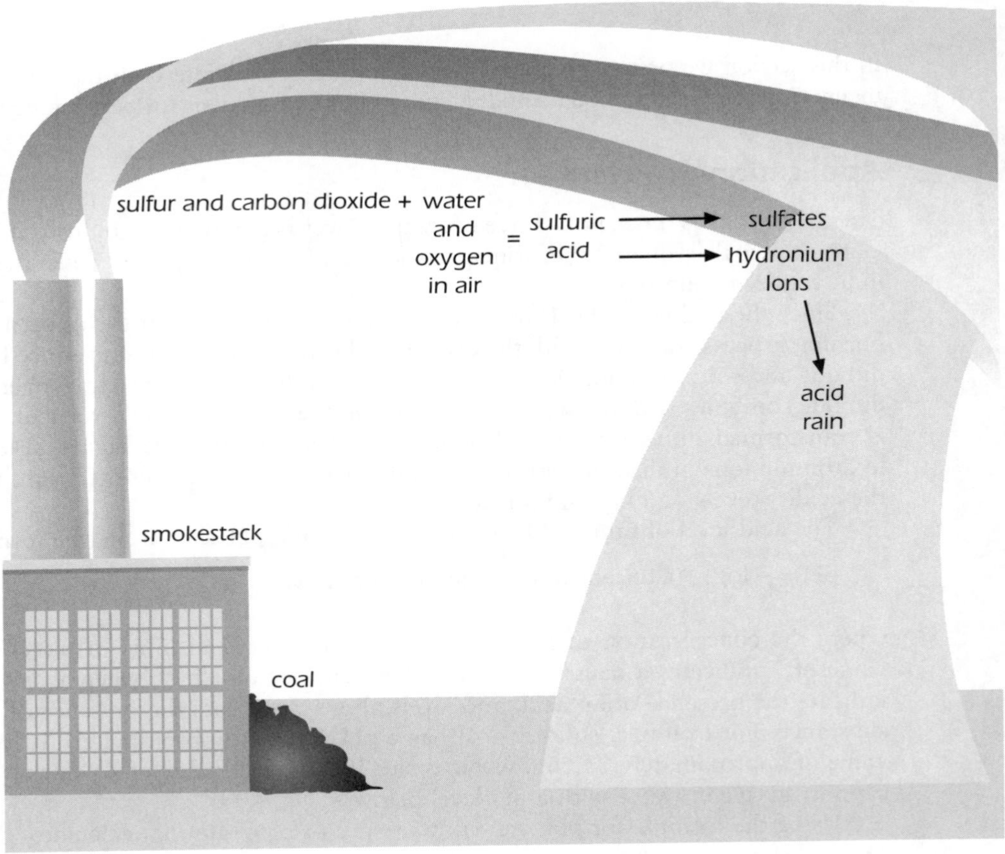

Figure 3.18 The formation of acid rain.

Step 2 Develop a Solution

The algorithm required to transform the input to the required output is a rather straightforward use of the pH formula that is provided. The pseudocode representation of the complete algorithm for entering the input data, processing the data to produce the desired output, and displaying the output is:

> *Display a prompt to enter an ion concentration level.*
> *Read a value for the concentration level.*
> *Calculate a pH level using the given formula.*
> *Display the calculated value.*

To ensure that we understand the formula used in the algorithm, we will do a hand calculation. The result of this calculation can then be used to verify the result produced by the program. Assuming a hydronium concentration of 0.0001 (any value would do), the pH level is calculated as $-\log_{10} 10^{-4}$. Either by knowing that the logarithm of 10 raised to a power is the power itself, or by using a log table, the value of this expressions is $-(-4) = 4$.

Step 3 Code the Solution

Program 3.16 describes the selected algorithm in C++. The choice of variable names is arbitrary.

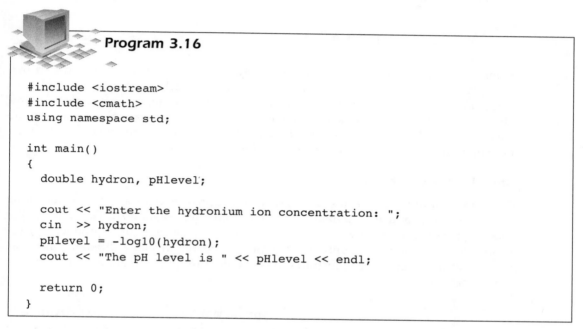

Program 3.16

```
#include <iostream>
#include <cmath>
using namespace std;

int main()
{
  double hydron, pHlevel;

  cout << "Enter the hydronium ion concentration: ";
  cin  >> hydron;
  pHlevel = -log10(hydron);
  cout << "The pH level is " << pHlevel << endl;

  return 0;
}
```

Program 3.16 begins with two `#include` preprocessor statements, followed by the function `main()`. Within `main()`, a declaration statement declares two floating-point variables, `hydron` and `pHlevel`. The program then displays a prompt requesting input data from the user. After the prompt is displayed, a `cin` statement is used to store the entered data in the variable `hydron`. Finally, a value for `pHlevel` is calculated, using the logarithmic library function, and displayed. As always, the program is terminated with a closing brace.

Step 4 Test and Correct the Program

A test run using Program 3.16 produced the following:

```
Enter the hydronium ion concentration level: 0.0001
The pH level is 4
```

Because the program performs a single calculation, and the result of this test run agrees with our previous hand calculation, the program has been completely tested. It can now be used to calculate the pH level of other hydronium concentrations with confidence that the results being produced are accurate.

Application 2: Approximating the Exponential Function

The exponential function e^x, where e is known as Euler's number (and has the value 2.718281828459045...) appears many times in descriptions of natural phenomena. For example, radioactive decay, population growth, and the normal (bell-shaped) curve used in statistical applications all can be described using this function.

The value of e^x can be approximated using the series[10]

$$1+\frac{x}{1}+\frac{x^2}{2}+\frac{x^3}{6}+\frac{x^4}{24}+\frac{x^5}{120}+\frac{x^6}{720}\cdots$$

Using this polynomial as a base, write a program that approximates e raised to a user input value of x using the first 4 terms of this series. For each approximation display the value calculated by C++'s exponential function, `exp()`, the approximate value, and the absolute difference between the two. Make sure to verify your program using a hand calculation. Once the verification is complete, use the program to approximate e^4. Using the development procedure described in Section 2.6 we perform the following steps.

Step 1 Analyze the Problem

The statement of the problem specifies that four approximations are to be made, using one, two, three, and four terms of the approximating polynomial, respectively. For each approximation three output values are required: the value of e^x produced by the exponential function, the approximated value, and the absolute difference between the two values. Figure 3.19 illustrates, in symbolic form, the structure of the required output display.

e^x	Approximation	Difference
library function value	1st approximate value	1st difference
library function value	2nd approximate value	2nd difference
library function value	3rd approximate value	3rd difference
library function value	4th approximate value	4th difference

Figure 3.19 Required output display.

The output indicated on Figure 3.19 can be used to get a "feel" for what the program must look like. Realizing that each line in the display can only be produced by executing a `cout` statement, it should be clear that four such statements must be executed. Additionally, since each output line contains three computed values, each `cout` statement will have three items in its expression list.

The only input to the program consists of the value of x. This will, of course, require a single prompt and a `cin` statement to input the necessary value.

[10]The formula from which this is derived is

$$e^x=\frac{x^0}{0!}+\frac{x^1}{1!}+\frac{x^2}{2!}+\frac{x^3}{3!}+\cdots+\frac{x^n}{n!}$$

Step 2 Develop a Solution

Before any output items can be calculated, it will be necessary to have the program prompt the user for a value of x and then have the program accept the entered value. The actual output display consists of two title lines followed by four lines of calculated data. The title lines can be produced using two `cout` statements. Now let's see how the actual data being displayed is produced.

The first item on the first data-output line illustrated on Figure 3.19 can be obtained using the `exp()` library function. The second item on this line, the approximation to e^x, can be obtained by using the first term in the polynomial that was given in the program specification. Finally, the third item on the line can be calculated using the `abs()` library function on the difference between the first two items. When all these items are calculated, a single `cout` statement can be used to display the three results on the same line.

The second output line illustrated in Figure 3.19 displays the same type of items as the first line, except that the approximation to e^x requires the use of two terms of the approximating polynomial. Notice also that the first item on the second line, the value obtained by the `exp()` function, is the same as the first item on the first line. This means that this item does not have to be recalculated and the value calculated for the first line can simply be displayed a second time. Once the data for the second line has been calculated, a single `cout` statement can be used to display the required values.

Finally, only the second and third items on the last two output lines shown in Figure 3.19 need to be recalculated, since the first item on these lines is the same as previously calculated for the first line.

Thus, for this problem, the complete algorithm described in pseudocode is

Display a prompt for the input value of x
Read the input value
Display the heading lines
Calculate the exponential value of x using the exp() function
Calculate the first approximation
Calculate the first difference
Print the first output line
Calculate the second approximation
Calculate the second difference
Print the second output line
Calculate the third approximation
Calculate the third difference
Print the third output line
Calculate the fourth approximation
Calculate the fourth difference
Print the fourth output line

To ensure that we understand the processing used in the algorithm we will do a hand calculation. The result of this calculation can then be used to verify the result produced by the program that we write. For test purposes we will use a value of 2 for x, which produces the following approximations.

Using the first term of the polynomial the approximation is

$$e^2 = 1$$

Using the first two terms of the polynomial the approximation is

$$e^2 = 1 + \frac{2}{1} = 3$$

Using the first three terms of the polynomial the approximation is

$$e^2 = 3 + \frac{2^2}{2} = 5$$

Using the first four terms of the polynomial the approximation is

$$e^2 = 5 + \frac{2^3}{6} = 6.3333$$

Notice that in using four terms of the polynomial it was not necessary to recalculate the value of the first three terms; instead, we used the previously calculated value.

Step 3 Code the Solution

Program 3.17 represents a description of the selected algorithm in C++.

Program 3.17

```
// this program approximates the function e raised to the x power
// using one, two, three, an four terms of an approximating polynomial
#include <iostream>
#include <iomanip>
#include <cmath>
using namespace std;

int main()
{
  double x, funcVal, approx, difference;

  cout << "\nEnter a value of x: ";
  cin  >> x;

    // print two title lines
  cout << " e to the x       Approximation      Difference\n";
  cout << "-------------     -------------      -------------\n";

  funcVal = exp(x);       // use the library function

    // calculate the first approximation
```

(Continued)

(Continued)

```
    approx = 1;
    difference = abs(funcVal - approx);
    cout << setw(10) << setiosflags(ios::showpoint) << funcVal
         << setw(18) << approx
         << setw(18) << difference << endl;

      // calculate the second approximation
    approx = approx + x;
    difference = abs(funcVal - approx);
    cout << setw(10) << setiosflags(ios::showpoint) << funcVal
         << setw(18) << approx
         << setw(18) << difference << endl;

      // calculate the third approximation
    approx = approx + pow(x,2)/2.0;
    difference = abs(funcVal - approx);
    cout << setw(10) << setiosflags(ios::showpoint) << funcVal
         << setw(18) << approx
         << setw(18) << difference << endl;

      // calculate the fourth approximation
    approx = approx + pow(x,3)/6.0;
    difference = abs(funcVal - approx);
    cout << setw(10) << setiosflags(ios::showpoint) << funcVal
         << setw(18) << approx
         << setw(18) << difference << endl;

    return 0;
}
```

In reviewing Program 3.17, notice that the input value of x is obtained first. The two title lines are then printed prior to any calculations being made. The value of the e^x is then computed using the `exp()` library function and assigned to the variable `funcVal`. This assignment permits this value to be used in the four difference calculations and displayed four times without the need for recalculation.

Since the approximation to the e^x is "built up" using more and more terms of the approximating polynomial, only the new term for each approximation is calculated and added to the previous approximation. Finally, to permit the same variables to be used over, the values in them are immediately printed before the next approximation is made. The following is a sample run produced by Program 3.17.

```
Enter a value of x: 2
 e to the x          Approximation         Difference
-------------        -------------        -------------
  7.38906               1.00000              6.38906
  7.38906               3.00000              4.38906
  7.38906               5.00000              2.38906
  7.38906               6.33333              1.05572
```

Step 4 Test and Correct the Program

The first two columns of output data produced by the sample run agree with our hand calculation. A hand check of the last column verifies that it also correctly contains the difference in values between the first two columns.

Because the program only performs nine calculations, and the result of the test run agrees with our hand calculations, it appears that the program has been completely tested. However, it is important to understand that this is because of our choice of test data. Selecting a value of 2 for x forced us to verify that the program was, in fact, calculating 2 raised to the required powers. A choice of 0 or 1 for our hand calculation would not have given us the verification that we need. Do you see why this is so?

Using these latter two values would not adequately test whether the program used the `pow()` function correctly, or even if it used it at all! That is, an incorrect program that did not use the `pow()` function could have been constructed to produce correct values for $x = 0$ and $x = 1$, but for no other values of x. Since the test data we used does adequately verify the program, however, we can use it with confidence in the results produced. Clearly, however, the output demonstrates that to achieve any level of accuracy with the program, more than four terms would be required.

Exercises 3.6

1. Enter, compile, and run Program 3.16 on your computer system.

2. **a.** Enter, compile, and run Program 3.17 on your computer system.
b. Determine how many terms of the approximating polynomial should be used to achieve an error of less than 0.0001 between the approximation and the value of e^2 as determined by the `exp()` function.

3. By mistake a student wrote Program 3.17 as follows:

```
// this program approximates the function e raised to the x power
// using one, two, three, an four terms of an approximating polynomial
#include <iostream>
#include <iomanip>
#include <cmath>
using namespace std;

int main()
{
  double x, funcVal, approx, difference;
```

```
    // print two title lines
  cout << " e to the x          Approximation         Difference\n";
  cout << "-------------        -------------         -------------\n";

  cout << "\nEnter a value of x: ";
  cin >> x;
  funcVal = exp(x);        // use the library function

    // calculate the first approximation
  approx = 1;
  difference = abs(funcVal - approx);
  cout << setw(10) << setiosflags(ios::showpoint) << funcVal
       << setw(18) << approx
       << setw(18) << difference << endl;

    // calculate the second approximation
  approx = approx + x;
  difference = abs(funcVal - approx);
  cout << setw(10) << setiosflags(ios::showpoint) << funcVal
       << setw(18) << approx
       << setw(18) << difference << endl;

    // calculate the third approximation
  approx = approx + pow(x,2)/2.0;
  difference = abs(funcVal - approx);
  cout << setw(10) << setiosflags(ios::showpoint) << funcVal
       << setw(18) << approx
       << setw(18) << difference << endl;

    // calculate the fourth approximation
  approx = approx + pow(x,3)/6.0;
  difference = abs(funcVal - approx);
  cout << setw(10) << setiosflags(ios::showpoint) << funcVal
       << setw(18) << approx
       << setw(18) << difference << endl;

  return 0;
}
```

Determine the output that will be produced by this program.

4. The value of π can be approximated by the series

$$4\left(1-\frac{1}{3}+\frac{1}{5}-\frac{1}{7}+\cdots\right)$$

Using this formula, write a program that calculates and displays the value of π using 2, 3, and 4 terms of the series.

5. a. The formula for the standard normal deviate, z, used in statistical applications is

$$z = \frac{x - \mu}{\sigma}$$

where μ refers to a mean value and σ to a standard deviation. Using this formula, write a program that calculates and displays the value of the standard normal deviate when $x = 85.3$, $\mu = 80$, and $\sigma = 4$.

b. Rewrite the program written in Exercise 5a to accept the values of x, μ, and σ as user inputs while the program is executing.

6. a. The equation of the normal (bell-shaped) curve used in statistical applications is

$$y = \frac{1}{\sigma\sqrt{2\pi}} e^{-\left(\frac{1}{2}\right)\left[(x-\mu)/\sigma\right]^2}$$

Using this equation, and assuming $\mu = 90$ and $\sigma = 4$, write a program that determines and displays the value of y when $x = 80$.

b. Rewrite the program written in Exercise 6a to accept the values of x, μ, and σ as user inputs while the program is executing.

7. a. Write, compile, and execute a C++ program that calculates and displays the voltage gain of a three-stage amplifier at a frequency of 1000 Hertz. The voltage gains of the stages are:

Stage 1 gain: $23/[2.3^2 + (0.044f)^2]^{1/2}$
Stage 2 gain: $12/[6.7^2 + (0.34f)^2]^{1/2}$
Stage 3 gain: $17/[1.9^2 + (0.45f)^2]^{1/2}$

where f is the frequency in Hertz. The voltage gain of the amplifier is the product of the gains of the individual stages.

b. Redo Exercise 7a assuming that the frequency will be entered when the program is run.

8. The volume of oil stored in a underground 200-foot deep cylindrical tank is determined by measuring the distance from the top of the tank to the surface of the oil. Knowing this distance and the radius of the tank, the volume of oil in the tank can be determined using the formula *volume* = π *radius*^{2} (200 – *distance*). Using this information, write, compile, and execute a C++ program that accepts the radius and distance measurements, calculates the volume of oil in the tank, and displays the two input values and the calculated volume. Verify the results of your program by doing a hand calculation using the following test data: radius equals 10 feet and distance equals 12 feet.

9. The perimeter, approximate surface area, and approximate volume of an in-ground pool are given by the following formulas:

perimeter = 2(*length* + *width*)
volume = *length* * *width* * *average depth*
underground surface area = 2(*length* + *width*)*average depth* + *length* * *width*

Using these formulas as a basis, write a C++ program that accepts the length, width, and average depth measurements, and then calculates the perimeter, volume, and underground surface area of the pool. In writing your program make the following two calculations immediately after the input data has been entered: *length * width* and *length + width*. The results of these two calculations should then be used, as appropriate, in the assignment statements for determining the perimeter, volume, and underground surface area without recalculating them for each equation. Verify the results of your program by doing a hand calculation using the following test data: length equals 25 feet, width equals 15 feet, and average depth equals 5.5 feet. When you have verified that your program is working, use it to complete the following table.

Length	Width	Depth	Perimeter	Volume	Underground Surface Area
25	10	5.0			
25	10	5.5			
25	10	6.0			
25	10	6.5			
30	12	5.0			
30	12	5.5			
30	12	6.0			
30	12	6.5			

3.7 COMMON PROGRAMMING ERRORS

In using the material presented in this chapter, be aware of the following possible errors:

1. Forgetting to assign or initialize values for all variables before the variables are used in an expression. Such values can be assigned by assignment statements, initialized within a declaration statement, or assigned interactively by entering values using the `cin` object.
2. Using a mathematical library function without including the preprocessor statement `#include <cmath>` (and on a UNIX based system forgetting to include the `-lm` argument on the `cc` command line).
3. Using a library function without providing the correct number of arguments having the proper data type.
4. Applying either the increment or decrement operator to an expression. For example, the expression

```
(count + n)++
```

is incorrect. The increment and decrement operators can only be applied to individual variables.

5. Forgetting to separate all variables passed to `cin` with an extraction symbol, >>.

6. Being unwilling to test a program in depth. After all, since you wrote the program, you assume it is correct or you would have changed it before it was compiled. It is extremely difficult to back away and honestly test your own software. As a programmer you must constantly remind yourself that just because you think your program is correct does not make it so. Finding errors in your own program is a sobering experience, but one that will help you become a master programmer.

7. A more exotic and less common error occurs when the increment and decrement operators are used with variables that appear more than once in the same expression. This error occurs because C++ does not specify the order in which operands are accessed within an expression. For example, the value assigned to result in the statement

   ```
   result = i + i++;
   ```

   is compiler dependent. If your compiler accesses the first operand, `i`, first, the above statement is equivalent to

   ```
   result = 2 * i;
   i++;
   ```

   However, if your compiler accesses the second operand, `i++`, first, the value of the first operand will be altered before it is used the second time and the value $2i + 1$ is assigned to result. As a general rule, therefore, do not use either the increment or decrement operator in an expression when the variable it operates on appears more than once in the expression.

3.8 CHAPTER SUMMARY

1. An expression is a sequence of one or more operands separated by operators. An operand is a constant, a variable, or another expression. A value is associated with an expression.

2. Expressions are evaluated according to the precedence and associativity of the operators used in the expression.

3. The assignment symbol, =, is an operator. Expressions using this operator assign a value to a variable; additionally, the expression itself takes on a value. Since assignment is an operation in C++, multiple uses of the assignment operator are possible in the same expression.

4. The increment operator, ++, adds one to a variable, while the decrement operator, `--`, subtracts one from a variable. Both of these operators can be used as prefixes or postfixes. In prefix operation the variable is incremented (or decremented) before its value is used. In postfix operation the variable is incremented (or decremented) after its value is used.

5. C++ provides library functions for calculating square root, logarithmic, and other mathematical computations. Each program using one of these mathematical functions must either include the statement `#include <cmath>` or have a function declaration for the mathematical function before it is called.

6. Every mathematical library function operates on its arguments to calculate a single value. To use a library function effectively, you must know what the function does, the name of the function, the number and data types of the arguments expected by the function, and the data type of the returned value.

7. Data passed to a function are called arguments of the function. Arguments are passed to a library function by including each argument, separated by commas, within the parentheses following the function's name. Each function has its own requirements for the number and data types of the arguments that must be provided.

8. Functions may be included within larger expressions.

9. The `cin` object is used for data input. This object accepts a stream of data from the keyboard and assigns the data to variables. The general form of a statement using `cin` is:

   ```
   cin >> var1 >> var2 . . . >> varn;
   ```

   The extraction symbol, >>, must be used to separate the variable names.

10. When a `cin` statement is encountered the computer temporarily suspends further statement execution until sufficient data has been entered for the number of variables contained in the `cin` statememt.

11. It is good programming practice to display a message, prior to a `cin` statement, that alerts the user as to the type and number of data items to be entered. Such a message is called a prompt.

12. Values can be equated to a single constant, using the `const` keyword. This creates a named constant that is read-only after it is initialized within the declaration statement. This declaration has the syntax

    `const` *dataType SymbolicName = initialValue;*

    and permits the constant to be used instead of the initial value anywhere in the program after the declaration.

3.9 A Closer Look: Programming Errors

The ideal in programming is to produce readable, error-free programs that work correctly and can be modified or changed with a minimum of testing. You can work toward this ideal by keeping in mind the different types of errors that can occur, when they are typically detected, and how to correct them.

You can detect an error in four ways:

1. Before a program is compiled
2. While the program is being compiled
3. While the program is being run
4. After the program has been executed and the output is being examined

And, oddly enough, in some cases, an error may not be detected at all.

The method for detecting errors before a program is compiled is called **desk checking.** Desk checking, which typically is performed while sitting at a desk with the code in front of you, refers to the process of checking the source code for mistakes immediately after it has been typed.

Errors detected by the compiler are formally referred to as **compile-time errors**, and errors that occur while the program is running are formally referred to as **run-time errors.** Other names for compile-time errors are **syntax errors** and **parse errors**, terms that emphasize the type of error being detected by the compiler.

By now, you have probably encountered numerous compile-time errors. Though beginning programmers tend to be frustrated by them, experienced programmers understand the compiler is doing a lot of valuable checking, and that correcting any errors the compiler does detect is usually easy. Because these errors occur while the program is being developed and not while a user is attempting to perform an important task, no one but the programmer ever knows they occurred; you fix them and they go away.

Run-time errors are more troubling because they occur while a user is executing the program; in most commercial systems, the user is not the programmer. Though many error types can cause a run-time error, such as a failure in the hardware, from a programming standpoint the majority of run-time errors are referred to as logic errors or faulty logic, which encompasses not thinking out what the program should do or not anticipating how a user can make the program fail. For example, if a user enters data that results in an attempt to divide a number by zero, a run-time error occurs. As a programmer, the only way to protect against run-time errors is to anticipate everything a person might do to cause errors and submit your program to rigorous testing. Though beginning programmers tend to blame a user for an error caused by entering incorrect data, professionals do not. They understand that a run-time error is a flaw in the final product that can cause damage to the reputation of program and programmer.

In terms of preventing compile-time and run-time errors, it is more fruitful to distinguish between them based on what causes them. As hs been noted, compile errors are also named syntax errors, which refer to errors in the structure or spelling of a statement.

For example, examine the following statements:

```
cout << "There are four syntax errors here\n
cot " Can you find tem";
```

They contain four syntax errors. These errors are the following:

1. A closing quote is missing in line 1.
2. A terminating semicolon (;) is missing in line 1.
3. The keyword `cout` is misspelled in line 2.
4. The insertion symbol, <<, is missing in line 2.

All of these errors will be detected by the compiler when the program is compiled. This is true of all syntax errors because they violate the basic rules of C++; if they are not discovered by desk checking, the compiler detects them and displays an error message.[11] In some cases, the error message is clear and the error is obvious; in other cases, it takes a little detective work to understand the error message displayed by the compiler. Because syntax errors are the only error type that can be detected at compile time, the terms compile-time errors and syntax errors are used interchangeably. Strictly speaking, however, compile-time refers to when the error was detected and syntax refers to the type of error detected.

The misspelling of the word "them" in the second statement is not a syntax error. Though this spelling error will result in an undesirable output line being displayed, it is not a violation of C++'s syntactical rules. It is a **typographical error**, commonly referred to as a "typo."

A logic error can cause a run-time error or produce incorrect results. Such errors are characterized by erroneous, unexpected, or unintentional output that is a direct result of some flaw in the program's logic. These errors, which are never caught by the compiler, may be detected by desk checking, by program testing, by accident when a user obtains an erroneous output while the program is executing, or not at all. If the error is detected while the program is executing, a run-time error can occur that results in an error message being generated, premature program termination, or both.

The most serious logic error is caused by an incorrect understanding of the full requirements of the program, because the logic within a program reflects on the logic upon which it is coded. For example, if the purpose of a program is to calculate the load bearing strength of a steel beam and the programmer does not fully understand how the calculation is to be made, what inputs are needed to perform the calculation, or what special conditions exist (such as how temperature effects the beam), a logic error will occur. Because such errors are not detected by the compiler and frequently may go undetected at run time, they are always more difficult to detect than syntax errors. If they are detected, a logic error typically appears in one of two predominant ways. In one instance,

[11]They may not, however, all be detected at the same time. Frequently, one syntax error masks another error, and the second error is detected after the first error is corrected.

the program executes to completion but produces incorrect results. Generally, logic errors of this type are revealed by the following:

- **No output**—This is caused by an omission of an output statement or a sequence of statements that inadvertently bypasses an output statement.
- **Unappealing or misaligned output**—This is caused by an error in an output statement.
- **Incorrect numerical results**—This is caused by incorrect values assigned to the variables used in an expression, the use of an incorrect arithmetic expression, an omission of a statement, a round-off error, or the use of an improper sequence of statements.

A second way that logic errors reveal themselves is by causing a run-time error. Examples of this type of logic error are attempts to divide by zero or to take the square root of a negative number.

You should plan your program testing carefully to maximize the possibility of locating errors. Always keep in mind that *although a single test can reveal the presence of an error, it does not verify the absence of another error.* That is, the fact that one error is revealed by testing, does not indicate that another error is not lurking somewhere else in the program; furthermore, *the fact that one test revealed no errors, does not mean there are no errors.*

Once you discover an error, however, you must locate where the error occurs and fix it. In computer jargon, a program error is referred to as a **bug,** and the process of isolating, correcting, and verifying the correction is called **debugging.**[12]

Although no hard-and-fast rules exist for isolating the cause of an error, some useful techniques can be applied. The first of these is a preventive technique. Frequently, many errors are introduced by the programmer in the rush to code and run a program before understanding what is required and how the result is to be achieved. A symptom of this haste to get a program entered into the computer is the lack of an outline of the proposed program or the lack of a detailed understanding of what is actually required. Many errors can be eliminated by desk checking a copy of the program before entering or compiling it.

A second useful technique is to imitate the computer and execute each statement by hand, as the computer would. This means writing down each variable, as it is encountered in the program, and listing the value that should be stored in the variable as each input and assignment statement is encountered. Doing this sharpens your programming skills because it requires that you understand what each statement in your program causes to happen. Such a check is called **program tracing.**

A third powerful debugging technique is to include some temporary code in your program that displays the values of selected variables. If the displayed values are incorrect, you can determine what part of your program generated them and make the necessary corrections.

---

[12]The derivation of this term is interesting. When a program stopped running on the MARK I computer at Harvard University in September 1945, the malfunction was traced to a dead insect that had gotten into the electrical circuits. The programmer, Grace Hopper, recorded the incident in her logbook as, "First actual case of bug being found."

In the same manner, you could add temporary code that displays the values of all input data. This technique is referred to as **echo printing**, and it is useful in establishing that the program is correctly receiving and correctly interpreting the input data.

The most powerful of all debugging and tracing techniques is to use a special program called a **debugger**. A debugger program can control the execution of a C++ program, can interrupt the C++ program at any point in its execution, and can display the values of all variables at the point of interruption.

Finally, no discussion of debugging is complete without mentioning the primary ingredient needed for successful isolation and correction of errors. This is the attitude and spirit you bring to the task. After you write a program, you naturally assume it is correct. Backing away and honestly testing and finding errors in your own software is difficult. As a programmer, you must constantly remind yourself that just because you think your program is correct does not make it so. Finding errors in your own programs is a sobering experience but one that will help you to become a master programmer. The process can be exciting and fun if you approach it as a detection problem with you as the master detective.

Looking at Career Choices

Mechanical Engineering

Generally speaking, mechanical engineers are concerned with machines or systems that produce or apply energy. The range of technological activities that are considered part of mechanical engineering is probably broader than in any other engineering field. The field can be roughly subdivided into four categories:

1. Power. Design of power-generating machines and systems such as boiler-turbine engines for generating electricity, solar power, heating systems, and heat exchanges.
2. Design. Innovative design of machine parts or components from the most intricate and small to the gigantic. For example, mechanical engineers work alongside electrical engineers to design automatic control systems such as robots.
3. Automotive. Design and testing of transportation vehicles and the machines used to manufacture them.
4. Heating, ventilation, air conditioning, and refrigeration. Design of systems to control our environment both indoors and out and to control pollution.

Mechanical engineers usually have a thorough background in subjects like thermodynamics, heat transfer, statics and dynamics, and fluid mechanics.

CHAPTER 4

Selection Structures

TOPICS

Many advances have occurred in the theoretical foundations of programming since the inception of high-level languages in the late 1950s. One of the most important of these advances was the recognition in the late 1960s that any algorithm, no matter how complex, could be constructed using combinations of four standardized ***flow of control*** *structures: sequential, selection, repetition, and invocation.*

The term ***flow of control*** *refers to the order in which a program's statements are executed. Unless directed otherwise, the normal flow of control for all programs is* ***sequential****. This means that statements are executed in sequence, one after another, in the order in which they are placed within the program.*

Selection, repetition and invocation structures permit the sequential flow of control to be altered in precisely defined ways. As you might have guessed, the selection structure is used to select which statements are to be performed next and the repetition structure is used to repeat a set of statements. In this chapter we present C++'s selection statements. Repetition and invocation techniques are presented in Chapters 5 and 6.

4.1 SELECTION CRITERIA

In the solution of many problems, different actions must be taken depending upon the value of the data. Examples of simple situations include calculating an area *only if* the measurements are positive, performing a division *only if* the divisor is not zero, printing different messages *depending upon* the value of a grade received, and so on.

The `if-else` statement in C++ is used to implement such a decision structure in its simplest form—that of choosing between two alternatives. The most commonly used pseudocode syntax of this statement is

```
if (condition)
  statement executed if condition is true;
else
  statement executed if condition is false;
```

When an executing program encounters the `if` statement, the condition is evaluated to determine its numerical value, which is then interpreted as either true or false. If the condition evaluates to any positive or negative non-zero numerical value, the condition is considered as a "true" condition and the statement following the `if` is executed. If the condition evaluates to a zero numerical value, the condition is considered as a "false" condition and the statement following the `else` is executed. The `else` part of the statement is optional and may be omitted.

The condition used in an `if` statement can be any valid C++ expression (including, as we will see, even an assignment expression). The most commonly used expressions, however, are called **relational expressions.** A **simple relational expression** consists of a relational operator that compares two operands, as shown in Figure 4.1.

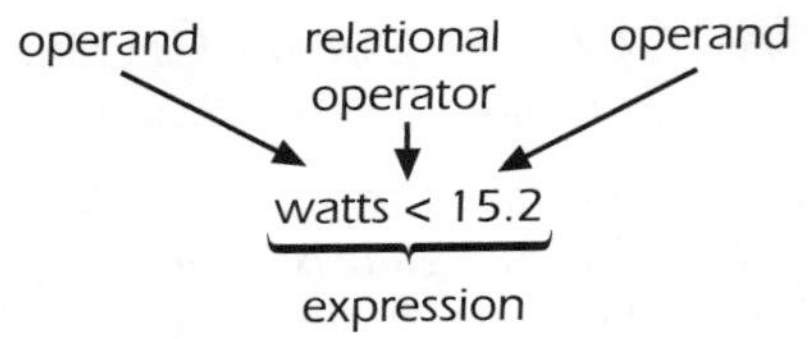

Figure 4.1 Anatomy of a simple relational expression.

While each operand in a relational expression can be either a variable or constant, the relational operators must be one of those listed in Table 4.1. These relational operators may be used with integer, float, double, or character operands, but must be typed exactly as given in Table 4.1. Thus, while the following examples are all valid:

```
age > 40        length <= 50      temp > 98.6
   3 < 4        flag == done      idNum == 682
day != 5        2.0 > 3.3         hours > 40
```

the following are invalid:

```
length =< 50     // operator out of order
2.0 >> 3.3       // invalid operator
flag = = done    // spaces are not allowed
```

Table 4.1

Relational operator	Meaning	Example
<	less than	`age < 30`
>	greater than	`height > 6.2`
<=	less than or equal to	`taxable <= 20000`
>=	greater than or equal to	`temp >= 98.6`
==	equal to	`grade == 100`
!=	not equal to	`number != 250`

Relational expressions are sometimes called **conditions** and we will use both terms to refer to these expressions. Like all C++ expressions, relational expressions are evaluated to yield a numerical result.[1] In the case of a relational expression, the value of the expression can only be the integer value of 1 or 0, which is interpreted as true and false, respectively. *A relational expression that we would interpret as true evaluates to an integer value of 1, and a false relational expression results in an integer value of 0.* For example, because the relationship 3 < 4 is always true, this expression has a value of 1, and because the relationship 2.0 > 3.3 is always false, the value of the expression itself is 0. This can be verified using the statements

```
cout << "The value of 3 < 4 is " << (3 < 4) << endl;
cout << "The value of 2.0 > 3.0 is " << (2.0 > 3.3) << endl;
cout << "The value of true is " << true << endl;
cout << "The value of false is " << false << endl;
```

[1]In this regard C++ differs from other high-level computer languages that yield a Boolean (true, false) result.

which results in the display

```
The value of 3 < 4 is 1
The value of 2.0 > 3.0 is 0
The value of true is 1
The value of false is 0
```

The value of a relational expression such as `hours > 40` depends on the value stored in the variable `hours`.

In a C++ program, a relational expression's value is not as important as the interpretation C++ places on the value when the expression is used as part of a selection statement. In these statements, which are presented in the next section, we will see that a zero value is used by C++ to represent a false condition and any non-zero value is used to represent a true condition. The selection of which statement to execute next is then based on the value obtained.

In addition to numerical operands, character data can be compared to using relational operators. For such comparisons, the `char` values are automatically coerced to `int` values for the comparison. For example, in the Unicode code, the letter 'A' is stored using a code that has a lower numerical value than the letter 'B,' the code for 'B' has a lower value than the code for 'C,' and so on. For character sets coded in this manner, the following conditions are evaluated as follows:

Expression	Value	Interpretation
`'A' > 'C'`	0	`false`
`'D' <= 'Z'`	1	`true`
`'E' == 'F'`	0	`false`
`'g' >= 'm'`	0	`false`
`'b' != 'c'`	1	`true`
`'a' == 'A'`	0	`false`
`'B' < 'a'`	1	`true`
`'b' > 'Z'`	1	`true`

Comparing letters is essential in alphabetizing names or using characters to select a particular choice in decision-making situations. Strings of characters may also be compared. Finally, two string expressions may be compared using relational operators or the `string` class' comparison methods (Chapter 7). In the ASCII character set, a blank precedes (and is considered "less than") all letters and numbers; the letters of the alphabet are stored in order from A to Z; and the digits are stored in order from 0 to 9. In this sequence, the lowercase letters come after (are considered "greater than") the uppercase letters, and the letter codes come after (are "greater than") the digit codes (see Appendix B).

When two strings are compared, their individual characters are compared one pair at a time (both first characters, then both second characters, and so on). If no differences are found, the strings are equal; if a difference is found, the string with the first lower character is considered the smaller string. Following are examples of string comparisons:

Expression	Value	Interpretation	Comment
`"Hello"> "Good-bye"`	1	`true`	The first 'H' in Hello is greater than the first 'G' in Good-bye.
`"SMITH" > "JONES"`	1	`true`	The first 'S' in SMITH is greater than the first 'J' in JONES.
`"123" > "1227"`	1	`true`	The third character, the '3' in 123 is greater than the third character, the '2' in 1227.
`"Behop" > "Beehive"`	1	`true`	The third character, the 'h', in Behop is greater than the third character 'e' in Beehive.
`"He" == "She"`	0	`false`	The first 'H' in He is not equal to the first 'S' in She.
`"plant" < "planet"`	0	`false`	The 't' in plant is greater than the 'e' in planet.

Logical Operators

In addition to using simple relational expressions as conditions, more complex conditions can be created using the logical operators AND, OR, and NOT. These operators are represented by the symbols `&&`, `||`, and `!`, respectively.

When the AND operator, `&&`, is used with two simple expressions, the condition is true only if both individual expressions are true by themselves. Thus, the logical condition

```
(voltage > 48) && (milliamp < 10)
```

is true only if `voltage` is greater than 48 and `milliamp` is less than 10. Since relational operators have a higher precedence than logical operators, the parentheses in this logical expression could have been omitted.

The logical OR operator, `||`, is also applied between two expressions. When using the OR operator, the condition is satisfied if either one or both of the two expressions is true. Thus, the condition

```
(voltage > 48) || (milliamp < 10)
```

is true if either `voltage` is greater than 48, `milliamp` is less than 10, or if both conditions are true. Again, the parentheses surrounding the relational expressions are included to make the expression easier to read. Because of the higher precedence of relational operators with respect to logical operators, the same evaluation would be made even if the parentheses were omitted.

For the declarations

```
int i, j;
double a, b, complete;
```

the following represent valid conditions:

```
a > b
(i == j) || (a < b) || complete
(a/b > 5) && (i <= 20)
```

Before these conditions can be evaluated, the values of `a`, `b`, `i`, `j`, and `complete` must be known. Assuming `a` = 12.0, `b` = 2.0, `i` = 15, `j` = 30, and `complete` = 0.0 the previous expressions yield the following results:

Expression	Value	Interpretation
`a > b`	1	`true`
`(i == j) || (a < b) || complete`	0	`false`
`(a/b > 5) && (i <= 20)`	1	`true`

The NOT operator is used to change an expression to its opposite state; that is, if the expression has any non-zero value (true), `!expression` produces a zero value (false). If an expression is false to begin with (has a zero value), `!expression` is true and evaluates to 1. For example, assuming the number 26 is stored in the variable `age`, the expression `age > 40` has a value of zero (it is false), while the expression `!(age > 40)` has a value of 1. Since the NOT operator is used with only one expression, it is a unary operator.

The relational and logical operators have a hierarchy of execution similar to the arithmetic operators. Table 4.2 lists the precedence of these operators in relation to the other operators we have used.

Table 4.2

Operator	Associativity
`!` unary `-` `++` `--`	right to left
`*` `/` `%`	left to right
`+` `-`	left to right
`<` `<=` `>` `>=`	left to right
`==` `!=`	left to right
`&&`	left to right
`||`	left to right
`=` `+=` `-=` `*=` `/=`	right to left

The following example illustrates the use of an operator's precedence and associativity to evaluate relational expressions, assuming the following declarations:

```
char key = 'm';
int i = 5, j = 7, k = 12;
double x = 22.5;
```

Expression	Equivalent Expression	Value	Interpretation
i + 2 == k - 1	(i + 2) == (k - 1)	0	false
3 * i - j < 22	(3 * i) - j < 22	1	true
i + 2 * j > k	(i + (2 * j)) > k	1	true
k + 3 <= -j + 3 * i	(k + 3) <= ((-j) + (3*i))	0	false
'a' + 1 == 'b'	('a' + 1) == 'b'	1	true
key - 1 > 'p'	(key - 1) > 'p'	0	false
key + 1 == 'n'	(key + 1) == 'n'	1	true
25 >= x + 1.0	25 >= (x + 1.0)	1	true

As with all expressions, parentheses can be used to alter the assigned operator priority and improve the readability of relational expressions. By evaluating the expressions within parentheses first, the following compound condition is evaluated as

```
(6 * 3 == 36 / 2) || (13 < 3 * 3 + 4) && !(6 - 2 < 5)
         (18 == 18) ||   (13 < 9 + 4)   && !(4 < 5)
                  1 ||   (13 < 13)      && !1
                  1 ||         0        &&  0
                  1 ||         0
                     1
```

A Numerical Accuracy Problem

A problem that can occur with C++'s relational expressions is a subtle numerical accuracy problem relating to single-precision and double-precision numbers. Due to the way computers store these numbers, tests for equality of single-precision and double-precision values and variables using the relational operator == should be avoided.

The reason for this is that many decimal numbers, such as 0.1, for example, cannot be represented exactly in binary using a finite number of bits. Thus, testing for exact equality for such numbers can fail. When equality of noninteger values is desired it is better to require that the absolute value of the difference between operands be less than some extremely small value. Thus, for single-precision and double-precision operands, the general expression

operandOne == operandTwo

should be replaced by the condition

abs(operandOne – operandTwo) < 0.000001

where the value 0.000001 can be altered to any other acceptably small value. Thus, if the difference between the two operands is less than 0.000001 (or any other user selected amount), the two operands are considered essentially equal. For example, if `x` and `y` are single-precision variables, a condition such as

```
x/y == 0.35
```

should be programmed as

```
abs(x/y - 0.35) < EPSILON
```

where `EPSILON` can be a constant set to any acceptably small value, such as 0.000001.[2] This latter condition ensures that slight inaccuracies in representing noninteger numbers in binary do not affect evaluation of the tested condition. Since all computers have an exact binary representation of zero, comparisons for exact equality to zero don't encounter this numerical accuracy problem.

Exercises 4.1

1. Determine the value of the following expressions. Assume `a` = 5, `b` = 2, `c` = 4, `d` = 6, and `e` = 3.
   a. `a > b`
   b. `a != b`
   c. `d % b == c % b`
   d. `a * c != d * b`
   e. `d * b == c * e`
   f. `!(a * b)`
   g. `!(a % b * c)`
   h. `!(c % b * a)`
   i. `b % c * a`

2. Using parentheses, rewrite the following expressions to correctly indicate their order of evaluation. Then evaluate each expression assuming `a` = 5, `b` = 2, and `c` = 4.
   a. `a % b * c && c % b * a`
   b. `a % b * c || c % b * a`
   c. `b % c * a && a % c * b`
   d. `b % c * a || a % c * b`

3. Write relational expressions to express the following conditions (use variable names of your own choosing):
   a. The distance is equal to 30 feet.
   b. The ambient temperature is 86.4.
   c. A speed is 55 MPH.
   d. The current month is 12 (December).
   e. The letter input is K.
   f. A length is greater than two feet and less than three feet.
   g. The current day is the 15th day of the 1st month.

[2]Using the `abs()` function requires inclusion of the `cmath` header file. This is done by placing the preprocessor statement `#include<cmath>` either immediately before or after the `#include<iostream>` preprocessor statement. UNIX based systems also require specific inclusion of the math library at compile time with a `-lm` command line argument.

h. The automobile's speed is 35 MPH and its acceleration is greater than 4 MPH per second.
i. An automobile's speed is greater than 50 MPH and it has been moving for at least 5 hours.
j. The code is less than 500 characters and takes more than 2 microseconds to transmit.

4. Determine the value of the following expressions, assuming `a = 5`, `b = 2`, `c = 4`, and `d = 5`.

a. `a == 5`
b. `b * d == c * c`
c. `d % b * c > 5 || c % b * d < 7`

4.2 THE `if-else` STATEMENT

The `if-else` structure directs the computer to perform a series of one or more instructions based on the result of a comparison. For example, suppose we are to calculate the area of a circle given the radius as an input value. If the input is a negative number we are to print a message that the radius cannot be a negative value; otherwise we are to calculate and print the circle's area. The `if-else` structure can be used in this situation to select the correct operation based on whether the radius is negative or not. The general syntax of the `if-else` statement is

```
if (expression) statement1;
else statement2;
```

The expression is evaluated first. If the value of the expression is non-zero, *statement1* is executed. If the value is zero, the statement after the keyword else is executed. Thus, one of the two statements (either *statement1* or *statement2*, but not both) is always executed depending on the value of the expression. Notice that the tested expression must be put in parentheses and a semicolon is placed after each statement

For clarity, the `if-else` statement is typically written on four lines using the form

```
if (expression) <—— no semicolon here
   statement1;
else <—— no semicolon here
   statement2;
```

The form of the `if-else` statement that is selected typically depends on the length of statements 1 and 2. However, when using the second form, do not put a semicolon after the parentheses or the keyword `else`. The semicolons go only after the ends of the statements.

The flowchart for the `if-else` statement is shown in Figure 4.2.

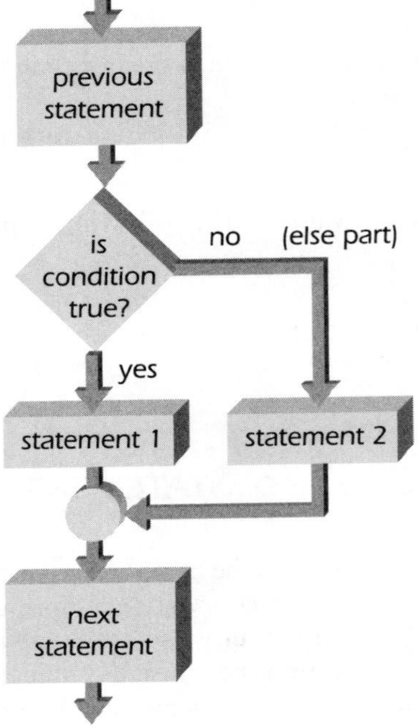

Figure 4.2 The `if-else` flowchart.

As a specific example of an `if-else` structure, we will construct a C++ program for determining the area of a circle by first examining the value of the radius. The condition to be tested is whether the radius is less than zero. An appropriate `if-else` statement for this situation is:

```
if (radius < 0.0)
  cout << "A negative radius is invalid" << endl;
else
  cout << "The area of this circle is " << 3.1416 * pow(radius,2) << endl;
```

Here we have used the relational operator < to represent the relation "less than." If the value of radius is less than 0, the condition is true (has a value of 1) and the statement `cout >> "A negative radius is invalid";` is executed. If the condition is not true, the value of the expression is zero, and the statement after the keyword `else` is executed. Program 4.1 illustrates the use of this statement in a complete program.

Program 4.1

```
#include <iostream>
#include <cmath>
using namespace std;

int main()
{
  double radius;

  cout << "Please type in the radius: ";
  cin  >> radius;

  if (radius < 0.0)
    cout << "A negative radius is invalid" << endl;
  else
    cout << "The area of this circle is " << 3.1416 * pow(radius,2) << endl;

  return 0;
}
```

A blank line was inserted before and after the `if-else` statement to highlight it in the complete program. We will continue to do this throughout the text to emphasize the statement being presented.

To illustrate selection in action, Program 4.1 was run twice with different input data. The results were

```
Please type in the radius: -2.5
A negative radius is invalid
```

and:

```
Please type in the radius: 2.5
The area of this circle is 19.635
```

In reviewing this output, observe that the radius in the first run of the program was less than 0 and the `if` part of the `if-else` structure correctly executed the `cout` statement, telling the user that a negative radius is invalid. In the second run, the radius is not negative and the `else` part of the `if-else` structure was used to yield a correct area computation of

$$3.1416 * (2.5)^2 = 19.635$$

Although any expression can be tested by an `if-else` statement, relational expressions are predominately used. However, statements such as

```
if (num)
  cout << "Bingo!";
```

```
else
  cout << "You lose!";
```

are valid. Since num, by itself, is a valid expression, the message `Bingo!` is displayed if num has any non-zero value and the message `You lose!` is displayed if num has a value of zero.

Compound Statements

Although only a single statement is permitted in both the `if` and `else` parts of the `if-else` statement, this statement can be a single compound statement. A **compound statement** is a sequence of single statements contained between braces, as shown in Figure 4.3.

```
{
   statement1;
   statement2;
   statement3;
        .
        .
        .
   last statement;
}
```

Figure 4.3 *A compound statement consists of individual statements enclosed within braces.*

The use of braces to enclose a set of individual statements creates a single block of statements, which may be used anywhere in a C++ program in place of a single statement. The next example illustrates the use of a compound statement within the general form of an `if-else` statement.

```
if (expression)
{
  statement1;     // as many statements as necessary
  statement2;     // can be put within the braces
  statement3;     // each statement must end with a ;

}
else
{
  statement4;
  statement5;
     .
     .
  statementn;
}
```

Program 4.2 illustrates the use of a compound statement in an actual program.

Program 4.2

```
#include <iostream>
#include <iomanip>
using namespace std;

// a temperature conversion program
int main()
{
  char tempType;
  double temp, fahren, celsius;

  cout << "Enter the temperature to be converted: ";
  cin  >> temp;
  cout << "Enter an f if the temperature is in Fahrenheit";
  cout << "\n or a c if the temperature is in Celsius: ";
  cin  >> tempType;

    // set output formats
  cout << setiosflags(ios::fixed)
       << setiosflags(ios::showpoint)
       << setprecision(2);

  if (tempType == 'f')
  {
    celsius = (5.0 / 9.0) * (temp - 32.0);
    cout << "\nThe equivalent Celsius temperature is "
         << celsius << endl;
  }
  else
  {
    fahren =  (9.0 / 5.0) * temp + 32.0;
    cout << "\nThe equivalent Fahrenheit temperature is "
         << fahren << endl;
  }

  return 0;
}
```

Program 4.2 checks whether the value in `tempType` is f. If the value is f, the compound statement corresponding to the `if` part of the `if-else` statement is executed. Any other letter results in execution of the compound statement corresponding to the `else` part. A sample run of Program 4.2 follows.

```
Enter the temperature to be converted: 212
Enter an f if the temperature is in Fahrenheit
 or a c if the temperature is in Celsius: f

The equivalent Celsius temperature is 100.00
```

Block Scope

All statements contained within a compound statement constitute a single block of code and any variable declared within such a block only has meaning between its declaration and the closing braces defining the block. For example, consider the following section of code, which consists of two blocks of code:

```
{   // start of outer block
   int a = 25;
   int b = 17;

   cout << "The value of a is " << a
        <<" and b is " << b << endl;

   {    // start of inner block
     float a = 46.25;
     int c = 10;

     cout << "a is now " << a
          << " b is now " << b
          << " and c is " << c << endl;
   }   // end of inner block

   cout << "a is now " << a
        << " and b is " << b << endl;

}   // end of outer block
```

The output that is produced by this section of code is:

```
The value of a is 25 and b is 17
a is now 46.25 b is now 17 and c is 10
a is now 25 and b is 17
```

This output is produced as follows: The first block of code defines two variables named `a` and `b`, which may be used anywhere within this block after their declaration, including any block contained inside of it. Within the inner block, two new variables have been declared, named `a` and `c`. At this stage then, we have created four different variables, two of which have the same name. Any referenced variable first results in an attempt to access a variable correctly declared within the block containing the reference. If no variable is defined within the block, an attempt is made to access a variable in the next immediate outside block until a valid access results.

Point of Information

Placement of Braces in a Compound Statement

A common practice for some C++ programmers is to place the opening brace of a compound statement on the same line as the `if` and `else` statements. Using this convention the `if` statement in Program 4.2 would appear as shown below. (This placement is a matter of style only—both styles are used and both are acceptable.)

```
if (tempType == 'f') {
  celsius = (5.0 / 9.0) * (temp - 32.0);
  cout << "\nThe equivalent Celsius temperature is "
       << celsius << endl;
}
else {
  fahren =  (9.0 / 5.0) * temp + 32.0;
  cout << "\nThe equivalent Fahrenheit temperature is "
       << fahren << endl;
}
```

Thus, the values of the variables `a` and `c` referenced within the inner block use the values of the variables `a` and `c` declared in that block. Since no variable named `b` was declared inside the inner block, the value of `b` displayed from within the inner block is obtained from the outer block. Finally, the last `cout` object, which is outside of the inner block, displays the value of the variable a declared in the outer block. If an attempt was made to display the value of `c` anywhere in the outer block, the compiler would issue an error message stating that `c` is an undefined symbol.

The area within a program where a variable can be used is formally referred to as the **scope** of the variable, and we will have much more to say on this subject in Chapter 6.

One-Way Selection

A useful modification of the `if-else` statement involves omitting the `else` part of the statement altogether. In this case, the `if` statement takes the shortened and frequently useful form

`if` *(expression)*
  statement;

The statement following `if (expression)` is only executed if the expression has a non-zero value (a true condition). As before, the statement may be a compound statement. The flowchart for this statement is illustrated in Figure 4.4.

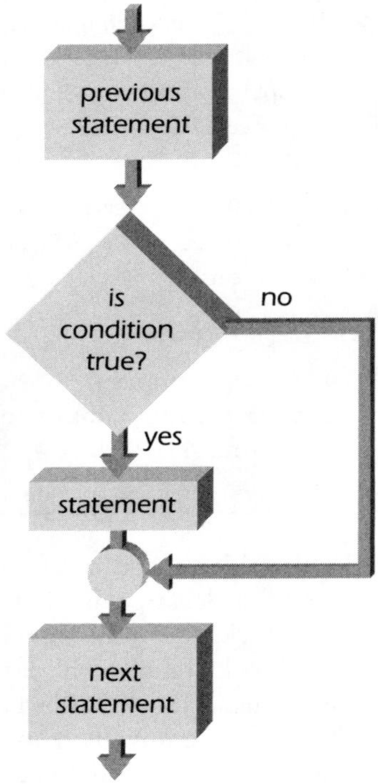

Figure 4.4 Flowchart for the one-way `if` statement.

This modified form of the `if` statement is called a one-way `if` statement. Program 4.3 uses this statement to selectively display a message for cars that have been driven more than 3000.0 miles.

Program 4.3

```
#include <iostream>
using namespace std;

int main()
{
  const double LIMIT = 3000.0;
  int idNum;
  double miles;

  cout << "Please type in car number and mileage: ";
  cin  >> idNum >> miles;

  if(miles > LIMIT)
    cout << "  Car " << idNum << " is over the limit.\n";

  cout << "End of program output.\n";

  return 0;
}
```

As an illustration of its one-way selection criteria in action, Program 4.3 was run twice, each time with different input data. Only the input data for the first run causes the message `Car 256 is over the limit` to be displayed.

```
Please type in car number and mileage: 256 3562.8
  Car 256 is over the limit.
End of program output.
```

and

```
Please type in car number and mileage: 23 2562.3
End of program output.
```

Problems Associated with the `if-else` Statement

Two of the most common problems encountered in initially using C++'s `if-else` statement are:

1. Misunderstanding the full implications of what an expression is, and
2. Using the assignment operator, =, in place of the relational operator ==.

Recall that an expression is any combination of operands and operators that yields a result. This definition is extremely broad and more encompassing than is initially apparent. For example, all of the following are valid C++ expressions:

```
age + 5
age = 30
age == 40
```

Assuming that the variables are suitably declared, each of the above expressions yields a result. Program 4.4 uses the `cout` object to display the value of these expressions when `age` = 18.

Program 4.4

```
#include <iostream>
using namespace std;

int main()
{
  int age = 18;

  cout << "The value of the first expression is " << (age + 5) << endl;
  cout << "The value of the second expression is " << (age = 30) << endl;
  cout << "The value of the third expression is " << (age == 40) << endl;

  return 0;
}
```

The display produced by Program 4.4 is:

```
The value of the first expression is 23
The value of the second expression is 30
The value of the third expression is 0
```

As the output of Program 4.4 illustrates, each expression, by itself, has a value associated with it. The value of the first expression is the sum of the variable `age` plus 5, which is 23. The value of the second expression is 30, which is also assigned to the variable `age`. The value of the third expression is zero, since `age` is not equal to 40, and a false condition is represented in C++ with a value of zero. If the value in `age` had been 40, the relational expression `a == 40` would be true and would have a value of 1.

Point of Information

The Boolean Data Type

Before the current ANSI/ISO C++ standard, C++ did not have a built-in Boolean data type with its two Boolean values, **true** and **false**. Since this data type was not originally a part of the language, a tested expression could not evaluate to a boolean value. Thus, the syntax

if(Boolean expression is true)
  execute this statement;

was also not built in to either C or C++. Rather, both C and C++ use the more encompassing syntax:

if(expression)
  execute this statement;

where *expression* is any expression that evalutes to a numeric value. If the value of the tested expression is a non-zero value it is considered as true, and only a zero value is considered as false.

As specified by the ANSI/ISO C++ standard, C++ has a built-in Boolean data type containing the two values, **true** and **false**. Boolean variables will be declared using the keyword **bool**. As currently implemented, the actual values represented by the two Boolean values, **true** and **false**, are the integer values 1 and 0, respectively. For example, consider the following program, which declares two Boolean variables.

```
#include <iostream>
using namespace std;
int main()
{
  bool t1, t2;

  t1 = true;
  t2 = false;

  cout <<"The value of t1 is " << t1
       << "\nand the value of t2 is " << t2 << endl;

  return 0;
}
```

The output produced by this program is:

```
The value of t1 is 1
and the value of t2 is 0
```

As seen by the output, the Boolean values **true** and **false**, are represented by the integer values 1 and 0, respectively. The Boolean values true and false have the following relationships.

```
!true= is false
!false= is true
```

Additionally, applying either a postfix or prefix ++ operator to a variable of type bool will set the Boolean value to **true**. the postfix and prefix -- operators cannot be applied to Boolean variables.

Boolean values can also be compared, as illustrated in the following code:

```
if (t1 == t2)
  cout << "The values are equal" << endl;
else
  cout << "The values are not equal" << endl;
```

Lastly, assigning any non-zero value to a Boolean variable results in the variable being set to **true**; that is, a value of 1, and assigning a zero value to a Boolean results in the variable being set to **false**; that is, a value of 0.

Now assume that the relational expression `age == 40` was intended to be used in the `if` statement

```
if (age == 40)
  cout << "Happy Birthday!";
```

but was mistyped as `age = 40`, resulting in

```
if (age = 40)
  cout << "Happy Birthday!";
```

Since the mistake results in a valid C++ expression, and any C++ expression can be tested by an `if` statement, the resulting `if` statement is valid and will cause the message `Happy Birthday!` to be printed regardless of what value was previously assigned to age. Can you see why?

The condition tested by the `if` statement does not compare the value in `age` to the number 40, but assigns the number 40 to `age`. That is, the expression `age = 40` is not a relational expression at all, but an assignment expression. At the completion of the assignment the expression itself has a value of 40. Since C++ treats any non-zero value as true, the `cout` statement is executed. Another way of looking at this is to realize that the `if` statement is equivalent to the following two statements:

```
age = 40;       // assign 40 to age
if (age)        // test the value of age
  cout << "Happy Birthday!";
```

Since a C++ compiler has no means of knowing that the expression being tested is not the desired one, you must be especially careful when writing conditions.

Exercises 4.2

1. Write appropriate `if` statements for each of the following conditions:
   a. If an angle is equal to 90 degrees print the message "The angle is a right angle," else print the message that "The angle is not a right angle."
   b. If the temperature is above 100 degrees display the message "above the boiling point of water" else display the message "below the boiling point of water."
   c. If the number is positive add the number to `possum`, else add the number to `negsum`.
   d. If the slope is less than 0.5 set the variable `flag` to zero, else set `flag` to one.
   e. If the difference between `volts1` and `volts2` is less than 0.001, set the variable `approx` to zero, else calculate `approx` as the quantity (`volts1 - volts2`) / 2.0.
   f. If the frequency is above 60, display the message "The frequency is too high."
   g. If the difference between `temp1` and `temp2` exceeds 2.3, calculate `error` as `(temp1 - temp2) * factor`.
   h. If x is greater than y and z is less than 20, read in a value for p.
   i. If distance is greater than 20 and it is less than 35, read in a value for time.

2. Write `if` statements corresponding to the conditions illustrated by each of the following flow charts.

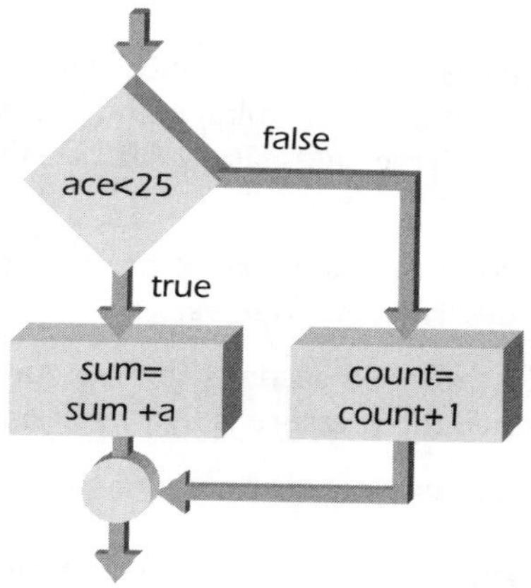

a.

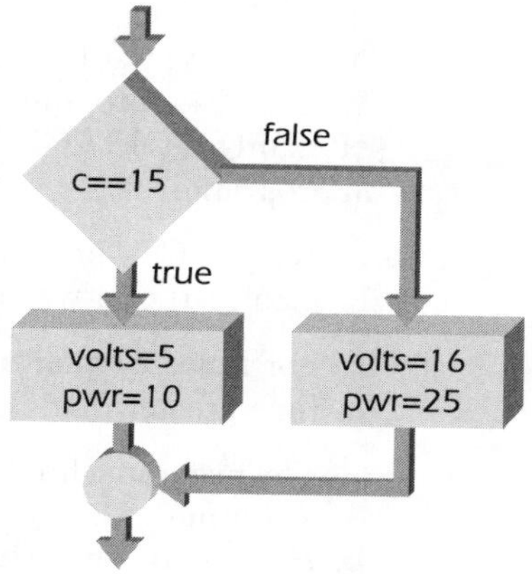

b.

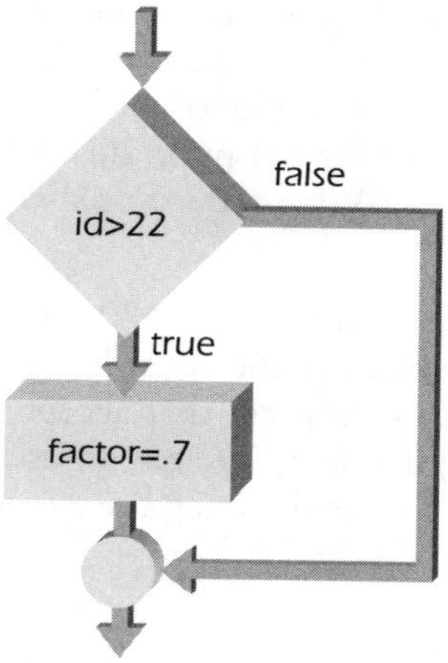

c.

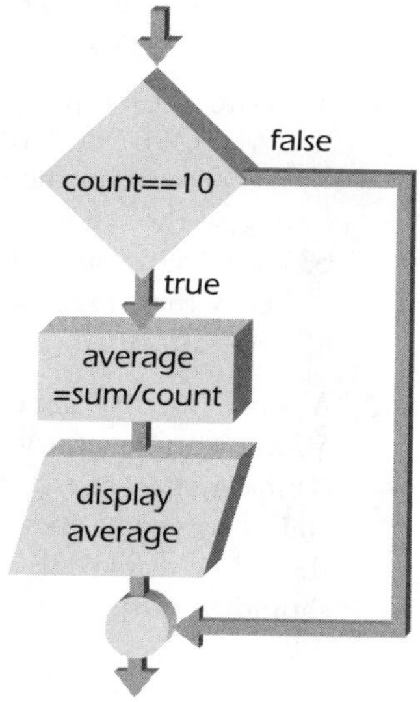

d.

3. Write a C++ program that asks the user to input two numbers. If the first number entered is greater than the second number the program should print the message "The first number is greater," else it should print the message "The first number is smaller." Test your program by entering the numbers 5 and 8 and then using the numbers 11 and 2. What do you think your program will display if the two numbers entered are equal? Test this case.

4. **a.** A certain waveform is 0 volts for time less than 2 seconds and 3 volts for time equal to or greater than 2 seconds (such waveforms are referred to as step functions). Write a C++ program that accepts time into the variable named `time` and display the appropriate voltage depending on the input value.

b. How many runs should you make for the program written in Exercise 4a to verify that it is operating correctly? What data should you input in each of the program runs?

5. An insulation test for a wire requires that the insulation withstand at least 600 volts. Write a C++ program that accepts a test voltage and prints either the message "PASSED VOLTAGE TEST" or the message "FAILED VOLTAGE TEST," as appropriate.

6. a. Write a C++ program to compute the value of pressure in pounds per square inch (psi) of a waveform described as follows:

For time, t, equal to or less than 35 seconds the pressure is $0.46t$ psi and for time greater than 35 seconds the pressure is $0.19t + 9.45$ psi.

The program should request the time as input and should display the pressure as output.

b. How many runs should you make for the program written in Exercise 6a to verify that it is operating correctly? What data should you input in each of the program runs?

7. a. Write a C++ program that displays either the message "PROCEED WITH TAKEOFF" or "ABORT TAKEOFF" depending on the input. If the character g is entered in the variable `code`, the first message should be displayed; otherwise the second message should be displayed.

b. How many runs should you make for the program written in Exercise 7a to verify that it is operating correctly? What data should you input in each of the program runs?

8. A small factory generates its own power with a 20-kilowatt generator and a 50-kilowatt generator. The plant manager indicates which generator is required by typing a character code. Write a C++ program that accepts this code as input. If code s is typed a message directing the plant foreman to use the smaller generator should be displayed; otherwise a message directing the use of the larger generator should be output.

4.3 NESTED `if` STATEMENTS

As we have seen, an `if-else` statement can contain simple or compound statements. Any valid C++ statement can be used, including another `if-else` statement. Thus, one or more `if-else` statements can be included within either part of an `if-else` statement. The inclusion of one or more `if` statements within an existing `if` statement is called a *nested* `if` statement. For example, substituting the one-way `if` statement

```
if (distance > 500)
  cout << "snap";
```

for `statement1` in the following `if` statement

```
if (hours < 9)
  statement1;
else
  cout << "pop";
```

results in the nested `if` statement

```
if (hours < 9)
{
  if (distance > 500)
    cout << "snap";
}
else
  cout << "pop";
```

The braces around the inner one-way `if` are essential because in their absence C++ associates an `else` with the closest unpaired `if`. Thus, without the braces, the above statement is equivalent to

```
if (hours < 9)
  if (distance > 500)
    cout << "snap";
  else
    cout << "pop";
```

Here the `else` is paired with the inner `if`, which destroys the meaning of the original `if-else` statement. Notice also that the indentation is irrelevant as far as the compiler is concerned. Whether the indentation exists or not, *the statement is compiled by associating the last* `else` *with the closest unpaired* `if`*, unless braces are used to alter the default pairing.*

The process of nesting `if` statements can be extended indefinitely, so that the `cout << "snap";` statement could itself be replaced by either a complete `if-else` statement or another one-way `if` statement.

Figure 4.5 illustrates the general form of a nested `if-else` statement when an `if-else` statement is nested (a) within the `if` part of an `if-else` statement and (b) within the `else` part of an `if-else` statement.

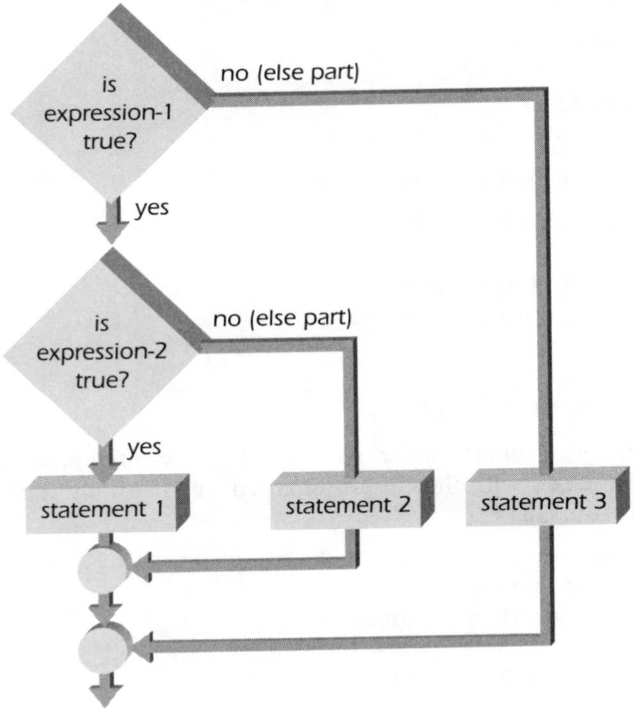

Figure 4.5a `if-else` statement nested in an `if`.

The `if-else` Chain

In general, the nesting illustrated in Figure 4.5a tends to be confusing and is best avoided in practice. However, an extremely useful construction occurs for the nesting illustrated in Figure 4.5b, which has the form

```
if (expression_1)
  statement1;
else
  if (expression_2)
    statement2;
  else
    statement3;
```

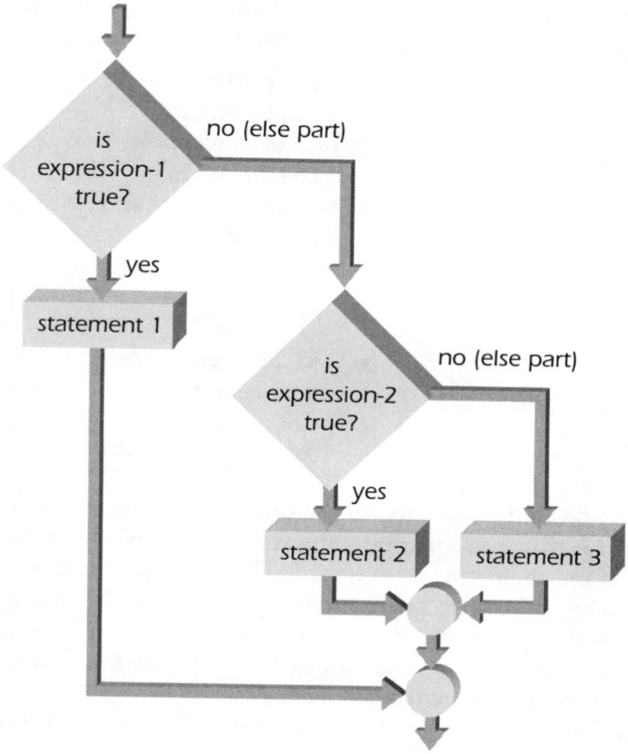

Figure 4.5b `if-else` *statement nested in an* `else`.

As with all C++ programs, since white space is ignored, the indentation shown is not required. More typically, the preceding construction is written using the following arrangement:

```
if (expression_1)
  statement1;
else if (expression_2)
  statement2;
else
  statement3;
```

This form of a nested `if` statement is extremely useful in practice, and is formally referred to as an `if-else chain`. Each condition is evaluated in order, and if any condition is true the corresponding statement is executed and the remainder of the chain is terminated. The statement associated with the final `else` is only executed if none of the previous conditions is satisfied. This serves as a default or catch-all case that is useful for detecting an impossible or error condition.

The chain can be continued indefinitely by repeatedly making the last statement another `if-else` statement. Thus, the general form of an `if-else` chain is:

```
if (expression_1)
  statement1;
else if (expression_2)
  statement2;
else if (expression_3)
  statement3;
      .
      .
      .
else if (expression_n)
  statement_n;
else
  last_statement;
```

Each condition is evaluated in the order it appears in the statement. For the first condition that is true, the corresponding statement is executed, and the remainder of the statements in the chain are not executed. Thus, if `expression_1` is true, only `statement1` is executed; otherwise `expression_2` is tested. If `expression_2` is then true, only `statement2` is executed; otherwise `expression_3` is tested, and so on. The final `else` in the chain is optional, and `last_statement` is only executed if none of the previous expressions were true.

To illustrate using an `if-else` chain, Program 4.5 displays an item's specification status corresponding to a letter input. The following letter codes are used:

Specification Status	Input Code
Space Exploration	S
Military Grade	M
Commercial Grade	C
Toy Grade	T

Program 4.5

```
#include <iostream>
using namespace std;

int main()
{
  char code;

  cout << "Enter a specification code: ";
  cin  >> code;

  if (code == 'S')
      cout << "The item is space exploration grade.";
  else if (code == 'M')
    cout << "The item is military grade.";
  else if (code == 'C')
    cout << "The item is commercial grade.";
  else if (code == 'T')
      cout << "The item is toy grade.";
  else
      cout << "An invalid code was entered.";
  cout << endl;

  return 0;
}
```

As a further example of an `if-else` chain, we determine the output of a digital converter unit using the following input/output relationship:

Input Weight	Output Reading
greater than or equal to 90 lbs	1111
less than 90 lbs but greater than 80 lbs	1110
less than 80 lbs but greater than or equal to 70 lbs	1101
less than 70 lbs but greater than or equal to 60 lbs	1100
less than 60 lbs	1011

The following statements can be used to determine the correct output reading, where the variable `inlbs` is used to store the input reading:

```
if (inlbs >= 90)
    digout = 1111;
```

```
else if (inlbs >= 80)
    digout = 1110;
else if (inlbs >= 70)
    digout = 1101;
else if (inlbs >= 60)
    digout = 1100;
else
    digout = 1011;
```

Notice that this example makes use of the fact that the chain is stopped once a true condition is found. This is accomplished by checking for the highest input weight first. If the input value is less than 90, the `if-else` chain continues checking for the next highest weight, and so on, until the correct weight category is obtained.

Program 4.6 uses an `if-else` chain to calculate and display the correct output reading corresponding to the weight input in the `cin` statement.

Program 4.6

```
#include <iostream>
using namespace std;

int main()
{
  int digout;
  double inlbs;

  cout << "Enter the input weight: ";
  cin  >> inlbs;

  if (inlbs >= 90)
      digout = 1111;
  else if (inlbs >= 80)
      digout = 1110;
  else if (inlbs >= 70)
    digout = 1101;
  else if (inlbs >= 60)
    digout = 1100;
  else
    digout = 1011;

  cout << "The digital output is " << digout << endl;

  return 0;
}
```

A sample run using Program 4.6 is illustrated below.

```
Enter the input weight: 72.5
The digital output is 1101
```

As with all C++ statements, each individual statement within an **if-else** chain can be replaced by a compound statement bounded by the braces { and }.

Exercises 4.3

1. Modify Program 4.5 to accept both lower and uppercase letters as codes. For example, if a user enters either an m or an M, the program should display the message "The item is military grade."

2. Write nested if statements corresponding to the conditions illustrated in each of the following flowcharts.

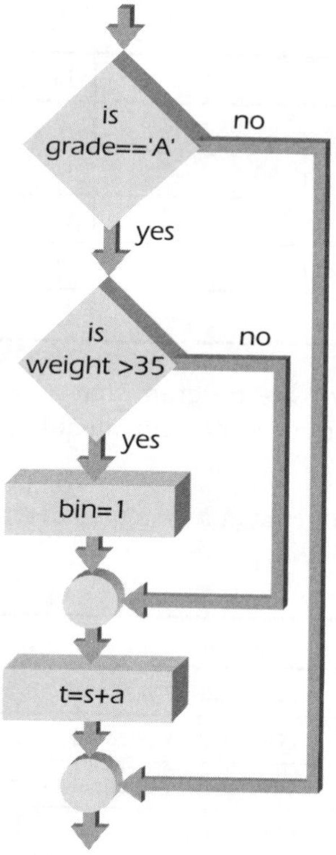

a.

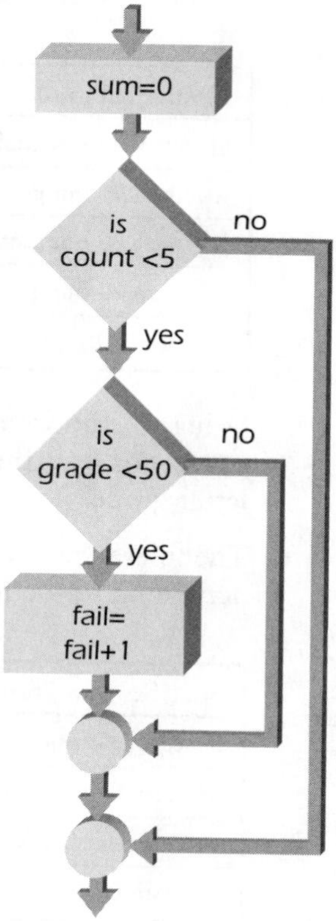

b.

3. An angle is considered acute if it is less than 90 degrees, obtuse if it is greater than 90 degrees, and a right angle if it is equal to 90 degrees. Using this information, write a C++ program that accepts an angle, in degrees, and displays the type of angle corresponding to the degrees entered.

4. The grade level of undergraduate college students is typically determined according to the following schedule:

Number of Credits Completed	Grade Level
less than 32	Freshman
32 to 63	Sophomore
64 to 95	Junior
96 or more	Senior

Using this information, write a C++ program that accepts the number of credits a student has completed, determines the student's grade level, and displays the grade level.

5. A student's letter grade is calculated according to the following schedule:

Numerical grade	Letter grade
greater than or equal to 90	A
less than 90 but greater than or equal to 80	B
less than 80 but greater than or equal to 70	C
less than 70 but greater than or equal to 60	D
less than 60	F

Using this information, write a C++ program that accepts a student's numerical grade, converts the numerical grade to an equivalent letter grade, and displays the letter grade.

6. The tolerance of critical components in a system is determined by the application according to the following schedule:

Specification Status	Tolerance
Space Exploration	Less than 0.1%
Military Grade	Greater than or equal to 0.1% and less than 1%
Commercial Grade	Greater than or equal to 1% and less than 10%
Toy Grade	Greater than or equal to 10%

Using this information, write a C++ program that accepts the tolerance reading of a component and determines the specification that should be assigned to the component.

7. Write a C++ program that accepts a number followed by one space and then a letter. If the letter following the number is f, the program is to treat the number entered as a temperature in degrees Fahrenheit, convert the number to the equivalent degrees Celsius, and print a suitable display message. If the letter following the number is c, the program is to treat the number entered as a temperature in Celsius, convert the number to the equivalent degrees Fahrenheit, and print a suitable display message. If the letter is neither an f or c, the program is to print a message that the data entered is incorrect and terminate. Use an `if-else` chain in your program and make use of the conversion formulas:

   $Celsius = (5.0 / 9.0) * (Fahrenheit - 32.0)$
   $Fahrenheit = (9.0 / 5.0) * Celsius + 32.0$

8. Using the relationships from Program 4.6, the following program calculates the digital output:

```
int main()
{
  int digout;
  double inlbs;

  cout << "Enter the input weight: ";
  cin  >> inlbs;

  if (inlbs >= 90) digout = 1111;
  if (inlbs >= 80) && (inlbs <= 90) digout = 1110;
  if (inlbs >= 70) && (inlbs <= 80) digout = 1101;
  if (inlbs >= 60) && (inlbs <= 70) digout = 1100;
  if (inlbs < 1000) digout = 1011;

  cout << "The digital output is " << digout << endl;

  return 0;
}
```

   a. Will this program produce the same output as Program 4.6?
   b. Which program is better and why?

9. The following program was written to produce the same result as Program 4.6:

```
int main()
{
  int digout;
  double inlbs;

  cout << "Enter the input weight: ";
  cin  >> inlbs;
```

```
    if (inlbs < 60)
        digout = 1011;
    else if (inlbs >= 60)
        digout = 1100;
    else if (inlbs >= 70)
      digout = 1101;
    else if (inlbs >= 80)
      digout = 1110;
    else if (inlbs >= 90)
      digout = 1111;

    cout << "The digital output is " << digout << endl;

    return 0;
  }
```

a. Will this program run?
b. What does this program do?
c. For what values of input pounds does this program calculate the correct digital output?

4.4 THE `switch` STATEMENT

The `if-else` chain is used in programming applications where one set of instructions must be selected from many possible alternatives. The `switch` statement provides an alternative to the `if-else` chain for cases that compare the value of an integer expression to a specific value. The general form of a `switch` statement is

```
switch (expression)
{    // start of compound statement
  case value_1:  <---------- terminated with a colon
    statement1;
    statement2;
        .
        .
    break;
  case value_2:  <---------- terminated with a colon
    statementm;
    statementn;
        .
        .
    break;
  .
  .
```

```
  case value_n:   <---------- terminated with a colon
    statementw;
    statementx;
        .
        .
    break;
  default:        <---------- terminated with a colon
    statementaa;
    statementbb;
        .
}    // end of switch and compound statement
```

The `switch` statement uses four new keywords: `switch`, `case`, `break`, and `default`. Let's see what each of these words does.

The keyword `switch` identifies the start of the `switch` statement. The expression in parentheses following this word is evaluated and the result of the expression compared to various alternative values contained within the compound statement. The expression in the `switch` statement must evaluate to an integer result or a compilation error results.

Internal to the `switch` statement, the keyword `case` is used to identify or label individual values that are compared to the value of the `switch` expression. The `switch` expression's value is compared to each of these `case` values in the order in which these values are listed until a match is found. When a match occurs, execution begins with the statement immediately following the match. Thus, as illustrated in Figure 4.6, the value of the expression determines where in the `switch` statement execution actually begins.

Any number of `case` labels may be contained within a `switch` statement, in any order. If the value of the expression does not match any of the `case` values, however, no statement is executed unless the keyword `default` is encountered. The word `default` is optional and operates the same as the last `else` in an `if-else` chain. If the value of the expression does not match any of the case values, program execution begins with the statement following the word `default`.

Once an entry point has been located by the `switch` statement, all further `case` evaluations are ignored and execution continues through the end of the compound statement unless a `break` statement is encountered. This is the reason for the `break` statement, which identifies the end of a particular `case` and causes an immediate exit from the `switch` statement. Thus, just as the word `case` identifies possible starting points in the compound statement, the `break` statement determines terminating points. If the `break` statements are omitted, all cases following the matching `case` value, including the `default` case, are executed.

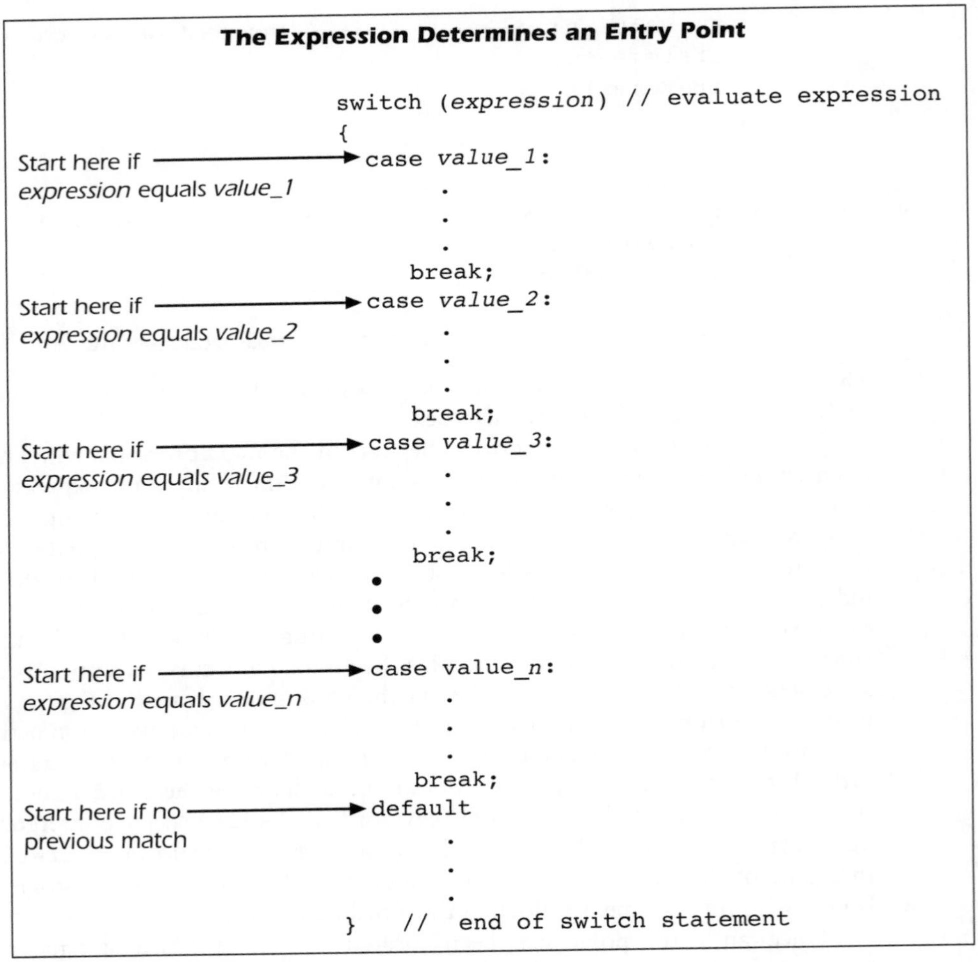
The Expression Determines an Entry Point
switch (expression) // evaluate expression
{
Start here if expression equals value_1
case value_1:
break;
Start here if expression equals value_2
case value_2:
break;
Start here if expression equals value_3
case value_3:
break;
Start here if expression equals value_n
case value_n:
break;
Start here if no previous match
default
} // end of switch statement

Figure 4.6 The expression determines an entry point.

When writing a `switch` statement, you can use multiple `case` values to refer to the same set of statements; the `default` label is optional. For example, consider the following:

```
switch (number)
{
  case 1:
    cout << "Have a Good Morning\n";
    break;
  case 2:
    cout << "Have a Happy Day\n";
    break;
  case 3:
  case 4:
  case 5:
    cout << "Have a Nice Evening\n";
}
```

If the value stored in the variable number is 1, the message `Have a Good Morning` is displayed. Similarly, if the value of number is 2, the second message is displayed. Finally, if the value of number is 3 or 4 or 5, the last message is displayed. Since the statement to be executed for these last three cases is the same, the cases for these values can be "stacked together," as shown in the example. Also, since there is no `default`, no message is printed if the value of number is not one of the listed `case` values. Although it is good programming practice to list `case` values in increasing order, this is not required by the `switch` statement. A `switch` statement may have any number of `case` values, in any order; only the values being tested for need be listed.

Program 4.7 uses a switch statement to select the arithmetic operation (addition, multiplication, or division) to be performed on two numbers depending on the value of the variable `opselect`.

Program 4.7 was run twice. The resulting display clearly identifies the case selected. The results are

```
Please type in two numbers: 12 3
Enter a select code:
          1 for addition
          2 for multiplication
          3 for division : 2
The product of the numbers entered is 36
```

and:

```
Please type in two numbers: 12 3
Enter a select code:
          1 for addition
          2 for multiplication
          3 for division : 3
The first number divided by the second is 4
```

In reviewing Program 4.7, notice the `break` statement in the last `case`. Although this `break` is not necessary, it is a good practice to terminate the last `case` in a `switch` statement with a `break`. This prevents a possible program error later if an additional `case` is subsequently added to the `switch` statement. With the addition of a new `case`, the `break` between `cases` becomes necessary; having the `break` in place ensures you will not forget to include it at the time of the modification.

Program 4.7

```
#include <iostream>
using namespace std;

int main()
{
  int opselect;
  double fnum, snum;

  cout << "Please type in two numbers: ";
  cin  >> fnum >> snum;
  cout << "Enter a select code: ";
  cout << "\n        1 for addition";
  cout << "\n        2 for multiplication";
  cout << "\n        3 for division : ";
  cin  >> opselect;

  switch (opselect)
  {
    case 1:
      cout << "The sum of the numbers entered is " << fnum+snum;
      break;
    case 2:
      cout << "The product of the numbers entered is " << fnum*snum;
      break;
    case 3:
      cout << "The first number divided by the second is " << fnum/snum;
      break;
  }     // end of switch

  cout << endl;

  return 0;
}
```

Because character data types are always converted to integers in an expression, a `switch` statement can also be used to "switch" based on the value of a character expression. For example, assuming that `choice` is a character variable, the following `switch` statement is valid:

```
switch(choice)
{
  case 'a':
  case 'e':
  case 'i':
```

```
    case 'o':
    case 'u':
      cout << "The character in choice is a vowel\n";
      break;
    default:
      cout << "The character in choice is not a vowel\n";
      break;    // this break is optional
  }    // end of switch statement
```

Exercises 4.4

1. Rewrite the following `if-else` chain using a `switch` statement:

```
if (letterGrade == 'A')
  cout << "The numerical grade is between 90 and 100\n";
else if (letterGrade == 'B')
  cout << "The numerical grade is between 80 and 89.9\n";
else if (letterGrade == 'C')
  cout << "The numerical grade is between 70 and 79.9\n";
else if (letterGrade == 'D')
  cout << "How are you going to explain this one\n";
else
{
  cout << "Of course I had nothing to do with my grade.\n";
  cout << "It must have been the professor's fault.\n";
}
```

2. Rewrite the following `if-else` chain using a `switch` statement:

```
if (factor == 1)
  pressure = 25.0;
else if (factor == 2)
  pressure = 36.0;
else if (factor == 3)
 pressure = 45.0;
else if (factor == 4) || (factor == 5) || (factor == 6)
  pressure = 49.0;
```

3. Each disk drive in a shipment of these devices is stamped with a code from 1 through 4, which indicates a drive of manufacturers as follows:

Code	Disk Drive Manufacturer
1	3M Corporation
2	Maxell Corporation
3	Sony Corporation
4	Verbatim Corporation

Write a C++ program that accepts the code number as an input and based on the value entered displays the correct disk drive manufacturer.

4. Rewrite Program 4.5 using a `switch` statement.
5. Determine why the `if-else` chain in Program 4.6 cannot be replaced with a `switch` statement.
6. Rewrite Program 4.7 using a character variable for the select code. (*Hint:* Review Section 3.4 if your program does not operate as you think it should.)

4.5 APPLICATIONS

Two major uses of C++'s `if` statements are to select appropriate processing paths and to prevent undesirable data from being processed at all. In this section, examples of both uses are provided.

Application 1: Data Validation

An important use of C++'s `if` statements is to validate data by checking for clearly invalid cases. For example, a date such as 5/33/06 contains an obviously invalid day. Similarly, the division of any number by zero within a program, such as 14/0, should not be allowed. Both of these examples illustrate the need for a technique called **defensive programming**, in which the program includes code to check for improper data before an attempt is made to process it further. The defensive programming technique of checking user input data for erroneous or unreasonable data is referred to as **input data validation.**

Consider the case where we are to write a C++ program to calculate the square root and the reciprocal of a user entered number. Before calculating the square root, validate that the number is not negative, and before calculating the reciprocal, check that the number is not zero.

Step 1 Analyze the Problem

The statement of the problem requires that we accept a single number as an input, validate the entered number, and based on the validation produce two possible outputs: If the number is non-negative we are to determine its square root, and if the input number is not zero we are to determine its reciprocal.

Step 2 Develop a Solution

Since the square root of a negative number does not exist as a real number, and the reciprocal of zero cannot be taken, our program must contain input data validation statements to screen the user input data and avoid these two cases. The pseudocode describing the processing required is:

Display a program purpose message
Accept a user input number

If the number is negative
print a message that the square root cannot be taken
Else
calculate and display the square root
Endif
If the number is zero then
print a message that the reciprocal cannot be taken
Else
calculate and display the reciprocal
Endif

Step 3 Code the Solution

The C++ code corresponding to our pseudocode solution is listed in Program 4.8.

Program 4.8

```
#include <iostream>
#include <cmath>
using namespace std;

int main()
{
  double usenum;

  cout << "This program calculates the square root and\n"
        << "reciprocal (1/number) of a number\n"
        << "\nPlease enter a number: ";
  cin  >> usenum;
  if (usenum < 0.0)
    cout << "The square root of a negative number does not exist.\n";
  else
    cout << "The square root of " << usenum
          << " is " << sqrt(usenum) << endl;
  if (usenum == 0.0)
    cout << "The reciprocal of zero does not exist.\n";
  else
    cout << "The reciprocal of " << usenum
          << " is " <<  (1.0/usenum) << endl;

  return 0;
}
```

Program 4.8 is a rather straightforward program containing two separate (non-nested) `if` statements. The first `if` statement checks for a negative input number; if the number is negative a message indicating that the square root of a negative number cannot be taken is displayed, else the square root is taken. The second `if` statement checks whether the entered number is zero; if it is a message indicating that the reciprocal of zero cannot be taken is displayed, else the reciprocal is taken.

Step 4 Test and Correct the Program

Test values should include a positive number, and values for the limiting cases, such as a negative and zero input value. Test runs follow for two of these cases:

```
This program calculates the square root and
reciprocal (1/number) of a number

Please enter a number: 5

The square root of 5 is 2.23607
The reciprocal of 5 is 0.2
```

and

```
This program calculates the square root and
reciprocal (1/number) of a number

Please enter a number: -6

The square root of a negative number does not exist
The reciprocal of -6 is -0.166667
```

Application 2: Solving Quadratic Equations

A **quadratic equation** is an equation that has the form $ax^2 + bx + c = 0$ or that can be algebraically manipulated into this form. In this equation x is the unknown variable, and a, b, and c are known constants. Although the constants b and c can be any numbers, including zero, the value of the constant a cannot be zero (if a is zero, the equation would become a **linear equation** in x). Examples of quadratic equations are

$$5x^2 + 6x + 2 = 0$$
$$x^2 - 7x + 20 = 0$$
$$34x^2 + 16 = 0$$

In the first equation $a = 5$, $b = 6$, and $c = 2$; in the second equation $a = 1$, $b = -7$, and $c = 20$; and in the third equation $a = 34$, $b = 0$, and $c = 16$.

The real roots of a quadratic equation can be calculated using the quadratic formula as:

$$\text{root } 1 = \frac{-b + \sqrt{b^2 - 4ac}}{2a}$$

and

$$\text{root } 2 = \frac{-b - \sqrt{b^2 - 4ac}}{2a}$$

Using these equations we will write a C++ program to solve for the roots of a quadratic equation.

Step 1 Analyze the Problem

The problem requires that we accept three inputs—the coefficients a, b, and c of a quadratic equation and compute the roots of the equation using the given formulas.

Step 2 Develop a Solution

A first attempt at a solution would be to use the user-entered values of a, b, and c to calculate directly a value for each of the roots. Thus, our first solution would be

Display a program purpose message
Accept user-input values for a, b, and c
Calculate the two roots
Display the values of the calculated roots

However, this solution must be refined further to account for a number of possible input conditions. For example, if a user entered a value of 0 for both a and b, the equation is neither quadratic nor linear and has no solution (this is referred to as a degenerate case). Another possibility is that the user supplies a non-zero value for b but makes a zero. In this case the equation becomes a linear one with a single solution of $-c / b$. A third possibility is that the value of the term $b^2 - 4ac$, which is called the **discriminant**, is negative. Since the square root of a negative number cannot be taken, this case will have no real roots. Finally, when the discriminant is zero, both roots are the same (this is referred to as the repeated roots case).

Taking into account all four of these limiting cases, a refined solution for correctly determining the roots of a quadratic equation is expressed by the following pseudocode:

Display a program purpose message
Accept user-input values for a, b, and c
If a = 0 and b = 0 then
    display a message saying that the equation has no solution
Else if a = zero then
    calculate the single root equal to –c/b
    display the single root
Else
    calculate the discriminant

If the discriminant > 0 then
solve for both roots using the given formulas
display the two roots
Else if the discriminant < 0 then
display a message that there are no real roots
Else
calculate the repeated root equal to –b/(2a)
display the repeated root
Endif
Endif

Notice in the pseudocode that we have used nested `if-else` statements. The outer `if-else` statement is used to validate the entered coefficients and determine that we have a valid quadratic equation. The inner `if-else` statement is then used to determine if the equation has two real roots (discriminant > 0), two imaginary roots (discriminant < 0), or repeated roots (discriminant = 0).

Step 3 Code the Solution

The equivalent C++ code corresponding to our pseudocode solution is listed in Program 4.9.

Step 4 Test and Correct the Program

Test values should include values for a, b, and c that result in two real roots, plus limiting values for a and b that result in either a linear equation ($a = 0, b \neq 0$), a degenerate equation ($a = 0, b = 0$), and a negative and zero discriminant. Two such test runs of Program 4.9 follow:

```
This program calculates the roots of a
   quadratic equation of the form
            2
         ax + bx + c = 0
Please enter values for a, b, and c: 1 2 -35

The two real roots are 5 and -7
```

and

```
This program calculates the roots of a
   quadratic equation of the form
            2
         ax + bx + c = 0

Please enter values for a, b, and c: 0 0 16

The equation is degenerate and has no roots.
```

Program 4.9

```
#include <iostream>
#include <cmath>
using namespace std;

// this program solves for the roots of a quadratic equation
int main()
{
  double a, b, c, disc, root1, root2;

  cout << "This program calculates the roots of a\n";
  cout << "   quadratic equation of the form\n";
  cout << "              2\n";
  cout << "            ax + bx + c = 0\n\n";
  cout << "Please enter values for a, b, and c: ";
  cin >>  a >>  b >> c;
  if ( a == 0.0 && b == 0.0)
    cout << "The equation is degenerate and has no roots.\n";
  else if (a == 0.0)
    cout << "The equation has the single root x = "
       << -c/b << endl;
  else
  {
    disc = pow(b,2.0) - 4 * a * c;    // calculate discriminant
    if (disc > 0.0)
    {
      disc = sqrt(disc);
      root1 = (-b + disc) / (2 * a);
      root2 = (-b - disc) / (2 * a);
      cout << "The two real roots are "
   << root1 << " and " << root2 << endl;
    }
    else if (disc < 0.0)
      cout << "Both roots are imaginary.\n";
    else
      cout << "Both roots are equal to " << -b / (2 * a) << endl;
  }

  return 0;
}
```

The first run solves the quadratic equation $x^2 + 2x - 35 = 0$, which has the real roots $x = 5$ and $x = -7$. The input data for the second run results in the equation $0x^2 + 0x + 16 = 0$. Because this degenerates into the mathematical impossibility of $16 = 0$, the program correctly identifies this as a degenerate equation. We leave it as an exercise to create test data for the other limiting cases checked for by the program.

Exercises 4.5

1. a. Write a program that accepts two real numbers from a user and a select code. If the entered select code is 1, have the program add the two previously entered numbers and display the result; if the select code is 2, the numbers should be multiplied, and if the select code is 3, the first number should be divided by the second number.

b. Determine what the program written in Exercise 1a does when the entered numbers are 3 and 0, and the select code is 3.

c. Modify the program written in Exercise 1a so that division by 0 is not allowed and an appropriate message is displayed when such a division is attempted.

2. a. Write a program to display the following two prompts:

```
Enter a month (use a 1 for Jan, etc.):
Enter a day of the month:
```

Have your program accept and store a number in the variable `month` in response to the first prompt, and accept and store a number in the variable `day` in response to the second prompt. If the month entered is not between 1 and 12 inclusive, print a message informing the user that an invalid month has been entered. If the day entered is not between 1 and 31, print a message informing the user that an invalid day has been entered.

b. What will your program do if the user types a number with a decimal point for the month? How can you ensure that your `if` statements check for an integer number?

c. In a non-leap year, February has 28 days, the months January, March, May, July, August, October, and December have 31 days, and all other months have 30 days. Using this information, modify the program written in Exercise 2a to display a message when an invalid day is entered for a user-entered month. For this program ignore leap years.

3. a. The quadrant in which a line drawn from the origin resides is determined by the angle that the line makes with the positive x axis as follows:

Angle from the positive x axis	Quadrant
Between 0 and 90 degrees	I
Between 90 and 180 degrees	II
Between 180 and 270 degrees	III
Between 270 and 360 degrees	IV

Using this information, write a C++ program that accepts the angle of the line as user input and determines and displays the quadrant appropriate to the input data. (*Note:* If the angle is exactly 0, 90, 180, or 270 degrees, the corresponding line does not reside in any quadrant but lies on an axis.)

b. Modify the program written for Exercise 3a so that a message is displayed that identifies an angle of zero degrees as the positive x axis, an angle of 90 degrees as the positive y axis, an angle of 180 degrees as the negative x axis, and an angle of 270 degrees as the negative y axis.

4. All years that are evenly divisible by 400 or are evenly divisible by four and not evenly divisible by 100 are leap years. For example, since 1600 is evenly divisible by 400, the year 1600 was a leap year. Similarly, since 1988 is evenly divisible by four but not by 100, the year 1988 was also a leap year. Using this information, write a C++ program that accepts the year as user input, determines if the year is a leap year, and displays an appropriate message that tells the user if the entered year is or is not a leap year.

5. Based on an automobile's model year and weight the state of New Jersey determines the car's weight class and registration fee using the following schedule:

Model Year	Weight	Weight Class	Registration Fee
1970 or earlier	Less than 2700 lbs	1	$16.50
	2700 to 3800 lbs	2	25.50
	More than 3800 lbs	3	46.50
1971 to 1979	Less than 2700 lbs	4	27.00
	2700 to 3800 lbs	5	30.50
	More than 3800 lbs	6	52.50
1980 or later	Less than 3500 lbs	7	19.50
	3500 or more lbs	8	52.50

Using this information, write a C++ program that accepts the year and weight of an automobile and determines and displays the weight class and registration fee for the car.

6. Modify Program 4.9 so that the imaginary roots are calculated and displayed when the discriminant is negative. For this case the two roots of the equation are:

$$x_1 = \frac{-b}{2a} + \frac{\text{sqrt}[-(b^2 - 4ac)]}{2a}i$$

and

$$x_2 = \frac{-b}{2a} - \frac{\text{sqrt}[-(b^2 - 4ac)]}{2a}i$$

where *i* is the imaginary number symbol for the square root of –1. (*Hint:* Calculate the real and imaginary parts of each root separately.)

7. In the game of blackjack, the cards 2 through 10 are counted at their face values, regardless of suit, all face cards (jack, queen, and king) are counted as 10, and an ace is counted as either a 1 or an 11, depending on the total count of all the cards in a player's hand. The ace is counted as 11 only if the resulting total value of all cards in a player's hand does not exceed 21, else it is counted as a 1. Using this information, write a C++ program that accepts three card values as inputs (a 1 corresponding to an ace, a 2 corresponding to a two, and so on), calculates the total value of the hand appropriately, and displays the value of the three cards with a printed message.

4.6 COMMON PROGRAMMING ERRORS

Three programming errors are common to C++'s selection statements.

1. Using the assignment operator, =, in place of the relational operator, ==. This can cause an enormous amount of frustration because any expression can be tested by an `if-else` statement. For example, the statement

```
if (opselect = 2)
   cout << "Happy Birthday";
else
   cout << "Good Day";
```

   always results in the message `Happy Birthday` being printed, regardless of the initial value in the variable `opselect`. The reason for this is that the assignment expression `opselect = 2` has a value of 2, which is considered a true value in C++. The correct expression to determine the value in `opselect` is `opselect == 2`.

2. Letting the `if-else` statement appear to select an incorrect choice. In this typical debugging problem, the programmer mistakenly concentrates on the tested condition as the source of the problem. For example, assume that the following `if-else` statement is part of your program:

```
if (key == 'F')
{
  contemp = (5.0/9.0) * (intemp - 32.0);
  cout << "Conversion to Celsius was done";
}
else
{
  contemp = (9.0/5.0) * intemp + 32.0;
  cout << "Conversion to Fahrenheit was done";
}
```

This statement will always display `Conversion to Celsius` was done when the variable `key` contains an `F`. Therefore, if this message is displayed when you believe `key` does not contain `F`, investigation of `key`'s value is called for. As a general rule, whenever a selection statement does not act as you think it should, test your assumptions about the values assigned to the tested variables by displaying their values. If an unanticipated value is displayed, you have at least isolated the source of the problem to the variables themselves, rather than the structure of the `if-else` statement. From there you will have to determine where and how the incorrect value was obtained.

3. Using nested `if` statements without including braces to indicate the desired structure. Without braces the compiler defaults to pairing `else`s with the closest unpaired `if`s, which sometimes destroys the original intent of the selection statement. To avoid this problem and to create code that is readily adaptable to change, it is useful to write all `if-else` statements as compound statements in the form

```
if (expression)
{
  one or more statements in here
}
else
{
  one or more statements in here
}
```

By using this form, no matter how many statements are added later, the original integrity and intent of the `if` statement is maintained.

4.7 Chapter Summary

1. Relational expressions, which are also called **conditions**, are used to compare operands. If a relational expression is true, the value of the expression is the integer 1. If the relational expression is false, it has an integer value of 0. Relational expressions are created using the following relational operators.

Relational Operator	Meaning	Example
<	Less than	`age < 30`
>	Greater than	`height > 6.2`
<=	Less than or equal to	`taxable <= 20000`
>=	Greater than or equal to	`temp >= 98.6`
==	Equal to	`grade == 100`
!=	Not equal to	`number != 250`

2. More complex conditions can be constructed from relational expressions using C++'s logical operators, `&&` (AND), `||` (OR), and `!` (NOT).

3. An `if-else` statement is used to select between two alternative statements based on the value of an expression. Although relational expressions are usually used for the tested expression, any valid expression can be used. In testing an expression, `if-else` statements interpret a non-zero value as true and a zero value as false. The general form of an `if-else` statement is:

```
if (expression)
  statement1;
else
  statement2;
```

   This is a two-way selection statement. If the expression has a non-zero value it is considered as true and `statement1` is executed; otherwise `statement2` is executed.

4. An `if-else` statement can contain other `if-else` statements. In the absence of braces, each `else` is associated with the closest preceding unpaired `if`.

5. The `if-else` chain is a multiway selection statement having the general form

```
if (expression_1)
  statement_1;
else if (expression_2)
  statement_2;
else if (expression_3)
  statement_3;
       .
       .
       .
else if (expression_m)
  statement_m;
else
  statement_n;
```

   Each expression is evaluated in the order in which it appears in the chain. Once an expression is true (has a non-zero value), only the statement between that expression and the next `else if` or `else` is executed, and no further expressions are tested. The final `else` is optional, and the statement corresponding to the final `else` is only executed if none of the previous expressions is true.

6. A compound statement consists of any number of individual statements enclosed within the brace pair, `{` and `}`. Compound statements are treated as a single unit and can be used anywhere a single statement is used.

7. The switch statement is a multiway selection statement. The general form of a switch statement is

```
switch (expression)
{     // start of compound statement
  case value_1:  <-------------- terminated with a colon
    statement1;
    statement2;
       .
       .
    break;
  case value_2:  <-------------- terminated with a colon
    statementm;
    statementn;
       .
       .
    break;
  .
  .
  case value_n:  <-------------- terminated with a colon
    statementw;
    statementx;
       .
       .
    break;
  default:       <-------------- terminated with a colon
    statementaa;
    statementbb;
       .
       .
}     // end of switch and compound statement
```

For this statement the value of an integer expression is compared to a number of integer or character constants or constant expressions. Program execution is transferred to the first matching case and continues through the end of the `switch` statement unless an optional `break` statement is encountered. The cases in a `switch` statement can appear in any order and an optional `default` case can be included. The `default` case is executed if none of the other cases is matched.

4.8 CHAPTER APPENDIX: A CLOSER LOOK AT PROGRAM TESTING

In theory, a comprehensive set of test runs would reveal all possible program errors and ensure that a program will work correctly for any and all combinations of input and computed data. In practice this requires checking all possible combinations of statement execution. Due to the time and effort required, this is an impossible goal except for extremely simple programs. Let us see why this is so. Consider Program 4.10.

Program 4.10

```
#include <iostream>
using namespace std;

int main()
{
  int num;

  cout << "Enter a number: ";
  cin  >> num;
  if (num == 5)
    cout << "Bingo!\n";
  else
    cout << "Bongo!\n";

  return 0;
}
```

Program 4.10 has two paths that can be traversed as the program progresses from its opening brace to its closing brace. The first path, which is executed when the input number is 5, is in the sequence

```
cout << "Enter a number";
cin  >> num;
cout << "Bingo!\n";
```

The second path, which is executed whenever any number except 5 is input, includes the sequence of instructions

```
cout << "Enter a number";
cin  >> num;
cout << "Bongo!\n";
```

To test each possible path through Program 4.10 requires two runs of the program, with a judicious selection of test input data to ensure that both paths of the `if` statement are exercised. The addition of one more `if` statement in the program increases the number of possible execution paths by a factor of two and requires four (2^2) runs of the program for complete testing. Similarly, two additional `if` statements increase the number of paths by a factor of four and requires eight (2^3) runs for complete testing and three additional `if` statements would produce a program that required sixteen (2^4) test runs.

Now consider a modestly sized application program consisting of only ten modules, each module containing five `if` statements. Assuming the modules are always called in the same sequence, there are 32 possible paths through each module (2 raised to the fifth power) and more than 1,000,000,000,000,000 (2 raised to the fiftieth power) possible paths through the complete program (all modules executed in sequence). The time needed to create individual test data to exercise each path and the actual computer run time required to check each path make the complete testing of such a program impossible to achieve.

The inability to fully test all combinations of statement execution sequences has led to the programming saying that "there is no error-free program." It has also led to the realization that any testing that is done should be well thought out to maximize the possibility of locating errors. At a minimum, test data should include appropriate values for input values, illegal input values that the program should reject, and limiting values that are checked by selection statements within the program.

Looking at Career Choices

Civil Engineering

The field of civil engineering is concerned primarily with large-scale structures and systems used by a community. A civil engineer designs, constructs, and operates bridges, dams, tunnels, buildings, airports, roads and other large-scale public works. Civil engineers are also responsible for the effects these large-scale systems have on society and the environment. Thus, civil engineers are involved in water resources, flood control, waste disposal, and overall urban planning. The field can be subdivided into three categories.

1. Structures. Design, construction, and operation of large-scale edifices such as dams, buildings, and roads. The properties of materials, geology, soil mechanics, and statics and dynamics are important elements of the background training. For example, how tall a building can be constructed before it will buckle under its own weight is a question involving all of these subjects.
2. Urban planning. Planning, design, and construction of transportation systems (road, railroads, river development, airports) and general land use. Surveying and mapmaking are necessary skills.
3. Sanitation. Waste treatment, water supply, and sewage systems. Fluid mechanics, hydrology, pollution control, irrigation, and economics are important considerations.

CHAPTER 5

Repetition Statements

TOPICS

The programs examined so far have illustrated the programming concepts involved in input, output, assignment, and selection capabilities. By this time you should have gained enough experience to be comfortable with these concepts and the mechanics of implementing them using C++. Many problems, however, require a repetition capability in which the same calculation or sequence of instructions is repeated, over and over, using different sets of data. Examples of such repetition include continual checking of user data entries until an acceptable entry, such as a valid password, is entered;

counting and accumulating running totals; and constant acceptance of input data and recalculation of output values that only stops upon entry of a sentinel value.

This chapter explores the different methods that programmers use in constructing repeating sections of code and how they can be implemented in C++. More commonly, a section of code that is repeated is referred to as a ***loop****, because after the last statement in the code is executed the program branches, or loops, back to the first statement and starts another repetition through the code. Each repetition is also referred to as an* ***iteration*** *or* ***pass through the loop****.*

5.1 BASIC LOOP STRUCTURES

The real power of a program is realized when the same type of operation must be made over and over. For example, consider Program 3.17 in Section 3.6, where the same set of instructions is repeated three times. Retyping this same set of instructions is tedious, time consuming, and subject to error. It certainly would be convenient if we could type such repeating instructions only once and then have a method of informing the program to repeat execution of the instructions three times. Such a method is available using repetitive sections of code.

Constructing a repetitive section of code requires that four elements be present. The first necessary element is a repetition statement. This **repetition statement** both defines the boundaries containing the repeating section of code and controls whether the code will be executed or not. In general, there are three different forms of repetition statments, all of which are provided in C++:

1. `while`
2. `for`
3. `do while`

Each of these statements requires a condition that must be evaluated, which is the second required element for constructing repeating sections of code. Valid conditions are identical to those used in selection statements. If the condition is true, the code is executed; otherwise, it is not.

The third required element is a statement that initially sets the condition. This statement must always be placed before the condition is first evaluated to ensure correct loop execution the first time the condition is evaluated.

Finally, there must be a statement within the repeating section of code that allows the condition to become false. This is necessary to ensure that, at some point, the repetitions stop.

Pretest and Posttest Loops

The condition being tested can be evaluated at either the beginning or the end of the repeating section of code. Figure 5.1 illustrates the case where the test occurs at the beginning of the loop. This type of loop is referred to as a **pretest loop** because the condition is tested before any statements within the loop are executed. If the condition is true, the executable statements within the loop are executed. If the initial value of the condition is false, the executable statements within the loop are never executed at all and control transfers to the first statement after the loop. To avoid infinite repetitions, the condition must be updated within the loop. Pretest loops are also referred to as **entrance-controlled loops**. Both the `while` and `for` loop structures are examples of such loops.

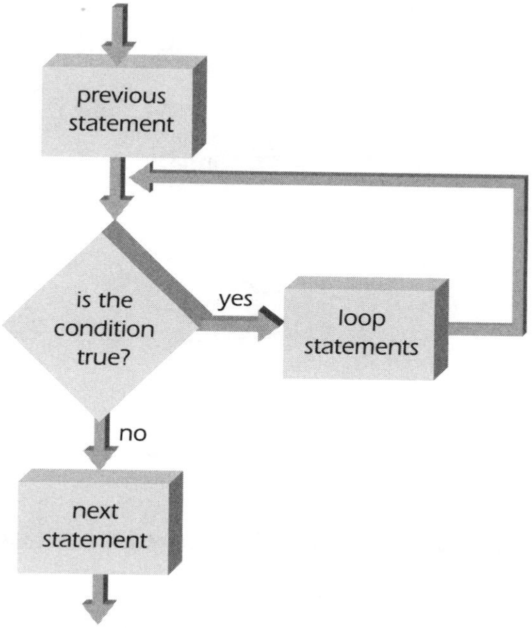

Figure 5.1 A pretest loop.

A loop that evaluates a condition at end of the repeating section of code, as illustrated in Figure 5.2, is referred to as **posttest** or **exit-controlled loop**. Such loops always execute the loop statements at least once before the condition is tested. Since the executable statements within the loop are continually executed until the condition becomes false, there always must be a statement within the loop that updates the condition and permits it to become false. The `do while` construct is an example of a posttest loop.

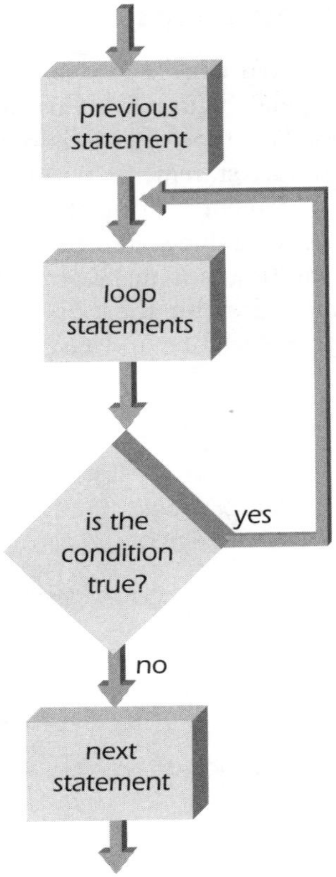

Figure 5.2 *A posttest loop.*

Fixed-Count versus Variable-Condition Loops

In addition to where the condition is tested (pretest or posttest), repeating sections of code are also classified as to the type of condition being tested. In a **fixed-count loop**, the condition is used to keep track of how many repetitions have occurred. For example, we might want to produce a table of 10 numbers, including their squares and cubes, or a fixed design such as

```
*************************
*************************
*************************
*************************
```

In each of these cases, a fixed number of calculations is performed or a fixed number of lines are printed, at which point the repeating section of code is exited. All of C++'s repetition statements can be used to produce fixed count loops.

In many situations the exact number of repetitions is not known in advance or the items are too numerous to count beforehand. For example, when entering a large amount of experimental data we might not want to take the time to count the number of actual data items that are to be entered. In cases like this a variable-condition loop is used. In a **variable-condition loop** the tested condition does not depend on a count being reached, but rather on a variable that can change interactively with each pass through the loop. When a specified value is encountered, regardless of how many iterations have occurred, repetitions stop. All of C++'s repetition statements can be used to create variable-condition loops.[1] In this chapter we will encounter examples of both fixed-count and variable-condition loops.

Exercises 5.1

1. List the three repetition statements that are provided in C++.
2. List the four elements that must be present in a repetition statement.
3. a. What is an entrance-controlled loop?
   b. Which of C++'s repetition statements produce entrance-controlled loops?
4. a. What is an exit-controlled loop?
   b. Which of C++'s repetition statements produce exit-controlled loops?
5. a. What is the difference between a pretest and posttest loop?
   b. If the condition being tested in a pretest loop is false to begin with, how many times will statements internal to the loop be executed?
   c. If the condition being tested in a posttest loop is false to begin with, how many times will statements internal to the loop be executed?
6. What is the difference between a fixed-count and variable-condition loop?

5.2 `while` LOOPS

In C++, a **`while` loop** is constructed using a `while` statement. The syntax of this statement is

while (expression)
  statement;

The ***`expression`*** contained within parentheses is the condition tested to determine if the ***`statement`*** following the parentheses is executed. The expression is evaluated in exactly the same manner as that contained in an `if-else` statement; the difference is in how the expression is used. As we have seen, when the expression is true (has a non-zero value) in an `if-else` statement, the statement following the expression is executed once. In a `while` statement, the statement following the expression is executed repeatedly as long as the expression evaluates to a non-zero value. Considering just the expression and the

[1] In this, both C and C++ differ from earlier high-level languages, in which the `for` statement (which was implemented using a `DO` statement in FORTRAN) could only be used to produce fixed-count loops. C++'s `for` statement, as we will see shortly, is virtually interchangeable with its `while` statement.

statement following the parentheses, the process used by the computer in evaluating a `while` statement is

1. *Test the expression*
2. *If the expression has a non-zero (true) value*
   a. *execute the statement following the parentheses*
   b. *go back to step 1*

   else

   exit the `while` *statement and execute the next executable statement following the* `while` *statement*

Notice that step 2b forces program control to be transferred back to step 1. This transfer of control back to the start of a `while` statement in order to re-evaluate the expression is what forms the program loop. The `while` statement literally loops back on itself to recheck the expression until it evaluates to zero (becomes false). This naturally means that somewhere in the loop provision must be made that permits the value of the tested expression to be altered. As we will see, this is indeed the case.

This looping process produced by a `while` statement is illustrated in Figure 5.3. A diamond shape is used to show the two entry and two exit points required in the decision part of the `while` statement.

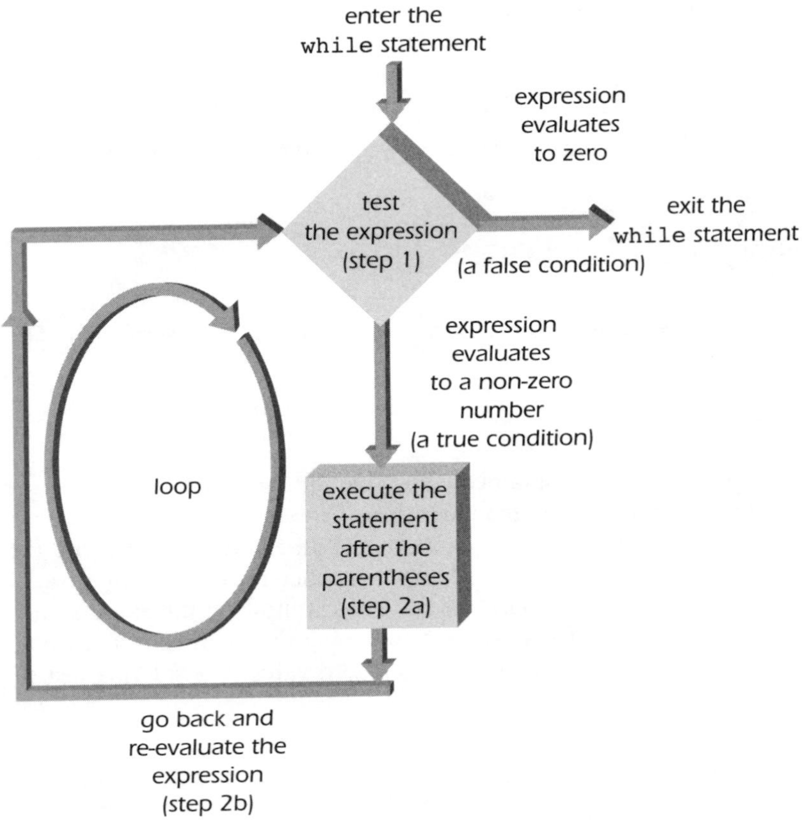

Figure 5.3 Anatomy of a `while` loop.

To make this a little more tangible, consider the relational expression `count <= 10` and the statement `cout << count;`. Using these, we can write the following valid `while` statement:

```
while (count <= 10)
  cout << count;
```

Although the above statement is valid, the alert reader will realize that we have created a situation in which the `cout` object either is called forever (or until we stop the program) or is not called at all. Let us see why this happens.

If `count` has a value less than or equal to 10 when the expression is first evaluated, the `cout` statement is executed. The `while` statement then automatically loops back on itself and retests the expression. Since we have not changed the value stored in `count`, the expression is still true and another call to `cout` is made. This process continues forever, or until the program containing this statement is prematurely stopped by the user. However, if `count` starts with a value greater than 10, the expression is false to begin with and the `cout` object is never used.

How do we set an initial value in `count` to control what the `while` statement does the first time the expression is evaluated? The answer, of course, is to assign values to each variable in the tested expression before the `while` statement is encountered. For example, the following sequence of instructions is valid:

```
count = 1;
while (count <= 10)
  cout << count;
```

Using this sequence of instructions, we have ensured that `count` starts with a value of 1. We could assign any value to `count` in the assignment statement—the important thing is to assign some value. In practice, the assigned value depends on the application.

We must still change the value of `count` so that we can finally exit the `while` statement. To do this requires an expression such as `count = count + 1` to increment the value of `count` each time the `while` statement is executed. The fact that a `while` statement provides for the repetition of a single statement does not prevent us from including an additional statement to change the value of `count`. All we have to do is replace the single statement with a compound statement. For example,

```
count = 1;          // initialize count
while (count <= 10)
{
  cout << count;
  count++;          // increment count
}
```

Note that, for clarity, we have placed each statement in the compound statement on a different line. This is consistent with the convention adopted for compound statements in the last chapter. Let us now analyze the above sequence of instructions.

The first assignment statement sets `count` equal to 1. The `while` statement is then entered and the expression is evaluated for the first time. Since the value of `count` is less than or equal to 10, the expression is true and the compound statement is executed. The first statement in the compound statement uses the `cout` object to display the value of count. The next statement adds 1 to the value currently stored in count, making this value equal to 2. The while statement now loops back to retest the expression. Since count is still less than or equal to 10, the compound statement is again executed. This process continues until the value of count reaches 11. Program 5.1 illustrates these statements in an actual program.

Program 5.1

```
#include <iostream>
using namespace std;

int main()
{
  int count;

  count = 1;                 // initialize count
  while (count <= 10)
  {
    cout << count << "   ";
    count++;                 // increment count
  }

  return 0;
}
```

The output for Program 5.1 is:

```
1  2  3  4  5  6  7  8  9  10
```

There is nothing special about the name count used in Program 5.1. Any valid integer variable could have been used.

Before we consider other examples of the while statement, two comments concerning Program 5.1 are in order. First, the statement count++ can be replaced with any statement that changes the value of count. A statement such as count = count + 2, for example, would cause every second integer to be displayed. Second, it is the programmer's responsibility to ensure that count is changed in a way that ultimately leads to a normal exit from the while. For example, if we replace the expression count++ with the expression count--, the value of count will never exceed 10 and an infinite loop will be created. An **infinite loop** is a loop that never ends; the program just keeps displaying numbers until you realize that the program is not working as you expected.

Now that you have some familiarity with the while statement, see if you can read and determine the output of Program 5.2.

Program 5.2

```
#include <iostream>
using namespace std;

int main()
{
  int i;

  i = 10;
  while (i >= 1)
  {
    cout << i << "  ";
    i--;              // subtract 1 from i
  }

  return 0;
}
```

The assignment statement in Program 5.2 initially sets the `int` variable `i` to 10. The `while` statement then checks to see if the value of `i` is greater than or equal to 1. While the expression is true, the value of `i` is displayed by the `cout` object and the value of `i` is decremented by 1. When `i` finally reaches zero, the expression is false and the program exits the `while` statement. Thus, the following display is obtained when Program 5.2 is run:

```
10  9  8  7  6  5  4  3  2  1
```

To illustrate the power of the `while` statement, consider the task of printing a table of numbers from 1 to 10 with their squares and cubes. This can be done with a simple `while` statement as illustrated by Program 5.3.

When Program 5.3 is run, the following display is produced:

```
NUMBER    SQUARE    CUBE
------    ------    ----
   1          1        1
   2          4        8
   3          9       27
   4         16       64
   5         25      125
   6         36      216
   7         49      343
   8         64      512
   9         81      729
  10        100     1000
```

Program 5.3

```
#include <iostream>
#include <iomanip>
using namespace std;

int main()
{
  int num;

  cout << "NUMBER    SQUARE    CUBE\n"
       << "------    ------    ----\n";

  num = 1;
  while (num < 11)
  {
    cout << setw(3) << num << "        "
         << setw(3) << num * num << "      "
         << setw(4) << num * num * num << endl;
    num++;          // increment num
  }
  return 0;
}
```

Note that the expression used in Program 5.3 is `num < 11`. For the integer variable `num`, this expression is exactly equivalent to the expression `num <= 10`. The choice of which to use is entirely up to you.

If we want to use Program 5.3 to produce a table of 1000 numbers, all we do is change the expression in the `while` statement from `num < 11` to `num < 1001`. Changing the 11 to 1001 produces a table of 1000 lines—not bad for a simple five-line `while` statement.

All the program examples illustrating the `while` statement are examples of fixed-count loops because the tested condition is a counter that checks for a fixed number of repetitions. A variation on the fixed-count loop can be made where the counter is not incremented by one each time through the loop, but by some other value. For example, consider the task of producing a Celsius to Fahrenheit temperature conversion table. Assume that Fahrenheit temperatures corresponding to Celsius temperatures ranging from 5 to 50 degrees are to be displayed in increments of five degrees. The desired display can be obtained with the series of statements

```
celsius = 5;     // starting Celsius value
while (celsius <= 50)
{
  fahren = (9.0/5.0) * celsius + 32.0;
  cout << celsius << "      "
       << fahren;
  celsius = celsius + 5;
}
```

As before, the `while` statement consists of everything from the word `while` through the closing brace of the compound statement. Prior to entering the `while` loop we have made sure to assign a value to the counter being evaluated, and there is a statement to alter the value of the counter within the loop (in increments of 5 Celsius) to ensure an exit from the `while` loop. Program 5.4 illustrates the use of similar code in a complete program.

Program 5.4

```
#include <iostream>
#include <iomanip>
using namespace std;

// a program to convert Celsius to Fahrenheit
int main()
{
  const int MAX_CELSIUS = 50;
  const int START_VAL = 5;
  const int STEP_SIZE = 5;
  int celsius;
  double fahren;

  cout << "DEGREES   DEGREES\n"
       << "CELSIUS  FAHRENHEIT\n"
       << "-------  ----------\n";

  celsius = START_VAL;

    // set output formats for floating point numbers only
  cout << setiosflags(ios::showpoint)
       << setprecision(2);
```

(Continued)

(Continued)

```
    while (celsius <= MAX_CELSIUS)
    {
      fahren = (9.0/5.0) * celsius + 32.0;
      cout << setw(4)  << celsius << fixed
           << setw(13) << fahren << endl;
      celsius = celsius + STEP_SIZE;
    }

    return 0;
  }
```

The display obtained when Program 5.4 is executed is

```
DEGREES    DEGREES
CELSIUS   FAHRENHEIT
-------   ----------
   5         41.00
  10         50.00
  15         59.00
  20         68.00
  25         77.00
  30         86.00
  35         95.00
  40        104.00
  45        113.00
  50        122.00
```

Exercises 5.2

1. Rewrite Program 5.1 to print the numbers 2 to 10 in increments of two. The output of your program should be

   ```
   2  4  6  8  10
   ```

2. Rewrite Program 5.4 to produce a table that starts at a Celsius value of –10 and ends with a Celsius value of 60, in increments of ten degrees.

3. **a.** For the following program determine the total number of items displayed. Also determine the first and last numbers printed.

```
#include <iostream>
using namespace std;

int main()
{
  int num = 0;
  while (num <= 20)
  {
    num++;
    cout << num << "  ";
  }

  return 0;
}
```

b. Enter and run the program from Exercise 3a on a computer to verify your answers to the exercise.

c. How would the output be affected if the two statements within the compound statement were reversed (that is, if the `cout` call were made before the `++n` statement)?

4. Write a C++ program that converts gallons to liters. The program should display gallons from 10 to 20 in one-gallon increments and the corresponding liter equivalents. Use the relationship that 1 gallon contains 3.785 liters.

5. Write a C++ program that converts feet to meters. The program should display feet from 3 to 30 in three-foot increments and the corresponding meter equivalents. Use the relationship that there are 3.28 feet to a meter.

6. A machine purchased for $28,000 is depreciated at a rate of $4000 a year for seven years. Write and run a C++ program that computes and displays a depreciation table for seven years. The table should have the form

Year	Depreciation	End-of-Year Value	Accumulated Depreciation
1	4000	24000	4000
2	4000	20000	8000
3	4000	16000	12000
4	4000	12000	16000
5	4000	8000	20000
6	4000	4000	24000
7	4000	0	28000

7. An automobile travels at an average speed of 55 miles per hour for four hours. Write a C++ program that displays the distance driven, in miles, that the car has traveled after, 1, 2, etc., hours until the end of the trip.

8. a. An approximate conversion formula for converting Fahrenheit to Celsius temperatures is

Celsius = (Fahrenheit – 30) / 2

Using this formula, and starting with a Fahrenheit temperature of zero degrees, write a C++ program that determines when the approximate equivalent Celsius temperature differs from the exact equivalent value by more than four degrees. (*Hint:* Use a `while` loop that terminates when the difference between approximate and exact Celsius equivalents exceeds four degrees.)

b. Using the approximate Celsius conversion formula given in Exercise 8a, write a C++ program that produces a table of Fahrenheit temperatures, exact Celsius equivalent temperatures, approximate Celsius equivalent temperatures, and the difference between the correct and approximate equivalent Celsius values. The table should begin at zero degrees Fahrenheit, use two-degree Fahrenheit increments, and terminate when the difference between exact and approximate values differs by more than four degrees.

9. The value of Euler's number, *e*, can be approximated using the formula

$$e = 1 + 1/1! + 1/2! + 1/3! + 1/4! + 1/5! + \cdots$$

Using this formula, write a C++ program that approximates the value of *e* using a `while` loop that terminates when the difference between two successive approximations differs by less than 10 e–9.

10. The value of sin *x* can be approximated using the formula

$$\sin x = x - \frac{x^3}{3!} + \frac{x^5}{5!} - \frac{x^7}{7!} + \frac{x^9}{9!} \cdots$$

Using this formula, determine how many terms are needed to approximate the value returned by the intrinsic `sin()` function with an error less than 1 e–6, when $x = 30$ degrees. (*Hints:* Use a `while` loop that terminates when the difference between the value returned by the intrinsic `sin()` function and the approximation is less than 1 e–6. Also note that *x* must first be converted to radian measure and that the alternating sign in the approximating series can be determined as $(-1)^*(n + 1)$ where *n* is the number of terms used in the approximation.)

5.3 INTERACTIVE `while` LOOPS

Combining interactive data entry with the repetition capabilities of the `while` statement produces very adaptable and powerful programs. To understand the concept involved, consider Program 5.5, where a `while` statement is used to accept and then display four user-entered numbers, one at a time. Although it uses a very simple idea, the program highlights the flow of control concepts needed to produce more useful programs.

Program 5.5

```
#include <iostream>
#include <iomanip>
using namespace std;

int main()
{
  const int MAXNUMS = 4;
  int count;
  double num;

  cout << "\nThis program will ask you to enter "
       << MAXNUMS << " numbers.\n";
  count = 1;
  while (count <= MAXNUMS)
  {
    cout << "\nEnter a number: ";
    cin  >> num;
    cout << "The number entered is " << num;
    count++;
  }
  cout << endl;

  return 0;
}
```

The following is a sample run of Program 5.5.

```
This program will ask you to enter 4 numbers.

Enter a number: 26.2
The number entered is 26.2
Enter a number: 5
The number entered is 5
Enter a number: 103.456
The number entered is 103.456
Enter a number: 1267.89
The number entered is 1267.89
```

Let us review the program so we clearly understand how the output was produced. The first message displayed is caused by execution of the first `cout` object call. This call is outside and before the `while` statement, so it is executed once before any statement in the `while` loop.

Once the `while` loop is entered, the statements within the compound statement are executed while the tested condition is true. The first time through the compound statement, the message `Enter a number:` is displayed. The program then calls `cin`, which forces the computer to wait for a number to be entered at the keyboard. Once a number is typed and the Return or Enter key is pressed, the `cout` object displays the number. The variable `count` is then incremented by one. This process continues until four passes through the loop have been made and the value of `count` is 5. Each pass causes the message `Enter a number:` to be displayed, causes one call to `cin` to be made, and causes the message `The number entered is` to be displayed. Figure 5.4 illustrates this flow of control.

Rather than simply displaying the entered numbers, Program 5.5 can be modified to use the entered data. For example, let us add the numbers entered and display the total. To do this, we must be very careful about how we add the numbers, since the same variable, `num`, is used for each number entered. Because of this the entry of a new number in Program 5.5 automatically causes the previous number stored in `num` to be lost. Thus, each number entered must be added to the total before another number is entered. The required sequence is

Enter a number
Add the number to the total

How do we add a single number to a total? A statement such as `total = total + num` does the job perfectly. This is the accumulating statement introduced in Section 3.1. After each number is entered, the accumulating statement adds the number into the total, as illustrated in Figure 5.5. The complete flow of control required for adding the numbers is illustrated in Figure 5.6.

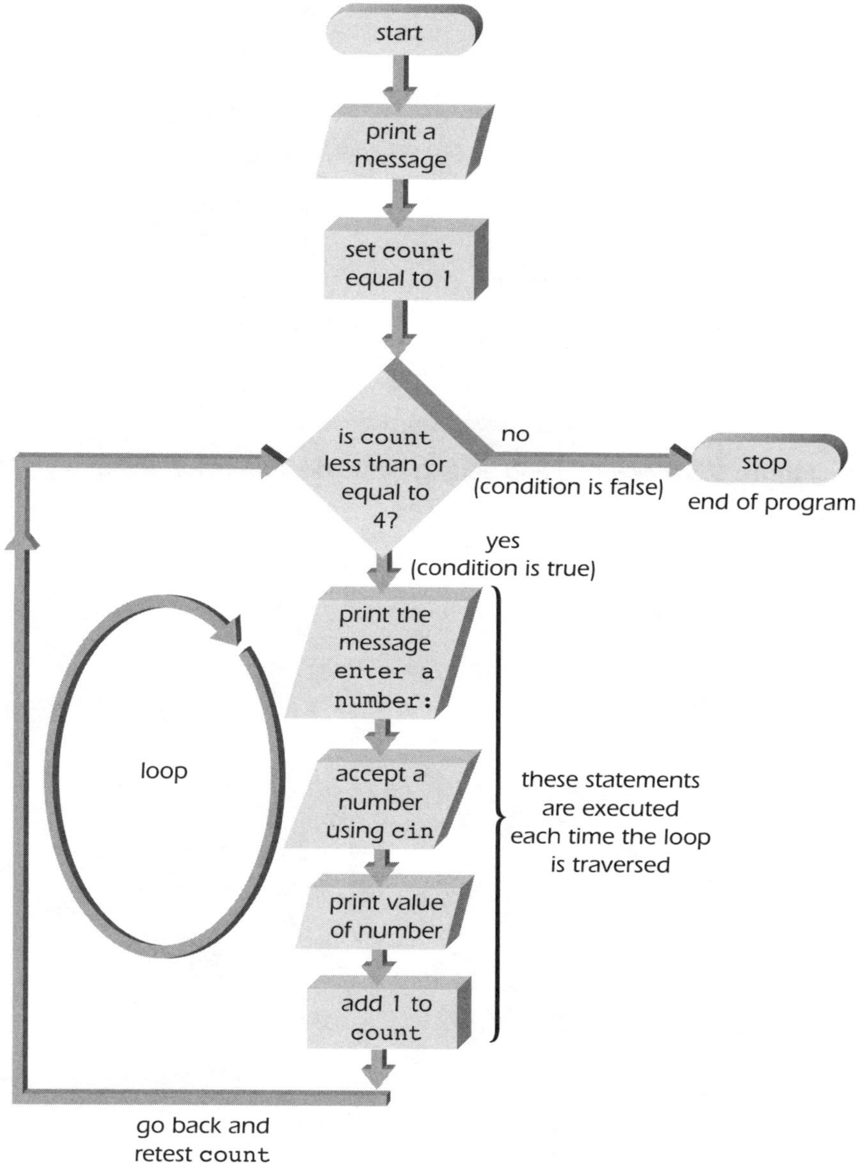

Figure 5.4 Flow of control diagram for Program 5.5.

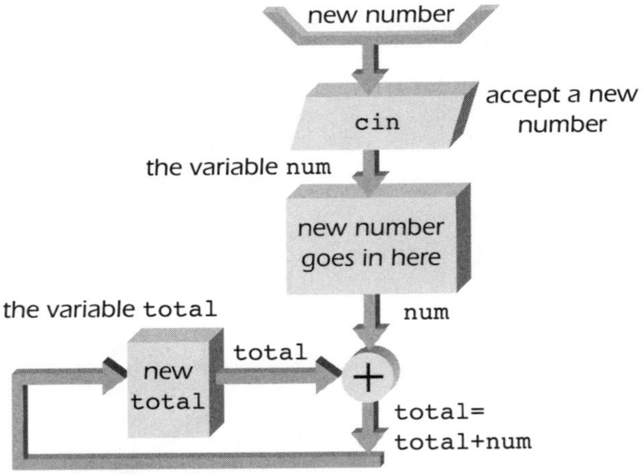

Figure 5.5 *Accepting and adding a number to a total.*

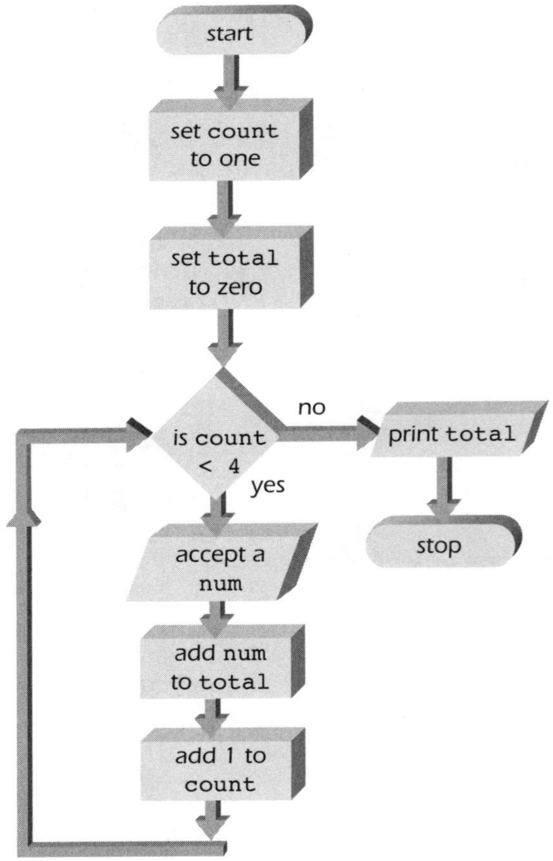

Figure 5.6 *Accumulation flow of control.*

In reviewing Figure 5.6, observe that we have made a provision for initially setting the total to zero before the `while` loop is entered. If we were to clear the total inside the `while` loop, it would be set to zero each time the loop was executed and any value previously stored would be erased.

Program 5.6 incorporates the necessary modifications to Program 5.5 to total the numbers entered. As indicated in the flow diagram shown in Figure 5.6, the statement `total = total + num;` is placed immediately after the `cin` statement. Putting the accumulating statement at this point in the program ensures that the entered number is immediately "captured" into the total.

Program 5.6

```
#include <iostream>
#include <iomanip>
using namespace std;

int main()
{
  const int MAXNUMS = 4;
  int count;
  double num, total;

  cout << "\nThis program will ask you to enter "
       << MAXNUMS << " numbers.\n";
  count = 1;
  total = 0;

  while (count <= MAXNUMS)
  {
    cout << "\nEnter a number: ";
    cin  >> num;
    total = total + num;
    cout << "The total is now " << setprecision(7) << total;
    count++;
  }

  cout << "\nThe final total is " << setprecision(7) << total << endl;

  return 0;
}
```

Let us review Program 5.6. The variable `total` was created to store the total of the numbers entered. Prior to entering the `while` statement the value of `total` is set to zero. This ensures that any previous value present in the storage location(s) assigned to the variable `total` is erased. Within the `while` loop the statement `total = total + num;` is used to add the value of the entered number into `total`. As each value is entered, it is added into the existing total to create a new total. Thus, `total` becomes a running subtotal of all the values entered. Only when all numbers are entered does `total` contain the final sum of all the numbers. After the `while` loop is finished, a `cout` statement is used to display this sum.

Using the same data we entered in the sample run for Program 5.5, the following sample run of Program 5.6 was made:

```
This program will ask you to enter 4 numbers.

Enter a number: 26.2
The total is now 26.2
Enter a number: 5
The total is now 31.2
Enter a number: 103.456
The total is now 134.656
Enter a number: 1267.89
The total is now 1402.546

The final total is 1402.546
```

Having used an accumulating assignment statement to add the numbers entered, we can now go further and calculate the average of the numbers. Where do we calculate the average—within the `while` loop or outside of it?

In the case at hand, calculating an average requires that both a final sum and the number of items in that sum be available. The average is then computed by dividing the final sum by the number of items. At this point, we must ask, "At what point in the program is the correct sum available, and at what point is the number of items available?" In reviewing Program 5.6 we see that the correct sum needed for calculating the average is available after the `while` loop is finished. In fact, the whole purpose of the `while` loop is to ensure that the numbers are entered and added correctly to produce a correct sum. After the loop is finished, we also have a count of the number of items used in the sum. However, due to the way the `while` loop was constructed, the number in `count` (5) when the loop is finished is 1 more than the number of items (4) used to obtain the total. Knowing this, we simply subtract one from `count` before using it to determine the average. With this as background, see if you can read and understand Program 5.7.

Program 5.7

```
#include <iostream>
#include <iomanip>
using namespace std;

int main()
{
  const int MAXNUMS = 4;
  int count;
  double num, total, average;

  cout << "\nThis program will ask you to enter "
       << MAXNUMS << " numbers.\n";
  count = 1;
  total = 0;

  while (count <= MAXNUMS)
  {
    cout << "Enter a number: ";
    cin  >> num;
    total = total + num;
    count++;
  }

  count--;
  average = total / count;
  cout << "\nThe average of the numbers is " << average << endl;

  return 0;
}
```

Program 5.7 is almost identical to Program 5.6, except for the calculation of the average. We have also removed the constant display of the total within and after the `while` loop. The loop in Program 5.7 is used to enter and add four numbers. Immediately after the loop is exited, the average is computed and displayed.

A sample run of Program 5.7 follows:

```
This program will ask you to enter 4 numbers.
Enter a number: 26.2
Enter a number: 5
Enter a number: 103.456
Enter a number: 1267.89

The average of the numbers is 350.637
```

Sentinels

All of the loops we have created thus far have been examples of fixed count loops, where a counter has been used to control the number of loop iterations. By means of a `while` statement, variable-condition loops may also be constructed. For example, when entering grades we may not want to count the number of grades that will be entered, but would prefer to enter the grades continuously and, at the end, type in a special data value to signal the end of data input.

In computer programming, data values used to signal either the start or end of a data series are called **sentinels**. The sentinel values must, of course, be selected so as not to conflict with legitimate data values. For example, if we were constructing a program to process a student's grades, and assuming that no extra credit is given that could produce a grade higher than 100, we could use any grade higher than 100 as a sentinel value. Program 5.8 illustrates this concept. In Program 5.8 data is continuously requested and accepted until a number larger than 100 is entered. Entry of a number higher than 100 alerts the program to exit the `while` loop and display the sum of the numbers entered.

We show a sample run using Program 5.8 below. As long as grades less than or equal to 100 are entered, the program continues to request and accept additional data. When a number less than or equal to 100 is entered, the program adds this number to the total. When a number greater than 100 is entered, the loop is exited and the sum of the grades that were entered is displayed.

```
To stop entering grades, type in any number
 greater than 100.

Enter a grade: 95
Enter a grade: 100
Enter a grade: 82
Enter a grade: 101

The total of the grades is 277
```

Program 5.8

```
#include <iostream>
using namespace std;

int main()
{
  const int HIGHGRADE = 100;
  double grade, total;

  grade = 0;
  total = 0;
  cout << "\nTo stop entering grades, type in any number";
  cout << "\n greater than 100.\n\n";

  while (grade <= HIGHGRADE)
  {
    total = total + grade;
    cout << "Enter a grade: ";
    cin  >> grade;
  }

  cout << "\nThe total of the grades is " << total << endl;
  return 0;
}
```

`break` and `continue` Statements

Two useful statements in connection with repetition statements are the **`break`** and **`continue`** statements. We have encountered the `break` statement in relation to the `switch` statement. The syntax of this statement is

break;

A `break` statement, as its name implies, forces an immediate break, or exit, from `switch`, `while`, and the `for` and `do-while` statements presented in the next sections.

For example, execution of the following `while` loop is immediately terminated if a number greater than 76 is entered.

```
while(count <= 10)
{
  cout << "Enter a number: ";
  cin  >> num;
  if (num > 76)
  {
    cout << "You lose!\n";
    break;        // break out of the loop
  }
  else
    cout << "Keep on trucking!\n";
  count++
}
// break jumps to here
```

The `break` statement violates pure structured programming principles because it provides a second, nonstandard exit from a loop. Nevertheless, the `break` statement is extremely useful and valuable for breaking out of loops when an unusual condition is detected. The `break` statement is also used to exit from a `switch` statement, but this is because the desired case has been detected and processed.

The `continue` statement is similar to the `break` statement but applies only to loops created with `while`, `do-while`, and `for` statements. The general format of a continue statement is

continue;

When `continue` is encountered in a loop, the next iteration of the loop is immediately begun. For `while` loops this means that execution is automatically transferred to the top of the loop and re-evaluation of the tested expression is initiated. Although the `continue` statement has no direct effect on a `switch` statement, it can be included within a `switch` statement that itself is contained in a loop. Here the effect of `continue` is the same: the next loop iteration is begun.

As a general rule, the `continue` statement is less useful than the `break` statement, but it is convenient for skipping over data that should not be processed while remaining in a loop. For example, invalid grades are simply ignored in the following section of code and only valid grades are added to the total:[2]

---

[2]The `continue` statement is not essential, however, and the selection could have been written as

```
if (grade >= 0 && grade <= 100)
{
  total = total + grade;
  count++;
}
```

```
while (count < 30)
{
  cout << "Enter a grade: ";
  cin  >> grade;
  if(grade < 0 || grade > 100)
    continue;
  total = total + grade;
  count++;
}
```

The Null Statement

All statements must be terminated by a semicolon. A semicolon with nothing preceding it is also a valid statement, called the null statement. Thus, the statement

```
;
```

is a null statement. This is a do-nothing statement that is used where a statement is syntactically required, but no action is called for. Null statements typically are used with either `while` or `for` statements. An example of a `for` statement using a null statement is found in Program 5.10c in the next section.

Exercises 5.3

1. Rewrite Program 5.6 to compute the total of eight numbers.

2. Rewrite Program 5.6 to display the prompt:

   `Please type in the total number of data values to be added:`

   In response to this prompt, the program should accept a user-entered number and then use this number to control the number of times the `while` loop is executed. Thus, if the user enters 5 in response to the prompt, the program should request the input of five numbers and display the total after five numbers have been entered.

3. a. Write a C++ program to convert Celsius degrees to Fahrenheit. The program should request the starting Celsius value, the number of conversions to be made, and the increment between Celsius values. The display should have appropriate headings and list the Celsius value and the corresponding Fahrenheit value. Use the relationship

   $$Fahrenheit = (9.0 / 5.0) * Celsius + 32.0$$

   b. Run the program written in Exercise 3a on a computer. Verify that your program starts at the correct starting Celsius value and contains the exact number of conversions specified in your input data.

4. a. Modify the program written in Exercise 3a to request the starting Celsius value, the ending Celsius value, and the increment. Thus, instead of the condition checking for a fixed count, the condition will check for the ending Celsius value.

b. Run the program written in Exercise 4a on a computer. Verify that your output starts at the correct beginning value and ends at the correct ending value.

5. Rewrite Program 5.7 to compute the average of ten numbers.

6. Rewrite Program 5.7 to display the following prompt:

```
Please type in the total number of data values to be averaged:
```

In response to this prompt, the program should accept a user-entered number and then use this number to control the number of times the `while` loop is executed. Thus, if the user enters 6 in response to the prompt, the program should request the input of six numbers and display the average of the next six numbers entered.

7. By mistake, a programmer put the statement `average = total / count;` within the `while` loop immediately after the statement `total = total + num;` in Program 5.7. Thus, the while loop becomes

```
while (count <= MAXNUMS)
{
  cout << "Enter a number: ";
  cin  >> num;
  total = total + num;
  average = total / count;
  count++;
}
```

Will the program yield the correct result with this `while` loop?
From a programming perspective, which `while` loop is better to use and why?

8. An arithmetic series is defined by

$$a + (a + d) + (a + 2d) + (a + 3d) + \cdots + [(a + (n - 1)d)]$$

where a is the first term, d is the "common difference," and n is the number of terms to be added. Using this information, write a C++ program that uses a `while` loop to both display each term and determine the sum of the arithmetic series having $a = 1$, $d = 3$, and $n = 100$. Make sure that your program displays the value it has calculated.

9. A geometric series is defined by

$$a + ar + ar^2 + ar^3 + \cdots + ar^{n-1}$$

where a is the first term, r is the "common ratio," and n is the number of terms in the series. Using this information, write a C++ program that uses a `while` loop to both display each term and determine the sum of a geometric series having $a = 1$, $r = .5$, and $n = 10$. Make sure that your program displays the value it has calculated.

10. In addition to the arithmetic average of a set of numbers, both a geometric and harmonic mean can be calculated. The geometric mean of a set of n numbers x_1, x_2, . . . x_n is defined as

$$\sqrt[n]{x_1 \cdot x_2 \cdot \cdots \cdot x_n}$$

and the harmonic mean as

$$\frac{n}{\frac{1}{x_1}+\frac{1}{x_2}+\cdots+\frac{1}{x_n}}$$

Using these formulas, write a C++ program that continues to accept numbers until the number 999 is entered and then calculates and displays both the geometric and harmonic means of the entered numbers. (*Hint:* It will be necessary for your program to correctly count the number of values entered.)

11. a. The following data were collected on a recent automobile trip.

Mileage	Gallons
22495	Full tank
22841	12.2
23185	11.3
23400	10.5
23772	11.0
24055	12.2
24434	14.7
24804	14.3
25276	15.2

Write a C++ program that accepts a mileage and gallons value and calculates the miles-per-gallon (mpg) achieved for that segment of the trip. The miles-per-gallon is obtained as the difference in mileage between fill-ups divided by the number of gallons of gasoline used in the fill-up.

b. Modify the program written for Exercise 11a to additionally compute and display the cumulative mpg achieved after each fill-up. The cumulative mpg is calculated as the difference between each fill-up mileage and the mileage at the start of the trip divided by the sum of the gallons used to that point in the trip.

5.4 `for` LOOPS

In C++, a **`for` loop** is constructed using a `for` statement. This statement performs the same functions as the `while` statement, but uses a different form. In many situations, especially those that use a fixed count condition, the `for` statement format is easier to use than its `while` statement equivalent.

The syntax of the `for` statement is

for (initializing list; expression; altering list)
statement;

Although the `for` statement looks a little complicated, it is really quite simple if we consider each of its parts separately.

Within the parentheses of the `for` statement are three items, separated by semicolons. Each of these items is optional and can be described individually, but the semicolons must always be present.

In its most common form, the *initializing* list consists of a single statement used to set the starting (initial value) of a counter, the *expression* contains the maximum or minimum value the counter can have and determines when the loop is finished, and the *altering* list provides the increment value that is added to or subtracted from the counter each time the loop is executed. Examples of simple `for` statements having this form are

```
for (count = 1; count < 10; count = count + 1)
  cout << count;
```

and

```
for (i = 5; i <= 15; i = i + 2)
  cout << i;
```

In the first `for` statement, the counter variable is named `count`, the initial value assigned to `count` is 1, the loop continues as long as the value in `count` is less than 10, and the value of `count` is incremented by one each time through the loop. In the next `for` statement, the counter variable is named `i`, the initial value assigned to `i` is 5, the loop continues as long as `i`'s value is less than or equal to 15, and the value of `i` is incremented by 2 each time through the loop. In both cases a `cout` statement is used to display the value of the counter. Another example of a `for` loop is given in Program 5.9.

When Program 5.9 is executed, the following display is produced:

```
NUMBER     SQUARE ROOT
------     -----------
  1          1.00000
  2          1.41421
  3          1.73205
  4          2.00000
  5          2.23607
```

The first two lines displayed by the program are produced by the two `cout` statements placed before the `for` statement. The remaining output is produced by the `for` loop. This loop begins with the `for` statement and is executed as follows.

The initial value assigned to the counter variable `count` is 1. Since the value in `count` does not exceed the final value of 5, the execution of the `cout` statement within the loop produces the display

```
1         1.00000
```

Control is then transferred back to the `for` statement, which then increments the value in `count` to 2, and the loop is repeated, producing the display

```
2         1.41421
```

Program 5.9

```
#include <iostream>
#include <iomanip>
#include <cmath>
using namespace std;

int main()
{
  const int MAXCOUNT = 5;
  int count;

  cout << "NUMBER    SQUARE ROOT\n";
  cout << "------    -----------\n";

  cout << setiosflags(ios::showpoint);
  for (count = 1; count <= MAXCOUNT; count++)
    cout << setw(4) << count
         << setw(15) << sqrt(double(count)) << endl;

  return 0;
}
```

This process continues until the value in `count` exceeds the final value of 5, producing the complete output table. For comparison purposes, a `while` loop equivalent to the `for` loop contained in Program 5.9 is:

```
count = 1
while (count <= MAXCOUNT)
{
  cout << setw(4) << count
       << setw(15) << sqrt(count) << endl;
  count++;
}
```

As seen in this example, the difference between the `for` and `while` loops is the placement of the initialization, condition test, and incrementing items. The grouping of these items in the `for` statement is very convenient when fixed-count loops must be constructed. See if you can determine the output produced by Program 5.10.

Program 5.10

```
#include <iostream>
using namespace std;

int main()
{
  int count;

  for (count = 2; count <= 20; count = count + 2)
    cout << count << "  ";

  return 0;
}
```

Did you figure it out? The loop starts with a `count` initialized to 2, stops when `count` exceeds 20, and increments `count` in steps of 2. The output of Program 5.10 is

```
2  4  6  8  10  12  14  16  18  20
```

The `for` statement does not require that any of the items in parentheses be present or that they be used for initializing or altering the values in the expression statements. However, the two semicolons must be present within the `for`'s parentheses. For example, the construction `for ( ; count <= 20 ;)` is valid.

If the initializing list is missing, the initialization step is omitted when the `for` statement is executed. This, of course, means that the programmer must provide the required initializations before the `for` statement is encountered. Similarly, if the altering list is missing, any expressions needed to alter the evaluation of the tested expression must be included directly within the statement part of the loop. The `for` statement only ensures that all expressions in the initializing list are executed once, before evaluation of the tested expression, and that all expressions in the altering list are executed at the end of the loop before the tested expression is rechecked. Thus, Program 5.10 can be rewritten in any of the three ways shown in Programs 5.10a, 5.10b, and 5.10c.

Program 5.10a

```
#include <iostream>
using namespace std;

int main()
{
  int count;

  count = 2;     // initializer outside for statement
  for ( ; count <= 20; count = count + 2)
    cout << count << "  ";

  return 0;
}
```

Program 5.10b

```
#include <iostream>
using namespace std;

int main()
{
  int count;

  count = 2;     // initializer outside for loop
  for( ; count <= 20; )
  {
    cout << count << "  ";
    count = count + 2;     // alteration statement
  }

  return 0;
}
```

Program 5.10c

```
#include <iostream>
using namespace std;

int main()   // all expressions within the for's parentheses
{
  int count;

  for (count = 2; count <= 20; cout << count << "   ", count = count + 2);

  return 0;
}
```

In Program 5.10a, `count` is initialized outside the `for` statement and the first list inside the parentheses is left blank. In Program 5.10b, both the initializing list and the altering list are removed from within the parentheses. Program 5.10b also uses a compound statement within the `for` loop, with the expression-altering statement included in the compound statement. Finally, Program 5.10c has included all items within the parentheses, so there is no need for any useful statement following the parentheses. Here the null statement satisfies the syntactical requirement of one statement to follow the `for`'s parentheses.

Observe also in Program 5.10c that the altering list (last set of items in parentheses) consists of two items, and that a comma has been used to separate these items. The use of commas to separate items in both the initializing and altering lists is required if either of these two lists contains more than one item. Last, note the fact that Programs 5.10a, 5.10b, and 5.10c are all inferior to Program 5.10, and although you may encounter them in your programming career, you should not use them. Adding items other than loop control variables and their updating conditions within the `for` statement tends to confuse its readability and can introduce unwanted effects. Keeping the loop control structure "clean," as is done in Program 5.10, is important and a good programming practice.

Although the initializing and altering lists can be omitted from a `for` statement, omitting the tested expression results in an infinite loop. For example, such a loop is created by the statement

```
for (count = 2; ; count = count + 1)
  cout << count;
```

As with the `while` statement, both `break` and `continue` statements can be used within a `for` loop. A `break` forces an immediate exit from the `for` loop, as it does in the `while` loop. A `continue`, however, forces control to be passed to the altering list in a `for` statement, after which the tested expression is re-evaluated. This differs from the action of a `continue` in a `while` statement, where control is passed directly to the re-evaluation of the tested expression.

Point of Information

Where to Place the Opening Braces

There are two styles of writing `for` loops that are used by professional C++ programmers. These styles only come into play when the `for` loop contains a compound statement. The style illustrated and used in the text takes the form

for (expression)
{
compound statement in here
}

An equally acceptable style that is used by many programmers places the initial brace of the compound statement on the first line. Using this style a `for` loop appears as

for (expression) {
compound statement in here
}

The advantage of the first style is that the braces line up under one another, making it easier to locate brace pairs. The advantage of the second style is that it makes the code more compact and saves a line, permitting more code to be viewed in the same display area. Both styles are used but are almost never intermixed. Select whichever style appeals to you and be consistent in its use. As always, the indentation you use within the compound statement (two or four spaces, or a tab) should also be consistent throughout all of your programs. The combination of styles that you select becomes a "signature" for your programming work.

Figure 5.7 illustrates the internal workings of a `for` loop. As shown, when the `for` loop is completed, control is transferred to the first executable statement following the loop. To avoid the necessity of always illustrating these steps, a simplified set of flowchart symbols is available for describing `for` loops. Using the fact that a `for` statement can be represented by the flowchart symbol

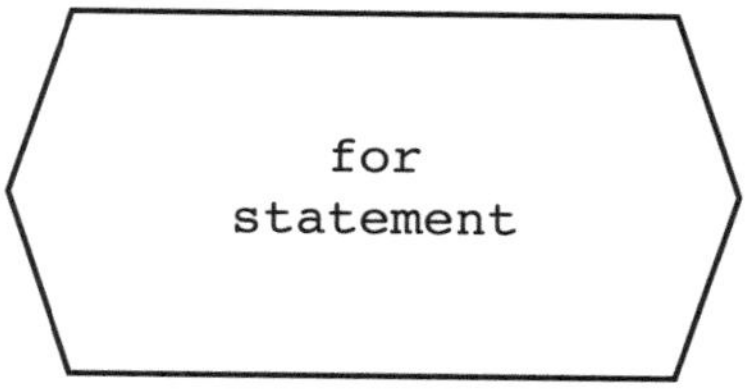

complete `for` loops can alternatively be illustrated as shown on Figure 5.8.

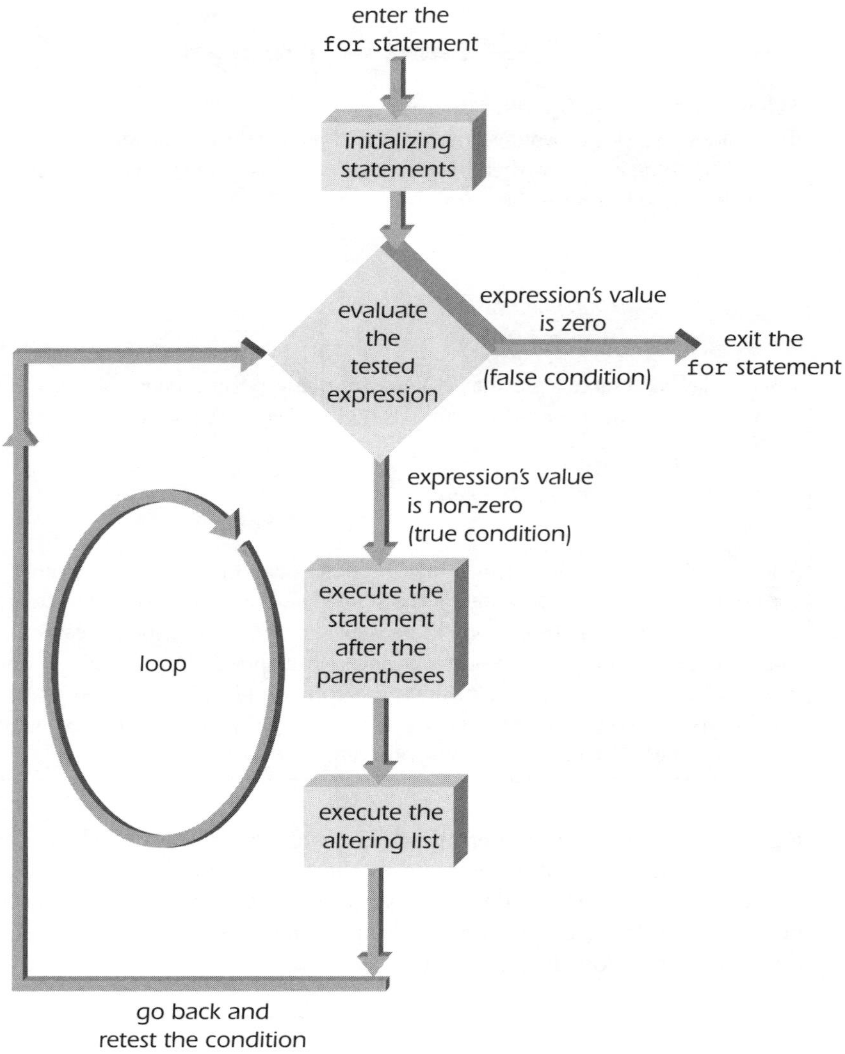

Figure 5.7 `for` loop flowchart.

Point of Information

Do You Use a `for` or `while` Loop?

A commonly asked question by beginning programmers is which loop structure should they use—a `for` or `while` loop. This is a good question because both of these loop structures are pretest loops that, in C++, can be used to construct both fixed-count and variable-condition loops.

In almost all other computer languages, including Visual Basic and Pascal, the answer is relatively straightforward, because the `for` statement can only be used to construct fixed-count loops. Thus, in these languages `for` statements are used to construct fixed-count loops and `while` statements are generally used only when constructing variable-condition loops.

In C++, this easy distinction does not hold, since each statement can be used to create each type of loop. The answer in C++, then, is really a matter of style. Since a `for` and `while` loop are interchangeable in C++, either loop is appropriate. Some professional programmers always use a `for` statement for every pretest loop they create and almost never use a `while` statement—others always use a `while` statement and rarely use a `for` statement. Still a third group tends to retain the convention used in other languages—a `for` loop is generally used to create fixed-count loops and a `while` loop is used to create variable-condition loops. In C++ it is all a matter of style and you will encounter all three styles in your programming career.

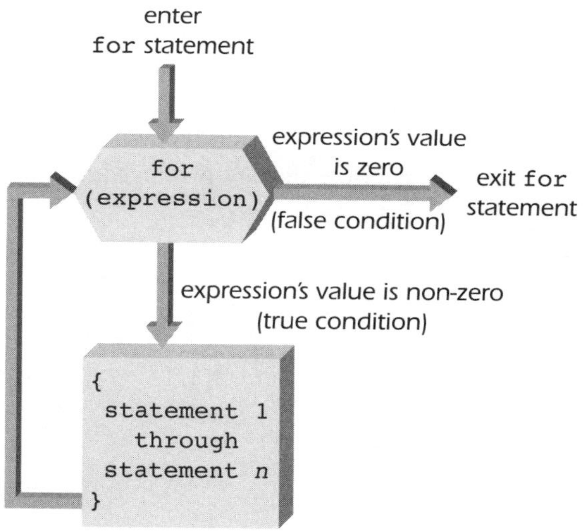

Figure 5.8 Simplified `for` loop flowchart.

To understand the enormous power of `for` loops, consider the task of printing a table of numbers from 1 to 10, including their squares and cubes, using this statement. Such a table was previously produced using a `while` loop in Program 5.3. You may wish to review Program 5.3 and compare it to Program 5.11 to get a further sense of the equivalence between `for` and `while` loops.

Program 5.11

```
#include <iostream>
#include <iomanip>
using namespace std;

int main()
{
  const int MAXNUMS = 10;
  int num;

  cout << "NUMBER    SQUARE    CUBE\n"
       << "------    ------    ----\n";

  for (num = 1; num <= MAXNUMS; num++)
    cout << setw(3) << num << "        "
         << setw(3) << num * num << "      "
         << setw(4) << num * num * num << endl;

  return 0;
}
```

When Program 5.11 is run, the display produced is

```
NUMBER      SQUARE     CUBE
------      ------     ----
   1            1         1
   2            4         8
   3            9        27
   4           16        64
   5           25       125
   6           36       216
   7           49       343
   8           64       512
   9           81       729
  10          100      1000
```

Simply changing the number 10 in the `for` statement of Program 5.11 to a 1000 creates a loop that is executed 1000 times and produces a table of numbers from 1 to 1000. As with the `while` statement, this small change produces an immense increase in the processing and output provided by the program. Notice also that the expression `num++` was used in the altering list in place of the usual `num = num + 1`.

Exercises 5.4

1. Write individual `for` statements for the following cases.
   a. Use a counter named `i` that has an initial value of 1, a final value of 20, and an increment of 1.
   b. Use a counter named `icount` that has an initial value of 1, a final value of 20, and an increment of 2.
   c. Use a counter named `j` that has an initial value of 1, a final value of 100, and an increment of 5.
   d. Use a counter named `icount` that has an initial value of 20, a final value of 1, and an increment of –1.
   e. Use a counter named `icount` that has an initial value of 20, a final value of 1, and an increment of –2.
   f. Use a counter named `count` that has an initial value of 1.0, a final value of 16.2, and an increment of 0.2.
   g. Use a counter named `xcnt` that has an initial value of 20.0, a final value of 10.0, and an increment of –0.5.

2. Determine the number of times that each `for` loop is executed for the `for` statements written for Exercise 1.

3. Determine the value in total after each of the following loops is executed.

   a.
   ```
   total = 0;
   for (i = 1; i <= 10; i = i + 1)
     total = total + 1;
   ```
   b.
   ```
   total = 1;
   for (count = 1; count <= 10; count = count + 1)
     total = total * 2;
   ```
   c.
   ```
   total = 0
   for (i = 10; i <= 15; i = i + 1)
     total = total + i;
   ```
   d.
   ```
   total = 50
   for (i = 1; i <=10; i = i + 1)
     total = total - i;
   ```
   e.
   ```
   total = 1
   for (icnt = 1; icnt <= 8; ++icnt)
     total = total * icnt;
   ```
   f.
   ```
   total = 1.0
   for (j = 1; j <= 5; ++j)
     total = total / 2.0;
   ```

4. Determine the output of the following program.

```
#include <iostream>
using namespace std;

int main()
{
  int i;

  for (i = 20; i >= 0; i = i - 4)
    cout << i << "  ";

  return 0;
}
```

5. Modify Program 5.11 to produce a table of the numbers zero through 20 in increments of 2, with their squares and cubes.

6. Modify Program 5.11 to produce a table of numbers from 10 to 1, instead of 1 to 10 as it currently does.

7. Write and run a C++ program that displays a table of 20 temperature conversions from Fahrenheit to Celsius. The table should start with a Fahrenheit value of 20 degrees and be incremented in values of 4 degrees. Recall that

Celsius = (5.0/9.0) * (*Fahrenheit* – 32)

8. Modify the program written for Exercise 7 to initially request the number of conversions to be made.

9. The expansion of a steel bridge as it is heated to a final Celsius temperature, T_F, from an initial Celsius temperature, T_0, can be approximated using the formula

$$\textit{Increase in length} = a * L * (T_F - T_0)$$

where a is the coefficient of expansion (which for steel is 11.7 e–6) and L is the length of the bridge at temperature T_0. Using this formula, write a C++ program that displays a table of expansion lengths for a steel bridge that is 7365 meters long at 0 degrees Celsius, as the temperature increases to 40 degrees in 5 degree increments.

10. The probability that an individual telephone call will last less than t minutes can be approximated by the exponential probability function

$$\textit{Probability that a call lasts less than t minutes} = 1 - e^{-t/a}$$

where a is the average call length and e is Euler's number (2.71828). For example, assuming that the average call length is 2 minutes, the probability that a call will last less than 1 minute is calculated as $1 - e^{-1/2} = 0.3297$.

Using this probability equation, write a C++ program that calculates and displays a list of probabilities of a call lasting less than 1 to less than 10 minutes, in one-minute increments.

11. a. The arrival rate of customers in a busy New York bank can be estimated using the Poisson probability function

$$P(x) = \frac{\lambda^x e^{-\lambda}}{x!}$$

where x = the number of customer arrivals per minute; λ = the average number of arrivals per minute; and e = Euler's number (2.71828). For example, if the average number of customers entering the bank is three customers per minute, then λ is equal to three. Thus, the probability of one customer arriving in any one minute is

$$P(x = 1) = \frac{3^1 e^{-3}}{1!} = 0.149561$$

and the probability of two customers arriving in any one minute is

$$P(x = 2) = \frac{3^2 e^{-3}}{2!} = 0.224454$$

Using the Poisson probability function, write a C++ program that calculates and displays the probability of 1 to 10 customer arrivals in any one minute when the average arrival rate is 3 customers per minute.

b. The formula given in Exercise 11a is also applicable for estimating the arrival rate of planes at a busy airport (here, an arriving "customer" is an incoming airplane). Using this same formula modify the program written in Exercise 11a to accept the average arrival rate as an input data item. Then run the modified program to determine the probability of 0 to ten planes attempting to land in any one minute period at an airport during peak arrival times. Assume that the average arrival rate for peak arrival times is two planes per minute.

12. A golf ball is dropped from an airplane. The distance, d, the ball falls in t seconds is given by the equation $d = (½)gt^2$, where g is the acceleration due to gravity and is equal to 32 ft/sec^2. Using this information, write and run a C++ program that displays the distance fallen in each one second interval for ten seconds and the total distance the golf ball falls at the end of each interval. The output should complete the following table:

Time	Distance in Current Interval	Total Distance
0	0.0	0.0
1	16.0	16.0
.	.	.
.	.	.
.	.	.
10	.	.

13. Assume the airplane in Exercise 12 is flying at a height of 50,000 feet. Modify the program written for Exercise 12 to determine how long it will take the ball to reach the ground. In order to increase the accuracy of your result without an undue number of calculations, decrease the time interval from 1 second to 0.1 second as the ball nears the ground.

14. The Fibonacci sequence is 0, 1, 1, 2, 3, 5, 8, 13, ... where the first two terms are 0 and 1, and each term thereafter is the sum of the two preceding terms; that is $Fib[n] = Fib[n-1] + Fib[n-2]$. Using this information, write a C++ program that calculates the nth number in a Fibonacci sequence, where n is interactively entered into the program by the user. For example, if $n = 6$, the program should display the value 5.

5.5 Loop Programming Techniques

In this section we present four common programming techniques associated with pretest (`for` and `while`) loops. All of these techniques are common knowledge to experienced programmers.

Technique 1: Interactive Input within a Loop

In Section 5.2 we presented the effect of including a `cin` statement within a `while` loop. Interactively entering data within a loop is a general technique that is equally applicable to `for` loops. For example, in Program 5.12 a `cin` statement is used to allow a user to interactively input a set of numbers. As each number is input, it is added to a total. When the `for` loop is exited, the average is calculated and displayed.

The `for` statement in Program 5.12 creates a loop that is executed four times. The user is prompted to enter a number each time through the loop. After each number is entered, it is immediately added to the total. Notice that `total` is initialized to zero as part of the initializing list of the `for` statement is executed. The loop in Program 5.12 is executed as long as the value in `count` is less than or equal to four and is terminated when `count` becomes five (the increment to five, in fact, is what causes the loop to end). The output produced by Program 5.12 is essentially the same as Program 5.7.

Program 5.12

```
#include <iostream>
using namespace std;

// This program calculates the average of MAXCOUNT
// user-entered numbers
int main()
{

  const int MAXCOUNT = 4;
  int count;
  double num, total, average;

  total = 0.0;

  for (count = 0; count < MAXCOUNT; count++)
  {
    cout << "Enter a number: ";
    cin  >> num;
    total = total + num;
  }

  average = total / MAXCOUNT;
  cout << "The average of the data entered is "
       << average << endl;
  return 0;
}
```

Technique 2: Selection within a Loop

Another common programming technique is to use either a `for` or `while` loop to cycle through a set of numbers and select those numbers that meet one or more criteria. For example, assume that we want to find both the positive and negative sum of a set of numbers. The criteria here is whether the number is positive or negative, and the logic for implementing this program is given by the pseudocode

While the loop condition is true
    Enter a number
    If the number is greater than zero
        add the number to the positive sum
    Else
        add the number to the negative sum
    Endif
Endwhile

Program 5.13 describes this algorithm in C++ for a fixed count loop where five numbers are to be entered.

Program 5.13

```
#include <iostream>
using namespace std;

// This program computes the positive and negative sums of a set
// of MAXNUMS user entered numbers
int main()
{
  const int MAXNUMS = 5;
  int i;
  double usenum, postot, negtot;

  postot = 0; // this initialization can be done in the declaration
  negtot = 0; // this initialization can be done in the declaration

  for (i = 1; i <= MAXNUMS; i++)
  {
    cout << "Enter a number (positive or negative) : ";
    cin  >> usenum;
    if (usenum > 0)
      postot = postot + usenum;
    else
      negtot = negtot + usenum;
   }
   cout << "The positive total is " << postot << endl;
   cout << "The negative total is " << negtot << endl;

   return 0;
}
```

The following is a sample run using Program 5.13.

```
Enter a number (positive or negative) : 10
Enter a number (positive or negative) : -10
Enter a number (positive or negative) : 5
Enter a number (positive or negative) : -7
Enter a number (positive or negative) : 11
The positive total is 26
The negative total is -17
```

Technique 3: Evaluating Functions of One Variable

Loops can be conveniently constructed to determine and display the values of a single variable mathematical function for a set of values over any specified interval. For example, assume that we want to know the values of the function

$$y = 10x^2 + 3x - 2$$

for x between 2 and 6. Assuming that x has been declared as an integer variable, the following `for` loop can be used to calculate the required values.

```
for (x = 2; x <= 6; x++)
{
  y = 10 * pow(x,2) + 3 * x - 2;
  cout << setw(4) << x
       << setw(11) << y << endl;
}
```

For this loop we have used the variable `x` as both the counter variable and the unknown (independent variable) in the function. For each value of `x` from two to five a new value of `y` is calculated and displayed. This `for` loop is contained within Program 5.14, which also displays appropriate headings for the values printed.

Program 5.14

```
#include <iostream>
#include <iomanip>
#include <cmath>
using namespace std;

int main()
{
  int x, y;

  cout << "x value    y value\n"
       << "-------    --------\n";
  for (x = 2; x <= 6; x++)
  {
    y = 10 * pow(x,2) + 3 * x - 2;
    cout << setw(4) << x
         << setw(11) << y << endl;
  }

  return 0;
}
```

The following is displayed when Program 5.14 is executed:

```
x value    y value
-------    --------
   2          44
   3          97
   4         170
   5         263
   6         376
```

Two items are of importance here. The first is that any equation with one unknown can be evaluated using a single `for` or an equivalent `while` loop. The method requires substituting the desired equation into the loop in place of the equation used in Program 5.14, and adjusting the counter values to match the desired solution range.

The second item of note is that we are not constrained to using integer values for the counter variable. For example, by specifying a noninteger increment, solutions for fractional values can be obtained. This is shown in Program 5.15, where the equation $y = 10x^2 + 3x - 2$ is evaluated in the range $x = 2$ to $x = 6$ in increments of 0.5.

Program 5.15

```
#include <iostream>
#include <iomanip>
#include <cmath>
using namespace std;

int main()
{
  double x, y;

  cout << "x value      y value\n";
       << "-------      ---------\n"
  cout << setiosflags(ios::fixed)
       << setiosflags(ios::showpoint)
       << setprecision(5);
  for (x = 2.0; x <= 6.0; x = x + 0.5)
  {
    y = 10.0 * pow(x,2.0) + 3.0 * x - 2.0;
    cout << setw(7) <<  x
         << setw(14) << y << endl;
  }

  return 0;
}
```

Notice that *x* and *y* have been declared as floating-point variables in Program 5.15 to allow these variables to take on fractional values. The following is the output produced by this program.

```
x value        y value
-------       ---------
2.00000        44.00000
2.50000        68.00000
3.00000        97.00000
3.50000       131.00000
4.00000       170.00000
4.50000       214.00000
5.00000       263.00000
5.50000       317.00000
6.00000       376.00000
```

Technique 4: Interactive Loop Control

Values used to control a loop may be set using variables rather than constant values. For example, the four statements

```
i = 5;
j = 10;
k = 1;
for (count = i; count <= j; count = count + k)
```

produce the same effect as the single statement

```
for (count = 5; count <= 10; count = count + 1)
```

Similarly, the statements

```
i = 5;
j = 10;
k = 1;
count = i;
while (count <= j)
  count = count + k;
```

produce the same effect as the following `while` loop

```
count = 5;
while (count <= 10)
  count = count + 1;
```

The advantage of using variables in the initialization, condition, and altering expressions is that it allows us to assign values for these expressions external to either the `for` or while statement. This is especially useful when a cin statement is used to set the actual values. To make this a little more tangible, consider Program 5.16.

Program 5.16

```
#include <iostream>
#include <iomanip>
using namespace std;

// this program displays a table of numbers, their squares and cubes
// starting from the number 1. The final number in the table is
// input by the user

int main()
{
  int num, final;

  cout << "Enter the final number for the table: ";
  cin  >> final;

  cout << "NUMBER SQUARE CUBE\n";
  cout << "------ ------ ----\n";

  for (num = 1; num <= final; num++)
    cout << setw(3) << num
         << setw(8) << num*num
         << setw(7) << num*num*num << endl;

  return 0;
}
```

In Program 5.16, we have used a variable to control the condition (middle) expression. Here a cin statement has been placed before the loop to allow the user to decide what the final value should be. Notice that this arrangement permits the user to set the size of the table at run time, rather than having the programmer set the table size at compile time. This also makes the program more general, since it now can be used to create a variety of tables without the need for reprogramming and recompiling.

Exercises 5.5

1. **`cin` within a loop:** Write and run a C++ program that accepts six Fahrenheit temperatures, one at a time, and converts each value entered to its Celsius equivalent before the next value is requested. Use a `for` loop in your program. The conversion required is *Celsius* = (5.0/9.0) · (*Fahrenheit* – 32).

2. **`cin` within a loop:** Write and run a C++ program that accepts 10 individual values of gallons, one at a time, and converts each value entered to its liter equivalent before the next value is requested. Use a `for` loop in your program. Use the fact that there are 3.785 liters in one gallon.

3. **Interactive loop control:** Modify the program written for Exercise 2 to initially request the number of data items that will be entered and converted.

4. **Interactive loop control:** Modify Program 5.13 so that the number of entries to be input is specified by the user when the program is executed.

5. **Selection:** Modify Program 5.13 so that it displays the average of the positive and negative numbers. (*Hint:* Be careful not to count the number zero as a negative number.) Test your program by entering the numbers 17, –10, 19, 0, –4. The positive average displayed by your program should be 18 and the negative average, –7.

6. **a. Selection:** Write a C++ program that selects and displays the maximum value of five numbers that are to be entered when the program is executed. (*Hint:* Use a `for` loop with both a `cin` and `if` statement internal to the loop.)
   b. Modify the program written for Exercise 6a so that it displays both the maximum value and the position in the input set of numbers where the maximum occurs.

7. **Selection:** Write a C++ program that selects and displays the first 20 integer numbers that are evenly divisible by 3.

8. **Selection:** A child's parents promised to give the child \$10 on her 12th birthday and double the gift on every subsequent birthday until the gift exceeded \$1000. Write a C++ program to determine how old the child will be when the last amount is given, and the total amount received.

9. **Mathematical functions:** Modify Program 5.15 to produce a table of y values for the following:
   a. $y = 3x^5 - 2x^3 + x$
   for x between 5 and 10 in increments of 0.2

   b. $y = 1 + x + \frac{x^2}{2} + \frac{x^3}{6} + \frac{x^4}{24}$
   for x between 1 and 3 in increments of 0.1

   c. $y = 2e^{0.8t}$ for t between 4 and 10 in increments of 0.2

10. Mathematical Functions: A model of worldwide population, in billions of people, is given by the equation

`Population = 6.0e`$^{0.02t}$`)`

where t is the time in years ($t = 0$ represents January 2000 and $t = 1$ represents January 2001). Using this formula, write a C++ program that displays a yearly population table for the years January 2005 though January 2010.

11. Mathematical Functions: The x and y coordinates, as a function of time, t, of a projectile fired with an initial velocity v at an angle of θ with respect to the ground is given by:

$x = v\ t \cos(\theta)$
$y = v\ t \sin(\theta)$

Using these formulas, write a C++ program that displays a table of x and y values for a projectile fired with an initial velocity of 500 ft/sec at an angle of 22.8 degrees. (*Hint:* Remember to convert to radian measure.) The table should contain values corresponding to the time interval 0 to 10 seconds in increments of $\frac{1}{2}$ seconds.

5.6 NESTED LOOPS

In many situations it is convenient to use a loop contained within another loop. Such loops are called **nested loops**. A simple example of a nested loop is

```
for(i = 1; i <= 5; i++)          // start of outer loop <─┐
{                                                          │
  cout << "\ni is now " << i << endl;                      │
                                                           │
  for(j = 1; j <= 4; j++)        // start of inner loop    │
    cout << "  j = " << j;       // end of inner loop      │
}                                // end of outer loop <────┘
```

The first loop, controlled by the value of `i`, is called the *outer loop*. The second loop, controlled by the value of `j`, is called the *inner loop*. Notice that all statements in the inner loop are contained within the boundaries of the outer loop and that we have used a different variable to control each loop. For each single trip through the outer loop, the inner loop runs through its entire sequence. Thus, each time the `i` counter increases by 1, the inner `for` loop executes completely. This situation is illustrated in Figure 5.9.

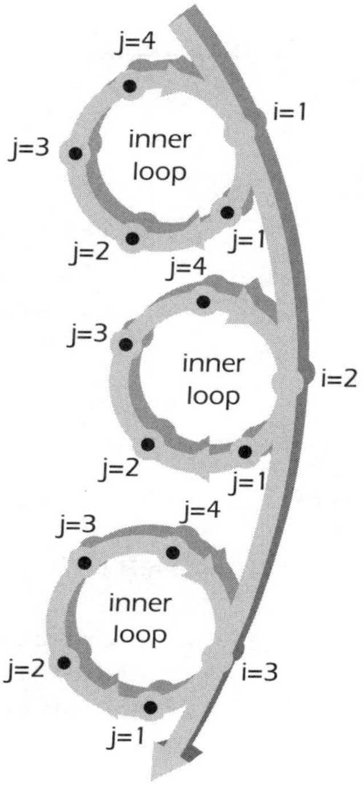

Figure 5.9 For each `i`, `j` loops.

Program 5.17 includes this type of code in a working program.

The output of a sample run of Program 5.17 is

```
i is now 1
  j = 1  j = 2  j = 3  j = 4
i is now 2
  j = 1  j = 2  j = 3  j = 4
i is now 3
  j = 1  j = 2  j = 3  j = 4
i is now 4
  j = 1  j = 2  j = 3  j = 4
i is now 5
  j = 1  j = 2  j = 3  j = 4
```

Program 5.17

```
#include <iostream>
using namespace std;

int main()
{
  const int MAXI = 5;
  const int MAXJ = 4;
  int i, j;

  for(i = 1; i <= MAXI; i++)      // start of outer loop <----+
  {                               //                          |
    cout << "\ni is now " << i << endl;  //                   |
                                  //                          |
    for(j = 1; j <= MAXJ; j++)    // start of inner loop      |
      cout << "  j = " << j;      // end of inner loop        |
  }                               // end of outer loop  <-----+

  cout << endl;

  return 0;
}
```

To illustrate the usefulness of a nested loop, we will use one to compute the average grade for each student in a class of 20 students. Each student has taken four exams during the course of the semester. The final grade is calculated as the average of these examination grades. The pseudocode describing how this computation can be done is

For 20 times
  Set the student grade total to zero
  For 4 times
    input a grade
    add the grade to the total
  Endfor // end of inner for loop
  Calculate student's average grade
  Print the student's average grade
Endfor // end of outer for loop

As described by the pseudocode, an outer loop consisting of 20 passes will be used to compute the average grade for each student. The inner loop will consist of 4 passes. One examination grade is entered in each inner loop pass. As each grade is entered it is added to the total for the student, and at the end of the loop the average is calculated and displayed.

Since both outer and inner loops are fixed count loops of 20 and 4, respectively, we will use `for` statements to create these loops. Program 5.18 provides the C++ code corresponding to the pseudocode.

Program 5.18

```
#include <iostream>
using namespace std;

int main()
{

  const int NUMGRADES = 4;
  const int NUMSTUDENTS = 20;
  int i, j;
  double grade, total, average;

  for (i = 1; i <= NUMSTUDENTS; i++) // start of outer loop
  {
    total = 0;                       // clear the total for this student
    for (j = 1; j <= NUMGRADES; j++) // start of inner loop
    {
      cout << "Enter an examination grade for this student: ";
      cin  >> grade;
      total = total + grade;         // add the grade into the total
    }                                // end of the inner for loop
    average = total / NUMGRADES;     // calculate the average
    cout << "\nThe average for student " << i
         << " is " << average << "\n\n";
  }                                  // end of the outer for loop

  return 0;
}
```

In reviewing Program 5.18, pay particular attention to the initialization of `total` within the outer loop, before the inner loop is entered. `total` is initialized 20 times, once for each student. Also notice that the average is calculated and displayed immediately after the inner loop is finished. Since the statements that compute and print the average are also contained within the outer loop, 20 averages are calculated and displayed. The entry and addition of each grade within the inner loop use techniques we have seen before, which should now be familiar to you.

Exercises 5.6

1. Four experiments are performed, each experiment consisting of six test results. The results for each experiment are given below. Write a program using a nested loop to compute and display the average of the test results for each experiment.

   1st experiment results: 23.2 31 16.9 27 25.4 28.6
   2nd experiment results: 34.8 45.2 27.9 36.8 33.4 39.4
   3rd experiment results: 19.4 16.8 10.2 20.8 18.9 13.4
   4th experiment results: 36.9 39 49.2 45.1 42.7 50.6

2. a. Modify the program written for Exercise 1 so that the number of test results for each experiment is entered by the user. Write your program so that a different number of test results can be entered for each experiment.
   b. Rewrite the program written for Exercise 2a to eliminate the inner loop.

3. a. An electrical manufacturer tests five generators by measuring their output voltages at three different times. Write a C++ program that uses a nested loop to enter each generator's test results and then computes and displays the average voltage for each generator. Assume the following generator test results:

   1st generator: 122.5 122.7 123.0
   2nd generator: 120.2 127.0 125.1
   3rd generator: 121.7 124.9 126.0
   4th generator: 122.9 123.8 126.7
   5th generator: 121.5 124.7 122.6

   b. Modify the program written for Exercise 3a to calculate and display the average voltage for all the generators. (*Hint:* Use a second variable to store the total of all the generator's voltages.)

4. Rewrite the program written for Exercise 3a to eliminate the inner loop. To do this, you will have to input three voltages for each generator rather than one at a time. Each voltage must be stored in its own variable name before the average is calculated.

5. Write a program that calculates and displays values for y when

   $$y = xz/(x - z)$$

   Your program should calculate y for values of x ranging between 1 and 5 and values of z ranging between 2 and 6. The x variable should control the outer loop and be incremented in steps of 1 and z should be incremented in steps of 1. Your program should also display the message `Function Undefined` when the x and z values are equal.

6. Assembly languages for some microprocessors do not have a multiply operation. While there are sophisticated algorithms for performing multiplication in such cases, a simple method multiplies by repeated addition. In this case the efficiency

of the algorithm can be increased by using nested loops. For example, to multiply a number by twelve, first add the number three times and then add the result four times. This requires only seven additions as opposed to twelve. Using this information write a C++ program that multiplies 33, 47, and 83 by 1001 using three loops and then displays the result. (*Hint:* 1001 = 7 · 11 · 13)

5.7 `do while` Loops

Both the `while` and `for` statements evaluate an expression at the start of the repetition loop; as such they are always used to create pretest loops. Posttest loops, which are also referred to as exit-controlled loops can also be constructed in C++. The basic structure of such a loop, which is referred to as a `do while` loop, is illustrated in Figure 5.10. Notice that a `do while` loop continues iterations through the loop while the condition is true and exits the loop when the condition is false.

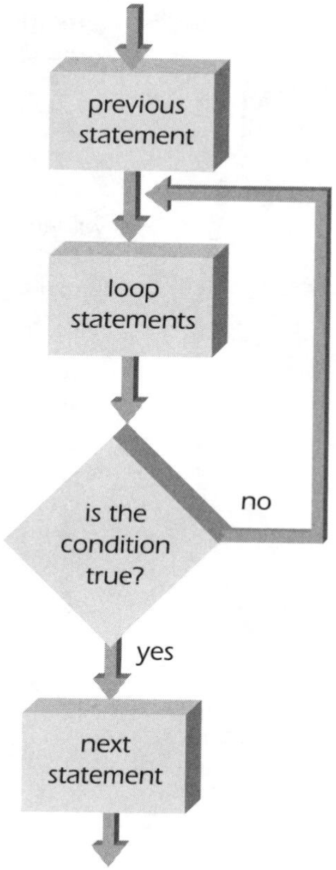

Figure 5.10 `do while` loop structure.

In C++, a posttest `do while` loop is created using a `do` statement. As its name implies, this statement allows us to do some statements before an expression is evaluated at the end of the loop. The general form of C++'s `do` statement is

```
do
  statement;
while (expression);  <———— don't forget the final ;
```

As with all C++ programs, the single statement in the `do` may be replaced with a compound statement. A flow-control diagram illustrating the operation of the `do` statement is shown in Figure 5.11.

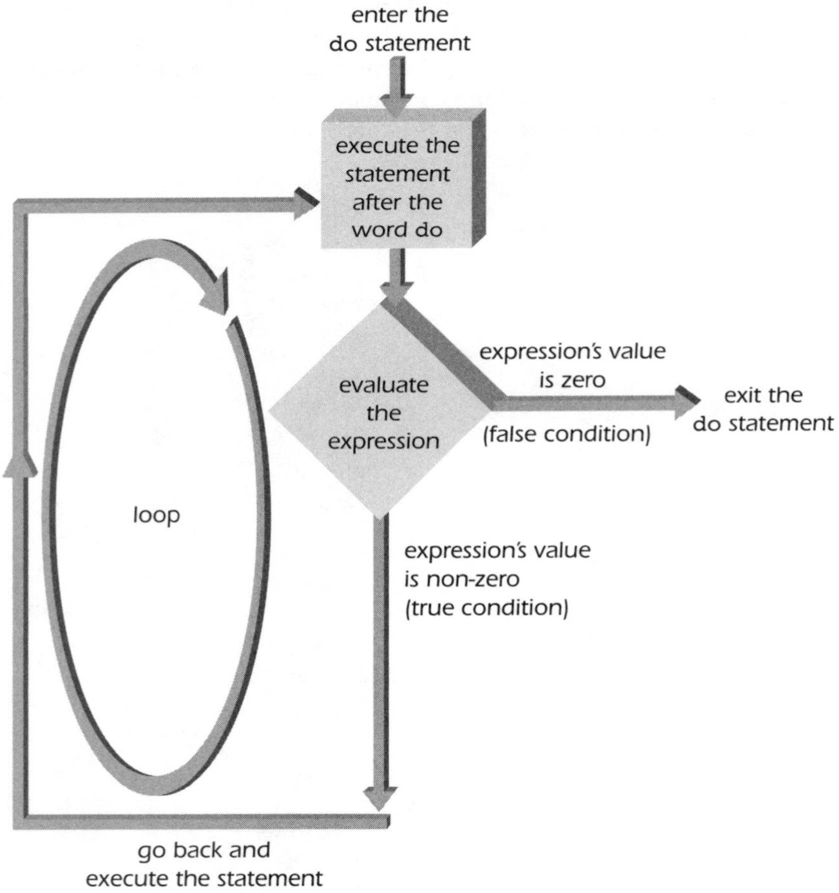

Figure 5.11 The `do` statement's flow of control.

As illustrated, all statements within the do statement are executed at least once before the expression is evaluated. Then, if the expression has a non-zero value, the statements are executed again. This process continues until the expression evaluates to zero (becomes false). For example, consider the following do statement:

```
do
{
  cout << "\nEnter a price: ";
  cin  >> price;
  if (abs(price - SENTINEL) < 0.0001)
    break;
  salestax = RATE * price;
  cout << setiosflags(ios::showpoint)
       << setprecision(2)
       << "The sales tax is $ " << salestax;
}
while (price != SENTINEL);
```

Observe that the prompt and `cin` statement are included within the loop because the tested expression is evaluated at the end of the loop.

As with all repetition statements, the do statement can always replace or be replaced by an equivalent `while` or `for` statement. The choice of which statement to use depends on the application and the style preferred by the programmer. In general, the `while` and `for` statements are preferred because they clearly let anyone reading the program know what is being tested "right up front" at the top of the program loop.

Validity Checks

The do statement is particularly useful in filtering user-entered input and providing data validation checks. For example, assume that an operator is required to enter a valid customer identification number between the numbers 1000 and 1999. A number outside this range is to be rejected and a new request for a valid number made. The following section of code provides the necessary data filter to verify the entry of a valid identification number:

```
do
{
  cout << "\nEnter an identification number: ";
  cin  >> id_num;
}
while (id_num < 1000 || id_num > 1999);
```

Here, a request for an identification number is repeated until a valid number is entered. This section of code is "bare bones" in that it neither alerts the operator to the cause of the new request for data nor allows premature exit from the loop if a valid identification number cannot be found. An alternative removing the first drawback is

```
do
{
  cout << "\nEnter an identification number: ";
  cin  >> id_num;
  if (id_num < 1000 || id_num > 1999)
  {
    cout << "An invalid number was just entered\n";
    cout << "Please check the ID number and re-enter\n";
  }
  else
    break;    // break if a valid id num was entered
} while(1);   // this expression is always true
```

Here we have used a `break` statement to exit from the loop. Since the expression being evaluated by the `do` statement is always 1 (true), an infinite loop has been created that is only exited when the `break` statement is encountered.

Exercises 5.7

1. a. Using a `do` statement, write a program to accept a grade. The program should request a grade continuously as long as an invalid grade is entered. An invalid grade is any grade less than 0 or greater than 100. After a valid grade has been entered, your program should display the value of the grade entered.

b. Modify the program written for Exercise 1a so that the user is alerted when an invalid grade has been entered.

c. Modify the program written for Exercise 1b so that it allows the user to exit the program by entering the number 999.

d. Modify the program written for Exercise 1b so that it automatically terminates after five invalid grades are entered.

2. a. Write a program that continuously requests a grade to be entered. If the grade is less than 0 or greater than 100, your program should print an appropriate message informing the user that an invalid grade has been entered, else the grade should be added to a total. When a grade of 999 is entered the program should exit the repetition loop and compute and display the average of the valid grades entered.

b. Run the program written in Exercise 2a on a computer and verify the program using appropriate test data.

3. a. Write a program to reverse the digits of a positive integer number. For example, if the number 8735 is entered, the number displayed should be 5378. (*Hint:* Use a `do` statement and continuously strip off and display the units digit of the number. If the variable `num` initially contains the number entered, the units digit is obtained as `(num % 10)`. After a units digit is displayed, dividing the number by 10 sets up the number for the next iteration. Thus, (8735 % 10) is 5 and

(8735 / 10) is 873. The do statement should continue as long as the remaining number is not zero.

b. Run the program written in Exercise 3a on a computer and verify the program using appropriate test data.

4. Repeat any of the exercises in Section 5.3 using a do statement rather than a `for` statement.

5. Given a number n, and an approximation for its square root, a closer approximation to actual square root can be obtained using the formula:

$$new\ approximation = \frac{(n\ /\ previous\ approximation) + previous\ approximation}{2}$$

Using this information, write a C++ program that prompts the user for a number and an initial guess at its square root. Using this input data your program should calculate an approximation to the square root that is accurate to 0.00001 (*Hint:* Stop the loop when the difference between two approximation is less than 0.00001.)

6. Here is a challenging problem for those who know a little calculus. The Newton–Raphson method can be used to find the roots of any equation $y(x) = 0$. In this method the $(i + 1)$st approximation, x_{i+1}, to a root of $y(x) = 0$ is given in terms of the ith approximation, x_i, by the formula

$$x_{i+1} = x_i - y(x_i)\ /\ y'(x_i)$$

For example, if $y(x) = 3x^2 + 2x - 2$, then $y'(x) = 6x + 2$, and the roots are found by making a reasonable guess for a first approximation x_1 and iterating using the equation

$$x_{i+1} = x_i - (3x_i^2 + 2x_i - 2)\ /\ (6x_i + 2)$$

a. Using the Newton–Raphson method, find the two roots of the equation $3x^2 + 2x - 2 = 0$. (*Hint:* There is one positive root and one negative root.)

b. Extend the program written for Exercise 6a so that it will find the roots of any function $y(x) = 0$, when the function for $y(x)$ and the derivative of $y(x)$ are placed in the code.

5.8 Common Programming Errors

Six errors are commonly made by beginning C++ programmers when using repetition statements. The most troublesome of these for new programmers is the "off by one" error, where the loop executes either one too many or one too few times than was intended. For example, the loop created by the statement `for(i = 1; i < 11; i++)` executes ten times, not eleven, even though the number 11 is used in the statement. Thus, an equivalent loop can be constructed using the statement `for(i = 1; i <= 10; i ++)`. However, if the loop is started with an initial value of i = 0, using the statement `for(i = 0; i < 11; i++)`, the loop will be traversed 11 times, as will a loop constructed with the statement `for(i = 0; i <= 10; i++)`. Thus, in constructing loops, you must pay particular attention to both initial and final conditions used to control the loop to ensure that number of loop traversals is not off by one too many or one too few executions.

The next two errors pertain to the tested expression, and have already been encountered with the `if` and `switch` statements. The first is the inadvertent use of the assignment operator, =, for the equality operator, ==, in the tested expression. An example of this error is typing the assignment expression a = 5 instead of the desired relational expression a==5. Since the tested expression can be any valid C++ expression, including arithmetic and assignment expressions, this error is not detected by the compiler.

As with the `if` statement, repetition statements should not use the equality operator, ==, when testing floating-point or double-precision operands. For example, the expression `fnum == 0.01` should be replaced by a test requiring that the absolute value of `fnum - 0.01` be less than an acceptable amount. The reason for this is that all numbers are stored in binary form. Using a finite number of bits, decimal numbers such as 0.01 have no exact binary equivalent, so that tests requiring equality with such numbers can fail.

The next two errors are particular to the `for` statement. The most common is to place a semicolon at the end of the `for`'s parentheses, which frequently produces a `do-nothing` loop. For example, consider the statements

```
for(count = 0; count < 10; count++);
  total = total + num;
```

Here the semicolon at the end of the first line of code is a null statement. This has the effect of creating a loop that is executed 10 times with nothing done except the incrementing and testing of `count`. This error tends to occur because C++ programmers are used to ending most lines with a semicolon.

The next error occurs when commas are used to separate the items in a `for` statement instead of the required semicolons. An example of this is the statement

```
for (count = 1, count < 10, count++)
```

Commas must be used to separate items within the initializing and altering lists, but semicolons must be used to separate these lists from the tested expression.

The last error occurs when the final semicolon is omitted from the `do` statement. This error is usually made by programmers who have learned to omit the semicolon after the parentheses of a `while` statement and carry over this habit when the reserved word `while` is encountered at the end of a `do` statement.

5.9 CHAPTER SUMMARY

1. A section of repeating code is referred to as a *loop*.

   The loop is controlled by a repetition statement that tests a condition to determine whether the code will be executed. Each pass through the loop is referred to as a *repetition* or *iteration*. The tested condition must always be explicitly set prior to its first evaluation by the repetition statement. Within the loop there must always be a statement that permits altering of the condition so that the loop, once entered, can be exited.

2. There are three basic type of loops:
   a. `while`
   b. `for`
   c. `do while`

   The `while` and `for` loops are *pretest* or *entrance controlled loops*. In this type of loop the tested condition is evaluated at the beginning of the loop, which requires that the tested condition be explicitly set prior to loop entry. If the condition is true, loop repetitions begin; otherwise the loop is not entered. Iterations continue as long as the condition remains true. In C++, `while` and `for` loops are constructed using `while` and `for` statements, respectively.

   The `do while` loop is a *posttest* or *exit controlled loop*, where the tested condition is evaluated at the end of the loop. This type of loop is always executed at least once. As long as the tested condition remains true, `do while` loops continue to execute.

3. Loops are also classified as to the type of tested condition. In a *fixed count loop*, the condition is used to keep track of how many repetitions have occurred. In a *variable condition loop* the tested condition is based on a variable that can change interactively with each pass through the loop.

4. In C++, a `while` loop is constructed using a `while` statement. The most commonly used form of this statement is

   while (expression)
   {
   statements;
   }

   The expression contained within parentheses is the condition tested to determine if the statement following the parentheses, which is generally a compound statement, is executed. The expression is evaluated in exactly the same manner as that contained in an `if-else` statement; the difference is how the expression is used. In a `while` statement the statement following the expression is executed repeatedly as long as the expression retains a non-zero value, rather than just once, as in an `if-else` statement. An example of a `while` loop is

```
count = 1;                // initialize count
while (count <= 10)
{
  cout << count << "  ";
  count++;                  // increment count
}
```

   The first assignment statement sets `count` equal to 1. The `while` statement is then entered and the expression is evaluated for the first time. Since the value of `count` is less than or equal to 10, the expression is true and the compound statement is executed. The first statement in the compound statement uses the `cout` object to display the value of `count`. The next statement adds 1 to the value currently stored in `count`, making this value equal to 2. The `while` statement now loops back to retest the expression. Since count is still less than or equal to 10, the compound statement is again executed. This process continues until the value of count reaches 11.

The while statement always checks its expression at the top of the loop. This requires that any variables in the tested expression must have values assigned before the while is encountered. Within the while loop there must be a statement that alters the tested expression's value.

5. In C++, a for loop is constructed using a for statement. This statement performs the same functions as the while statement, but uses a different form. In many situations, especially those that use a fixed-count condition, the for statement format is easier to use than its while statement equivalent. The most commonly used form of the for statement is

```
for (initializing list; expression; altering list)
{
  statements;
}
```

Within the parentheses of the for statement are three items, separated by semicolons. Each of these items is optional but the semicolons must be present.

The initializing list is used to set any initial values before the loop is entered; generally it is used to initialize a counter. Statements within the initializing list are only executed once. The expression in the for statement is the condition being tested: It is tested at the start of the loop and prior to each iteration. The altering list contains loop statements that are not contained within the compound statement: generally it is used to increment or decrement a counter each time the loop is executed. Multiple statements within a list are separated by commas. An example of a for loop is

```
for (total = 0, count = 1; count < 10; count++)
{
  cout << "Enter a grade: ";
  total = total + grade;
}
```

In this for statement, the initializing list is used to initialize both total and count. The expression determines that the loop will execute as long as the value in count is less than 10, and the value of count is incremented by one each time through the loop.

6. The for statement is extremely useful in creating fixed-count loops. This is because the initializing statements, the tested expression, and statements affecting the tested expression can all be included in parentheses at the top of a for loop for easy inspection and modification.

7. The do statement is used to create posttest loops because it checks its expression at the end of the loop. This ensures that the body of a do loop is executed at least once. Within a do loop there must be at least one statement that alters the tested expression's value.

Looking at Career Choices

Industrial Engineering

Each of the traditional engineering disciplines (civil, mechanical, electrical, chemical, and metallurgical/mining) relies on a particular area of natural science for its foundation. Industrial engineering, however, incorporates the knowledge of the social sciences into designing improvements in human-machine systems. Industrial engineers are responsible for designing, installing, and evaluating machines and systems and also for monitoring their interface with people to improve overall productivity. This job may involve understanding human behavioral characteristics and their effects on the design of machines or the workplace. Industrial engineers draw heavily on knowledge in economics, business management, and finance, as well as in the natural sciences. The areas of specialization of the industrial engineer may be divided into four categories:

1. Operations research. This area involves the application of analytical techniques and mathematical models to phenomena such as inventory control, simulation, decision theory, and queuing theory to optimize the total systems necessary for the production of goods.
2. Management or administrative engineering. The increasingly complex interplay of management and production skills in modern industrial operations has resulted in a need for technically trained managers. These managers evaluate and plan corporate ventures and interact with labor, engineering departments, and subcontractors. A management engineer may also participate in the financial operations of a company, drawing on knowledge in economics, business management, and law.
3. Manufacturing and production engineering. Before a product is produced, the complete manufacturing process must be designed and set up to optimize the economics involved and the final quality of the item. This task requires a broad knowledge of process design, plant layouts, tool design, robotics, and human-machine interactions.
4. Information systems. This area involves the use of computers to gather and analyze data for decision making and planning and to improve human–machine activity.

The following list includes the most common responsibilities of industrial engineers who responded to a recent survey by the American Institute of Industrial Engineers:

Facilities planning and design
Methods engineering
Work systems design
Production engineering
Management information and control systems
Organization analysis and design
Work measurement
Wage administration
Quality control
Project management
Cost control
Inventory control
Energy conservation
Computerized process control
Product packaging, handling, and testing
Tool and equipment selection
Production control
Product improvement study
Preventive maintenance
Safety programs
Training programs

CHAPTER 6

Modularity Using Functions

TOPICS

Professional programs are designed, coded, and tested very much like hardware: as a set of modules that are integrated to perform a completed whole. A good analogy of this is an automobile where one major module is the engine, another is the transmission, a third the braking system, a fourth the body, and so on. Each of these modules are linked together and ultimately placed under the control of the driver, which can be compared to a supervisor or main program module. The whole now operates as a complete unit, able to do useful work, such as driving to the store. During the assembly process, each module is individually constructed, tested, and found to be free of defects (bugs) before it is installed in the final product.

Now think of what you might do if you wanted to improve your car's performance. You might alter the existing engine or remove it altogether and bolt in a new engine. Similarly, you might change the transmission or tires or shock absorbers, making each modification individually as your time and budget allowed. In each case, the majority of the other modules can stay the same, but the car now operates differently.

In this analogy, each of the major components of a car can be compared to a function. For example, the driver calls on the engine when the gas pedal is pressed. The engine accepts inputs of fuel, air, and electricity to turn the driver's request into a useful product—power—and then sends this output to the transmission for further processing. The transmission receives the output of the engine and converts it to a form that can be used by the drive axle. An additional input to the transmission is the driver's selection of gears (drive, reverse, neutral, etc.).

In each case, the engine, transmission, and other modules only "know" the universe bounded by their inputs and outputs. The driver need know nothing of the internal operation of the engine, transmission, air-conditioning, and other modules that are being controlled. All that is required is an understanding of what *each unit does and* how *to use it. The driver simply "calls" on a module, such as the engine, brakes, air conditioning, and steering when that module's output is required. Communication between modules is restricted to passing needed inputs to each module as it is called upon to perform its task, and each module operates internally in a relatively independent manner. This same modular approach is used by engineers to create and maintain reliable C++ programs using functions.*

As we have seen, each C++ program must contain a `main()` *function. In addition to this required function, C++ programs may also contain any number of additional functions. In this chapter we learn how to write these functions, pass data to them, process the passed data, and return a result.*

6.1 FUNCTION AND PARAMETER DECLARATIONS

In creating C++ functions, we must be concerned with both the function itself and how it interacts with other functions, such as `main()`. This includes correctly passing data into a function when it is called and in returning values from a function. In this section we describe the first part of the interface, passing data to a function and having the function correctly receive, store, and process the transmitted data.

As we have already seen with mathematical functions, a function is called, or used, by giving the function's name and passing any data to it, as arguments, in the parentheses following the function name (see Figure 6.1).

function-name (data passed to function);

function-name	(data passed to function)
This identifies the called function	This passes data to the function

Figure 6.1 Calling and passing data to a function.

The called function must be able to accept the data passed to it by the function doing the calling. Only after the called function successfully receives the data can the data be manipulated to produce a useful result.

To clarify the process of sending and receiving data, consider Program 6.1, which calls a function named `findMax()`. The program, as shown, is not yet complete. Once the function `findMax()` is written and included in Program 6.1, the completed program, consisting of the functions `main()` and `findMax()`, can be compiled and executed.

Program 6.1

```
#include <iostream>
using namespace std;

void findMax(int, int);  // the function declaration (prototype)

int main()
{
  int firstnum, secnum;

  cout << "\nEnter a number: ";
  cin  >> firstnum;
  cout << "Great! Please enter a second number: ";
  cin  >> secnum;

  findMax(firstnum, secnum); // the function is called here

  return 0;
}
```

Let us examine the declaration and calling of the function `findMax()` from `main()`. We will then write `findMax()` to accept the data passed to it and determine the largest or maximum value of the two passed values.

The function `findMax()` is referred to as the **called function**, since it is called or summoned into action by its reference in `main()`. The function that does the calling, in this case `main()`, is referred to as the **calling function**. The terms called and calling come from standard telephone usage, where one party calls the other on a telephone. The party initiating the call is referred to as the calling party, and the party receiving the call is referred to as the called party. The same terms describe function calls. The called function, in this case `findMax()`, is declared as a function that expects to receive two integer numbers and to return no value (a void) to `main()`. This declaration is formally referred to as a function prototype. The function is then called by the last statement in the program.

Function Prototypes

Before a function can be called, it must be declared to the function that will do the calling. The declaration statement for a function is referred to as a **function prototype**. The function prototype tells the calling function the type of value that will be formally returned, if any, and the data type and order of the values that the calling function should transmit to the called function. For example, the function prototype previously used in Program 6.1

```
void findMax(int, int);
```

declares that the function `findMax()` expects two integer values to be sent to it, and that this particular function formally returns no value (void). Function prototypes may be placed with the variable declaration statements of the calling function, above the calling function name, as in Program 6.1, or in a separate header file that will be included using an `#include` preprocessor statement. Thus, the function prototype for `findMax()` could have been placed either before or after the statement `#include <iostream>`, prior to `main()`, or within `main()`. (The reasons for the choice of placement are presented in Section 6.3.) The general form of function prototype statements is:

returnDataType functionName(list of argument data types);

where the data type refers to the type of the value that will be formally returned by the function. Examples of function prototypes are

```
int fmax(int, int);
double swap(int, char, char, double);
void display(double, double);
```

The function prototype for `fmax()` declares that this function expects to receive two integer arguments and will formally return an integer value. The function prototype for `swap()` declares that this function requires four arguments consisting of an integer, two characters, and a double-precision argument, in this order, and will formally return a double-precision number. Finally, the function prototype for `display()` declares that this function requires two double-precision arguments and does not return any value. Such a function might be used to display the results of a computation directly, without returning any value to the called function.

The use of function prototypes permits error-checking of data types by the compiler. If the function prototype does not agree with data types defined when the function is written, a compiler warning will occur. The prototype also serves another task: it ensures conversion of all arguments passed to the function to the declared argument data type when the function is called.

Calling a Function

Calling a function is a rather easy operation. The only requirements are that the name of the function be used and that any data passed to the function be enclosed within the parentheses following the function name using the same order and type as declared in the function prototype. The items enclosed within the parentheses are called **arguments** of the called function (see Figure 6.2).

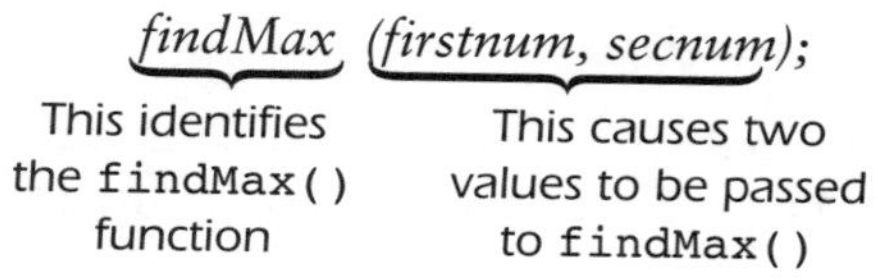

Figure 6.2 Calling and passing two values to `findMax()`.

If a variable is one of the arguments in a function call, the called function receives a copy of the value stored in the variable. For example, the statement `findMax(firstnum, secnum);` calls the function `findMax()` and causes the values currently residing in the variables `firstnum` and `secnum` to be passed to `findMax()`. The variable names in parentheses are arguments that provide values to the called function. After the values are passed, control is transferred to the called function.

As illustrated in Figure 6.3, the function `findMax()` *does not receive the variables named* `firstnum` *and* `secnum` *and has no knowledge of these variable names.*[1] The function simply receives the values in these variables and must itself determine where to store these values before it does anything else. Although this procedure for passing data to a function may seem surprising, it is really a safety procedure for ensuring that a called function does not inadvertently change data stored in a variable. The function gets a copy of the data to use. It may change its copy and, of course, change any variables declared inside itself. However, unless specific steps are taken to do so, a function is not allowed to change the contents of variables declared in other functions.

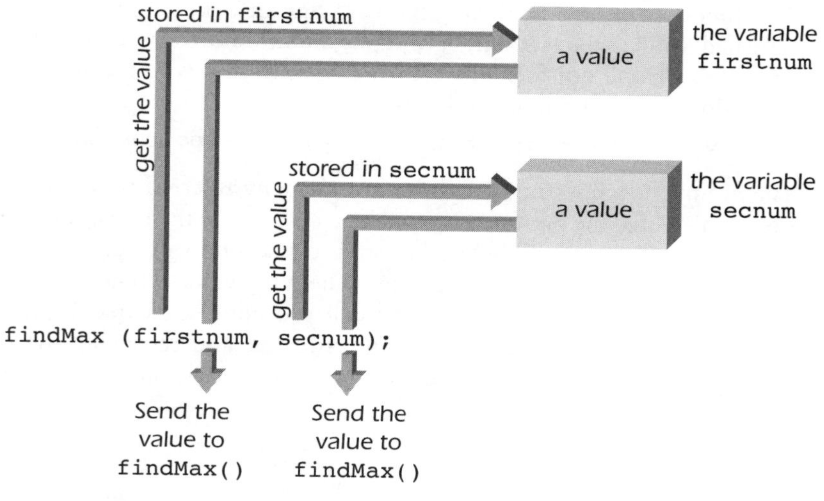

Figure 6.3 `findMax()` receives actual values.

Now we will begin writing the function `findMax()` to process the values passed to it.

[1]In Section 6.3 we will see how, using reference variables, that C++ also permits direct access to the calling function's variables.

Defining a Function

A function is defined when it is written. Each function is defined once (that is, written once) in a program and can then be used by any other function in the program that suitably declares it.

Like the `main()` function, every C++ function consists of two parts, a **function header** and a **function body**, as illustrated in Figure 6.4. The purpose of the function header is to identify the data type of the value returned by the function, provide the function with a name, and specify the number, order, and type of arguments expected by the function. The purpose of the function body is to operate on the passed data and directly return, at most, one value back to the calling function. (We will see, in Section 6.3, how a function can be made to return multiple values.)

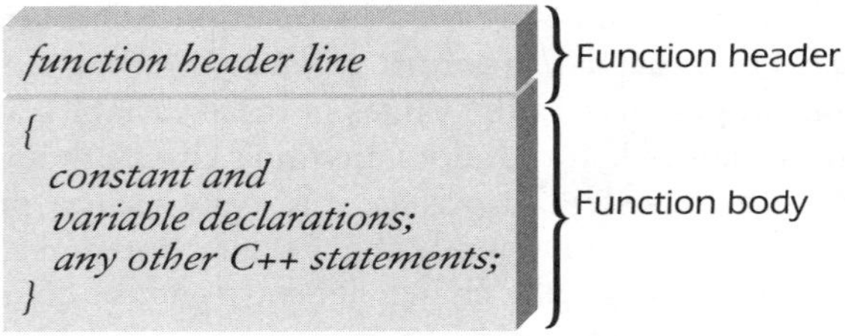

Figure 6.4 General format of a function.

The function header is always the first line of a function and contains the function's returned value type, its name, and the names and data types of its arguments. Since `findMax()` will not formally return any value and is to receive two integer arguments, the following header line can be used:

```
void findMax(int x, int y)  <---- no semicolon
```

The argument names in the header are formally referred to as **formal parameters** of the function.[2] Thus, the parameter `x` will be used to store the first value passed to `findMax()` and the parameter `y` will be used to store the second value passed at the time of the function call. The function does not know where the values come from when the call is made from `main()`. The first part of the call procedure executed by the computer involves going to the variables `firstnum` and `secnum` and retrieving the stored values. These values are then passed to `findMax()` and ultimately stored in the parameters `x` and `y` (see Figure 6.5).

[2]The portion of the function header that contains the function name and parameters is formally referred to as a *function declarator*.

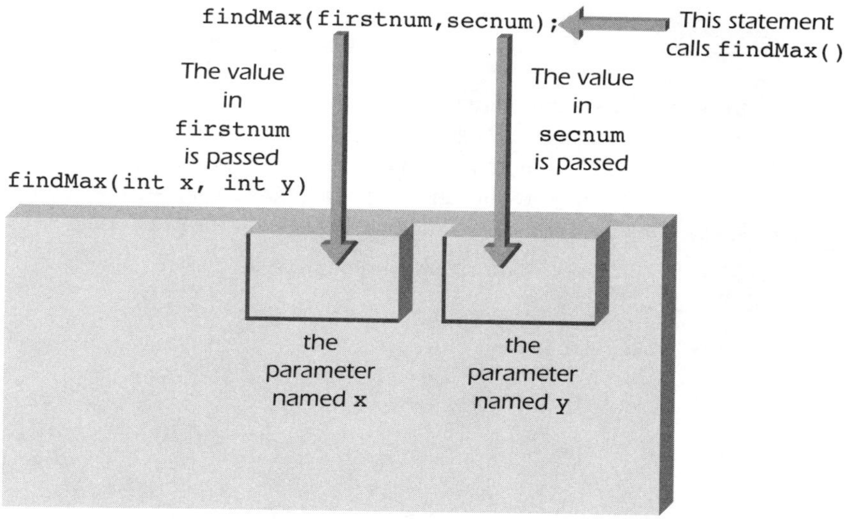

Figure 6.5 Storing values into parameters.

The function name and all parameter names in the header, in this case `findMax`, `x`, and `y`, are chosen by the programmer. Any names selected according to the rules used to choose variable names can be used. All parameters listed in the function header line must be separated by commas and must have their individual data types declared separately.

Now that we have written the function header for the `findMax()` function, we can construct its body. Let us assume that the `findMax()` function selects and displays the larger of the two numbers passed to it.

As illustrated in Figure 6.6, a function body begins with an opening brace, `{`, contains any necessary declarations and other C++ statements, and ends with a closing brace, `}`. This should be familiar to you because it is the same structure used in all the `main()` functions we have written. This should not be a surprise because `main()` is itself a function and must adhere to the rules required for constructing all legitimate functions.

{
symbolic constant declarations,
variable declarations, and
other C++ statements
}

Figure 6.6 Structure of a function body.

Point of Information

Function Definitions and Function Prototypes

When you write a function, you are formally creating a function definition. Each definition begins with a header line that includes a parameter list, if any, enclosed in parentheses and ends with the closing brace that terminates the function's body. The parentheses are required whether or not the function uses any parameters. A commonly used syntax for a function definition is:

```
returnDataType functionName(parameter list)
{
  constant declarations
  variable declarations

  other C++ statements

  return value
}
```

A **function prototype** declares a function. The syntax for a function prototype, which provides the return data type of the function, the function's name, and the function's argument list is:

```
returnDataType functionName(list of parameter data types);
```

As such, the prototype along with pre- and postcondition comments (see the next Point of Information box) should provide a user with all the programming information needed to successfully call the function.

Generally, all functions prototypes are placed at the top of the program, and all definitions are placed after the `main()` function. However, this placement can be changed. The only requirement in C++ is that a function cannot be called before it has been either declared or defined.

In the body of the `findMax()` function, we will declare one variable to store the maximum of the two numbers passed to it. We will then use an `if-else` statement to find the maximum of the two numbers. Finally, a `cout` statement will be used to display the maximum. The complete function definition for the `findMax()` function is:

```
void findMax(int x, int y)
{                       // start of function body
  int maxnum;           // variable declaration

  if (x >= y)           // find the maximum number
    maxnum = x;
  else
    maxnum = y;

  cout << "\nThe maximum of the two numbers is "
       << maxnum << endl;

}  // end of function body and end of function
```

Point of Information

Preconditions and Postconditions

Preconditions are any set of conditions required by a function to be true if it is to operate correctly. For example, if a function uses the symbolic constant `MAXCHARS`, which must have a positive value, a precondition is that `MAXCHARS` be declared with a positive value before the function is called.

Similarly, a postcondition is a condition that will be true after the function is executed, assuming that the preconditions are met.

Pre- and postconditions are typically documented as user comments. For example, consider the following declaration and comments:

```
bool leapyr(int)
// Preconditions: the integers must represent a year in a four
//              : digit form, such as 2006
// Postcondition: a value of true is be returned if the year is a leap year;
//              : otherwise false will be returned
```

Pre- and postcondition comments should be included with both function prototypes and function definitions whenever clarification is needed.

Notice that the parameter declarations are made within the header line and the variable declaration is made immediately after the opening brace of the function's body. This is in keeping with the concept that parameter values are passed to a function from outside the function, and that variables are declared and assigned values from within the function body.

Program 6.2 includes the `findMax()` function within the program code previously listed in Program 6.1.

Program 6.2 can be used to select and print the maximum of any two integer numbers entered by the user. A sample run using Program 6.2 follows:

```
Enter a number: 25
Great! Please enter a second number: 5

The maximum of the two numbers is 25
```

The placement of the `findMax()` function after the `main()` function in Program 6.2 is a matter of choice. We will usually list `main()` first because it is the driver function that should give anyone reading the program an idea of what the complete program is about before encountering the details of each function. In no case, however, can the definition of `findMax()` be placed inside `main()`. This is true for all C++ functions, which must be defined by themselves outside any other function. Each C++ function is a separate and independent entity with its own parameters and variables; *nesting of functions is never permitted.*

Program 6.2

```
#include <iostream>
using namespace std;

void findMax(int, int);  // the function prototype

int main()
{
  int firstnum, secnum;

  cout << "\nEnter a number: ";
  cin  >> firstnum;
  cout << "Great! Please enter a second number: ";
  cin  >> secnum;

  findMax(firstnum, secnum); // the function is called here

  return 0;
}

// following is the function FindMax()

void findMax(int x, int y)
{                    // start of function body
  int maxnum;        // variable declaration

  if (x >= y)        // find the maximum number
    maxnum = x;
  else
    maxnum = y;

  cout << "\nThe maximum of the two numbers is "
       << maxnum << endl;

  return;
} // end of function body and end of function
```

Placement of Statements

C++ does not impose a rigid statement-ordering structure on the programmer. The general rule for placing statements in a C++ program is simply that all preprocessor directives, named constants, variables, and functions must be either declared or defined before they can be used. As we have noted previously, although this rule permits both preprocessor directives and declaration statements to be placed throughout a program, doing so results in a very poor program structure.

As a matter of good programming form, the following statement ordering should form the basic structure around which all of your C++ programs are constructed.

```
preprocessor directives

function prototypes

int main()
{
  symbolic constants
  variable declarations

  other executable statements

  return value
}

function definitions
```

As always, comment statements can be freely intermixed anywhere within this basic structure.

Function Stubs

An alternative to completing each function required in a complete program is to write the `main()` function first, and add the functions later, as they are developed. The problem that arises with this approach, however, is the same problem that occurred with Program 6.1; that is, the program cannot be run until all the functions are included. For convenience we have reproduced the code for Program 6.1 below.

```
#include <iostream>
using namespace std;

void findMax(int, int);  // the function declaration (prototype)

int main()
{
  int firstnum, secnum;

  cout << "\nEnter a number: ";
  cin  >> firstnum;
  cout << "Great! Please enter a second number: ";
  cin  >> secnum;

  findMax(firstnum, secnum); // the function is called here

  return 0;
}
```

Point of Information

Isolation Testing

One of the most successful software testing methods known is to always embed the code being tested within an environment of working code. For example, assume you have two untested functions that are called in the order shown below, and the result returned by the second function is incorrect.

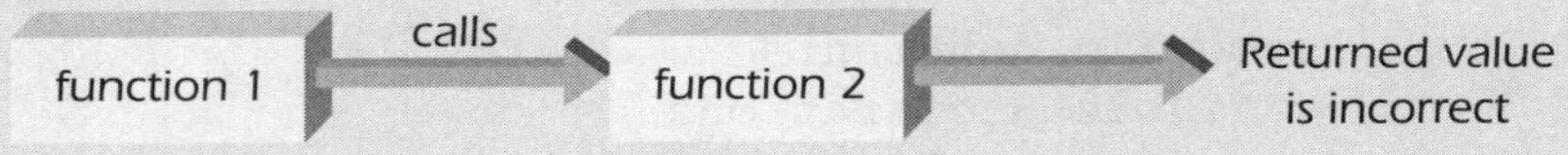

From the information shown on this figure, one or possibly both of the functions could be operating incorrectly. The first order of business is to isolate the problem to a specific function.

One of the most powerful methods of performing this code isolation is to decouple the functions. This is done by either testing each function individually or by testing one function first and, only when you know it is operating correctly, reconnecting it to the second function. Then, if an error occurs, you have isolated the error to either the transfer of data between functions or the internal operation of the second function.

This specific procedure is an example of the *basic rule of testing*, which states that each function should only be tested in a program in which all other functions are known to be correct. This means that one function must first be tested by itself, using stubs if necessary for any called functions, and a second tested function should be tested either by itself or with a previously tested function, and so on. This ensures that each new function is isolated within a test bed of correct functions, with the final program effectively built up of tested function code.

This program would be complete if there were a function definition for `findMax`. But we really don't need a *correct* `findMax` function to test and run what has been written, we just need a function that *acts* like it is: A "fake" `findMax` that accepts the proper number and types of parameters and returns values of the proper form for the function call is all we need to allow initial testing. This fake function is called a stub. A **stub** is the beginning of a final function that can be used as a placeholder for the final unit until the unit is completed. A stub for `findMax` is as follows:

```
void findMax(int x, int y)
{
  cout << "In findMax()\n";
  cout << "The value of x is " << x << endl;
  cout << "The value of x is " << y << endl;
}
```

This stub function can now be compiled and linked with the previously completed code to obtain an executable program. The code for the function can then be further developed with the "real" code when it is completed, replacing the stub portion.

The minimum requirement of a stub function is that it compiles and links with its calling module. In practice, it is a good idea to have a stub display a message that it has been entered successfully and the value(s) of its received parameters, as in the stub for `findMax()`.

As the function is refined, you let it do more and more, perhaps allowing it to return intermediate or incomplete results. This incremental, or stepwise, refinement is an important concept in efficient program development that provides you with the means to run a program that does not yet meet all its final requirements.

Functions with Empty Parameter Lists

Although useful functions having an empty parameter list are extremely limited (one such function is provided in Exercise 11), they can occur. The function prototype for such a function requires either writing the keyword `void` or nothing at all between the parentheses following the function's name. For example, both prototypes

```
int display();
```

and

```
int display(void);
```

indicate that the `display()` function takes no parameters and returns an integer. A function with an empty parameter list is called by its name with nothing written within the required parentheses following the function's name. For example, the statement `display();` correctly calls the `display()` function whose prototype is given above.

Default Arguments[3]

A convenient feature of C++ is its flexibility of providing default arguments in a function call. The primary use of default arguments is to extend the parameter list of existing functions without requiring any change in the calling argument lists already in place within a program.

Default argument values are listed in the function prototype and are automatically transmitted to the called function when the corresponding arguments are omitted from the function call. For example, the function prototype

```
void example(int, int = 5, double = 6.78);
```

provides default values for the last two arguments. If any of these arguments are omitted when the function is actually called, the C++ compiler will supply these default values. Thus, all the following function calls are valid:

```
example(7, 2, 9.3)   // no defaults used
example(7, 2)        // same as example(7, 2, 6.78)
example(7)           // same as example(7, 5, 6.78)
```

Four rules must be followed when using default parameters. The first is that default values should be assigned in the function prototype.[4] The second is that if any parameter is given a default value in the function prototype, all parameters following it must also be supplied with default values. The third rule is that if one argument is omitted in the actual function call, then all arguments to its right must also be omitted. These two rules make it clear to the C++ compiler which arguments are being omitted and permits the compiler to

[3]This topic may be omitted on first reading without loss of subject continuity.

[4]Some compilers accept default assignments in the function definition.

supply correct default values for the missing arguments, starting with the rightmost argument and working in toward the left. The last rule specifies that the default value used in the function prototype may be an expression consisting of both constants and previously declared variables. If such an expression is used, it must pass the compiler's check for validly declared variables, even though the actual value of the expression is evaluated and assigned at run time.

Default arguments are extremely useful when extending an existing function to include more features that require additional arguments. Adding the new arguments to the right of the existing arguments and providing each new argument with a default value permits all existing function calls to remain as they are. Thus, the effect of the new changes are conveniently isolated from existing code in the program.

Reusing Function Names (Overloading)[5]

C++ provides the capability of using the same function name for more than one function, which is referred to as **function overloading**. The only requirement in creating more than one function with the same name is that the compiler must be able to determine which function to use based on the data types of the parameters (not the data type of the return value, if any). For example, consider the three following functions, all named `cdabs()`.

```
void cdabs(int x)  // compute and display the absolute value of an integer
{
  if ( x < 0 )
    x = -x;
  cout << "The absolute value of the integer is " << x << endl;
}

void cdabs(float x)  // compute and display the absolute value of a float
{
  if ( x < 0 )
    x = -x;
  cout << "The absolute value of the float is " << x << endl;
}

void cdabs(double x)  // compute and display the absolute value of a double
{
  if ( x < 0 )
   x = -x;
  cout << "The absolute value of the double is " << x << endl;
}
```

[5]This topic may be omitted on first reading without loss of subject continuity.

Which of the three functions named `cdabs()` is actually called depends on the argument types supplied at the time of the call. Thus, the function call `cdabs(10);` would cause the compiler to use the function named `cdabs()` that expects an integer argument, and the function call `cdabs(6.28f);` would cause the compiler to use the function named `cdabs()` that expects a single-precision argument.[6]

Notice that overloading a function's name simply means using the same name for more than one function. Each function that uses the name must still be written and exists as a separate entity. The use of the same function name does not require that the code within the functions be similar, although good programming practice dictates that functions with the same name should perform essentially the same operations. All that is formally required in using the same function name is that the compiler can distinguish which function to select based on the data types of the arguments when the function is called. Clearly, however, if all that is different about the overloaded functions is the argument types, a better programming solution is to simply create a function template. The use of overloaded functions, however, is extremely useful with constructor functions, a topic that is presented in Section 8.3.

Function Templates[7]

In most high-level languages, including C++'s immediate predecessor, C, each function requires its own unique name. In theory this makes sense, but in practice it can lead to a profusion of function names, even for functions that perform essentially the same operations. For example, consider determining and displaying the absolute value of a number. If the number passed into the function can be either an integer, a single-precision, or a double-precision value, three distinct functions must be written to correctly handle each case. Certainly, we could give each of these functions a unique name, such as `abs()`, `fabs()`, and `dabs()`, respectively, having the function prototypes:

```
void abs(int);
void fabs(float);
void dabs(double);
```

Clearly, each of these three functions performs essentially the same operation, but on different parameter data types. A much cleaner and more elegant solution is to write a general function that handles all cases, but whose parameters, variables, and even return type can be set by the compiler based on the actual function call. This is possible in C++ using function templates.

---

[6]This is accomplished by a process referred to as *name mangling*. Using this process the function name actually generated by the C++ compiler differs from the function name used in the source code. The compiler appends information to the source code function name depending on the type of data being passed, and the resulting name is said to be a mangled version of the source code name.

[7]This topic may be omitted on first reading without loss of subject continuity.

A **function template** is a single, complete function that serves as a model for a family of functions. Which function from the family that is actually created depends on subsequent function calls. To make this more concrete, consider a function template that computes and displays the absolute value of a passed argument. An appropriate function template is:

```
template <class T>
void showabs(T number)
{
  if (number < 0)
    number = -number;
  cout << "The absolute value of the number "
       << " is " << number << endl;

  return
}
```

For the moment, ignore the first line `template <class T>`, and look at the second line, which consists of the function header `void showabs(T number)`. Notice that this header line has the same syntax that we have been using for all our function definitions, except for the `T` in place of where a data type is usually placed. For example, if the header line were `void showabs(int number)`, you should recognize this as a function named `showabs` that expects one integer argument to be passed to it, and that returns no value. Similarly, if the header line were `void showabs(float number)`, you should recognize it as a function that expects one floating point argument to be passed when the function is called.

The advantage in using the `T` within the function template header line is that it represents a general data type that is replaced by an actual data type, such as `int`, `float`, `double`, etc., when the compiler encounters an actual function call. For example, if a function call with an integer argument is encountered, the compiler will use the function template to construct the code for a function that expects an integer parameter. Similarly, if a call is made with a floating-point argument, the compiler will construct a function that expects a floating-point parameter. As a specific example of this, consider Program 6.3.

First notice the three function calls made in the `main()` function shown in Program 6.3, which call the function `showabs()` with an integer, float, and double value, respectively. Now review the function template for `showabs()` and let us consider the first line `template <class T>`. This line, which is called a **template prefix**, is used to inform the compiler that the function immediately following is a template that uses a data type named `T`. Within the function template the `T` is used in the same manner as any other data type, such as `int`, `float`, `double`, etc. Then, when the compiler encounters an actual function call for `showabs()`, the data type of the argument passed in the call is substituted for `T` throughout the function. In effect, the compiler creates a specific function, using the template, that expects the argument type in the call. Since Program 6.3 makes three calls to `showabs`, each with a different argument data type, the compiler will create three separate

Program 6.3

```
#include <iostream>
using namespace std;

template <class T>
void showabs(T number)
{

  if (number < 0)
    number = -number;
  cout << "The absolute value of the number is "
       << number << endl;

  return;
}

int main()
{
  int num1 = -4;
  float num2 = -4.23f;
  double num3 = -4.23456;

  showabs(num1);
  showabs(num2);
  showabs(num3);

  return 0;
}
```

`showabs()` functions. The compiler knows which function to use based on the arguments passed at the time of the call. The output displayed when Program 6.3 is executed is:

```
The absolute value of the number is 4
The absolute value of the number is 4.23
The absolute value of the number is 4.23456
```

The letter `T` used in the template prefix `template <class T>` is simply a placeholder for a data type that is defined when the function is actually invoked. As such, any letter or non-keyword identifier can be used instead. Thus, the `showabs()` function template could just as well have been defined as:

```
template <class DTYPE>
void abs(DTYPE number)
{
  if (number < 0)
    number = -number;
  cout << "The absolute value of the number is "
       << number << endl;

  return;
}
```

In this regard, it is sometimes simpler and clearer to read the word *class* in the template prefix as the words *data type*. Thus, the template prefix `template <class T>` can be read as "we are defining a function template that has a data type named `T`." Then, within both the header line and body of the defined function the data type `T` (or any other letter or identifier defined in the prefix) is used in the same manner as any built-in data type, such as `int`, `float`, `double`, etc..

Now suppose, we would like to create a function template to include both a return type and an internally declared variable. For example, consider the following function template:

```
template <class T> // template prefix
T abs(T value)    //header line
{
  T absnum;  // variable declaration

  if (value < 0)
    absnum = -value;
  else
    absnum = value;

  return absnum;
}
```

In this template definition, we have used the date type `T` to declare three items: the return type of the function, the data type of a single function parameter named `value`, and one variable declared within the function. Program 6.4 illustrates how this function template could be used within the context of a complete program.

Program 6.4

```
#include <iostream>
using namespace std;

template <class T> // template prefix
T abs(T value)    // header line
{
  T absnum;  // variable declaration

  if (value < 0)
    absnum = -value;
  else
    absnum = value;

  return absnum;
}
int main()
{
  int num1 = -4;
  float num2 = -4.23f;
  double num3 = -4.23456;

  cout << "The absolute value of " << num1
       << " is " << abs(num1) << endl;
  cout << "The absolute value of " << num2
       << " is " << abs(num2) << endl;
  cout << "The absolute value of " << num3
       << " is " << abs(num3) << endl;

  return 0;
}
```

In the first call to `abs()` made within `main()`, an integer value is passed as an argument. In this case, the compiler substitutes an `int` data type for the `T` data type in the function template and creates the following function:

```
int abs(int value) // header line
{
  int absnum;  // variable declaration

  if (value < 0)
    absnum = -value;
```

```
    else
      absnum = value;

    return absnum;
  }
```

Similarly, in the second and third function calls, the compiler creates two more functions, one in which the data type `T` is replaced by the keyword `float`, and one in which the data type `T` is replaced by the keyword `double`. The output produced by Program 6.4 is:

```
The absolute value of -4 is 4
The absolute value of -4.23 is 4.23
The absolute value of -4.23456 is 4.23456
```

The value of using the function template is that one function definition has been used to create three different functions, each of which uses the same logic and operations but operates on different data types.

Finally, although both Programs 6.3 and 6.4 define a function template that uses a single placeholder data type, function templates with more than one data type can be defined. For example, the template prefix

```
template <class DTYPE1, class DTYPE2, class DTYPE3>
```

can be used to create a function template that requires three different data types. As before, within the header and body of the function template the data types `DTYPE1`, `DTYPE2`, and `DTYPE3` would be used in the same manner as any built-in data type, such as an `int`, `float`, `double`, etc. Additionally, as noted previously, the names `DTYPE1`, `DTYPE2`, and `DTYPE3` can be any non-keyword identifier. Conventionally, the letter `T` followed by zero or more digits would be used, such as `T`, `T1`, `T2`, `T3`, etc.

Exercises 6.1

1. For the following function headers, determine the number, type, and order (sequence) of the values that must be passed to the function:
   a. `void factorial(int n)`
   b. `void volts(int res, double induct, double cap)`
   c. `void power(int type, double induct, double cap)`
   d. `void flag(char type, double current, double time)`
   e. `void total(double amount, double rate)`
   f. `void roi(int a, int b, char c, char d, double e, double f)`
   g. `void getVal(int item, int iter, char decflag, char delim)`

2. a. Write a function named `check()` that has three parameters. The first parameter should accept an integer number, the second parameter a double-precision number, and the third parameter a double-precision number. The body of the function should just display the values of the data passed to the function when it is called. (*NOTE*: When tracing errors in functions, it is very helpful to have the function display the values it has been passed. Quite frequently, the error is not in what the body of the function does with the data, but in the data received and stored.)

b. Include the function written in Exercise 2a in a working program. Make sure your function is called from `main()`. Test the function by passing various data to it.

3. a. Write a function named `findAbs()` that accepts a double-precision number passed to it, computes its absolute value, and displays the absolute value. The absolute value of a number is the number itself if the number is positive and the negative of the number if the number is negative.
b. Include the function written in Exercise 3a in a working program. Make sure your function is called from `main()`. Test the function by passing various data to it.

4. a. Write a function called `mult()` that accepts two floating-point numbers as parameters, multiplies these two numbers, and displays the result.
b. Include the function written in Exercise 4a in a working program. Make sure your function is called from `main()`. Test the function by passing various data to it.

5. a. Write a function named `sqrIt()` that computes the square of the value passed to it and displays the result. The function should be capable of squaring numbers with decimal points.
b. Include the function written in Exercise 5a in a working program. Make sure your function is called from `main()`. Test the function by passing various data to it.

6. a. Write a function named `powfun()` that raises an integer number passed to it to a positive integer power and displays the result. The positive integer should be the second value passed to the function. Declare the variable used to store the result as a long-integer data type to ensure sufficient storage for the result.
b. Include the function written in Exercise 6a in a working program. Make sure your function is called from `main()`. Test the function by passing various data to it.

7. a. Write a C++ program that returns the fractional part of any user entered number. For example, if the number 256.879 is entered, the number 0.879 should be displayed. (*Hint:* Use an `int` cast.)
b. Enter, compile, and execute the program written for Exercise 7a.

8. a. Write a C++ program that accepts an integer argument and determines whether the passed integer is even or odd. (*Hint:* Use the `%` operator.)
b. Enter, compile, and execute the program written for Exercise 8a.

9. a. Write a function that produces a table of the numbers from 1 to 10, their squares, and their cubes. The function should produce the same display as that produced by Program 5.11.
b. Include the function written in Exercise 9a in a working program. Make sure your function is called from `main()`. Test the function by passing various data to it.

10. a. Modify the function written for Exercise 9 to accept the starting value of the table, the number of values to be displayed, and the increment between values. If the increment is not explicitly sent, the function should use a default value of 1. Name your function `selTab()`. A call to `selTab(6,5,2);` should produce a table of five lines, the first line starting with the number 6 and each succeeding number increasing by 2.

b. Include the function written in Exercise 10a in a working program. Make sure your function is called from `main()`. Test the function by passing various data to it.

11. A useful function that uses no parameters can be constructed to return a value for π that is accurate to the maximum number of decimal places allowed by your computer. This value is obtained by taking the arcsine of 1.0, which is $\pi/2$, and multiplying the result by 2. In C++, the required expression is 2.0 * asin(1.0), where the `asin()` function is provided in the standard C++ mathematics library (remember to include `cmath`). Using this expression, write a C++ function named `pi()` that calculates and displays the value of π.

12. a. Write a function template named `display()` that displays the value of the single argument that is passed to it when the function is called.

b. Include the function template created in Exercise 12a within a complete C++ program that calls the function three times: once with a character argument, once with an integer argument, and once with a double-precision argument.

13. a. Write a function template named `whole()` that returns the integer value of any argument that is passed to it when the function is called.

b. Include the function template created in Exercise 13a within a complete C++ program that calls the function three times: once with a character argument, once with an integer argument, and once with a double-precision argument.

14. a. Write a function template named `maximum()` that returns the maximum value of three arguments that are passed to the function when it is called. Assume that all three arguments will be of the same data type.

b. Include the function template created for Exercise 14a within a complete C++ program that calls the function with three integers and then with three double-precision numbers.

15. a. Write a function template named `square()` that computes and returns the square of the single argument passed to the function when it is called.

b. Include the function template created for Exercise 15a within a complete C++ program.

6.2 Returning a Single Value

Using the method of passing data into a function presented in the previous section, the called function only receives copies of the values contained in the arguments at the time of the call (review Figure 6.3 if this is unclear to you). When a value is passed to a called function in this manner, the passed argument is referred to as **passed by value** and is a distinct advantage of C++.[8] Since the called function does not have direct access to the variables used as arguments by the calling function, it cannot inadvertently alter the value stored in one of these variables.

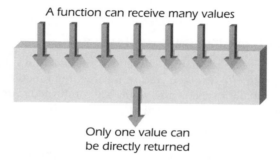

The function receiving the passed by value arguments may process the values sent to it in any fashion desired and directly return at most one, and only one, "legitimate" value to the calling function (see Figure 6.7). In this section we see how such a value is returned to the calling function. As you might expect, given C++'s flexibility, there is a way of returning more than a single value, but that is the topic of the next section.

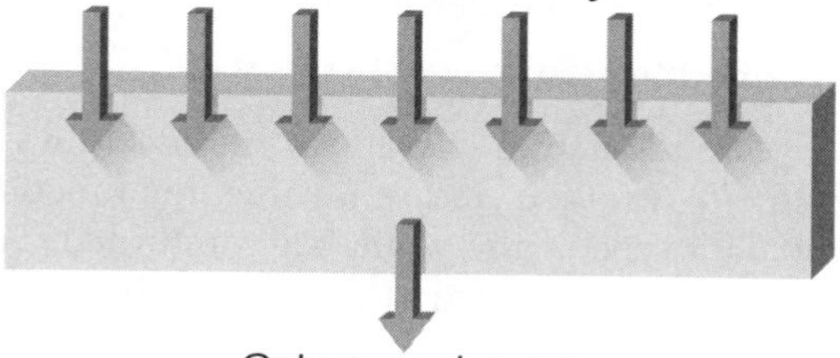
A function can receive many values
Only one value can
be directly returned

Figure 6.7 A function directly returns at most one value.

As with the calling of a function, directly returning a value requires that the interface between the called and calling functions be handled correctly. From its side of the return transaction, the called function must provide the following items:

- the data type of the returned value
- the actual value being returned

A function returning a value must specify, in its header line, the data type of the value that will be returned. Recall that the function header line is the first line of the function, which includes both the function's name and a list of parameter names. As an example, consider the `findMax()` function written in the last section. It determined the maximum

[8]This is also referred to as a **call by value**. The term, however, does not refer to the function call as a whole, but to how an individual argument is passed when the call to a function is made.

value of two numbers passed to the function. For convenience, the `findMax()` code is listed again:

```
void findMax(int x, int y)
{                           // start of function body
  int maxnum;               // variable declaration

  if (x >= y)               // find the maximum number
    maxnum = x;
  else
    maxnum = y;

  cout << "\nThe maximum of the two numbers is "
       << maxnum << endl;

}  // end of function body and end of function
```

As written, the function's header line is

```
void findMax(int x,  int y)
```

where `x` and `y` are the names chosen for the function's parameters.

If `findMax()` is now to return a value, the function's header line must be amended to include the data type of the value being returned. For example, if an integer value is to be returned, the proper function header line is

```
int findMax(int x, int y)
```

Similarly, if the function is to receive two single-precision parameters and return a single-precision value the correct function header line is

```
float findMax(float x, float y)
```

and if the function is to receive two double-precision parameters and return a double-precision value the header line would be[9]

```
double findMax(double x, double y)
```

Let us now modify the function `findMax()` to return the maximum value of the two numbers passed to it. To do this, we must first determine the data type of the value that is to be returned and include this data type in the function's header line.

Since the maximum value determined by `findMax()` is stored in the integer variable `maxnum`, it is the value of this variable that the function should return. Returning an integer value from `findMax()` requires that the function declaration be

```
int findMax(int x, int y)
```

Observe that this is the same as the original function header line for `findMax()` with the substitution of the keyword `int` for the keyword `void`.

[9]The return data type is only related to the parameter data types in as much as the returned value is computed from parameter values. In this case, since the function is used to return the maximum value of its parameters, it would make little sense to return a data type that did not match the function's parameter types.

Having declared the data type that `findMax()` will return, all that remains is to include a statement within the function to cause the return of the correct value. To return a value, a function must use a **return statement**, which has the form:[10]

return expression;

When the return statement is encountered, the expression is evaluated first. The value of the expression is then automatically converted to the data type declared in the function header before being sent back to the calling function. After the value is returned, program control reverts to the calling function. Thus, to return the value stored in `maxnum`, all we need to do is add the statement `return maxnum;` before the closing brace of the `findMax()` function. The complete function code is:

These should be the same data type

```
int findMax(int x, int y)  // function header line
{                          // start of function body
  int maxnum;              // variable declaration

   if (x >= y)
     maxnum = x;
   else
     maxnum = y;

   return maxnum;          // return statement
}
```

In this new code for the function `findMax()`, note that the data type of the expression contained in the return statement correctly matches the data type in the function's header line. It is up to the programmer to ensure that this is so for every function returning a value. Failure to exactly match the return value with the function's declared data type may not result in an error when your program is compiled, but it may lead to undesired results because the return value is always converted to the data type declared in the function declaration. Usually this is a problem only when the fractional part of a returned floating-point or double-precision number is truncated because the function was declared to return an integer value.

Having taken care of the sending side of the return transaction, we must now prepare the calling function to receive the value sent by the called function. On the calling (receiving) side, the calling function must

- be alerted to the type of value to expect
- properly use the returned value

[10]Many programmers place the expression within parentheses, yielding the statement `return (expression);`. Although either form can be used, for consistency only one should be adopted.

Alerting the calling function as to the type of return value to expect is properly taken care of by the function prototype. For example, including the function prototype

```
int findMax(int, int);
```

before the `main()` function is sufficient to alert `main()` that `findMax()` is a function that will return an integer value.

To actually use a returned value we must either provide a variable to store the value or use the value directly in an expression. Storing the returned value in a variable is accomplished using a standard assignment statement. For example, the assignment statement

```
max = findMax(firstnum, secnum);
```

can be used to store the value returned by `findMax()` in the variable named `max`. This assignment statement does two things. First, the right-hand side of the assignment statement calls `findMax()`, then the result returned by `findMax()` is stored in the variable `max`. Since the value returned by `findMax()` is an integer, the variable `max` should also be declared as an integer variable within the calling function's variable declarations.

The value returned by a function need not be stored directly in a variable, but can be used wherever an expression is valid. For example, the expression `2 * findMax(firstnum, secnum)` multiplies the value returned by `findMax()` by two, and the statement

```
cout << findMax(firstnum, secnum);
```

displays the returned value.

Program 6.5 illustrates the inclusion of both prototype and assignment statements for `main()` to correctly declare, call, and store a returned value from `findMax()`. As before, and in keeping with our convention of placing the `main()` function first, we have placed the `findMax()` function after `main()`.

In reviewing Program 6.5 it is important to note the four items we have introduced in this section. The first item is the prototype for `findMax()`. This statement, which ends with a semicolon, as all declaration statements do, alerts `main()` and any subsequent functions that use `findMax()` to the data type that `findMax()` will be returning. The second item to notice in `main()` is the use of an assignment statement to store the returned value from the `findMax()` call into the variable `maxnum`. We have also made sure to correctly declare `maxnum` as an integer within `main()`'s variable declarations so that it matches the data type of the returned value.

The last two items of note concern the coding of the `findMax()` function. The first line of `findMax()` declares that the function will return an integer value, and the expression in the return statement evaluates to a matching data type. Thus `findMax()` is internally consistent in sending an integer value back to `main()`, and `main()` has been correctly alerted to receive and use the returned integer.

In writing your own functions you must always keep these four items in mind. For another example, see if you can identify these four items in Program 6.6.

Program 6.5

```
#include <iostream>
using namespace std;

int findMax(int, int);  // the function prototype

int main()
{
  int firstnum, secnum, max;


  cout << "\nEnter a number: ";
  cin  >> firstnum;
  cout << "Great! Please enter a second number: ";
  cin  >> secnum;

  max = findMax(firstnum, secnum); // the function is called here

  cout << "\nThe maximum of the two numbers is " << max << endl;

  return 0;
}

int findMax(int x, int y)
{                       // start of function body
  int maxnum;           // variable declaration

  if (x >= y)           // find the maximum number
    maxnum = x;
  else
    maxnum = y;

  return maxnum;        // return statement
}
```

Program 6.6

```
#include <iostream>
using namespace std;

double tempvert(double);  // function prototype

int main()
{
  const CONVERTS = 4;  // number of conversions to be made
  int count;
  double fahren;

  for(count = 1; count <= CONVERTS; count++)
  {
    cout << "\nEnter a Fahrenheit temperature: ";
    cin  >> fahren;
    cout << "The Celsius equivalent is "
         << tempvert(fahren) << endl;
  }

  return 0;
}

// convert fahrenheit to celsius
double tempvert(double inTemp)
{
  return (5.0/9.0) * (inTemp - 32.0);
}
```

In reviewing Program 6.6, let us first analyze the `tempvert()` function. The complete definition of the function begins with the function's header line and ends with the closing brace after the return statement. The function is declared as a `double`; this means the expression in the function's return statement must evaluate to a double-precision number, which it does. Since a function header line is not a statement but the start of the code defining the function, the function header line does not end with a semicolon.

On the receiving side, `main()` has a prototype for the function `tempvert()` that agrees with `tempvert()`'s function definition. No variable is declared in `main()` to store the returned value from `tempvert()` because the returned value is immediately passed to `cout` for display.

One further point is worth mentioning here. One of the purposes of declarations, as we learned in Chapter 2, is to alert the computer to the amount of internal storage reserved for the data. The prototype for `tempvert()` performs this task and alerts the compiler to the type of storage needed for the returned value. Since we have chosen always to list `main()` as the first function in a file, we must include function prototypes for all functions called by `main()`and any subsequent functions.

`inline` Functions[11]

Calling a function places a certain amount of overhead on a computer. This consists of placing argument values in a reserved memory region that the function has access to (this memory region is referred to as the **stack**), passing control to the function, providing a reserved memory location for any returned value (again, the stack region of memory is used for this purpose), and finally returning to the proper point in the calling program. Paying this overhead is well justified when a function is called many times, because it can significantly reduce the size of a program. Rather than repeating the same code each time it is needed, the code is written once, as a function, and called whenever it is needed.

For small functions that are not called many times, however, paying the overhead for passing and returning values may not be warranted. It still would be convenient, though, to group repeating lines of code together under a common function name and have the compiler place this code directly into the program wherever the function is called. This capability is provided by `inline` functions.

Telling the C+ compiler that a function is `inline` causes a copy of the function code to be placed in the program at the point the function is called. For example, consider the function `tempvert()` defined in Program 6.6. Since this is a relatively short function, it is an ideal candidate to be an `inline` function. To make this, or any other function, an `inline` one, simply requires placing the reserved word `inline` before the function name and defining the function before any calls are made to it. This is done for the `tempvert()` function in Program 6.7.

[11]This section is optional and may be omitted on first reading without loss of subject continuity.

Program 6.7

```
#include <iostream>
using namespace std;

inline double tempvert(double inTemp)  // an inline function
{
  return (5.0/9.0) * (inTemp - 32.0);
}

int main()
{
  const CONVERTS = 4;   // number of conversions to be made
  int count;
  double fahren;

  for(count = 1; count <= CONVERTS; count++)
  {
    cout << "\nEnter a Fahrenheit temperature: ";
    cin  >> fahren;
    cout << "The Celsius equivalent is "
         << tempvert(fahren) << endl;
  }

  return 0;
}
```

Observe in Program 6.7 that the `inline` function is placed ahead of any calls to it. This is a requirement of all `inline` functions and obviates the need for a function prototype before any subsequent calling function. Since the function is now an `inline` one, its code will be expanded directly into the program wherever it is called.

The advantage of using an `inline` function is an increase in execution speed. Since the `inline` function is directly expanded and included in every expression or statement calling it, there is no execution time loss due to the call and return overhead required by a non-`inline` function. The disadvantage is the increase in program size when an `inline` function is called repeatedly. Each time an `inline` function is referenced, the complete function code is reproduced and stored as an integral part of the program. A non-`inline` function, however, is stored in memory only once. No matter how many times the function is called, the same code is used. Therefore, `inline` functions should only be used for small functions that are not extensively called in a program.

Exercises 6.2

1. Rewrite Program 6.5 so that the function `findMax()` accepts two double-precision arguments and returns a double-precision value to `main()`. Make sure to modify `main()` in order to pass two floating-point values to `findMax()` and accept and store the double-precision value returned by `findMax()`.

2. For the following function headers, determine the number, type, and order (sequence) of values that should be passed to the function when it is called and the data type of the value returned by the function.
   a. `int factorial(int n)`
   b. `double volts(int res, double induct, double cap)`
   c. `double power(int type, double induct, double cap)`
   d. `char flag(char type, float current, float time)`
   e. `int total(float amount, float rate)`
   f. `float roi(int a, int b, char c, char d, float e, float f)`
   g. `void getVal(int item, int iter, char decflag, char delim)`

3. Write function headers for the following:
   a. a function named `check` that has three parameters. The first parameter should accept an integer number, the second parameter a double-precision number, and the third parameter a double-precision number. The function returns no value.
   b. a function named `findAbs()` that accepts a double-precision number passed to it and returns its absolute value.
   c. a function named `mult` that accepts two floating-point numbers as parameters, multiplies these two numbers, and returns the result.
   d. a function named `sqrIt()` that computes and returns the square of the integer value passed to it.
   e. a function named `powfun()` that raises an integer number passed to it to a positive integer (as an argument) power and returns the result as an integer.
   f. a function that produces a table of the numbers from 1 to 10, their squares, and their cubes. No arguments are to be passed to the function and the function returns no value.

4. a. Write a function named `rightTriangle()` that accepts the lengths of two sides of a right triangle as the arguments a and b, respectively. The subroutine should determine and return the hypotenuse, c, of the triangle. (*Hint:* Use Pythagoras' theorem, $c^2 = a^2 + b^2$).
   b. Include the function written for Exercise 4a in a working program. The `main()` function unit should correctly call `rightTriangle()` and display the value returned by the function.

5. a. Write a C++ function named `findAbs()` that accepts a double-precision number passed to it, computes its absolute value, and returns the absolute value to the calling function. The absolute value of a number is the number itself if the number is positive and the negative of the number if the number is negative.
   b. Include the function written in Exercise 5a in a working program. Make sure your function is called from `main()` and correctly returns a value to `main()`. Have `main()` use a `cout` statement to display the value returned. Test the function by passing various data to it.

6. a. The volume, v, of a cylinder is given by the formula

   $$v = \pi r^2 l$$

   where r is the cylinder's radius and l is its length. Using this formula, write a C++ function named `cylvol()` that accepts the radius and length of a cylinder and returns its volume.
   b. Include the function written in Exercise 6a in a working program. Make sure your function is called from `main()` and correctly returns a value to `main()`. Have `main()` use a `cout` statement to display the value returned. Test the function by passing various data to it.

7. a. The surface area, s, of a cylinder is given by the formula

   $$s = 2\pi rl$$

   where r is the cylinder's radius and l is its length. Using this formula write a C++ function named `surfarea()` that accepts the radius and length of a cylinder and returns its surface.
   b. Include the function written in Exercise 7a in a working program. Make sure your function is called from `main()` and correctly returns a value to `main()`. Have `main()` use a `cout` statement to display the value returned. Test the function by passing various data to it.

8. A second-degree polynomial in x is given by the expression $ax^2 + bx + c$, where a, b, and c are known numbers and a is not equal to zero. Write a C++ function named *polyTwo(a, b, c, x)* that computes and returns the value of a second-degree polynomial for any passed values of a, b, c, and x.

9. a. The maximum allowable deflection of a beam depends on its function. For a floor, the typical maximum allowable deflection, in inches, is $D_{max} = L / 240$, while for a roof beam $D_{max} = L / 180$, where L is the length of the beam in inches. Using these formulas, write and test a function named `maxDeflect()` that accepts the length of a beam, in feet, and the type of beam (floor or roof) as a character code, and returns the maximum allowable deflection.
   b. Include the function written in Exercise 9a in a working program. Make sure your function is called from `main()` and correctly returns a value to `main()`. Have `main()` use a `cout` statement to display the value returned. Test the function by passing various data to it.

10. a. The load, P_{cr}, in units of kips, applied to a column that will cause the column to buckle is referred to as the critical buckling load. This load can be determined using the equation

$$P_{cr} = \pi^2 E A / (L / r)^2$$

where E is the modulus of elasticity of the material used in the column, A is the cross-sectional area, L is the length of the column, and r is its radius of gyration. Using this formula, write a C++ function named `cLoad()` that accepts values of E, A, L, and r, and returns the critical load.

b. Include the function written in Exercise 10a in a working program. Make sure your function is called from `main()` and correctly returns a value to `main()`. Have `main()` use a `cout` statement to display the value returned. Test the function by passing various data to it.

11. a. An extremely useful programming algorithm for rounding a real number to n decimal places is

Step 1: Multiply the number by 10^n
Step 2: Add 0.5
Step 3: Delete the fractional part of the result
Step 4: Divide by 10^n

For example, using this algorithm to round the number 78.374625 to three decimal places yields:

Step 1: $78.374625 \times 10^3 = 78374.625$
Step 2: $78374.625 + 0.5 = 78375.125$
Step 3: Retaining the integer part = 78375
Step 4: 78375 divided by $10^3 = 78.375$

Using this algorithm, write a C++ function that accepts a user-entered value and returns the result rounded to two decimal places.

b. Enter, compile, and execute the program written for Exercise 11a.

12. a. Write a C++ function named `whole()` that returns the integer part of any number passed to the function. (*Hint:* Assign the passed argument to an integer variable.)

b. Include the function written in Exercise 12a in a working program. Make sure your function is called from `main()` and correctly returns a value to `main()`. Have `main()` use a `cout` statement to display the value returned. Test the function by passing various data to it.

13. a. Write a C++ function named `fracpart()` that returns the fractional part of any number passed to the function. For example, if the number 256.879 is passed to `fracpart()`, the number 0.879 should be returned. Have the function `fracpart()` call the function `whole()` that you wrote in Exercise 12. The number returned can then be determined as the number passed to `fracpart()`

less the returned value when the same argument is passed to `whole()`. The completed program should consist of `main()` followed by `fracpart()` followed by `whole()`.

b. Include the function written in Exercise 13a in a working program. Make sure your function is called from `main()` and correctly returns a value to `main()`. Have `main()` use a `cout` statement to display the value returned. Test the function by passing various data to it.

14. All years that are evenly divisible by 400 or are evenly divisible by four and not evenly divisible by 100 are leap years. For example, since 1600 is evenly divisible by 400, the year 1600 was a leap year. Similarly, since 1988 is evenly divisible by four but not by 100, the year 1988 was also a leap year. Using this information, write a C++ function that accepts the year as a user input and returns a one if the passed year is a leap year or a zero if it is not.

6.3 RETURNING MULTIPLE VALUES

In a typical function invocation, the called function receives values from its calling function, stores and manipulates the passed values, and directly returns at most one single value. When data is passed in this manner it is referred to as a **pass by value**.

Calling a function and passing arguments by value is a distinct advantage of C++. It allows functions to be written as independent entities that can use any variable or parameter name without concern that other functions may also be using the same name. It also alleviates any concern that altering a parameter or variable in one function may inadvertently alter the value of a variable in another function. Under this approach, parameters can be considered as either initialized variables or variables that will be assigned values when the function is executed. At no time, however, does the called function have direct access to any variable defined in the calling function, even if the variable is used as an argument in the function call.

There are times, however, when it is necessary to alter this approach by giving a called function direct access to the variables of its calling function. This allows one function, which is the called function, to use and change the value of variables that have been defined in the calling function. To do this requires that the address of the variable be passed to the called function. Once the called function has the variable's address, it "knows where the variable lives," so to speak, and can access and change the value stored there directly.

Passing addresses is referred to as a function **pass by reference**,[12] since the called function can reference, or access, the variable whose address has been passed. C++ provides two types of address parameters, references and pointers. In this section we describe the method that uses reference parameters.

[12] It is also referred to as a **call by reference**, where again, the term applies only to the arguments whose address has been passed.

Passing and Using Reference Parameters

As always, in exchanging data between two functions we must be concerned with both the sending and receiving sides of the data exchange. From the sending side, however, calling a function and passing an address as an argument that will be accepted as a reference parameter is exactly the same as calling a function and passing a value; the called function is summoned into action by giving its name and a list of arguments. For example, the statement `newval(firstnum, secnum);` both calls the function named `newval` and passes two arguments to it. Whether a value or an address is actually passed depends on the parameter types declared for `newval()`. Let us now write the `newval` function and prototype so that it receives the addresses of the variables `firstnum` and `secnum`, which we will assume to be double-precision variables, rather than their values.

One of the first requirements in writing `newval()` is to declare two reference parameters for accepting passed addresses. In C++ a reference parameter is declared using the syntax

dataType& referenceName

For example, the reference declaration

```
double& num1;
```

declares that `num1` is a reference parameter that will be used to store the address of a `double`. Similarly, `int& secnum` declares that `secnum` is a reference to an integer and `char& key` declares that `key` is a reference to a character.

Recall from Section 2.4 that the ampersand, &, symbol in C++ means "the address of." Additionally, when an & symbol is used within a declaration it refers to "the address of" the preceding data type. Using this information, declarations such as `double& num1` and `int& secnum` are sometimes more clearly understood if they are read backward. Reading the declaration `double& num1` in this manner yields the information that "num1 is the address of a double-precision value."

Since we need to accept two addresses in the parameter list for `newval()`, the declarations `double& num1, double& num2` can be used. Including these declarations within the parameter list for `newval()`, and assuming that the function returns no value (`void`), the function header for `newval()` becomes:

```
void newval(double& num1, double& num2)
```

For this function header line, an appropriate function prototype is

```
void newval(double&, double&);
```

This prototype and header line are included in Program 6.8, which includes a completed `newval()` function body that both displays and directly alters the values stored in these reference variables from within the called function.

Program 6.8

```
#include <iostream>
using namespace std;

void newval(double&, double&);  // prototype with two references parameters

int main()
{
  double firstnum, secnum;

  cout << "Enter two numbers: ";
  cin  >> firstnum >> secnum;
  cout << "\nThe value in firstnum is: " << firstnum << endl;
  cout << "The value in secnum is: " << secnum << "\n\n";

  newval(firstnum, secnum);   // call the function

  cout << "The value in firstnum is now: " << firstnum << endl;
  cout << "The value in secnum is now: " << secnum << endl;

  return 0;
}

void newval(double& xnum, double& ynum)
{
  cout << "The value in xnum is: " << xnum << endl;
  cout << "The value in ynum is: " << ynum << "\n\n";
  xnum = 89.5;
  ynum = 99.5;

  return;
}
```

In calling the `newval()` function within Program 6.8, it is important to understand the connection between the arguments, `firstnum` and `secnum`, used in the function call and the parameters, `xnum` and `ynum`, used in the function header. *Both refer to the same data items.* The significance of this is that the values in the arguments (`firstnum` and `secnum`) can now be altered from within `newval()` by using the parameter names (`xnum` and `ynum`). Thus, the parameter `xnum` and `ynum` do not store copies of the values in `firstnum` and `secnum`, but directly access the locations in memory set aside for these two arguments. The equivalence of argument names in Program 6.8, which is the essence of a pass by reference, is illustrated in Figure 6.8. As illustrated in this figure, the argument names and their matching parameter names are simply different names referring to the same memory storage areas. In `main()` these memory locations are referenced by the names `firstnum` and secnum, respectively, while in newval() the same locations are referenced by the parameter names xnum and ynum, respectively.

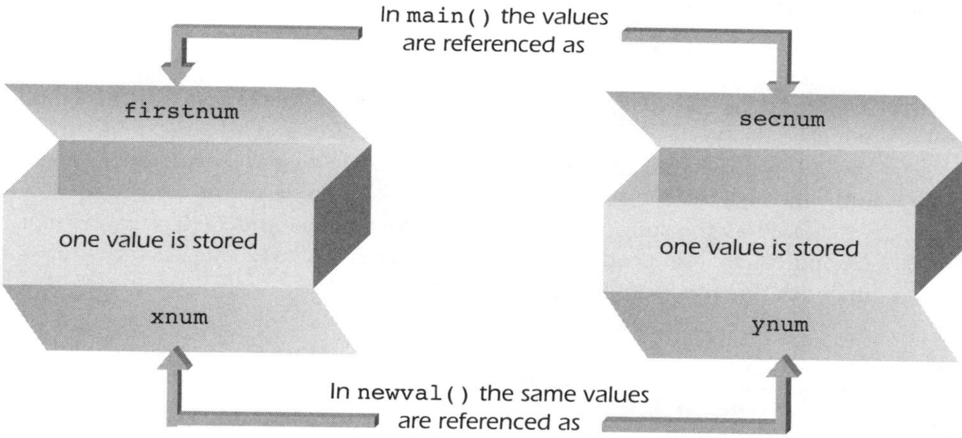

Figure 6.8 *The equivalence of arguments and parameters in Program 6.8.*

The following sample run was obtained using Program 6.8:

```
Enter two numbers: 22.5 33.0

The value in firstnum is: 22.5
The value in secnum is:   33

The value in xnum is: 22.5
The value in ynum is: 33

The value in firstnum is now: 89.5
The value in secnum is now: 99.5
```

In reviewing this output, notice that the values initially displayed for the parameters xnum and ynum are the same as those displayed for the arguments firstnum and secnum. Since xnum and ynum are reference parameters, however, newval() now has direct access to the arguments firstnum and secnum. Thus, any change to xnum within newval() directly alters the value of firstnum in main() and any change to ynum directly changes secnum's value. As illustrated by the final displayed values, the assignment of values to xnum and ynum within newval() is reflected in main() as the altering of firstnum's and secnum's values.

The equivalence between actual calling arguments and function parameters illustrated in Program 6.8 provides the basis for returning multiple values from within a function. For example, assume that a function is required to accept three values, compute these values' sum and product, and return these computed results to the calling routine. By naming the function calc() and providing five parameters (three for the input data and two references for the returned values), the following function can be used.

```
void calc(double num1, double num2, double num3, double& total, double& product)
{
  total = num1 + num2 + num3;
  product = num1 * num2 * num3;
  return;
}
```

This function has five parameters, named num1, num2, num3, total, and product, of which only the last two are declared as references. Thus, the first three arguments are passed by value and the last two arguments are passed by reference. Within the function only the last two parameters are altered. The value of the fourth parameter, total, is calculated as the sum of the first three parameters and the last parameter, product, is computed as the product of the parameters num1, num2, and num3. Program 6.9 includes this function in a complete program.

Program 6.9

```
#include <iostream>
using namespace std;

void calc(double, double, double, double&, double&);  // prototype

int main()
{
  double firstnum, secnum, thirdnum, sum, product;

  cout << "Enter three numbers: ";
  cin  >> firstnum >> secnum >> thirdnum;

  calc(firstnum, secnum, thirdnum, sum, product);  // function call

  cout << "\nThe sum of the numbers is: " << sum << endl;
  cout << "The product of the numbers is: " << product << endl;

  return 0;
}

void calc(double num1, double num2, double num3, double& total, double& product)
{
  total = num1 + num2 + num3;
  product = num1 * num2 * num3;
  return;
}
```

Within main(), the function calc() is called using the five arguments firstnum, secnum, thirdnum, sum, and product. As required, these arguments agree in number and data type with the parameters declared by calc(). Of the five arguments passed, only firstnum, secnum, and thirdnum have been assigned values when the call to calc() is made. The remaining two arguments have not been initialized and will be used to receive values back from calc(). Depending on the compiler used in compiling the program, these arguments will initially contain either zeros or "garbage" values. Figure 6.9 illustrates the relationship between actual and parameter names and the values they contain after the return from calc().

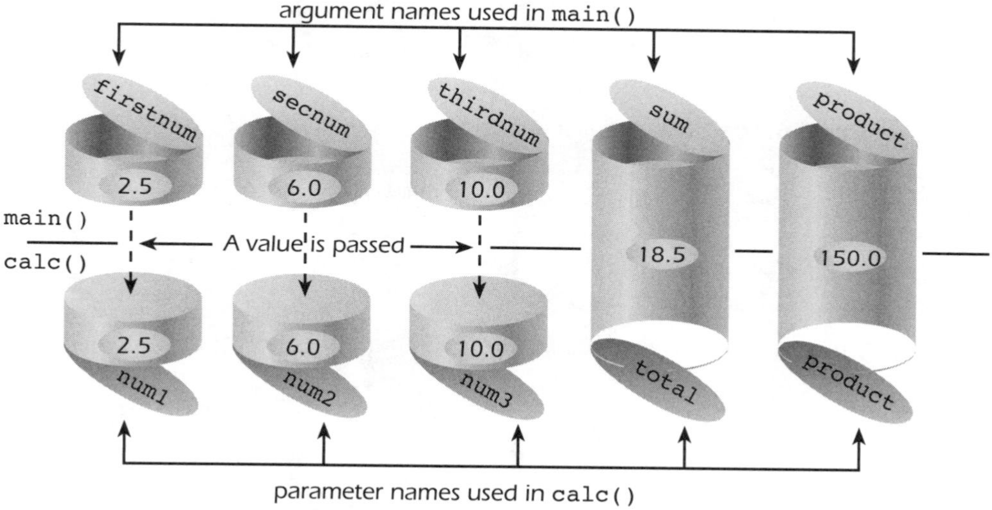

Figure 6.9 Relationship between argument and parameter names.

Once calc() is called, it uses its first three parameters to calculate values for total and product and then returns control to main(). Because of the order of its actual calling arguments, main() knows the values calculated by calc() as sum and product, which are then displayed. Following is a sample run using Program 6.9.

```
Enter three numbers: 2.5 6.0 10.0

The sum of the entered numbers is: 18.5
The product of the entered numbers is: 150
```

As a final example illustrating the usefulness of passing references to a called function, we will construct a function named swap() that exchanges the values of two of main()'s double-precision variables. Such a function is useful when sorting a list of numbers.

Since the value of more than a single variable is affected, swap() cannot be written as a pass by value function that returns a single value. The desired exchange of main()'s variables by swap() can only be obtained by giving swap() access to main()'s variables. One way of doing this is using reference parameters.

We have already seen how to pass references to two variables in Program 6.8. We will now construct a function to exchange the values in the passed reference arguments. Exchanging values in two variables is accomplished using the three-step exchange algorithm:

1. Save the first parameter's value in a temporary location (see Figure 6.10a).
2. Store the second parameter's value in the first variable (see Figure 6.10b).
3. Store the temporary value in the second parameter (see Figure 6.10c).

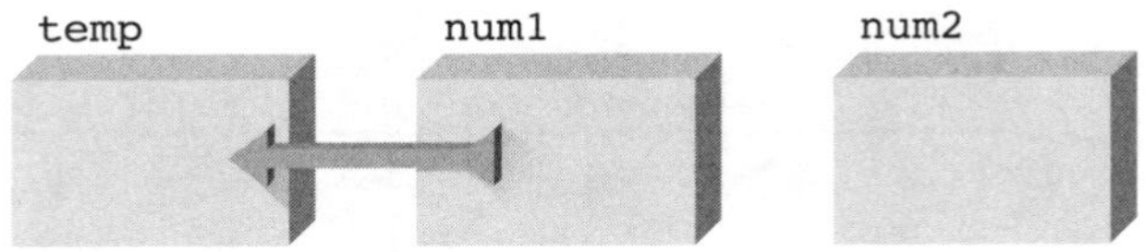

Figure 6.10a Save the first value.

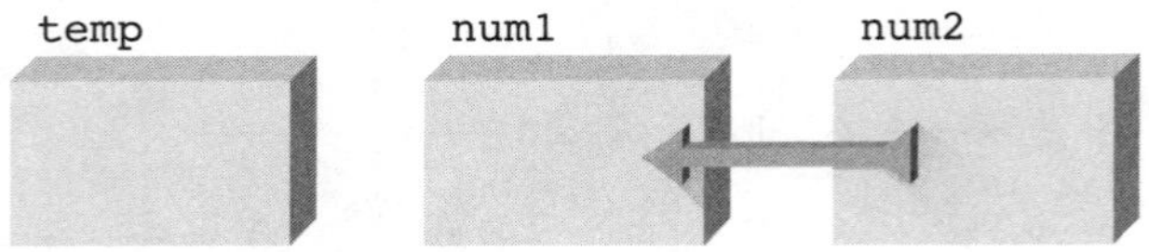

Figure 6.10b Replace the first value with the second value.

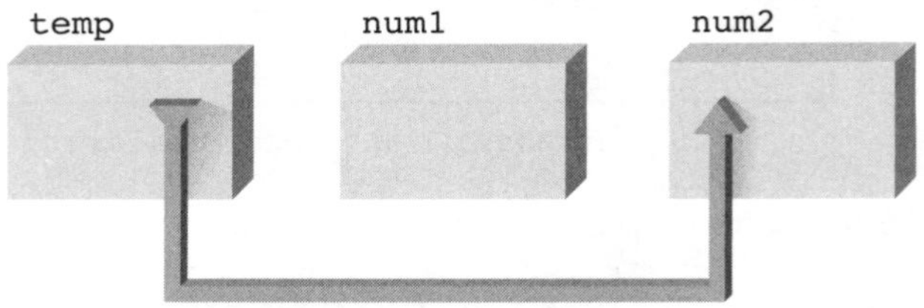

Figure 6.10c Change the second value.

Following is the function `swap()` written according to these specifications:

```
void swap(double& num1, double& num2)
{
  double temp;

  temp = num1;      // save num1's value
  num1 = num2;      // store num2's value in num1
  num2 = temp;      // change num2's value

  return;
}
```

Notice that the use of references in `swap()`'s header line gives `swap()` access to the equivalent arguments in the calling function. Thus, any changes to the two reference parameters in `swap()` automatically changes the values in the calling function's arguments. Program 6.10 contains `swap()` in a complete program.

Program 6.10

```
#include <iostream>
using namespace std;

void swap(double&, double&);   // function receives 2 references

int main()
{
  double firstnum = 20.5, secnum = 6.25;

  cout << "The value stored in firstnum is: " << firstnum << endl;
  cout << "The value stored in secnum is: "<< secnum << "\n\n";

  swap(firstnum, secnum);   // call the function with references

  cout << "The value stored in firstnum is now: "
       << firstnum << endl;
  cout << "The value stored in secnum is now: "
       << secnum << endl;

  return 0;
}

void swap(double& num1, double& num2)
{
  double temp;

  temp = num1;      // save num1's value
  num1 = num2;      // store num2's value in num1
  num2 = temp;      // change num2's value

  return;
}
```

The following sample run was obtained using Program 6.10:

```
The value stored in firstnum is: 20.5
The value stored in secnum is: 6.25

The value stored in firstnum is now: 6.25
The value stored in secnum is now: 20.5
```

As illustrated by this output, the values stored in `main()`'s variables have been modified from within `swap()`, which was made possible by the use of reference parameters. If a pass by value had been used instead, the exchange within `swap()` would only affect `swap()`'s parameters and would accomplish nothing with respect to `main()`'s variables. Thus, a function such as `swap()` can only be written using references or some other means that provides access to `main()`'s variables (this other means is by pointers, the topic of Chapter 12).

In using reference arguments, two cautions need to be mentioned. The first is that reference arguments must be variables (that is, they *cannot* be used to change constants). For example, calling `swap()` with two constants, such as in the call `swap(20.5, 6.5)` passes two constants to the function. Although `swap()` may execute, it will not change the values of these constants.[13]

The second caution to note is that a function call itself gives no indication that the called function will be using reference arguments. The default in C++ is to make passes by value rather than passes by reference, precisely to limit a called function's ability to alter variables in the calling function. This calling procedure should be adhered to whenever possible, which means that reference parameters should only be used in very restricted situations that actually require multiple return values, such as in the `swap()` function illustrated in Program 6.10. The `calc()` function, included in Program 6.9, while useful for illustrative purposes, could also be written as two separate functions, each returning a single value.

Exercises 6.3

1. Write parameter declarations for the following:
   a. a parameter named `amount` that will be a reference to a double-precision value.
   b. a parameter named `price` that will be a reference to a double-precision number.
   c. a parameter named `minutes` that will be a reference to an integer number.
   d. a parameter named `key` that will be a reference to a character.
   e. a parameter named `yield` that will be a reference to a double-precision number.

2. Three integer arguments are to be used in a call to a function named `time()`. Write a suitable function header for `time()`, assuming that `time()` accepts these variables as the reference parameters `sec`, `min`, and `hours`, and returns no value to its calling function.

3. Rewrite the `findMax()` function in Program 6.5 so that the variable `max`, declared in `main()`, is used to store the maximum value of the two passed numbers. The value of `max` should be set directly from within `findMax()`. (*Hint:* A reference to `max` will have to be accepted by `findMax()`.)

4. Write a function named `change()` that has an integer parameter and six integer reference parameters named `hundreds`, `fifties`, `twenties`, `tens`, `fives` and `ones`, respectively. The function is to consider the passed integer value as a dollar amount and convert the value into the fewest number of equivalent bills. Using

[13]Most compilers will catch this error.

the references, the function should directly alter the respective arguments in the calling function.

5. Write a function named `time()` that has an integer parameter named `seconds` and three integer reference parameters named `hours`, `min`, and `sec`. The function is to convert the passed number of seconds into an equivalent number of hours, minutes, and seconds. Using the references the function should directly alter the respective arguments in the calling function.

6. Write a function named `yearCalc()` that has an integer parameter representing the total number of days from the date 1/1/1900 and reference parameters named `year`, `month`, and `day`. The function is to calculate the current year, month, and day for the given number of days passed to it. Using the references, the function should directly alter the respective arguments in the calling function. For this problem assume that each year has 365 days and each month has 30 days.

7. The following program uses the same argument and parameter names in both the calling and called function. Determine if this causes any problem for the computer.

```
#include <iostream>
using namespace std;

void time(int&, int&);  // function prototype

int main()
{
  int min, hour;

  cout << "Enter two numbers :";
  cin  >> min >> hour;
  time(min, hour);

  return 0;
}

void time(int& min, int& hour)   // accept two references
{
  int sec;

  sec = (hour * 60 + min) * 60;
  cout << "The total number of seconds is " << sec << endl;

  return;
}
```

6.4 APPLICATIONS

Preparing a well-designed computer program is very much like preparing a well-designed term paper, in that both should start with an outline. This outline can either be written down or, for very small programs, may simply be kept in mind as the program is being developed. As with a term-paper outline, however, which lists the paper's main topics, a computer program's initial outline must provide a listing of the primary tasks that the program must accomplish.

In written form, a computer program's initial outline is typically either a pseudocode description (see Section 1.3) or a first-level structure diagram (see Section 1.2). This initial outline begins the process of defining a more complicated problem into a set of smaller, more manageable tasks. Each of these tasks can be further subdivided or refined, into even smaller tasks, if required. Once the tasks are well defined, the actual work of coding can begin, starting with any task, in any order. If there are more tasks than can be handled by one programmer, they can be distributed among as many programmers as required. This is equivalent to having many people work on a large research project, with each person responsible for an individual topic. A general outline applicable to many engineering and scientific tasks is the following algorithm:

Get the inputs to the problem
Calculate the desired result
Report the results of the calculation

These three tasks are the primary responsibilities of every program, and we shall refer to this algorithm as the **Problem-Solver Algorithm**. A first-level structure diagram of this algorithm is shown in Figure 6.11.

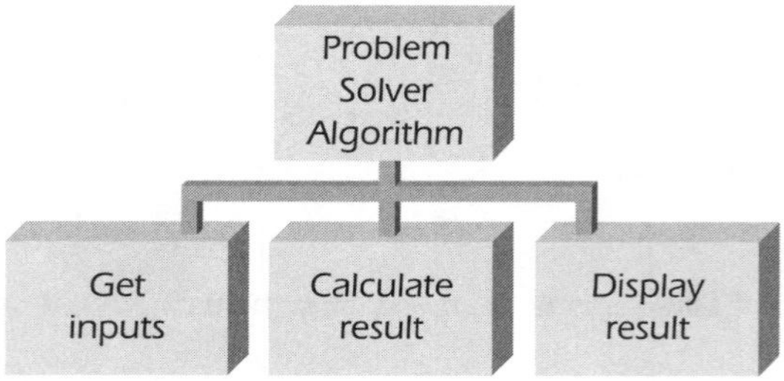

Figure 6.11 *First-level structure diagram of the Problem-Solver Algorithm.*

Each task in the Problem-Solver Algorithm can be worked on independently as a function—a sort of "mini" C++ program that typically is easier to complete than a whole program. Each of these function tasks can be refined and coded in any desired order, although completing the input section first usually makes testing and development easier. We now apply this development procedure to an actual programming problem.

Application 1: Rectangular to Polar Coordinate Conversion

Assume that we must write a C++ program to convert the rectangular (x,y) coordinates of a point into polar form. That is, given an x and y position on a Cartesian coordinate system, as illustrated in Figure 6.12, we must calculate the distance from the origin, r, and the angle from the x axis, θ, specified by the point. The values of r and θ are referred to as the point's *polar coordinates*.

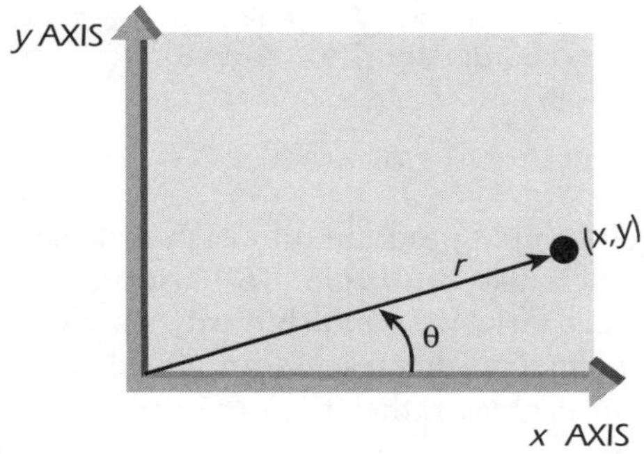

Figure 6.12 Correspondence between polar (distance and angle) and Cartesian (x,y) coordinates.

When the x and y coordinates of a point are known, the equivalent r and θ coordinates can be calculated using the formulas:

$$r = \sqrt{x^2 + y^2}$$

$$\theta = \tan^{-1}(y / x) \quad x \neq 0$$

We begin the development of our program with an outline of what the program is to accomplish. An initial pseudocode description of the desired program can be constructed using our Problem-Solver Algorithm as it pertains to the specifics of this application. For this application the required inputs are an x and y coordinate, the calculation is to convert the input values to their polar coordinate form, and the display is the calculated polar coordinates. Thus the initial pseudocode description is

Get the x and y coordinate values
Calculate the polar (r and θ) coordinate values
Display the polar coordinate values

The equivalent first- or top-level structure diagram for this algorithm is illustrated in Figure 6.13.

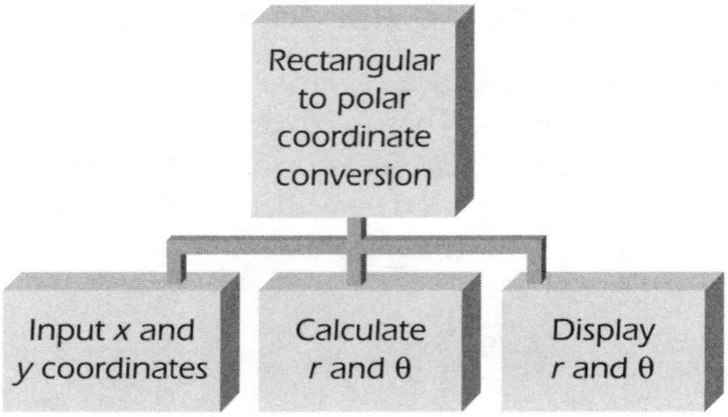

Figure 6.13 *Top-level structure diagram.*

As this is a relatively simple program and each task described by the algorithm is well defined, coding of each task can begin. To illustrate that any task may be coded independently of any other task, we will arbitrarily start coding the function that performs the calculation of polar coordinates. As an added feature, we will have this function return the angle θ in degrees rather than the radian measure returned by the intrinsic `atan()` function. Since this function must receive two inputs, the *x* and *y* coordinates, and return two outputs, the *r* and θ coordinates, we provide the function with four parameters, two for its inputs and two for its outputs. Arbitrarily selecting the parameter names of `x`, `y`, `r`, and `theta`, and naming the function `polar()`, the following code performs the required calculation of polar coordinates.

```
void polar(double x, double y, double& r, double& theta)
{
  const double TODEGREES = 180.0/3.141593;

  r = sqrt(x * x + y * y);
  theta = atan(y/x) * TODEGREES;

  return;
}
```

The `polar()` function is rather straightforward. The function's header line declares that the function will directly return no value and each of its parameters is declared as a floating-point data type. The first two parameters will be used to accept an *x* and *y* value, while the last two parameters, which are reference parameters, will be used to pass the converted distance and angle values back to the calling function. Within the function's body a named constant `TODEGREES` is defined as the factor 180.0 / 3.142593. The next two assignment statements use the two parameters, `x` and `y`, to assign values to the `r` and `theta` parameters. The `TODEGREES` named constant is used to convert the returned radian value from the `atan()` function into degrees. As written, the `polar()` function may be compiled to check for any compile-time errors.

To understand how the return values are passed it is helpful to think of the reference parameters `r` and `theta` as containers (or variables) through which values may be passed in either direction. This situation is shown in Figure 6.14, which is helpful in understanding the fundamental characteristics of reference parameters: *they simply provide the ability for both a called and a calling function to access the same storage area using different names.*

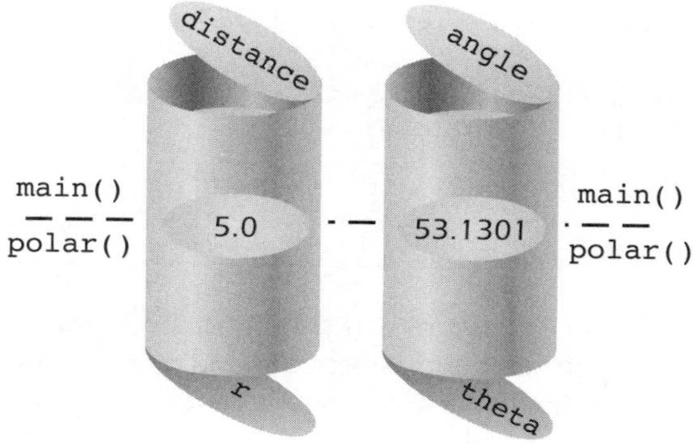

Figure 6.14 Parameter values when `polar()` is called.

As shown in Figure 6.14, the values assigned to `r` and `theta` within `polar()` can be accessed by the calling function using the argument names `distance` and `angle`, or any other programmer selected argument names.

Testing the Function

Once `polar()` is written it can be tested independently of any other function. This is done by writing a dedicated driver function that only calls `polar()`, as is done in Program 6.11.

Program 6.11

```
#include <iostream>
#include <cmath>
using namespace std;

void polar(double, double, double&, double&); // function prototype

int main()
{
  double distance, angle;
  polar(3.0, 4.0, distance, angle);
  cout << "r = " << distance << endl;
  cout << "angle = " << angle << endl;

  return 0;
}
```

(Continued)

(Continued)

```
void polar(double x, double y, double& r, double& theta)
{
  const double TODEGREES = 180.0/3.141593;

  r = sqrt(x * x + y * y);
  theta = atan(y/x) * TODEGREES;

  return;
}
```

Notice that in `main()` we pass the constants 3.0 and 4.0 into `polar()`. The function accepts these inputs as the parameters `x` and `y`, and uses these parameters in calculating values for the parameters `r` and `theta`. Within `main()`, these last two parameters are known as `distance` and `angle`, whose values are displayed immediately after the call to `polar()` is made. The output produced when Program 6.11 is executed is

```
r = 5
angle = 53.1301
```

These are the same results that would be obtained from a hand calculation. As the function performs only two calculations, and the result displayed by our test program agrees with those obtained from a hand calculation, the function has been completely tested by itself. It still remains to be group tested with the remaining two functions required for the complete program to ensure that correct argument values are exchanged between each function.

Completing the Program

The structure diagram for our complete program (Figure 6.13) requires that functions also be written for accepting two rectangular coordinates and displaying the calculated polar coordinates, respectively. The following function, `getrec()`, can be used to accept the input data.

```
void getrec(double& x, double& y)
{
  cout << "Rectangular to  Polar Coordinate"
       << " Conversion Program\n" << endl;
  cout << "Enter the x coordinate: ";
  cin  >> x;
  cout << "Enter the y coordinate: ";
  cin  >> y;

  return;
}
```

In this function the reference parameters `x` and `y` are used to return the values that are entered in response to the two `cin` prompts. As with the `polar()` function, this function may be tested by itself using a small dedicated driver program. The function with its driver program is illustrated in Program 6.12.

Program 6.12

```
#include <iostream>
using namespace std;

void getrec(double&, double&); // function prototype

int main()
{
  double xcoord, ycoord;

  getrec(xcoord, ycoord);
  cout << "The entered value for x is " << xcoord << endl;
  cout << "The entered value for y is " << ycoord << endl;

  return 0;
}


void getrec(double& x, double& y)
{
  cout << "Rectangular to Polar Coordinate"
       << " Conversion Program\n" << endl;
  cout << "Enter the x coordinate: ";
  cin  >> x;
  cout << "Enter the y coordinate: ";
  cin  >> y;

  return;
}
```

Notice that the dedicated driver program, which is also referred to as a "front-end" driver, has been used to both call `getrec()` and display the values returned by this function. The following output produced by Program 6.12 verifies the correct operation of the `getrec()` function:

```
Rectangular to Polar Coordinate Conversion Program

Enter the x coordinate: 3
Enter the y coordinate: 4
```

```
The entered value for x is 3
The entered value for y is 4
```

In a similar manner, the function for displaying polar coordinates is constructed. Program 6.13 contains both the function, which we have named `showit()`, and a front-end driver used for testing the function. Notice that the parameter names used in the header line for `showit()` need not be the same as those used in any other function. `showit()` is constructed to simply display the values in its two parameters, which in this case have been named `radius` and `angle`.

Program 6.13

```
#include <iostream>
using namespace std;

void showit(double, double); // function prototype

int main()
{
  showit(5.0, 53.1301);

  return 0;
}

void showit(double radius, double angle)
{
  cout << "\nThe polar coordinates are: " << endl;
  cout << "  Distance from origin: " << radius << endl;
  cout << "  Angle (in degrees) from x-axis: " << angle << endl;

  return;
}
```

The output of Program 6.13, which follows, verifies that `showit()` correctly displays the values passed to it.

```
The polar coordinates are:
  Distance from origin: 5
  Angle (in degrees) from x-axis: 53.1301
```

It now remains to create one `main()` program that calls each of the developed functions in the correct order. This is done in Program 6.14, which also includes the functions `getrec()`, `polar()`, and `showit()`.

Program 6.14

```
// This program converts rectangular coordinates to polar coordinates
// Functions used: getrec() - obtain the rectangular coordinates
//                : polar() - calculate the polar coordinates
//                : showit() - display the polar coordinates
//
#include <iostream>
#include <cmath>
using namespace std;

void getrec(double&, double&);                    // function prototype
void polar(double, double, double&, double&);     // function prototype
void showit(double, double);                      // function prototype

int main()
{
  double x, y, distance, angle;

  getrec(x, y);
  polar(x, y, distance, angle);
  showit(distance, angle);

  return 0;
}

void getrec(double& x, double& y)
{
  cout << "Rectangular to Polar Coordinate"
       << " Conversion Program\n" << endl;
  cout << "Enter the x coordinate: ";
  cin  >> x;
  cout << "Enter the y coordinate: ";
  cin  >> y;

  return;
}
```

(Continued)

(Continued)

```
void polar(double x, double y, double& r, double& theta)
{
  const double TODEGREES = 180.0/3.141593;

  r = sqrt(x * x + y * y);
  theta = atan(y/x) * TODEGREES;

  return;
}

void showit(double radius, double angle)
{
  cout << "\nThe polar coordinates are: " << endl;
  cout << "  Distance from origin: " << radius << endl;
  cout << "  Angle (in degrees) from x-axis: " << angle << endl;

  return;
}
```

The following output was produced from one run using Program 6.14:

```
Rectangular to Polar Coordinate Conversion Program

Enter the x coordinate: 3
Enter the y coordinate: 4

The polar coordinates are:
  Distance from origin: 5
  Angle (in degrees) from x-axis: 53.1301
```

Before leaving Program 6.14, it should be noted that an alternative to writing driver programs for each subroutine as the subroutine was developed is to write a `main()` program first and add the subroutines later as they are developed. This is accomplished by using stubs for each function (see Section 6.1) and then replacing each stub, one at a time, with the completed function.

Application 2: Simulation

There are many scientific and engineering simulation problems in which probability must be considered or statistical sampling techniques must be used. For example, in simulating automobile traffic flow or telephone usage patterns, statistical models are required. Additionally, applications such as simple computer games and more involved engineering scenarios can only be described statistically. All of these statistical models require the generation of **random numbers**; that is, a series of numbers whose order cannot be predicted.

In practice, there are no truly random numbers. Dice are never perfect; cards are never shuffled completely randomly; the supposedly random motions of molecules are influenced by the environment; and digital computers can handle numbers only within a finite range and with limited precision. The best one can do is generate **pseudorandom** numbers, which are sufficiently random for the task at hand.

Some computer languages contain a library function that produces random numbers; others do not. The functions provided by C++ are named `rand()`, which generates random numbers, and `srand()`, which sets initial random "seed" values. We present these two functions and then use them in an application that simulates the tossing of a coin to determine the number of resulting heads and tails.

Generating Pseudorandom Numbers

Two functions are provided by C++ compilers for creating random numbers: `rand()` and `srand()`. The `rand()` function produces a series of random numbers in the range 0 ≤ `rand()` ≤ `RAND_MAX`, where the constant `RAND_MAX` is defined in the `cmath` header file. The `srand()` function provides a starting "seed" value for `rand()`. If `srand()` or some other equivalent "seeding" technique is not used, `rand()` will always produce the same series of random numbers.

The general procedure for creating a series of *n* random numbers using C++'s library functions is illustrated by the following code:

```
srand(time(NULL));   // this generates the first "seed" value

for (int i = 1; i <= N; i++)   // this generates N random numbers
{
  rvalue = rand();
  cout << rvalue << endl;
}
```

Here, the argument to the `srand()` function is a call to the `time()` function with a `NULL` argument. With this argument the `time()` function reads the computer's internal clock time, in seconds. The `srand()` function then uses this time, converted to an unsigned `int`, to initialize the random number generator function `rand()`.[14] Program 6.15 uses this code to generate a series of 10 random numbers.

---

[14]Alternatively, many C++ compilers have a `randomize()` routine that is defined using the `srand()` function. If this routine is available, the call `randomize()` can be used in place of the call `srand(time(NULL))`. In either case, the initializing "seed" routine is called only once, after which the `rand()` function is used to generate a series of numbers.

Program 6.15

```
#include <iostream>
#include <iomanip>
#include <cmath>
#include <ctime>
using namespace std;

// this program generates ten pseudo-random numbers
// using C++'s rand() function

int main()
{
  const int NUMBERS = 10;

  double randvalue;
  int i;

  srand(time(NULL));
  for (i = 1; i <= NUMBERS; i++)
  {
    randvalue = rand();
    cout << randvalue << endl;
  }

  return 0;
}
```

The following is the output produced by one run of Program 6.15:

```
20203
21400
15265
26935
 8369
10907
31299
15400
 5074
20663
```

Because of the `srand()` function call in Program 6.15, the series of ten random numbers will differ each time the program is executed. Without the randomizing "seeding" effect of this function, the same series of random numbers would be always be produced.

Note also the inclusion of the `cmath` and `ctime` header files. The `cmath` file contains the function prototypes for the `srand()` and `rand()` functions, while the `ctime` header file contains the function prototype for the `time()` function.

Scaling

One modification to the random number produced by the `rand()` function typically must be made in practice. In most applications, either the random numbers are required to be floating-point values within the range 0.0 to 1.0 or to be integers within a specified range, such as 1 to 100. The method for adjusting the random numbers produced by a random number generator to reside within such ranges is called **scaling**.

Scaling random numbers to reside within the range 0.0 to 1.0 is accomplished easily by dividing the returned value of `rand()` by `RAND_MAX`. Thus, the expression `double(rand())/RAND_MAX` produces a double-precision random number between 0.0 and 1.0.

Scaling a random number as an integer value between 0 and *N*–1 is accomplished by using either of the expressions `rand() % N` or `int(double(rand())/RAND_MAX * N)`. For example, the expression `int(double(rand())/RAND_MAX * 100)` produces a random integer between 0 and 99.

To produce an integer random number between 1 and *N* the expression `1 + rand() % N` can be used. For example, in simulating the roll of a die, the expression `1 + rand() % 6` produces a random integer between 1 and 6. The more general scaling expression `a + rand() % (b + 1 - a)` can be used to produce a random integer between the numbers *a* and *b*.

A common use of random numbers is to simulate events using a program, rather than going through the time and expense of constructing a real-life experiment. For example, statistical theory tells us that the probability of having a single tossed coin turn up heads is $\frac{1}{2}$. Similarly, there is a 50% probability of having a single tossed coin turn up tails.

Using these probabilities we would expect a single coin that is tossed 1000 times to turn up heads 500 times and tails 500 times. In practice, however, this is never exactly realized for a single experiment consisting of 1000 tosses. Instead of actually tossing a coin 1000 times we can use a random number generator to simulate these tosses.

Step 1 Analyze the Problem

For this problem two outputs are required: the percentage of heads and the percentage of tails that result when a simulated coin is tossed 1000 times. No input item will be required for the random number generator function.

Step 2 Develop a Solution

The percentage of heads and tails are determined as

$$\text{percentage of heads} = \frac{\text{number of heads}}{1000} \times 100\%$$

$$\text{percentage of tails} = \frac{\text{number of tails}}{1000} \times 100\%$$

To determine the number of heads and tails, we will have to simulate 1000 random numbers in such a manner that we can define a result of "heads" or "tails" from each generated number. There are a number of ways to do this.

One way is to use the `rand()` function to generate integers between 0 and `RAND_MAX`. Knowing that any single toss has a 50% chance of being either a head or a tail, we could designate a "head" as an even random number and a "tail" as an odd random number. Another method would be to scale the return value from `rand()` to reside between 0.0 and 1.0 as described above. Then we could define a "head" as any number greater than 0.5 and any other result as a "tail." This is the algorithm we will adopt.

Having defined how we will create a single toss that has a 50% chance of turning up heads or tails, the generation of 1000 tosses is rather simple: we use a fixed-count loop that generates 1000 random numbers. For each generation we identify the result as either a head or tail and accumulate the results in a heads and tails counter. Thus, the complete simulation algorithm is given by the pseudocode

```
Initialize a heads count to zero
Initialize a tails count to zero
For 1000 times
  generate a random number between 0 and 1
  If the random number is greater than 0.5
    consider this as a head and
    add one to the heads count
  Else
    consider this as a tail and
    add one to the tails count
  Endif
Endfor
Calculate the percentage of heads as the number of heads divided by 1000 × 100%
Calculate the percentage of tails as the number of tails divided by 1000 × 100%
Print the percentage of heads and tails obtained
```

Step 3 Code the Solution

Program 6.16 codes this algorithm in C++.

Program 6.16

```
#include <iostream>
#include <iomanip>
#include <cmath>
#include <ctime>
using namespace std;

// a program to simulate the tossing of a coin NUMTOSSES times
int main()
{
  const int NUMTOSSES = 1000;

  int heads = 0;  // initialize heads count
  int tails = 0;  // initialize tails count
  int i;
  double flip, perheads, pertails;

    // simulate NUMTOSSES tosses of a coin
  srand(time(NULL));
  for (i = 1; i <= NUMTOSSES; i++)
  {
    flip = double(rand())/RAND_MAX;   // scale the number between 0 and 1
    if (flip > 0.5)
      heads = heads + 1;
    else
      tails = tails + 1;
  }
  perheads = (heads / double (NUMTOSSES)) * 100.0;  // calculate heads percentage
  pertails = (tails / double (NUMTOSSES)) * 100.0;  // calculate tails percentage
  cout << "\nHeads came up " << perheads << " percent of the time";
  cout << "\nTails came up " << pertails << " percent of the time" << endl;

  return 0;
}
```

Following are two sample runs using Program 6.16.

```
Heads came up 50.9 percent of the time
Tails came up 49.1 percent of the time
```

and

```
Heads came up 49.7 percent of the time
Tails came up 50.3 percent of the time
```

Writing and executing Program 6.16 is certainly easier than manually tossing a coin 1000 times. It should be noted that the validity of the results produced by the program depends on how random the numbers produced by `rand()` actually are.

Step 4 Test and Debug the Program

There are really two tests that Program 6.16 must pass. The more important test concerns the randomness of each generated number. This, of course, is really a test of the random number function. For our purposes, we have used a previously written function supplied by the compiler. So at this point we accept the "randomness" of the generator. (See Exercise 13 for a method of verifying the function's randomness.)

Once the question of the random number generator has been settled, the second test requires that we correctly generate 1000 numbers and accumulate a head and tail count. That this is correctly accomplished is adequately verified by a simple desk check of the `for` loop within Program 6.16. Also, we do know that the result of the simulation must be close to 50% heads and 50% tails. The results of the simulation verify this to be the case.

Exercises 6.4

1. The volume, v, and surface area, s, of a cylinder are given by the formulas $v = \pi r^2 l$ and $s = 2\pi r l$, where r is the cylinder's radius and l is its length. Using these formulas, write and test a function named `cylinder()` that accepts the radius and length of a cylinder and returns its volume and surface area.

2. Write and test a C++ function that calculates the radius, r, and area, a, of a circle when its circumference, c, is given. The relevant formulas are $r = c/(2\pi)$ and $a = \pi r^2$. Test your function using a program having a dedicated driver function.

3. Fluid flowing in a pipe will either flow in a smooth pattern known as *laminar* flow or in a turbulent pattern known as *turbulent* flow. The velocities that clearly produce each type of flow within the pipe can be determined using the formulas:

   $v_{lam} = 2100\mu \,/\, \rho\, d$ and $v_{tur} = 4000\mu \,/\, \rho\, d$,

   where

   v_{lan} is the velocity of the fluid, in feet/sec, that produces a definite laminar flow

   v_{tur} is the velocity of the fluid, in feet/sec, that produces a definite turbulent flow

   μ is the viscosity of the fluid, in foot-pound sec /ft^2

   ρ is the density of the fluid, in slug/ft^3

   d is the inside diameter of the pipe, in feet

   Using these formulas, write and test a C++ function named `flow()` that returns both the laminar flow velocity, v_{lan}, and the turbulent flow velocity, v_{tur}, using reference parameters. The function should calculate these velocities for water, which has a viscosity, μ, of 1.9×10^5 foot-pound sec /ft^2 and a density, ρ, of 1.94 slug/ft^3. The pipe diameter should be passed by value into the `flow()` function.

4. The viscosity and densities of three common fluids are listed below:

	Viscosity (foot-pound sec /ft^2)	Density (slug/ft^3)
Ethyl alcohol	2.29×10^5	1.527
Methyl alcohol	1.17×10^5	1.531
Propyl alcohol	4.01×10^5	1.556

Using this data, write and test a C++ function named `viscDen()` that returns the viscosity and density of the selected fluid using reference parameters. The type of fluid should be input to the function as a character that is passed by value.

5. Write a C++ program that accepts the rectangular coordinates of two points (x_1, y_1) and (x_2, y_2), calculates the distance of each point from the origin, and the distance between the two points. The distance, d, between two points is given by the formula

$$d = \sqrt{(x_2 - x_1)^2 + (y_2 - y_1)^2}$$

6. Modify Program 6.16 so that it requests the number of tosses from the user. (*Hint:* Make sure to have the program correctly determine the percentages of heads and tails obtained.)

7. Many algorithms have been developed for generating pseudorandom numbers. Some of these algorithms utilize a counting scheme, such as counting bits beginning at some arbitrary location in a changing memory. Another scheme, which creates pseudorandom numbers by performing a calculation, is the power residue method.

The **power residue method** begins with an odd n-digit integer, which is referred to as the "seed" number. The seed is multiplied by the value $(10^{n/2} - 3)$. Using the lowest n digits of the result (the "residue") produces a new seed. Continuing this procedure produces a series of random numbers, with each new number used as the seed for the next number. If the original seed has four or more digits (n equal to or greater than 4) and is not divisible by either two or five, this procedure yields $5 \times 10^{(n-2)}$ random numbers before a sequence of numbers repeats itself. For example, starting with a six-digit seed ($n = 6$), such as 654321, a series of $5 \times 10^4 = 50{,}000$ random numbers can be generated.

As an algorithm, the specific steps in generating pseudorandom numbers using a power-residue procedure consists of the following steps:

Step 1: Have a user enter a six-digit integer seed that is not divisible by 2 or 5—this means the number should be an odd number not ending in 5.
Step 2: Multiply the seed number by 997, which is $10^3 - 3$.
Step 3: Extract the lower six digits of the result produced by Step 2. Use this random number as the next seed.
Step 4: Repeat Steps 2 and 3 for as many random numbers as needed.

Thus, if the user entered seed number is 654321 (Step 1), the first random number generated is calculated as follows:

Step 2: 654321 * 997 = 652358037
Step 3: Extract the lower six digits of the number obtained in Step 2. This is accomplished using a standard programming "trick."

The trick involves:

Step 3a: Dividing the number by 10^6 = 1000000.
For example, 652358037 / 1000000 = 652.358037
Step 3b: Taking the integer part of the result of Step 3a.
For example, the integer part of 652.358037 = 652
Step 3c: Multiplying the previous result by 10^6
For example, 652 $\times$ 10^6 = 652000000
Step 3d: Subtracting this result from the original number.
For example, 652358037 – 652000000 = 358037

The integer part of a floating-point number can either be taken by assigning the floating-point number to an integer variable, or by a C++ cast (see Section 3.3). In our procedure we will use the cast mechanism. Thus, the algorithm for producing a random number can be accomplished using the following code:

```
i = int(997.0 * x / 1.e6);    // take the integer part
x = 997.0 * x - i * 1.e6;
```

Using this information,

a. Create a function named `randnum()` that accepts a floating-point "seed" as a parameter and returns a floating-point random number between 0 and 1.e6.
b. Incorporate the `randnum()` function created in Exercise 7a into a working C++ program that produces ten random numbers between 0 and 1.e6.
c. Test the randomness of the `randnum()` function created in Exercise 7a using the method described in Exercise 13. Try some even seed values and some odd seed values that end in 5 to determine whether these affect the randomness of the numbers.

8. Write a C++ function that determines in which quadrant a line drawn from the origin resides. The determination of the quadrant is made using the angle that the line makes with the positive *x* axis as follows:

Angle from the positive *x* axis	Quadrant
Between 0 and 90 degrees	1
Between 90 and 180 degrees	2
Between 180 and 270 degrees	3
Between 270 and 360 degrees	4

NOTE: If the angle is exactly 0, 90, 180, or 270 degrees the corresponding line does not reside in any quadrant but lies on an axis. For this case your function should return a zero.

9. Write a program to simulate the roll of two dice. If the total of the two dice is 7 or 11 you win; otherwise, you lose. Embellish this program as much as you like, with betting, different odds, different combinations for win or lose, stopping play when you have no money left or reach the house limit, displaying the dice, etc. (*Hint:* Calculate the dots showing on each die by the expression `dots = (int)(6.0 * random number + 1)`, where the random number is between 0 and 1.)

10. A value that is sometimes useful is the greatest common divisor of two integers $n1$ and $n2$. A famous mathematician, Euclid, discovered an efficient method to do this over two thousand years ago. Right now, however, we'll settle for a stub. Write the integer function `stub gcd(n1, n2)`. Simply have it return a value that suggests it received its parameters correctly. (*Hint:* $n1 + n2$ is a good choice of return values. Why isn't $n1/n2$ a good choice?).

11. Euclid's method for finding the greatest common divisor (GCD) of two positive integers consists of the following steps:
    a. Divide the larger number by the smaller and retain the remainder.
    b. Divide the smaller number by the remainder, again retaining the remainder.
    c. Continue dividing the prior remainder by the current remainder until the remainder is zero, at which point the last non-zero remainder is the greatest common divisor.

    For example, assume the two positive integers are 84 and 49, we have:

    Step a: 84/49 yields a remainder of 35
    Step b: 49/35 yields a remainder of 14
    Step c: 35/14 yields a remainder of 7
    Step d: 14/7 yields a remainder of 0

    Thus, the last non-zero remainder, which is 7, is the greatest common divisor of 84 and 49.

    Using Euclid's algorithm, replace the stub function written for Exercise 10 with an actual function that determines and returns the GCD of its two integer parameters.

12. The following program uses the same variable names in both the calling and called function. Determine if this causes any problem for the compiler.

```
#include <iostream.h>

int time(int, int);  // function prototype

int main()
```

```
{
  int min, hour, sec;

  cout << "Enter two numbers: ";
  cin  >> min, hour;
  sec = time(min, hour);
  cout << "The total number of seconds is " << sec << endl;

  return 0;
}

int time(int min, int hour)
{
  int sec;

  sec = (hour * 60 + min) * 60;
  return sec;
}
```

13. Write a program that tests the effectiveness of the `rand()` library function. Start by initializing 10 counters, such as `zerocount`, `onecount`, `twocount`,..., `ninecount` to 0. Then generate a large number of pseudorandom integers between 0 and 9. Each time a 0 occurs increment `zerocount`, when a 1 occurs increment `onecount`, etc. Finally, print out the number of 0s, 1s, 2s, etc., that occured and the percentage of the time they occured.

14. The determinant of the 2-by-2 matrix

$$\begin{vmatrix} a_{11} & a_{12} \\ a_{21} & a_{22} \end{vmatrix}$$

is $a_{11}a_{22} - a_{21}a_{12}$.

Similarly, the determinant of a 3-by-3 matrix

$$\begin{vmatrix} a_{11} & a_{12} & a_{13} \\ a_{21} & a_{22} & a_{23} \\ a_{31} & a_{32} & a_{33} \end{vmatrix} =$$

$$a_{11}\begin{vmatrix} a_{22} & a_{23} \\ a_{32} & a_{33} \end{vmatrix} - a_{21}\begin{vmatrix} a_{12} & a_{13} \\ a_{32} & a_{33} \end{vmatrix} + a_{31}\begin{vmatrix} a_{12} & a_{13} \\ a_{22} & a_{23} \end{vmatrix}$$

Using this information, write and test two functions, named `det2()` and `det3()`. The `det2()` function should accept the four coefficients of a 2-by-2 matrix and return its determinant. The `det3()` function should accept the nine coefficients of a 3-by-3 matrix and return its determinant by calling `det2()` to calculate the required 2-by-2 determinants.

6.5 Variable Scope

Now that we have begun to write programs containing more than one function, we can look more closely at the variables declared within each function and their relationship to variables in other functions.

By their very nature, C++ functions are constructed to be independent modules. As we have seen, values are passed to a function using the function's parameter list and a value is returned from a function using a return statement. Seen in this light, a function can be thought of as a closed box, with slots at the top to receive values and a single slot at the bottom of the box to return a value (see Figure 6.15).

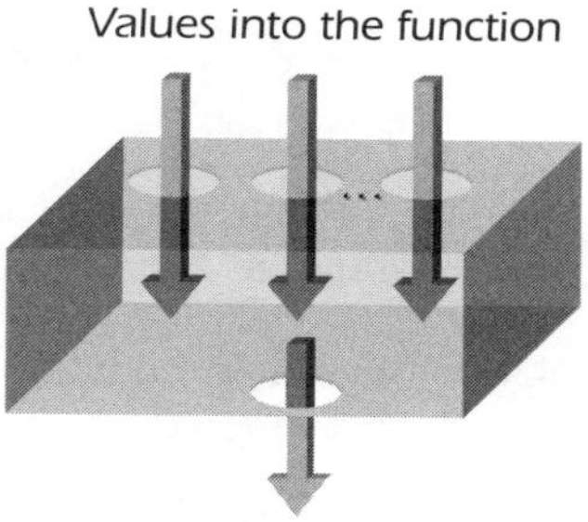

Figure 6.15 A function can be considered a closed box.

The metaphor of a closed box is useful because it emphasizes the fact that what goes on inside the function, including all variable declarations within the function's body, are hidden from the view of all other functions. Since the variables created inside a function are conventionally available only to the function itself, they are said to be local to the function or **local variables**. This term refers to the scope of an identifier, where **scope** is defined as the section of the program where the identifier, such as a variable, is valid or "known." This section of the program is also referred to as where the variable is visible. A variable can have either a local scope or a global scope. A variable with a **local scope** is simply one that has had storage locations set aside for it by a declaration statement made within a function body. Local variables are only meaningful when used in expressions or statements inside the function that declared them. This means that the same variable name can be declared and used in more than one function. For each function that declares the variable, a separate and distinct variable is created.

All the variables we have used until now have been local variables. This is a direct result of placing our declaration statements inside functions and using them as definition statements that cause the computer to reserve storage for the declared variable. As we shall see, declaration statements can be placed outside functions and also need not act as definitions that cause new storage areas to be reserved for the declared variable.

A variable with **global scope**, more commonly termed a **global variable**, is one whose storage has been created for it by a declaration statement located outside any function.

These variables can be used by all functions that are physically placed after the global variable declaration. This is shown in Program 6.17, where we have purposely used the same variable name inside both functions contained in the program.

Program 6.17

```
#include <iostream>
using namespace std;

int firstnum;     // create a global variable named firstnum

void valfun();    // function prototype (declaration)

int main()
{
  int secnum;           // create a local variable named secnum

  firstnum = 10; // store a value into the global variable
  secnum = 20;   // store a value into the local variable

  cout << "From main(): firstnum = " << firstnum << endl;
  cout << "From main(): secnum =  " << secnum << endl;

  valfun();      // call the function valfun

  cout << "\nFrom main() again: firstnum = " << firstnum << endl;
  cout << "From main() again: secnum = " << secnum << endl;

  return 0;
}

void valfun()   // no values are passed to this function
{
  int secnum;  // create a second local variable named secnum

  secnum = 30; // this only affects this local variable's value

  cout << "\nFrom valfun(): firstnum = " << firstnum << endl;
  cout << "From valfun(): secnum = " << secnum << endl;

  firstnum = 40;    // this changes firstnum for both functions

  return;
}
```

The variable `firstnum` in Program 6.17 is a global variable because its storage is created by a definition statement located outside a function. Since both functions, `main()` and `valfun()`, follow the definition of `firstnum`, both of these functions can use this global variable with no further declaration needed.

Program 6.17 also contains two separate local variables, both named `secnum`. Storage for the `secnum` variable named in `main()` is created by the definition statement located in `main()`. A different storage area for the `secnum` variable in `valfun()` is created by the definition statement located in the `valfun()` function. Figure 6.16 illustrates the three distinct storage areas reserved by the three definition statements found in Program 6.17.

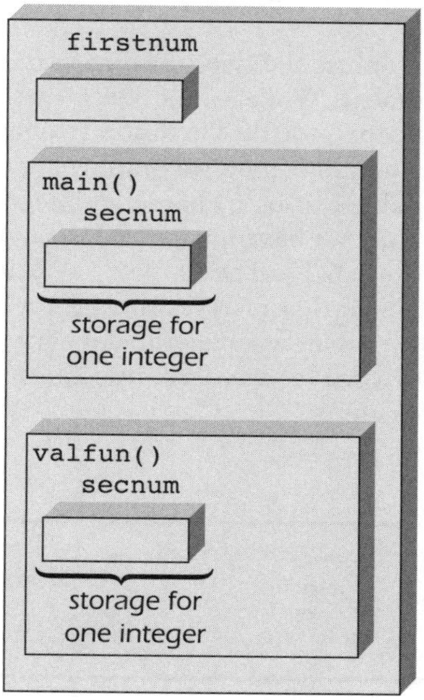

Figure 6.16 The three storage areas created by Program 6.17.

Each of the variables named `secnum` are local to the function in which their storage is created, and each of these variables can only be used from within the appropriate function. Thus, when `secnum` is used in `main()`, the storage area reserved by `main()` for its `secnum` variable is accessed, and when `secnum` is used in `valfun()`, the storage area reserved by `valfun()` for its `secnum` variable is accessed. The following output is produced when Program 6.17 is run:

```
From main(): firstnum = 10
From main(): secnum = 20

From valfun(): firstnum = 10
From valfun(): secnum = 30
```

```
From main() again: firstnum = 40
From main() again: secnum = 20
```

Let's analyze this output. Since `firstnum` is a global variable, both the `main()` and `valfun()` functions can use and change its value. Initially, both functions print the value of 10 that `main()` stored in `firstnum`. Before returning, `valfun()` changes the value of `firstnum` to 40, which is the value displayed when the variable `firstnum` is next displayed from within `main()`.

Because each function only "knows" its own local variables, `main()` can only send the value of its `secnum` to the `cout` object, and `valfun()` can only send the value of its `secnum` to the `cout` object. Thus, whenever `secnum` is obtained from `main()` the value of 20 is displayed, and whenever `secnum` is obtained from `valfun()` the value 30 is displayed.

C++ does not confuse the two `secnum` variables because only one function can execute at a given moment. While a function is executing, only those variables and parameters that are "in scope" for that function (global and local) can be accessed.

The scope of a variable in no way influences or restricts the data type of the variable. Just as a local variable can be a character, integer, Boolean, double, or any of the other data types (long/short) we have introduced, so can global variables be of these data types, as illustrated in Figure 6.17. The scope of a variable is determined by the placement of the definition statement that reserves storage for it and optionally by a declaration statement that makes it visible, whereas the data type of the variable is determined by using the appropriate keyword (`char`, `int`, `bool`, `double`, etc.) before the variable's name in a declaration statement.

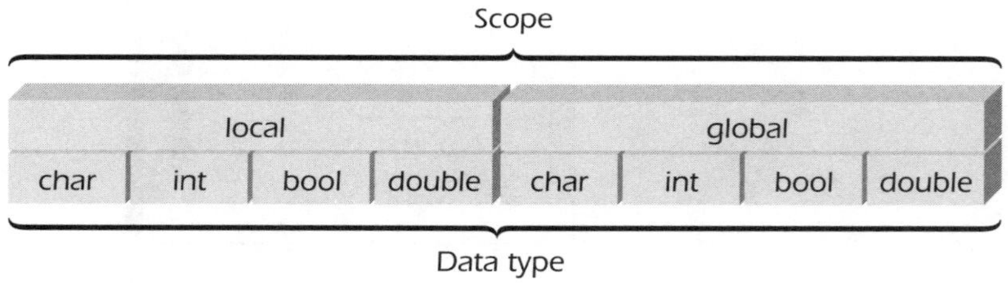

Figure 6.17 Relating the scope and type of a variable.

Scope Resolution Operator

When a local variable has the same name as a global variable, all references to the variable name made within the scope of the local variable refer to the local variable. This situation in illustrated in Program 6.18, where the variable name `number` is defined as both a global and local variable.

Program 6.18

```
#include <iostream>
using namespace std;

double number = 42.8;          // a global variable named number

int main()
{
  double number = 26.4;        // a local variable named number

  cout << "The value of number is " << number << endl;

  return 0;
}
```

When Program 6.18 is executed, the following output is displayed.

```
The value of number is 26.4
```

As shown by this output, the local variable name takes precedence over the global variable. In such cases, we can still access the global variable by using C++'s scope resolution operator. This operator, which has the symbol `::`, must be placed immediately before the variable name, as in `::number`. When used in this manner, the `::` tells the compiler to use the global variable. As an example, the scope resolution operator is used in Program 6.18a.

Program 6.18a

```
#include <iostream>
using namespace std;

double number = 42.5;          // a global variable named number

int main()
{
  double number = 26.4;        // a local variable named number

  cout << "The value of number is " << ::number << endl;

  return 0;
}
```

The output produced by Program 6.18a is:

```
The value of number is 42.5
```

As indicated by this output, the scope resolution operator causes the global, rather than the local variable to be accessed.

Misuse of Globals

Global variables allow the programmer to "jump around" the normal safeguards provided by functions. Rather than passing variables to a function, it is possible to make all variables global ones. **Do not do this.** By indiscriminately making all variables global, you instantly destroy the safeguards C++ provides to make functions independent and insulated from each other, including the necessity of carefully designating the type of arguments needed by a function, the variables used in the function, and the value returned.

Using only global variables can be especially disastrous in larger programs that have many user-created functions. Since all variables in a function must be declared, creating functions that use global variables requires that you remember to write the appropriate global declarations at the top of each program using the function—they no longer come along with the function. More devastating than this, however, is the horror of trying to track down an error in a large program using global variables. Since a global variable can be accessed and changed by any function following the global declaration, it is a time-consuming and frustrating task to locate the origin of an erroneous value.

Global definitions, however, are sometimes useful in creating variables and constants that must be shared between many functions. Rather than passing the same variable to each function, it is easier to define the variable once as a global. Doing so also alerts anyone reading the program that many functions use the variable. Most large programs almost always make use of a few global variables or constants. Smaller programs containing a few functions, however, should almost never contain global variables.

The misuse of globals does not apply to function prototypes, which typically are global. It should be noted that all the function prototypes we have used have been of global scope, which declares the prototype to all subsequent functions. Placing a function prototype within a function makes the prototype a local declaration available only to the function it is declared within.

Exercises 6.5

1. a. For the following section of code, determine the data type and scope of all declared variables. To do this, use a separate sheet of paper and list the three column headings that follow (we have filled in the entries for the first variable):

Variable name	Data type	Scope
`volts`	`int`	`global to main, roi, and step`

```
#include <iostream>
using namespace std;

int volts;
long int resistance;
double current;

int main()
{
  int power;
  double factor, time;
      .
      .
  return 0;
}

double roi(int mat1, int mat2)
{
  int count;
  double weight;
       .
       .
  return weight;
}

int step(double first, double last)
{
  int hours;
  double fracpart;
       .
       .
  return 10*hours;
}
```

b. Draw boxes around the appropriate section of the above code to enclose the scope of each variable.

c. Determine the data type of the parameters that the functions `roi` and `step` expect, and the data type of the value returned by these functions.

2. a. For the following section of code, determine the data type and scope of all declared variables. To do this, use a separate sheet of paper and list the three column headings that follow (we have filled in the entries for the first variable):

Variable name	Data type	Scope
`key`	`char`	`global to main, func1, and func2`

```
#include <iostream>
using namespace std;

char key;
long int number;

int main()
{
  int a,b,c;
  double x,y;
      .
      .
  return 0;
}

double secnum;

int func1(int num1, int num2)
{
  int o,p;
  float q;
      .
      .
  return p;
}

double func2(double first, double last)
{
  int a,b,c,o,p;
  double r;
  double s,t,x;
      .
      .
  return s * t;
}
```

b. Draw a box around the appropriate section of the above code to enclose the scope of the variables `key`, `secnum`, `y`, and `r`.

c. Determine the data type of the arguments that functions `func1` and `func2` expect, and the data type of the value returned by these functions.

3. Besides speaking about the scope of a variable, we can also apply the term to a function's parameters. What do you think is the scope of all function parameters?

4. Consider the following program structure:

```
#include <iostream>
using namespace std;

int a, b;
double One(float);
void Two(void);
int main()
{
  int c, d;
  double e, f;
    .
    .
  return 0;
}

double One(double p2)
{
  char m, n;
    .
    .
}

void Two(void)
{
  int p, d;
  double q, r;
    .
    .
}
```

Define the scope of the parameter `p2` and the variables `a`, `b`, `c`, `d`, `m`, `n`, `p`, `d`, `q`, and `r`.

5. Determine the values displayed by each cout statement in the following program:

```
#include <iostream>
using namespace std;

int firstnum = 10;  // declare and initialize a global variable
void display();  // function prototype
int main()
{
  int firstnum = 20;    // declare and initialize a local variable
  cout << "\nThe value of firstnum is " << firstnum << endl;
  display();

  return 0;
}
```

```
void display(void)
{
  cout << "The value of firstnum is now " << firstnum << endl;
  return;
}
```

6.6 VARIABLE STORAGE CATEGORY

The scope of a variable defines the location within a program where that variable can be used. Given a program, you could take a pencil and draw a box around the section of the program where each variable is valid. The space inside the box would represent the scope of a variable. From this viewpoint, the scope of a variable can be thought of as the space within the program where the variable is valid.

In addition to the space dimension represented by its scope, variables also have a time dimension. The time dimension refers to the length of time that storage locations are reserved for a variable. This time dimension is referred to as the variable's "lifetime." For example, all variable storage locations are released back to the computer when a program is finished running. However, while a program is still executing, interim variable storage areas are reserved and subsequently released back to the computer. Where and how long a variable's storage locations are kept before they are released can be determined by the **storage category** of the variable.

Besides having a data type and scope, every variable also has a storage category. The four available storage categories are called `auto`, `static`, `extern`, and `register`. If one of these category names is used, it must be placed before the variable's data type in a declaration statement. Examples of declaration statements that include a storage category designation are

```
auto int num;       // auto storage category and int data type
static int miles;   // static storage category and int data type
register int dist;  // register storage category and int data type
extern int volts;   // extern storage category and int data type
auto float coupon;  // auto storage category and float data type
static double yrs;  // static storage category and double data type
extern float yld;   // extern storage category and float data type
auto char inKey;    // auto storage category and char variable
```

To understand what the storage category of a variable means, we will first consider local variables (those variables created inside a function) and then global variables (those variables created outside a function).

Local Variable Storage Categories

Local variables can only be members of the `auto`, `static`, or `register` storage classes. If no class description is included in the declaration statement, the variable is automatically assigned to the `auto` category. Thus, `auto` is the default category used by C++. All the local variables we have used, since the storage category designation was omitted, have been `auto` variables.

The term `auto` is short for **automatic**. Storage for automatic local variables is automatically reserved or created each time a function declaring automatic variables is called. As long as the function has not returned control to its calling function, all automatic variables local to the function are "alive"—that is, storage for the variables is available. When the function returns control to its calling function, its local automatic variables "die"—that is, the storage for the variables is released back to the computer. This process repeats itself each time a function is called. For example, consider Program 6.19, where the function `testauto()` is called three times from `main()`.

Program 6.19

```
#include <iostream>
using namespace std;

void testauto();    // function prototype

int main()
{
  int count;                   // count is a local auto variable

  for(count = 1; count <= 3; count++)
    testauto();

  return 0;
}

void testauto()
{
  int num = 0;      // num is a local auto variable
                    // initialized to zero
  cout << "The value of the automatic variable num is "
       << num << endl;
  num++;

  return;
}
```

The output produced by Program 6.19 is:

```
The value of the automatic variable num is 0
The value of the automatic variable num is 0
The value of the automatic variable num is 0
```

Each time `testauto()` is called, the automatic variable `num` is created and initialized to zero. When the function returns control to `main()`, the variable `num` is destroyed along with any value stored in `num`. Thus, the effect of incrementing `num` in `testauto()`, before the function's return statement, is lost when control is returned to `main()`.

For most applications, the use of automatic variables works just fine. There are cases, however, where we would like a function to remember values between function calls. This is the purpose of the `static` storage class. A local variable that is declared as `static` causes the program to keep the variable and its latest value even when the function that declared it is through executing. Examples of `static` variable declarations are

```
static int rate;
static double resistance;
static char inKey;
```

A local `static` variable is not created and destroyed each time the function declaring the `static` variable is called. Once created, local `static` variables remain in existence for the life of the program. This means that the last value stored in the variable when the function is finished executing is available to the function the next time it is called.

Because local `static` variables retain their values, they are not initialized within a declaration statement in the same way as automatic variables. To understand why, consider the automatic declaration `int num = 0;`, which causes the automatic variable `num` to be created and set to zero each time the declaration is encountered. This is called a **run-time initialization** because initialization occurs each time the declaration statement is encountered. This type of initialization would be disastrous for a `static` variable, because resetting the variable's value to zero each time the function is called would destroy the very value we are trying to save.

The initialization of `static` variables (both local and global) is done only once, when the program is first compiled. At compilation time the variable is created and any initialization value is placed in it.[15] Thereafter, the value in the variable is kept without further initialization. To see how this works, consider Program 6.20.

---

[15]Some compilers initialize static local variables the first time the definition statement is executed rather than when the program is compiled.

Program 6.20

```
#include <iostream>
using namespace std;

void teststat();    // function prototype

int main()
{
  int count;               // count is a local auto variable

  for(count = 1; count <= 3; count++)
    teststat();

  return 0;
}

void teststat()
{
  static int num = 0;     // num is a local static variable
  cout << "The value of the static variable num is now "
       << num << endl;
  num++;

  return;
}
```

The output produced by Program 6.20 is

```
The value of the static variable num is now 0
The value of the static variable num is now 1
The value of the static variable num is now 2
```

As illustrated by this output, the `static` variable `num` is set to zero only once. The function `teststat()` then increments this variable just before returning control to `main()`. The value that `num` has when leaving the function `teststat()` is retained and displayed when the function is next called.

Unlike automatic variables that can be initialized by either constants or expressions using both constants and previously initialized variables, `static` variables can only be initialized using constants or constant expressions, such as `3.2 + 8.0`. Also, unlike automatic variables, all `static` variables are set to zero when no explicit initialization is given. Thus, the specific initialization of `num` to zero in Program 6.19 is not required.

The remaining storage class available to local variables, the `register` class, is not used as extensively as either `auto` or `static` variables. Examples of `register` variable declarations are

```
register int time;
register double diffren;
register float coupon;
```

The `register` variables have the same time duration as `auto` variables; that is, a local `register` variable is created when the function declaring it is entered and is destroyed when the function completes execution. The only difference between `register` and `auto` variables is where the storage for the variable is located.

Storage for all variables (local and global), except `register` variables, is reserved in the computer's memory area. Most computers have a few additional high-speed storage areas located directly in the computer's processing unit that can also be used for variable storage. These special high-speed storage areas are called **registers**. Since registers are physically located in the computer's processing unit, they can be accessed faster than the normal memory storage areas located in the computer's memory unit. Also, computer instructions that reference registers typically require less space than instructions that reference memory locations because there are fewer registers that can be accessed than there are memory locations. When the compiler substitutes the location of a register for a variable during program compilation, less space in the instruction is needed than is required to address a memory having millions of locations.

Besides decreasing the size of a compiled C++ program, using register variables can increase the execution speed of a C++ program if your computer supports this data type. Applications programs intended to be executed on various computers should not use registers. Attempts to do so will generally be foiled by the compiler by automatically switching variables declared with the register storage category to the auto storage category.

The only restriction in using the `register` storage class is that the address of a `register` variable, using the address operator `&`, cannot be taken. This is easily understood when you realize that registers do not have standard memory addresses.

Global Variable Storage Classes

Global variables are created by definition statements external to a function. By their nature, these externally defined variables do not come and go with the calling of any function. Once a global variable is created, it exists until the program in which it is declared is finished executing. Thus, global variables cannot be declared as either `auto` or `register` variables that are created and destroyed as the program is executing. Global variables may additionally be declared as members of the `static` or `extern` storage classes (but not both). Examples of declaration statements including these two class descriptions are

```
extern int sum;
extern double volts;
static double current;
```

The `static` and `extern` classes affect only the scope, not the time duration, of global variables. As with `static` local variables, all global variables are initialized to zero at compile time.

The purpose of the `extern` storage class is to extend the scope of a global variable beyond its normal boundaries. To understand this, we must first note that all of the programs we have written so far have always been contained together in one file. Thus, when you have saved or retrieved programs you have only needed to give the computer a single name for your program. This is not required by C++.

Larger programs typically consist of many functions that are stored in multiple files. An example of this is shown in Figure 6.18, where the three functions `main()`, `func1()`, and `func2()` are stored in one file and the two functions `func3()` and `func4()` are stored in a second file.

file1

```
int volts;
double current;
static double power;
    .
    .
    .
int main( )
{
    func1( );
    func2( );
    func3( );
    func4( );
}
int func1( )
{
    .
    .
    .
}
int func2( )
{
    .
    .
    .
}
```

file2

```
double factor;
int func3( )
{
    .
    .
    .
}
int func4( )
    .
    .
    .
}
```

Figure 6.18 A program may extend beyond one file.

For the files illustrated in Figure 6.18, the global variables `volts`, `current`, and `power` declared in file1 can only be used by the functions `main()`, `func1()`, and `func2()` in this file. The single global variable, `factor`, declared in file2 can only be used by the functions `func3()` and `func4()` in file2.

Although the variable `volts` has been created in file1, we may want to use it in file2. Placing the declaration statement `extern int volts;` in file2, as shown in Figure 6.19, allows us to do this. Putting this statement at the top of file2 extends the scope of the variable `volts` into file2 so that it may be used by both `func3()` and `func4()`. Thus, the `extern` designation simply declares a global variable that is defined in another file. So placing the statement `extern double current;` in `func4()` extends the scope of this global variable, created in file1, into `func4()`, and the scope of the global variable `factor`, created in file2, is extended into `func1()` and `func2()` by the declaration statement `extern double factor;` placed before `func1()`. Notice that `factor` is not available to `main()`.

file1

```
int volts;
double current;
static double power;
    .
    .
    .
int main( )
{
   func1( );
   func2( );
   func3( );
   func4( );
}
extern double factor;
int func1( )
{
    .
    .
    .
}
int func2( )
{
    .
    .
    .
}
```

file2

```
double factor;
extern int volts;
int func3( )
{
     .
     .
     .
}
int func4( )
{
   extern double current;
     .
     .
     .
}
```

Figure 6.19 Extending the scope of global variables.

A declaration statement that specifically contains the word `extern` is different from every other declaration statement in that it does not cause the creation of a new variable by reserving new storage for the variable. An `extern` declaration statement simply informs the computer that a global variable already exists and can now be used. The actual storage for the variable must be created somewhere else in the program using one,

Point of Information

Storage Categories

Variables of type `auto` and `register` are always local variables. Only non-static global variables may be declared using the `extern` keyword. Doing so extends the variable's scope into another file or function.

Making a global variable `static` makes the variable private to the file in which it is declared. Thus, `static` variables *cannot* use the `extern` keyword. Except for `static` variables, all variables are initialized each time they come into scope. `static` variables are only initialized once when they are defined.

and only one, global declaration statement in which the word `extern` has not been used. Initialization of the global variable can, of course, be made with the original declaration of the global variable. Initialization within an `extern` declaration statement is not allowed and will cause a compilation error.

The existence of the `extern` storage class is the reason we have been so careful to distinguish bsetween the creation and declaration of a variable. Declaration statements containing the word `extern` do not create new storage areas; they only extend the scope of existing global variables.

The last global class, `static` global variables, is used to prevent the extension of a global variable into a second file. Global `static` variables are declared in the same way as local `static` variables, except that the declaration statement is placed outside any function.

The scope of a global `static` variable cannot be extended beyond the file in which it is declared. This provides a degree of privacy for `static` global variables. Since they are only "known" and can only be used in the file in which they are declared, other files cannot access or change their values. Thus, `static` global variables cannot be subsequently extended to a second file using an `extern` declaration statement. Trying to do so will result in a compilation error.

Exercises 6.6

1. **a.** List the storage classes available to local variables.
   b. List the storage classes available to global variables.
2. Describe the difference between a local `auto` variable and a local `static` variable.
3. What is the difference between the following functions?

```
void init1()
{
  static int yrs = 1;
  cout << "The value of yrs is " << yrs << endl;
  yrs = yrs + 2;
}
```

```
void init2()
{
  static int yrs;
  yrs = 1;
  cout << "The value of yrs is " << yrs << endl;
  yrs = yrs + 2;
}
```

4. a. Describe the difference between a `static` global variable and an `extern` global variable.
   b. If a variable is declared with an `extern` storage class, what other declaration statement must be present somewhere in the program?

5. The declaration statement `static double resistance;` can be used to create either a local or global `static` variable. What determines the scope of the variable `resistance`?

6. For the function and variable declarations illustrated in Figure 6.20, place an `extern` declaration to individually accomplish the following:
   a. Extend the scope of the global variable `choice` into all of file2.
   b. Extend the scope of the global variable `flag` into function `average()` only.
   c. Extend the scope of the global variable `date` into `average()` and `variance()`.
   d. Extend the scope of the global variable `date` into `roi()` only.
   e. Extend the scope of the global variable `factor` into `roi()` only.
   f. Extend the scope of the global variable `bondtype` into all of file1.
   g. Extend the scope of the global variable `resistance` into both `watts()` and `thrust()`.

file1

```
char choice;
int flag;
long date, time;
int main( )
{
     .
     .
     .
}
double factor;
double watts( )
{
     .
     .
     .
}
double thrust( )
{
     .
     .
     .
}
```

file2

```
char bondtype;
double resistance;
double roi( )
{
     .
     .
     .
}
double average( )
{
     .
     .
     .
}
double variance
{
     .
     .
     .
}
```

Figure 6.20 Files for Exercise 6.

6.7 COMMON PROGRAMMING ERRORS

An extremely common programming error related to functions is passing incorrect data types. The values passed to a function must correspond to the data types of the parameters declared for the function. One way to verify that correct values have been received is to display all passed values within a function's body before any calculations are made. Once this verification has taken place, the display can be dispensed with.[16]

Another common error can occur when the same variable is declared locally within both the calling and called functions. Even though the variable name is the same, a change to one local variable *does not* alter the value in the other local variable.

Related to this error is the error that can occur when a local variable has the same name as a global variable. Within the function declaring it, the use of the variable's name only affects the local variable's contents unless the scope resolution operator, **::**, is used.

---

[16] In practice a good debugger program should be used.

Another common error is omitting the called function's prototype either before or within the calling function. The called function must be alerted to the type of value that will be returned, and this information is provided by the function prototype. The prototype can be omitted if the called function is physically placed in a program before its calling function. Although it is also permissible to omit the prototype and return type for functions returning an integer, it is poor documenting practice to do so. The actual value returned by a function can be verified by displaying it both before and after it is returned.

The last two common errors are terminating a function's header line with a semicolon and forgetting to include the data type of a function's parameters within the header line.

6.8 CHAPTER SUMMARY

1. A function is called by giving its name and passing any data to it in the parentheses following the name. If a variable is one of the arguments in a function call, the called function receives a copy of the variable's value.

2. The commonly used form of a user-written function is

   returnDataType functionName(parameter list)

   {

       declarations and other C++ statements;

       return expression;

   }

   The first line of the function is called the **function header**. The opening and closing braces of the function and all statements in between these braces constitute the function's **body**. The returned data type is, by default, an integer when no returned data type is specified. The parameter list is a comma separated list of parameter declarations.

3. A function's return type is the data type of the value returned by the function. If no type is declared the function is assumed to return an integer value. If the function does not return a value it should be declared as a `void` type.

4. Functions can directly return at most a single data type value to their calling functions. This value is the value of the expression in the return statement.

5. Using reference arguments, a function can be passed the address of a variable. If a called function is passed an address it has the capability of directly accessing the respective calling function's variable. Using passed addresses permits a called function to effectively return multiple values.

6. Functions can be declared to all calling functions by means of a **function prototype.** The prototype provides a declaration for a function that specifies the data type returned by the function, its name, and the data types of the arguments expected by the function. As with all declarations, a function prototype is terminated with a semicolon and may be included within local variable declarations or as a global declaration. The most common form of a function prototype is:

   dataType functionName(parameter data type list);

   If the called function is placed physically above the calling function, no further declaration is required because the function's definition serves as a global declaration to all following functions.

7. Every variable used in a program has a **scope**, which determines where in the program the variable can be used. The scope of a variable is either local or global and is determined by where the variable's definition statement is placed. A local variable is defined within a function and can only be used within its defining function or block. A global variable is defined outside a function and can be used in any function following the variable's definition. All global variables that are not specifically initialized by the user are initialized to zero by the compiler and can be shared between files using the keyword `extern`.

8. Every variable has a **category**. The category of a variable determines how long the value in the variable will be retained, which is also known as the variable's duration: `auto` variables are local variables that exist only while their defining function is executing; `register` variables are similar to `auto` variables but are stored in a computer's internal registers rather than in memory; `static` variables can be either global or local and retain their values for the duration of a program's execution. All `static` variables are set to zero when they are defined if they are not explicitly initialized by the user.

Looking at Career Choices

Chemical Engineering

Chemical engineering is the application of the knowledge or techniques of science, particularly chemistry, to industry. Chemical engineers are responsible for the design and operation of large-scale manufacturing plants for materials that undergo chemical changes in their production. These materials include all the new and improved products that have so profoundly affected society such as petrochemicals, rubbers and polymers, new metal alloys, industrial and fine chemicals, foods, paints, detergents, cements, pesticides, industrial gases, and medicines. Chemical engineers also play an important role in pollution abatement and the management of existing energy resources. Because the field of chemical engineering has grown to be so broad, it is difficult to classify the activities of chemical engineers. A rough subdivision is into large-scale production systems, or chemical processing, and smaller scale, or molecular, systems.

Chemical Processing

Chemical processing concerns all aspects of the design and operation of large chemical-processing plants. It includes the following areas.

1. Petrochemicals. The distillation and refinement of fuels such as gasoline, synthetic natural gas, coal liquefaction and gasification, and the production of an infinite variety of products made from petroleum, from cosmetics to pharmaceuticals.
2. Synthetic materials The process of polymerization, a joining of simpler molecules into large complex molecules, is responsible for many modern materials such as nylon, synthetic rubbers, polystyrene, and a great variety of plastics and synthetic fibers.
3. Food and biochemical engineering. The manufacture of packaged food, improved food additives, sterilization, and the utilization of industrial bacteria, fungi, and yeasts in processes like fermentation.
4. Unit operations. The analysis of the transport of heat or fluid, such as the pumping of chemicals through a pipeline or the transfer of heat between substances. This area also includes the effect of heat transfer on chemical reactions such as oxidation, chlorination, and so on.
5. Cryogenic engineering. The design of plants operating at temperatures near absolute zero.
6. Electrochemical engineering. The use of electricity to alter chemical reactions, such as electroplating, or the design of batteries or energy cells.
7. Pollution control. A rapidly growing field that seeks to monitor and reduce the harmful effects of chemical processing on the environment. Topics of concern are waste-water control, air pollution abatement, and the economics of pollution control.

(Continued)

Looking at Career Choices

Molecular Systems

This field involves the application of laboratory techniques to large-scale processes. It includes the following areas:

1. Biochemical engineering. Application of enzymes, bacteria, and so on to improve large-scale chemical processes.
2. Polymer synthesis. Molecular basis for polymer properties and the chemical synthesis of new polymers adapted for large-scale production.
3. Research and development in all areas of chemical processing.

Preparation for a career in chemical engineering requires a thorough background in physics, chemistry, and mathematics and a knowledge of thermodynamics and physical, analytic, and organic chemistry. Although extensively trained in chemistry, chemical engineers differ from chemists in that their main concern is the adaptation of laboratory techniques to large-scale manufacturing plants.

CHAPTER 7

Completing the Basics

TOPICS

The current ANSI/ISO standard for C++ introduces two new features that were not part of the original C++ specification: exception handling and a `string` *class. Both of these new features are presented in this chapter.*

Exception handling is a means of error detection and processing, which has gained increasing acceptance in programming technology. It permits detecting an error at the point in the code at which the error has occurred and provides a means of processing the error and returning control to the line that generated the error. Although such error detection and code correction is possible using `if` *statements and functions, exception handling provides one more useful programming tool targeted at error detection and processing.*

With the new ANSI/ISO C++ standard, a class named `string` *is now part of the standard C++ library. This class provides a greatly expanded set of class functions that includes easy insertion and removal of characters from a string, automatic string expansion whenever a string's original capacity is exceeded, string contraction when characters are removed from the string, and range checking to detect invalid character positions.*

In addition to presenting these two new C++ features, this chapter shows how exception handling, when applied to strings, provides a very useful means of validating user input.

7.1 EXCEPTION HANDLING

The traditional C++ approach to error handling uses a function to return a specific value to indicate specific operations. Typically, a return value of 0 or 1 is used to indicate a successful completion of the function's task, whereas a negative value is used to indicate an error condition. For example, if a function were used to divide two numbers, a return value of –1 could be used to indicate that the denominator was zero and that the division could not be performed. When multiple error conditions can occur, different return values would be used to indicate specific errors.

Though this approach is still available and often used, a number of problems can occur with this method. First, the programmer must check the return value to detect if an error did occur. Next, the error handling code that checks the return value frequently becomes intermixed with normal processing code, making it sometimes difficult to determine which part of the code is handling errors as opposed to normal program processing. Finally, returning an error condition from a function means that the condition must be the same data type as a valid returned value; hence, the error code must be a specially identified value that can be identified as an error alert. This means that the error code is effectively imbedded as one of the possible non-error values that may be required from the function and is only available at the point where the function returns a value. A function that returns a Boolean value has no additional values that can be used to report an error condition.

None of this is insurmountable and many times this approach is simple and effective. However, in the latest versions, C++ compilers have added a technique specifically designed for error detection and handling referred to as exception handling.

In **exception handling**, when an error occurs while a function is executing, the method creates a value, variable, or object, which is referred to as an **exception**, that contains information about the error at the point the error occurs. This exception is immediately passed, at the point it was generated, to code that is referred to as the **exception handler**, which is designed to deal with the exception. The process of generating and passing the exception at the point the error was detected is referred to as **throwing an exception**. The exception is thrown from within the function while it is still executing. This permits handling the error and then returning control back to the function so that it can complete its assigned task.

In general, two fundamental types of errors can cause C++ exceptions: those that result from a program's inability to obtain a required resource and those that result from flawed data. Examples of the first error type are attempts to obtain a system resource, such as locating and finding a file for input. These types of errors are the result of external resources over which the programmer has no control.

The second type of error can occur when a program prompts the user to enter an integer, and the user enters a string, such as e234, that cannot be converted to a numerical value. Another example is the attempt to divide two numbers when the denominator has a 0 value. This latter condition is referred to as a division by zero error. Each of these errors can always be checked and handled in a manner that does not result in a program crash. Before seeing how this is accomplished using exception handling, review Table 7.1 to familiarize yourself with the terminology used in relation to processing exceptions.

Table 7.1 Exception Handling Terminology

Terminology	Description
Exception	A value, variable, or object that identifies a specific error that has occurred while a program is executing
Throw an exception	Sends the exception to a section of code that processes the detected error
Catch or handle an exception	Receives a thrown exception and processes it
Catch clause	The section of code that processes the error
Exception handler	The code that throws and catches an exception

The general syntax of the code required to throw and catch an exception is the following:

```
try
{
  // one or more statements,
  // at least one of which should
  // be capable of throwing an exception;
}
catch(exceptionDataType parameterName)
{
  // one or more statements
}
```

The example here uses two new keywords: `try` and `catch`.

The keyword `try` identifies the start of an exception handling block of code. At least one of the statements within the braces defining this block of code should be capable of throwing an exception. As an example, examine the `try` block in the following section of code:

```
try
{
  cout << "Enter the numerator (whole numbers only): ";
  cin  >> numerator;
  cout << "Enter the denominator (whole numbers only):";
  cin  >> denominator;
  result = numerator/denominator;
}
```

The `try` block contains five statements, three of which may result in an error that you want to catch. In particular, a professionally written program would ensure that valid integers are entered in response to both prompts and that the second entered value is not a zero. For this example, you will only check that the second value entered is not zero. (In Appendix C you will find the exception handling code that can be used to validate both inputs to ensure that both entered data are integers.)

From the standpoint of the `try` block, only the value of the second number matters. The `try` block will be altered to say "try all of the statements within me to see if an exception, which in this particular case is a zero second value, occurs." To check that the second value is not a zero, you add a `throw` statement within the `try` block, as follows:

```
try
{
  cout << "Enter the numerator: (whole number only): ";
  cin  >> numerator;
  cout << "Enter the denominator: (whole number only): ";
  cin  >> denominator;
  if (denominator == 0)
    throw denominator;
  else
    result = numerator/denominator;
}
```

In this `try` block, the thrown item is an integer value. A string literal, a variable, or an object could have been used, but only one of these items can be thrown by any single `throw` statement. The first four statements in the `try` block do not have to be included in the code; however, doing so keeps all the relevant statements together. Keeping related statements together can facilitate adding throw statements within the same `try` block to ensure that both input values are integer values, so it is more convenient to have all the relevant code available within the same `try` block.

A `try` block must be followed by one or more `catch` blocks, which serve as exception handlers for any exceptions thrown by the statements in the `try` block. Here is a `catch` block that handles the thrown exception, which is an integer:

```
catch(int e)
  {
    cout << "A denominator value of " << e << " is invalid." << endl;
    exit (1);
  }
```

The exception handling provided by this `catch` block is an output statement that identifies the particular caught exception and then terminates program execution. Notice the parentheses following the `catch` keyword. Listed within the parentheses is the data type of the exception that is thrown and a parameter name (which is `e`) used to receive it. This identifier, which is programmer-selected but conventionally uses the letter `e` for exception, is used to hold the exception value generated when an exception is thrown.

Multiple catch blocks can be provided as long as each block catches a unique data type. The only requirement is that at least one `catch` block be provided for each `try` block. The more exceptions that can be caught with the same `try` block, the better.

Program 7.1 provides a complete program that includes a `try` block and a `catch` block to detect a division by zero error.

Program 7.1

```
#include <iostream>
using namespace std;

int main()
{
      int numerator, denominator;

  try
  {
    cout << "Enter the numerator (whole number only): ";
    cin  >> numerator;
    cout << "Enter the denominator(whole number only): ";
    cin  >> denominator;
      if (denominator == 0)
        throw denominator;  // an integer value is thrown
    else
        cout << numerator <<'/' << denominator
             << " = " << double(numerator)/ double(denominator) << endl;
  }
  catch(int e)
  {
    cout << "A denominator value of " << e << " is invalid." << endl;
    exit (1);
  }

  return 0;
}
```

Following are two sample runs using Program 7.1. Note the second output indicates that an attempt to divide by a zero denominator has been successfully detected before the operation is performed.

```
Enter the numerator (whole number only): 12
Enter the denominator(whole number only): 3
12/3 = 4
```

and

```
Enter the numerator (whole number only): 12
Enter the denominator(whole number only): 0
A denominator value of 0 is invalid.
```

Having detected a zero denominator, rather than terminating program execution, a more robust program can provide the user with the opportunity to re-enter a non-zero value. This can be accomplished by including the `try` block within a `while` statement and then having the `catch` block return program control to the `while` statement after informing the user that a zero value has been entered. The following code accomplishes this:

Program 7.2

```
#include <iostream>
using namespace std;

int main()
{
  int numerator, denominator;
  bool needDenominator = true;

  cout << "Enter a numerator (whole number only): ";
  cin  >> numerator;

  cout << "Enter a denominator (whole number only): ";
  while(needDenominator)
  {
    cin  >> denominator;
    try
    {
      if (denominator == 0)
        throw denominator;  // an integer value is thrown
    }
    catch(int e)
    {
      cout << "A denominator value of " << e << " is invalid." << endl;
      cout << "Please re-enter the denominator (whole number only): ";
      continue;  // this sends control back to the while statement
    }
    cout << numerator <<'/' << denominator
         << " = " << double(numerator)/ double(denominator) << endl;
      needDenominator = false;
  }

  return 0;
}
```

In reviewing this code, notice that it is the `continue` statement within the `catch` block that returns control to the top of the `while` statement (see Section 6.3 for a review of the `continue` statement). Following is a sample run using Program 7.2:

```
Enter a numerator (whole number only): 12
Enter a denominator (whole number only): 0
A denominator value of 0 is invalid.
Please re-enter the denominator (whole number only): 5
12/5 = 2.4
```

One caution should be mentioned when throwing string literals as opposed to numeric values. Whenever a string literal is thrown, it is a C-string, not a `string` class object, that is thrown. This means that the `catch` statement must declare the received argument as a C-string, which is a character array, rather than as a string. As an example, consider that rather than throwing the value of the `denominator` variable in both Programs 7.1 and 7.2, the following statement was used:

```
throw "***Invalid input - A denominator value of zero is not permitted***";
```

Here is a correct `catch` statement for the preceding `throw` statement:

```
catch(char e[])
```

An attempt to declare the exception as a `string` class variable will result in a compiler error.

Exercises 7.1

1. Define the following terms:

exception
`try` block
`catch` block
exception handler
throw an exception
catch an exception

2. Enter and execute Program 7.1.

3. Replace the statement

```
cout << numerator <<'/' << denominator
     << " = " << double (numerator)/ double (denominator) << endl;
```

in Program 7.1 with the statement

```
cout << numerator <<'/' << denominator
     << " = " << numerator/denominator << endl;
```

and execute the modified program. Enter the values 12 and 5, and explain why the result is incorrect from the user's viewpoint.

4. Modify Program 7.1 so it throws and catches the message `***Invalid input - A denominator value of zero is not permitted***`. (*Hint:* Review the caution presented at the end of this section.)

5. Enter and execute Program 7.2.

6. Modify Program 7.2 so it continues to divide two numbers until the user enters the character q (as a numerator or denominator) to terminate program execution.

7. Include the exception handling code provided in this section within Program 7.1 to ensure the user enters a valid integer value for both the numerator and denominator.

7.2 THE `string` CLASS

The programs in this text have used the `istream` class' `cout` object extensively without having investigated this class or how the `cout` object is created. This is one of the advantages of object-oriented program design; thoroughly tested classes can be used without knowing the internals of how the class is constructed. In this section, we will use another class provided by C++'s standard library, the `string` class. However, in this case, we will create objects from the class before using them, rather than use an existing object, such as `cout`.

A class is a user-created data type. Like the built-in data types, a class defines a valid set of data values and a set of operations that can be used on them. The difference between a user-created class and a built-in type is how the class is constructed. A built-in data type is provided as an integral part of the compiler, and a class is constructed by a programmer using C++ code. Other than that and the terminology used, the two types are used in much the same manner. The key difference in terminology is that storage areas for built-in types are referred to as variables, whereas storage areas declared for a class are referred to as objects.

The values permitted by the `string` class are referred to as sting literals. A string literal is any sequence of characters enclosed in double quotation marks. A string literal is also referred to as a string value, a string constant, and more conventionally, a string. Examples of strings are `"This is a string"`, `"Hello World!"`, and `"xyz 123 *!#@&"`. The double quotation marks indicate the beginning and ending points of the string and are never stored with the string.

Figure 7.1 shows the programming representation of the string `Hello` whenever this string is created as an object of the `string` class. By convention, the first character in a string is always designated as position 0. This position value is also referred to as both the character's index value and its offset value.

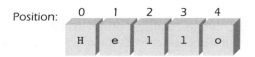

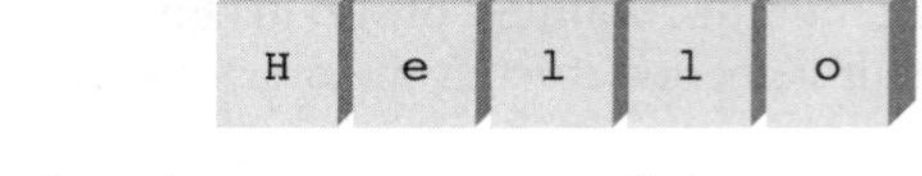

Figure 7.1 The storage of a string as a sequence of characters.

string Class Functions

The `string` class provides a number of functions for declaring, creating, and initializing a string. In the earlier versions of C++, the process of creating a new object is referred to as instantiating an object, which in this case becomes instantiating a string object, or creating a string, for short. Table 7.2 lists the functions provided by the `string` class for creating and initializing a string object. In class terminology, functions are formally referred to as methods, and the methods that perform this task are referred to as constructor methods, or constructors, for short.

Table 7.2 `string` Class Constructors (Requires the Header File `string`)

Constructor	Description	Examples

`string objectName = value`	Creates and initializes a string object to a value that can be a string literal, a previously declared string object, or an expression containing string literals and string objects	`string str1 = "Good Morning";`
		`string str2 = str1;`
		`string str3 = str1 +  str2;`

`string objectName(stringValue)`	Produces the same initialization as above	`string str1("Hot");` `string str1(str1 +  " Dog");`
`string objectName(str, n)`	Creates and initializes a string object with a substring of string object `str`, starting at index position `n` of `str`	`string str1(str2, 5)` If `str2` contains the string `Good Morning`, then `str1` becomes the string `Morning`
`string objectName(str, n, p)`	Creates and initializes a string object with a substring of string object `str`, starting at index position `n` of `str` and containing `p` characters	`string str1(str2, 5,2)` If `str2` contains the string `Good Morning`, then `str1` becomes the string `Mo`
`string objectName(n, char)`	Creates and initializes a string object with `n` copies of `char`	`string str1(5,'*')` This makes `str1` = `"*****"`
`string objectName;`	Creates and initializes a string object to represent an empty character sequence (Same as string `objectName = "";` The length of the string is `0`)	`string message;`

Program 7.3 illustrates examples of each of the constructor methods provided by the `string` class.

Program 7.3

```
#include <iostream>
#include <string>
using namespace std;

int main()
{
  string str1; // an empty string
  string str2("Good Morning");
  string str3 = "Hot Dog";
  string str4(str3);
  string str5(str4, 4);
  string str6 = "linear";
  string str7(str6, 3, 3);

  cout << "str1 is: " << str1 << endl;
  cout << "str2 is: " << str2 << endl;
  cout << "str3 is: " << str3 << endl;
  cout << "str4 is: " << str4 << endl;
  cout << "str5 is: " << str5 << endl;
  cout << "str6 is: " << str6 << endl;
  cout << "str7 is: " << str7 << endl;

  return 0;
}
```

Here is the output created by Program 7.3:

```
str1 is:
str2 is: Good Morning
str3 is: Hot Dog
str4 is: Hot Dog
str5 is: Dog
str6 is: linear
str7 is: ear
```

Although this output is straightforward, `str1` is an empty string consisting of no characters; because the first character in a string is designated as position zero, not one, the character position of the `D` in the string `Hot Dog` is located at position four, which is shown in Figure 7.2.

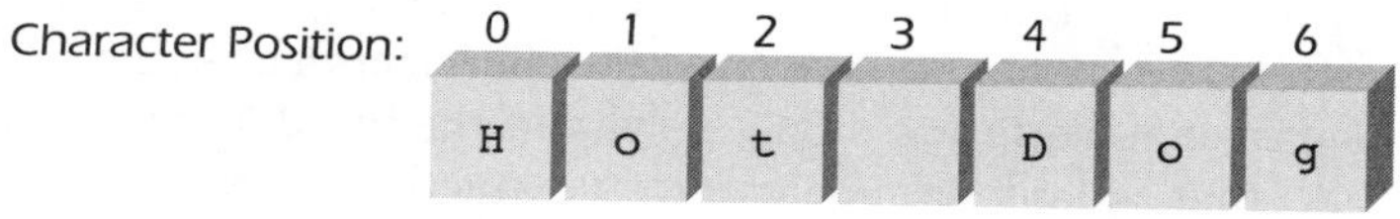

Figure 7.2 The character positions of the string `Hot Dog`.

`string` Input and Output

In addition to a string being initialized using the constructor methods listed in Table 7.2, strings can be input from the keyboard and displayed on the screen. Table 7.3 lists the basic methods and objects that can be used to input and output string values.

Table 7.3 `string` Class Input and Output Routines

C++ Routine	Description
`cout`	General purpose screen output
`cin`	General purpose terminal input that stops reading when a white space is encountered
`getline(cin, strObj)`	General purpose terminal input that inputs all characters entered into the string, `strObj`, and stops accepting characters when it receives a newline character (\n)

In addition to the standard `cout` and `cin` streams, the `string` class provides the `getline()` method for string input. For example, the expression `getline(cin, message)` will continuously accept and store characters typed at the terminal until the Enter key is pressed. Pressing the Enter key at the terminal generates a newline character, `'\n'`, which is interpreted by `getline()` as the end-of-line entry. All the characters encountered by `getline()`, except the newline character, are stored in the string, `message`, as illustrated in Figure 7.3.

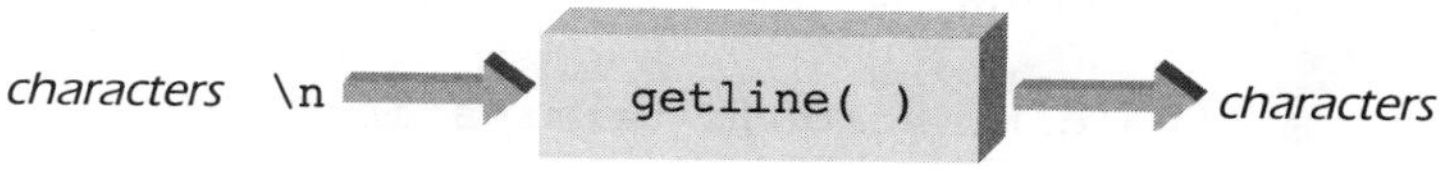

Figure 7.3 Inputting a string with `getline()`.

Program 7.4 illustrates using the `getline()` method and `cout` stream to input and output a string, respectively, that is entered at the user's terminal.

The following is a sample run of Program 7.4:

```
Enter a string:
This is a test input of a string of characters.
The string just entered is:
This is a test input of a string of characters.
```

Though the `cout` stream object is used in Program 7.4 for string output, the `cin` stream input object generally cannot be used in place of `getline()`for string input. This is because the `cin` object reads a set of characters up to either a blank space or a newline character. Thus, attempting to enter the characters `This is a string` using the statement `cin >> message;` only results in the word `This` being assigned to `message`. The fact that a blank terminates a `cin` extraction operation restricts the usefulness of the `cin` object for entering string data and is the reason for using `getline()`.

Program 7.4

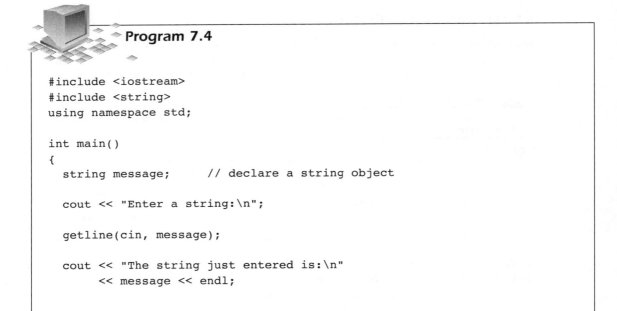

```
#include <iostream>
#include <string>
using namespace std;

int main()
{
  string message;      // declare a string object

  cout << "Enter a string:\n";

  getline(cin, message);

  cout << "The string just entered is:\n"
       << message << endl;


  return 0;
}
```

In its most general form, the `getline()` method has the syntax

```
getline(cin, strObj, terminatingChar)
```

where ***`strObj`*** is a string variable name and ***`terminatingChar`*** is an optional character constant, or variable, specifying the terminating character. For example, the expression `getline(cin, message, '!')` will accept all characters entered at the keyboard, including a newline character, until an exclamation point is entered. The exclamation point will not be stored as part of the string.

If the optional third argument is omitted when `getline()` is called, the default terminating character is the newline (`'\n'`) character. Thus, the statement `getline(cin, message,'\n');` can be used in place of the statement `getline(cin, message);`. Both of these statements stop reading characters when the Enter key is pressed. For all the programs used from this point forward, you can assume that input is terminated by pressing the Enter key, which generates a newline character. As such, the optional third argument passed to `getline()`, which is the terminating character, will be omitted.

Caution: The Phantom Newline Character

Seemingly strange results can be obtained when either the `cin` input stream and `getline()`method are used together to accept data or when the `cin` input stream is used, by itself, to accept individual characters. To see how this can occur, consider Program 7.5, which uses `cin` to accept an integer entered at the keyboard, storing it in the variable `value`, and is followed by a `getline()` method call.

Program 7.5

```
#include <iostream>
#include <string>
using namespace std;

int main()
{
  int value;
  string message;

  cout << "Enter a number: ";
  cin  >> value;
  cout << "The number entered is:\n"
       << value << endl;

  cout << "Enter text:\n";
  getline(cin, message);
  cout << "The text entered is:\n"
       << message << endl;
  cout << int(message.length());


  return 0;
}
```

Point of Information

The `string` and `char` Data Types

A string can consist of zero, one, or more characters. When the string has no characters, it is said to be an empty string with a length of zero. A string with a single character, such as `"a"`, is a string of length one and is stored differently than a `char` data type, such as `'a'`. However, for many practical purposes, a string of length one and a `char` respond in the same manner; for example, `cout >> "\n"` and `cout >> '\n'` produce a new line on the screen. It is important to understand that they are different data types; for example, both declarations

```
string s1 = 'a';   // INVALID INITIALIZATION
char key = "\n"; // INVALID INITIALIZATION
```

produce a compiler error because they attempt to initialize one data type with literal values of another type.

When Program 7.5 is run, the number entered in response to the prompt `Enter a number:` is stored in the variable `value`. At this point, everything seems to be working fine. Notice, however, that in entering a number, you enter a number and press the Enter key. On almost all computer systems, these entered data are stored in a temporary holding area called a buffer immediately after the characters are entered, as illustrated in Figure 7.4.

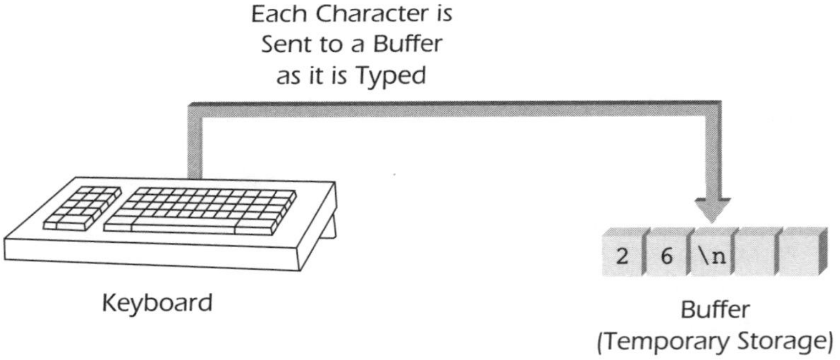

Figure 7.4 Typed keyboard characters are first stored in a buffer.

The `cin` input stream in Program 7.5 first accepts the number entered but leaves the `'\n'` in the buffer. The next input statement, which is a call to `getline()`, picks up the code for the Enter key as the next character and terminates any further input. Following is a sample run for Program 7.5:

```
Enter a number: 26
The number entered is 26
Enter text:
The text entered is
```

In this output, no text is accepted in response to the prompt `Enter text:`. No text occurs because, after the number 26 has been accepted by the program, the code for the Enter key, which is a newline escape sequence, remains in the buffer and is picked up and interpreted by the `getline()` method as the end of its input. This will occur whether an integer, as in Program 7.5, a string, or any other input is accepted by `cin` and then followed by a `getline()` method call.

There are three separate solutions to this "phantom" Enter key problem:

- Do not mix `cin` with `getline()` inputs in the same program.
- Follow the `cin` input with the call to `cin.ignore()`.
- Accept the Enter key into a character variable and then ignore it.

The preferred solution is the first one. All solutions, however, center on the fact that the Enter key is a legitimate character input and must be recognized as such. You will encounter this problem again when you consider accepting `char` data types in the next section.

String Processing

Strings can be manipulated using `string` class methods or the character at-a-time methods described in the next section. Table 7.4 lists the most commonly used `string` class methods. These include `accessor` and `mutator` methods plus methods and operator functions that use the standard arithmetic and comparison operators.

Table 7.4 The `string` class processing methods (Require the Header File `string`)

Method/Operation	Description	Example
`int length()`	Returns the length of the implicit string	`string.length()`
`int size()`	Same as above	`string.size()`
`at(int index)`	Returns the character at the specified index, and throws an exception if the index is non-existent	`string.at(4)`
`int compare(string)`	Compares two strings; returns a negative value if the implied string is less than `str`, zero if they are equal, and a positive value if the implied string is greater than `str`	`string1.compare(string2)`
`c_str()`	Returns the string as a `null` terminated C-string	`string1.c_str()`

Table 7.4 The `string` class processing methods (Require the Header File `string`) (continued)

Method/Operation	Description	Example
`bool empty`	Returns `true` if the implied string is empty; otherwise, returns `false`	`string1.empty()`
`erase(ind,n);`	Removes `n` characters from the implied string, starting at index `ind`.	`string1.erase(2,3)`
`erase(ind)`	Removes all characters from the implied string, starting from index `ind` until the end of the string. The length of the remaining string becomes `ind`.	`string1.erase(4)`
`int find(str)`	Returns the index of the first occurrence of `str` within the implied object.	`string1.find("the")`
`int find(str, ind)`	Returns the index of the first occurrence of `str` within the implied object, with the search beginning at index `ind`.	`string1.find("the", 5)`
`int find_first_of(str, ind)`	Returns the index of the first occurrence of any character in `str` within the implied object, with the search starting at index `ind`.	`string1.find_first_of("lt", 6)`
`int find_first_not_of(str, ind)`	Returns the index of the first occurrence of any character not in `str` within the implied object, with the search starting at index `ind`.	`string1.find_first_not_of("lt ,6)`
`void insert(ind, str)`	Inserts the string `str` into the implied string, starting at index `ind`.	`string.insert(4, "there")`

Table 7.4 The `string` class processing methods (Require the Header File `string`) (continued)

Method/Operation	Description	Example
`void replace(ind, n, str)`	Removes n characters in the implied object, starting at index position `ind`, and insert the string `str` at index position `ind`	`string1.replace(2,4,"okay")`
`string substr(ind,n)`	Returns a string consisting of n characters extracted from the implied string starting at index `ind`. If `n` is greater than the remaining number of characters, the rest of the implied string is used	`string2 = string1.substr(0,10)`
`void swap(str)`	Swaps characters in `str` with the implied object.	`string1.swap(string2)`
`[ind]`	Returns the character at index `x`, without checking if `ind` is a valid index	`string1[5]`
=	Assignment (also converts a C-string to a string)	`string1 = string`
+	Concatenates two strings	`string1 + string2`
+=	Concatenation and assignment	`string2 += string1`

`==` `!=`
`<` `<=`
`>` `>=`
	Relational operators. Returns `true` if the relation is satisfied; otherwise returns `false`	`string1 == string2`
		`string1 <= string2`
		`string1 > string2`

The most commonly used method in Table 7.4 is the `length()` method. This returns the number of characters in the string, which is referred to as the string's length. For example, the value returned by the method call `"Hello World!".length()` is 12. As always, the double quotation marks surrounding a string value are not considered part of the string. Similarly, if the string referenced by `string1` contains the value `"Have a good day."`, the value returned by the call `string1.length()` is 16.

Two string expressions may be compared for equality using the standard relational operators. Each character in a string is stored in binary using the ASCII or UNICODE code. Though these codes are different, they have some characteristics in common. In each of them, a blank precedes (is less than) all letters and numbers; the letters of the alphabet are stored in order from A to Z; and the digits are stored in order from 0 to 9. In both character codes, the digits come before (that is, are less than) the uppercase characters, which are followed by the lowercase characters. Thus, the uppercase characters are mathematically less than the lowercase characters. When two strings are compared, their individual characters are compared a pair at a time (both first characters, then both second characters, and so on). If no differences are found, the strings are equal; if a difference is found, the string with the first lower character is considered the smaller string.

- "Hello" is greater than "Good Bye" because the first H in Hello is greater than the first G in Good Bye.
- "Hello" is less than "hello" because the first 'H' in Hello is less than the first 'h' in hello.
- "SMITH" is greater than "JONES" because the first 'S' in SMITH is greater than the first 'J' in JONES.
- "123" is greater than "1227" because the third character, the '3', in 123 is greater than the third character, the '2' in 1227.
- "Behop" is greater than "Beehive" because the third character, the 'h', in Behop is greater than the third character, the 'e', in Beehive.

Program 7.6 uses `length()` and several relational expressions within the context of a complete program.

Program 7.6

```
#include <iostream>

#include <string>
using namespace std;

int main()
{
  string string1 = "Hello";
  string string2 = "Hello there";

  cout << "string1 is the string: " <<  string1 << endl;
  cout << "The number of characters in string1 is " <<  int(string1.length())
       << endl << endl;

  cout << "string2 is the string: " <<  string2 << endl;
  cout << "The number of characters in string2 is " <<  int(string2.length())
       << endl << endl;

  if (string1 < string2)
    cout << string1 <<  " is less than " <<  string2 << endl << endl;
  else if (string1 == string2)
    cout << string1 <<  " is equal to " <<  string2 << endl << endl;
  else
    cout << string1 <<  " is greater than " <<  string2 << endl << endl;

  string1 = string1 + " there world!";
  cout << "After concatenation, string1 contains the characters: " << string1 << endl;
  cout << "The length of this string is " <<  int(string1.length()) << endl;

  return 0;
}
```

Following is a sample output produced by Program 7.6:

```
string1 is the string: Hello
The number of characters in string1 is 5
```

```
string2 is the string: Hello there
The number of characters in string2 is 11

Hello is less than Hello there

After concatenation, string1 contains the characters: Hello there world!
The length of this string is 18
```

When reviewing this output, refer to Figure 7.5, which shows how the characters in `string1` and `string2` are stored in memory. The length of each string refers to the total number of characters in the string, and the first character in each string is located at index position 0. Thus, the length of a string is always one more than the index number of the last character's position in the string.

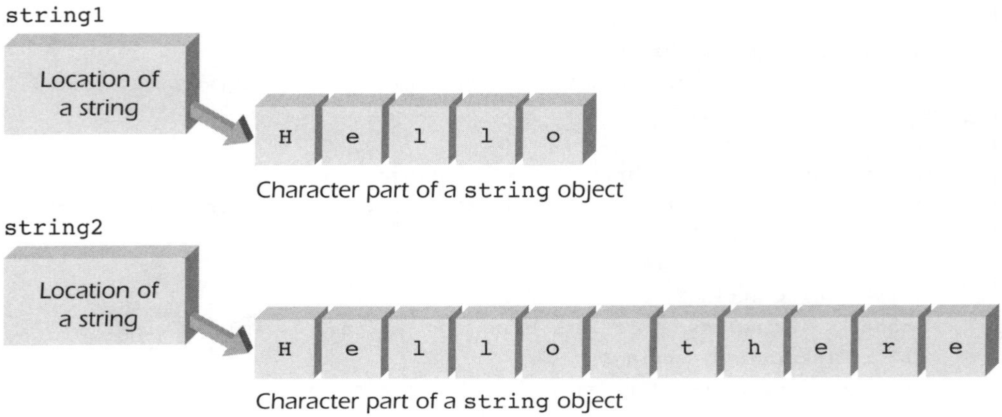

Figure 7.5 *The initial strings used in Program 7.6.*

Though you will mostly use the concatenation operator and `length()` method, there are times when you will find the other string methods, which are described in Table 7.4, useful. One of the more useful of these is the `at()` method, which permits you to retrieve individual characters in a string. Program 7.7 uses this method to select one character at a time from the string, starting at string position zero and ending at the index of the last character in the string. This last index value is always one less than the number of characters (that is, the string's length) in the string.

Program 7.7

```
#include <iostream>
#include <string>
using namespace std;

int main()
{

  string str = "Counting the number of vowels";
  int i, numChars;
  int vowelCount = 0;

  cout << "The string: " <<  str << endl;

  numChars = int(str.length());
  for (i = 0; i < numChars; i++)
  {
    switch(str.at(i))   // here is where a character is retrieved
    {
      case 'a':
      case 'e':
      case 'i':
      case 'o':
      case 'u':
        vowelCount++;
    }
  }
  cout << "has " <<  vowelCount <<  " vowels." << endl;


  return 0;
}
```

The expression `str.at(i)` in the `switch` statement above retrieves the character at position `i` in the string. This character is then compared to five different character values. The `switch` statement uses the fact that selected cases "drop through" in the absence of break statements. Thus, all selected cases result in an increment to `vowelCount`. The output displayed by Program 7.7 is the following:

```
The string: Counting the number of vowels
has 9 vowels.
```

As an example of inserting and replacing characters in a string, using methods listed in Table 7.4, assume that you start with a string created by the following statement:

```
string str = "This cannot be";
```

Figure 7.6 illustrates how this string is stored in the buffer created for it. As indicated, the initial length of the string is 14 characters.

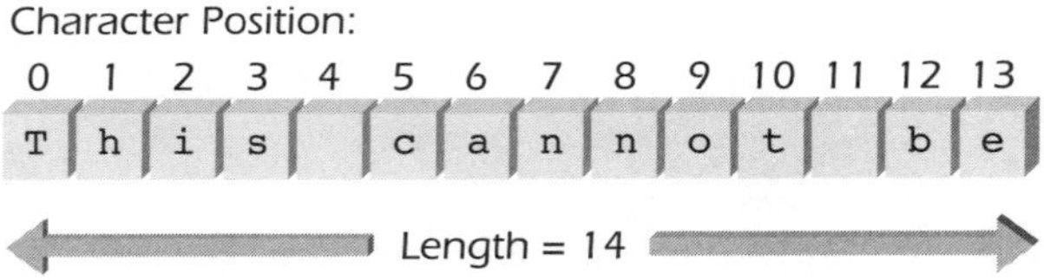

Figure 7.6 *Initial storage of a string object.*

Now assume that the following statement is executed:

```
str.insert(4," I know");
```

This statement causes the designated seven characters, beginning with a blank, to be inserted, starting at index position 4, in the existing string. The resulting string, after the insertion, is as shown in Figure 7.7.

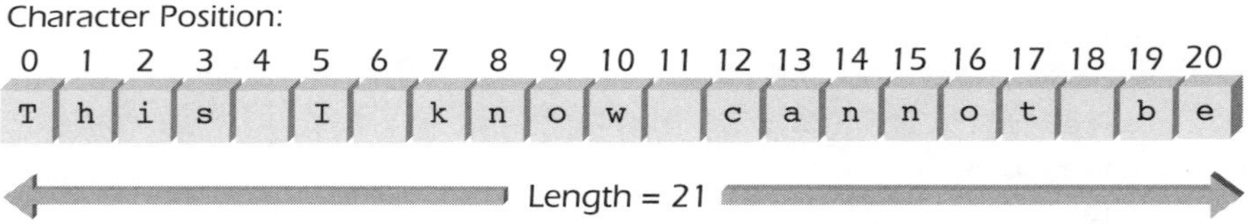

Figure 7.7 *The string after the insertion.*

If the statement `str.replace(12, 6, "to");` is now executed, the existing characters in index positions 12 through 17 will be deleted and the two characters `to` inserted starting at index position 12. Thus, the net effect of the replacement is as shown in Figure 7.8. The number of replacement characters, which in this particular case is two, can be fewer than, equal to, or greater than the characters that are being replaced, which in this case is six.

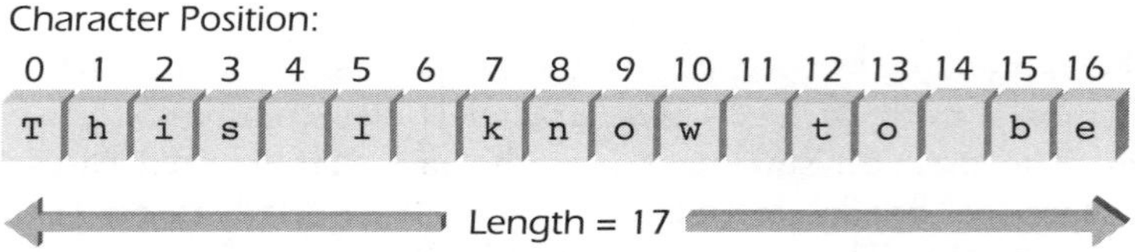

Figure 7.8 *The string after the replacement.*

Finally, if you append the string `"correct"` to the string shown in Figure 7.8 using the concatenation operator, +, the string illustrated in Figure 7.9 is obtained.

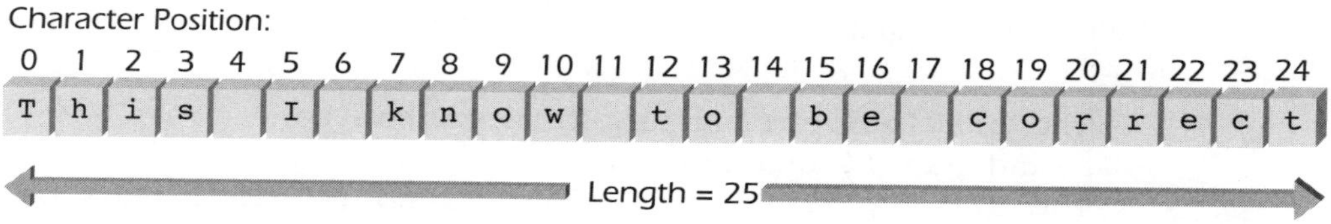

Figure 7.9 The string after the append.

Program 7.8 illustrates using the statements within the context of a complete program.

Program 7.8

```
#include <iostream>
#include <string>
using namespace std;

int main()
{
  string str = "This cannot be";

  cout << "The original string is: " << str << endl
       << "  and has " << int(str.length()) << " characters." << endl;

  // insert characters
  str.insert(4," I know");
  cout << "The string, after insertion is : " << str << endl
       << "  and has " << int(str.length()) << " characters." << endl;

  // replace characters
  str.replace(12, 6, "to");
  cout << "The string, after replacement is: " << str << endl
       << "  and has " << int(str.length()) << " characters." << endl;

  // append characters
  str = str + " correct";
  cout << "The string, after appending is: " << str << endl
       << "  and has " << int(str.length()) << " characters." << endl;

   return 0;
}
```

The following output produced by Program 7.8 matches the strings shown in Figures 7.6 to 7.9:

```
The original string is: This cannot be
  and has 14 characters.
The string, after insertion, is now: This I know cannot be
  and has 21 characters.
The string, after replacement, is: This I know to be
  and has 17 characters.
The string, after appending, is: This I know to be correct
  and has 25 characters.
```

Of the remaining string methods listed in Table 7.4, the most commonly used are those that locate specific characters in a string and create substrings. Program 7.9 presents examples of how some of these other methods are used.

Program 7.9

```
#include <iostream>
#include <string>
using namespace std;

int main()
{

  string string1 = "LINEAR PROGRAMMING THEORY";
  string s1, s2, s3;
  int j, k;

  cout << "The original string is " <<  string1 << endl;

  j = int(string1.find('I'));
  cout << "  The first position of an 'I' is " <<  j << endl;

  k = int(string1.find('I', (j+1)));
  cout << "  The next position of an 'I' is " <<  k << endl;

  j = int(string1.find("THEORY"));
  cout << "  The first location of \"THEORY\" is " <<  j << endl;

  k = int(string1.find("ING"));
  cout << "  The first index of \"ING\" is " <<  k << endl;
```

(Continued)

(Continued)

```
    s1 = string1.substr(2,5);
    s2 = string1.substr(19,3);
    s3 = string1.substr(6,8);

    cout << s1 + s2 + s3 << endl;


    return 0;
}
```

Here is the output produced by Program 7.9:

```
The original string is LINEAR PROGRAMMING THEORY
  The first position of an 'I' is 1
  The next position of an 'I' is 15
  The first location of "THEORY" is 19
  The first index of "ING" is 15
NEAR THE PROGRAM
```

The main point illustrated in Program 7.9 is that individual characters and sequences of characters can be located and extracted from a string.

Exercises 7.2

1. Enter and execute Program 7.4.
2. Determine the value of `text.at(0)`, `text.at(3)`, and `text.at(10)`, assuming that text is, individually, each of the following strings:
   a. now is the time
   b. rocky raccoon welcomes you
   c. Happy Holidays
   d. The good ship
3. Enter and execute Program 7.7.
4. Modify Program 7.7 to count and display the individual numbers of each vowel contained in the string.
5. Modify Program 7.7 to display the number of vowels in a user-entered string.
6. Using the `at()` method, write a C++ program that reads in a string using `getline()` and then displays the string out in reverse order. (*Hint:* Once the string has been entered and saved, retrieve and display characters starting from the end of the string.)
7. Write a C++ program that accepts both a string and a single character from the user. The program should determine how many times the character is contained

in the string. (*Hint:* Search the string using the `find(str, ind)` method. This method should be used in a loop that starts the index value at zero and then changes the index to one value past the index of where the char was last found.)

8. Enter and execute Program 7.8.

9. Enter and execute Program 7.9.

10. Write a C++ program that accepts a string from the user and then replaces all occurrences of the letter e with the letter x.

11. Modify the program written for Exercise 10 to search for the first occurrence of a user-entered sequence of characters and to replace this sequence, when it is found in the string, with a second set of a user-entered sequence. For example, if the entered string is `Figure 4-4 illustrates the output of Program 4-2` and the user enters that `4-` is to be replaced by `3-`, the resulting string will be `Figure 3-4 illustrates the output of Program 4-2`. (Only the first occurrence of the searched for sequence has been changed.)

12. Modify the program written for Exercise 11 to replace all occurrences of the designated sequence of characters with the new sequence of characters. For example, if the entered string is `Figure 4-4 illustrates the output of Program 4-2` and the user enters that `4-` is to be replaced by `3-`, the resulting string will be `Figure 3-4 illustrates the output of Program 3-2`.

7.3 CHARACTER MANIPULATION METHODS

In addition to the `string` methods provided by the `string` class, the C++ language provides a number of useful `character` class functions. These functions are listed in Table 7.5. The function declarations (prototypes) for each of these routines are contained in the header file string and `cctype`, which must be included in any program that uses these functions.

Table 7.5 Character Library Functions (Requires the Header File String or `cctype`)

Function Prototype	Description	Example
`int isalpha(charExp)`	Returns a `true` (non-zero integer) if `charExp` evaluates to a letter; otherwise, it returns a `false` (zero integer)	`isalpha('a')`

`int isalnum(charExp)`	Returns a `true` (non-zero integer) if `charExp` evaluates to a letter or a digit; otherwise, it returns a `false` (zero integer)	`char key;`
		`cin >> key;`
		`isalnum(key);`

Table 7.5 Character Library Functions (Requires the Header File String or `cctype`) (continued)

Function Prototype	Description	Example
`int isupper(charExp)`	Returns a `true` (non-zero integer) if `charExp` evaluates to an uppercase letter; otherwise it returns a `false` (zero integer)	`isupper('a')`
`int islower(charExp)`	Returns a `true` (non-zero integer) if `charExp` evaluates to a lowercase letter; otherwise it returns a `false` (zero integer)	`islower('a')`
`int isdigit(charExp)`	Returns a `true` (non-zero integer) if `charExp` evaluates to a digit (0 through 9); otherwise it returns a `false` (zero integer)	`isdigit('a')`
`int isascii(charExp)`	Returns a `true` (non-zero integer) if `charExp` evaluates to an ASCII character; otherwise returns a false (zero integer)	`isascii('a')`
`int isspace(charExp)`	Returns a `true` (non-zero integer) if `charExp` evaluates to a space; otherwise, returns a `false` (zero integer)	`isspace(' ')`
`int isprint(charExp)`	Returns a `true` (non-zero integer) if `charExp` evaluates to a printable character; otherwise, returns a `false` (zero integer)	`isprint('a')`
`int isctrl(charExp)`	Returns a `true` (non-zero integer) if `charExp` evaluates to a control character; otherwise, it returns a false (zero integer)	`isctrl('a')`
`int ispunct(charExp)`	Returns a `true` (non-zero integer) if `charExp` evaluates to a punctuation character; otherwise, returns a `false` (zero integer)	`ispucnt('!')`
`int isgraph(charExp)`	Returns a `true` (non-zero integer) if `charExp` evaluates to a printable character other than whitespace; otherwise `false` (zero integer)	`isgraph(' ')`
`int toupper(charExp)`	Returns the uppercase equivalent if `charExp` evaluates to a lowercase character; otherwise it returns the character code without modification	`toupper('a')`
`int tolower(charExp)`	Returns the lowercase equivalent if `charExp` evaluates to a uppercase character; otherwise it returns the character code without modification	`tolower('A')`

Because all of the `istype( )` functions listed in Table 7.5 return a non-zero integer (which is interpreted as a Boolean `true` value) when the character meets the desired condition and a zero integer (or Boolean `false` value) when the condition is not met, these functions are typically used directly within an `if` statement. For example, consider the following code segment, which assumes that `ch` is a character variable:

```
if(isdigit(ch))
  cout << "The character just entered is a digit" << endl;
else if(ispunct(ch))
  cout << "The character just entered is a punctuation mark" << endl;
```

In this example, if `ch` contains a digit character, the first `cout` statement is executed; if the character is a letter, the second `cout` statement is executed. In both cases, however, the character to be checked is included as an argument to the appropriate method. Program 7.10 illustrates this type of code within a program that counts the number of letters, digits, and other characters in a string. The individual characters to be checked are obtained using the `string` class' `at()` method. In Program 7.10, this method is used in a `for` loop that cycles through the string from the first character to the last.

Program 7.10

```
#include <iostream>
#include <string>
#include <cctype>
using namespace std;

int main()
{
    string str = "This -123/ is 567 A ?<6245> Test!";
    char nextChar;
    int i;
    int numLetters = 0, numDigits = 0, numOthers = 0;

    cout << "The original string is: " <<  str
         << "\nThis string contains " <<  int(str.length())
            <<  " characters," <<  " which consist of" << endl;

    // check each character in the string
    for (i = 0; i < int(str.length()); i++)
    {
      nextChar = str.at(i);  // get a character
      if (isalpha(nextChar))
        numLetters++;
      else if (isdigit(nextChar))
        numDigits++;
```

(Continued)

(Continued)

```
        else
          numOthers++;
      }

      cout << "       " << numLetters << " letters" << endl;
      cout << "       " << numDigits << " digits" << endl;
      cout << "       " << numOthers << " other characters." << endl;

    cin.ignore();
    return 0;
}
```

The output produced by Program 7.10 is the following:

```
The original string is: This -123/ is 567 A ?<6245> Test!
This string contains 33 characters, which consist of
     11 letters
     10 digits
     12 other characters.
```

As indicated by this output, each of the 33 characters in the string has correctly been categorized as a letter, digit, or other character.

Typically, as in Program 7.10, each of the functions in Table 7.5 is used in a character-by-character manner on each character in a string. This is again illustrated in Program 7.11, where each lowercase string character is converted to its uppercase equivalent using the `toupper()` function. This function only converts lowercase letters, leaving all other characters unaffected.

A sample run of Program 7.11 produced the following output:

```
Type in any sequence of characters: this is a test OF 12345.
The characters just entered, in uppercase are: THIS IS A TEST OF 12345.
```

In Program 7.11, pay particular attention to the statement `for (i = 0; i < int(str.length()); i++)`that is used to cycle through each of the characters in the string. This is typically how each element in a string is accessed, using the `length()` method to determine when the end of the string has been reached. (Review Program 7.10 to see that it is used in the same way.) The only real difference is that in Program 7.11 each element is accessed using the subscript notation `str[i]`; in Program 7.10, the `at()` method was used. Though these two notations are interchangeable, and which you use is a matter of choice, the two notations should not be mixed in the same program for consistency.

Program 7.11

```
#include <iostream>
#include <string>
using namespace std;

int main()
{
  int i;
  string str;

  cout << "Type in any sequence of characters: ";
  getline(cin,str);

  // cycle through all elements of the string
  for (i = 0; i < int(str.length()); i++)
    str[i] = toupper(str[i]);

  cout << "The characters just entered, in uppercase, are: "
       << str << endl;

  cin.ignore();
  return 0;
}
```

Character I/O

Although you have used `cin` and `getline()` to accept data entered from the keyboard in a more or less "cookbook" manner, you need to understand what data are being sent to the program and how the program must react to process the data. At a fundamental level, all input (as well as output) is done on a character-by-character basis, as illustrated in Figure 7.10.

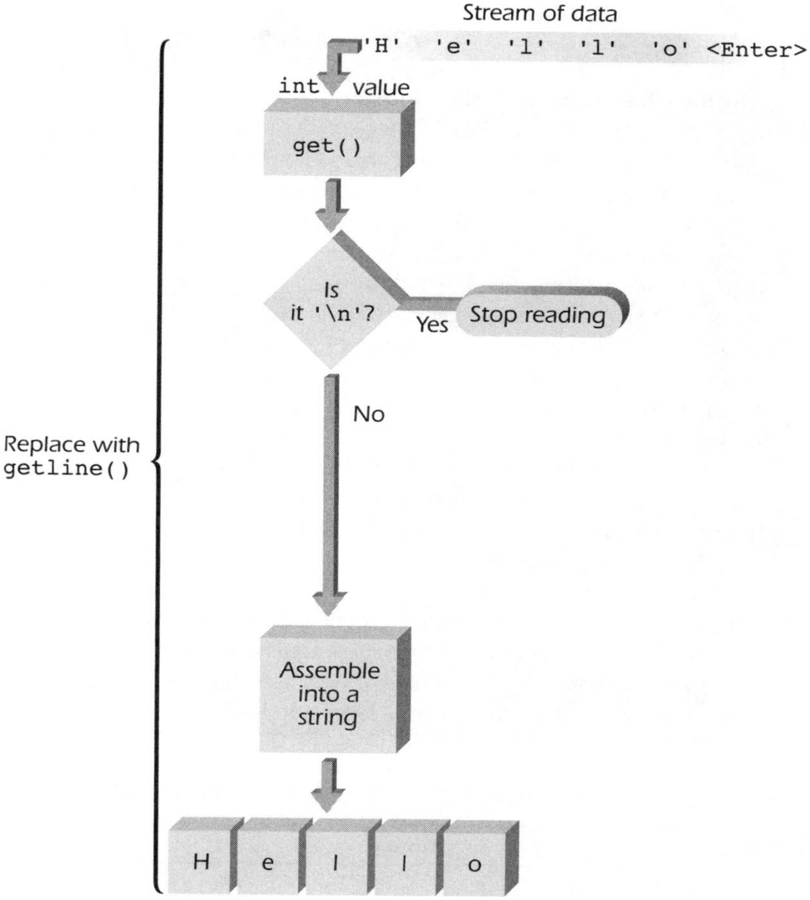

Figure 7.10 Accepting keyboard-entered characters.

As illustrated in Figure 7.10, the entry of every piece of data, be it string or a number, consists of typing individual characters. For example, the entry of the string `Hello` consists of pressing and releasing the five keys `H`, `e`, `l`, `l`, `o`, and the Enter key. Similarly, the output of the number `26.95` consists of the display of the five characters `2`, `6`, `.`, `9`, and `5`. Though the programmer typically does not think of data in this manner, the program is restricted to this character-by-character I/O, and all of C++'s higher-level I/O methods and streams are based on lower-level character I/O methods. These more elemental character methods, which can be used directly by a programmer, are listed in Table 7.6.

Point of Information

Why the `char` Data Type Uses Integer Values

In C++, a character is stored as an integer value, which is sometimes confusing to beginning programmers. The reason for this is that, in addition to the standard English letters and characters, a program needs to store special characters that have no printable equivalents. One of these is the end-of-file sentinel that all computer systems use to designate the end of a file of data. These end-of-file sentinels can be transmitted from the keyboard. For example, on Unix-based systems, it is generated by pressing the Ctrl button and, while holding it down, pressing the D key; on Windows-based systems, it is generated by pressing the Ctrl and, while holding it down, pressing the Z key. Both of these sentinels are stored as the integer number –1, which has no equivalent character value. (You can check this by displaying the integer value of each entered character (see Program 7.12), and typing the Ctrl + D combination or the Ctrl + Z combination, depending on the system you are using)

By using a 16-bit integer value, over 64,000 different characters can be represented. This provides sufficient storage for multiple character sets that can include Arabic, Chinese, Hebrew, Japanese, Russian, and almost all known language symbols. Thus, storing a character as an integer value has a practical value.

An important consequence of using integer codes for string characters is that characters can easily be compared for alphabetical ordering. For example, as long as each subsequent letter in an alphabet has a higher value than its preceding letter, the comparison of character values is reduced to the comparison of numeric values. If characters are stored in sequential numerical order, it ensures that adding one to a letter will produce the next letter in the alphabet.

Table 7.6 Basic Character I/O Methods (Require the Header File `cctype`)

Method	Description	Example
`cout.put(charExp)`	Places the character value of `charExp` on the output stream	`cout.put('A');`
`cin.get(charVar)`	Extracts the next character from the input stream and assigns it to the variable `charVar`	`cin.get(key);`
`cin.peek(charVar)`	Assigns the next character from the input stream to the variable `charVar` *without* extracting the character from the stream	`cin.peek(nextKey);`
`cin.putback(charExp)`	Pushes a character value of `charExp` back onto the input stream	`cin.putback(cKey);`
`cin.ignore(n, char)`	Ignores a maximum of the next `n` input characters, up and including the detection of `char`. If no arguments are specified, ignores the next single character on input stream	`cin.ignore(80,'\n');` `cin.ignore();`

A Bit of Background

A Notational Inconsistency

All of the character class methods listed in Table 7.6 use the standard object-oriented notation of preceding the method's name with an object name, as in `cin.get()`. This is not the case with the string class `getline()` method, which uses the notation `getline(cin, strVar)`. In this notation, the object, `cin` for example, appears as an argument, which is how procedural-based functions pass variables. In terms of achieving consistency, you can expect `getline()` to be called as `cin.getline()`.

Unfortunately, the proper notation is in use for a `getline()` method originally created for C-style strings (see Section 10.1); hence, a notational inconsistency was created.

The `get()` function reads the next character in the input stream and assigns it to the function's character variable. For example, examine the statement below:

```
cin.get(nextChar);
```

It causes the next character entered at the keyboard to be stored in the character variable `nextChar`. This function is useful in inputting and checking individual characters before they are assigned to a complete string or C++ data type.

The character output function corresponding to `get()` is `put()`. This function expects a single-character argument and displays the character passed to it on the terminal. For example, the statement `cout.put('A')` causes the letter `A` to be displayed on the screen.

Of the last three functions listed in Table 7.6, the `cin.ignore()` function is the most useful. This function permits skipping over input until a designated character, such as `'\n'`, is encountered. For example, the statement `cin.ignore(80, '\n')` will skip up to a maximum of the next 80 characters or will stop the skipping if the newline character is encountered. Such a statement can be useful in skipping all further input on a line, up to a maximum of 80 characters, or until the end of the current line is encountered. Input would begin with the next line.

The `peek()` function returns the next character on the stream but does not remove it from the stream's buffer (see Figure 7.6). For example, the expression `cin.peek(nextChar)` returns the next character input by the keyboard but leaves it in the buffer. This is sometimes useful for peeking ahead and seeing what the next character is, while leaving it in place for the next input.

Finally, the `putback()` function places a character back on the stream so it will be the next character read. The argument passed to `putback()` can be any character expression that evaluates to a legitimate character value and need not be the last input character.

The Phantom Newline Revisited

As you saw in the previous section, seemingly strange results are sometimes obtained when a `cin` stream input is followed by a `getline()` method call. This same result can occur when characters are inputted using the `get()` character method. To see how this can occur, consider Program 7.12, which uses the `get()` method to accept the next character entered at the keyboard and stores the character in the variable `fkey`.

Program 7.12

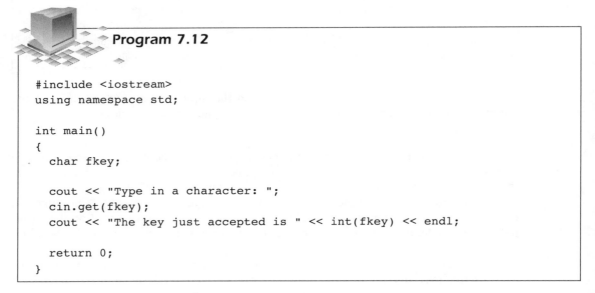

```
#include <iostream>
using namespace std;

int main()
{
  char fkey;

  cout << "Type in a character: ";
  cin.get(fkey);
  cout << "The key just accepted is " << int(fkey) << endl;

  return 0;
}
```

When Program 7.12 is run, the character entered in response to the prompt `Type in a character:` is stored in the character variable `fkey` and the decimal code for the character is displayed by explicitly casting the character into an integer, to force its display as an integer value. The following sample run illustrates this:

```
Type in a character: m
The key just accepted is 109
```

At this point, everything seems to be working, though you might be wondering why the decimal value of `m` is displayed rather than the character itself. The reason for this will become apparent.

In typing `m`, two keys are usually pressed, the m key and the Enter key. As in the previous section, these two characters are stored in a buffer after they are pressed (see Figure 7.4).

The first key pressed, `m` in this case, is taken from the buffer and stored in `fkey`. This, however, still leaves the code for the Enter key in the buffer. Thus, a subsequent call to `get()` for a character input will automatically pick up the code for the Enter key as the next character. For example, consider Program 7.13.

Program 7.13

```
#include <iostream>
using namespace std;

int main()
{
  char fkey, skey;

  cout << "Type in a character: ";
  cin.get(fkey);
  cout << "The key just accepted is " << int(fkey) << endl;

  cout << "Type in another character: ";
  cin.get(skey);
  cout << "The key just accepted is " << int(skey) << endl;

  return 0;
}
```

The following is a sample run for Program 7.13.

```
Type in a character: m
The key just accepted is 109
Type in another character: The key just accepted is 10
```

After entering the letter `m` in response to the first prompt, the Enter key is also pressed. From a character standpoint, this represents the entry of two distinct characters. The first character is `m`, which is coded and stored as the integer 109. The second character also gets stored in the buffer with the numerical code for the Enter key. The second call to `get()` picks up this code immediately, without waiting for any additional key to be pressed. The last `cout` stream displays the code for this key. The reason for displaying the numerical code rather than the character itself is because the Enter key has no printable character associated with it that can be displayed.

Remember that every key has a numerical code, including the Enter, Spacebar, Escape, and Control keys. These keys generally have no effect when entering numbers because the input methods ignore them as leading or trailing input with numerical data. Nor do these keys affect the entry of a single character requested as the first user data to be inputted, as is the case in Program 7.12. Only when a character is requested after the user has already input some other data, as in Program 7.13, does the usually invisible Enter key become noticeable.

In Section 9.1, you learned some ways to prevent the Enter key from being accepted as a legitimate character input when the `getline()` method was used. The following ways can be used when the `get()` method is used within a program:

- Follow the `cin.get()` input with the call `cin.ignore()`.
- Accept the Enter key into a character variable, and then do not use further.

Program 7.14 applies the first solution to Program 7.13. Ignoring the Enter key after the first character is read and displayed clears the buffer of the Enter key and gets it ready to store the next valid input character as its first character.

Program 7.14

```
#include <iostream>
using namespace std;

int main()
{
  char fkey, skey;

  cout << "Type in a character: ";
  cin.get(fkey);
  cout << "The key just accepted is " << int(fkey) << endl;
  cin.ignore();

  cout << "Type in another character: ";
  cin.get(skey);
  cout << "The key just accepted is " << int(skey) << endl;

  cin.ignore();
  return 0;
}
```

In Program 7.14, observe that when the user types the letter m and presses the Enter key, the m is assigned to `fkey` and the code for the Enter key is ignored. The next call to `get()` stores the code for the next key pressed in the variable `skey`. From the user's standpoint, the Enter key has no effect except to signal the end of each character input. The following is a sample run for Program 7.14:

```
Type in a character: m
The key just accepted is 109
Type in another character: b
The key just accepted is 98
```

A Second Look at User-Input Validation

As mentioned during the first look at user-input validation (Section 3.4), programs that respond effectively to unexpected user input are formally referred to as robust programs and informally as "bulletproof" programs. Code that validates user input and ensures that a program does not produce unintended results due to unexpected input is a sign of a well-constructed, robust program. One of your jobs, as a programmer, is to produce such programs. To see how such unintended results can occur, consider the following two code examples. First, assume that your program contains the following statements:

```
cout << "Enter an integer: ";
cin  >> value;
```

Now assume that, by mistake, a user enters the characters e4. In earlier versions of C++, this would cause the program to unexpectedly terminate, or **crash**. While a crash can still occur with the current ANSI/ISO standard (see, for example, Exercise 9), it will not occur in this case. Rather, a meaningless integer value will be assigned to the variable `value`. This, of course, will invalidate any results obtained using this variable.

As a second example, consider the following code, which will cause an infinite loop to occur if the user enters a non-numeric value (the program can be halted by pressing the Ctrl button and, while holding it down, pressing the c key):

```
double value;

  do
  {
    cout << "Enter a number (enter 0 to exit): ";
    cin  >> value;

    cout << "The square root of this number is: " << sqrt(value) << endl;
  }while (value !=0);
```

The basic technique for handling invalid data input and preventing seemingly innocuous code, such as in the two previous examples, from producing unintended results is referred to as **user-input validation**. This means validating the entered data during or after data entry and providing the user with a way of re-entering any invalid data. User-input validation is an essential part of any commercially viable program, and if done correctly, it will protect a program from attempting to process data types that can cause a program to crash, create infinite loops, or produce more invalid results

The central element in user-input validation is the checking of each entered character to verify that it qualifies as a legitimate character for the expected data type. For example, if an integer is required, the only acceptable characters are a leading plus (+) or minus (–) sign and the digits 0 through 9. These characters can be checked as they are being typed, which means the `get()` function is used to input a character at a time, or after all the characters can be accepted in a string, and then each string character checked for validity. Once all the entered characters have been validated, the entered string can be converted into the correct data type.

Two basic means exist for accomplishing the validity of the entered characters. Section 7.4 initially presents one of these ways: character-by-character checking. A second technique, which encompasses a broader scope of data processing tasks using exception handling, is presented at the end of Section 7.4.

Exercises 7.3

1. Enter and execute Program 7.10.

2. Enter and execute Program 7.11.

3. Write a C++ program that counts the number of words in a string. A word is encountered whenever a transition from a blank space to a non-blank character is encountered. Assume the string contains only words separated by blank spaces.

4. Generate ten random numbers in the range 0 to 129. If the number represents a printable character, print the character with an appropriate message that indicates the following:

The character is a lowercase letter
The character is an uppercase letter
The character is a digit
The character is a space

If the character is none of these, display its value in integer format.

5. **a.** Write a function, `length()`, that determines and returns the length of a string without using the string class `length()` method.
b. Write a simple `main()`function to test the `length()` function written for Exercise 5a.

6. **a.** Write a function, `countlets()`, that returns the number of letters in a string passed as an argument. Digits, spaces, punctuation, tabs, and newline characters should not be included in the returned count.
b. Include the `countlets()` method written for Exercise 6a in an executable C++ program and use the program to test the method.

7. Write a program that accepts a string from the console and displays the hexadecimal equivalent of each character in the string.

8. Write a C++ program that accepts a string from the console and displays the string one word per line.

9. In response to the following code suppose a user enters the data 12e4:

```
cout << "Enter an integer: ";
cin  >> value;
```

What value will be stored in the integer variable `value`?

10. a. Write a C++ program that stops reading a line of text when a period is entered and displays the sentence with correct spacing and capitalization. For this program, correct spacing means that there should only one space between words and that all letters should be in lowercase, except for the first letter. For example, if the user entered the text `i am          going   to     Go TO   THe moVies.`, the displayed sentence should be `I am going to go to the movies.`
    b. Determine what characters, if any, are not correctly displayed by the program you created for Exercise 10a.
11. Write a C++ program that accepts a name as first name last name and then displays the name as last name, first name. For example, if the user entered Gary Bronson, the output should be Bronson, Gary.
12. Modify the program written for Exercise 11 to include an array of five names.

7.4 INPUT DATA VALIDATION

One of the major uses of strings in programs is for user-input validation. The necessity for validating user input is essential: though a program prompts the user to enter a specific type of data, such as an integer, this does not ensure the user will comply. What a user enters is, in fact, totally out of the programmer's control. What is in your control is how you deal with the entered data.

It certainly does no good to tell a frustrated user that, "The program clearly tells you to enter an integer and you entered a date." Rather, successful programs always anticipate invalid data and isolate such data from being accepted and processed. This is typically accomplished by first validating that the data are of the correct type; if it is, the data is accepted; otherwise, the user is requested to re-enter the data, with an explanation of why the entered data was invalid.

One of the most common methods of validating numerical input data is to accept all numbers as strings. Each character in the string can then be checked to ensure it complies with the requested data type. After this check is made and the data is verified for the correct type, the string converted to an integer or double-precision value using the conversion functions listed in Table 7.7. (For data accepted using `string` class objects, the `c_str()` method must be applied to the string before the conversion function is invoked.)

As an example, consider the input of an integer number. To be valid, the data entered must adhere to the following conditions:

- The data must contain at least one character.
- If the first character is a + or – sign, the data must contain at least one digit.
- Only digits from 0 to 9 are acceptable following the first character.

Table 7.7 C-string Conversion Functions

Function	Description	Example
`int atoi(stringExp)`	Converts `stringExp` to an integer. Conversion stops at the first noninteger character.	`atoi("1234")`
`double atof(stringExp)`	Converts `stringExp` to a double precision number. Conversion stops at the first character that cannot be interpreted as a double.	`atof("12.34")`
`char[] itoa(integerExp)`	Converts `integerExp` to a character array. The space allocated for the returned characters must be large enough for the converted value.	`itoa(1234)`

The following function, `isvalidInt()`, can be used to check that an entered string complies with these conditions. This function returns the Boolean value of `true` if the conditions are satisfied; otherwise, it returns a Boolean `false` value.

```
bool isvalidInt(string str)
{
  int start = 0;
  int i;
  bool valid = true;  // assume a valid
  bool sign = false;  // assume no sign


  // check for an empty string
  if (int(str.length()) == 0)  valid = false;

  // check for a leading sign
  if (str.at(0) == '-'|| str.at(0) == '+')
  {
    sign = true;
    start = 1;  // start checking for digits after the sign
  }

  // check that there is at least one character after the sign
  if (sign && int(str.length() == 1)) valid = false;

  // now check the string, which we know has at least one non-sign char
  i = start;
```

```
  while(valid && i < int(str.length()))
  {
    if(!isdigit(str.at(i))) valid = false;  //found a non-digit character
    i++;  // move to next character
  }

  return valid;
}
```

In the code for the `isvalidInt()` method, pay attention to the conditions that are being checked. These are commented in the code and consist of checking the following:

- The string is not empty.
- A valid sign symbol (+ or –) is present.
- If a sign symbol is present, at least one digit follows it.
- All the remaining characters in the string are digits.

Only if all of these conditions are met does the function return a Boolean `true` value. Once this value is returned, the string can be safely converted into an integer with the assurance that no unexpected value will result to hamper further data processing. Program 7.15 uses this method within the context of a complete program.

Program 7.15

```
#include <iostream>
#include <string>
using namespace std;

int main()
{
  bool isvalidInt(string);  // function prototype (declaration)
  string value;
  int number;

  cout << "Enter an integer: ";
  getline(cin, value);
```

(Continued)

(Continued)

```
  if (!isvalidInt(value))
   cout << "The number you entered is not a valid integer.";
  else
  {
      number = atoi(value.c_str());
    cout << "The integer you entered is " << number;
  }


  return 0;
}

bool isvalidInt(string str)
{
  int start = 0;
  int i;
  bool valid = true;  // assume a valid
  bool sign = false;  // assume no sign


  // check for an empty string
  if (int(str.length()) == 0)  valid = false;

  // check for a leading sign
  if (str.at(0) == '-'|| str.at(0) == '+')
  {
    sign = true;
    start = 1;  // start checking for digits after the sign
  }

  // check that there is at least one character after the sign
  if (sign && int(str.length()) == 1) valid = false;

  // now check the string, which we know has at least one non-sign char
  i = start;
  while(valid && i < int(str.length()))
  {
    if(!isdigit(str.at(i))) valid = false;  //found a non-digit character
    i++;  // move to next character
  }

  return valid;
}
```

Two sample runs using Program 7.15 produced the following:

```
Enter an integer: 12e45
The number you entered is not a valid integer.
```

and

```
Enter an integer: -12345
The integer you entered is -12345
```

As illustrated by this output, the program successfully determines that an invalid character was entered in the first run.

A second line of defense is to provide error-processing code within the context of exception handling code. This type of code is typically provided to permit the user to correct a problem such as invalid data entry by re-entering a new value. The means of providing this in C++ is referred to as exception handling and is presented next.

Using exception handling, a complete means of ensuring that an integer number is entered by a user in response to a request for an integer value can be constructed. The technique we will use extends the `isvalidInt()` function included in Program 7.15 to ensure that an invalid integer value is not only detected, but that the program provides the user with the option of re-entering values until a valid integer is obtained. This technique can easily be applied to ensure the entry of a valid double-precision number, which is the other numerical data type frequently requested as user-entered data.

Using the `isvalidInt()`function provided in Program 7.15, we now develop a more comprehensive function named `getanInt()` that uses exception processing to continuously accept a user input until a string that corresponds to a valid integer is detected. Once such a string is entered, the `getanInt()` function converts the string to an integer and returns the integer value. This ensures that the program requesting an integer actually receives an integer and prevents any unwarranted effects, such as a program crash due to an invalid data type being entered.

The algorithm that we will use to perform this task is:

```
Set a Boolean variable named notanint to true
while (notanint is true)
    try
        Accept a string value
        If the string value does not correspond to an integer throw an
        exception
    catch the exception
        Display the error message "Invalid integer - Please re-enter: "
        Send control back to the while statement
        Set notanint to false (this causes the loop to terminate)
  End while
  Return the integer corresponding to the entered string
```

The code corresponding to this algorithm is highlighted in Program 7.16.

Program 7.16

```
#include <iostream>
#include <string>
using namespace std;

int main()
{
  int getanInt();  // function declaration (prototype)
  int value;

  cout << "Enter an integer value: ";
  value = getanInt();
  cout << "The integer entered is: " << value << endl;

  return 0;
}

int getanInt()
{
  bool isvalidInt(string);  // function declaration (prototype)
  bool notanint = true;
  string svalue;

  while (notanint)
  {
    try
    {
      cin >> svalue;  // accept a string input
      if (!isvalidInt(svalue)) throw svalue;
      }
    catch (string e)
    {
      cout << "Invalid integer - Please re-enter: ";
        continue; // send control to the while statement
    }
    notanint = false;
  }
  return atoi(svalue.c_str());  // convert to an integer
}
```

(Continued)

(Continued)

```
  bool isvalidInt(string str)
  {
    int start = 0;
    int i;
    bool valid = true;  // assume a valid
    bool sign = false;  // assume no sign

    // check for an empty string
    if (int(str.length()) == 0)  valid = false;

    // check for a leading sign
    if (str.at(0) == '-'|| str.at(0) == '+')
    {
      sign = true;
      start = 1;  // start checking for digits after the sign
    }

    // check that there is at least one character after the sign
    if (sign && int(str.length()) == 1) valid = false;

    // now check the string, which we know has at least one non-sign char
    i = start;
    while(valid && i < int(str.length()))
    {
      if(!isdigit(str.at(i))) valid = false;  //found a non-digit character
      i++;  // move to next character
    }

   return valid;
 }
```

Following is a sample output produced by Program 7.16:

```
Enter an integer value: abc
Invalid integer - Please re-enter: 12.
Invalid integer - Please re-enter: 12e
Invalid integer - Please re-enter: 120
The integer entered is: 120
```

As shown by this output, the `getanInt()` function works correctly. It continuously requests input until a valid integer is entered.

Exercises 7.4

1. Write a C++ program that prompts the user to type in an integer. Have your program accept the number, as an integer, using `cin` and, using `cout`, display the value your program actually accepted from the data entered. Run your program four times. The first time you run the program, enter a valid integer number, the second time enter a double-precision number, and the third time enter a character. Next, enter the value 12e34.

2. Modify the program you wrote for Exercise 1 but have your program use a double-precision variable. Run the program four times. The first time enter an integer, the second time enter a decimal number, the third time enter a decimal number with an f as the last character entered, and the fourth time enter a character. Using the output display, keep track of what number your program actually accepted from the data you entered. What happened, if anything, and why?

3. a. Why do you think that successful application programs contain extensive data input validity checks? (*Hint:* Review Exercises 1 and 2.)
   b. What do you think is the difference between a data type check and a data reasonableness check?
   c. Assume that a program requests that the user enter a month, day, and year. What are some reasonable checks that could be made on the data entered?

4. a. Enter and execute Program 7.15.
   b. Run Program 7.15 four times, using the data referred to in Exercise 1 for each run.

5. Modify Program 7.15 to display any invalid characters that were entered.

6. Modify Program 7.15 to request an integer continually until a valid number is entered.

7. Modify Program 7.15 to remove all leading and trailing spaces from the entered string before it is checked for validity.

8. Write a function that checks each digit as it is entered, rather than checking the completed string, as done in Program 7.15.

9. Enter and execute Program 7.16.

10. Modify the `isvalidInt()` function used in Program 7.16 to remove all leading and trailing blank spaces from its string argument before determining if the string corresponds to a valid integer.

11. Modify the `isvalidInt()` function used in Program 7.16 to accept a string that ends in a decimal point. For example, input 12. should be accepted and converted to the integer number twelve.

12. a. Write a C++ function named `isvalidReal()` that checks for a valid double-precison number. This kind of number can have an optional + or – sign, at most one decimal point, which can be the first character, and at least one digit between 0 and 9 inclusive. The function should return a Boolean value of true

if the entered number is a real number; otherwise, it should return a Boolean value of false.

b. Modify the `isvalidReal()` function written for Exercise 12a to remove all leading and trailing blank spaces from its string argument before determining if the string corresponds to a valid real number.

13. Write and execute a C++ function, named `getareal()`, that uses exception handling to continuously accept an input string until a string that can be converted to a real number is entered. The function should return a double value corresponding to the string value entered by the user.

7.5 NAMESPACES AND CREATING A PERSONAL LIBRARY

Until the introduction of personal computers in the early 1980s, with their extensive use of integrated circuits and microprocessors, both the speed of computers and their available memory were severely restricted. For example, the most advanced computers of the time had speeds measured in milliseconds (one-thousandth of a second); current computers have speeds measured in nanoseconds (one-billionth of a second) and higher. Similarly, the memory capacity of early desktop computers consisted of 32 thousand locations, with each location consisting of eight bits. Today's computer memories consist of millions of memory locations, each consisting of from 32 to 64 bits.

These early hardware restrictions made it imperative that programmers use every possible trick to save memory space and make programs run more efficiently. Almost every program was hand-crafted and included what was referred to as "clever code" to minimize run time and maximize the use of memory storage. Unfortunately, this individualized code, over time, became a liability. New programmers had to expend considerable time understanding the existing code; even the original programmer had trouble figuring out code that had been written only months before. This made modifications extremely time-consuming and costly, and precluded cost-effective use of existing code for new installations.

The inability to reuse code efficiently, combined with expanded hardware capabilities, provided the incentive for discovering more efficient programming. Initially this led to the structured programming concepts incorporated into procedural languages, such as Pascal, and currently to the object-oriented techniques that form the basis of C++. One of the early criticisms of C++, however, was that it did not provide a comprehensive library of classes. This has changed dramatically with the current ANSI/ISO standard and the inclusion of an extensive C++ library.

No matter how many useful classes and methods that are provide, however, each major type of programming application, such as engineering, scientific, and financial areas have their own specialized requirements. For example, C++ provides rather good date and time functions in its `ctime` header file. For specialized needs, such as those encountered in scheduling problems, however, these functions must be expanded. Thus, a more complete set of functions would include finding the number of working days between two dates that took into account weekends and holidays. It would also require functions that implemented prior and next-day algorithms that accounted for leap years and the actual days in each month. These could be provided as part of a more complete `Date` class or as non-class functions.

In situations like this, programmers create and share their own libraries of classes and functions with other programmers working on the same or similar projects. Once the classes and functions have been tested, they can be incorporated into any program without further coding time expenditures.

At this stage in your programming career, you can begin to build your own library of specialized functions and classes. Section 7.4 described how this can be accomplished by using the input validation functions, `isvalidInt()`, and `getanInt()`, which are reproduced next for convenience:

```
bool isvalidInt(string str)
{
  int start = 0;
  int i;
  bool valid = true;  // assume a valid
  bool sign = false;  // assume no sign

  // check for an empty string
  if (int(str.length()) == 0)  valid = false;

  // check for a leading sign
  if (str.at(0) == '-'|| str.at(0) == '+')
  {
    sign = true;
    start = 1;  // start checking for digits after the sign
  }

  // check that there is at least one character after the sign
  if (sign && int(str.length()) == 1) valid = false;

  // now check the string, which we know has at least one non-sign char
  i = start;
  while(valid && i < int(str.length()))
  {
    if(!isdigit(str.at(i))) valid = false;  //found a non-digit character
    i++;  // move to next character
  }

  return valid;
}

int getanInt()
{
  bool isvalidInt(string);  // function declaration (prototype)
  bool notanint = true;
  string svalue;
```

```
    while (notanint)
    {
      try
      {
        cin >> svalue;  // accept a string input
        if (!isvalidInt(svalue)) throw svalue;
      }
      catch (string e)
      {
        cout << "Invalid integer - Please re-enter: ";
           continue; // send control to the while statement
      }
      notanint = false;
    }
    return atoi(svalue.c_str());  // convert to an integer
  }
```

The first step in creating a library is to encapsulate all of the preferred functions and classes into one or more namespaces and then store the complete code (with or without using a namespace) into one or more files. For example, you can create one namespace, `dataChecks`, and save it in the file named `dataChecks.cpp`. It is important to note thet the file name under which the namespace is saved *need not be* the same as the namespace name used in the code.

The syntax for creating a namespace is the following:

```
namespace name
{
  functions and/or classes in here
}  // end of namespace
```

Including the two functions `isvalidInt()` and `getanInt()` within a namespace, `dataChecks`, and adding the appropriate `include` files and `using` declaration statement needed by the new namespace yield the following code. For convenience, the syntax required to create the namespace has been highlighted:

```
#include <iostream>
#include <string>
using namespace std;

namespace dataChecks
{
  bool isvalidInt(string str)
  {
    int start = 0;
    int i;
    bool valid = true;  // assume a valid
    bool sign = false;  // assume no sign
```

```
    // check for an empty string
    if (int(str.length()) == 0)  valid = false;

    // check for a leading sign
    if (str.at(0) == '-'|| str.at(0) == '+')
    {
      sign = true;
      start = 1;  // start checking for digits after the sign
    }

    // check that there is at least one character after the sign
    if (sign && int(str.length()) == 1) valid = false;

    // now check the string, which we know has at least one non-sign char
    i = start;
    while(valid && i < int(str.length()))
    {
      if(!isdigit(str.at(i))) valid = false;  //found a non-digit character
      i++;  // move to next character
    }
    return valid;
  }

  int getanInt()
  {
    bool isvalidInt(string);  // function declaration (prototype)
    bool notanint = true;
    string svalue;

    while (notanint)
    {
      try
      {
        cin >> svalue;  // accept a string input
        if (!isvalidInt(svalue)) throw svalue;
      }
      catch (string e)
      {
        cout << "Invalid integer - Please re-enter: ";
        continue; // send control to the while statement
      }
      notanint = false;
    }
    return atoi(svalue.c_str());  // convert to an integer
  }
} // end of dataChecks namespace
```

Once the namespace has been created and stored in a file, it can be included within another file by supplying a preprocessor directive to inform the compiler where the desired namespace is to be found and to include a `using` directive instructing the compiler to the particular namespace in the file to use. For the `dataChecks` namespace, which is stored in a file named, `dataChecks.cpp` this is accomplished by the following statements:

```
#include <c:\\mylibrary\\dataChecks>
using namespace dataChecks;
```

The first statement provides the full path name for the source code file. Notice that a full path name has been used and that two slashes are used to separate path names. The double backslashes are required whenever providing a relative or full path name. The only time that backslashes are not required is when the library code resides in the same directory as the program being executed. As indicated, the `dataChecks` source file is saved within a folder named `mylibrary`. The second statement tells the compiler to use the `dataChecks` namespace within the designated file. Program 7.17 includes these two statements within an executable program.

Program 7.17

```
#include <c:\\mylibrary\\dataChecks.cpp>
using namespace dataChecks;

int main()
{
  int value;

  cout << "Enter an integer value: ";
  value = getanInt();
  cout << "The integer entered is: " << value << endl;

  return 0;
}
```

The only requirement for the include statement in Program 7.17 is that the file name and location must correspond to an existing file having the same name in the designated path; otherwise, a compiler error will occur. Should you want to name the source code file using a file extension, any extension can be used as long as the following rules are maintained:

1. The file name under which the code is stored includes the extension.
2. The same file name, including extension, is used in the `include` statement.

Thus, if the file name used to store the functions were `dataLib.cpp`, the `include` statement in Program 7.17 would be

```
#include<c::\\mylibrary\\dataLib.cpp>
```

Additionally, a namespace is not required within the file. Using a namespace permits us to isolate the data checking functions into one area and allows us to add additional namespaces to the file as the need arises. The designation of a namespace in the `using` statement tells the compiler to include only the code in the specified namespace, rather than all of the code in the file. In Program 7.17, if the data checking functions were not enclosed within a namespace, the `using` statement for the `dataChecks` namespace would have to be omitted.

Including the previously written and tested data checking functions within Program 7.17 as a separate file allows you to focus on the code within the program that uses these functions, rather than being concerned with the function code itself. This permits you to concentrate on using these functions as opposed to re-examining or seeing the previously written and tested function code. In Program 7.17, the `main()` method exercises the data checking functions and produces the same output as Program 7.17. In creating the `dataChecks` namespace, you have included source code for the two functions. This is not required, and a compiled version of the source code can be saved instead. Finally, additions to a namespace defined in one file can be made in another file by using the same namespace name in the new file and including a `using` statement for the first file's namespace.

Exercises 7.5

1. Enter and compile Program 7.17. (*Hint:* The namespace header file `dataChecks` and the program file are available with the source code provided on the Course Technology Web site for this text. See Exercise 4 for the downloading procedure.)

2. Why would a programmer supply a namespace file in its compiled form rather than as source code?

3. **a.** What is an advantage of namespaces?
b. What is a possible disadvantage of namespaces?

4. What types of classes and functions would you include in a personal library? Why?

5. **a.** Write a C++ function. `whole()`, that returns the integer part of any number passed to the function. (*Hint:* Assign the passed argument to an integer variable.)
b. Include the function written in Exercise 5a in a working program. Make sure your function is called from `main()` and correctly returns a value to `main()`. Have `main()` use a `cout` statement to display the value returned. Test the function by passing various data to it.
c. When you are confident that the `whole()` function written for Exercise 5a works correctly, save it in a namespace and a personal library of your choice.

6. **a.** Write a C++ function, `fracpart()`, that returns the fractional part of any number passed to the function. For example, if the number 256.879 is passed to `fracpart()`, the number .879 should be returned. Have the function `fracpart()` call the `whole()` function that you wrote in Exercise 5a. The number returned can then be determined as the number passed to `fracpart()` less the returned value when the same argument is passed to `whole()`.

b. Include the function written in Exercise 6a in a working program. Make sure the function is called from `main()` and correctly returns a value to `main()`. Have `main()` use a `cout` statement to display the value returned. Test the function by passing various data to it.

c. When you are confident the `fracpart()` function written for Exercise 6a works correctly, save it in the same namespace and personal library selected for Exercise 5c.

7.6 Common Programming Errors

Here are the common errors associated with defining and processing strings:

1. Forgetting to include the `string` header file when using `string` class objects.
2. Forgetting that the newline character, `'\n'`, is a valid data input character.
3. Forgetting to convert a string class object using the `c_str()` method when converting `string` class objects to numerical data types.

7.7 Chapter Summary

1. A string literal is any sequence of characters enclosed in double quotation marks. A string literal is referred to as a string value, a string constant, and more conventionally, a string.
2. A string can be constructed as an object of the `string` class.
3. The `string` class is commonly used for constructing strings for input and output purposes, such as for prompts and displayed messages. Because of the provided capabilities, this class is used when strings need to be compared or searched, or individual characters in a string need to be examined or extracted as a substring. It is used in more advanced situations when characters within a string need to be replaced, inserted, or deleted on a regular basis.
4. Strings can be manipulated using the methods of the class they are objects of or using the general purpose string and character methods.
5. The `cin` object, by itself, tends to be of limited usefulness for string input because it terminates input when a blank is encountered.
6. For `string` class data input, use the `getline()` method.
7. The `cout` object can be used to display `string` class strings.

Looking at Career Choices

Materials Science and Metallurgical Engineering

To a large extent, advances in many areas of engineering in the twentieth century have been made possible by discoveries of new materials and a better understanding of the properties of existing materials. Knowledge of the physical and chemical principles determining the electrical properties of exotic materials called semiconductors have resulted in the fantastic progress in the field of solid-state devices, from transistors to integrated-circuit chips to large computers. Better understanding of the origins of metallic properties such as hardness, strength, ductility, corrosiveness, and others have led to improved design of automobiles, aircraft, spacecraft, and all types of machinery. The field is basically subdivided into metals and nonmetals, although there is often considerable overlap of interests and activities.

Materials Science

Materials science concerns the behavior and properties of materials, both metals and nonmetals, from both microscopic and macroscopic perspectives. It includes the following areas:

1. Ceramics. Noncrystalline materials, such as glass, that are nonmetallic and that require high temperatures in their processing. Ceramics can be made brittle or flexible, hard or soft, or stronger than steel. They can be made to have a variety of chemical properties.
2. Polymers. Structural and physical properties of organic, inorganic, and natural polymers that are useful in engineering applications.
3. Materials fabrication, processing, and treatment. All aspects of the manufacture of ceramics, metals, and polymer synthesis, from the growth of crystals and fibers to metal forming.
4. Corrosion. Reaction mechanism and thermodynamics of corrosion of metals in the atmosphere or submerged under water or chemicals, whether standing or under stress.
5. Stress-strain, and fatigue-fracture of engineering materials. Physical properties governing the deformation and fracture of materials and their improvement and use in construction and design.

(*Continued*)

Looking at Career Choices

Metallurgical Engineering

Metallurgical engineering is the branch engineering responsible for the production of metals and metal alloys, from the discovery of ore deposits to the fabrication of the refined metal into useful products. Metallurgical engineers are important in every step in the production of metal from metal ore. Metallurgical engineering includes the following areas

1. Mining engineering. Usually a separate branch of engineering. However, the concerns of mining engineers and metallurgists frequently overlap in the processes of extraction of metals from metal ores and the refinement into usable products. Extraction metallurgy makes use of physical and chemical reactions to optimize metal production.
2. Metals fabrication. Metal forming into products such as cans, wires, and tubes; casting and joining of metals—for example, by welding.
3. Physical metallurgy. Analysis of stress-strain, fatigue-fracture characteristics of metals and metal alloys to prevent engineering component failures.

Part Two
Object-Oriented Programming

CHAPTERS

CHAPTER 8

I/O Files Streams and Data Files

TOPICS

The data for the programs we have used so far have been assigned internally within the programs or entered by the user during program execution. As such, the data used in these programs are stored in the computer's main memory and cease to exist once the program using it finishes executing. This type of data entry is fine for small amounts of data. However, imagine a company having to pay someone to type in the names and addresses of hundreds or thousands of customers every month each time bills are prepared and sent.

As you will learn in this chapter, storing such data outside of a program on a convenient storage medium is more sensible. Data stored together under a common name on a storage medium other than the computer's main memory are called a data file. Typically, data files are stored on disks, tapes, or CD-ROMs. Besides providing a permanent storage for the data, data files can be shared between programs, so the data output by one program can be input directly to another program. You will begin this chapter by learning how data files are created and maintained in C++. One major concern about using data files is ensuring that your programs open and connect correctly to them before any data processing begins. For this reason, you will learn how to use exception handling for this task. This type of error detection and correction is a major concern of all professionally written programs.

8.1 I/O FILE STREAM OBJECTS AND METHODS

To store and retrieve data outside a C++ program, you need two things:

- A file
- A file stream object

You will learn about these important topics in the following two sections.

Files

A **file** is a collection of data stored together under a common name, usually on a disk, magnetic tape, or CD-ROM. For example, the C++ programs that you store on disk are examples of files. The stored data in a program file are the program code that becomes input data to the C++ compiler. In the context of data processing, however, the C++ program is not usually considered data, and the term "file," or "data file," typically refers only to external files that contain the data used in a C++ program.

A file is physically stored on an external medium such as a disk. Each file has a unique file name referred to as the file's **external name**. The external name is how the file is known by the operating system. When you review the contents of a directory or folder (for example, in Windows Explorer), you see files listed by their external names. Each computer operating system has its own specification as to the maximum number of characters permitted for an external file name. Table 8.1 lists these specifications for the more commonly used operating systems.

Table 8.1 Maximum Allowable File Name Characters

Operating System	Maximum File Name Length
DOS	8 characters plus an optional period and 3-character extension
Windows 98, 2000, XP	255 characters
UNIX	
Early Versions	14 characters
Current Versions	255 characters

A Bit of Background

Privacy, Security, and Files

Data files were around long before computers were used but were primarily stored as paper records in filing cabinets. Terms such as *open, close, records,* and *lookup* that are used in handling computer files are reminders of these older techniques for accessing paper files stored in drawers.

Today, most files are stored electronically, and the amount of collected and stored information proliferates wildly. The ease of sharing large amounts of data electronically has led to increasing problems with privacy and security.

Whenever a person fills out a government form or a credit application, submits a mail order, applies for a job, writes a check, or uses a credit card, an electronic data trail is created. Each time those files are shared among government agencies or private enterprises, the individual loses more of his or her privacy.

To help protect U.S. citizens' constitutional rights, the Fair Credit Reporting Act was passed in 1970, followed by the Federal Privacy Act in 1974. These acts specify it is illegal for a business to keep secret files, that you are entitled to examine and correct any data collected about you, and government agencies and contractors must show justification for accessing your records. Efforts continue to create mechanisms that will serve to preserve an individual's security and privacy.

To ensure that the examples presented in this text are compatible with all the operating systems listed in Table 8.1, we will generally, but not exclusively, adhere to the more restrictive DOS specifications. If you are using one of the other operating systems, however, you should take advantage of the increased length specification to create descriptive file names. Long file names should be avoided because they take more time to type and can result in typing errors. A manageable length for a file name is 12 to 14 characters, with a maximum of 25 characters.

Using the DOS convention, the following are all valid computer data file names:

```
prices.dat     records       info.txt
exper1.dat     scores.dat    math.mem
```

Choose file names that indicate the type of data in the file and the application for which it is used. Frequently, the first eight characters describe the data, and an extension (the characters after the decimal point) describes the application. For example, the Excel spreadsheet program automatically applies an extension of "xls" to all spreadsheet files, Microsoft's Word and the WordPerfect word processing programs use the extensions "doc" and "wp*x*" (where *x* refers to the version number), respectively, and C++ compilers require a program file to have the extension "cpp." When creating your own file names, you should adhere to this practice.

Using the DOS convention, the name "exper1.dat" is appropriate in describing a file of data corresponding to experiment number 1.

Point of Information

Input and Output Streams

A *stream* is a one-way transmission path between a source and a destination. A stream of bytes gets sent down this transmission path. A good analogy to this stream of bytes is a stream of water that provides a one-way path for water to travel from a source to a destination.

Stream objects are created from stream classes. Two stream objects we have used extensively are the input stream object named `cin` and the output stream object named `cout`. The `cin` object provides a transmission path from keyboard to program, and the `cout` object provides a transmission path from program to terminal screen. These two objects are created from the stream classes `istream` and `ostream`, respectively, which are parent classes to the `iostream` class. When the `iostream` header file is included in a program using the `#include <iostream>` directive, the `cin` and `cout` stream objects are automatically declared and opened by the C++ compiler for the compiled program.

File stream objects provide the same capabilities as the `cin` and `cout` objects, except they connect a program to a file rather than the keyboard or terminal screen. File stream objects must be explicitly declared. File stream objects used for input must be declared as objects of the class `ifstream`. File stream objects used for output must be declared as objects of the class `ofstream`. The classes `ifstream` and `ofstream` are made available to a program by inclusion of the `fstream` header file, using the directive `#include <fstream>`. The `fstream` class is derived from the `ifstream` and `ofstream` classes (see Section 8.8).

Two basic types of files exist: **text files**, which are known as **character-based files**, and **binary-based** files. Both file types store data using a binary code; the difference is in what the codes represent. Briefly, text-based files store each individual character, such as a letter, digit, dollar sign, decimal point, etc., using an individual character code (typically ASCII or UNICODE). The use of a character code allows a word processing program or text editor to display the files so a person can read them. Binary-based files use the same code as your C++ compiler uses for its primitive data types. This means that numbers appear in their true binary form, while strings retain their ASCII or UNICODE form. The advantage of binary-based files is compactness because less space is used to store most numbers using their binary code than as individual character values. In general, the majority of files used by programmers are text files because the file's data can be displayed by word processing programs and simple text editors. The default file type in C++ is always a text file and is the file type presented in this chapter.

File Stream Objects

A **file stream** is a one-way transmission path used to connect a file stored on a physical device, such as a disk or CD-ROM, to a program. Each file stream has its own mode, which determines the direction of data on the transmission path, that is, whether the path will move data from a file into a program or whether the path will move data from a program to a file. A file stream that receives or reads data from a file into a program is referred to as an **input file stream**. A file stream that sends or writes data to a file is referred to as an **output file stream**. The direction, or mode, is defined in relation to the program and not the file; data that go into a program are considered input data, and data sent out from the program are considered output data. Figure 8.1 illustrates the data flow from and to a file using input and output streams.

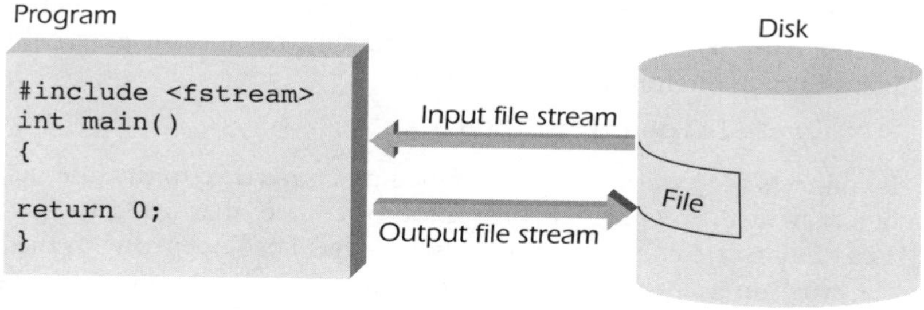

Figure 8.1 Input and output file streams.

For each file your program uses, regardless of the file's type (text or binary), a distinct file stream object must be created. If you want your program to read and write to a file, an input and output file stream object are required. Input file stream objects are declared to be of type `ifstream`, and output file streams are declared to be of type `ofstream`. For example, examine the following declaration statement:

```
ifstream inFile;
```

This statement declares an input file stream object named `inFile` to be an object of the class `ifstream`. Similarly, examine the next declaration statement:

```
ofstream outFile;
```

This statement declares an output file stream object named `outFile` to be an object of the class `ofstream`. Within a C++ program, a file stream is accessed by its appropriate stream object name: one name for reading the file and one name for writing to the file. Object names, such as `inFile` and `outFile`, can be any programmer-selected names that conform to C++'s identifier rules.

File Stream Methods

Each file stream object has access to the methods defined for its respective `ifstream` or `ofstream` class. These methods include connecting a stream object name to an external file name (called **opening a file**), determining if a successful connection has been made, closing a connection (called **closing a file**), getting the next data item into the program from an input stream, putting a new data item from the program onto an output stream, and detecting when the end of a file has been reached.

Opening a file connects each file stream object to a specific external file name. This is accomplished using a file stream's open method, which accomplishes two purposes. First, opening a file establishes the physical connecting link between a program and a file. Since details of this link are handled by the computer's operating system and are transparent to the program, the programmer normally does not need to consider them.

From a coding perspective, the second purpose of opening a file is more relevant. Besides establishing the actual physical connection between a program and a data file, opening a file connects the file's external computer name to the stream object name used internally by the program. The method that performs this task is named `open()` and is provided by the `ifstream` and `ofstream` classes.

In using the `open()` method to connect the file's external name to its internal object stream name, only one argument is required, which is the external file name. For example, examine the following statement:

```
inFile.open("prices.dat");
```

It connects the external text file named `prices.dat` to the internal program file stream object named `inFile`. This assumes, of course, that `inFile` has been declared as an `ifstream` or `ofstream` object. If a file has been opened with the preceding statement, the program accesses the file using the internal object name `inFile`, and the computer saves the file under the external name `prices.dat`. The external file name argument passed to `open()` is a string contained between double quotation marks. Calling the `open()` method requires the standard object notation where the name of the desired method, in this case `open()`, is preceded by a period and an object name.

When an existing file is connecting to an input file stream, the file's data are made available for input, starting at the first data item in the file. Similarly, a file connected to an output file stream creates a new file and makes the file available for output. If a file exists with the same name as a file opened in output mode, the old file is erased and all its data are lost.

When opening a file, for input or output, good programming practice requires that you check the connection has been established before attempting to use the file. You can do this via the `fail()` method, which will return a `true` value if the file was unsuccessfully opened (that is, it is true the open failed) or a `false` value if the open succeeded. Typically, the `fail()` method is used in code similar to the following, which attempts to open a file named `prices.dat` for input, checks that a valid connection was made, and reports an error message if the file was not successfully opened for input:

```
ifstream inFile;  // any object name can be used here
inFile.open("prices.dat");  // open the file

// check that the connection was successfully opened
if (inFile.fail())
{
  cout << "\nThe file was not successfully opened"
       << "\n Please check that the file currently exists."
       << endl;
  exit(1);
}
```

If the `fail()` method returns a `true`, which indicates that the open failed, a message is displayed by this code. In addition, the `exit()` function, which is a request to the operating system to end program execution immediately, is called. The `exit()` function requires inclusion of the `cstdlib` header function in any program that uses this function, and `exit()`'s single-integer argument is passed directly to the operating system for possible further operating system program action or user inspection. Throughout the remainder of the text we will include this type of error checking whenever a file is opened. (Section 8.3 shows how to use exception handling for the same type of error checking.)

In addition to the `fail()` method, C++ provides three other methods, listed in Table 8.2, that can be used to detect a file's status. The use of these additional methods is presented at the end of the next section.

Table 8.2 File Status Methods

Prototype	Description
`fail()`	Returns a Boolean `true` if the file has not been successfully opened; otherwise, returns a Boolean `false` value.
`eof()`	Returns a Boolean `true` if a read has been attempted past the end-of-file; otherwise, returns a Boolean `false` value. The value becomes true only when the first character after the last valid file character is read.
`good()`	Returns a Boolean `true` value while the file is available for program use. Returns a Boolean `false` value if a read has been attempted past the end-of-file. The value becomes false only when the first character after the last valid file character is read.
`bad()`	Returns a Boolean `true` value if a read has been attempted past the end-of-file; otherwise, returns a `false`. The value becomes true only when the first character after the last valid file character is read.

Program 8.1 illustrates the statements required to open a file for input, including an error-checking routine to ensure that a successful open was obtained. A file opened for input is said to be in **read mode**.

Program 8.1

```
#include <iostream>
#include <fstream>
#include <cstdlib>   // needed for exit()
using namespace std;

int main()
{
  ifstream inFile;

  inFile.open("prices.dat");  // open the file with the
                              // external name prices.dat
  if (inFile.fail())  // check for a successful open
  {
    cout << "\nThe file was not successfully opened"
         << "\n Please check that the file currently exists."
         << endl;
    exit(1);
  }

  cout << "\nThe file has been successfully opened for reading."
       << endl;

  // statements to read data from the file would be placed here

  return 0;
}
```

A sample run using Program 8.1 produced the following output:

```
The file has been successfully opened for reading.
```

A different check is required for output files because, if a file exists having the same name as the file to be opened in output mode, the existing file is erased and all its data are lost. To avoid this situation, the file is first opened in input mode to see if it exists. If it does, the user is given the choice of explicitly permitting it to be overwritten when it is later opened in output mode. The code used to accomplish this is highlighted in Program 8.2.

Program 8.2

```
#include <iostream>
#include <fstream>
#include <cstdlib>   // needed for exit()
using namespace std;

int main()
{
  ifstream inFile;
  ofstream outFile;

  inFile.open("prices.dat");  // attempt to open the file for input

  char response;

  if (!inFile.fail())  // if it doesn't fail, the file exists
  {
    cout << "A file by the name prices.dat exists.\n"
         << "Do you want to continue and overwrite it\n"
         << " with the new data (y or n): ";
    cin >> response;
    if (tolower(response) == 'n')
    {
      cout << "The existing file will not be overwritten." << endl;
       exit(1);  //terminate program execution
    }
  }
  outFile.open("prices.dat"); // now open the file for writing

  if (inFile.fail())  // check for a successful open
  {
    cout << "\nThe file was not successfully opened"
         << endl;
    exit(1);
  }

  cout << "The file has been successfully opened for output."
       << endl;

  // statements to write to the file would be placed here

  return 0;
}
```

Point of Information

Using C-strings as File Names

If you choose to use a C-string to store an external file name, you must be aware of the following restrictions:

The maximum length of the C-string must be specified within brackets immediately after it is declared. For example, examine the following declaration:

```
char filename[21] = "prices.dat";
```

The number 21 limits the number of characters that can be stored in the C-string. The number in brackets (21) represents one more than the maximum number of characters that can be assigned to the variable. This is because the compiler adds a final end-of-string character to terminate the string. Thus, the string value `"prices.dat"`, which consists of ten characters, is actually stored as 11 characters. The extra character is an end-of-string marker supplied by the compiler. In our example, the maximum string value assignable to the string variable file name is a string value consisting of 20 characters.

The following two runs were made with Program 8.2:

```
A file by the name prices.dat exists.
Do you want to continue and overwrite it
 with the new data (y or n): n
The existing file will not be overwritten.
```

and

```
A file by the name prices.dat exists.
Do you want to continue and overwrite it
 with the new data (y or n): y
The file has been successfully opened for output.
```

Although Programs 8.1 and 8.2 can be used to open an existing file for reading and writing, respectively, both programs lack statements to perform a read or write and close the file. These topics are discussed shortly. Before moving on, however, it is possible to combine the declaration of an `ifstream` or `ofstream` object and its associated open statement into one statement. For example, examine the following two statements in Program 8.1:

```
ifstream inFile;
inFile.open("prices.dat");
```

They can be combined into a single statement:

```
ifstream inFile("prices.dat");
```

Embedded and Interactive File Names

Programs 8.1 and 8.2 have two problems:

1. The external file name is embedded within the program code.
2. There is no provision for a user to enter the desired file name while the program is executing.

As both programs are written, if the file name is to change, a programmer must modify the external file name in the call to `open()` and recompile the program. Both of these problems can be alleviated by assigning the file name to a string variable.

A string variable as we have used it throughout the text (see Chapter 9) is a variable that can hold a string value, which is any sequence of zero or more characters enclosed within double quotation marks. For example, `"Hello World"`, `"prices.dat"`, and `""` are all strings. Notice that strings are written with double quotation marks that delimit the beginning and end of a string but are not stored as part of the string.

In declaring and initializing a string variable for use in an `open()` method, the string is considered as a C-string. (See the Point of Information on the prior page for precautions that must be understood when using a C-string.) A safer alternative, and one that we will use throughout this text, is to use a string class object and convert this object to a C-string using the `c_str()` method.

Once a string variable is declared to store a file name, it can be used in one of two ways. First, as shown in Program 8.3a, it can be placed at the top of a program to clearly identify a file's external name, rather than embedding it within an `open()` method call.

Program 8.3a

```
#include <iostream>
#include <fstream>
#include <cstdlib>   // needed for exit()
#include <string>
using namespace std;

int main()
{
  string filename = "prices.dat"; // place the file name up front
  ifstream inFile;

  inFile.open(filename.c_str());  // open the file

  if (inFile.fail())  // check for successful open
  {
    cout << "\nThe file named " << filename << " was not successfully opened"
         << "\n Please check that the file currently exists."
         << endl;
    exit(1);
  }

  cout << "\nThe file has been successfully opened for reading.\n";

  return 0;
}
```

Program 8.3a shows we have declared and initialized the string object with the following name:

```
filename
```

We use this name at the top of `main()` for easy file identification. When a string object is used, as opposed to a string literal, the variable name is not enclosed within double quotation marks in the `open()` method call. Within the `open()` call, the string object is converted to a C-string using the following expression:

```
filename.c_str().
```

Finally, in the `fail()` method code the file's external name is easily displayed by inserting the string object's name in the `cout` output stream. For these reasons, we will continue to identify the external names of files in this manner.

Another useful role played by string objects is to permit the user to enter the file name as the program is executing:. For example, the code:

```
string filename;

cout << "Please enter the name of the file you wish to open: ";
cin  >> filename;
```

allows a user to enter a file's external name at run time. The only restriction in this code is that the user must not enclose the entered string value in double quotation marks, and the entered string value cannot contain any blanks. The reason for this is that when using `cin`, the compiler will terminate the string when it encounters a blank. Program 8.3b uses this code in the context of a complete program.

The following is a sample output provided by Program 8.3b:

```
Please enter the name of the file you wish to open: foobar

The file named foobar was not successfully opened
 Please check that the file currently exists.
```

Closing a File

A file is closed using the `close()` method. This method breaks the connection between the file's external name and the file stream object, which can be used for another file. Examine the following statement:

```
inFile.close();
```

This statement closes the `inFile` stream's connection to its current file. As indicated, the `close()` method takes no argument.

Because all computers have a limit on the maximum number of files that can be opened at one time, closing files no longer needed makes good sense. Any open files existing at the end of normal program execution will be automatically closed by the operating system.

Program 8.3b

```
#include <iostream>
#include <fstream>
#include <cstdlib>    // needed for exit()
#include <string>
using namespace std;
int main()
{
  string filename;
  ifstream inFile;

  cout << "Please enter the name of the file you wish to open: ";
  cin  >> filename;

  inFile.open(filename.c_str());  // open the file

  if (inFile.fail())  // check for successful open
  {
    cout << "\nThe file named " << filename << " was not successfully opened"
         << "\n Please check that the file currently exists."
         << endl;
    exit(1);
  }
  cout << "\nThe file has been successfully opened for reading.\n";

  return 0;
}
```

Point of Information

Using `fstream` Objects

In using `ifstream` and `ofstream` objects, the input or output mode is implied by the object. Thus, `ifstream` objects must be used for input, and `ofstream` objects must be used for output.

Another means of creating file streams is to use `fstream` objects that can be used for input or output, but this method requires an explicit mode designation. An `fstream` object is declared using the following syntax:

```
fstream objectName;
```

When using the `fstream` class's `open()` method, two arguments are required: a file's external name and a mode indicator. Here are the permissible mode indicators:

Indicator	Description
`ios::in`	Open a text file in input mode
`ios::out`	Open a text file in output mode
`ios::app`	Open a text file in append mode
`ios::ate`	Go to the end of the opened file
`ios::binary`	Open a binary file in input mode (default is text file)
`ios::trunc`	Delete file contents if it exists
`ios::nocreate`	If file does not exist, open fails
`ios::noreplace`	If file exists, open for output fails

As with `ofstream` objects, an `fstream` object in output mode creates a new file and makes the file available for writing. If a file exists with the same name as a file opened for output, the old file is erased. For example, assume `file1` has been declared as an object of type `fstream` using the following statement:

```
fstream file1;
```

The statement below attempts to open the text file named `prices.dat` for output:

```
file1.open("prices.dat",ios::out);
```

Once this file has been opened, the program accesses the file using the internal object name `file1`, and the computer saves the file under the external name `prices.dat`.

An `fstream` file object opened in append mode means that an existing file is available for data to be added to the end of the file. If the file opened for appending does not exist, a new file with the designated name is created and made available to receive output from the program. For example, assume `file1` has been declared to be of type `fstream`:

```
file1.open("prices.dat",ios::app);
```

The above statement attempts to open a text file named `prices.dat` and makes it available for data to be appended to the end of the file.

Finally, an `fstream` object opened in input mode means that an existing external file has been connected and its data are available as input. For example, assume `file1` has been declared to be of type `fstream`:

```
file1.open("prices.dat",ios::in);
```

(Continued)

(Continued)

The above statement attempts to open a text file named `prices.dat` for input. The mode indicators can be combined by the bit `or` operation (see Section 15.2).

```
file1.open("prices.dat", ios::in | ios::binary)
```

The above statement opens the `file1` stream, which can be an `fstream` or `ifstream`, as an input binary stream. If the mode indicator is omitted as the second argument for an `ifstream` object, the stream is, by default, opened as a text input file; if the mode indicator is omitted for an `ofstream` object, the stream is opened, by default, as a text output file.

Exercises 8.1

1. Write individual declaration and open statements that link the following external data file names to their corresponding internal object names. Assume all the files are text-based.

External Name	Object Name	Mode
`coba.mem`	`memo`	`output`
`book.let`	`letter`	`output`
`coupons.bnd`	`coups`	`append`
`yield.bnd`	`yield`	`append`
`prices.dat`	`priFile`	`input`
`rates.dat`	`rates`	`input`

2. a. Write a set of two statements that first declares the following objects as `ifstream` objects and then opens them as text input files: `inData.txt`, `prices.txt`, `coupons.dat`, and `exper.dat`.
   b. Rewrite the two statements for Exercise 2a using a single statement.
3. a. Write a set of two statements that first declares the following objects as `ofstream` objects and then opens them as text output files: `outDate.txt`, `rates.txt`, `distance.txt`, and `file2.txt`.
   b. Rewrite the two statements for Exercise 3a using a single statement.
4. Enter and execute Program 8.1 on your computer.
5. Enter and execute Program 8.2 on your computer.
6. a. Enter and execute Program 8.3a on your computer.
   b. Add a `close()` method to Program 8.3a and then execute the program.
7. a. Enter and execute Program 8.3b on your computer.
   b. Add a `close()` method to Program 8.3b and then execute the program.

Point of Information

Checking for a Successful Connection

You must check the `open()` method successfully established a connection between a file stream and an external file. This is because the `open()` call is a request to the operating system that can fail for various reasons. Chief among these reasons is a request to open an existing file for reading that the operating system cannot locate or a request to open a file for output in a non-existent folder.) If the operating system cannot satisfy the open request, you need to know about it and terminate your program. Failure to do so can result in abnormal program behavior or a subsequent program crash.

There are two styles of coding for checking the return value. The most common method for checking that a fail did not occur when attempting to use a file for input is the one coded in Program 8.1. It is used to distinguish the `open()` request from the check made via the `fail()` call and is repeated below for convenience:

```
inFile.open("prices.dat");  // request to open the file

if (inFile.fail())    // check for a failed connection
{
  cout << "\nThe file was not successfully opened"
       << "\n Please check that the file currently exists."
       << endl;
  exit(1);
}
```

Similarly, the check made in Program 8.2 is typically included when a file is being opened in output mode.

Alternatively, you may encounter programs that use `fstream` objects in place of `ifstream` and `ofstream` objects (see the previous Point of Information box). When using `fstream`'s `open()` method, two arguments are required: a file's external name and an explicit mode indication. Using an `fstream` object, the open request and check for an input file typically appear as follows:

```
fstream inFile;

inFile.open("external file name", ios::in);
if (inFile.fail())
{
  cout << "\nThe file was not successfully opened"
       << "\n Please check that the file currently exists."
       << endl;
  exit(1);
}
```

Many times the conditional expression `inFile.fail()` is replaced by the equivalent expression `!inFile`. Though we always use `ifstream` and `ofstream` objects, be prepared to encounter the styles that use `fstream` objects.

8. Using the reference manuals provided with your computer's operating system, determine the following:
   a. the maximum number of characters that can be used to name a file for storage by the computer system
   b. the maximum number of data files that can be open at the same time

9. Would it be appropriate to call a saved C++ program a file? Why or why not?

10. a. Write individual declaration and open statements to link the following external data file names to their corresponding internal object names. Use only `ifstream` and `ofstream` objects.

External Name	Object Name	Mode
`coba.mem`	`memo`	`binary and output`
`coupons.bnd`	`coups`	`binary and append`
`prices.dat`	`priFile`	`binary and input`

   b. Redo Exercise 10a using only `fstream` objects.
   c. Write close statements for each of the files opened in Exercise 10a.

8.2 READING AND WRITING CHARACTER-BASED FILES

Reading or writing character-based files involves almost the identical operations for reading input from a keyboard and writing data to a display screen. For writing to a file, the `cout` object is replaced by the `ofstream` object name declared in the program. For example, if `outFile` is declared as an object of type `ofstream`, the following output statements are valid:

```
outFile << 'a';
outFile << "Hello World!";
outFile << descrip << ' ' << price;
```

The file name in each of these statements, in place of `cout`, directs the output stream to a specific file instead of to the standard display device. Program 8.4 illustrates the use of the insertion operator, <<, to write a list of descriptions and prices to a file.

Program 8.4

```
#include <iostream>
#include <fstream>
#include <cstdlib>   // needed for exit()
#include <string>
#include <iomanip>  // needed for formatting
using namespace std;

int main()
{
  string filename = "prices.dat";  // put the filename up front
  ofstream outFile;

  outFile.open(filename.c_str());

  if (outFile.fail())
  {
    cout << "The file was not successfully opened" << endl;
    exit(1);
  }

  // set the output file stream formats
  outFile << setiosflags(ios::fixed)
          << setiosflags(ios::showpoint)
          << setprecision(2);

  // send data to the file
  outFile << "Mats " << 39.95 << endl
          << "Bulbs "  << 3.22 << endl
          << "Fuses " << 1.08 << endl;

  outFile.close();
  cout << "The file " << filename
       << " has been successfully written." << endl;

  return 0;
}
```

Point of Information

Formatting Text File Output Stream Data

Output file streams can be formatted in the same manner as the `cout` standard output stream. For example, if an output stream named `fileOut` has been declared, the statement below formats all data inserted in the `fileOut` stream in the same way that these parameterized manipulators work for the `cout` stream:

```
fileOut << setiosflags(ios::fixed)
        << setiosflags(ios::showpoint)
        << setprecision(2);
```

The first manipulator parameter, `ios::fixed`, causes the stream to output all numbers as if they were floating-point values. The next parameter, `ios::showpoint`, tells the stream to provide a decimal point. Thus, a value such as 1.0 will appear as 1.0, and not 1. Finally, the `setprecision` manipulator tells the stream to display two decimal values after the decimal point. Thus, the number 1.0, for example, will appear as 1.00.

Instead of using manipulators, you can also use the stream methods `setf()` and `precision()`. For example, the previous formatting can be accomplished using the following code:

```
fileOut.setf(ios::fixed);
fileOut.setf(ios::showpoint);
fileOut.precision(2);
```

Which style you select is a matter of preference. In both cases, the formats need only be specified once, and remain in effect for every number subsequently inserted into the file stream.

When Program 8.4 is executed, a file, `prices.dat`, is created and saved by the computer as a text file. The file is a sequential file consisting of the following data:

```
Mats 39.95
Bulbs 3.22
Fuses 1.08
```

The actual storage of characters in the file depends on the character codes used by the computer. Though only 30 characters appear to be stored in the file—corresponding to the descriptions, blanks, and prices written to the file—the file contains 36 characters.

The extra characters consist of the newline escape sequence at the end of each line created by the `endl` manipulator, which is created as a carriage return character (`cr`) and linefeed (`lf`). Assuming characters are stored using the ASCII code, the `prices.dat` file is physically stored as illustrated in Figure 8.2. For convenience, the character corresponding to each hexadecimal code is listed below the code. A code of 20 represents the blank character. Additionally, C and C++ append the low-value hexadecimal byte 0x00 as the end-of-file (EOF) sentinel when the file is closed. This EOF sentinel is never counted as part of the file.

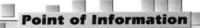

Point of Information

The `put()` Method

All output streams have access to the `fstream` class's `put()` method, which permits character-by-character output to a stream. This method works in the same manner as the character insertion operator, <<. The syntax of this method call is the following:

```
ofstreamName.put(characterExpression);
```

The *`characterExpression`* can be a character variable or literal value. For example, the following code can be used to output an 'a' to the standard output stream:

```
cin.put('a');
```

In a similar manner, if `outFile` is an `ofstream` object file that has been opened, the following code outputs the character value in the character variable named `keycode` to this output:

```
char keycode;
  .
  .
outFile.put(keycode);
```

```
4D 61 74 73 20 33 39 2E 39 35 0D 0A 42 75 6C 62 73 20
 M  a  t  s     3  9  .  9  5 cr 1f  B  u  l  b  s

33 2E 32 32 0D 0A 46 75 73 65 73 20 31 2E 30 38 0D 0A
 3  .  2  2 cr 1f  F  u  s  e  s     1  .  0  8 cr 1f
```

Figure 8.2 *The* `prices.dat` *file as stored by the computer.*

Reading from a Text File

Reading data from a character-based file is almost identical to reading data from a standard keyboard, except that the `cin` object is replaced by the `ifstream` object declared in the program. For example, if `inFile` is declared as an object of type `ifstream` that is opened for input, the input following statement will read the next two items in the file and store them in the variables `descrip` and `price`:

```
inFile >> descrip >> price;
```

The file stream name in this statement, in place of `cin`, directs the input to come from the file stream rather than the standard input device stream. Other methods that can be used for stream input are listed in Table 8.3. Each of these methods must be preceded by a stream object name.

Table 8.3 `fstream` Methods

Method Name	Description
`get()`	Returns the next character extracted from the input stream as an `int`.
`get(charVar)`	Overloaded version of `get()` that extracts the next character from the input stream and assigns it to the specified character variable, `charVar`.
`getline( strObj, termChar)`	Extracts characters from the specified input stream, `strObj` until the terminating character, `termChar`, is encountered. Assigns the characters to the specified string class object, `strObj`.
`peek()`	Returns the next character in the input stream without extracting it from the stream.
`ignore(int n)`	Skips over the next *n* characters. If n is omitted, the default is to skip over the next single character.

Program 8.5 illustrates how the `prices.dat` file that was created in Program 8.4 can be read. The program illustrates one method of detecting the EOF marker using the `good()` function (see Table 8.2). Because this function returns a Boolean `true` value before the EOF marker has been read or passed over, it can be used to verify the data read are valid file data. Only after the EOF marker has been read or passed over does this function return a Boolean `false`. Thus, the notation `while(infile.good())` used in Program 8.5 ensures the data are from the file before the EOF has been read.

The display produced by Program 8.5 is the following:

```
Mats 39.95
Bulbs 3.22
Fuses 1.08
```

Examine the expression `inFile.good()` used in the `while` statement. This expression is `true` as long as the EOF marker has not been read. Thus, as long as the item read was good, the loop continues to read the file. Within the loop, the items just read are displayed, and then a new string and a double-precision number are input to the program. When the EOF has been detected, the expression returns a Boolean value of `false` and the loop terminates. This ensures data are read and displayed up to, but not including, the EOF marker.

A direct replacement for the statement `while(inFile.good())` is the statement `while(!inFile.eof())`, which is read as "while the end of file *has not* been reached." This works because the `eof()` function returns a `true` only after the EOF marker has been read or passed over. In effect, the relational expression checks that the EOF has not been read; hence, the use of the NOT`, !,` operator.

Another means of detecting the EOF is to use the fact that the extraction operation, >>, returns a Boolean value of `true` if data are extracted from a stream; otherwise, it returns a Boolean `false` value. Using this return value, the following code can be used within Program 8.5 to read the file.

Program 8.5

```
#include <iostream>
#include <fstream>
#include <cstdlib>   // needed for exit()
#include <string>
using namespace std;

int main()
{
  string filename = "prices.dat";  // put the filename up front
  string descrip;
  double price;

  ifstream inFile;

  inFile.open(filename.c_str());

  if (inFile.fail())  // check for successful open
  {
    cout << "\nThe file was not successfully opened"
         << "\n Please check that the file currently exists."
         << endl;
    exit(1);
  }

  // read and display the file's contents
  inFile >> descrip >> price;
  while (inFile.good()) // check next character
  {
    cout << descrip << ' ' << price << endl;
    inFile >> descrip >> price;
  }

  inFile.close();

  return 0;
}
```

Point of Information

A Way to Identify a File's Name and Location

During program development, test files are usually placed in the same directory as the program. Therefore, a method call such as `inFile.open("exper.dat")` causes no problems to the operating system. In production systems, however, it is not uncommon for data files to reside in one directory while program files reside in another. For this reason it is always a good idea to include the full path name of any file opened.

For example, if the `exper.dat` file resides in the directory `C:\test\files`, the `open()` call should include the full path name: `inFile.open("C:\\test\\files\\exper.dat")`. Then, no matter where the program is run from, the operating system will know where to locate the file. Note the use of double slashes, which is required.

Another important convention is to list all file names at the top of a program instead of embedding the names deep within the code. This can easily be accomplished by string variables to store each file name.

For example, if the statements:

```
string filename = "c:\\test\\files\\exper.dat";
```

are placed at the top of a program file, the declaration statement clearly lists both the name of the desired file and its location. Then, if some other file is to be tested, all that is required is a simple one-line change at the top of the program.

Using a string variable for the file's name is also useful for the `fail()` method check. For example, consider the following code:

```
string filename;
ifstream infile;

inFile.open(filename.c_str());

if (inFile.fail())
{
  cout << "\n The file named " << filename
       << was not successfully opened"
       <<\n Please check that this file currently exists."
       exit(1);
}
```

In this code, the name of the file that failed to open is directly displayed within the error message without the name being embedded as a string value.

```
// read and display the file's contents
  while (inFile >> descrip >> price) // check next character
    cout << descrip << ' ' << price << endl;
```

Though initially a bit cryptic, this code makes perfect sense when you understand that the expression being tested extracts data from the file and returns a Boolean value to indicate if the extraction was successful.

Finally, in the previous `while` statement or in Program 8.5, the expression `inFile >> descrip >> price` can be replaced by a `getline()` method (see Section 7.2). For file input, this method has the following syntax:

`getline(`*`fileObject, strObj, terminatingChar`*`)`

`fileObject` is the name of the `ifstream` file, *`strObj`* is a string class object , and *`terminatingChar`* is an optional character constant or variable specifying the terminating character. If this optional third argument is omitted, the default terminating character is the newline (`'\n'`) character. Program 8.6 illustrates using `getline()` within the context of a complete program.

Program 8.6

```
#include <iostream>
#include <fstream>
#include <cstdlib>   // needed for exit()
#include <string>
using namespace std;

int main()
{
  string filename = "prices.dat";  // put the filename up front
  string line;
  ifstream inFile;

  inFile.open(filename.c_str());

  if (inFile.fail())  // check for successful open
  {
    cout << "\nThe file was not successfully opened"
         << "\n Please check that the file currently exists."
         << endl;
    exit(1);
  }

  // read and display the file's contents
  while (getline(inFile,line))
    cout << line << endl;

  inFile.close();

  return 0;
}
```

Point of Information

The `get()` and `putback()` Methods

All input streams have access to the `fstream` class's `get()` method, which permits character-by-character input from an input stream. This method works in a similar manner to character extraction, using the >> operator with two important differences: If a newline character, `'\n'`, or a blank character, `' '`, is encountered, each of these characters is read in the same manner as any other alphanumeric character. The syntax of this method call is the following:

```
istreamName.get(characterVariable);
```

For example, the following code can be used to read the next character from the standard input stream and store the character into the variable `ch`:

```
char ch;
cin.get(ch);
```

In a similar manner, if `inFile` is an `ifstream` object that has been opened to a file, the following code reads the next character in the stream and assigns it to the character `keycode`:

```
char keycode;
inFile.get(keycode);
```

In addition to the `get()` method, all input streams have a `putback()` method that can be used to put the last character read from an input stream back on the stream. This method has the following syntax:

```
ifstreamName.putback(characterExpression);
```

`characterExpression` can be any character variable or character value.

The `putback()` method provides an output capability to an input stream. The putback character need not be the last character read; rather, it can be any character. All putback characters, however, have no effect on the data file but only on the open input stream. Thus, the data file characters remain unchanged though the characters subsequently read from the input stream can change.

Program 8.6 is a line-by-line text-copying program, which reads a line of text from the file and then displays it on the terminal. The output of Program 8.6 is the following:

```
Mats 39.95
Bulbs 3.22
Fuses 1.08
```

If it were necessary to obtain the description and price as individual variables, either Program 8.5 should be used or the string returned by `getline()` in Program 8.6 must be processed further to extract the individual data items. (See Section 8.7 for parsing procedures.)

Standard Device Files

The file stream objects we have used have been logical file objects. A logical file object is a stream that connects a file of logically related data, such as a data file, to a program. In addition to logical file objects, C++ supports physical file objects. A physical file object is a stream that connects to a hardware device, such as a keyboard, screen, or printer.

The actual physical device assigned to your program for data entry is formally called the **standard input file.** Usually, this is the keyboard. When a `cin` object method call is encountered in a C++ program, it is a request to the operating system to go to this standard input file for the expected input. Similarly, when a `cout` object method call is encountered, the output is automatically displayed or "written to" a device that has been assigned as the **standard output file.** For most systems, this is a computer screen, though it can be a printer.

When a program is executed, the standard input stream `cin` is connected to the standard input device. Similarly, the standard output stream `cout` is connected to the standard output device. These two object streams are available for programmer use, as are the standard error stream, `cerr`, and the standard log stream, `clog`. Both of these streams connect to the terminal screen.

Other Devices

The keyboard, display, error-reporting, and logging streams are automatically connected to the stream objects named `cin`, `cout`, `cerr`, and `clog` respectively when the `iostream` header file is included in a program. Other devices can be used for input or output if the name assigned by the system is known. For example, most IBM or IBM-compatible personal computers assign the name `prn` to the printer connected to the computer. For these computers, a statement such as `outFile.open("prn")` connects the printer to the `ofstream` object named `outFile`. A subsequent statement, such as `outFile << "Hello World!";` would cause the string `Hello World!` to be output directly on the printer. As the name of an actual file, `prn`, must be enclosed in double quotation marks in the `open()` function call.

Exercises 8.2

1. a. Enter and execute Program 8.5.
   b. Modify Program 8.5 to use the expression `!inFile.eof()` in place of the expression `inFile.good()`, and execute the program to see that it operates correctly.
2. a. Enter and execute Program 8.6.
   b. Modify Program 8.6 by replacing the identifier `cout` with `cerr`, and verify the output for the standard error file stream is the screen.
   c. Modify Program 8.6 by replacing the identifier `cout` with `clog`, and verify the output for the standard log stream is the screen.

3. a. Write a C++ program that accepts lines of text from the keyboard and writes each line to a file named `text.dat` until an empty line is entered. An empty line is a line with no text that is created by pressing the Enter (or Return) key.
   b. Modify Program 8.6 to read and display the data stored in the `text.dat` file created in Exercise 3a.

4. Determine the operating system command or procedure provided by your computer to display the contents of a saved file.

5. a. Create a text file named `employee.dat` containing the following data:

Anthony	A	10031	7.82	12/18/05
Burrows	W	10067	9.14	6/ 9/04
Fain	B	10083	8.79	5/18/04
Janney	P	10095	10.57	9/28/04
Smith	G	10105	8.50	12/20/03

   b. Write a C++ program to read the `employee.dat` file created in Exercise 5a and produce a duplicate copy of the file named `employee.bak`.
   c. Modify the program written in Exercise 5b to accept the names of the original and duplicate files as user input.
   d. The program written for Exercise 5c always copies data from an original file to a duplicate file. What is a better method of accepting the original and duplicate file names, other than prompting the user for them each time the program is executed?

6. a. Write a C++ program that opens a file and displays the contents of the file with associated line numbers. That is, the program should print the number 1 before displaying the first line, print the number 2 before displaying the second line, and so on for each line in the file.
   b. Modify the program written in Exercise 6a to list the contents of the file on the printer assigned to your computer.

7. a. Create a text file containing the following data (without the headings):

Names	Social Security Number	Hourly Rate	Hours Worked
B Caldwell	555-88-2222	7.32	37
D Memcheck	555-77-4444	8.32	40
R Potter	555-77-6666	6.54	40
W Rosen	555-99-8888	9.80	35

   b. Write a C++ program that reads the data file created in Exercise 7a and computes and displays a payroll schedule. The output should list the Social Security number, name, gross pay for each individual, and where gross pay is calculated as *Hourly Rate x Hours Worked*.

8. a. Create a text file containing the following car numbers, number of miles driven, and number of gallons of gas used in each car (do not include the headings):

Car Number	Miles Driven	Gallons Used
54	250	19
62	525	38
71	123	6
85	1,322	86
97	235	14

b. Write a C++ program that reads the data in the file created in Exercise 8a and displays the car number, miles driven, gallons used, and the miles per gallon for each car. The output should contain the total miles driven, total gallons used, and average miles per gallon for all the cars. These totals should be displayed at the end of the output report.

9. a. Create a text file with the following data (without the headings):

Part Number	Initial Amount	Quantity Sold	Minimum Amount
QA310	95	47	50
CM145	320	162	200
MS514	34	20	25
EN212	163	150	160

b. Write a C++ program to create an inventory report based on the data in the file created in Exercise 9a. The display should consist of the part number, current balance, and the amount that is necessary to bring the inventory to the minimum level.

10. a. Create a text file containing the following data (without the headings):

Name	Rate	Hours
Callaway,G.	6.00	40
Hanson,P.	5.00	48
Lasard,D.	6.50	35
Stillman,W.	8.00	50

b. Write a C++ program that uses the information contained in the file created in Exercise 10a to produce the following pay report for each employee:

```
Name  Pay Rate  Hours  Regular Pay  Overtime Pay  Gross Pay
```

Regular pay is to be computed as any hours worked up to and including 40 hours multiplied by the pay rate. Overtime pay is to be computed as any hours worked above 40 hours times a pay rate of 1.5 multiplied by the regular rate, and the gross pay is the sum of regular and overtime pay. At the end of the report, the program should display the totals of the regular, overtime, and gross pay columns.

11. a. Store the following data in a file:

    5 96 87 78 93 21 4 92 82 85 87 6 72 69 85 75 81 73

    b. Write a C++ program to calculate and display the average of each group of numbers in the file created in Exercise 11a. The data is arranged in the file so that each group of numbers is preceded by the number of data items in the group. Thus, the first number in the file, 5, indicates that the next five numbers should be grouped together. The number 4 indicates that the following four numbers are a group, and the 6 indicates that the last six numbers are a group. (*Hint:* Use a nested loop. The outer loop should terminate when the end-of-file has been encountered.)

8.3 EXCEPTIONS AND FILE CHECKING[1]

Error detection and processing with exception handling is used extensively within C++ programs that use one or more files. For example, if a user deletes or renames a file using an operating system command, this action will cause a C++ program to fail when an `open()` function call attempts to open the file under its original name.

Recall from Section 7.1 that the code for general exception handling looks like this:

```
try
{
  // one or more statements,
  // at least one of which should
  // throw an exception
}
catch(exceptionDataType parameterName)
{
  // one or more statements
}
```

In this code, the `try` block statements are executed. If no error occurs, the `catch` block statements are omitted and processing continues with the statement following the `catch` block. However, if any statement within the `try` block throws an exception, the `catch` block whose exception data type matches the exception is executed. If no `catch` block is defined for a `try` block, a compiler error occurs. If no `catch` block exists that catches a thrown data type, a program crash occurs if the exception is thrown. Most times, the `catch` block displays an error message and terminates processing with a call to the `exit()` function. Program 8.7 illustrates the statements required to open a file in read mode that includes exception handling.

[1]This section may be omitted on first reading without loss of subject continuity.

Program 8.7

```
#include <iostream>
#include <fstream>
#include <cstdlib>   // needed for exit()
#include <string>
using namespace std;

int main()
{
  string filename = "prices.dat";  // put the filename up front
  string descrip;
  double price;

  ifstream inFile;

  try  // this block tries to open the file, read, and display the file's data
  {
    inFile.open(filename.c_str());

    if (inFile.fail()) throw filename; // this is the exception being checked

    // read and display the file's contents
    inFile >> descrip >> price;
    while (inFile.good()) // check next character
    {
      cout << descrip << ' ' << price << endl;
      inFile >> descrip >> price;
    }
    inFile.close();

    return 0;
  }
  catch (string e)
  {
    cout << "\nThe file "<< e << " was not successfully opened"
         << "\n Please check that the file currently exists."
         << endl;
     exit(1);
  }
}
```

Point of Information

Checking That a File Was Opened Successfully

Using exception handling, the most common method for checking that the operating system located the designated file is the one coded in Program 8.7, the key coding points of which are repeated here for convenience:

```
try // this block tries to open the file, read, and display the file's data
{
  // open the file, throwing an exception if the open fails
  // perform all required file processing
  // close the file
}
catch (string e)
{
  cout << "\nThe file "<< e << " was not successfully opened"
       << "\n Please check that the file currently exists." << endl;
  exit(1);
}
```

The exception message produced by Program 8.7 when the `prices.dat` file was not found is the following:

```
The file prices.dat was not successfully opened.
 Please check that the file currently exists.
```

Although the exception handling code in Program 8.7 can be used to check for a successful file open for input and output, a more rigorous check is usually required for output files because, on output, the file is almost guaranteed to be found. If it exists, the file will be found; if it does not exist, the operating system will create it (unless append mode is specified and the file exists, or the operating system cannot find the indicated folder). Knowing that the file has been found and opened, however, is insufficient for output purposes when an existing output file must not be overwritten. For these cases, the file can be opened for input, and, if the file is found, a further check can be made to ensure that the user explicitly provides approval for overwriting it. How this is accomplished is illustrated in highlighted code within Program 8.8.

Program 8.8

```
#include <iostream>
#include <fstream>
#include <cstdlib>   // needed for exit()
#include <string>
#include <iomanip>  // needed for formatting
using namespace std;

int main()
{
  char response;
  string filename = "prices.dat";  // put the filename up front
  ifstream inFile;
  ofstream outFile;

  try // open a basic input stream simply to check if the file exists
  {
    inFile.open(filename.c_str());
    if (inFile.fail()) throw 1; // this means the file doesn't exist
      // only get here if the file was found;
      // otherwise the catch block takes control
    cout << "A file by the name " << filename << " currently exists.\n"
         << "Do you want to overwrite it with the new data (y or n): ";
    cin >> response;
    if (tolower(response) == 'n')
    {
      inFile.close();
      cout << "The existing file has not been overwritten." << endl;
      exit(1);
    }
   }
   catch(int e) {};  // a do-nothing block that permits
                     // processing to continue
   try
   {
     // open the file in write mode and continue with file writes
     outFile.open(filename.c_str());
     if (outFile.fail()) throw filename;
     // set the output file stream formats
```

(Continued)

(Continued)

```
      outFile << setiosflags(ios::fixed)
                << setiosflags(ios::showpoint)
                << setprecision(2);
      // write the data to the file
      outFile << "Mats " << 39.95 << endl
              << "Bulbs "  << 3.22 << endl
              << "Fuses " << 1.08 << endl;
      outFile.close();
      cout << "The file " << filename
           << " has been successfully written." << endl;


      return 0;
    }
    catch(string e)
    {
      cout << "The file " << filename
           << " was not opened for output and has not been written."
           << endl;
    }
}
```

In Program 8.8, the `try` blocks are separate. Because a `catch` block is affiliated with the closest previous `try` block, there is no ambiguity about unmatched `try` and `catch` blocks.

Opening Multiple Files

As an example of applying exception handling to the opening of two files at the same time, assume we wish to read the data from a character-based file named `info.txt`, one character at a time, and write this data to a file named `info.bak`. Essentially, this application is a file-copy program that reads the data from one file in a character-by-character manner and writes the data to a second file. For purposes of illustration, assume that the characters stored in the input file are as shown in Figure 8.3.

```
Now is the time for all good people
  to come to the aid of their party.
Please call (555) 888-6666 for
  further information.
```

Figure 8.3 *The data stored in the* `info.txt` *file.*

Figure 8.4 illustrates the structure of the streams that are necessary for producing our file copy. In this figure, an input stream object referenced by the variable `inFile` will read data from the `info.txt` file, and an output stream object referenced by the variable `outFile` will write data to the `info.bak` file.

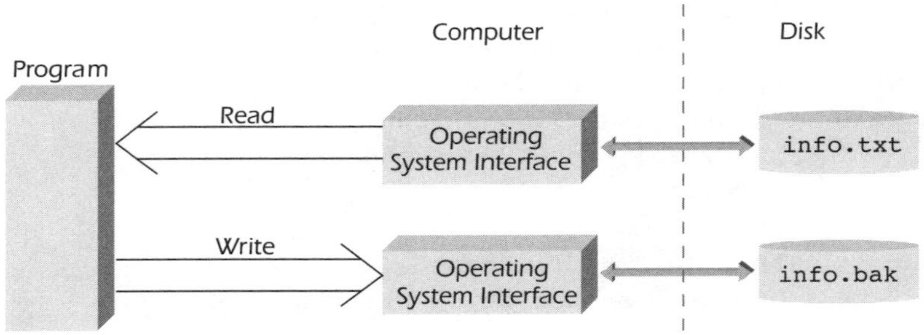

Figure 8.4 *The file copy stream structure.*

Now consider Program 8.9, which creates the `info.bak` file as an exact duplicate of the `info.txt` file using the procedure illustrated in Figure 8.4.

Program 8.9

```
#include <iostream>
#include <fstream>
#include <cstdlib>   // needed for exit()
#include <string>
using namespace std;

int main()
{
  string fileOne = "info.txt";  // put the filename up front
  string fileTwo = "info.bak";
  char ch;
  ifstream inFile;
  ofstream outFile;

  try  //this block tries to open the input file
  {
    // open a basic input stream
    inFile.open(fileOne.c_str());
      if (inFile.fail()) throw fileOne;
  } // end of outer try block
  catch (string in)  // catch for outer try block
```

(Continued)

(Continued)

```
    {
      cout << "The input file " << in
           << " was not successfully opened." << endl
           << " No backup was made." << endl;
      exit(1);
    }

    try  // this block tries to open the output file and
    {    // perform all file processing

      outFile.open(fileTwo.c_str());
      if (outFile.fail())throw fileTwo;
      while ((ch = inFile.get())!= EOF)
         outFile.put(ch);

      inFile.close();
      outFile.close();
     }
     catch (string out)  // catch for inner try block
     {
       cout << "The backup file " << out
            << " was not successfully opened." << endl;
       exit(1);
     }

    cout << "A successful backup of " << fileOne
         << " named " << fileTwo << " was successfully made." << endl;

    return 0;
  }
```

For simplicity, Program 8.9 attempts to open the input and output files within separate and non-nested `try` blocks. More generally, the second file would be opened in a nested inner `try` block so the attempt to open this second file would not be made if the opening of the first file threw an exception. (The Point of Information on nesting `try` blocks explains how this is accomplished.)

Point of Information

Nesting `try` Blocks

When more than one file stream is involved, opening each file stream in its own `try` block permits exact isolation and identification of which file caused an exception, should one occur. The `try` blocks can be nested. For example, consider Program 8.9, which is rewritten here using nested `try` blocks. Notice that in this case the `catch` block for the inner `try` block must be nested in the same block scope as its `try` block.

```
#include <iostream>
#include <fstream>
#include <cstdlib>   // needed for exit()
#include <string>
using namespace std;

int main()
{
  string fileOne = "info.txt";  // put the filename up front
  string fileTwo = "info.bak";

  char ch;
  ifstream inFile;
  ofstream outFile;

  try  //this block tries to open the input file
  {
    // open a basic input stream
    inFile.open(fileOne.c_str());
    if (inFile.fail()) throw fileOne;
    try  // this block tries to open the output file and
    {    // perform all file processing

         // open a basic output stream
      outFile.open(fileTwo.c_str());
      if (outFile.fail())throw fileTwo;
      while ((ch = inFile.get()) != EOF)
        outFile.put(ch);

      inFile.close();
      outFile.close();
    }  // end of inner try block
    catch (string out)  // catch for inner try block
```

(Continued)

(Continued)

```
      {
        cout << "The backup file " << out
             << " was not successfully opened." << endl;
        exit(1);
      }
    } // end of outer try block
    catch (string in)  // catch for outer try block
    {
      cout << "The input file " << in
           << " was not successfully opened." << endl
           << " No backup was made." << endl;
      exit(1);
    }

    cout << "A successful backup of " << fileOne
         << " named " << fileTwo << "was successfully made." << endl;

    return 0;
}
```

The important point to notice in this program is the nesting of the `try` blocks. If the two `try` blocks were not nested and the input stream declaration, `ifstream inFile;`, was placed in the first block, it could not be used in the second `try` block without producing a compiler error. The reason for this is that all variables declared in a block of code, which is defined by an opening and closing brace pair, are local to the block in which they are declared.

In reviewing Program 8.9, pay particular attention to the statement:

```
while((ch = inFile.get())!= EOF)
```

This statement continually reads a value from the input stream until the EOF value is detected. As long as the returned value does not equal the EOF value, the value is written to the output object stream. The parentheses surrounding the expression `(ch = inFile.get())` are necessary to ensure that a value is first read and assigned to the variable `ch` before the retrieved value is compared to the EOF value. In their absence, the complete expression would be `ch = inFile.get()!= EOF`. Due to the precedence of operations, the relational expression `inFile.get()!= EOF` would be executed first. Because this is a relational expression, its result is a Boolean `true` or `false` value based on the data retrieved by the `get()` method. Attempting to assign this Boolean result to the character variable `ch` is an invalid conversion across an assignment operator.

Exercises 8.3

1. List two conditions that will cause a fail condition when a file is opened for input.
2. List two conditions that will cause a fail condition when a file is opened for output.
3. If a file that exists is opened for output in write mode, what will happen to the data currently in the file?
4. Modify Program 8.7 to use an identifier of your choice, in place of the letter `e`, for the `catch` block's exception parameter name.
5. Enter and execute Program 8.8.
6. Determine why the two `try` blocks in Program 8.8, which are not nested, cause no problems in compilation or execution. (*Hint:* Place the declaration for the file name within the first `try` block and compile the program.)
7. a. If the nested `try` blocks in the Point of Information on nested `try` blocks are separated into non-nested blocks, the program will not compile. Determine why this is so.
   b. What additional changes would have to be made to the program in Exercise 7a that would allow it to be written with non-nested blocks? (*Hint:* See Exercise 6.)
8. Enter the data for the `info.txt` file in Figure 8.3 or obtain it from this text's web site (see Preface for the URL). Then enter and execute Program 8.9 and verify that the backup file was written.
9. Modify Program 8.9 to use a `getline()` method in place of the `get()` method currently in the program.

8.4 RANDOM FILE ACCESS

The term **file access** refers to the process of retrieving data from a file. There are two types of file access: sequential access and random access. To understand file access types, you need to understand some concepts related to how data is organized within a file.

The term **file organization** refers to the way data are stored in a file. The files we have used, and will continue to use, have a **sequential organization**. This means that the characters within the file are stored in a sequential manner.

In addition to being sequentially organized, we have read each open file in a sequential manner. That is, we have accessed each character sequentially. This is referred to as **sequential access**. Though characters in the file are stored sequentially, however, this does not force us to access them sequentially. In fact, we can skip over characters and read a sequentially organized file in a non-sequential manner.

In **random access**, any character in the opened file can be read directly without first having to sequentially read all the characters stored ahead of it. To provide random access to files, each `ifstream` object automatically creates a file position marker. This marker is a long integer that represents an offset from the beginning of each file and keeps track of where the next character is to be read from or written to. The functions used to access and change the file position marker are listed in Table 8.4. The suffixes `g` and `p` in these function names denote `get` and `put`, respectively, where `get` refers to an input (get from) file and `put` refers to an output (put to) file.

Table 8.4 File Position Marker Functions

Name	Description
`seekg(offset, mode)`	For input files, move to the offset position as indicated by the mode.
`seekp(offset, mode)`	For output files, move to the offset position as indicated by the mode.
`tellg(void)`	For input files, return the current value of the file position marker.
`tellp(void)`	For output files, return the current value of the file position marker.

The `seek()` functions allow the programmer to move to any position in the file. To understand this method, you must understand how data are referenced in the file using the file position marker.

Each character in a data file is located by its position in the file. The first character in the file is located at position 0, the next character at position 1, etc. A character's position is referred to as its offset from the start of the file. Thus, the first character has a 0 offset, the second character has an offset of 1, etc., for each character in the file.

The `seek()` functions require two arguments: the first is the offset, as a long integer, into the file; the second is where the offset is to be calculated from, as determined by the mode. The three possible alternatives for the mode are `ios::beg`, `ios::cur`, and `ios::end`, which denote the beginning, current position, and the end of the file, respectively. Thus, a mode of `ios::beg` means the offset is the true offset from the start of the file. A mode of `ios::cur` means the offset is relative to the current position in the file, and an `ios::end` mode means the offset is relative to the end of the file. A positive offset means move forward in the file and a negative offset means move backward. Examples of `seek()` function calls are shown below. In these examples, assume that `inFile` has been opened as an input file and `outFile` as an output file. In these examples, the offset passed to `seekg()` and `seekp()` must be a long integer.

```
inFile.seekg(4L,ios::beg);     // go to the fifth character in the input file
outFile.seekp(4L,ios::beg);    // go to the fifth character in the output file
inFile.seekg(4L,ios::cur);     // move ahead five characters in the input file
outFile.seekp(4L,ios::cur);    // move ahead five characters in the output file
inFile.seekg(-4L,ios::cur);    // move back five characters in the input file
```

```
outFile.seekp(-4L,ios::cur);  // move back five characters in the output file
inFile.seekg(0L,ios::beg);    // go to start of the input file
outFile.seekp(0L,ios::beg);   // go to start of the output file
inFile.seekg(0L,ios::end);    // go to end of the input file
outFile.seekp(0L,ios::end);   // go to end of the output file
inFile.seekg(-10L,ios::end);  // go to 10 characters before the input file's end
outFile.seekp(-10L,ios::end); // go to 10 characters before the output file's end
```

As opposed to the `seek()` functions that move the file position marker, the `tell()` functions return the offset value of the file position marker. For example, if ten characters have been read from an input file named `inFile`, the function call returns the long integer 10:

```
inFile.tellg();
```

This means the next character to be read is offset ten byte positions from the start of the file and is the eleventh character in the file.

Program 8.10 illustrates the use of `seekg()` and `tellg()` to read a file in reverse order, from last character to first. As each character is read, it is also displayed.

Program 8.10

```
#include <iostream>
#include <fstream>
#include <string>
#include <cstdlib>
using namespace std;

int main()
{
  string filename = "test.dat";
  char ch;
  long offset, last;

  ifstream inFile(filename.c_str());

  if (inFile.fail())   // check for successful open
  {
    cout << "\nThe file was not successfully opened"
         << "\n Please check that the file currently exists"
         << endl;
    exit(1);
  }
```

(Continued)

(Continued)

```
  inFile.seekg(0L,ios::end);    // move to the end of the file
  last = inFile.tellg();        // save the offset of the last character

  for(offset = 1L; offset <= last; offset++)
  {
    inFile.seekg(-offset, ios::end);
    ch = inFile.get();
    cout << ch << " : ";
  }

  inFile.close();

  cout << endl;

  return 0;
}
```

Assume the file `test.dat` contains the following data:

```
The grade was 92.5
```

The output of Program 8.10 is the following:

```
5 : . : 2 : 9 :   : s : a : w :   : e : d : a : r : g :   : e : h : T :
```

Program 8.10 initially goes to the last character in the file. The offset of this character, the EOF character, is saved in the variable `last`. Since `tellg()` returns a long integer, `last` has been declared as a long integer.

Starting from the end of the file, `seekg()` is used to position the next character to be read, referenced from the end of the file. As each character is read, the character is displayed and the offset adjusted to access the next character. The first offset used is `-1`, which represents the character immediately preceding the EOF marker.

Exercises 8.4

1. **a.** Create a file named `test.dat` that contains the data in the `test.dat` file used in Program 8.10. You can do this by using a text editor or by copying the file `test.dat` on the data disk provided with this book.
   b. Enter and execute Program 8.10 on your computer.
2. Rewrite Program 8.10 so that the origin for the `seekg()` function used in the `for` loop is the start of the file rather than the end.
3. Modify Program 8.10 to display an error message if `seekg()`attempts to reference a position beyond the end of the file.

4. Write a program that will read and display every second character in a file named `test.dat`.

5. Using the `seek()` and `tell()` functions, write a function named `fileChars()` that returns the total number of characters in a file.

6. a. Write a function named `readBytes()` that reads and displays *n* characters starting from any position in a file. The function should accept three arguments: a file object name, the offset of the first character to be read, and the number of characters to be read. (*Note:* The prototype for `readBytes()` should be `void readBytes(fstream&, long, int)`.)
   b. Modify the `readBytes()` function written in Exercise 6a to store the characters read into a string or an array. The function should accept the address of the storage area as a fourth argument.

8.5 FILE STREAMS AS FUNCTION ARGUMENTS

A file stream object can be used as a function argument. The only requirement is that the function's formal parameter be a reference (see Section 6.3) to the appropriate stream, either as `ifstream&` or `ofstream&`. For example, in Program 8.11, an `ofstream` object named `outFile` is opened in `main()` and this stream object is passed to the function `inOut()`. The function prototype and header line for `inOut()` declare the formal parameter as a reference to an `ostream` object type. The `inOut()` function is then used to write five lines of user-entered text to the file.

Program 8.11

```
#include <iostream>
#include <fstream>
#include <cstdlib>
#include <string>
using namespace std;


int main()
{
  string fname = "list.dat";  // here is the file we are working with

  void inOut(ofstream&);    // function prototype

  ofstream outFile;
```

(*Continued*)

(Continued)

```
  outFile.open(fname.c_str());
  if (outFile.fail())   // check for a successful open
  {
    cout << "\nThe output file " << fname << " was not successfully opened"
         << endl;
    exit(1);
  }

  inOut(outFile);  // call the function

  return 0;
}

void inOut(ofstream& fileOut)
{

  const int NUMLINES = 5;  // number of lines of text
  string line;
  int count;

  cout << "Please enter five lines of text:" << endl;
  for (count = 0; count < NUMLINES; count++)
  {
    getline(cin,line);
    fileOut << line << endl;
  }

  cout << "\nThe file has been successfully written." << endl;
  return;
}
```

Within `main()`, the file is an `ostream` object named `outFile`. This object is passed to the `inOut()` function and is accepted as the formal parameter named `fileOut`, which is declared to be a reference to an `ostream` object type. The function `inOut()` then uses its reference parameter `outFile` as an output file stream name in the same manner as `main()` would use the `fileOut` stream object. Program 8.11 uses the `getline()` method introduced in Section 8.2 (see Table 8.3).

In Program 8.12, we have expanded on Program 8.11 by adding a `getOpen()` function to perform the open. `getOpen()`, like `inOut()`, accepts a reference argument to an `ofstream` object. After the `getOpen()` function completes execution, this reference is passed to `inOut()`, as it was in Program 8.11. Though you might be tempted to write `getOpen()` to return a reference to an `ofstream`, this will not work because it results in an attempt to assign a returned reference to an existing one.

Program 8.12

```
#include <iostream>
#include <fstream>
#include <cstdlib>
#include <string>
using namespace std;

int main()
{
  int getOpen(ofstream&);  // pass a reference to an fstream
  void inOut(ofstream&);   // pass a reference to an fstream

  ofstream outFile;    // filename is an fstream object

  getOpen(outFile);   // open the file
  inOut(outFile);     // write to it

  return 0;
}

int getOpen(ofstream& fileOut)
{
  string name;

  cout << "\nEnter a file name: ";
  getline(cin,name);

  fileOut.open(name.c_str());      // open the file

  if (fileOut.fail())      // check for successful open
  {
    cout << "Cannot open the file" << endl;
    exit(1);
  }
  else
    return 1;
}
```

(Continued)

(Continued)

```
void inOut(ofstream& fileOut)
{
  const int NUMLINES = 5;  // number of lines
  int count;
  string line;

  cout << "Please enter five lines of text:" << endl;
  for (count = 0; count < NUMLINES; ++count)
  {
    getline(cin,line);
    fileOut << line << endl;
  }
  cout << "\nThe file has been successfully written.";
  return;
}
```

Program 8.12 is a modified version of Program 8.11 that allows the user to enter a file name from the standard input device and then opens the `ofstream` connection to the external file. If the name of an existing data file is entered, the file will be destroyed when it is opened for output. A useful trick you may employ to prevent this type of mishap is to open the entered file using an input file stream. If the file exists, the `fail()` method will indicate a successful open (i.e., the open does not fail), which indicates that the file is available for input. This can be used to alert the user that a file with the entered name exists in the system and to request confirmation that the data in the file can be destroyed and the file opened for output. Before the file is reopened for output, the input file stream should be closed. The implementation of this algorithm is left as an exercise.

Exercises 8.5

1. A function named `pFile()` is to receive a file name as a reference to an `ifstream` object. What declarations are required to pass a file name to `pFile()`?

2. Write a function, named `fcheck()`, that checks if a file exists. The function should accept an `ifstream` object as a formal reference parameter. If the file exists, the function should return a value of 1; otherwise, the function should return a value of zero.

3. Assume that a data file consisting of a group of individual lines has been created. Write a function named `printLine()` that will read and display any desired line of the file. For example, the function call `printLine(fstream& fName,5);` should display the fifth line of the passed object stream.

4. Rewrite the function `getOpen()` used in Program 8.12 to incorporate the file-checking procedures described in this section. Specifically, if the entered file name exists, an appropriate message should be displayed. The user should be presented

with the option of entering a new file name or allowing the program to overwrite the existing file. Use the function written for Exercise 2 in your program.

8.6 COMMON PROGRAMMING ERRORS

The common programming errors with respect to files are:

1. Using a file's external name in place of the internal file stream object name when accessing the file. The only stream method that uses the data file's external name is the `open()` function. As always, all stream methods presented in this chapter must be preceded by a stream object name and the dot operator.
2. Opening a file for output without first checking that a file with the given name already exists. Not checking for a pre-existing file name ensures that the file will be overwritten.
3. Not understanding that the end of a file is detected only after the EOF sentinel has been read or passed over.
4. Attempting to detect the end of a file using character variables for the EOF marker. Any variable used to accept the EOF must be declared as an integer variable. For example, if `ch` is declared as a character variable, the following expression produces an infinite loop.[2]

   ```
   while ( (ch = in.file.peek()) != EOF )
   ```

   This occurs because a character variable can never take on an EOF code. EOF is an integer value (usually -1) that has no character representation. This ensures that the EOF code can never be confused with any legitimate character encountered as normal data in the file. To terminate the loop created by the above expression, the variable `ch` must be declared as an integer variable.
5. Using an integer argument with the `seekg()` and `seekp()` functions. This offset must be a long integer constant or variable. Any other value passed to these functions can result in an unpredictable effect.

8.7 CHAPTER SUMMARY

1. A data file is any collection of data stored together in an external storage medium under a common name.
2. A data file is connected to a file stream using `fstream`'s `open()` method. This function connects a file's external name with an internal object name. After the file is opened, all subsequent accesses to the file require the internal object name.

---

[2]This will not occur on UNIX systems, where characters are stored as signed integers.

3. A file can be opened in input or output mode. An opened output file stream creates a new data file or erases the data in an existing opened file. An opened input file stream makes an existing file's data available for input. An error condition results if the file does not exist and can be detected using the `fail()` method.

4. All file streams must be declared as objects of either the `ifstream` or `ofstream` classes. This means that a declaration similar to either of the following must be included with the declarations in which the file is opened:

```
ifstream inFile;
ofstream outFile;
```

   The stream object names `inFile` and `outFile` can be replaced with any user-selected object name.

5. In addition to any files opened within a function, the standard stream objects `cin`, `cout`, and `cerr` are automatically declared and opened when a program is run. `cin` is the object name of an input file stream used for data entry (usually from the keyboard), `cout` is the object name of an output file stream used for default data display (usually the computer screen), and `cerr` is the object name of an output file stream used for displaying system error messages (usually the computer screen).

6. Data files can be accessed randomly using the `seekg()`, `seekp()`, `tellg()`, and `tellp()` methods. The `g` versions of these functions are used to alter and query the file position marker for input file streams, and the `p` versions do the same for output file streams.

7. Table 8.5 lists the methods supplied by the `fstream` class for file manipulation.

Table 8.5 `fstream` Methods

Method Name	Description
`get()`	Extract the next character from the input stream and return it as an `int`.
`get(chrVar)`	Extract the next character from the input stream and assign it to `chrVar`.
`getline(fileObj, string, termChar)`	Extract the next string of characters from the input file stream object and assign them to string until the specified terminating character is detected. If omitted, the default terminating character is a newline.
`getline(C-stringVar,int n,'\n')`	Extract and return characters from the input stream until either `n-1` characters are read or a newline is encountered (terminates the input with a `'\0'`)
`peek()`	Return the next character in the input stream without extracting it from the stream.
`put(chrExp)`	Put the character specified by `chrExp` on the output stream.
`putback(chrExp)`	Push the character specified by `chrExp` back onto the input stream. Does not alter the data in the file.

Table 8.5 `fstream` Methods (continued)

Method Name	Description
`ignore(int n)`	Skip over the next *n* characters; if `n` is omitted, the default will be to skip over the next single character.
`eof()`	Returns a Boolean `true` value if a read has been attempted past the end-of-file; otherwise, it returns a Boolean `false` value. The value becomes `true` only when the first character after the last valid file character is read.
`good()`	Returns a Boolean `true` value while the file is available for program use. Returns a Boolean `false` value if a read has been attempted past the end-of-file. The value becomes `false` only when the first character after the last valid file character is read.
`bad()`	Returns a Boolean `true` value if a read has been attempted past the end-of-file; otherwise, it returns a `false`. The value becomes `true` only when the first character after the last valid file character is read.
`fail()`	Returns a Boolean `true` if the file has not been opened successfully; otherwise, it returns a Boolean `false` value.

8.8 CHAPTER SUPPLEMENT: THE `iostream` CLASS LIBRARY

As we have seen, the classes contained within the `iostream` class library access files using entities called streams. For most systems, the data bytes transferred on a stream represent ASCII characters or binary numbers.

The mechanism for reading a byte stream from a file or writing a byte stream to a file is hidden when using a high-level language such as C++. Nevertheless, it is useful to understand this mechanism so we can place the services provided by the `iostream` class library in their appropriate context.

File Stream Transfer Mechanism

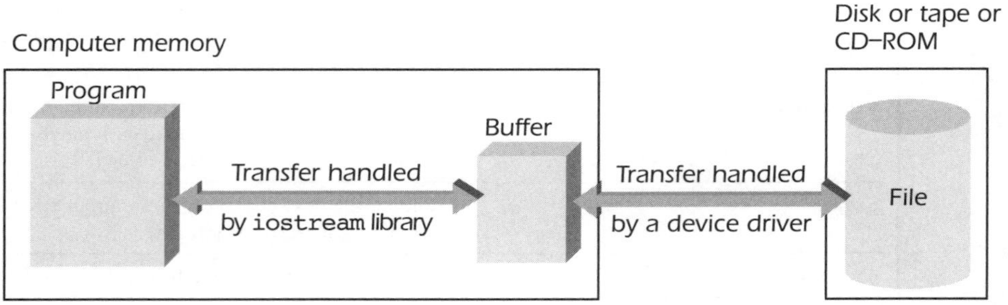

Figure 8.5 The data transfer mechanism.

The mechanism for transferring data between a program and a file is illustrated in Figure 8.5. As shown, transferring data between a program and a file involves an intermediate file buffer contained in the computer's memory. Each opened file is assigned its own file buffer, which is a storage area used by the data being transferred between the program and the file.

From its side, the program either writes a set of data bytes to the file buffer or reads a set of data bytes from the file buffer using a stream object. On the other side of the buffer, the transfer of data between the device storing the actual data file (usually a tape, disk, or CD-ROM) and the file buffer is handled by special operating system programs that are referred to as device drivers. Device drivers are not stand-alone programs but are an integral part of the operating system. A **device driver** is a section of operating system code that accesses a hardware device, such as a disk unit, and handles the data transfer between the device and the computer's memory. As such, it must correctly synchronize the speed of the data transferred between the computer and the device sending or receiving the data. This is because the computer's internal data transfer rate is generally much faster than any device connected to it.

Typically, a disk device driver will only transfer data between the disk and file buffer in fixed sizes, such as 1024 bytes at a time. Thus, the file buffer provides a convenient means of permitting a device driver to transfer data in blocks of one size, and the program can access them using a different size (typically, as individual characters or as a fixed number of characters per line).

Components of the `iostream` Class Library

The `iostream` class library consists of two primary base classes: the `streambuf` class and the `ios` class. The `streambuf` class provides the file buffer, illustrated in Figure 8.5, and a number of general routines for transferring binary data. The `ios` class contains a pointer to the file buffers provided by the `streambuf` class and a number of general routines for transferring text data. From these two base classes, a number of other classes are derived and included in the `iostream` class library.

Figure 8.6 illustrates an inheritance diagram for the `ios` family of classes as it relates to the `ifstream`, `ofstream`, and `fstream` classes. The inheritance diagram for the `streambuf` family of classes is shown in Figure 8.7. The convention adopted for inheritance diagrams is that the arrows point from a derived class to a base class.

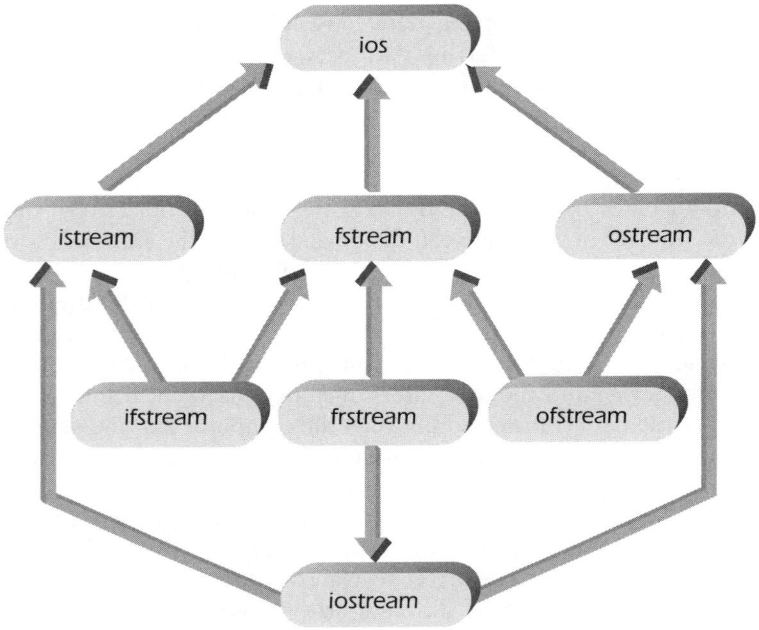

Figure 8.6 The base class `ios` and its derived classes.

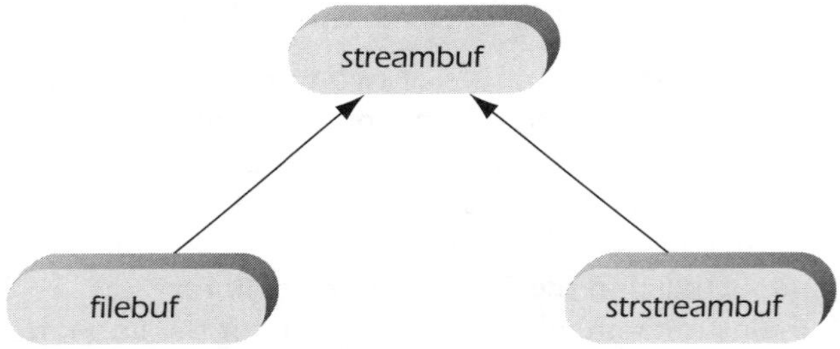

Figure 8.7 The base class `streambuf` and its derived classes.

The correspondence between the classes illustrated in Figures 8.6 and 8.7, including the header files that define these classes, is listed in Table 8.6.

Table 8.6 Correspondence between Classes Illustrated in Figures 8.6 and 8.7

ios Class	streambuf Class	Header File
istream ostream iostream	streambuf	iostream or fstream
iftream oftream fstream	filebuf	fstream

Thus, the `ifstream`, `ofstream`, and `fstream` classes that we have used for file access all use a buffer provided by the `filebuf` class, defined in the `fstream` header file. Similarly, the `cin`, `cout`, `cerr`, and `clog` `iostream` objects that we have been using throughout the text use a buffer provided by the `streambuf` class and defined in the `iostream` header file.

In-Memory Formatting

In addition to the classes illustrated in Figure 8.6, a class named `strstream` is also derived from the `ios` class. This class uses the `strstreambuf` class illustrated in Figure 8.7, requires the `strstream` header file, and provides capabilities for writing and reading strings to and from in-memory defined streams.

As an output stream, such streams are typically used to "assemble" a string from smaller pieces until a complete line of characters is ready to be written, either to `cout` or to a file. Attaching a `strstream` object to a buffer for this purpose is done in a similar manner as attaching an `fstream` object to an output file. For example, the statement

```
strstream inmem(buf, 72, ios::out);
```

attaches a `strstream` object to an existing buffer of 72 bytes in output mode. Program 8.13 illustrates how this statement is used within the context of a complete program.

Program 8.13

```
#include <iostream>
#include <strstream>
#include <iomanip>
using namespace std;

int main()
{
  const int MAXCHARS = 81;  // one more than the maximum characters in a line
  int units = 10;
  double price = 36.85;
  char buf[MAXCHARS];

  strstream inmem(buf, MAXCHARS, ios::out);  // open an in memory stream

  // write to the buffer through the stream
  inmem << "No. of units = "
        << setw(3) << units
        << "  Price per unit = $"
        << setw(6) << setprecision(2) << fixed << price << '\0';

  cout << '|' << buf << '|';

  cout << endl;

  return 0;
}
```

The output produced by Program 8.13 is the following:

```
|No. of units =  10  Price per unit = $  36.85|
```

This output illustrates that the character buffer has been correctly filled in by insertions to the `inmem` stream. (Note that the end-of-string `NULL, '\0'`, which is the last insertion to the stream, is required to correctly close off the C-string.) Once the desired character array has been filled, it would be written out to a file as a single string.

In a similar manner, a `strstream` object can be opened in input mode. Such a stream would be used as a working storage area, or buffer, for storing a complete line of text from a file or standard input. Once the buffer has been filled, the extraction operator would be used to "disassemble" the string into component parts and convert each data item into its designated data type. Doing this permits inputting data from a file on a line-by-line basis prior to assigning individual data items to their respective variables.

CHAPTER 9

Introduction to Classes

TOPIC

Besides being an improved version of C, the distinguishing characteristic of C++ is its support of object-oriented programming. Central to this object orientation is the concept of an abstract data type, which is a programmer-defined data type. In this chapter we explore the implications of permitting programmers to define their own data types and then present C++'s mechanism for constructing them. As we will see, the construction of a data type is based on both variables and functions; variables provide the means for creating new data configurations and functions provide the means for preforming operations on these structures. What C++ provides is a unique way of combining variables and functions together in a self-contained, cohesive unit from which objects can be created.

Point of Information

Procedural, Hybrid, and Pure Object-Oriented Languages

Most high-level programming languages can be categorized into one of three main categories: procedural, hybrid, or object-oriented. FORTRAN, which was the first commercially available high-level programming language, is procedural. This makes sense because FORTRAN was designed to perform mathematical calculations that used standard algebraic formulas. These formulas were described as algorithms and then the algorithms were coded using function and subroutine procedures. Other procedural languages that followed FORTRAN included BASIC, COBOL, and Pascal.

Currently there are only two pure object-oriented languages: Smalltalk and Eiffel. The first requirement of a pure object-oriented language is that it contain three specific features: classes, inheritance, and polymorphism (each of these features is described in this and the next chapter). In addition to providing these features, however, a "pure" object-oriented language must, as a minimum, always use classes. In a pure object-oriented language all data types are constructed as classes, all data values are objects, all operators can be overloaded, and every data operation can only be executed using a class member function. *It is impossible in a pure object-orientated language not to use object-oriented features* throughout a program. This is not the case in a hybrid language.

In a hybrid language, such as C++, *it is impossible not to use elements of a procedural program.* This is because the use of any built-in data type or operation effectively violates the pure object-oriented paradigm. Although a hybrid language must have the ability to define classes, the distinguishing feature of a hybrid language is that it is possible to write a complete program using only procedural code. Additionally, hybrid languages need not even provide inheritance and polymorphic features—but they must provide classes. Languages that use classes but do not provide inheritance and polymorphic features are referred to as *object-based* languages rather than *object-oriented*.

9.1 ABSTRACT DATA TYPES IN C++ (classes)

We live in a world full of objects—planes, trains, cars, telephones, books, computers, etc. Until quite recently, however, programming techniques have not reflected this at all. The primary programming paradigm[1] has been procedural, defining a program as an algorithm written in a machine-readable language. The reasons for this emphasis on procedural programming are primarily historical.

When computers were developed in the 1940s they were used by mathematicians for military purposes—for computing bomb trajectories and decoding enemy orders and diplomatic transmissions. After World War II, computers were still primarily used by mathematicians for mathematical computations. This reality was reflected in the name of the first commercially available high-level language introduced in 1957. The language's name was FORTRAN, which was an acronym for FORmula TRANslation.

[1] A *paradigm* is a standard way of thinking about or doing something.

Further reflecting this predominant use was the fact that in the 1960s almost all computer courses were taught in either engineering or mathematics departments. The term computer science was not yet in common use and computer science departments were just being formed.

This situation has changed dramatically, primarily for two reasons. One of the reasons for disenchantment with procedural-oriented programs has been the failure of traditional procedural languages to provide an adequate means of containing software costs. Software costs include all costs associated with initial program development and subsequent program maintenance. As illustrated in Figure 9.1, the major cost of most computer projects today, whether technical or commercial, is for software.

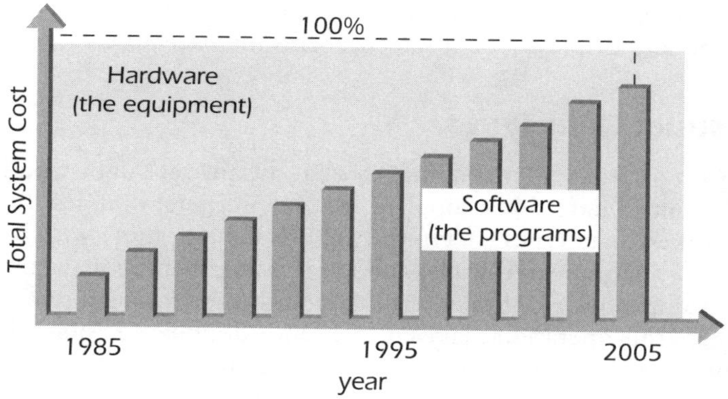

Figure 9.1 Software is the major cost of most computer projects.

Software costs contribute so heavily to total project costs because they are directly related to human productivity (they are labor intensive), while the equipment associated with hardware costs is related to manufacturing technologies. For example, microchips that cost over $500 ten years ago can now be purchased for less than $1.

It is far easier, however, to dramatically increase manufacturing productivity a thousandfold, with the consequent decrease in hardware costs, than it is for programmers to double either the quantity or quality of the code they produce. So as hardware costs have plummeted, software productivity and its associated costs have remained relatively constant. Thus, the ratio of software costs to total system costs (hardware plus software) has increased dramatically.

One way to significantly increase programmer productivity is to create code that can be reused without extensive revision, retesting, and revalidation. The inability of procedurally structured code to provide this type of reusability has led to the search for other software approaches.

The second reason for disenchantment with procedural-based programming has been the emergence of graphical screens and the subsequent interest in window applications. Providing a graphical user interface (GUI) where a user can easily move around in even a single window is a challenge using procedural code. Programming multiple and possibly overlapping windows on the same graphical screen increases the complexity enormously when procedural code is used.

Unlike a procedural approach, however, an object-oriented approach fits well to graphically windowed environments, where each window can be specified as a self-contained rectangular object that can be moved and resized in relation to other objects on the screen. Additionally, within each window other graphical objects, such as check boxes, option buttons, labels, and text boxes can easily be placed and moved.

To provide this object-creation capability, extensions to the procedural language C were developed. This extension became the new language named C++, which permits a programmer to both use and create new objects.

Central to the creation of objects is the concept of an abstract data type, which is simply a user-defined data type, as opposed to the built-in data types provided by all languages (such as integer and floating-point types). Permitting a programmer to define new data types, such as a rectangular type, out of which specific rectangular objects can be created and displayed on a screen, forms the basis of C++'s object orientation.

Abstract Data Types

To gain a clear understanding of what an abstract data type is, consider the following four built-in data types supplied in C++: integers, doubles, Boolean, and characters. In using these data types we typically declare one or more variables of the desired type, use them in their accepted ways, and avoid using them in ways that are not specified. Thus, for example, we would not use the modulus operator on two double-precision numbers. Because this operation makes no sense for double-precision numbers, it is never defined, in any programming language, for such numbers. Thus, although we typically don't consider it, each data type consists of *both* a type of data, such as integer or double, *and* specific operational capabilities provided for each type.

In computer terminology, the combination of data and their associated operations is defined as a **data type**. That is, a data type defines *both* the types of data and the types of operations that can be performed on the data. Seen in this light, the integer data type, the double-precision data type, and the character data type provided in C++ are all examples of **built-in** data types that are defined by a type of data and specific operational capabilities provided for initializing and manipulating the type. In a simplified form this relationship can be described as

Data Type = Allowable Data Values + Operational Capabilities

Thus, the operations that we have been using in C++ are an inherent part of each data type we have been using. For each of these data types the designers of C++ had to carefully consider, and then implement, specific operations.

To understand the importance of the operational capabilities provided by a programming language, let's take a moment to list some of those supplied with C++'s built-in data types (`int`s, `double`s, `bool`s, and `char`s). The minimum set of the capabilities provided by C++'s built-in data types is listed in Table 9.1.[2]

---

[2]You might notice the absence of reading and writing operations. In both C and C++, except for very primitive operations, input and output is provided by standard library routines and class functions.

Table 9.1 C++ Built-In Data Type Capabilities

Capability	Example
Define one or more variables of the data type	`int a, b;`
Initialize a variable at definition	`int a = 5;`
Assign a value to a variable	`a = 10;`
Assign one variable's value to another variable	`a = b;`
Perform mathematical operations	`a + b`
Perform relational operations	`a > b`
Convert from one data type to another	`a = int (7.2);`

Now let's see how all of this relates to abstract data types (ADTs). By definition an **abstract data type** is simply a user-defined type that defines both a type of data and the operations that can be performed on them. Such user-defined data types are required when we wish to create objects that are more complex than simple integers and characters. If we are to create our own data types we must be aware of both the type of data we are creating and the capabilities that we will provide to initialize and manipulate the data.

As a specific example, assume that we are programming an application that uses dates extensively. Clearly, from a data standpoint, a date must be capable of accessing and storing a month, day, and year designation. Although from an implementation standpoint there are a number of means of storing a date, from a user viewpoint the actual implementation is not relevant. For example, a date can be stored as three integers, one for the month, day, and year, respectively. Alternatively, a single long integer in the form *yyyymmdd* can also be used. Using the long integer implementation the date 5/16/08 would be stored as the integer 20080516. For sorting dates, the long integer format is very attractive because the numerical sequence of the dates corresponds to their calendar sequence.

The method of internally structuring the date, unfortunately, supplies only a partial answer to our programming effort. We must still supply a set of operations that can be used with dates. Clearly, such operations could include assigning values to a date, subtracting two dates to determine the number of days between them, comparing two dates to determine which is earlier and which is later, and displaying a date in a form such as 12/03/06 rather than as 12/3/6.

Notice that the details of how each operation works is dependent on how we choose to store a date (formally referred to as its data structure) and is only of interest to us as we develop each operation. For example, the implementation of comparing two dates will differ if we store a date using a single long integer as opposed to using separate integers for the month, day, and year, respectively.

The combination of the storage structure used for dates with a set of available operations appropriate to dates would then define an abstract Date data type. Once this date type is developed, programmers that want to use it need never be concerned with *how* dates are stored or *how* the operations are performed. All that they need to know is *what* each operation does and how to invoke it, much as they use C++'s built-in operations.

For example, we don't really care how the addition of two integers is performed but only that it is done correctly.

In C++ an abstract data type is referred to as a **class**. Construction of a class is inherently easy and we already have all the necessary tools in variables and functions. What C++ provides is a mechanism for packaging these two items together in a self-contained unit. Let's see how this is done.

Class Construction

A class defines both data and functions. This is usually accomplished by constructing a class in two parts, consisting of a declaration section and an implementation section. As illustrated in Figure 9.2, the declaration section declares both the data types and functions for the class. The implementation section is then used to define the functions whose prototypes have been declared in the declaration section.[3] When a function is part of a class, it is formally referred to as a method to denote class membership. By convention, however, the terms class method and class function are used interchangeably in C++.

```
// class declaration section
class className
{
  data members // the variables
  function member // prototypes
};
// class implementation section
function definitions
```

Figure 9.2 Format of a `class` definition.

Both the variables and functions listed in the class declaration section are collectively referred to as **class members**. Individually, the variables are referred to as both **data members** and **instance variables** (the terms are synonymous), while the functions are referred to as **member functions**. A member function name may not be the same as a data member name.

As a specific example of a class, consider the following definition of a class named `Date`. This type of class is very important in applications where equipment delivery dates and interest payments all depend on date determinations. Using such a class, the determination of whether a date falls on a weekend or holiday, for example, are easily answered.

---

[3]This separation into two parts is not mandatory as the implementation can be included within the declaration section, as described in the next section.

```
//--- class declaration section

class Date
{
  private:          // notice the colon after the word private
     int month;     // a data member
     int day;       // a data member
     int year;      // a data member
   public:          // again, notice the colon here
     Date(int = 7, int = 4, int = 2005); // a member function - the constructor
     void setDate(int, int, int);      // a member function
     void showDate();                  // a member function
};

//--- class implementation section

Date::Date(int mm, int dd, int yyyy)
{
  month = mm;
  day = dd;
  year = yyyy;
}

void Date::setDate(int mm, int dd, int yyyy)
{
  month = mm; day = dd; year = yyyy;

  return;
}

void Date::showDate()
{
  cout << "The date is ";
  cout << setfill('0')
       << setw(2) << month << '/'
       << setw(2) << day << '/'
       << setw(2) << year % 100; // extract the last 2 year digits
  cout << endl;

  return;
}
```

Because this definition may initially look overwhelming, first notice that it does consist of two sections—a declaration section and an implementation section. Now consider each of these sections individually.

The class declaration section begins with the keyword `class` followed by a class name. Following the class name are the class's variable declarations and function prototypes, enclosed in a brace pair that is terminated with a semicolon. Thus, the general structure of the form that we have used is[4]

```
class Name
{
  private:
    a list of variable declarations
  public:
    a list of function prototypes
};
```

Notice that this format is followed by our `Date` class, which for convenience we have listed below with no internal comments.

```
//--- class declaration section

class Date
{
  private:
     int month;
     int day;
     int year;
 public:
     Date(int = 7, int = 4, int = 2005);
     void setDate(int, int, int);
     void showDate();
};  // this is a declaration - don't forget the semicolon
```

The name of this class is `Date`. Although the initial capital letter is not required, it is conventionally used to designate a class. The body of the declaration section, which is enclosed within braces, consists of variable and function declarations. In this case the data members `month`, `day`, and `year` are declared as integers and three functions named `Date()`, `setDate()`, and `showDate()` are declared via prototypes. The keywords `private` and `public` are access specifiers that define access rights. The `private` keyword specifies that the class members following, in this case the data members `month`, `day`, and `year`, may only be accessed by using the class functions (or friend functions, as will be discussed in Section 9.2).[5] The purpose of the `private` designation is specifically meant to enforce data security by requiring all access to `private` data members through the provided member functions. This type of access, which restricts a user from seeing how the data is actually stored, is referred to as **data hiding**. Once a class category such as `private` is designated, it remains in force until a new category is listed.

---

[4]Other forms are possible. As this form is one of the most commonly used and easily understood, it will serve as our standard model throughout the text.

[5]Note that the default membership category in a class is `private`, which means that this keyword can be omitted. In this text we will explicitly use the `private` designation to reinforce the idea of access restrictions inherent in class membership.

Specifically, we have chosen to store a date using three integers: one for the month, day, and year, respectively. We will also always store the year as a four-digit number. Thus, for example, we will store the year 1998 as 1998 and not as 98. Making sure to store all years with their correct century designation will eliminate a multitude of problems that can crop up if only the last two digits, such as 98, are stored. For example, the number of years between 2006 and 1999 can be quickly calculated as 2006 – 1999 = 7 years, while this same answer is not so easily obtained if only the year values 06 and 99 are used. Additionally, we are sure of what the year 2006 refers to, while a two-digit value such as 06 could refer to either 1906 or 2006.

Following the `private` class data members, the function prototypes listed in the `Date` class have been declared as `public`. This means that these class functions *can* be called by any objects and functions not in the class (outside). In general, all class functions should be `public`; as such they furnish capabilities to manipulate the class variables from outside of the class. For our `Date` class we have initially provided three functions named `Date()`, `setDate()`, and `showDate()`. Notice that one of these member functions has the same name, `Date`, as the class name. This particular function is referred to as a **constructor** function, and it has a specially defined purpose: it can be used to initialize class data members with values. The default values that are used for this function are the numbers 7, 4, and 2001, which, as we will shortly see, are used as the default `month`, `day`, and `year` values, respectively. The only point to notice here is that the default year is correctly represented as a four-digit integer that retains the century designation. Also notice that the constructor function has no return type, which is a requirement for this special function. The two remaining functions declared in our declaration example are `setdate()` and `showdate()`, both of which have been declared as returning no value (`void`). In the implementation section of the class these three member functions will be written to permit initialization, assignment, and display capabilities, respectively.

The **implementation section** of a class is where the member functions declared in the declaration section are written.[6] Figure 9.3 illustrates the general form of functions included in the implementation section. This format is correct for all functions except the constructor, which, as we have stated, has no return type.

```
returnType  className::functionName(parameter list)
{
    function body
}
```

Figure 9.3 Format of a member function.

[6]It is also possible to define these functions within the declaration section by declaring and writing them as inline functions. Examples of inline member functions are presented in Section 9.2.

As shown in Figure 9.3, member functions defined in the implementation section have the same format as all user-written C++ functions with the addition of the class name and scope resolution operator, `::`, that identifies the function as a member of a particular class. Let us now reconsider the implementation section of our `Date` class, which is repeated below for convenience.

```
//--- class implementation section

Date::Date(int mm, int dd, int yyyy)
{
  month = mm;
  day = dd;
  year = yyyy;
}

void Date::setDate(int mm, int dd, int yyyy)
{
  month = mm;
  day = dd;
  year = yyyy;

  return;
}

void Date::showDate()
{
  cout << "The date is ";
  cout << setfill('0')
       << setw(2) << month << '/'
       << setw(2) << day << '/'
       << setw(2) << year % 100; // extract the last 2 year digits
  cout << endl;

  return;
}
```

Notice that the first function in this implementation section has the same name as the class, which makes it a constructor function. As such, it has no return type. The `Date::` included at the beginning of the function header line identifies this function as a member of the `Date` class. The rest of the header line,

```
Date(int mm, int dd, int yyyy)
```

defines the function as having three integer parameters. The body of this function simply assigns the data members `month`, `day`, and `year` with the values of the parameters `mm`, `dd`, and `yyyy`, respectively.

The next function header line

```
void Date::setDate(int mm, int dd, int yyyy)
```

defines this as the `setDate()` function belonging to the `Date class (Date::)`. This function returns no value (`void`) and expects three integer parameters, `mm`, `dd`, and `yyyy`. In a manner similar to the `Date()` function, the body of this function assigns the data members month, day, and year with the values of its parameters.

Finally, the last function header line in the implementation section defines a function named `showDate()`. This function has no parameters, returns no value, and is a member of the `Date` class. The body of this function, however, needs a little more explanation.

Although we have chosen to internally store all years as four-digit values that retain century information, users are accustomed to seeing dates where the year is represented as a two-digit value, such as 12/15/99. To display the last two digits of the year value, the expression `year % 100` can be used. For example, if the year is 1999, the expression `1999 % 100` yields the value 99, and if the year is 2006, the expression `2006 % 100` yields the value 6. Notice that if we had used an assignment such as `year = year % 100;` we would actually be altering the stored value of `year` to correspond to the last two digits of the year. Since we want to retain the year as a four-digit number, we must be careful to only manipulate the displayed value using the expression `year % 100` within the `cout` stream. The `setfill` and `setw` manipulators are used to ensure that the displayed values correspond to conventionally accepted dates. For example, the date March 9, 2006, should appear as either 3/9/06 or 03/09/06. The `setw` manipulator forces each value to be displayed in a field width of 2. Since this manipulator only remains in effect for the next insertion, we have included it before the display of each date value. As the `setfill` manipulator, however, remains in effect until the fill character is changed, we only have to include it once. We have used the `setfill` manipulator here to change the fill character from its default of a blank space to the character 0. Doing this ensures that a date such as December 9, 2006, will appear as `12/09/06` and not `12/ 9/ 6`.

To see how our `Date` class can be used within the context of a complete program, consider Program 9.1. To make the program easier to read it has been shaded in light and darker areas. The lighter area contains the class declaration and implementation sections that we have already considered. The darker area contains the header and `main()` function. For convenience we will retain this shading convention for all programs using classes.[7]

[7]This shading is not accidental. In practice the lighter shaded region containing the class definition would be placed in a separate file. A single `#include` statement would then be used to include this class declaration in the program. Thus, the final program would consist of the two darker shaded regions illustrated in Program 9.1 with the addition of one more `#include` statement in the first region.

Program 9.1

```
#include <iostream>
#include <iomanip>
using namespace std;

// class declaration

class Date
{
  private:
    int month;
    int day;
    int year;
  public:
    Date(int = 7, int = 4, int = 2005);  // constructor
    void setDate(int, int, int);          // member function to copy a date
    void showDate();                    // member function to display a date
};

// implementation section

Date::Date(int mm, int dd, int yyyy)
{
  month = mm;
  day = dd;
  year = yyyy;
}
void Date::setDate(int mm, int dd, int yyyy)
{
  month = mm;
  day = dd;
  year = yyyy;

  return;
}
void Date::showDate()
{
   cout << "The date is ";
   cout << setfill('0')
        << setw(2) << month << '/'
        << setw(2) << day << '/'
        << setw(2) << year % 100; // extract the last 2 year digits
   cout << endl;
```

(Continued)

(Continued)

```
    return;
}

int main()
{
    Date a, b, c(4,1,2000);   // declare 3 objects

    b.setDate(12,25,2006);   // assign values to b's data members
    a.showDate();            // display object a's values
    b.showDate();            // display object b's values
    c.showDate();            // display object c's values

    return 0;
}
```

The declaration and implementation sections contained in the lighter shaded region of Program 9.1 should look familiar to you, as they contain the class declaration and implementation sections that we have already discussed. Notice, however, that this region only declares the class; it does not create any variables of this class type. This is true of all C++ types, including the built-in types such as integers and doubles. Just as a variable of an integer type must be defined, variables of a user-declared class must also be defined. Variables defined to be of a user-declared class are referred to as **objects**.

Using this new terminology, the first statement in the Program 9.1 `main()` function, contained in the darker area, defines three objects, named `a`, `b`, and `c`, to be of class type `Date`. In C++ whenever a new object is defined, memory is allocated for the object and its data members are automatically initialized. This is done by an automatic call to the `class` constructor function. For example, consider the definition `Date a, b, c(4,1,2000);` contained in `main()`. When the object named `a` is defined, the constructor function `Date` is automatically called. Because no parameters have been assigned to `a`, the default values of the constructor function are used, resulting in the initialization:

```
a.month = 7
a.day = 4
a.year = 2005
```

Notice the notation that we have used here. It consists of an object name and an attribute name separated by a period. This is the standard syntax for referring to an object's attribute, namely

`objectName.attributeName`

where *`objectName`* is the name of a specific object and *`attributeName`* is the name of a data member defined for the object's class.

Thus, the notation `a.month = 7` refers to the fact that object `a`'s month data member has been set to the value `7`. Similarly, the notation `a.day = 4` and `a.year = 2005` refers to the fact that `a's` day and year data members have been set to the values 4 and 2005, respectively. In the same manner, when the object named b is defined, the same default parameters are used, resulting in the initialization of b's data members as

```
b.month = 7
b.day = 4
b.year = 2005
```

The object named c, however, is defined with the arguments 4, 1, and 2000. These three arguments are passed into the constructor function when the object is defined, resulting in the initialization of c's data members as

```
c.month = 4
c.day = 1
c.year = 2000
```

The next statement in `main()`, `b.setDate(12,25,2006)`, calls b's `setDate` function, which assigns the argument values 12, 25, 2006 to b's data members, resulting in the assignment

```
b.month = 12
b.day = 25
b.year = 2006
```

Notice the syntax for referring to an object's method. This syntax is

objectName.methodName(parameters)

where *objectName* is the name of a specific object and *methodName* is the name of one of the functions defined for the object's class. Since we have defined all class functions as public, a statement such as `b.setDate(12,25,2006)` is valid inside the `main()` function and is a call to the `class`' `setDate()` function. This statement tells the `setDate()` function to operate on the b object with the arguments 12, 25, and 2006. It is important to understand that because all class data members were specified as `private`, a statement such as `b.month = 12` would be invalid from within `main()`. We are, therefore, forced to rely on member functions to access data member values.

The last three statements in `main()` call the `showDate()` function to operate on the a, b, and c objects. The first call results in the display of a's data values, the second call in the display of b's data values, and the third call in the display of c's data values. Thus, the output of Program 9.1 is

```
The date is 07/04/05
The date is 12/25/06
The date is 04/01/00
```

Notice that a statement such as `cout << a;` is invalid within `main()` because `cout` does not know how to handle an object of `class Date`. Thus, we have supplied our class with a function that can be used to access and display an object's internal values.

Point of Information

Interfaces, Implementations, and Information Hiding

The terms interface and implementation are used extensively in object-oriented programming literature. Each of these terms can be equated to specific parts of a class's declaration and implementation sections.

An *interface* consists of a `class`' `public` member function declarations and any supporting comments. As such, the interface should be all that is required to tell a programmer how to use the `class`.

The *implementation* consists of both the class's implementation section, which consists of both `private` and `public` member definitions *and* the `class`' `private` data members, which is contained in a class's declaration section.

The implementation is the essential means of providing information hiding. In its most general context *information hiding* refers to the principal that *how* a class is internally constructed is not relevant to any programmer who wishes to use the class. That is, the implementation can and should be hidden from all class users precisely to ensure that the class is not altered or compromised in any way. All that a programmer needs to know to correctly use class should be provided by the interface.

Terminology

As there is sometimes confusion about the terms classes, objects, and other terminology associated with object-oriented programming, we will take a moment to clarify and review the terminology.

A **class** is a programmer-defined data type out of which objects can be created. **Objects** are created from classes; they have the same relationship to classes as variables do to C++'s built-in data types. For example, in the declaration

```
int a;
```

`a` is said to be a variable, while in the Program 9.1 declaration

```
Date a;
```

`a` is said to be an object. If it initially helps you to think of an object as a variable, do so.

Objects are also referred to as **instances** of a class and the process of creating a new object is frequently referred to as an **instantiation** of the object. Each time a new object is instantiated (created), a new set of data members belonging to the object is created.[8] The particular values contained in these data members determines the object's **state**.

Seen in this way, a class can be thought of as a blueprint out of which particular instances (objects) can be created. Each instance (object) of a class will have its own set of particular values for the set of data members specified in the class declaration section.

[8]Note that only one set of class functions is created. These functions are shared between objects.

In addition to the data types allowed for an object, a class also defines **behavior**—that is, the operations that are permitted to be performed on an object's data members. Users of the object need to know *what* these functions can do and how to activate them through function calls, but unless runtime or space implications are relevant, they do not need to know *how* the operation is done. The actual implementation details of an object's operations are contained in the class implementation, which can be hidden from the user. Other names for the operations defined in a class implementation section are procedures, functions, services, and methods. We will use these terms interchangeably throughout the remainder of the text.

Exercises 9.1

1. Define the following terms:

a. class
b. object
c. declaration section
d. implementation section
e. instance variable
f. member function
g. data member
h. constructor
i. class instance
j. services
k. methods
l. interface
m. state
n. behavior

2. a. In place of specifying a rectangle's location by listing the position of two diagonal corner points, what other attributes could be used?

b. What other attributes, besides length and width, might be used to describe a rectangle if the rectangle is to be drawn on a color monitor?

c. Describe a set of attributes that could be used to define circles that are to be drawn on a black and white monitor?

d. What additional attributes would you add to those selected in response to Exercise 2c if the circles were to be drawn on a color monitor?

3. a. The attributes of a class represent how objects of the class appear to the outside world. The behavior represents how an object of a class reacts to an external stimulus. Given this, what do you think is the mechanism by which one object "triggers" the designated behavior in another object?

b. If behavior in C++ is constructed by defining an appropriate function, how do you think the behavior is activated in C++?

4. Write a class declaration section for each of the following specifications. In each case include a prototype for a constructor and a member function named `showdata()` that can be used to display member values.

a. A class named `Time` that has integer data members named `secs`, `mins`, and `hours`.

b. A class named `Complex` that has double-precision data members named `real` and `imaginary`.

c. A class named `Circle` that has integer data members named `xcenter` and `ycenter` and a double-precision data member named `radius`.

d. A class named `System` that has character data members named `computer`, `printer`, and `screen`, each capable of holding 30 characters (including the end of string `NULL`), and double-precision data members named `compPrice`, `printPrice`, and `scrnPrice`.

5. a. Construct a class implementation section for the constructor and `showdata()` function members corresponding to the class declaration created for Exercise 4a.
b. Construct a class implementation section for the constructor and `showdata()` function members corresponding to the class declaration created for Exercise 4b.
c. Construct a class implementation section for the constructor and `showdata()` function members corresponding to the class declaration created for Exercise 4c.
d. Construct a class implementation section for the constructor and `showdata()` function members corresponding to the class declaration created for Exercise 4d.

6. a. Include the class declaration and implementation sections prepared for Exercises 4a and 5a in a complete working program.
b. Include the class declaration and implementation sections prepared for Exercises 4b and 5b in a complete working program.
c. Include the class declaration and implementation sections prepared for Exercises 4c and 5c in a complete working program.
d. Include the class declaration and implementation sections prepared for Exercises 4d and 5d in a complete working program.

7. Determine the errors in the following class declaration section:

```
class employee
  {
  public:
    int empnum;
    char code;
  private:
    class(int = 0);
    void showemp(int, char);
  };
```

8. a. Construct a class named `Rectangle` that has double-precision data members named `length` and `width`. The class should have a member function named `perimeter()` and `area()` to calculate the perimeter and area of a rectangle, a member function named `setdata()` to set a rectangles `length` and `width`, and a member function named `showdata()` that displays a rectangle's `length`, `width`, `perimeter`, and `area`.
b. Include the `Rectangle` class constructed in Exercise 8a within a working C++ program.

9. a. Modify the `Date` class defined in Program 9.1 to include a `nextDay()` function that increments a date by one day. Test your function to ensure that it correctly increments days into a new month and into a new year.

b. Modify the `Date` class defined in Program 9.1 to include a `priorDay()` function that decrements a date by one day. Test your function to ensure that it correctly decrements days into a prior month and into a prior year.

10. Modify the `Date` class in Program 9.1 to contain a method that compares two `Date` objects and returns the larger of the two. The method should be written according to the following algorithm:

Comparison function
Accept two `Date` *values as parameters*
Determine the later date using the following procedure:
Convert each date into an integer value having the form yyyymmdd
This can be accomplished using the formula year*100000 + month*100 + day
Compare the corresponding integers for each date
The larger integer corresponds to the later date
Return the later date

11. a. Add a member function to Program 9.1's class definition that determines the day of the week for any date object. An algorithm for determining the day of the week, known as Zeller's algorithm, is the following:

For dates in the form of mm/dd/ccyy, where mm is the month, dd is the day, cc is the century, and yy is the year in the century. For example, with 12/28/2006, mm = 12, dd = 28, cc = 20, and yy = 6.

If mm is less than 3
Set mm = mm + 12 and ccyy = ccyy−1
Endif
Set cc = int(ccyy/100)
Set yy = ccyy % 100
*Set the variable T = dd + int(26 * (mm + 1)/10) + yy + int(yy/4) – 2 * cc*
dayOfWeek = T %7
If dayOFWeek is less than 0
dayOfWeek = dayOfWeek + 7
Endif

Using this algorithm, the `Day-of-week` will have a value of 0 if the date is a Saturday, 1 if a Sunday, etc.

b. Include the class definition constructed for Exercise 11a in a complete C++ program. The `main()` function should display the name of the day (Sun, Mon, Tue, etc.) for the `Date` object being tested.

9.2 CONSTRUCTORS

A **constructor** function is any function that has the same name as its class. Multiple constructors can be defined for each class as long as they are distinguishable by the number and types of their parameters.

The intended purpose of a constructor is to initialize a new object's data members. As such, depending on the number and types of supplied arguments, one constructor function is automatically called each time an object is created. If no constructor function is written, the compiler supplies a default constructor. In addition to its initialization role, a constructor function may also perform other tasks when it is called and can be written in a variety of ways. In this section we present the possible variations of constructor functions and introduce another function, the destructor, which is automatically called whenever an object goes out of existence.

Figure 9.4 illustrates the general format of a constructor. As shown in this figure, a constructor

- must have the same name as the class to which it belongs
- must have no return type (not even void)

```
className::className(parameter list)
{
  function body
}
```

Figure 9.4 Constructor format.

If you do not include a constructor in your class definition, the compiler supplies a do-nothing default one for you. For example, consider the following class declaration:

```
class Date
{
  private:
    int month, day, year;
  public:
    void setDate(int, int, int);
    void showDate(void)
};
```

Because no user-defined constructor has been declared here, the compiler creates a default constructor. For our `Date` class this default constructor is equivalent to the implementation `Date::Date(void){}`—that is, the compiler-supplied default constructor expects no parameters and has an empty body. Clearly this default constructor is not very useful, but it does exist if no other constructor is declared.

Point of Information

Constructors

A **constructor** is any function that has the same name as its class. The primary purpose of a constructor is to initialize an object's member variables when an object is created. As such, a constructor is automatically called when an object is declared.

A `class` can have multiple constructors provided that each constructor is distinguishable by having a different formal parameter list. A compiler error results when unique identification of a constructor is not possible. If no constructor is provided the compiler will supply a do-nothing default constructor.

Every constructor function must be declared *with no return type* (not even void). Since they are functions, constructors may also be explicitly called in nondeclarative statements. When used in this manner, the function call requires parentheses following the constructor name, even if no parameters are used. However, when used in a declaration, parentheses *must not* be included for a zero parameter constructor. For example, the declaration `Date a();` is incorrect. The correct declaration is `Date a;`. When parameters are used, however, they must be enclosed within parentheses in both declarative and nondeclarative statements. Default parameter values should be included within the constructor's prototype.

The term **default constructor** is used quite frequently in C++. It refers to any constructor that does not require any arguments when it is called. This can be because no arguments are declared, which is the case for the compiler-supplied default, or because all arguments have been given default values. For example, the constructor `Date(int mm = 7, int dd = 4, int yyyy = 2001)` is a valid prototype for a default constructor also. Here, each argument has been given a default value, and an object can be declared as type `Date` without supplying any further arguments. Using such a constructor, the declaration `Date a;` initializes the `a` object with the default values `7`, `4`, and `2001`.

To verify that a constructor function is automatically called whenever a new object is created, consider Program 9.2. Notice that in the implementation section the constructor function uses `cout` to display the message `Created a new object with data values`. Thus, whenever the constructor is called this message is displayed. Since the `main()` function creates three objects, the constructor is called three times and the message is displayed three times.

The following output is produced when Program 9.2 is executed:

```
Created a new data object with data values 7, 4, 2005
Created a new data object with data values 7, 4, 2005
Created a new data object with data values 4, 1, 2006
```

Although any legitimate C++ statement can be used within a constructor function, such as the `cout` statement used in Program 9.2, it is best to keep constructors simple and use them only for initializing purposes. One further point needs to be made with respect to the constructor function contained in Program 9.2. According to the rules of C++, object members are initialized in the order they are declared in the class declaration section and *not* in the order they may appear in the function's definition within the implementation section. Usually this will not be an issue, unless one member is initialized using another data member's value.

Program 9.2

```
#include <iostream>
using namespace std;

// class declaration section

class Date
{
  private:
    int month;
    int day;
    int year;
  public:
    Date(int = 7, int = 4, int = 2005);     // constructor
};

// implementation section

Date::Date(int mm, int dd, int yyyy)
{
  month = mm;
  day = dd;
  year = yyyy;
  cout << "Created a new data object with data values "
       << month << ", " << day << ", " << year << endl;
}

int main()
{
  Date a;             // declare an object
  Date b;             // declare an object
  Date c(4,1,2006);   // declare an object

  return 0;
}
```

Calling Constructors

As we have seen, constructors are called whenever an object is created. The actual declaration, however, can be made in a variety of ways.

For example, the declaration

```
Date c(4,1,2006);
```

used in Program 9.2 could also have been written as

```
Date c = Date(4,1,2006);
```

This second form declares `c` as being of type `Date` and then makes a direct call to the constructor function with the arguments 4, 1, and 2006. This second form can be simplified when only one argument is passed to the constructor. For example, if only the month data member of the `c` object needed to be initialized with the value 8 and the day and year members can use the default values, the object can be created using the declaration

```
Date c = 8;
```

Since this resembles declarations in C, it and its more complete form using the equal sign is referred to as the **C style of initialization**. The form of declaration used in Program 9.2 is referred to as the **C++ style of initialization**, and is the form we will use predominantly throughout the remainder of the text.

Regardless of which initialization form you use, in no case should an object be declared with empty parentheses. For example, the declaration `Date a();` is not the same as the declaration `Date a;`. The latter declaration uses the default constructor values while the former declaration results in no object being created.

Overloaded and Inline Constructors

The primary difference between a constructor and other user-written functions is how the constructor is called: Constructors are called automatically each time an object is created, while other functions must be explicitly called by name.[9] As a function, however, a constructor must still follow all of the rules applicable to user-written functions that were presented in Chapter 6. This means that constructors may have default arguments, as was illustrated in Program 9.1, may be overloaded, and may be written as inline functions.

Recall from Section 6.1 that function overloading permits the same function name to be used with different argument lists. Based on the supplied argument types the compiler determines which function to use when the call is encountered. Let's see how this can be applied to our `Date` class. For convenience the appropriate class declaration is repeated below:

```
// class declaration section
class Date
{
  private:
    int month;
```

[9] This is true for all functions except destructors, which are described later in this section. A destructor function is automatically called each time an object is destroyed.

```
      int day;
      int year;
    public:
      Date(int = 7, int = 4, int = 2005);      // constructor
  };
```

Here, the constructor prototype specifies three integer parameters, which are used to initialize the month, day, and year data members.

An alternate method of specifying a date is to use a long integer in the form $year \cdot 10000 + month \cdot 100 + day$. For example, the date 12/24/1998 using this form is 19981224 and the date 2/5/2006 is 20060205.[10] A suitable prototype for a constructor that uses dates of this form is:

```
Date(long);    // an overloaded constructor
```

Here, the constructor is declared as receiving one long integer argument. The code for this new `Date` function must, of course, correctly convert its single argument into a month, day, and year, and would be included within the class implementation section. The actual code for such a constructor is:

```
Date::Date(long yyyymmdd)    // a second constructor
{
  year = int(yyyymmdd/10000.0);      // extract the year
  month = int( (yyyymmdd - year * 10000.0) / 100.00 ); // extract the month
  day = int(yyyymmdd - year * 10000.0 - month * 100.0); // extract the day
}
```

Do not be overly concerned with the actual conversion code used within the function's body. The important point here is the concept of overloading the `Date()` function to provide two constructors. Program 9.3 contains the complete class definition within the context of a working program.

Program 9.3

```
#include <iostream>
#include <iomanip>
using namespace std;
```

(Continued)

[10] The reason for specifying dates in this manner is that only one number needs to be used per date and that sorting the numbers automatically puts the corresponding dates into chronological order.

(Continued)

```
// class declaration

class Date
{
  private:
    int month;
    int day;
    int year;
  public:
    Date(int = 7, int = 4, int = 2005);   // constructor
    Date(long);                    // another constructor
    void showDate();               // member function to display a date
};

// implementation section

Date::Date(int mm, int dd, int yyyy)
{
  month = mm;
  day = dd;
  year = yyyy;
}

Date::Date(long yyyymmdd)
{
  year = int(yyyymmdd/10000.0);     // extract the year
  month = int( (yyyymmdd - year * 10000.0)/100.00 ); // extract the month
  day = int(yyyymmdd - year * 10000.0 - month * 100.0); // extract the day
}

void Date::showDate()
{
  cout << "The date is ";
  cout << setfill('0')
       << setw(2) << month << '/'
       << setw(2) << day << '/'
       << setw(2) << year % 100; // extract the last 2 year digits
  cout << endl;

  return;
}
```

(Continued)

(Continued)

```
int main()
{
  Date a, b(4,1,1998), c(20060515L); // declare three objects

  a.showDate();           // display object a's values
  b.showDate();           // display object b's values
  c.showDate();           // display object c's values

  return 0;
}
```

The output provided by Program 9.3 is:

```
The date is 07/04/05
The date is 04/01/98
The date is 05/15/06
```

Three objects are created in the Program 9.3 `main()` function. The first object, `a`, is initialized with the default constructor using its default arguments. Object `b` is also initialized with the default constructor but uses the arguments 4, 1, and 1998. Finally, object `c`, which is initialized with a long integer, uses the second constructor in the class implementation section. The compiler knows to use this second constructor because the argument specified, 20020515L, is clearly designated as a long integer. It is worthwhile pointing out that a compiler error would occur if both `Date` constructors had default values. In such a case a declaration such as `Date d;` would be ambiguous to the compiler, as it would not be able to determine which constructor to use. Thus, in each implementation section only one constructor can be written as the default.

Just as constructors may be overloaded, they may also be written as inline functions. Doing so simply means defining the function in the class declaration section. For example, making both of the constructors contained in Program 9.3 inline is accomplished by the declaration section:

```
// class declaration

class Date
{
  private:
    int month;
    int day;
    int year;
  public:
    Date(int mm = 7, int dd = 4, int yyyy = 2005)
    {
      month = mm;
      day = dd;
      year = yyyy;
    }
```

Point of Information

Accessor Functions

An *accessor function* is any non-constructor member function that accesses a class's private data members. For example, the function `showDate()` in the `Date class` is an accessor function. Such functions are extremely important because they provide a means of displaying `private` data member's stored values.

When you construct a `class` make sure to provide a complete set of accessor functions. Each accessor function does not have to return a data member's exact value, but it should return a useful representation of the value. For example, assume that a date such as 12/25/2006 is stored as a long-integer member variable in the form 20062512. Although an accessor function could display this value, a more useful representation would typically be either 12/25/06, or December 25, 2006.

```
    Date(long yyyymmdd)    // here is the overloaded constructor
    {
      year = int(yyyymmdd/10000.0);      // extract the year
      month = int( (yyyymmdd - year * 10000.0)/100.00 );  // extract the month
      day = int(yyyymmdd - year * 10000.0 - month * 100.0); // extract the day
    }
};
```

The keyword inline is not required in this declaration because member functions defined inside the `class` declaration are inline by default.

Generally, only functions that can be coded on a single line are good candidates for inline functions. This reinforces the convention that inline functions should be small. Thus, the first constructor is more conventionally written as

```
Date(int mm = 7, int dd = 4, int yyyy = 2005)
  { month = mm; day = dd; year = yyyy; }
```

The second constructor, which extends over three lines, should not be written as an inline function.

Destructors

The counterpart to constructor functions are destructor functions. Destructors are functions having the same class name as constructors, but preceded with a tilde(~). Thus, for our `Date` class, the destructor name is `~Date()`. Like constructors, a default do-nothing destructor is provided by the C++ compiler in the absence of an explicit destructor. Unlike constructors, however, there can only be one destructor function per class. This is because destructors take no parameters—they also return no values.

Destructors are automatically called whenever an object goes out of existence and are meant to "clean up" any undesirable effects that might be left by the object. Generally such effects only occur when an object contains a pointer member.

Programming Note

Mutator Methods

A **mutator method**, more commonly called a mutator, is any non-constructor class method that changes an object's data values. Mutators are used to alter an object's data values after the object has been created and automatically initialized by a constructor method. A class can contain multiple mutators as long as each mutator has a unique name or parameter list. For example, in our `Date` class, a mutator could exist for changing a `Date` object's month, day, and year values.

Constructors, whose primary purpose is to initialize an object's member variables when an object is created, are not considered to be mutators.

Exercises 9.2

1. Determine whether the following statements are true or false.
   a. A constructor function must have the same name as its class.
   b. A class can only have one constructor function.
   c. A class can only have one default constructor function.
   d. A default constructor can only be supplied by the compiler.
   e. A default constructor can have no parameters or all parameters must have default values.
   f. A constructor must be declared for each `class`.
   g. A constructor must be declared with a return type.
   h. A constructor is automatically called each time an object is created.
   i. A class can only have one destructor function.
   j. A destructor must have the same name as its class, preceded by a tilde(~).
   k. A destructor can have default arguments.
   l. A destructor must be declared for each class.
   m. A destructor must be declared with a return type.
   n. A destructor is automatically called each time an object goes out of existence.
   o. Destructors are not useful when the class contains a pointer data member.
2. For Program 9.3, what date would be initialized for object `c` if the declaration `Date c(15);` were used in place of the declaration `Date c(20060515L);`?
3. Modify Program 9.3 so that the only data member of the class is a long integer named `yyyymmdd`. Do this by substituting the declaration

   ```
   long yyyymmdd;
   ```

   for the existing declarations

   ```
   int month;
   int day;
   int year;
   ```

Then, using the same constructor function prototypes currently declared in the class declaration section, rewrite them so that the `Date(long)` function becomes the default constructor and the `Date(int, int, int)` function converts a month, day, and year into the proper form for the class data member.

4. a. Construct a `Time` class containing integer data members `seconds`, `minutes`, and `hours`. Have the class contain two constructors: the first should be a default constructor having the prototype `time(int, int, int)`, which uses default values of 0 for each data member. The second constructor should accept a long integer representing a total number of seconds and disassemble the long integer into `hours`, `minutes`, and `seconds`. The final function member should display the class data members.

b. Include the class written for Exercise 4a within the context of a complete program.

5. a. Construct a class named `Student` consisting of an integer student identification number, an array of five double-precision grades, and an integer representing the total number of grades entered. The constructor for this class should initialize all `Student` data members to zero. Included in the class should be member functions to (1) enter a student ID number, (2) enter a single test grade and update the total number of grades entered, and (3) compute an average grade and display the student ID followed by the average grade.

b. Include the class constructed in Exercise 5a within the context of a complete program. Your program should declare two objects of type `Student` and accept and display data for the two objects to verify operation of the member functions.

6. a. In Exercise 4 you were asked to construct a `Time` class. For such a class include a `tick()` function that increments the time by one second. Test your function to ensure that it correctly increments into a new minute and a new hour.

b. Modify the `Time` class written for Exercise 6a to include a `detick()` function that decrements the time by one second. Test your function to ensure that it correctly decrements time into a prior hour and into a prior minute.

9.3 APPLICATIONS

Now that you have an understanding of how classes are constructed and the terminology used in describing them, let us apply this knowledge to two new applications. In the first application we develop a class for determining the floor area of a rectangular-shaped room. In the second application we simulate the operation of a gas pump.

Application 1: Constructing a Room Object

In this application, we will create a class from which room type objects can be constructed. The room's floor area must be calculated for any size room when its length and width are known. For modeling purposes, assume every room is rectangular.

Step 1 Analyze the Problem

In this application, we have one type of object, which is a rectangular-shaped room. Because of this, the floor of the room can be designated by its length and width. Once these attributes have been assigned for a room, its floor area can be calculated as the room's length multiplied by its width.

Step 2 Develop a Solution

For this application, the length and width of a room are the only attributes of interest. These can be represented by double-precision variables we will name length and width. The service required of the class is a constructor to set a room's length and width attributes, an accessor to display a room's attribute values, a mutator to change a room's attribute values, and a function to determine a room's floor area from its length and width values. We will arbitrarily name our class `RoomType`, name the accessor function `showRoomValues()`, name the mutator function `setNewRoomValues()`, and name the area calculation function `calculateRoomArea()`.

Step 3 Code the Class

From the design and the choice of attribute and class function names, a suitable class declaration is the following:

```
class RoomType
{
  // data declaration section
  private:
    double length;  // declare length as a double variable
    double width;   // declare width as a double variable

  public:
    RoomType(); // the constructor's declaration statement
    void showRoomValues();
    void setNewRoomValues();
    void calculateRoomArea();
};
```

We have declared two data members, `length` and `width`, and four class functions. The data members' length and width will store a room's length and width, respectively. The services provided by the class are a constructor to create a room object, an accessor to display a room's object's length and width values, a mutator to change a room's length and width values, and finally, a calculation function for calculating the a room's floor area. To accomplish these services, a suitable class implementation section is the following:

```
// methods implementation section
RoomType::RoomType(double l, double w)  // this is a constructor
{
  length = l;
```

```
  width = w;
  cout << "Created a new room object using the default constructor.\n\n";
}

void RoomType::showRoomValues()   // this is an accessor
{
  cout << "  length = " << length
       << "\n   width = " << width << endl;
}

void RoomType::setNewRoomValues(double l, double w)   // this is a mutator
{
  length = l;
  width = w;
}

void RoomType::calculateRoomArea()  // this performs a calculation
{
  cout << (length * width);
}
```

Each of these functions is straightforward. When a room object is declared, it will be initialized with a length and width of zero unless specific values are provided in the declaration. The accessor function displays the values stored in length and width, and the mutator permits reassigning values after a room object has been created. Finally, the calculation function displays the area of a room by multiplying its length by its width.

Step 4 Test and Correct the Program

Testing the `RoomType` class entails testing each class function. To do this, we include the `RoomType` class within the context of a working program, which is listed as Program 9.4.

Program 9.4

```
#include <iostream>
using namespace std;
class RoomType
{
  // data declaration section
  private:
    double length;  // declare length as a double variable
    double width;   // declare width as a double variable
```

(Continued)

(Continued)

```
  public:
    RoomType(double = 0.0, double = 0.0); // the constructor's declaration
statement
    void showRoomValues();
    void setNewRoomValues(double, double);
    void calculateRoomArea();
};

// methods implementation section
RoomType::RoomType(double l, double w)  // this is a constructor
{
  length = l;
  width = w;
  cout << "Created a new room object using the default constructor.\n\n";
}

void RoomType::showRoomValues()  // this is an accessor
{
  cout << "  length = " << length
       << "\n   width = " << width << endl;
}

void RoomType::setNewRoomValues(double l, double w)   // this is a mutator
{
  length = l;
  width = w;
}

void RoomType::calculateRoomArea()  // this performs a calculation
{
  cout << (length * width);
}
```

```
int main()
{
  RoomType roomOne(12.5, 18.2);  // declare a variable of type RoomType

  cout << "The values for this room are:\n";
  roomOne.showRoomValues();        // use a class method on this object
  cout << "\nThe floor area of this room is: ";
  roomOne.calculateRoomArea();     // use another class method on this object

  roomOne.setNewRoomValues(5.5, 9.3);   // call the mutator

  cout << "\n\nThe values for this room have been changed to:\n";
  roomOne.showRoomValues();
```

(Continued)

(Continued)

```
  cout << "\nThe floor area of this room is: ";
  roomOne.calculateRoomArea();

  cout << endl;
  return 0;
}
```

The lightly shaded portion of Program 9.4 contains the class construction that we have already described. To see how this class is used, concentrate on the darker section of the program that contains the `main()` function. This function creates a room object having a length of 12.5 and a width of 18.2. These room dimensions are displayed using the `showRoomValues()` function, and the area is calculated and displayed using the `calculateRoomArea()` function. The room's dimensions are reset, displayed, and the room's area recalculated. The output produced by Program 9.4 is the following:

```
Created a new room object using the default constructor.

The values for this room are:
  length = 12.5
   width = 18.2

The floor area of this room is: 227.5

The values for this room have been changed to:
  length = 5.5
   width = 9.3

The floor area of this room is: 51.15
```

The basic requirements of object-oriented programming are evident in even as simple a program as Program 9.4. Before the `main()` function can be written, a useful class must be constructed. This is typical of programs that use objects. For such programs the design process is front-loaded with the requirement that careful consideration of the class—its declaration and implementation—be given. Code contained in the implementation section effectively removes code that would otherwise be part of `main()`'s responsibility. Thus, any program that uses the object does not have to repeat the implementation details within its `main()` function. Rather, the `main()` function and any function called by `main()` is only concerned with sending messages to its objects to activate them appropriately. How the object responds to the messages and how the state of the object is retained is not `main()`'s concern—these details are hidden within the `class` construction.

Application 2: A Single Object Gas Pump Simulation

In this section, we present the first class required for a simulation that requires two separate classes. The first class, and the one developed in this section, models a gas pump. The second class, which completes the simulation and is developed in Section 9.6, models the arrival of multiple customers, each with various requests for differing amounts of gas to be pumped. The complete simulation is based on the following requirement:

We have been requested to write a program that simulates the operation of a gas pump. At any time during the simulation, we should be able to determine, from the pump, the price per gallon of gas and the amount remaining in the supply tank from which the gas is pumped. If the amount of gas in the supply tank is greater than or equal to the amount of gas requested, the request should be filled; otherwise, only the available amount in the supply tank should be used. Once the gas is pumped, the total price of the gallons pumped should be displayed and the amount of gas in gallons that was pumped should be subtracted from the supply tank amount.

For the simulation, assume that the pump is randomly idle between 1 to 15 minutes between customer arrivals and that a customer randomly requests between 3 and 20 gallons of gas. Though the default supply tank capacity is 500 gallons, assume the initial amount of gas in the tank for this simulation is only 300 gallons. Initially, the program should simulate a one-half hour time frame.

Additionally, for each arrival and request for gas, we want to know the idle time before the customer arrived, how many gallons of gas were pumped, and the total price of the transaction. The pump itself must keep track of the price per gallon of gas and the amount of gas remaining in the supply tank. Typically, the price per gallon is $1.80, but the price for the simulation should be $2.00.

For this part of the simulation, we will construct a gas pump class that can be used in the final simulation, which is completed in Section 10.5.

Step 1 Analyze the Problem

This problem involves two distinct object types. The first is a person who can arrive randomly between 1 and 15 minutes and can randomly request between 3 and 20 gallons of gas. The second object type is the gas pump. For this part of the problem, our goal will be to create a suitable gas pump class that can be used in the final simulation, which is completed in the next application.

The model for constructing a gas pump class that meets the requirements of the simulation is described in pseudocode as the following:

Put `Pump` *in Service*
  Initialize the amount of gas in the supply tank
  Initialize the price per gallon of gas

Display Values
  Display the amount of gas in the supply tank
  Display the price per gallon

`Pump` *an Amount of Gas*
If the amount in the supply tank is greater than or equal to the requested amount
Set the pumped amount of gas equal to the requested amount
Else
Set the pumped amount equal to the amount in the supply tank
EndIf
Subtract the pumped amount from the amount in the supply tank
Calculate the total price as the price per gallon times the pumped amount
Display the gallons of gas requested
Display the gallons of gas pumped
Display the amount remaining in the supply tank
Display the total price for the amount of gas pumped

Step 2 Develop a Solution

From the pseudocode description, the implementation of a `Pump` class is straightforward. The attributes of interest for the pump are the amount of gallons in the supply tank and the price per gallon. The required operations include supplying initial values for the pump's attributes, interrogating the pump for its attribute values, and satisfying a request for gas.

Because the two attributes, the amount in the tank and the price per gallon, can have fractional values, making them double-precision values is appropriate. Additionally, three services need to be provided. The first consists of initializing a pump's attributes, which consists of setting values for the amount in the supply tank and the price per gallon. The second consists of satisfying a request for gas, and the third service provides a reading of the pump's current attribute values.

Step 3 Code the Solution

A suitable class declaration is the following:

```
const double AMOUNT_IN_TANK = 500;  // initial gallons in the tank
const double DEFAULT_PRICE = 1.80;  // price per gallon

class Pump
{
  // data declaration section
  private:
    double amtInTank;
    double price;

  // method declarations
  public:
    Pump(double = DEFAULT_PRICE, double = AMOUNT_IN_TANK);   // constructor
    void getValues();
    void request(double);
};
```

Let's analyze this class declaration by individually inspecting its data and method members. First, notice we have declared two symbolic constants and two private instance variables. As private members, these data attributes can only be accessed through the class's member methods: `Pump()`, `getValues()`, and `request()`. It is these functions that provide the external services available to each `Pump` object.

The `Pump()` function, which has the same name as its class, is the constructor function that is automatically called when an object of type `Pump` is created. The `getValues()` function provides a readout of the current attribute values, and the `request()` function handles the logic of fulfilling a customer's request for gas. To accomplish these services, a suitable class implementation section is the following:

```
// methods implementation section

Pump::Pump(double todaysPrice, double amountInTank)
{
  amtInTank = amountInTank;
  price = todaysPrice;
}

void Pump::getValues()
{
  cout << "The gas tank has " << amtInTank << " gallons of gas." << endl;
  cout << "The price per gallon of gas is $" << setiosflags(ios::showpoint)
       << setprecision(2) << setiosflags(ios::fixed) << price << endl;
}

void Pump::request(double pumpAmt)
{
  double pumped;

  if (amtInTank >= pumpAmt)
     pumped = pumpAmt;
  else
     pumped = amtInTank;

  amtInTank -= pumped;
  cout << pumpAmt << " gallons were requested " << endl;
  cout << pumped << " gallons were pumped" << endl;
  cout << amtInTank << " gallons remain in the tank" << endl;
  cout << "The total price is $" << setiosflags(ios::showpoint)
       << setprecision(2) << (pumped * price) << endl;

  return;
}
```

The constructor function is straightforward. When a `Pump` object is declared, it will be initialized to a given amount of gas in the supply tank and a given price per gallon. If no values are given, the defaults of $1.80 per gallon and 500 gallons are used; if only the price per gallon is provided, the constructor uses the default value of 500 for the missing second argument.

The `getvalues()` function defined in the implementation section provides a readout of the current attribute values. It is the `request()` function that is the most complicated because it provides the primary pump service. The code following the requirements of the pump provides all of the gas required unless the amount remaining in the supply tank is less than the requested amount. Finally, it subtracts the amount pumped from the amount in the tank and calculates the total dollar value of the transaction.

Step 4 Test and Correct the Class

Testing the `Pump` class requires testing each class function. To do this, consider Program 9.5.

Program 9.5

```
#include <c:\\cpcode\\Pump.cpp>

int main()
{
  Pump a(2.00, 300), b;   // declare 2 objects of type Pump

  a.getValues();
  cout << endl;
  a.request(20.0);
  cout << endl;
  a.request(290.0);
  b.getValues();

  return 0;
}
```

In Program 9.5, we have included the `Pump` class using the following statement:

```
#include <c:\\cpcode\\Pump.cpp>
```

This assumes the `Pump` class resides in the folder named `cpcode` on the C drive, and is saved as the file named `Pump.cpp`. An equivalent statement is the following:

```
#include "c:\\cpcode\\Pump.cpp"
```

In both include statements, the double slashes are required because a single slash would be interpreted as an escape character.

Point of Information

Encapsulation

The term **encapsulation** refers to the packaging of a number of items into a single unit. For example, a function is used to encapsulate the details of an algorithm. Similarly, a class encapsulates both variables and functions together in a single package.

Although the term encapsulation is sometimes used to refer to the process of information hiding, this usage is technically not accurate. The correct relationship between terms is that information hiding refers to the encapsulation and hiding of all implementation details.

Within the `main()` method, eight statements are included. The first statement creates an object of type `Pump`. The supply tank for the first `Pump` object contains 300 gallons and the price per gallon is set to $2.00; the second `Pump` object uses the default values AMOUNT_IN_PUMP and DEFAULT_PRICE, which are 500 and 1.80, respectively.

A call is made to `getValues()` to display the first pump's attribute values. The next statement is a request for gas of 20 gallons from the first `Pump` object. This is followed by a request for 290 gallons, which exceeds the remaining gas in the supply tank. Finally, the attribute values for the second pump are displayed. The output produced by Program 9.5 is the following:

```
The gas tank has 300 gallons of gas.
The price per gallon of gas is $2.00

20.00 gallons were requested
20.00 gallons were pumped
280.00 gallons remain in the tank
The total price is $40.00

290.00 gallons were requested
280.00 gallons were pumped
0.00 gallons remain in the tank
The total price is $560.00

The gas tank has 500 gallons of gas.
The price per gallon of gas is $1.80
```

As indicated by this output, all of the `Pump` class methods provide the correct functionality. Specifically, both `Pump` objects are initialized correctly by the constructor, and the `request()` method supplies the requested amount of gas at the correct price until the supply tank has been emptied.

Exercises 9.3

1. Enter Program 9.4 in your computer and execute it.

2. Modify the `main()` function in Program 9.4 to create a second room having a length of 9 and a width of 12. Have the program calculate this new room's area.

3. a. Modify the `main()` function in Program 9.4 to create four rooms: hall, kitchen, dining room, and living room. The dimensions for these rooms are as follows:

```
Hall: length = 12.40, width = 3.5
Kitchen: length = 14, width = 14
Living Room: length = 12.4, width = 20
Dining Room: length = 14, width = 9.5.
```

Your program should display the area of each room and the total area of all four rooms combined.

b. The total area of all rooms can be calculated and saved using a class variable. To do this, what type of variable do you think this class variable would have to be?

4. a. Modify the `main()` function in Program 9.5 to use a `while` loop that calls the `Pump`'s request function with a random number between 3 and 20. The `while` loop should terminate after 5 requests have been made.

b. Modify the `main()` function written for Exercise 4a to provide a 30-minute simulation of the gas pump's operation. To do this you will have to modify the `while` loop to select a random number between 1 and 15 that represents the idle time between customer requests. Have the simulation stop once the idle time exceeds 30 minutes.

5. a. Construct a class definition of a `Person` object type. The class is to have no attributes, a single constructor function and two additional member functions named `arrive()` and `gallons()`.The constructor function should simply call `srand()` with the argument `time(NULL)` to initialize the `rand()` function. The `arrive()` function should provide a random number between 1 and 15 as a return value, while the `gallons()` function should provide a random number between 3 and 20.

b. Test the `Person` class functions written for Exercise 5a in a complete working program.

c. Use the `Person` class function to simulate a random arrival of a `Person` and a random request for gallons of gas within the program written for Exercise 4b.

6. Modify Program 9.5 so that the `Pump` class definition resides in a file named `Pump.h`. Then have Program 9.5 use an `#include` statement to include the `class` definition within the program. Make sure to use a full path name in the `#include` statement. For example, if `Pump.h` resides in the directory named `foo` on the C drive, the `include` statement should be

```
#include <c:\\foo\\Pump.h>.
```

7. Construct a class named `Light` that simulates a traffic light. The color attribute of the class should change from `Green` to `Yellow` to `Red` and then back to `Green` by the `class`' `change()` function. When a new `Light` object is created its initial color should be `Red`.

8. a. Construct a class definition that can be used to represent an employee of a company. Each employee is defined by an integer ID number, a floating-point pay rate, and the maximum number of hours the employee should work each week. The services provided by the class should be the ability to enter data for a new employee, the ability to change data for a new employee, and the ability to display the existing data for a new employee.
   b. Include the class definition created for Exercise 8a in a working C++ program that asks the user to enter data for 3 employees and displays the entered data.
   c. Modify the program written for Exercise 8b to include a menu that offers the user the following choices:

      1. Add an employee
      2. Modify employee data
      3. Delete an employee
      4. Exit this menu

      In response to a choice the program should initiate appropriate action to implement the choice.

9. a. Construct a class definition that can be used to represent types of food. A type of food is classified as basic or prepared. Basic foods are further classified as either `Dairy`, `Meat`, `Fruit`, `Vegetable`, or `Grain`. The services provided by the class should be the ability to enter data for a new food, the ability to change data for a new food, and the ability to display the existing data for a new food.
   b. Include the class definition created for Exercise 9a in a working C++ program that asks the user to enter data for four food items and displays the entered data.
   c. Modify the program written for Exercise 9b to include a menu that offers the user the following choices:

      1. Add a food item
      2. Modify a food item
      3. Delete a food item
      4. Exit this menu

      In response to a choice the program should initiate appropriate action to implement the choice.

9.4 Common Programming Errors

The more common programming errors initially associated with the construction of classes are

1. Failing to terminate the class declaration section with a semicolon.
2. Including a return type with the constructor's prototype or failing to include a return type with the other functions' prototypes.

3. Using the same name for a data member as for a member function.
4. Defining more than one default constructor for a class.
5. Forgetting to include the class name and scope operator, `::`, in the header line of all member functions defined in the class implementation section.

All of these errors will result in a compiler error message.

9.5 CHAPTER SUMMARY

1. A **class** is a programmer-defined data type. **Objects** of a class may be defined and have the same relationship to their class as variables do to C++'s built-in data types.
2. A class definition consists of a declaration and implementation section. The most common form of a class definition is

```
// class declaration section
class name
{
  private:
   a list of variable declarations;
  public:
   a list of function prototypes;
};

// class implementation section
class function definitions
```

   The variables and functions declared in the class declaration section are collectively referred to as **class members**. The variables are individually referred to as class data members and the functions as class member functions. The terms `private` and `public` are access specifiers. Once an access specifier is listed it remains in force until another access specifier is given. The `private` keyword specifies that the class members following it are `private` to the class and can only be accessed by member functions. The `public` keyword specifies that the class members following may be accessed from outside the class. Generally, all data members should be specified as `private` and all member functions as `public`.
3. Class functions listed in the declaration section may either be written inline or their definitions included in the class implementation section. Except for constructor and destructor functions, all class functions defined in the class implementation section have the header line form

   returnType className::functionName(parameter list);

Except for the addition of the class name and scope operator, `::`, which are required to identify the function name with the class, this header line is identical to the header line used for any user-written function.

4. A **constructor function** is a special function that is automatically called each time an object is declared. It must have the same name as its class and cannot have any return type. Its purpose is to initialize each declared object.

5. If no constructor is declared for a class the compiler will supply a default constructor. This is a do-nothing function having the definition `className::className(void){}`.

6. The term **default constructor** refers to any constructor that does not require any arguments when it is called. This can be because no parameters are declared (as is the case for the compiler-supplied default constructor) or because all parameters have been given default values.

7. Each class may only have one default constructor. If any user-defined constructor is defined the compiler will not create its default constructor.

8. Objects are created using either a C++ or C style of declaration. The C++ style of declaration has the form:

   className list-of-objectNames(list of initializers);

   where the list of initializers is optional. An example of this style of declaration, including initializers, for a class named `Date` is

   ```
   Date a, b, c(12,25,2006);
   ```

   Here the objects `a` and `b` are declared to be of type `Date` and are initialized using the default constructor while the object `c` is initialized with the values 12, 25, and 2006.

   The equivalent C style of declaration, including the optional list of initializers, has the form

   className objectName = className(list of initializers);

   An example of this style of declaration for a class named `Date` is

   ```
   Date c = Date(12,25,2006)
   ```

   Here the object `c` is created and initialized with the values 12, 25, and 2006.

9. Constructors may be overloaded in the same manner as any other user-written C++ function.

10. If a constructor is defined for a class, a user-defined default constructor also should be written, as the compiler will not supply it.

11. A destructor function is called each time an object goes out of scope. Destructors must have the same name as their class, but preceded with a tilde (~). There can only be one destructor per class.

12. A **destructor function** takes no arguments and returns no value. If a user-defined destructor is not included in a class the compiler will provide a do-nothing destructor.

Chapter 10

Class Functions and Conversions

Topics

The creation of a class requires that we provide the capability to declare, initialize, assign, manipulate, and display data members. In the previous chapter the declaration, initialization, and display of objects were presented. In this chapter we continue our construction of classes by providing the ability to create operator and conversion capabilities similar to those inherent in C++'s built-in types. With these additions our user-defined types will have all of the functionality of built-in types.

10.1 ASSIGNMENT

In Chapter 3 we saw how C++'s assignment operator, =, performs assignment between variables. In this section we see how assignment works when it is applied to objects and how to define our own assignment operator to override the default provided for user-defined classes.

For a specific assignment example, consider the `main()` function of Program 10.1.

Notice that the implementation section of the `Date` class in Program 10.1 contains no assignment function. Nevertheless, we would expect the assignment statement `a = b;` in `main()` to assign `b`'s data member values to their counterparts in `a`. This is, in fact, the case and is verified by the output produced when Program 10.1 is executed:

```
The date stored in a is originally 04/01/07
After assignment the date stored in a is 12/18/08
```

The type of assignment illustrated in Program 10.1 is referred to as **memberwise assignment**. In the absence of any specific instructions to the contrary, the C++ compiler builds this type of default assignment operator for each class. If the class *does not* contain any pointer data members this default assignment operator is adequate and can be used without further consideration. Before considering the problems that can occur with pointer data members, let's see how to construct our own explicit assignment operators.

Assignment operators, like all class members, are declared in the class declaration section and defined in the class implementation section. For the declaration of operators, however, the keyword `operator` must be included in the declaration. Using this keyword, a simple **assignment operator** declaration has the form:

```
void operator=(ClassName&);
```

Here the keyword `void` indicates that the assignment returns no value, the `operator=` indicates that we are overloading the assignment operator with our own version, and the class name and ampersand within the parentheses indicates that the argument to the `operator` is a class reference. For example, to declare a simple assignment operator for our `Date` class, the declaration:

```
void operator=(Date&);
```

can be used.

The actual implementation of the assignment operator is defined in the implementation section. For our declaration, a suitable implementation is

```
void Date::operator=(Date& newdate)
{
  day = newdate.day;      // assign the day
  month = newdate.month;  // assign the month
  year = newdate.year;    // assign the year
}
```

Program 10.1

```
#include <iostream>
#include <iomanip>
using namespace std;

// class declaration
class Date
{
  private:
    int month;
    int day;
    int year;
  public:
    Date(int = 7, int = 4, int = 2005);      // constructor
    void showDate();     // member function to display a Date
};

// implementation section
Date::Date(int mm, int dd, int yyyy)
{
  month = mm;
  day = dd;
  year = yyyy;
}

void Date::showDate()
{
  cout << setfill('0')
       << setw(2) << month << '/'
       << setw(2) << day << '/'
       << setw(2) << year % 100;
  return;
}

int main()
{
  Date a(4,1,2007), b(12,18,2008); // declare two objects

  cout << "\nThe date stored in a is originally ";
  a.showDate();  // display the original date
  a = b;         // assign b's value to a
  cout << "\nAfter assignment the date stored in a is ";
  a.showDate();  // display a's values
  cout << endl;
  return 0;
}
```

The use of the reference argument in the definition of this operation is not accidental. In fact, one of the primary reasons for adding reference variables to C++ was to facilitate the construction of overloaded operators and make the notation more natural.[1] In this definition `newdate` is defined as a reference to a `Date` class. Within the body of the definition the `day` member of the object referenced by `newdate` is assigned to the `day` member of the current object, which is then repeated for the `month` and `year` members. Assignments such as `a.operator=(b);` can then be used to call the overloaded assignment operator and assign `b`'s member values to `a`. For convenience, the expression `a.operator=(b)` can be replaced with `a = b;`. Program 10.2 contains our new assignment `operator` within the context of a complete program.

Except for the addition of the overloaded assignment operator declaration and definition, Program 10.2 is identical to Program 10.1 and produces the same output. Its usefulness to us is that it illustrates how we can explicitly construct our own assignment definitions. Before moving on, however, two simple modifications to our assignment operator need to be made.

Program 10.2

```
#include <iostream>
#include <iomanip>
using namespace std;

// class declaration
class Date
{
  private:
    int month;
    int day;
    int year;
  public:
    Date(int = 7, int = 4, int = 2005);      // constructor
    void operator=(Date&);    // define assignment of a date
    void showDate();      // member function to display a date
};

// implementation section
Date::Date(int mm, int dd, int yyyy)
{
  month = mm;
  day = dd;
  year = yyyy;
}
```

(Continued)

[1] Passing a reference is preferable to passing an object by value because it reduces the overhead required in making a copy of each object's data members.

(Continued)

```
void Date::operator=(Date& newdate)
{
  day = newdate.day;          // assign the day
  month = newdate.month;      // assign the month
  year = newdate.year;        // assign the year
  return;
}

void Date::showDate()
{
  cout << setfill('0')
       << setw(2) << month << '/'
       << setw(2) << day << '/'
       << setw(2) << year % 100;
  return;
}
```

```
int main()
{
  Date a(4,1,2007), b(12,18,2008); // declare two objects

  cout << "\nThe date stored in a is originally ";
  a.showDate();  // display the original date
  a = b;         // assign b's value to a
  cout << "\nAfter assignment the date stored in a is ";
  a.showDate();  // display a's values
  cout << endl;

  return 0;
}
```

First, to preclude any inadvertent alteration to the object used on the right-hand side of the assignment, a constant reference argument should be used. For our `Date` class, this takes the form:

```
void Date::operator=(const Date& newdate);
```

The final modification concerns the operation's return value. As constructed, our simple assignment operator returns no value, which precludes us from using it in multiple assignments such as `a = b = c`. The reason for this is that overloaded operators retain the same precedence and associativity as their equivalent built-in versions. Thus, an expression such as `a = b = c` is evaluated in the order `a = (b = c)`. As we have defined assignment, unfortunately, the expression `b = c` returns no value, making subsequent assignment to `a` an error. To provide for multiple assignments, a more complete assignment operation would return a reference to its class type. As the implementation of such an assignment requires a special class pointer, the presentation of this more complete assignment operator is deferred until the material presented in Chapter 11 is introduced. Until then, our simple assignment operator will be more than adequate for our needs.

Copy Constructors

Although assignment looks similar to initialization, it is worthwhile noting that they are two entirely different operations. In C++ an initialization occurs every time a new object is created. In an assignment no new object is created—the value of an existing object is simply changed. Figure 10.1 illustrates this difference.

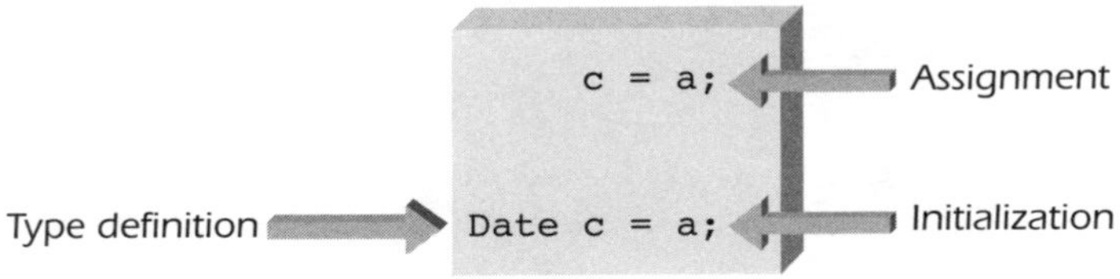

Figure 10.1 *Initialization and assignment.*

One type of initialization that closely resembles assignment occurs in C++ when one object is initialized using another object of the same class. For example, in the declaration

```
Date b = a;
```

or its entirely equivalent form

```
Date b(a);
```

the `b` object is initialized to a previously declared `a` object. The constructor that performs this type of initialization is called a **copy constructor**, and if you do not declare one the compiler will construct one for you. The compiler's **default copy constructor** performs in a similar manner to the default assignment `operator` by doing a memberwise copy between objects. Thus, for the declaration `Date b = a;` the default copy constructor sets `b`'s month, day, and year values to their respective counterparts in `a`. As with default assignment operators, default copy constructors work just fine unless the class contains pointer data members. Before considering the complications that can occur with pointer data members and how to handle them, it will be helpful to see how to construct our own copy constructors.

Copy constructors, like all class functions, are declared in the class declaration section and defined in the class implementation section. The declaration of a copy constructor has the general form:

```
ClassName(const ClassName&);
```

As with all constructors, the function name must be the class name. As further illustrated by the declaration, the argument is a reference to the class, which is a characteristic of all copy constructors.[2] To ensure that the argument is not inadvertently altered, it is always specified as a constant. Applying this general form to our `Date` class, a copy constructor can be explicitly declared as

```
Date(const Date&);
```

[2] A copy constructor is frequently defined as a constructor whose first argument is a reference to its class type, with any additional arguments being defaults.

The actual implementation of this constructor, if it were to perform the same memberwise initialization as the default copy constructor, would take the form:

```
Date:: Date(const Date& olddate)
{
  month = olddate.month;
  day = olddate.day;
  year = olddate.year;
}
```

As with the assignment operator, the use of a reference argument for the copy constructor is no accident: The reference argument again facilitates a simple notation within the body of the function. Program 10.3 contains this copy constructor within the context of a complete program.

Program 10.3

```
#include <iostream>
#include <iomanip>
using namespace std;

// class declaration

class Date
{
  private:
    int month;
    int day;
    int year;
  public:
    Date(int = 7, int = 4, int = 2005);     // constructor
    Date(const Date&);    // copy constructor
    void showDate();      // member function to display a date
};

// implementation section

Date::Date(int mm, int dd, int yyyy)
{
  month = mm;
  day = dd;
  year = yyyy;
}
```

(Continued)

(Continued)

```
Date::Date(const Date& olddate)
{
  month = olddate.month;
  day = olddate.day;
  year = olddate.year;
}

void Date::showDate()
{
  cout << setfill('0')
       << setw(2) << month << '/'
       << setw(2) << day << '/'
       << setw(2) << year % 100;

  return;
}
```

```
int main()
{
  Date a(4,1,2007), b(12,18,2008); // use the constructor
  Date c(a);    // use the copy constructor
  Date d = b;   // use the copy constructor

  cout << "\nThe date stored in a is ";
  a.showDate();
  cout << "\nThe date stored in b is ";
  b.showDate();
  cout << "\nThe date stored in c is ";
  c.showDate();
  cout << "\nThe date stored in d is ";
  d.showDate();
  cout << endl;

  return 0;
}
```

The output produced by Program 10.3 is:

```
The date stored in a is 04/01/07
The date stored in b is 12/18/08
The date stored in c is 04/01/07
The date stored in d is 12/18/08
```

As illustrated by this output, c's and d's data members have been initialized by the copy constructor to a's and b's values, respectively. Although the copy constructor defined in Program 10.3 adds nothing to the functionality provided by the compiler's default copy constructor, it does provide us with the fundamentals of defining our own copy constructors.

Base/Member Initialization[3]

Except for the reference names `olddate` and `newdate`, a comparison of Program 10.3's copy constructor to Program 10.2's assignment operator shows them to be essentially the same function. The difference in these functions is that the copy constructor first creates an object's data members before the body of the constructor uses assignment to specify member values. Thus, the copy constructor does not perform a true initialization, but rather a creation followed by assignment.

A true initialization would have no reliance on assignment whatsoever and is possible in C++ using a **base/member initialization list**. Such a list can only be applied to constructor functions and may be written in two ways.

The first way to construct a base/member initialization list is within a class's declaration section using the form

```
ClassName(argument list) : list of data members(initializing values) {}
```

For example, using this form, a default constructor that performs true initialization is

```
// class declaration section

public:
  Date(int mo = 4, int da = 1, int yr = 2006) : month(mo), day(da), year(yr) {}
```

The second way is to declare a function prototype with defaults in the class's declaration section followed by the initialization list in the implementation section. For our `Date` constructor this takes the form:

```
// class declaration section

public:
  Date(int = 4, int = 1, int = 2006);   // prototype with defaults

// class implementation section

Date::Date(int mo, int da, int yr) : month(mo), day(da), year(yr) {}
```

Notice that in both forms the body of the constructor function is empty. This is not a requirement, and the body can include any subsequent operations that you would like the constructor to perform. The interesting feature of this type of constructor is that it clearly differentiates between the initialization tasks performed in the member initialization list contained between the colon and the braces, and any subsequent assignments that might be contained within the function's body. Although we will not be using this type of initialization subsequently, it is required whenever there is a `const class` instance variable.

[3]The material in this section is presented for completeness only and may be omitted without loss of subject continuity.

Exercises 10.1

1. Describe the difference between assignment and initialization.

2. a. Construct a class named `Time` that contains three integer data members named `hours`, `mins`, and `secs` that will be used to store the hours, minutes, and seconds. The function members should include a constructor that provides default values of 0 for each data member, a display function that prints an object's data values, and an assignment operator that performs a memberwise assignment between two time objects.
   b. Include the `Time` class developed in Exercise 2a in a working C++ program that creates and displays two `Time` objects, the second of which is assigned the values of the first object.

3. a. Construct a class named `Complex` that contains two double-precision data members named `real` and `imag`, which will be used to store the real and imaginary parts of a complex number. The function members should include a constructor that provides default values of 0 for each member function, a display function that prints an object's data values, and an assignment operator that performs a memberwise assignment between two complex number objects.
   b. Include the class written for Exercise 3a in a working C++ program that creates and displays the values of two `Complex` objects, the second of which is assigned the values of the first object.

4. a. Construct a class named `Cartesian` that contains two double-precision data members named `x` and `y`, which will be used to store the `x` and `y` values of a point in rectangular coordinates. The function members should include a constructor that initializes the `x` and `y` values of an object to 0 and functions to input and display an object's `x` an `y` values. Additionally, there should be an assignment function that performs a memberwise assignment between two `Cartesian` objects.
   b. Include the class written for Exercise 4a in a working C++ program that creates and displays the values of two `Cartesian` objects, the second of which is assigned the values of the first object.

5. a. Construct a class named `Car` that contains the following three data members: a double-precision variable named `engineSize`, a character variable named `bodyStyle`, and an integer variable named `colorCode`. The class functions should include a constructor that provides default values of 0 for each numeric data member and an `X` for each character variable; a display function that prints the engine size, body style, and color code; and an assignment operator that performs a memberwise assignment between two `Car` objects for each instance variable.
   b. Include the class written for Exercise 5a in a working C++ program that creates and displays two `Car` objects, the second of which is assigned the values of the first object.

Point of Information

Values and Identities

Apart from any behavior that an object is supplied with, a characteristic feature of objects that they share with variables is that they always have a unique identity. It is an object's identity that permits distinguishing one object from another. This is not true of a value, such as the number 5, because all occurrences of 5 are indistinguishable from one another. As such, values are not considered as objects in object-oriented programming languages such as C++.

Another distinguishing feature between an object and a value is that a value can never be a container whose value can change, while an object clearly can. A value is simply an entity that stands for itself.

Now consider a string such as "Chicago." As a string this is a value. However, since Chicago could also be a specific and identifiable object of type `City`, the context in which the name is used is important. Notice that if the string "Chicago" were assigned to an object's name attribute, it reverts to being a value.

10.2 Additional Class Features

This section presents additional features pertaining to classes. These include the scope of a class, creating static class members, and granting access privileges to nonmember functions. Each of these topics may be read independently of the others.

Class Scope

We have already encountered local and global scope in Section 6.5. As we saw, the scope of a variable defines the portion of a program where the variable can be accessed.

For local variables, this scope is defined by any block contained within a brace pair, `{}`. This includes both the complete function body and any internal sub-blocks. Additionally, all parameters of a function are considered as local function variables.

Global variables are accessible from their point of declaration throughout the remaining portion of the file containing them, with three exceptions:

1. If a local variable has the same name as a global variable, the global variable can only be accessed within the scope of the local variable by using the scope resolution operator, `::`.
2. The scope of a global variable can be extended into another file by using the keyword `extern`.
3. The same global name can be reused in another file to define a separate and distinct variable by using the keyword `static`. `static` global variables are unknown outside of their immediate file.

In addition to local and global scopes, each class also defines an associated **class scope.** That is, the names of the data and function members are local to the scope of their class. Thus, if a global variable name is reused within a class, the global variable is hidden by the class data member in the same manner as a local function variable hides a global variable of the same name. Similarly, member function names are local to the class they are declared in and can only be used by objects declared for the class. Additionally, local function variables also hide the names of class data members having the same name. Figure 10.2 illustrates the scope of the variables and functions for the following declarations.

```
double rate;     // global
// class declaration
class Test
{
  private:
    double amount, price, total;   // class scope
  public:
    double extend(double, double);   // class scope
};
```

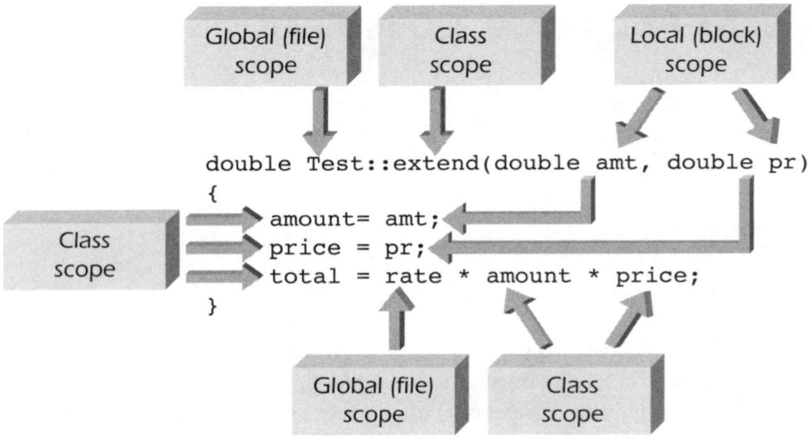

Figure 10.2 Example of scopes.

Static Class Members

As each class object is created it gets its own block of memory for its data members. In some cases, however, it is convenient for every instantiation of a class to share the *same* memory location for a specific variable. For example, consider a class consisting of employee payment information, where each employee is subject to the same social security tax rate. Clearly we could make the sales tax a global variable, but this is not very safe. Such data could be modified anywhere in the program, could conflict with an identical variable name within a function, and certainly violates C++'s principle of data hiding.

This type of situation is handled in C++ by declaring a class variable to be static. `Static` class data members share the same storage space for all objects of the class; as such, they act as global variables for the class and provide a means of communication between objects.

C++ requires that such `static` variables be declared within the class's declaration section. To create such variables, the declared static variable must be re-declared, with or without an initial value (this defines the variable in contrast to a formal declaration statement that does not physically allocate storage for the variable) outside of the class's declaration sections.

For example, assume the class declaration:

```
//class declaration

class Employee
{
  private:
    static double taxRate;
    int idNum;
  public:
    Employee(int);    //constructor
    void display();
};
```

The definition and initialization of the `static` variable `taxRate` is accomplished using a statement such as the following:

```
double Employee::taxRate = 0.07;  // this defines taxRate
```

Here the scope resolution operator, `::`, is used to identify `taxRate` as a member of the class `Employee` and the keyword `static` is not included. Program 10.4 uses this definition within the context of a complete program.

The output produced by Program 10.4 is

```
Employee number 11122 has a tax rate of 0.07
Employee number 11133 has a tax rate of 0.07
```

Although it might appear that the initialization of `taxRate` is global, it is not. Once the definition is made, any other definition will result in an error. Thus, the actual definition of a `static` member remains the responsibility of the class creator. The storage sharing produced by the `static` data member and the objects created in Program 10.4 is illustrated in Figure 10.3.

Program 10.4

```
#include <iostream>
using namespace std;

// class declaration

class Employee
{
  private:
    static double taxRate;
    int idNum;
  public:
    Employee(int = 0);     // constructor
    void display();   // access function
};

// static member definition
double Employee::taxRate = 0.07;   // this defines taxRate

// implementation section

Employee::Employee(int num)
{
  idNum = num;
}

void Employee::display()
{
  cout << "Employee number " << idNum
       << " has a tax rate of " << taxRate << endl;

  return;
}

int main()
{
  Employee emp1(11122), emp2(11133);

  emp1.display();
  emp2.display();

  return 0;
}
```

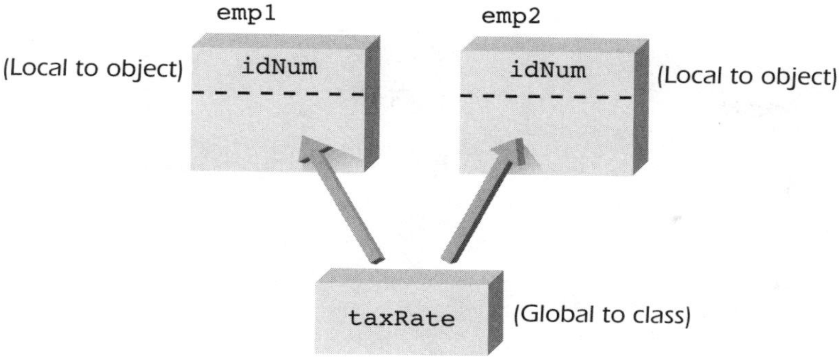

Figure 10.3 *Sharing the* `static` *data member* `taxRate`.

In addition to `static` data members, `static` member functions can also be created. Such functions apply to a class as a whole rather than for individual class objects and can only access static data members and other static member functions of the class. An example of such a function is provided by Program 10.5.

Program 10.5

```
#include <iostream>
using namespace std;

// class declaration

class Employee
{
  private:
    static double taxRate;
    int idNum;
  public:
    Employee(int = 0);     // constructor
    void display();       // access function
    static void disp();  // static function
};
// static member definition
double Employee::taxRate = 0.07;
```

(Continued)

(Continued)

```
// implementation section

Employee::Employee(int num)
{
  idNum = num;
}

void Employee::display()
{
  cout << "Employee number " << idNum
       << " has a tax rate of " << taxRate << endl;

  return;
}

void Employee::disp()
{
  cout << "The static tax rate is " << taxRate << endl;

  return;
}
```

```
int main()
{
  Employee::disp();   // call the static functions
  Employee emp1(11122), emp2(11133);

  emp1.display();
  emp2.display();

  return 0;
}
```

The output produced by Program 10.5 is

```
The static tax rate is 0.07
Employee number 11122 has a tax rate of 0.07
Employee number 11133 has a tax rate of 0.07
```

Once the definition (as opposed to the declaration) of a static class variable is made, any other definition will result in an error. Thus, the actual definition of a `static` member remains the responsibility of the class creator. A compiler error will occur if this definition is omitted.

Friend Functions

The only method we currently have for accessing and manipulating a class's private variables is through the class's member functions. Conceptually, this arrangement can be viewed as illustrated in Figure 10.4a. There are times, however, when it is useful to provide such access to selected nonmember functions.

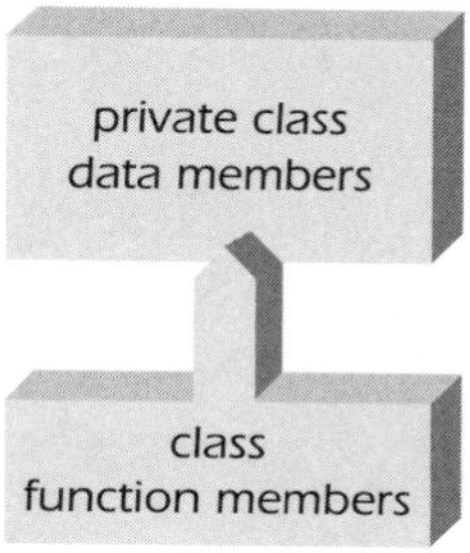

Figure 10.4a Direct access is provided to member functions.

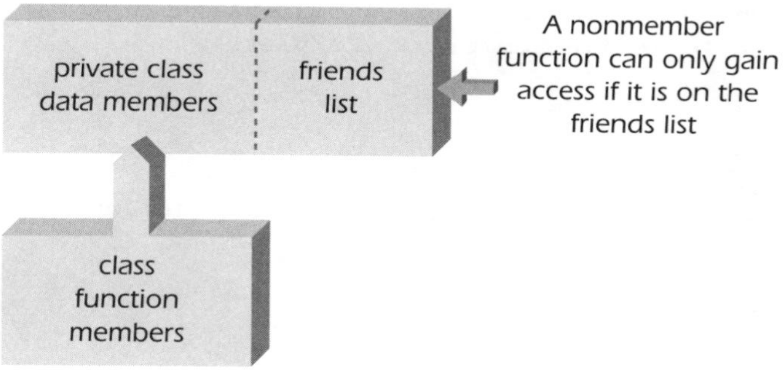

Figure 10.4b Access provided to nonmember functions.

The procedure for providing this external access is rather simple—the class maintains its own approved list of nonmember functions that are granted the same privileges as a class's functions. The nonmember functions on the list are called **friend functions**, and the list is referred to as a **friends list.**

Figure 10.4b conceptually illustrates the use of such a list for nonmember access. Any function attempting access to an object's private variables is first checked against the friends list: If the function is on the list, access is approved; otherwise access is denied.

From a coding standpoint the friends list is simply a series of function prototype declarations that are preceded with the keyword `friend` and included in the class's declaration section. For example, if the functions named `addreal()` and `addimag()` are to be allowed access to the private members of a class named `Complex`, the following prototypes would be included within `Complex`'s declaration section.

```
friend double addreal(Complex&, Complex&);
friend double addimag(Complex&, Complex&);
```

Here the friends list consists of two declarations. The prototypes indicate that each function returns a floating-point number and expects two references to objects of type `Complex` as arguments. Program 10.6 includes these two friend declarations in a complete program.

Program 10.6

```
#include <iostream>
#include <cmath>
using namespace std;

// class declaration

class Complex
{
  // friends list
  friend double addreal(Complex&, Complex&);
  friend double addimag(Complex&, Complex&);
  private:
    double real;
    double imag;
  public:
    Complex(double = 0, double = 0);  // constructor
    void display();

};

// implementation section

Complex::Complex(double rl, double im)
{
  real = rl;
  imag = im;
}

void Complex::display()
{
  char sign = '+';

  if(imag < 0) sign = '-';
  cout << real << sign << abs(imag) << 'i';

  return;
}
```

(Continued)

(Continued)

```
// friend implementations

double addreal(Complex &a, Complex &b)
{
  return(a.real + b.real);
}

double addimag(Complex &a, Complex &b)
{
  return(a.imag + b.imag);
}
```

```
int main()
{
  Complex a(3.2, 5.6), b(1.1, -8.4);
  double re, im;

  cout << "\nThe first complex number is ";
  a.display();
  cout << "\nThe second complex number is ";
  b.display();

  re = addreal(a,b);
  im = addimag(a,b);
  Complex c(re,im);   // create a new Complex object
  cout << "\n\nThe sum of these two complex numbers is ";
  c.display();

  return 0;
}
```

The output produced by Program 10.6 is

```
The first complex number is 3.2+5.6i
The second complex number is 1.1-8.4i

The sum of these two complex numbers is 4.3-2.8i
```

In reviewing Program 10.6 notice four items. The first is that since friends are not class members, they are unaffected by the access section in which they are declared—*they may be declared anywhere within the declaration section.* The convention we have followed is to include all `friend` declarations immediately following the class header. The second item to notice is that the keyword `friend` (like the keyword `static`) is used only within the class declaration and not in the actual function definition. Third, since a `friend` function is intended to have access to an object's private variables, at least one of the friend's arguments should be a reference to an object of the class that has made it a friend. Finally, as illustrated by Program 10.6, it is the class that grants `friend` status to a function and not the other way around. The function can never confer `friend` status on itself, because to do so would violate the concepts of data hiding and access provided by a class.

Exercises 10.2

1. a. Rewrite Program 10.5 to include an integer `static` variable named `numemps`. This variable should act as a counter that is initialized to zero and is incremented by the class constructor each time a new object is declared. Rewrite the `static` function `disp()` to display the value of this counter.
   b. Test the program written for Exercise 1a. Have the `main()` function call `disp()` after each `Employee` object is created.

2. a. Construct a class named `Circle` that contains two integer variables named `xCenter` and `yCenter`, and a double-precision variable named `radius`. Additionally, the class should contain `static` data member named `scaleFactor`. Here the `xCenter` and `yCenter` values represent the center point of a circle, `radius` represents the circle's actual radius, and `scaleFactor` represents a scale factor that will be used to scale the circle to fit on a variety of display devices.
   b. Include the class written for Exercise 2a in a working C++ program.

3. a. Could the following three statements in Program 10.6

```
re = addreal(a,b);
im = addimag(a,b);
Complex c(re,im);   // create a new complex object
```

   be replaced by the single statement

```
Complex c(addreal(a,b), addimag(a,b));
```

   b. Verify your answer to Exercise 3a by running Program 10.6 with the suggested replacement statement.

4. a. Rewrite the program written for Exercise 2a, but include a `friend` function that multiples an object's `radius` by a static `scaleFactor` and then displays the actual radius value and the scaled value.
   b. Test the program written for Exercise 4a.

5. Rewrite Program 10.6 to have only one `friend` function named `addComplex()`. This function should accept two complex objects and return a complex object. The real and imaginary parts of the returned object should be the sum of the real and imaginary parts, respectively, of the two objects passed to `addComplex()`.

6. **a.** Construct a class named `Coord` that contains two double-precision variables named `xval` and `yval`, which will be used to store the `x` and `y` values of a point in rectangular coordinates. The class functions should include appropriate constructor and display functions and a `friend` function named `convPol()`. The `convPol()` function should accept two floating-point numbers that represent a point in polar coordinates and convert them into rectangular coordinates. For conversion from polar to rectangular coordinates use the formulas

   $x = r \cos \theta$
   $y = r \sin \theta$

   b. Include the class written for Exercise 6a in a working C++ program.

7. **a.** Construct two classes named `RecCoord` and `PolCoord`. The class named `RecCoord` should contain two double-precision variables named `xval` and `yval`, which will be used to store the `x` and `y` values of a point in rectangular coordinates. The class functions should include appropriate constructor and display functions and a `friend` function named `convPol()`.

   The class named `PolCoord` should contain two double-precision data members named `dist` and `theta`, which will be used to store the distance and angle values of a point represented in polar coordinates. The class functions should include appropriate constructor and display functions and a `friend` function named `convPol()`. The `friend` function should accept an integer argument named `dir`; two double-precision arguments named `val1` and `val2`; and two reference arguments named `recref` and `polref`, the first of which should be a reference to an object of type `recCoord`, and the second to an object of type `polCoord`. If the value of `dir` is 1, `val1` and `val2` are to be considered as `x` and `y` rectangular coordinates that are to be converted to polar coordinates; if the value of `dir` is any other value, `val1` and `val2` are to be considered as distance and angle values that are to be converted to rectangular coordinates. For conversion from rectangular to polar, coordinates are

   $r = \sqrt{x^2 + y^2}$

   $\theta = \tan (y/x)^{-1}$

   For conversion from polar to rectangular coordinates, use the formulas:

   $x = r \cos \theta$
   $y = r \sin \theta$

   b. Include the class written for Exercise 7a in a working C++ program.

10.3 OPERATOR FUNCTIONS

A simple assignment operator was constructed in Section 10.1. In this section we extend this capability and show how to broaden C++'s built-in operators to work with class objects. As we will discover, class operators are themselves either member or friend functions.

The only symbols permitted for user-defined purposes are the subset of C++'s built-in symbols listed in Table 10.1. Each of these symbols may be adopted for class use with no limitation as to its meaning.[4] This is done by making each operation a function that can be overloaded like any other function.

The operation of the symbols listed in Table 10.1 can be redefined as we see fit for our classes, subject to the following restrictions:

- Symbols not in Table 10.1 cannot be redefined. For example, the `.`, `::`, and `?:` symbols cannot be redefined.
- New operator symbols cannot be created. For example, since `%%` is not an operator in C++, it cannot be defined as a class operator.
- Neither the precedence nor the associativity of C++'s operators can be modified. Thus, you cannot give the addition operator a higher precedence than the multiplication operator.
- Operators cannot be redefined for C++'s built-in types.
- A C++ operator that is unary cannot be changed to a binary operator and a binary operator cannot be changed to a unary operator.
- The operator must either be a member of a class or defined to take at least one class member as an operand.

The first step in providing a class with operators from Table 10.1 is to decide which operations make sense for the class and how they should be defined. As a specific example, we continue to build on the `Date` class introduced previously. For this class a small, meaningful set of class operations is defined.

Clearly, the addition of two dates is not meaningful. The addition of a date with an integer, however, does make sense if the integer is taken as the number of days to be added to the date. Likewise, the subtraction of an integer from a date makes sense. Also, the subtraction of two dates is meaningful if we define the difference to mean the number of days between the two dates. Similarly, it makes sense to compare two dates and determine if the dates are equal or one date occurs before or after another date. Let's now see how these operations can be implemented using C++'s operator symbols.

---

[4]The only limitation is that the syntax of the operator cannot be changed. Thus, a binary operator must remain binary and a unary operator must remain unary. Within this syntax restriction an operator symbol can be used to produce any operation, whether or not the operation is consistent with the symbol's accepted usage. For example, we could redefine the addition symbol to provide multiplication. Clearly, this violates the intent and spirit of making these symbols available to us. We shall be very careful to redefine each symbol in a manner consistent with its accepted usage.

Table 10.1 Operators Available for Class Use

<table>
<tr><th>Operator</th><th>Description</th></tr>
<tr><td>()</td><td>Function call</td></tr>
<tr><td>[]</td><td>Array element</td></tr>
<tr><td>-></td><td>Structure member pointer reference</td></tr>
<tr><td>new</td><td>Dynamically allocate memory</td></tr>
<tr><td>delete</td><td>Dynamically deallocate memory</td></tr>
<tr><td>++</td><td>Increment</td></tr>
<tr><td>--</td><td>Decrement</td></tr>
<tr><td>-</td><td>Unary minus</td></tr>
<tr><td>!</td><td>Logical negation</td></tr>
<tr><td>~</td><td>One's complement</td></tr>
<tr><td>*</td><td>Indirection</td></tr>
<tr><td>*</td><td>Multiplication</td></tr>
<tr><td>/</td><td>Division</td></tr>
<tr><td>%</td><td>Modulus (remainder)</td></tr>
<tr><td>+</td><td>Addition</td></tr>
<tr><td>-</td><td>Subtraction</td></tr>
<tr><td><<</td><td>Left shift</td></tr>
<tr><td>>></td><td>Right shift</td></tr>
<tr><td><</td><td>Less than</td></tr>
<tr><td><=</td><td>Less than or equal to</td></tr>
<tr><td>></td><td>Greater than</td></tr>
<tr><td>>=</td><td>Greater than or equal to</td></tr>
<tr><td>==</td><td>Equal to</td></tr>
<tr><td>!=</td><td>Not equal to</td></tr>
<tr><td>&&</td><td>Logical AND</td></tr>
<tr><td>||</td><td>Logical OR</td></tr>
<tr><td>&</td><td>Bit-by-bit AND</td></tr>
<tr><td>^</td><td>Bit-by-bit exclusive OR</td></tr>
<tr><td>|</td><td>Bit-by-bit inclusive OR</td></tr>
<tr><td>=</td><td>Assignment</td></tr>
<tr><td>+= -= *=</td><td>Assignment</td></tr>
<tr><td>/= %= &=</td><td>Assignment</td></tr>
<tr><td>^= |=</td><td>Assignment</td></tr>
<tr><td><<= >>=</td><td>Assignment</td></tr>
<tr><td>,</td><td>Comma</td></tr>
</table>

A user-defined operation is created as a function that redefines C++'s built-in operator symbols for class use. Functions that define operations on class objects and use C++'s built-in operator symbols are referred to as **operator functions.**

Operator functions are declared and implemented in the same manner as all member functions, with one exception: It is the function's name that connects the appropriate operator symbol to the operation defined by the function. An operator function's name is always of the form operator<symbol> where <symbol> is one of the operators listed in Table 10.1. For example, the function name `operator+` is the name of the addition function, while the function name `operator==` is the name of the equal-to comparison function.

Once the appropriate function name is selected, the process of writing the function simply amounts to having it accept the desired inputs and produce the correct returned value.[5] For example, in comparing two `Date` objects for equality we would select C++'s equality operator. Thus, the name of our function becomes `operator==`. We would want our comparison operation to accept two `Date` objects, internally compare them, and return an integer value indicating the result of the comparison: `true` for equality and `false` for inequality. As a member function, a suitable prototype that could be included in the class declaration section is

```
bool operator==(Date&);
```

This prototype indicates that the function is named `operator==`, that it returns a Boolean value, and that it accepts a reference to a `Date` object.[6] Only one `Date` object is required here because the second `Date` object will be the object that calls the function. Let's now write the function definition to be included in the class implementation section. Assuming our class is named `Date`, a suitable definition is

```
bool Date::operator==(Date& Date2)
{
  if( day == date2.day && month == date2.month && year == date2.year)
    return true;
  else
    return false;
}
```

Once this function has been defined, it may be called using the same syntax as for C++'s built-in types. For example, if `a` and `b` are objects of type `Date`, the expression `if (a == b)` is valid. Program 10.7 includes this if statement as well as the declaration and definition of this operator function within the context of a complete program.

The output produced by Program 10.7 is

```
Dates a and b are not the same.
Dates a and c are the same.
```

The first new feature to be illustrated in Program 10.7 is the declaration and implementation of the function named `operator==()`. Except for its name, this operator function is constructed in the same manner as any other member function: It is declared in the declaration section and defined in the implementation section. The second new feature is how the function is called. Operator functions may be called using their associated symbols rather than in the way other functions are called. Since operator functions are true functions, however, the traditional method of calling them can also be used—by specifying their name and including appropriate arguments. Thus, in addition to being called by the expression `a == b` in Program 10.7, the call `a.operator==(b)` could also have been used.

---

[5] As previously noted, this implies that the specified operator can be redefined to perform any operation. Good programming practice, however, dictates against such redefinitions.

[6] The prototype `bool operator==(Date)` also works. Passing a reference, however, is preferable to passing an object because it reduces the function call's overhead. This is because passing an object means that a copy of the object must be made for the called function, while passing a reference gives the function direct access to the object whose address is passed.

Program 10.7

```
#include <iostream>
using namespace std;

// class declaration
class Date
{
  private:
    int month;
    int day;
    int year;
  public:
    Date(int = 7, int = 4, int = 2005);  // constructor
    bool operator==(Date &);  // declare the operator== function
};

// implementation section
Date::Date(int mm, int dd, int yyyy)
{
  month = mm;
  day = dd;
  year = yyyy;
}

bool Date::operator==(Date &date2)
{
  if(day == date2.day && month == date2.month && year == date2.year)
    return true;
  else
    return false;
}

int main()
{
  Date a(4,1,2007), b(12,18,2008), c(4,1,2007); // declare 3 objects

  if (a == b)
    cout << "Dates a and b are the same." << endl;
  else
    cout << "Dates a and b are not the same." << endl;

  if (a == c)
    cout << "Dates a and c are the same." << endl;
  else
    cout << "Dates a and c are not the same." << endl;

  return 0;
}
```

Let's now create another operator for our `Date` class—an addition operator. As before, creating this operator requires that we specify three items:

1. The name of the operator function
2. The processing that the function is to perform
3. The data type, if any, that the function is to return

Clearly, for addition we will use the operator function named `operator+`. Having selected the function's name we must now determine what we want this function to do, as it specifically relates to `Date` objects. As we noted previously, the sum of two dates makes no sense. Adding an integer to a date is meaningful, however, when the integer represents the number of days either before or after the given date. Here the sum of an integer to a `Date` object is simply another `Date` object, which should be returned by the addition operation. Thus, a suitable prototype for our addition function is

```
Date operator+(int);
```

This prototype would be included in the class declaration section. It specifies that an integer is to be added to a class object and the operation returns a `Date` object. Thus, if `a` is a `Date` object, the function call `a.operator+(284)`, or its more commonly used alternative, `a + 284`, should cause the number `284` to be correctly added to `a`'s date value. We must now construct the function to accomplish this.

Constructing the function requires that we first select a specific date convention. For simplicity we will adopt the financial date convention that considers each month to consist of 30 days and each year to consist of 360 days. Using this convention, our function will first add the integer number of days to the `Date` object's day value and then adjust the resulting day value to lie within the range 1 to 30 and the month value to lie within the range 1 to 12. A function that accomplishes this is

```
Date Date::operator+(int days)
{
  Date temp;  // a temporary Date to store the result

  temp.day = day + days;  // add the days
  temp.month = month;
  temp.year = year;
  while (temp.day > 30)    // now adjust the months
  {
    temp.month++;
    temp.day -= 30;
  }
  while (temp.month > 12)  // adjust the years
  {
    temp.year++;
    temp.month -= 12;
  }
  return temp;     // the values in temp are returned
}
```

The important feature to notice here is the use of the `temp` object. The purpose of this object is to ensure that none of the function's arguments, which become the operator's operands, are altered. To understand this consider a statement such as `b = a + 284;` that uses this operator function, where `a` and `b` are `Date` objects. This statement should never modify `a`'s value. Rather, the expression `a + 284` should yield a `Date` value that is then assigned to `b`. The result of the expression is, of course, the `temp Date` object returned by the `operator+()` function. Program 10.8 uses this function within the context of a complete program.

Program 10.8

```
#include <iostream>
#include <iomanip>
using namespace std;

// class declaration

class Date
{
  private:
    int month;
    int day;
    int year;
  public:
    Date(int = 7, int = 4, int = 2005);      // constructor
    Date operator+(int);       // overload the + operator
    void showDate();      // member function to display a date
};
// implementation section
Date::Date(int mm, int dd, int yyyy)
{
  month = mm;
  day = dd;
  year = yyyy;
}

Date Date::operator+(int days)
{
  Date temp;  // a temporary date to store the result

  temp.day = day + days;  // add the days
  temp.month = month;
  temp.year = year;
  while (temp.day > 30)    // now adjust the months
```

(Continued)

(Continued)

```
  {
    temp.month++;
    temp.day -= 30;
  }
  while (temp.month > 12)  // adjust the years
  {
    temp.year++;
    temp.month -= 12;
  }
  return temp;     // the values in temp are returned
}
void Date::showDate()
{
  cout << setfill('0')
       << setw(2) << month << '/'
       << setw(2) << day << '/'
       << setw(2) << year % 100
  return;
}
```

```
int main()
{
  Date a(4,1,2007), b; // declare two objects

  cout << "The initial date is ";
  a.showDate();
  b = a + 284;    // add in 284 days = 9 months and 14 days
  cout << "The new date is ";
  b.showDate();

  return 0;
}
```

The output produced by Program 10.8 is

```
The initial date is 04/01/07
The new date is 01/15/08
```

Operator Functions as Friends

The operator functions in Programs 10.7 and 10.8 have been constructed as class members. An interesting feature of operator functions is that, except for the operator functions =, `()`, `[]`, and `->`, they may also be written as friend functions. For example, if the `operator+()` function used in Program 10.8 were written as a friend, a suitable declaration section prototype is

```
friend Date operator+(Date& , int);
```

Notice that the friend version contains a reference to a `Date` object that is not contained in the member function version. In all cases the equivalent friend version of a member operator function *must* contain an additional class reference that is not required by the member function.[7] This equivalence is listed in Table 10.2 for both unary and binary operators.

Table 10.2 Operator Function Argument Requirements

	Member Function	Friend Function
Unary operator	1 implicit	1 explicit
Binary operator	1 implicit and 1 explicit	2 explicit

Program 10.8's `operator+()` function, written as a friend function, is

```
Date operator+(Date& op1, int days)
{
  Date temp;  // a temporary Date to store the result

  temp.day = op1.day + days;  // add the days
  temp.month = op1.month;
  temp.year = op1.year;
  while (temp.day > 30)     // now adjust the months
  {
    temp.month++;
    temp.day -= 30;
  }
  while (temp.month > 12)  // adjust the years
  {
    temp.year++;
    temp.month -= 12;
  }
  return temp;       // the values in temp are returned
}
```

The only difference between this version and the member version is the explicit use of a `Date` argument named `op1` (the choice of this name is entirely arbitrary) in the friend version. This means that within the body of the friend function the first three assignment statements explicitly reference `op1`'s data members as `op1.day`, `op1.month`, and `op1.year`, whereas the member function simply refers to its arguments as `day`, `month`, and `year`.

In making the determination to overload a binary operator as either a friend or member operator function, the following convention can be applied: *Friend functions are more appropriate for binary functions that modify neither of their operands, such as ==, +, -, etc., while member functions are more appropriate for binary functions, such as =, +=, -=, etc., that are used to modify one of their operands.*

[7]This extra argument is necessary to identify the correct object. This argument is not needed when using a member function because the member function "knows" which object it is operating on. The mechanism of this "knowing" is supplied by an implied member function argument named `this`.

Exercises 10.3

1. a. Define a *greater than* relational operator function named `operator>()` that can be used with the `Date` class declared in Program 10.7.
   b. Define a *less than* operator function named `operator<()` that can be used with the `Date` class declared in Program 10.7.
   c. Include the operator functions written for Exercises 1a and 1b in a working C++ program.

2. a. Define a subtraction operator function named `operator-()` that can be used with the `Date` class defined in Program 10.7. The subtraction should accept a long-integer argument that represents the number of days to be subtracted from an object's date and return a `Date`. In doing the subtraction use the assumption that all months consist of 30 days and all years of 360 days. Additionally, an end-of-month adjustment should be made, if necessary, that converts any resulting day of 31 to a day of 30, except if the month is February. If the resulting month is February and the day is either 29, 30, or 31, it should be changed to 28.
   b. Define another subtraction operator function named `operator-()` that can be used with the `Date` class defined in Program 10.7. The subtraction should yield a long integer that represents the difference in days between two dates. In calculating the day difference use the financial-day count basis that assumes that all months have 30 days and all years have 360 days.
   c. Include the overloaded operators written for Exercises 2a and 2b in a working C++ program.

3. a. Determine if the following addition operator function provides the same result as the function used in Program 10.8.

```
Date Date::operator+(int days)   // return a Date object
{
  Date temp;

  temp.day = day + days;    // add the days in
  temp.month = month + int(day/30);  // determine total months
  temp.day = temp.day % 30;          // determine actual day
  temp.year = year + int(temp.month/12);  // determine total years
  temp.month = temp.month % 12;      // determine actual month

  return temp;
}
```

   b. Verify your answer to Exercise 3a by including the function in a working C++ program.

4. a. Rewrite the equality relational operator function in Program 10.7 as a friend function.
   b. Verify the operation of the friend operator function written for Exercise 4a by including it within a working C++ program.
5. a. Construct an addition operator for the `Complex` class declared in Program 10.6. This should be a member function that adds two complex numbers and returns a complex number.
   b. Add a member multiplication operator function to the class used in Exercise 5a that multiplies two complex numbers and returns a complex number.
   c. Verify the operation of the operator functions written for Exercises 5a and 5b by including them within a working C++ program.
6. a. Rewrite the addition operator function in Program 10.8 to account for the actual days in a month, neglecting leap years. (*NOTE:* This requires an array to store the days in each month.)
   b. Verify the operation of the operator function written for Exercise 6a by including it within a working C++ program.

10.4 DATA TYPE CONVERSIONS

The conversion from one built-in data type to another was described in Section 3.2. With the introduction of user-defined data types, the possibilities for conversion between data types expand to the following cases:

- Conversion from built-in type to built-in type
- Conversion from built-in type to class type
- Conversion from class type to built-in type
- Conversion from class type to class type

The first conversion is handled either by C++'s built-in implicit conversion rules or its explicit cast operator. The second conversion type is made using a **type conversion constructor**. The third and fourth conversion types are made using a **conversion operator function.** In this section the specific means of performing each of these conversions are presented.

Built-in to Built-in Conversion

The conversion from one built-in data type to another has already been presented in Section 3.1 and 3.3. To review this case briefly, this type of conversion is either implicit or explicit.

An implicit conversion occurs in the context of one of C++'s operations. For example, when a floating-point value is assigned to an integer variable, only the integer portion of the value is stored. The conversion is implied by the operation and is performed automatically by the compiler.

An explicit conversion occurs whenever a cast is used. In C++ two cast notations exist. Using the older C notation, a cast has the form *(dataType) expression* while the newer C++ notation has the function-like form *dataType(expression)*. For example, both of the expressions `(int)24.32` and `int(24.32)` cause the double-precision value 24.32 to be truncated to the integer value 24.

Built-In to Class Conversion

User-defined casts for converting a built-in to a class data type are created using constructor functions. A constructor whose first argument is not a member of its `class` and whose remaining arguments, if any, have default values is a **type conversion constructor**. If the first argument of a type conversion constructor is a built-in data type, the constructor can be used to cast the built-in data type to a class object. Clearly, one restriction of such functions is that, as constructors, they must be member functions.

Although this type of cast occurs when the constructor is invoked to initialize an object, it is actually a more general cast than might be evident at first glance. This is because a constructor function can be explicitly invoked after all objects have been declared, whether or not it was invoked previously as part of an object's declaration. Before exploring this further, let's first construct a type conversion constructor. We will then see how to use it as a cast independent of its initialization purpose.

The cast we will construct will convert a long integer into a `Date` object. Our `Date` object will consist of dates in the form month/day/year and use our now familiar `Date` class. The long integer will be used to represent dates in the form `year` * 10000 + `month` * 100 + `day`. For example, using this representation the date 12/31/2000 becomes the long integer 20001231. Dates represented in this fashion are very useful for two reasons: First, it permits a date to be to stored as a single integer, and second, such dates are in numerically increasing date order, making sorting extremely easy. For example, the date 01/03/2002, which occurs after 12/31/2001 becomes the integer 20020103, which is larger than 20011231. Since the integers representing dates can exceed the size of a normal integer, the integers are always declared as longs.

A suitable constructor function for converting from a long-integer date to a date stored as a month, day, and year is

```
// type conversion constructor from long to Date

Date::Date(long findate)
{
  year = int(findate/10000.0);
  month = int((findate - year * 10000.0)/100.0);
  day = int(findate - year * 10000.0 - month * 100.0);
}
```

Program 10.9 uses this type conversion constructor both as an initialization function at declaration time and as an explicit cast later on in the program.

Program 10.9

```
#include <iostream>
#include <iomanip>
using namespace std;

// class declaration

class Date
{
  private:
    int month, day, year;
  public:
    Date(int = 7, int = 4, int = 2005);  // constructor
    Date(long);            // type conversion constructor
    void showDate();
};

// implementation section

// constructor
Date::Date(int mm, int dd, int yyyy)
{
  month = mm;
  day = dd;
  year = yyyy;
}

// type conversion constructor from long to date
Date::Date(long findate)
{
  year = int(findate/10000.0);
  month = int((findate - year * 10000.0)/100.0);
  day = int(findate - year * 10000.0 - month * 100.0);
}

// member function to display a date
void Date::showDate()
{
  cout << setfill('0')
       << setw(2) << month << '/'
       << setw(2) << day << '/'
       << setw(2) << year % 100;

  return;
}
```

(Continued)

(Continued)

```
int main()
{
  Date a, b(20061225L), c(4,1,2007);  // declare 3 objects - initialize 2 of them

  cout << "Dates a, b, and c are ";
  a.showDate();
  cout << ", ";
  b.showDate();
  cout << ", and ";
  c.showDate();
  cout << ".\n";

  a = Date(20080103L);  // cast a long to a date

  cout << "Date a is now ";
  a.showDate();
  cout << ".\n";

  return 0;
}
```

The output produced by Program 10.9 is

```
Dates a, b, and c are 07/04/05, 12/25/06, and 04/01/07.
Date a is now 01/03/08.
```

The change in `a`'s date value illustrated by this output is produced by the assignment expression `a = Date(20080103L)`, which uses a type conversion constructor to perform the cast from long to `Date`.

Class to Built-in Conversion

Conversion from a user-defined data type to a built-in data type is accomplished using a conversion operator function. A **conversion operator function** is a member operator function having the name of a built-in data type or class. When the operator function has a built-in data type name it is used to convert from a class to a built-in data type. For example, a conversion operator function for casting a class object to a long integer would have the name `operator long()`. Here the name of the operator function indicates that a conversion to a long will take place. If this function were part of a `Date` class it would be used to cast a `Date` object into a long integer. This usage is illustrated by Program 10.10.

The output produced by Program 10.10 is

```
a's date is 04/01/07
This date, as a long integer, is 20070401
```

Program 10.10

```
#include <iostream>
#include <iomanip>
using namespace std;

// class declaration

class Date
{
  private:
    int month, day, year;
  public:
    Date(int = 7, int = 4, int = 2005);    // constructor
    operator long();         // conversion operator function
    void showDate();
};

// implementation section

// constructor
Date::Date(int mm, int dd, int yyyy)
{
  month = mm;
  day = dd;
  year = yyyy;
}

// conversion operator function converting from Date to long
Date::operator long()   // must return a long
{
  long yyyymmdd;

  yyyymmdd = year * 10000 + month * 100 + day;

  return(yyyymmdd);
}

// member function to display a date
void Date::showDate()
{
   cout << setfill('0')
        << setw(2) << month << '/'
        << setw(2) << day << '/'
        << setw(2) << year % 100;
   return;
}
```

(Continued)

(Continued)

```
int main()
{
  Date a(4,1,2007);  // declare and initialize one object of type date
  long b;            // declare an object of type long

  b = a;             // a conversion takes place here

  cout << "a's date is ";
  a.showDate();
  cout << "\nThis date, as a long integer, is " << b << endl;

  return 0;
}
```

The change in `a`'s date value to a long integer illustrated by this output is produced by the assignment expression `b = a`. This assignment, which also could have been written as `b = long(a)`, calls the conversion operator function `long()` to perform the cast from `Date` to `long`. In general, since explicit conversion more clearly documents what is happening, its use is preferred to implicit conversion.

Notice that the conversion operator has no explicit argument and has no explicit return type. This is true of all conversion operators: The implicit argument will always be an object of the class being cast from, and the return type is implied by the name of the function. Additionally, as previously indicated, a conversion operator function *must* be a member function.

Class to Class Conversion

Converting from a class data type to a class data type is performed in the same manner as a cast from a class to built-in data type—it is done using a member **conversion operator function**. In this case, however, the operator function uses the class name being converted to rather than a built-in data name. For example, if two classes named `Date` and `Intdate` exist, the operator function named operator `Intdate()` could be placed in the `Date` class to convert from a `Date` object to an `Intdate` object. Similarly, the operator function named `Date()` could be placed in the `Intdate` class to convert from an `Intdate` to a `Date`.

Notice that as before, in converting from a class data type to a built-in data type, *the operator function's name determines the result of the conversion*; the class containing the operator function determines the data type being converted from.

Before providing a specific example of a class to class conversion, one additional point must be noted. Converting between classes clearly implies that we have two classes, one of which is always defined first and one of which is defined second. Having, within the second class, a conversion operator function with the name of the first class poses no problem because the compiler knows of the first class's existence. However, including a conversion operator function with the second class's name in the first class does pose a problem because the second class has not yet been defined. This is remedied by including a declaration for the second class prior to the first class's definition. This declaration, which is formally referred to as a **forward declaration**, is illustrated in Program 10.11, which also includes conversion operators between the two defined classes.

Program 10.11

```
#include <iostream>
#include <iomanip>
using namespace std;

// forward declaration of class Intdate
class Intdate;

// class declaration for Date
class Date
{
  private:
    int month, day, year;
  public:
    Date(int = 7, int = 4, int = 2005);    // constructor
    operator Intdate();     // conversion operator Date to Intdate
    void showDate();
};
// class declaration for Intdate
class Intdate
{
  private:
    long yyyymmdd;
  public:
    Intdate(long = 0);    // constructor
    operator Date();  // conversion operator intdate to date
    void showint();
};

// implementation section for Date
Date::Date(int mm, int dd, int yyyy)  // constructor
{
  month = mm;
  day = dd;
  year = yyyy;
}
// conversion operator function converting from Date to Intdate class
Date::operator Intdate()   // must return an Intdate object
```

(Continued)

(Continued)

```
{
  long temp;

  temp = year * 10000 + month * 100 + day;
  return(Intdate(temp));
}
// member function to display a Date
void Date::showDate()
{
  cout << setfill('0')
        << setw(2) << month << '/'
        << setw(2) << day << '/'
        << setw(2) << year % 100;
  return;
}

// implementation section for Intdate
Intdate::Intdate(long ymd)  // constructor
{
  yyyymmdd = ymd;
}
// conversion operator function converting from Intdate to Date class
Intdate::operator Date()    // must return a Date object
{
  int mo, da, yr;

  yr = int(yyyymmdd/10000.0);
  mo = int((yyyymmdd - yr * 10000.0)/100.0);
  da = int(yyyymmdd - yr * 10000.0 - mo * 100.0);
  return(Date(mo,da,yr));
}
// member function to display an Intdate
void Intdate::showint()
{
  cout << yyyymmdd;
  return;
}
```

```
int main()
{
  Date a(4,1,2007), b;      // declare two Date objects
  Intdate c(20081215L), d;  // declare two Intdate objects

  b = Date(c);       // cast c into a Date object
  d = Intdate(a);    // cast a into an Intdate object
```

(Continued)

(Continued)

```
    cout << " a's date is ";
    a.showDate();
    cout << "\n   as an Intdate object this date is ";
    d.showint();

    cout << "\n c's date is ";
    c.showint();
    cout << "\n   as a Date object this date is ";
    b.showDate();
    cout << endl;

    return 0;
}
```

The output produced by Program 10.11 is

```
a's date is 04/01/07
  as an Intdate object this date is 20070401
c's date is 20081215
  as a Date object this date is 12/15/08
```

As illustrated by Program 10.11, the cast from `Date` to `Intdate` is produced by the assignment `b = Date(c)` and the cast from `Intdate` to `Date` is produced by the assignment `d = Intdate(a)`. Alternatively, the assignments `b = c` and `d = a` would produce the same results. Notice also the forward declaration of the `Intdate` class prior to the `Date` class's declaration. This is required so that the `Date` class can reference `Intdate` in its operator conversion function.

Exercises 10.4

1. a. Define the four data type conversions available in C++ and the method of accomplishing each conversion.
   b. Define the terms type conversion constructor and conversion operator function and describe how they are used in user-defined conversions.

2. Write a C++ program that declares a class named `Time` having integer data members named `hours`, `minutes`, and `seconds`. Include in the program a type conversion constructor that converts a long integer, representing the elapsed seconds from midnight, into an equivalent representation as hours:minutes:seconds. For example, the long integer 30336 should convert to the time 8:25:36. Use a military representation of time so that 2:30 pm is represented as 14:30:00. The relationship between time representations is

   *elapsed seconds = hours * 3600 + minutes * 60 + seconds.*

3. A Julian date is a date represented as the number of days from a known base date. One algorithm for converting from a Gregorian date, in the form month/day/year, to a Julian date with a base date of 00/00/0000 is given below. All of the calculations in this algorithm use integer arithmetic, which means that the fractional part of all divisions must be discarded. In this algorithm M = month, D = day, and Y = year.

If M is less than or equal to 2
  Set the variable MP = 0 and YP = Y–1
Else
  *Set MP = int(0.4 * M + 2.3) and YP = Y*
EndIf
T = int(YP/4) – int(YP/100) + int(YP/400)
*Julian date = 365 * Y + 31 * (M – 1) + D + T – MP*

Using this algorithm, modify Program 10.10 to cast from a Gregorian date object to its corresponding Julian representation as a long integer. Test your program using the Gregorian dates 1/31/2005 and 3/16/2006, which correspond to the Julian dates 732342 and 732751, respectively.

4. Modify the program written for Exercise 2 to include a member conversion operator function that converts an object of type `Time` into a long integer representing the number of seconds from twelve midnight.

5. Write a C++ program that has a `Date` class and a `Julian` class. The `Date` class should be the same `Date` class as that used in Program 10.11, while the `Julian` class should represent a date as a long integer. For this program include a member conversion operator function within the `Date` class that converts a `Date` object to a `Julian` object, using the algorithm presented in Exercise 3. Test your program by converting the dates 1/31/2006 and 3/16/2007, which correspond to the Julian dates 732707 and 733116, respectively.

6. Write a C++ program that has a `Time` class and an `Ltime` class. The `Time` class should have integer data members named `hours`, `minutes`, and `seconds`, while the `Ltime` class should have a long data member named `elsecs`, which represents the number of elapsed seconds since midnight. For the `Time` class include a member conversion operator function named `Ltime()` that converts a `Time` object to an `Ltime` object. For the `Ltime` class include a member conversion operator function named `Time()` that converts an `Ltime` object to a `Time` object.

10.5 APPLICATION–A MULTI-OBJECT GAS PUMP SIMULATION

In Application 2 of Section 8.4, a requirement was made to construct a C++ program that simulated a gas pump's operation over the course of any 30-minute period. For convenience, this requirement is restated below:

We have been requested to write a program that simulates the operation of a gas pump. At any time during the simulation, we should be able to determine, from the pump, the price per gallon of gas, and the amount remaining in the supply tank from which the gas is pumped. If the amount of gas in the supply tank is greater than or equal to the amount of gas requested, the request should be filled; otherwise, only the available amount in the supply tank should be used. Once the gas is pumped, the total price of the gallons pumped should be displayed and the amount of gas in gallons that was pumped should be subtracted from the supply tank amount.

For the simulation, assume that the pump is randomly idle between 1 to 15 minutes between customer arrivals and that a customer randomly requests between 3 and 20 gallons of gas. Though the default supply tank capacity is 500 gallons, assume the initial amount of gas in the tank for this simulation is 300 gallons. Initially, the program should simulate a one-half hour time frame.

Additionally, for each arrival and request for gas, we want to know the idle time before the customer arrived, how many gallons of gas were pumped, and the total price of the transaction. The pump itself must keep track of the price per gallon of gas and the amount of gas remaining in the supply tank. Typically, the price per gallon is $1.80, but the price for the simulation should be $2.00.

Having constructed a `Pump` class to model the operation of a gas pump, we can use this class within the context of a complete simulation. We do so by providing a `Customer` class and then controlling the interaction between these two classes using a `main()` function to create an actual multi-class simulation program.

Step 1 Analyze the Problem

As specified, the problem entails two types of objects: a gas pump and a customer. Let's consider these object types separately.

The Pump. A `Pump` class was designed and implemented in Section 9.4 and is repeated here for convenience:

```
#include <iostream>
#include <iomanip>
using namespace std;

const double AMOUNT_IN_TANK = 500;  // initial gallons in the tank
const double DEFAULT_PRICE = 1.80;  // price per gallon

class Pump
{
  // data declaration section
  private:
    double amtInTank;
    double price;

  // method declarations
  public:
    Pump(double = DEFAULT_PRICE, double = AMOUNT_IN_TANK);   // constructor
    void getValues();
    void request(double);
};
```

```
// methods implementation section


Pump::Pump(double todaysPrice, double amountInTank)
{
  amtInTank = amountInTank;
  price = todaysPrice;
}

void Pump::getValues()
{
  cout << "The gas tank has " << amtInTank << " gallons of gas." << endl;
  cout << "The price per gallon of gas is $" << setiosflags(ios::showpoint)
        << setprecision(2) << setiosflags(ios::fixed) << price << endl;
}

void Pump::request(double pumpAmt)
{
  double pumped;

  if (amtInTank >= pumpAmt)
     pumped = pumpAmt;
  else
   pumped = amtInTank;

  amtInTank -= pumped;
  cout << pumpAmt << " gallons were requested " << endl;
  cout << pumped << " gallons were pumped" << endl;
  cout << amtInTank << " gallons remain in the tank" << endl;
  cout << "The total price is $" << setiosflags(ios::showpoint)
       << setprecision(2) << (pumped * price) << endl;

  return;
}
```

You should review Problem 2 in Section 8.4 if the data or member methods of this `Pump` class are unclear. For later convenience in writing the required simulation program, assume the code for the `Pump` class has been named `Pump.cpp` and is stored within a folder, `cpcode`, on the `C` drive. Once this is done, you can include the `Pump` class definition with a program by using the single-line preprocessor directive:

`#include <C:\\cpcode\\Pump.cpp>`.[8]

The Customer. For this simulation, there are multiple instances of customers arriving randomly between 1 and 15 minutes and requesting gas in amounts that vary between 3 and

[8] The reason for using a full path name in the `#include` statement is to ensure that the preprocessor accesses the `Pump.cpp` class that we have placed in the named folder. We do not want the preprocessor to search its default folder and possibly locate some other `Pump.cpp` class that we do not know about or be unable to locate the `Pump.cpp` files at all.

20 gallons. From an object viewpoint, however, we are not interested in storing the arrival and number of gallons requested by each customer. We need a customer object to present us with an arrival time and a request for gas in gallons. Therefore, our `Customer` object type need have no attributes but must provide two operations. The first operation, `arrive()`, will provide a random arrival time between 1 and 15 minutes. The second operation, `gallons()`, will provide a random request of between 3 and 20 gallons of gas. This class is simple and its design and implementation are coded as the following:

```
#include <ctime>
#include <cmath>
using namespace std;

//class declaration and implementation
class Customer
{
  public:
    Customer() {srand(time(NULL));};
    int arrive() {return(1 + rand() % 15);};
    int gallons() {return(3 + rand() % 18);};
};
```

The class constructor is used to randomize the `rand()` function. (Review Section 6.7 if you are unfamiliar with the `srand()` or `rand()` functions.) The `arrive()` function returns a random integer between 1 and 15, and the `gallons()` function returns a random integer between 3 and 20. (We leave it as an exercise for you to rewrite the `gallons()` function to return a non-integer value.) Since all of the functions are single line, we have included their definitions within the declaration section as inline functions.

Again, for later convenience in writing the complete simulation program, assume that the code for the `Customer` class is placed in a file named `Customer.cpp` within a folder named `cpcode` on the `C` drive. Once this is done, including the `Customer` class within a program requires the following statement:

```
#include <C:\\cpcode\\Customer.cpp
```

Program Logic. Having analyzed and defined the two classes we will be using, we need to analyze and define the logic to control the interaction between `Customer` and `Pump` objects for a valid simulation. In this particular case, the only interaction between a `Customer` object and a `Pump` object is that a customer's arrival, followed by a request, determines when the `Pump` is activated and how much gas is requested. Thus, each interaction between a `Customer` and a `Pump` can be expressed by the following pseudocode:

Obtain a Customer arrival time
Obtain a Customer request for gas
Activate the `Pump` *with the request*

Though this repetition of events takes place continuously over the course of a day, we are interested in a one-half hour period. Therefore, we must place these three events in a loop that is executed until the required simulation time has elapsed.

Point of Information

Program and Class Libraries

The concept of a program library began with FORTRAN, which was the first commercial high-level language introduced in 120054. The FORTRAN library consisted of a group of completely tested and debugged mathematical routines provided with the compiler. Since then, every programming language has provided its own library of functions. In C and C++, this library is referred to as the standard program library and includes more than 12,000 functions declared in fifteen different header files. Examples of standard library functions include `sqrt()`, `pow()`, `abs()`, `rand()`, `srand()`, and `time()`. The advantage of library functions is they enhance program development and design by providing code known to work without the need for additional testing and debugging.

With the introduction of object-oriented languages, the concept of a program library has been extended to include class libraries. A *class library* is a library of tested and debugged classes.

One of the key practical features of class libraries is that they help realize the goal of code reuse in a significant way. By providing tested and debugged code consisting of data and function members, class libraries furnish large sections of pre-written and reusable code ready for incorporation within new applications. This shifts the focus of writing application programs from the creation of new code to understanding how to use predefined objects and stitch them together in a cohesive and useful way.

Step 2 Develop a Solution

Having developed and coded the two required classes, `Pump` and `Customer`, what remains to be developed is the control logic within the `main()` function for activating class events. This will require a loop controlled by the total arrival time for all customers. A suitable control structure for `main()` is described by the following algorithm:

Create a Pump *object with the required initial supply of gas*
Display the values in the initialized `Pump`
Set the total time to 0
Obtain a Customer arrival time // first arrival
Add the arrival time to the total time
While the total time does not exceed the simulation time
    Display the total time
    Obtain a Customer request for gas
    Activate the Pump *with the request*
    Obtain a Customer arrival time // next arrival
    Add the arrival time to the total time
EndWhile
Display a message that the simulation is over

Step 3 Code the Solution

The C++ code corresponding to our design is listed as Program 10.12.

Program 10.12

```
#include <C:\\cpcode\\Pump.cpp>      // note use of full path name here
#include <C:\\cpcode\\Customer.cpp>    // again - a full path name is used

const double SIMTIME = .5;          // simulation time in hours
const int MINUTES = 60;             // number of minutes in an hour

int main()
{
  Pump a(2.00, 300);   // declare 1 object of type Pump
  Customer b;          // declare 1 object of type Customer
  int totalTime = 0;
  int idleTime;
  int amtRequest;
  int SimMinutes;  // simulation time in minutes


  SimMinutes = SIMTIME * MINUTES;
  cout << "\nStarting a new simulation-simulation time is "
       << SimMinutes << " minutes" << endl << endl;
  a.getValues();

  // get the first arrival
  idleTime = b.arrive();
  totalTime += idleTime;

  while (totalTime <= SimMinutes)
  {
    cout << "\nThe idle time is " << idleTime << " minutes" << endl
       << "   and we are " << totalTime
       << " minutes into the simulation." << endl;
    amtRequest = b.gallons();
    a.request(double(amtRequest));

    // get the next arrival
    idleTime = b.arrive();
    totalTime += idleTime;
  }
  cout << "\nThe idle time is " << idleTime << " minutes." << endl
       << "As the total time now exceeds the simulation time, " << endl
       << "   this simulation run is over." << endl;

  return 0;
}
```

Step 4 Test and Correct the Program

Assuming the `Pump` and `Customer` classes have been thoroughly tested and debugged, testing and debugging Program 10.12 is restricted to testing and debugging the `main()` method. This specificity of testing is precisely one of the advantages of an object-oriented approach. Using previously written and tested class definitions allows us to focus our attention on the remaining code that controls the flow of events between objects, which in Program 10.12 centers on the `main()` method.

By itself, the `main()` method in Program 10.12 is a straightforward `while` loop where the `Pump` idle time corresponds to the time between customer arrivals. The output of a sample run, shown below, verifies that the loop is operating correctly:

```
Starting a new simulation - simulation time is 30 minutes

The gas tank has 300 gallons of gas.
The price per gallon of gas is $2.00

The idle time is 2 minutes
   and we are 2 minutes into the simulation.
7.00 gallons were requested
7.00 gallons were pumped
293.00 gallons remain in the tank
The total price is $14.00

The idle time is 1 minutes
   and we are 3 minutes into the simulation.
15.00 gallons were requested
15.00 gallons were pumped
278.00 gallons remain in the tank
The total price is $30.00

The idle time is 11 minutes
   and we are 14 minutes into the simulation.
13.00 gallons were requested
13.00 gallons were pumped
265.00 gallons remain in the tank
The total price is $26.00

The idle time is 8 minutes
   and we are 22 minutes into the simulation.
20.00 gallons were requested
20.00 gallons were pumped
245.00 gallons remain in the tank
The total price is $40.00

The idle time is 9 minutes.
As the total time now exceeds the simulation time,
   this simulation run is over.
```

Exercises 10.5

1. Enter Program 10.12 on your computer and execute it.

2. a. Remove the `inline` functions in the `Customer` class declaration and implementation section by constructing individual declaration and implementation sections. Discuss which form of the `Customer` class you prefer and why.
   b. Rewrite the `gallons()` function in the `Customer` class so that it returns a floating-point number between 3.0 and 20.0 gallons.

3. In place of the `main()` function used in Program 10.12, a student proposed the following:

```
int main()
{
  Pump a(AMT_IN_TANK, TODAYS_PRICE);    // declare 1 object of type Pump
  Customer b;                         // declare 1 object of type Customer
  int totalTime = 0;
  int idleTime;
  int amtRequest;
  int SimMinutes;  // simulation time in minutes

  SimMinutes = SIMTIME * MINUTES;
  cout << "\nStarting a new simulation - simulation time is "
       << SimMinutes << " minutes" << endl;
  a.values();

  do
  {
    idleTime = b.arrive();
    totalTime += idleTime;
    if (totalTime > (SIMTIME * MINUTES))
    {
      cout << "\nThe idle time is " << idleTime << " minutes." << endl
           << "As the total time now exceeds the simulation time, " << endl
           << "    this simulation run is over." << endl;
      break;
    }
    else
    {
      cout << "\nThe idle time is " << idleTime << " minutes" << endl
         << "    and we are " << totalTime
         << " minutes into the simulation." << endl;
      amtRequest = b.gallons();
      a.request(double(amtRequest));
    }
  } while (1);  // always true

  return 0;
}
```

Determine if this `main()` function produces a valid simulation. If it does not, discuss why not. If it does, discuss which version you prefer and why.

4. Construct a class named `Elevator` that can be used to create an `elevator` object. For this problem, the only attribute of interest is the location of the elevator. Represent this location, which corresponds to the elevator's current floor position, by an integer variable named `currentFloor`. The functions that should be provided for this class are a constructor to set the initial floor position of a new `elevator` object to the first floor and a mutator function to change the elevator's position (state) to a new floor. Here is the algorithm describing the mutator function:

   If a request is made for a floor above 15 or for the current floor,
       Do nothing
   ElseIf the request is for a floor above the current floor
       Display the current floor number
       While not at the designated floor
           Increment the floor number
           Display the new floor number
       EndWhile
       Display the ending floor number
   Else // the request must be for a floor below the current floor
       Display the current floor number
       While not at the designated floor
           Decrement the floor number
           Display the new floor number
       EndWhile
       Display the ending floor number
   EndIf

   This algorithm consists of an `if-else` statement having three parts: If an incorrect service is requested, no action is taken; if a floor above the current position is selected, the elevator moves up; and if a floor below the current position is selected, the elevator moves down. For movement up or down, a `while` loop can be used to increment or decrement the elevator's position one floor at a time and report the movement using a `cout` statement.

5. Using the `Elevator` class defined in Exercise 4 and defining a new class named `Person`, construct a simulation whereby a person randomly arrives at any time from 1 to 10 minutes on any floor and calls the elevator. If the elevator is not on the floor that the person is, it must move to the floor that the person is on. Once inside the elevator the person can select any floor. Run the simulation for three randomly arriving people and have the simulation display the movement of the elevator.

10.6 Class Inheritance

The ability to create new classes from existing ones is the underlying motivation and power behind class- and object-oriented programming techniques. Doing so facilitates reusing existing code in new ways without the need for retesting and validation. It permits the designers of a class to make it available to others for additions and extensions without relinquishing control over the existing class features.

Constructing one class from another is accomplished using a capability called inheritance. Related to this capability is an equally important feature named polymorphism. Polymorphism provides the ability to redefine how member functions of related classes operate based on the class object being referenced. In fact, for a programming language to be classified as an object-oriented language it must provide the features of classes, inheritance, and polymorphism. In this section we describe the inheritance and polymorphism features provided in C++.

Inheritance is the capability of deriving one class from another class. The initial class used as the basis for the derived class is referred to as either the **base**, **parent**, or **superclass**. The derived class is referred to as either the **derived**, **child**, or **subclass**.

A derived class is a completely new class that incorporates all of the data and member functions of its base class. However, it can, and usually does, add its own additional new data and function members and can override any base class function.

As an example of inheritance, consider three geometric shapes consisting of a circle, a cylinder, and a sphere. All of these shapes share a common characteristic, a radius. Thus, for these shapes we can make the circle a base type for the other two shapes, as illustrated in Figure 10.5. By convention, arrows always point from the derived class to the base class. Reformulating these shapes as class types we would make the circle the base class and derive the cylinder and sphere classes from it.

The relationships illustrated in Figure 10.5 are examples of simple inheritance. In **simple inheritance** each derived type has only one immediate base type. The complement to simple inheritance is multiple inheritance. In **multiple inheritance** a derived type has two or more base types. Figure 10.6 illustrates an example of multiple inheritance. In this text we will only consider simple inheritance.

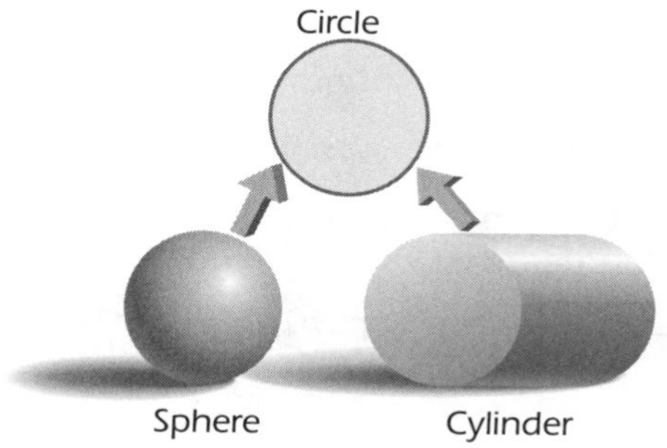

Figure 10.5 Relating object types.

Point of Information

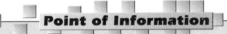

Object-Based versus Object-Oriented Languages

An ***object-based*** language is one in which data and operations can be incorporated together in such a way that data values can be isolated and accessed through the specified class functions. The ability to bind the data members with operations in a single unit is referred to as ***encapsulation***. In C++ encapsulation is provided by its class capability.

For a language to be classified as ***object-oriented*** it must also provide inheritance and polymorphism. ***Inheritance*** is the capability to derive one class from another. A derived class is a completely new data type that incorporates all of the data members and member functions of the original class with any new data and function members unique to itself. The class used as the basis for the derived type is referred to as the ***base*** or ***parent*** class and the derived data type is referred to as the ***derived*** or ***child*** class.

Polymorphism permits the same method name to invoke one operation in objects of a parent class and a different operation in objects of a derived class.

C++, which provides encapsulation, inheritance, and polymorphism, is a true object-oriented language. Because C, which is C++'s predecessor, does not provide these features, it is neither an object-based nor object-oriented language.

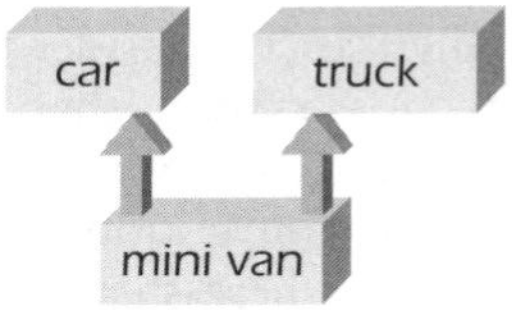

Figure 10.6 *An example of multiple inheritance.*

The class derivations illustrated in both Figures 10.5 and 10.6 are formally referred to as **class hierarchies** because they illustrate the hierarchy, or order, in which one class is derived from another. Let's now see how to derive one class from another.

A derived class has the same form as any other class in that it consists of both a declaration and an implementation. The only difference is in the first line of the declaration section. For a derived class, this line is extended to include an access specification and a base class name and has the form:

class derivedClassName : classAccess baseClassName

For example, if `Circle` is the name of an existing class, a new class named `Cylinder` can be derived as follows:

```
class Cylinder : public Circle
{
    // add any additional data and
    // function members in here
};  // end of Cylinder class declaration
```

Except for the class-access specifier after the colon and the base class name, there is nothing inherently new or complicated about the construction of the `Cylinder` class. Before providing a description of the `Circle` class and adding data and function members to the derived `Cylinder` class, we will need to reexamine access specifiers and how they relate to derived classes.

Access Specifications

Until now we have only used private and public access specifiers within a class. Giving all data members private status ensured that they can only be accessed by either class member functions or friends. This restricted access prevents access by any non-class functions (except friends), *which also precludes access by any derived class functions*. This is a sensible restriction because if it did not exist anyone could "jump around" the private restriction by simply deriving a class.

To retain a restricted type of access across derived classes, C++ provides a third access specification—protected. A protected access behaves identically to private access in that it only permits member or friend function access, but it permits this restriction to be inherited by any derived class. The derived class then defines the type of inheritance it is willing to take on, subject to the base class's access restrictions. This is done by the class-access specifier, which is listed after the colon at the start of its declaration section. Table 10.3 lists the resulting derived class member access based on the base class member specifications and the derived class-access specifier.

Table 10.3 Inherited Access Restrictions

Base Class Member	Derived Class Access	Derived Class Member
`private` →	`: private` →	`inaccessible`
`protected` →	`: private` →	`private`
`public` →	`: private` →	`private`
`private` →	`: public` →	`inaccessible`
`protected` →	`: public` →	`protected`
`public` →	`: public` →	`public`
`private` →	`: protected` →	`inaccessible`
`protected` →	`: protected` →	`protected`
`public` →	`: protected` →	`protected`

Using Table 10.3 it can be seen (shaded region), that if the base class member has a protected access and the derived class specifier is `public`, then the derived class member will be protected to its class. Similarly, if the base class has a public access and the derived class specifier is `public`, the derived class member will be public. As this is the most commonly used type of specification for base class data and function members respectively, it is the one we will use. This means that for all classes intended for use as a base class we will use a `protected` data member access in place of a `private` designation.

An Example

To illustrate the process of deriving one class from another we will derive a `Cylinder` class from a base `Circle` class. The definition of the `Circle` class is:

```
// class declaration

class Circle
{
  protected:
    double radius;
  public:
    Circle(double = 1.0);  // constructor
    double calcval();
};

// class implementation

// constructor
Circle::Circle(double r)  // constructor
{
  radius = r;
}

// calculate the area of a circle
double Circle::calcval()
{
  return(PI * radius * radius);
}
```

Except for the substitution of the access specifier `protected` in place of the usual `private` specifier for the data member, this is a standard class definition. The only variable not defined is `PI`, which is used in the `calcval()` function. We will define this as

```
const double PI = 2.0 * asin(1.0);
```

This is simply a "trick" that forces the computer to return the value of `PI` accurate to as many decimal places as allowed by your computer. This value is obtained by taking the arcsin of 1.0, which is $\pi/2$, and multiplying the result by 2.

Having defined our base class, we can now extend it to a derived class. The definition of the derived class is

```
// class declaration where
// Cylinder is derived from Circle

class Cylinder : public Circle
{
  protected:
    double length;  // add one additional data member and
  public:           // two additional function members
```

```
  Cylinder(double r = 1.0, double l = 1.0) : Circle(r), length(l) {}
  double calcval();
};

// class implementation

double Cylinder::calcval()   // this calculates a volume
{
  return (length * Circle::calcval()); // note the base function call
}
```

This definition encompasses several important concepts relating to derived classes. First, as a derived class, `Cylinder` contains all of the data and function members of its base class, `Circle`, plus any additional members that it may add. In this particular case the `Cylinder` class consists of a `radius` data member, inherited from the `Circle` class, plus an additional `length` member. Thus, each `Cylinder` object contains *two* data members, as is illustrated in Figure 10.7.

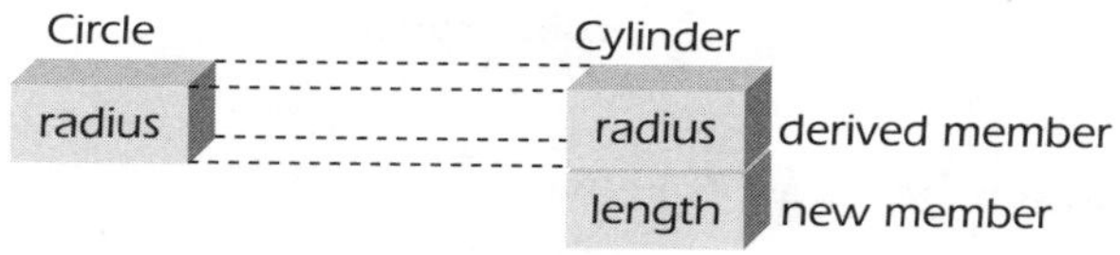

Figure 10.7 *Relationship between* `circle` *and* `cylinder` *data members.*

In addition to having two data members, the `Cylinder` class also inherits `Circle`'s function members. This is illustrated in the `Cylinder` constructor, which uses a base member initialization list (see Section 10.1) that specifically calls the `Circle` constructor. It is also illustrated in `Cylinder`'s `calcval()` function, which makes a call to `Circle::calcval()`.

In both classes the same function name, `calcval()`, has been specifically used to illustrate the overriding of a base function by a derived function. When a `Cylinder` object calls `calcval()` it is a request to use the `Cylinder` version of the function, while a `Circle` object call to `calcval()` is a request to use the `Circle` version. In this case the `Cylinder` class can only access the class version of `calcval()` using the scope resolution operator, as is done in the call `Circle::calcval()`. Program 10.13 uses these two classes within the context of a complete program. The output produced by Program 10.13 is:

```
The area of circle_1 is 3.14159
The area of circle_2 is 12.5664
The volume of cylinder_1 is 113.097

The area of circle_1 is now 28.2743
```

Program 10.13

```
#include <iostream>
#include <cmath>
using namespace std;

const double PI = 2.0 * asin(1.0);

// class declaration

class Circle
{
  protected:
    double radius;
  public:
    Circle(double = 1.0);  // constructor
    double calcval();
};
// implementation section for Circle

// constructor
Circle::Circle(double r)
{
  radius = r;
}

// calculate the area of a circle
double Circle::calcval()
{
  return(PI * radius * radius);
}

// class declaration for the derived class
// Cylinder which is derived from Circle
class Cylinder : public Circle
{
  protected:
    double length;  // add one additional data member and
  public:           // two additional function members
    Cylinder(double r = 1.0, double l = 1.0) : Circle(r), length(l) {}
    double calcval();
};
```

(Continued)

(Continued)

```
// implementation section for Cylinder

double Cylinder::calcval()   // this calculates a volume
{
  return (length * Circle::calcval()); // note the base function call
}
```

```
int main()
{
  Circle circle_1, circle_2(2);  // create two Circle objects
  Cylinder cylinder_1(3,4);      // create one Cylinder object

  cout << "The area of circle_1 is " << circle_1.calcval() << endl;
  cout << "The area of circle_2 is " << circle_2.calcval() << endl;
  cout << "The volume of cylinder_1 is " << cylinder_1.calcval() << endl;

  circle_1 = cylinder_1;  // assign a cylinder to a Circle

  cout << "\nThe area of circle_1 is now " << circle_1.calcval() << endl;

  return 0;
}
```

The first three output lines are all straightforward and are produced by the first three `cout` statements in the program. As the output shows, a call to `calcval()` using a `Circle` object activates the `Circle` version of this function, while a call to `calcval()` using a `Cylinder` object activates the `Cylinder` version.

The assignment statement `circle_1 = cylinder_1;` introduces another important relationship between a base and derived `class`: *A derived class object can be assigned to a base class object*. This should not be surprising because both base and derived classes share a common set of data member types. In this type of assignment it is only this set of data members, which consists of all the base class data members, that is assigned. Thus, as illustrated in Figure 10.8, our `Cylinder` to `Circle` assignment results in the following memberwise assignment:

```
circle_1.radius = cylinder_1.radius;
```

The length member of the `Cylinder` object is not used in the assignment because it has no equivalent variable in the `Circle` class. The reverse cast, from base to derived class, is not as simple and requires a constructor to correctly initialize the additional derived class members not in the base class.

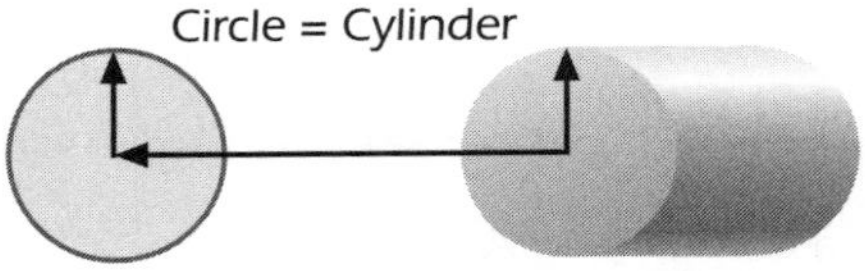

Figure 10.8 *Assignment from derived to base class.*

Before leaving Program 10.13, one additional point should be made. Although the `Circle` constructor was explicitly called using a base/member initialization list for the `Cylinder` constructor, an implicit call could also have been made. In the absence of an explicit derived class constructor the compiler will automatically call the default base class constructor first, before the derived class constructor is called. This works because the derived class contains all of the base class data members. In a similar fashion the destructor functions are called in the reverse order—first derived class and then base class.

Exercises 10.6

1. Define the following terms:
   a. inheritance
   b. base class
   c. derived class
   d. simple inheritance
   e. multiple inheritance
   f. class hierarchy
2. Describe the difference between a `private` and a `protected` class member.
3. What three features must a programming language provide for it to be classified as an object-oriented language?
4. a. Modify Program 10.13 to include a derived class named `Sphere` from the base `Circle` class. The only additional class members of `Sphere` should be a constructor and a `calcval()` function that returns the volume of the sphere. (NOTE: *volume* = 4/3 $\pi radius^3$)
   b. Include the class constructed for Exercise 4a in a working C++ program. Have your program call all of the member functions in the `Sphere` class.
5. a. Create a base class named `Point` that consists of an `x` and `y` coordinate. From this class derive a class named `Circle` having an additional data member named `radius`. For this derived class the `x` and `y` data members represent the center coordinates of a circle. The function members of the first class should consist of a constructor, an area function named area that returns zero, and a distance function that returns the distance between two points, where

$$\text{distance} = \sqrt{(x_2 - x_1)^2 + (y_2 - y_1)^2}$$

   Additionally, the derived class should have a constructor and an override function named `area` that returns the area of a circle.

b. Include the classes constructed for Exercise 5a in a working C++ program. Have your program call all of the member functions in each class. In addition call the base class `distance` function with two `Circle` objects and explain the result returned by the function.

6. a. Using the classes constructed for Exercise 5a, derive a class named `Cylinder` from the derived `Circle` class. The `Cylinder` class should have a constructor and a member function named `area` that determines the surface area of the cylinder. For this function use the algorithm $surface\ area = 2\ \pi\ r\ (l + r)$, where r is the radius of the cylinder and l is the length.

b. Include the classes constructed for Exercise 6a in a working C++ program. Have your program call all of the member functions in the `Cylinder` class.

c. What do you think might be the result if the base class `distance()` function was called with two `Cylinder` objects?

7. a. Create a base class named `Rectangle` that contains length and width data members. From this class derive a class named `Box` having an additional data member named `depth`. The function members of the base `Rectangle` class should consist of a constructor and an area function. The derived `Box` class should have a constructor, a volume function, and an override function named `area` that returns the surface area of the box.

b. Include the classes constructed for Exercise 7a in a working C++ program. Have your program call all of the member functions in each class and explain the result when the `distance()` function is called using a `Box` object.

10.7 POLYMORPHISM

The overriding of a base member function using an overloaded derived member function, as was illustrated by the `calcval()` function in Program 10.13, is an example of polymorphism. **Polymorphism** permits the same function name to invoke one response in objects of a base class and another response in objects of a derived class. In some cases, however, this method of overriding does not work as one might desire. To understand why this is so, consider Program 10.14.

Program 10.14

```
#include <iostream>
#include <cmath>
using namespace std;
```

(Continued)

(Continued)

```
// class declaration for the base class

class One
{
  protected:
    double a;
  public:
    One(double = 2.0);    // constructor
    double f1(double);    // a member function
    double f2(double);    // another member function
};

// class implementation for One

One::One(double val)   // constructor
{
  a = val;
}

double One::f1(double num)  // a member function
{
  return(num/2);
}
double One::f2(double num)  // another member function
{
  return( pow(f1(num),2) );  // square the result of f1()
}

// class declaration for the derived class

class Two : public One
{
  public:
    double f1(double);    // this overrides class One's f1()
};

// class implementation for Two

double Two::f1(double num)
{
  return(num/3);
}
```

(Continued)

(Continued)

```
int main()
{
  One object_1;  // object_1 is an object of the base class
  Two object_2;  // object_2 is an object of the derived class

    // call f2() using a base class object call
  cout << "The computed value using a base class object call is "
       << object_1.f2(12) << endl;

    // call f2() using a derived class object call
  cout << "The computed value using a derived class object call is "
       << object_2.f2(12) << endl;

  return 0;
}
```

The output produced by this program is

```
The computed value using a base class object call is 36
The computed value using a derived class object call is 36
```

As this output shows, the same result is obtained no matter which object type calls the `f2()` function. This result is produced because the derived class does not have an override to the base class `f2()` function. Thus, both calls to `f2()` result in the base class `f2()` function being called.

Once invoked, the base class `f2()` function will always call the base class version of `f1()` rather than the derived class override version. This behavior is due to a process referred to as **function binding**. In normal function calls static binding is used. In **static binding** the determination of which function is called is made at compile time. Thus, when the compiler first encounters the `f1()` function in the base class it makes the determination that whenever `f2()` is called, either from a base or derived class object, it will subsequently call the base class `f1()` function.

In place of static binding we would like a binding method that is capable of determining which function should be invoked at run time, based on the object type making the call. This type of binding is referred to as **dynamic binding**. To achieve dynamic binding C++ provides virtual functions.

A **virtual function** specification tells the compiler to create a pointer to a function, but to not fill in the value of the pointer until the function is actually called. Then, at run time, *and based on the object making the call*, the appropriate function address is used. Creating a **virtual** function is extremely easy—all that is required is that the keyword `virtual` be placed before the function's return type in the declaration section. For example, consider Program 10.15, which is identical to Program 10.14 except for the virtual declaration of the `f1()` function.

Program 10.15

```
#include <iostream>
#include <cmath>
using namespace std;

// class declaration for the base class

class One
{
  protected:
    double a;

  public:
    One(double = 2.0);    // constructor
    virtual double f1(double);    // a member function
    double f2(double);    // another member function
};

// class implementation for One

One::One(double val)    // constructor
{
  a = val;
}

double One::f1(double num)  // a member function
{
  return(num/2);
}

double One::f2(double num)  // another member function
{
  return( pow(f1(num),2) );  // square the result of f1()
}

// class declaration for the derived class

class Two : public One
{
  public:
    virtual double f1(double);    // this overrides class One's f1()
};

// class implementation for Two
```

(Continued)

(Continued)

```
double Two::f1(double num)
{
  return(num/3);
}

int main()
{
  One object_1;  // object_1 is an object of the base class
  Two object_2;  // object_2 is an object of the derived class

    // call f2() using a base class object call
  cout << "The computed value using a base class object call is "
       << object_1.f2(12) << endl;

    // call f2() using a derived class object call
  cout << "The computed value using a derived class object call is "
       << object_2.f2(12) << endl;

  return 0;
}
```

The output produced by Program 10.15 is

```
The computed value using a base class object call is 36
The computed value using a derived class object call is 16
```

As illustrated by this output, the `f2()` function now calls different versions of the overloaded `f1()` function based on the object type making the call. This selection, based on the object making the call, is the classic definition of polymorphic function behavior and is caused by the dynamic binding imposed on `f1()` by virtue of its being a virtual function.

Once a function is declared as virtual *it remains virtual for the next derived class with or without a virtual declaration in the derived class*. Thus, the second virtual declaration in the derived class is not strictly needed, but should be included both for clarity and to ensure that any subsequently derived classes correctly inherit the function. Consider the inheritance diagram illustrated in Figure 10.9, where class `C` is derived from class `B` and class `B` is derived from class `A`.[9] In this situation, if function `f1()` is virtual in class `A`, but is not declared in class `B`, it will not be virtual in class `C`. The only other requirement is that once a function has been declared as virtual the return type and parameter list of all subsequent derived class override versions *must be* the same.

[9] By convention, as previously noted in Section 10.6, arrows always point from the derived class to the base class.

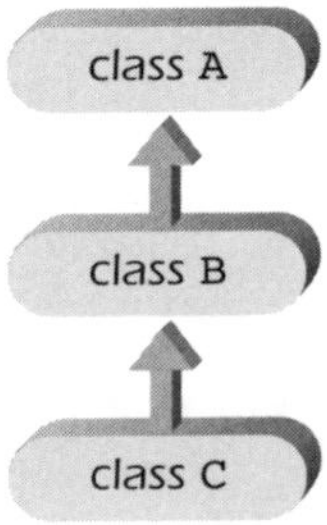

Figure 10.9 *An inheritance diagram.*

Exercises 10.7

1. Enter and execute both Program 10.14 and 10.15 on your computer so that you understand the relationship between function calls in each program.
2. Describe the two methods C++ provides for implementing polymorphism.
3. Describe the difference between static binding and dynamic binding.
4. Describe the difference between a virtual function and a nonvirtual function.
5. Describe what polymorphism is and provide an example of polymorphic behavior.
6. Discuss, with reasons, whether the multiplication operator provided for both the integer and double-precision built-in types is an example of overloading or polymorphism.

10.8 COMMON PROGRAMMING ERRORS

1. Using a user-defined assignment operator in a multiple assignment expression when the operator has not been defined to return an object.
2. Using the keyword `static` when defining either a static data or function member. Here, the `static` keyword should be used only within the class declaration section.
3. Using the keyword `friend` when defining a friend function. The `friend` keyword should be used only within the class declaration section.
4. Failing to instantiate static data members before creating class objects that must access these data members.
5. Attempting to redefine an operator's meaning as it applies to C++'s built-in data types.
6. Redefining an overloaded operator to perform a function not indicated by its conventional meaning. Although this will work, it is an example of extremely bad programming practice.

7. Attempting to make a conversion operator function a friend, rather than a member function.

8. Attempting to specify a return type for a member conversion operator function.

9. Attempting to override a virtual function without using the same type and number of arguments as the original function.

10. Using the keyword `virtual` in the class implementation section. Functions are only declared as `virtual` in the class declaration section.

10.9 CHAPTER SUMMARY

1. An assignment operator may be declared for a class with the function prototype

   ```
   void operator=(className&);
   ```

   Here, the argument is a reference to the class name. The return type of void precludes using this operator in multiple assignment expressions such as `a = b = c`.

2. A type of initialization that closely resembles assignment occurs in C++ when one object is initialized using another object of the same class. The constructor that performs this type of initialization is called a *copy constructor* and has the function prototype

   ```
   className(const className& );
   ```

   This is frequently represented using the notation *X(X&)*.

3. Each class has an associated class scope, which is defined by the brace pair, `{}`, containing the class declaration. Data and function members are local to the scope of their class and can only be used by objects declared for the class. If a global variable name is reused within a class, the global variable is hidden by the class variable. Within the scope of the class variable the global variable may be accessed using the scope resolution operator, `::`.

4. For each class object a separate set of memory locations is reserved for all data members, except those declared as `static`. A static data member is a shared by all class objects and provides a means of communication between objects. Static data members must be declared as such within the class declaration section and are defined outside of the declaration section.

5. `static` function members apply to the class as a whole, rather than individual objects. As such, a `static` function member can access only `static` data members and other `static` function members. Any `static` function members must be declared as such within the class declaration section and are defined outside of the declaration section.

6. A nonmember function may access a class's `private` data members if it is granted friend status by the class. This is accomplished by declaring the function as a friend within the class's declaration section. Thus, it is always the class that determines which nonmember functions are friends; a function can never confer friend status on itself.

7. User-defined operators can be constructed for classes using member operator functions. An operator function has the form *operator<symbol>*, where <symbol> is one of the following:

```
()   []   ->   new   delete   ++   --   !   ~   *   /   %   +   -
<<   >>   <   <=   >   >=   ++ !=   &&  ||   &   ^   |   =   +=
-=   *=   /=   %=   &=   ^=   |=   <<= >>=   ,
```

   For example, the function prototype `Date operator+(int);` declares that the addition operator will be defined to accept an integer and return a `Date` object.

8. User-defined operators may be called in either of two ways—as a conventional function with arguments or as an operator expression. For example, for an operator having the header line

```
Date Date::operator+(int)
```

   if `dte` is an object of type `Date`, the following two calls produce the same effect:

```
dte.operator+(284)
dte + 284
```

9. Operator functions may also be written as friend functions. The equivalent friend version of a member operator function will always contain an additional class reference that is not required by the member function.

10. There are four categories of data type conversions. They are conversions from

   - Built-in types to built-in types
   - Built-in types to user-defined (class) types
   - User-defined (class) types to built-in types
   - User-defined (class) types to user-defined (class) types

   Built-in to built-in type conversions are done using C++'s implicit conversion rules or explicitly using casts. Built-in to user-defined type conversions are done using type conversion constructors. Conversions from user-defined types to either built-in or other user-defined types are done using conversion operator functions.

11. A **type conversion constructor** is a constructor whose first argument is not a member of its class and whose remaining arguments, if any, have default values.

12. A **conversion operator function** is a member operator function having the name of a built-in data type or class. It has no explicit arguments or return type; rather, the return type is the name of the function.

13. **Inheritance** is the capability of deriving one class from another class. The initial class used as the basis for the derived class is referred to as the base, parent, or superclass. The derived class is referred to as either the derived, child, or subclass.

14. Base class functions can be overridden by derived class functions with the same name. The override function is simply an overloaded version of the base member function defined in the derived class.

15. **Polymorphism** is the capability of having the same function name invoke different responses based on the object making the function call. It can be accomplished using either override functions or virtual functions.

16. In **static binding** the determination of which function is invoked is made at compile time. In **dynamic binding** the determination is made at run time.

17. A **virtual function** specification designates that dynamic binding should take place. The specification is made in the function's prototype by placing the keyword `virtual` before the function's return type. Once a function has been declared as `virtual` it remains so for all derived classes as long as there is a continuous trail of function declarations through the derived chain of classes.

Part Three
Data Structures

CHAPTERS

CHAPTER 11

Arrays

TOPICS

The variables that we have used so far have all had a common characteristic: each variable could only be used to store a single value at a time. For example, although the variables `key`, `count`, *and* `grade` *declared in the statements*

```
char key;
int count;
double grade;
```

are of different data types, each variable can only store one value of the declared data type. These types of variables are called atomic variables. An **atomic variable**, *which is also referred to as a* **scalar variable**, *is a variable whose value cannot be further subdivided or separated into a legitimate data type.*

Frequently we may have a set of values, all of the same data type, that form a logical group. For example, Figure 11.1 illustrates three groups of items. The first group is a list of five double-precision temperatures, the second group is a list of four character codes, and the last group is a list of six integer voltages.

Temperatures	Codes	Voltages
95.75	Z	98
83.0	C	87
97.625	K	92
72.5	L	79
86.25		85
		72

Figure 11.1 Three lists of items.

A simple list containing individual items of the same data type is called a one-dimensional array. In this chapter we describe how one-dimensional arrays are declared, initialized, stored inside a computer, and used. Additionally, we explore the use of one-dimensional arrays with example programs and present the procedures for declaring and using multidimensional arrays.

11.1 ONE-DIMENSIONAL ARRAYS

A **one-dimensional array**, which is also referred to as a **single-dimensional array**, is a list of related values with the same data type that is stored using a single group name.[1] In C++, as in other computer languages, the group name is referred to as the **array name**. For example, consider the list of temperatures illustrated in Figure 11.2.

Temperatures
95.75
83.0
97.625
72.5
86.25

Figure 11.2 A list of temperatures.

[1]Note that lists can be implemented in a variety of ways. An array is simply one implementation of a list in which all of the list elements are of the same type and each element is stored consecutively in a set of contiguous memory locations.

All the temperatures in the list are floating-point numbers and must be declared as such. However, the individual items in the list do not have to be declared separately. The items in the list can be declared as a single unit and stored under a common variable name called the array name. For convenience, we will choose `temp` as the name for the list shown in Figure 11.2. To specify that `temp` is to store five individual floating-point values requires the declaration statement `double temp[5]`. Notice that this declaration statement gives the array (or list) name, the data type of the items in the array, and the number of items in the array. It is a specific example of the general array declaration statement having the syntax:

dataType arrayName[number-of-items]

Good programming practice requires defining the number-of-items in the array as a constant before declaring the array. Thus, the previous array declaration for `temp` would, in practice, be declared using two statements, such as:

```
const int NUMELS = 5; // define a constant for the number of items
double temp[NUMELS];   // declare the array
```

Other examples of array declarations using this two-line syntax are:

```
const int NUMELS = 6;
int volts[NUMELS];

const int ARRAYSIZE = 4;
char code[ARRAYSIZE];

const int SIZE = 100;
double amount[SIZE];
```

In these declaration statements, each array is allocated sufficient memory to hold the number of data items given in the declaration statement. Thus, the array named `volts` has storage reserved for six integers, the array named `code` has storage reserved for four characters, and the array named `amount` has storage reserved for 100 double-precision numbers. The constant identifiers, `NUMELS`, `ARRAYSIZE`, and `SIZE` are programmer-selected names.

Figure 11.3 illustrates the storage reserved for the `volts` and `code` arrays.

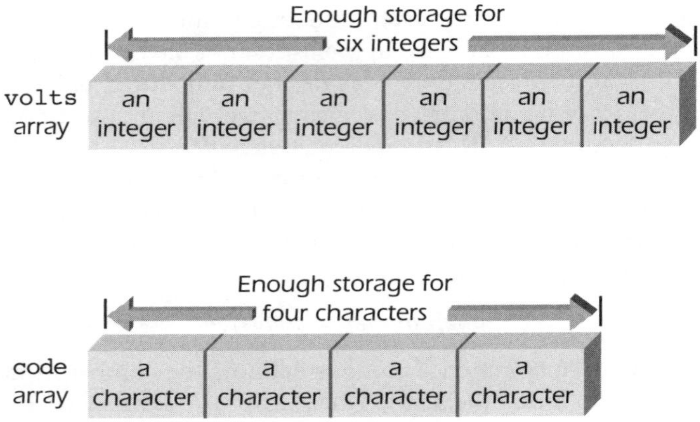

Figure 11.3 *The `volts` and `code` arrays in memory.*

Each item in an array is called an **element** or **component** of the array. The individual elements stored in the arrays illustrated in Figure 11.3 are stored sequentially, with the first array element stored in the first reserved location, the second element stored in the second reserved location, and so on until the last element is stored in the last reserved location. This contiguous storage allocation for the list is a key feature of arrays because it provides a simple mechanism for easily locating any single element in the list.

Since elements in the array are stored sequentially, any individual element can be accessed by giving the name of the array and the element's position. This position is called the element's ***index*** or ***subscript*** value (the two terms are synonymous). For a single-dimensional array, the first element has an index of 0, the second element has an index of 1, and so on. In C++, the array name and index of the desired element are combined by listing the index in braces after the array name. For example, given the declaration `double temp[5],`

`temp[0]` refers to the first temperature stored in the `temp` array

`temp[1]` refers to the second temperature stored in the `temp` array

`temp[2]` refers to the third temperature stored in the `temp` array

`temp[3]` refers to the fourth temperature stored in the `temp` array

`temp[4]` refers to the fifth temperature stored in the `temp` array

Figure 11.4 illustrates the `temp` array in memory with the correct designation for each array element. Each individual element is referred to as an **indexed variable** or a **subscripted variable**, since both a variable name and an index or subscript value must be used to reference the element. Remember that the index or subscript value gives *the position* of the element in the array.

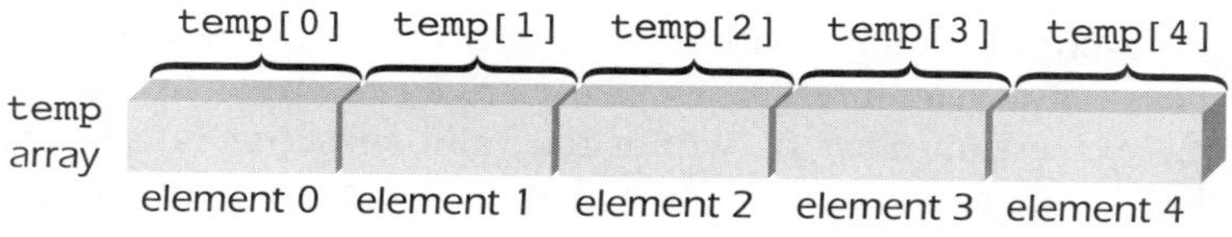

Figure 11.4 Identifying individual array elements.

The subscripted variable, `temp[0]`, is read as "`temp sub zero`" or "`tempzero`." This is a shortened way of saying "the temp array subscripted by zero." Similarly, `temp[1]` is read as either "`temp sub one`" or "`tempone`," `temp[2]` as either "`temp sub two`" or "`temptwo`," and so on.

Although it may seem unusual to reference the first element with an index of zero, doing so increases the computer's speed when it accesses array elements. Internally, unseen by the programmer, the computer uses the index as an offset from the array's starting position. As illustrated in Figure 11.5, the index tells the computer how many elements to skip, starting from the beginning of the array, to get to the desired element.

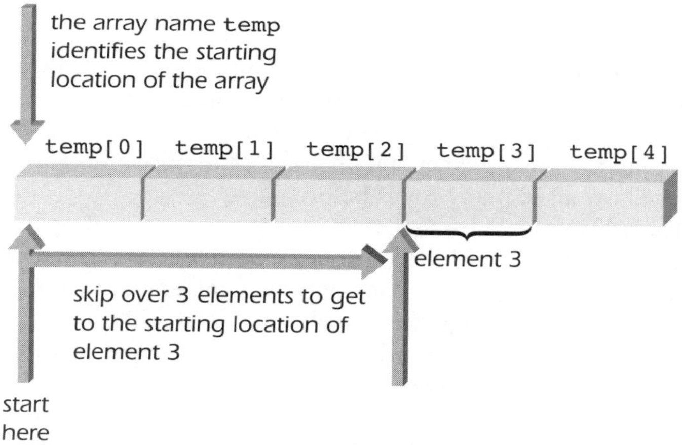

Figure 11.5 Accessing an individual array element—element 3.

Subscripted variables can be used anywhere that scalar variables are valid. Examples using the elements of the temp array are:

```
temp[0] = 95.75;
temp[1] = temp[0] - 11.0;
temp[2] = 5.0 * temp[0];
temp[3] = 79.0;
temp[4] = (temp[1] + temp[2] - 3.1) / 2.2;
sum = temp[0] + temp[1] + temp[2] + temp[3] + temp[4];
```

The subscript contained within brackets need not be an integer constant; any expression that evaluates to an integer may be used as a subscript.[2] In each case, of course, the value of the expression must be within the valid subscript range defined when the array is declared. For example, assuming that `i` and `j` are `int` variables, the following subscripted variables are valid:

```
temp[i]
temp[2*i]
temp[j-i]
```

One extremely important advantage of using integer expressions as subscripts is that it allows sequencing through an array by using a loop. This makes statements like

```
sum = temp[0] + temp[1] + temp[2] + temp[3] + temp[4];
```

unnecessary. The subscript values in this statement can be replaced by a `for` loop counter to access each element in the array sequentially. For example, the code

```
sum = 0;                      // initialize the sum to zero
for (i = 0; i < 5; i++)
  sum = sum + temp[i];        // add in a value
```

sequentially retrieves each array element and adds the element to `sum`. Here the variable `i` is used both as the counter in the `for` loop and as a subscript. As `i` increases by one each time through the loop, the next element in the array is referenced. The procedure for adding the array elements within the `for` loop is similar to the accumulation procedure we have used many times before.

The advantage of using a `for` loop to sequence through an array becomes apparent when working with larger arrays. For example, if the `temp` array contained 100 values rather than just five, simply changing the number 5 to 100 in the `for` statement is sufficient to sequence through the 100 elements and add each temperature to the sum.

As another example of using a `for` loop to sequence through an array, assume that we want to locate the maximum value in an array of 1000 elements named `volts`. The procedure we will use to locate the maximum value is to assume initially that the first element in the array is the largest number. Then, as we sequence through the array, the maximum is compared to each element. When an element with a higher value is located, that element becomes the new maximum. The following code does the job.

```
const int NUMELS = 1000;

maximum = volts[0];              // set the maximum to element zero
for (i = 1; i < NUMELS; i++)     // cycle through the rest of the array
  if (volts[i] > maximum)        // compare each element to the maximum
    maximum = volts[i];          // capture the new high value
```

In this code the `for` statement consists of one `if` statement. The search for a new maximum value starts with element 1 of the array and continues through the last element. Each element is compared to the current maximum, and when a higher value is encountered it becomes the new maximum.

[2]Note: Some compilers permit floating-point variables as subscripts; in these cases the floating-point value is truncated to an integer value.

Input and Output of Array Values

Individual array elements can be assigned values interactively using a `cin` stream object. Examples of individual data entry statements are:

```
cin >> temp[0];
cin >> temp[1] >> temp[2] >> temp[3];
cin >> temp[4] >> volts[6];
```

In the first statement a single value will be read and stored in the variable named `temp[0]`. The second statement will cause three values to be read and stored in the variables `temp[1]`, `temp[2]`, and `temp[3]`, respectively. Finally, the last `cin` statement can be used to read values into the variables `temp[4]` and `volts[6]`.

Alternatively, a `for` loop can be used to cycle through the array for interactive data input. For example, the code

```
const int NUMELS = 5;

for (i = 0; i < NUMELS; i++)
{
  cout << "Enter a temperature: ";
  cin  >> temp[i];
}
```

prompts the user for five temperatures. The first temperature entered is stored in `temp[0]`, the second temperature entered in `temp[1]`, and so on until five temperatures have been input.

One caution should be mentioned about storing data in an array. C++ does not check the value of the index being used (called a **bounds check**). If an array has been declared as consisting of 10 elements, for example, and you use an index of 12, which is outside the bounds of the array, C++ will not notify you of the error when the program is compiled. The program will attempt to access element 12 by skipping over the appropriate number of bytes from the start of the array. Usually this results in a program crash, but not always. If the referenced location itself contains a value of the correct data type, the new value will simply overwrite the value in the referenced memory locations. This leads to more errors, which are particularly troublesome to locate when the variable legitimately assigned to the storage location is used at a different point in the program.

During output, individual array elements can be displayed using the `cout` object or complete sections of the array can be displayed by including a `cout` statement within a for loop. Examples of this are

```
cout << volts[6];
```

and

```
cout << "The value of element " << i << " is " << temp[i];
```

Point of Information

Aggregate Data Types

In contrast to atomic types, such as integer and floating-point data, there are aggregate types. An aggregate type, which is also referred to as both a *structured type* and a *data structure*, is any type whose values can be decomposed and are related by some defined structure. Additionally, operations must be available for retrieving and updating individual values in the data structure.

Single-dimensional arrays are examples of a structured type. In a single-dimensional array, such as an array of integers, the array is composed of individual integer values, where integers are related by their position in the list. Indexed variables provide the means of accessing and modifying values in the array.

and

```
const int NUMELS = 20;

for (k = 5; k < NUMELS; k++)
  cout <<  k << "   " << amount[k] << endl;
```

The first statement displays the value of the subscripted variable `volts[6]`. The second statement displays the value of the subscript `i` and the value of `temp[i]`. Before this statement can be executed, `i` would have to have an assigned value. Finally, the last example includes a `cout` object within a `for` loop. Both the value of the index and the value of the elements from 5 to 20 are displayed.

Program 11.1 illustrates these input and output techniques using an array named `temp` that is defined to store five integer numbers. Included in the program are two `for` loops. The first `for` loop is used to cycle through each array element and allows the user to input individual array values. After five values have been entered, the second `for` loop is used to display the stored values.

Program 11.1

```
#include <iostream>
using namespace std;

int main()
{
  const int MAXTEMPS = 5;
  int i, temp[MAXTEMPS];

  for (i = 0; i < MAXTEMPS; i++)     // Enter the temperatures
  {
    cout << "Enter a temperature: ";
    cin  >> temp[i];
  }

  cout << endl;

  for (i = 0; i < MAXTEMPS; i++)     // Print the temperatures
    cout << "temperature " << i << " is " << temp[i] << endl;

  return 0;
}
```

A sample run of Program 11.1 follows:

```
Enter a temperature: 85
Enter a temperature: 90
Enter a temperature: 78
Enter a temperature: 75
Enter a temperature: 92

temperature 0 is 85
temperature 1 is 90
temperature 2 is 78
temperature 3 is 75
temperature 4 is 92
```

In reviewing the output produced by Program 11.1, pay particular attention to the difference between the index value displayed and the numerical value stored in the corresponding array element. The index value refers to the location of the element in the array, while the subscripted variable refers to the value stored in the designated location.

In addition to simply displaying the values stored in each array element, the elements can also be processed by appropriately referencing the desired element. For example, in Program 11.2, the value of each element is accumulated in a total, which is displayed upon completion of the individual display of each array element.

Program 11.2

```
#include <iostream>
using namespace std;

int main()
{
  const int MAXTEMPS = 5;
  int i, temp[MAXTEMPS], total = 0;

  for (i = 0; i < MAXTEMPS; i++)      // Enter the temperatures
  {
    cout << "Enter a temperature: ";
    cin  >> temp[i];
  }

  cout << "\nThe total of the temperatures";

  for (i = 0; i < MAXTEMPS; i++)      // Display and total the temperatures
  {
    cout << "   " << temp[i];
    total =  total + temp[i];
  }

  cout << " is " << total << endl;

  return 0;
}
```

A sample run of Program 11.2 follows:

```
Enter a temperature: 85
Enter a temperature: 90
Enter a temperature: 78
Enter a temperature: 75
Enter a temperature: 92

The total of the temperatures  85  90  78  75  92 is 420
```

Notice that in Program 11.2, unlike Program 11.1, only the values stored in each array element are displayed and not the index numbers. Although the second `for` loop was used to accumulate the total of each element, the accumulation could also have been accomplished in the first loop by placing the statement `total = total + temp[i];` after the `cin` statement used to enter a value. Also notice that the `cout` statement used to display the total is made outside of the second `for` loop, so that the total is displayed only once, after all values have been added to the total. If this `cout` statement were placed inside of the `for` loop, five totals would be displayed, with only the last displayed total containing the sum of all of the array values.

Exercises 11.1

1. Write array declarations for the following:
   a. a list of 100 double-precision voltages
   b. a list of 50 double-precision temperatures
   c. a list of 30 characters, each representing a code
   d. a list of 100 integer years
   e. a list of 32 double-precision velocities
   f. a list of 1000 double-precision distances
   g. a list of 6 integer code numbers

2. Write appropriate notation for the first, third, and seventh elements of the following arrays:
   a. `int grades[20]`
   b. `double volts[10]`
   c. `double amps[16]`
   d. `int dist[15]`
   e. `double velocity[25]`
   f. `double time[100]`

3. a. Write individual input statements using `cin` that can be used to enter values into the first, third, and seventh elements of each of the arrays declared in Exercises 2a through 2f.
   b. Write a `for` loop that can be used to enter values for the complete array declared in Exercises 2a through 2f.

4. a. Write individual output statements using `cout` that can be used to print the values from the first, third, and seventh elements of each of the arrays declared in Exercises 2a through 2f.
   b. Write a `for` loop that can be used to display values for the complete array declared in Exercises 2a through 2f.

5. List the elements that will be displayed by the following sections of code:
   a.
   ```
   for (m = 1; m <= 5; m++)
     cout << a[m] << " ";
   ```
   b.
   ```
   for (k = 1; k <= 5; k = k + 2)
     cout <<  a[k] << " ";
   ```
   c.
   ```
   for (j = 3; j <= 10; j++)
      cout << b[j] << " ";
   ```
   d.
   ```
   for (k = 3; k <= 12; k = k + 3)
      cout << b[k] << " ";
   ```
   e.
   ```
   for (i = 2; i < 11; i = i + 2)
      cout << c[i] << " ";
   ```

6. a. Write a program to input the following values into an array named `volts`: 11.95, 16.32, 12.15, 8.22, 15.98, 26.22, 13.54, 6.45, 17.59. After the data has been entered, have your program display the values.
   b. Repeat Exercise 6a, but after the data has been entered, have your program display it in the following form:

11.95	16.32	12.15
8.22	15.98	26.22
13.54	6.45	17.59

7. Write a program to input eight integer numbers into an array named `temp`. As each number is input, add the numbers into a total. After all numbers are input, display the numbers and their average.

8. a. Write a program to input 10 integer numbers into an array named `fmax` and determine the maximum value entered. Your program should contain only one loop and the maximum should be determined as array element values are being input. (*Hint*: Set the maximum equal to the first array element, which should be input before the loop used to input the remaining array values.)
   b. Repeat Exercise 8a, keeping track of both the maximum element in the array and the index number for the maximum. After displaying the numbers, print these two messages

```
The maximum value is:
This is element number ______ in the list of numbers
```

   Have your program display the correct values in place of the underlines in the messages.
   c. Repeat Exercise 8b, but have your program locate the minimum of the data entered.

9. a. Write a program to input the following integer numbers into an array named `grades`: 89, 95, 72, 83, 99, 54, 86, 75, 92, 73, 79, 75, 82, 73. As each number is input, add the numbers to a total. After all numbers are input and the total is obtained, calculate the average of the numbers and use the average to determine the deviation of each value from the average. Store each deviation in an array named `deviation`. Each deviation is obtained as the element value less the average of all the data. Have your program display each deviation alongside its corresponding element from the `grades` array.
   b. Calculate the variance of the data used in Exercise 9a. The variance is obtained by squaring each individual deviation and dividing the sum of the squared deviations by the number of deviations.

10. Write a program that specifies three one-dimensional arrays named `current`, `resistance`, and `volts`. Each array should be capable of holding 10 elements. Using a `for` loop, input values for the `current` and `resistance` arrays. The entries in the `volts` array should be the product of the corresponding values in the `current` and `resistance` arrays (thus, `volts[i] = current[i] * resistance[i]`). After all of the data has been entered, display the following output:

```
Current          Resistance          Volts
```

Under each column heading display the appropriate value.

11.2 Array Initialization

Array elements can be initialized within their declaration statements in the same manner as scalar variables, except that the initializing elements must be included in braces. Examples of such initializations are

```
int temp[5] = {98, 87, 92, 79, 85};
char codes[6] = {'s', 'a', 'm', 'p', 'l', 'e'};
double slopes[7] = {11.96, 6.43, 2.58, .86, 5.89, 7.56, 8.22};
```

Initializers are applied in the order they are written, with the first value used to initialize element 0, the second value used to initialize element 1, and so on, until all values have been used. Thus, in the declaration

```
int temp[5] = {98, 87, 92, 79, 85};
```

`temp[0]` is initialized to 98, `temp[1]` is initialized to 87, `temp[2]` is initialized to 92, `temp[3]` is initialized to 79, and `temp[4]` is initialized to 85.

Because white space is ignored in C++, initializations may be continued across multiple lines. For example, the declaration

```
int gallons[20] = {19, 16, 14, 19, 20, 18,   // initializing values
                   12, 10, 22, 15, 18, 17,   // may extend across
                   16, 14, 23, 19, 15, 18,   // multiple lines
                   21, 5};
```

uses four lines to initialize all of the array elements.

If the number of initializers is less than the declared number of elements listed in square brackets, the initializers are applied starting with array element 0. Thus, in the declaration

```
double length[7] = {7.8, 6.4, 4.9, 11.2};
```

only `length[0]`, `length[1]`, `length[2]`, and `length[3]` are initialized with the listed values. The other array elements will be initialized to zero.

Unfortunately, there is no method of either indicating repetition of an initialization value or initializing later array elements without first specifying values for earlier elements.

A unique feature of initializers is that the size of an array may be omitted when initializing values are included in the declaration statement. For example, the declaration

```
int gallons[] = {16, 12, 10, 14, 11};
```

reserves enough storage room for five elements. Similarly, the following two declarations are equivalent:

```
char codes[6] = {'s', 'a', 'm', 'p', 'l', 'e'};
char codes[] = {'s', 'a', 'm', 'p', 'l', 'e'};
```

Both of these declarations set aside six character locations for an array named `codes`. An interesting and useful simplification can also be used when initializing character arrays. For example, the declaration

```
char codes[] = "sample";   // no braces or commas
```

uses the string `"sample"` to initialize the `codes` array. Recall that a string is any sequence of characters enclosed in double quotes. This last declaration creates an array named `codes` having seven elements and fills the array with the seven characters illustrated in Figure 11.6. The first six characters, as expected, consist of the letters `s`, `a`, `m`, `p`, `l`, and `e`. The last character, which is the escape sequence `\0`, is called the **null character**. The null character is automatically appended to all strings that are used to initialize a character array and is what distinguishes a C-string from a `string` class string. This character has an internal storage code that is numerically equal to zero (the storage code for the zero character has a numerical value of decimal 48, so the two cannot be confused by the computer), and is used as a marker, or sentinel, to mark the end of a string.

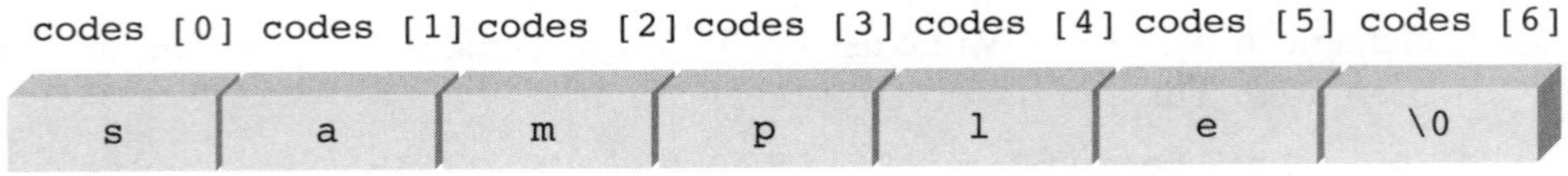

Figure 11.6 Initializing a character array with a string adds a terminating \0 character.

Once values have been assigned to array elements, either through initialization within the declaration statement or using interactive input, the array elements can be processed as described in the previous section. For example, Program 11.3 illustrates the initialization of array elements within the declaration of the array and then uses a `for` loop to locate the maximum value stored in the array.

Program 11.3

```
#include <iostream>
using namespace std;

int main()
{
  const int MAXELS = 5;

  int i, max, nums[MAXELS] = {2, 18, 1, 27, 16};

  max = nums[0];

  for (i = 1; i < MAXELS; i++)
    if (max < nums[i])
      max = nums[i];

  cout << "The maximum value is " << max << endl;

  return 0;
}
```

The output produced by Program 11.3 is

```
The maximum value is 27
```

Exercises 11.2

1. Write array declarations, including initializers, for the following
   a. a list of 10 integer voltages: 89, 75, 82, 93, 78, 95, 81, 88, 77, 82
   b. a list of five double-precision slopes: 11.62, 13.98, 18.45, 12.68, 14.76
   c. a list of 100 double-precision distances; the first six distances are 6.29, 6.95, 7.25, 7.35, 7.40, 7.42
   d. a list of 64 double-precision temperatures; the first 10 temperatures are 78.2, 69.6, 68.5, 83.9, 55.4, 67.0, 49.8, 58.3, 62.5, 71.6
   e. a list of 15 character codes; the first seven codes are f, j, m, q, t, w, z
2. Write an array declaration statement that stores the following values in an array named `volts`: 16.24, 18.98, 23.75, 16.29, 19.54, 14.22, 11.13, 15.39. Include these statements in a program that displays the values in the array.
3. Write a program that uses an array declaration statement to initialize the following numbers in an array named `slopes`: 17.24, 25.63, 5.94, 33.92, 3.71, 32.84, 35.93, 18.24, 6.92. Your program should locate and display both the maximum and minimum values in the array.
4. Write a program that stores the following prices in an array named `resistance`: 16, 27, 39, 56, and 81. Your program should also create two arrays named `current` and `power`, each capable of storing five double-precision numbers. Using a `for` loop and a `cin` statement, have your program accept five user-input numbers into the `current` array when the program is run. Your program should store the product of the corresponding values of the square of the `current` array and the `resistance` array in the `power` array (for example, `power[1] = resistance[1] * pow(current[1],2)` and display the following output (fill in the table appropriately):

```
Resistance          Current          Power
16                     .               .
27                     .               .
39                     .               .
56                     .               .
81                     .               .
                                     ---------
Total:                                 .
```

5. a. Write a declaration to store the string `"This is a test"` into an array named `strtest`. Include the declaration in a program to display the message using the following loop:

   ```
   for (i = 0; i < NUMDISPLAY; i++)
     cout << strtest[i];
   ```

   where `NUMDISPLAY` is a named constant for the number 14.

   b. Modify the `for` statement in Exercise 5a to display only the array characters t, e, s, and t.

c. Include the array declaration written in Exercise 5a in a program that uses the `cout` object to display characters in the array. For example, the statement `cout << strtest;` will cause the string stored in the `strtest` array to be displayed. Using this statement requires that the last character in the array is the end of string marker `\0`.

d. Repeat Exercise 5a using a `while` loop. (*Hint:* Stop the loop when the `\0` escape sequence is detected. The expression `while (strtest[i] != '\0')` can be used.)

11.3 DECLARING AND PROCESSING TWO-DIMENSIONAL ARRAYS

A **two-dimensional array,** which is sometimes referred to as a table, consists of both rows and columns of elements. For example, the array of numbers

8	16	9	52
3	15	27	6
14	25	2	10

is called a two-dimensional array of integers. This array consists of three rows and four columns. To reserve storage for this array, both the number of rows and the number of columns must be included in the array's declaration. Calling the array `val`, the correct specification for this two-dimensional array is

```
int val[3][4];
```

Similarly, the declarations

```
double volts[10][5];
char code[6][26];
```

declare that the array `volts` consists of 10 rows and 5 columns of floating-point numbers and that the array `code` consists of 6 rows and 26 columns, with each element capable of holding one character.

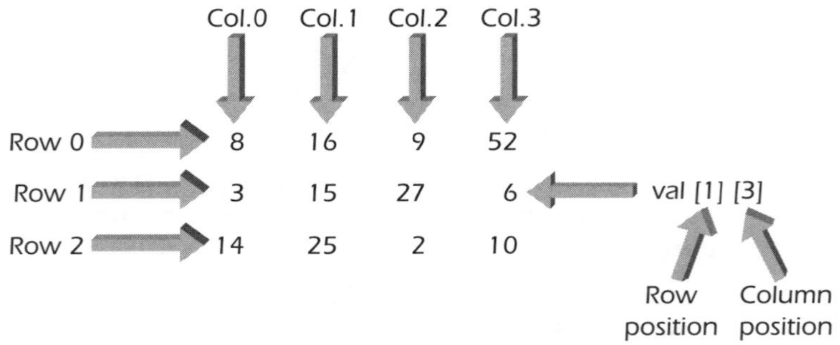

Figure 11.7 Each array element is identified by its row and column position.

To locate each element in a two-dimensional array, an element is identified by its position in the array. As illustrated in Figure 11.7, the term `val[1][3]` uniquely identifies the element in row 1, column 3. As with single-dimensional array variables, double-dimensional array variables can be used anywhere that scalar variables are valid. Examples using elements of the `val` array are

```
watts = val[2][3];
val[0][0] = 62;
newnum = 4 * (val[1][0] - 5);
sumRow0 = val[0][0] + val[0][1] + val[0][2] + val[0][3];
```

The last statement causes the values of the four elements in row 0 to be added and the sum to be stored in the scalar variable `sumRow0`.

As with single-dimensional arrays, two-dimensional arrays can be initialized from within their declaration statements. This is done by listing the initial values within braces and separating them by commas. Additionally, braces can be used to separate individual rows. For example, the declaration

```
int val[3][4] = { {8,16,9,52},
                  {3,15,27,6},
                  {14,25,2,10} };
```

declares `val` to be an array of integers with three rows and four columns, with the initial values given in the declaration. The first set of internal braces contains the values for row 0 of the array, the second set of internal braces contains the values for row 1, and the third set of braces the values for row 2.

Although the commas in the initialization braces are always required, the inner braces can be omitted. Thus, the initialization for `val` may be written as

```
int val[3][4] = {8,16,9,52,
                  3,15,27,6,
                 14,25,2,10};
```

The separation of initial values into rows in the declaration statement is not necessary since the compiler assigns values beginning with the `[0][0]` element and proceeds row by row to fill in the remaining values. Thus, the initialization

```
int val[3][4] = {8,16,9,52,3,15,27,6,14,25,2,10};
```

is equally valid but does not clearly illustrate to another programmer where one row ends and another begins.

As illustrated in Figure 11.8, the initialization of a two-dimensional array is done in row order. First, the elements of the first row are initialized, then the elements of the second row are initialized, and so on, until the initializations are completed. This row ordering is also the same ordering used to store two-dimensional arrays. That is, array element `[0][0]` is stored first, followed by element `[0][1]`, followed by element `[0][2]` and so on. Following the first row's elements are the second row's elements, and so on for all the rows in the array.

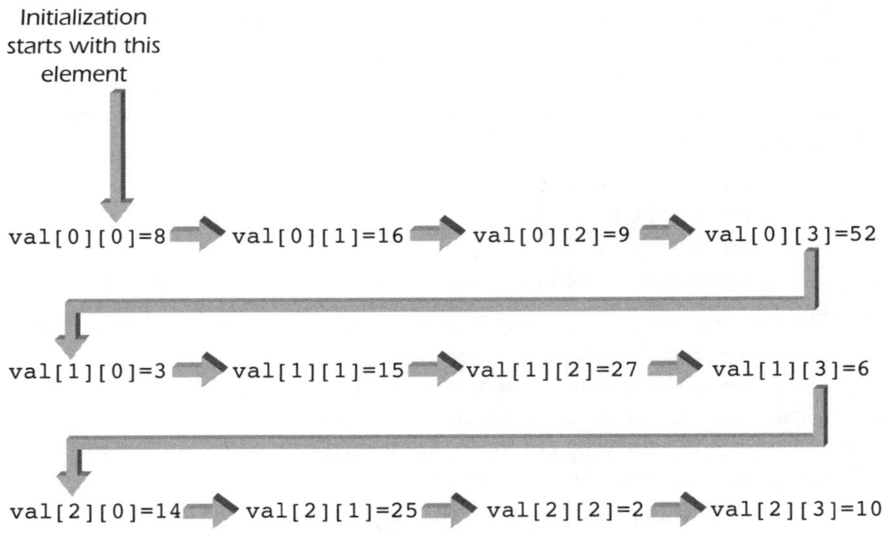

Figure 11.8 Storage and initialization of the `val` array.

As with single-dimensional arrays, two-dimensional arrays may be displayed by individual element notation or by using loops (either `while` or `for`). This is illustrated by Program 11.4, which displays all of the elements of a 3-by-4 two-dimensional array using two different techniques. Notice in Program 11.4 that we have used constants to define the array's rows and columns.

The display produced by Program 11.4 follows.

```
Display of val array by explicit element
   8  16   9  52
   3  15  27   6
  14  25   2  10
Display of val array using a nested for loop
   8  16   9  52
   3  15  27   6
  14  25   2  10
```

The first display of the `val` array produced by Program 11.4 is constructed by explicitly designating each array element. The second display of array element values, which is identical to the first, is produced using a nested `for` loop. Nested loops are especially useful when dealing with two-dimensional arrays because they allow the programmer to designate and cycle through each element easily. In Program 11.4, the variable `i` controls the outer loop and the variable `j` controls the inner loop. Each pass through the outer loop corresponds to a single row, with the inner loop supplying the appropriate column elements. After a complete row is printed, a new line is started for the next row. The effect is a display of the array in a row-by-row fashion.

Program 11.4

```
#include <iostream>
#include <iomanip>
using namespace std;

int main()
{

  const int NUMROWS = 3;
  const int NUMCOLS = 4;

  int i, j;
  int val[NUMROWS][NUMCOLS] = {8,16,9,52,3,15,27,6,14,25,2,10};

  cout << "\nDisplay of val array by explicit element"
       << endl << setw(4) << val[0][0] << setw(4) << val[0][1]
       << setw(4) << val[0][2] << setw(4) << val[0][3]
       << endl << setw(4) << val[1][0] << setw(4) << val[1][1]
       << setw(4) << val[1][2] << setw(4) << val[1][3]
       << endl << setw(4) << val[2][0] << setw(4) << val[2][1]
       << setw(4) << val[2][2] << setw(4) << val[2][3];

  cout << "\n\nDisplay of val array using a nested for loop";

  for (i = 0; i < NUMROWS; i++)
  {
    cout << endl;       // print a new line for each row
    for (j = 0; j < NUMCOLS; j++)
      cout << setw(4) <<  val[i][j];
  }

  cout << endl;

  return 0;
}
```

Once two-dimensional array elements have been assigned, array processing can begin. Typically, `for` loops are used to process two-dimensional arrays because, as was previously noted, they allow the programmer to designate and cycle through each array element easily. For example, the nested `for` loop illustrated in Program 11.5 is used to multiply each element in the `val` array by the scalar number 10 and display the resulting value.

Following is the output produced by Program 11.5:

```
Display of multiplied elements
   80  160   90  520
   30  150  270   60
  140  250   20  100
```

Program 11.5

```
#include <iostream>
#include <iomanip>
using namespace std;

int main()
{
  const int NUMROWS = 3;
  const int NUMCOLS = 4;

  int i, j;
  int val[NUMROWS][NUMCOLS] = {8,16,9,52,
                                3,15,27,6,
                               14,25,2,10};

// multiply each element by 10 and display it
  cout << "\nDisplay of multiplied elements";
  for (i = 0; i < NUMROWS; i++)
  {
    cout << endl;   // start each row on a new line
    for (j = 0; j < NUMCOLS; j++)
    {
      val[i][j] = val[i][j] * 10;
      cout << setw(5) << val[i][j];
    }  // end of inner loop
  }    // end of outer loop
  cout << endl;

  return 0;
}
```

Larger Dimensional Arrays

Although arrays with more than two dimensions are not commonly used, C++ does allow any number of dimensions to be declared. This is done by listing the maximum size of all dimensions for the array. For example, the declaration `int response [4][10][6];` declares a three-dimensional array. The first element in the array is designated as `response[0][0][0]` and the last element as `response[3][9][5]`.

Conceptually, as illustrated in Figure 11.9, a three-dimensional array can be viewed as a book of data tables. Using this visualization, the first index can be thought of as the location of the desired row in a table, the second index value as the desired column, and the third index value, which is often called the "rank," as the page number of the selected table.

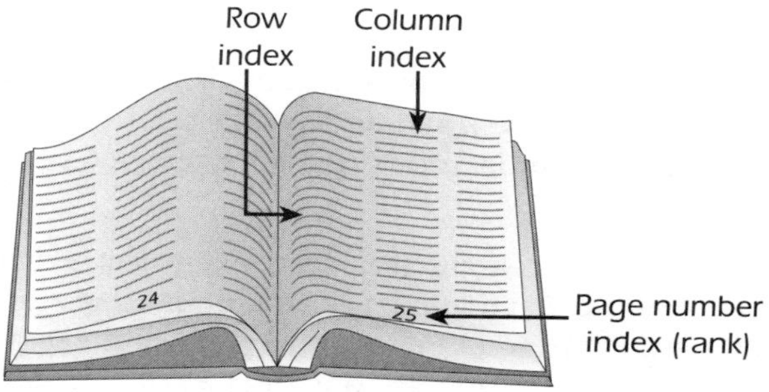

Figure 11.9 *Representation of a three-dimensional array.*

Similarly, arrays of any dimension can be declared. Conceptually, a four-dimensional array can be represented as a shelf of books, where the fourth dimension is used to declare a desired book on the shelf, and a five-dimensional array can be viewed as a book case filled with books where the fifth dimension refers to a selected shelf in the book case. Using the same analogy, a six-dimensional array can be considered as a single row of book cases where the sixth dimension references the desired bookcase in the row; a seven-dimensional array can be considered as multiple rows of book cases where the seventh dimension references the desired row, and so on. Alternatively, arrays of three, four, five, six, etc. dimensional arrays can be viewed as mathematical *n*-tuples of order three, four, five, six, etc., respectively.

Exercises 11.3

1. Write appropriate specification statements for

a. an array of integers with 6 rows and 10 columns
b. an array of integers with 2 rows and 5 columns
c. an array of characters with 7 rows and 12 columns
d. an array of characters with 15 rows and 7 columns
e. an array of double-precision numbers with 10 rows and 25 columns
f. an array of double-precision numbers with 16 rows and 8 columns

2. Determine the output produced by the following program:

```
#include <iostream>
using namespace std;

int main()
{
  int i, j, val[3][4] = {8,16,9,52,3,15,27,6,14,25,2,10};
```

```
    for (i = 0; i < 3; ++i)
      for (j = 0; j < 4; ++j)
        cout << "    " << val[i][j];

    return 0;
  }
```

3. a. Write a C++ program that adds the values of all elements in the `val` array used in Exercise 2 and displays the total.
   b. Modify the program written for Exercise 3a to display the total of each row separately.

4. Write a C++ program that adds equivalent elements of the two-dimensional arrays named `first` and `second`. Both arrays should have two rows and three columns. For example, element `[1][2]` of the resulting array should be the sum of `first[1][2]` and `second[1][2]`. The `first` and `second` arrays should be initialized as follows:

```
      FIRST                    SECOND
16    18    23           24    52    77
54    91    11           16    19    59
```

5. a. Write a C++ program that finds and displays the maximum value in a two-dimensional array of integers. The array should be declared as a 4-by-5 array of integers and initialized with the data 16, 22, 99, 4, 18, –258, 4, 101, 5, 98, 105, 6, 15, 2, 45, 33, 88, 72, 16, 3
   b. Modify the program written in Exercise 5a so that it also displays the maximum value's row and column subscript numbers.

6. Write a C++ program to select the values in a four by five array of positive integers in increasing order and store the selected values in the single-dimensional array named sort. Use the data statement given in Exercise 5a to initialize the two-dimensional array.

7. a. An engineer has constructed a two dimensional array of real numbers having 3 rows and 5 columns. This array currently contains the test voltages of an amplifier. Write a C++ program that interactively inputs 15 array values and then determines the total number of voltages in the ranges less than 60, greater than or equal to 60 and less than 70, greater than or equal to 70 and less than 80, greater than or equal to 80 and less than 90, and greater or equal to 90.
   b. Entering 15 voltages each time the program written for Exercise 7a is run is cumbersome. What method, therefore, is appropriate for initializing the array during the testing phase?
   c. How might the program you wrote for Exercise 7a be modified to include the case of no voltage being present? That is, what voltage could be used to indicate an invalid voltage and how would your program have to be modified to exclude counting such a voltage?

11.4 APPLICATIONS

Arrays are extremely useful in any application that requires multiple passes through the same set of data elements. Two such applications are presented in this section. The first application is a statistical data analysis requiring two passes through the data. The first pass is used to input the list and determine the average of the data, while the second pass uses the average to determine a standard deviation. The second application presents a simple but elegant method of plotting data on either a video screen or standard printer. Here a first pass is used to both initialize the array with the data points that are to be plotted and to determine maximum and minimum array values. These values are then used to calculate an appropriate scaling factor to ensure that the final plot fits within the area of the video screen or paper. Finally, a second pass through the array is made to produce the plot.

Application 1: Statistical Analysis

A program is to be developed that accepts a list of a maximum of 100 voltages as input, determines both the average and standard deviation of the input voltages, and then displays the results.

Step 1 Analyze the Problem

The statement of the problem indicates that two output values are required: an average and a standard deviation. In Step 2 we will verify that we know how these values are to be calculated. The input item defined in the problem statement is a maximum of 100 voltages. This means that any number of voltages, from zero to 100 could be input by the user when the program is executed. To accommodate for this, we will have to ask the user how many voltages he or she intends to input. Thus, the first input will be the number of voltages that will subsequently be entered.

Step 2 Develop a Solution

The I/O specifications determined in Step 1 define that the user will enter two types of input: the number of voltages followed by the actual data. Based on this input the program is to calculate and display the average and standard deviation of the data. These output items are determined as follows:

Calculate the average by adding the voltages and dividing by the number of voltages that were added
Determine the standard deviation by

1. *Subtracting the average from each individual voltage: This results in a set of new numbers, each of which is called a **deviation***
2. *Square each deviation found in the previous step*
3. *Add the squared deviations and divide the sum by the number of deviations*
4. *The square root of the number found in the previous step is the standard deviation*

Notice that the calculation of the standard deviation requires the average, which means that the standard deviation can be calculated only after the average has been computed. This is the advantage of specifying the algorithm, in detail, before any coding is done; it ensures that all necessary inputs and requirements are discovered early in the programming process.

To ensure that we understand the required processing, we will do a hand calculation. For this calculation we will arbitrarily assume that the average and standard deviation of the following 10 voltages are to be determined: 98, 82, 67, 54, 78, 83, 95, 76, 68, and 63.

The average of this data is determined as

$$
\begin{aligned}
\text{Average} &= (98 + 82 + 67 + 54 + 78 + 83 + 95 + 76 + 68 + 63)/10 \\
&= 76.4
\end{aligned}
$$

The standard deviation is calculated by first determining the sum of the squared deviations. The standard deviation is then obtained by dividing the resulting sum by 10 and taking its square root.

$$
\begin{aligned}
\text{Sum of squared deviations} &= (98 - 76.4)^2 \\
&+ (82 - 76.4)^2 \\
&+ (67 - 76.4)^2 \\
&+ (54 - 76.4)^2 \\
&+ (78 - 76.4)^2 \\
&+ (83 - 76.4)^2 \\
&+ (95 - 76.4)^2 \\
&+ (76 - 76.4)^2 \\
&+ (68 - 76.4)^2 \\
&+ (63 - 76.4)^2 \\
&= 1730.4007 \\
\text{Standard deviation} &= \sqrt{1730.4007 / 10} \\
&= \sqrt{173.04007} \\
&= 13.154470
\end{aligned}
$$

Having specified the algorithm required of each function, we are now in a position to code them.

Step 3 Code the Solution

Program 11.6 presents the C++ version of the selected algorithm. Notice that the program uses one `for` loop to enter and sum the individual voltages and a second `for` loop to determine the sum of the squared deviations. Because calculation of the squared deviations requires the average, the standard deviation can be calculated only after the average has been computed. Notice also that the termination value of the loop counter in both `for` loops is `numvolts`, which is the number of voltages input by the user. The use of this argument gives the program its generality and allows it to be used for lists of any number of voltages, up to `NUMELS`, which is defined as 100 by the `const` statement.

Program 11.6

```
#include <iostream>
#include <iomanip>
#include <cmath>
using namespace std;

int main()
{

  const int NUMELS = 100;

  int i, numvolts;
  double volt[NUMELS];
  double average, stddev;
  double sumvolts = 0.0, sumdevs = 0.0;

  cout << "Enter the number of voltages to be analyzed: ";
  cin  >> numvolts;

  // read the input voltages and total them
  for (i = 0; i < numvolts; i++)
  {
      cout << "Enter voltage " << i+1 << ": ";
      cin  >> volt[i];
    sumvolts = sumvolts + volt[i];
  }
  // calculate and display the average
  average = sumvolts / numvolts;
  cout << "\nThe average of the voltages is "
       << setw(11) << setiosflags(ios::showpoint)
       << setprecision(8) << average << endl;

  // calculate and display the standard deviation
  for (i = 0; i < numvolts; i++)
     sumdevs = sumdevs + pow((volt[i] - average),2);
  stddev = sqrt(sumdevs/numvolts);
  cout << "The standard deviation of the voltages is "
       << setw(11) << setiosflags(ios::showpoint)
       << setprecision(8) << stddev << endl;

  return 0;

}
```

Step 4 Test and Correct the Program

A test run using Program 11.6 produced the following display:

```
Enter the number of voltages to be analyzed: 10
Enter voltage 1: 98
Enter voltage 2: 82
Enter voltage 3: 67
Enter voltage 4: 54
Enter voltage 5: 78
Enter voltage 6: 83
Enter voltage 7: 95
Enter voltage 8: 76
Enter voltage 9: 68
Enter voltage 10: 63

The average of the voltages is   76.400000
The standard deviation of the voltages is 13.154467
```

Although this result agrees with our previous hand calculation, testing is really not complete without verifying the calculation at the boundary points. In this case such a test consists of checking the calculation with all of the same values, such as all 0s and all 100s. Another simple test would be to use five 0s and five 100s. We leave these tests as an exercise.

Application 2: List Maintenance[3]

A common programming problem is to maintain a list in numerical or alphabetical order. For example, inventory part numbers are typically kept in numerical order, but telephone lists are kept in alphabetical order.

For this application, write a function that inserts a three-digit part number code within a list of part numbers. The list is maintained in increasing numerical order, and duplicate part number codes are not allowed. A maximum list size of 100 values is to be allocated and a sentinel value of 9999 will be used to indicate the end of the list. For example, if the current list contains nine part number codes, the tenth position in the list will contain the sentinel value.

Step 1 Analyze the Problem

The required output is an updated list of three-digit codes in which the new code has been inserted into the existing list. The input items for this function are the existing array of identification codes and the new code that is to be inserted into the list.

[3]This topic requires an understanding of passing arrays into a function (see Section 11.5).

Step 2 Develop a Solution

Insertion of a new part number into the existing list requires the following processing:

Determine where in the list the new code should be placed
This is done by comparing the new code to each value in the current list until a match is found, an identification code larger than the new code is located, or the end of the list is encountered
If the new code matches an existing code,
display a message that the code exists
Else
To make room for the new element in the array, move each element down one position. This is done by starting from the sentinel value and moving each item down one position until the desired position in the list is vacated
Insert the new code in the vacated position
Endif

To ensure we understand this algorithm, we will do a hand calculation. For this calculation, assume the list of identification codes consists of the numbers illustrated in Figure 11.10a. If the number code 142 is to be inserted into this list, it must be placed in the fourth position in the list after the number 136. To make room for the new code, all of the codes from the fourth position to the end of the list must be moved one position down as illustrated in Figure 11.10b. The move is always started from the end of the list and proceeds from the sentinel value back until the desired position in the list is reached. (If the copy proceeded forward from the fourth element, the number 144 would be reproduced in all subsequent locations until the sentinel value was reached.) After the movement of the necessary elements, the new code is inserted in the correct position. This creates the updated list shown in Figure 11.10c.

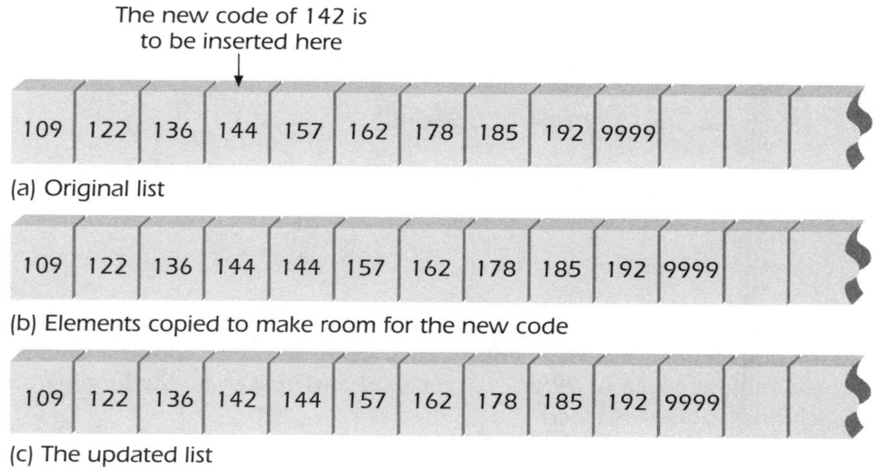

Figure 11.10 Updating an ordered list of identification numbers.

Step 3 Code the Solution

For this problem, we use the argument name `idcode` for the passed array of identification numbers and the argument name `newcode` for the new code number to be inserted into the array. Here, the passed array is used for receiving the original array of numbers and as the final, updated array. Internal to the function, we will use a variable named `newpos` to hold the position in the list where the new code is to be inserted and the variable named `endpos` to hold the position value of the sentinel. The variable `i` will be used as an index value.

Using these argument and variable names, the function named `insert()` performs the required processing. After accepting the array and the new code value as arguments, `insert()` performs the four major tasks described by the pseudocode selected in Step 2.

```
void insert(int idcode[], int newcode)
{
  int i, newpos, endpos;

  // find correct position to insert the new code
  i = 0;
  while (idcode[i] < newcode)
    i++;
  if (idcode[i] == newcode)
    cout << "\nThis identification code is already in the list";
  else
  {
    newpos = i;     // found the position for the new code

    // find the end of the list
    while (idcode[i] != 9999)
      i++;
    endpos = i;

    // move idcodes over one position
    for (i = endpos; i >= newpos; --i)
      idcode[i+1] = idcode[i];

    // insert the new code
    idcode[newpos] = newcode;
  }
}
```

The function's first task is to determine the new code's correct position. This is done by cycling through the list as long as each value encountered is less than the new code. Since the sentinel value of 9999 is larger than any new code, the looping must stop when the sentinel value is reached.

After the correct position is determined, the position of the sentinel value, which is the last element in the list, is found. Starting from this last position, each element in the list is moved down by one position until the value in the required new position is reached. Finally, the new identification code is inserted in the correct position.

Step 4 Test and Debug the Function

Program 11.7 incorporates the `insert()` function within a complete program. This allows us to test the function with the same data used in our hand calculation.

Program 11.7

```
#include <iostream>
using namespace std;

void insert(int [], int);      // function prototype

int main()
{
  const int MAXNUM = 100;
  int newcode, i;
  int id[MAXNUM] = {109, 122, 136, 144, 157, 162, 178, 185, 192, 9999};

  cout << "\nEnter the new identification code: ";
  cin  >> newcode;

  insert(id, newcode);

  cout << "\nThe updated list is:";
  i = 0;
  while(id[i] != 9999)
  {
    cout << " " << id[i];
    i++;
  }
  cout << endl;

  return 0;
}
```

(Continued)

(Continued)

```
void insert(int idcode[], int newcode)
{
  int i, newpos, endpos;

  // find correct position to insert the new code
  i = 0;
  while (idcode[i] < newcode)
    i++;
  if (idcode[i] == newcode)
    cout << "\nThis identification code is already in the list";
  else
  {
    newpos = i;    // found the position for the new code

    // find the end of the list
    while (idcode[i] != 9999)
      i++;
    endpos = i;

    // move idcodes over one position
    for (i = endpos; i >= newpos; i--)
      idcode[i+1] = idcode[i];

    // insert the new code
    idcode[newpos] = newcode;
  }

  return;
}
```

A sample run of Program 11.7 follows:

```
Enter the new identification code: 142
The updated list is: 109 122 136 142 144 157 162 178 185 192
```

Though this result agrees with our previous hand calculation, it does not constitute full testing of the program. To be sure that the program works for all cases, test runs should be made that do the following:

1. Enter a new identification code that duplicates an existing code
2. Place a new identification code at the beginning of the list
3. Place a new identification code at the end of the list

Finally, the restriction of the maximum array size of 100 part numbers designated in the original problem specification is unrealistic in practice. Typically, the maximum size is never known with certainty because conditions change that make the original size unrealistic. The solution to this uncertainty is to declare a large array that anticipates possible changes, which wastes computer memory, or to create an array that can dynamically and automatically expand as new part numbers are added. How this second solution can be implemented is presented in Section 11.6.

Exercises 11.4

1. Enter and run Program 11.6 on your computer.
2. Run Program 11.6 to determine the average and standard deviation of the following list of 15 voltages: 68, 72, 78, 69, 85, 98, 95, 75, 77, 82, 84, 91, 89, 65, 74.
3. Enter and run Program 11.7 on your computer system.
4. **a.** Test Program 11.7 using a part number of 86, which should place this new code at the beginning of the existing list.

   b. Test Program 11.7 using a part number of 200, which should place this new part number at the end of the existing list.
5. **a.** Determine an algorithm for deleting an entry from an ordered list of numbers.

   b. Write a function, `delete()`, which uses the algorithm selected in Exercise 5a, to delete an identification code from the list of numbers illustrated in Figure 11.10a.
6. Assume the following letters are stored in an alphabet array: B, J, K, M, S, Z. Write and test a function, `adlet()`, which accepts the alphabet array and a new letter as arguments and then inserts the new letter in the correct alphabetical order in the alphabet array.

11.5 ARRAYS AS ARGUMENTS

Individual array elements are passed to a called function in the same manner as individual scalar variables; they are simply included as subscripted variables when the function call is made. For example, the function call

```
findMin(volts[2], volts[6]);
```

passes the values of the elements `volts[2]` and `volts[6]` to the function `findMin()`.

Passing a complete array of values to a function is in many respects an easier operation than passing individual elements. The called function receives access to the actual array, rather than a copy of the values in the array. For example, if `volts` is an array, the function call `findMax(volts);` makes the complete `volts` array available to the `findMax()` function. This is different from passing a single variable to a function.

Recall that when a single scalar argument is passed to a function, the called function only receives a copy of the passed value, which is stored in one of the function's parameters. If arrays were passed in this manner, a copy of the complete array would have to be created. For large arrays, making duplicate copies of the array for each function call would be wasteful of computer storage and would frustrate the effort to return multiple-element changes made by the called program. (Recall that a function returns at most one direct value.) To avoid these problems, the called function is given direct access to the original array.[4] Thus, any changes made by the called function are made directly to the array itself. For the following specific examples of function calls, assume that the arrays `nums`, `keys`, `volts`, and `current` are declared as:

```
int nums[5];                          // an array of five integers
char keys[256];                       // an array of 256 characters
double vots[500], current[500];       // two arrays of 500 doubles
```

For these arrays, the following function calls can be made:

```
     findMax(nums);
     findCh(keys);
     calcTot(nums, volts, current);
```

In each case, the called function receives direct access to the named array.

On the receiving side, the called function must be alerted that an array is being made available. For example, suitable function header lines for the previous functions are

```
int findMax(int vals[5])
char findCh(char in_keys[256])
void calcTot(int arr1[5], double arr2[500], double arr3[500])
```

In each of these function header lines, the names in the parameter list are chosen by the programmer. However, the parameter names used by the functions still refer to the original array created outside the function. This is made clear in Program 11.8.

---

[4]This is accomplished because the starting address of the array is actually passed as an argument. The formal parameter receiving this address argument is a pointer. The intimate relationship between array names and pointers is presented in Chapter 12.

Program 11.8

```
#include <iostream>
using namespace std;

const int MAXELS = 5;
int findMax(int [MAXELS]);        // function prototype

int main()
{
  int nums[MAXELS] = {2, 18, 1, 27, 16};

  cout << "The maximum value is " << findMax(nums) << endl;

  return 0;
}

// find the maximum value
int findMax(int vals[MAXELS])
{
  int i, max = vals[0];
  for (i = 1; i < MAXELS; i++)
    if (max < vals[i]) max = vals[i];

  return max;
}
```

Notice that the function prototype for `findMax()` declares that `findMax` will return an integer and expects an array of five integers as an actual argument. It is also important to know that only one array is created in Program 11.9. In `main()` this array is known as `nums`, and in `findMax()` the array is known as `vals`. As illustrated in Figure 11.11, both names refer to the same array. Thus, in Figure 11.11 `vals[3]` is the same element as `nums[3]`.

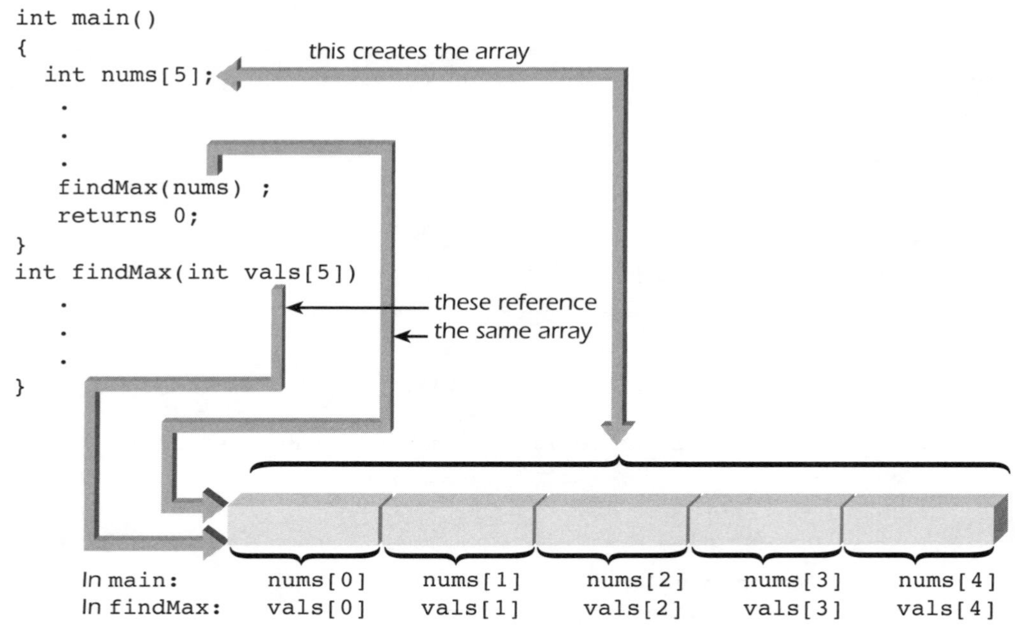
int main()
{
int nums[5];
.
.
.
findMax(nums) ;
returns 0;
}
int findMax(int vals[5])
.
.
.
}
this creates the array
these reference
the same array
In main: nums[0] nums[1] nums[2] nums[3] nums[4]
In findMax: vals[0] vals[1] vals[2] vals[3] vals[4]

Figure 11.11 *Only one array is created.*

The parameter declaration in the `findMax()` header line actually contains extra information that is not required by the function. All that `findMax()` must know is that the parameter `vals` references an array of integers. Since the array has been created in `main()` and no additional storage space is needed in `findMax()`, the declaration for `vals` can omit the size of the array. Thus, an alternative function header line is

```
int findMax(int vals[])
```

This form of the function header makes more sense when you realize that only one item is actually passed to `findMax` when the function is called, the starting address of the `num` array. This is illustrated in Figure 11.12.

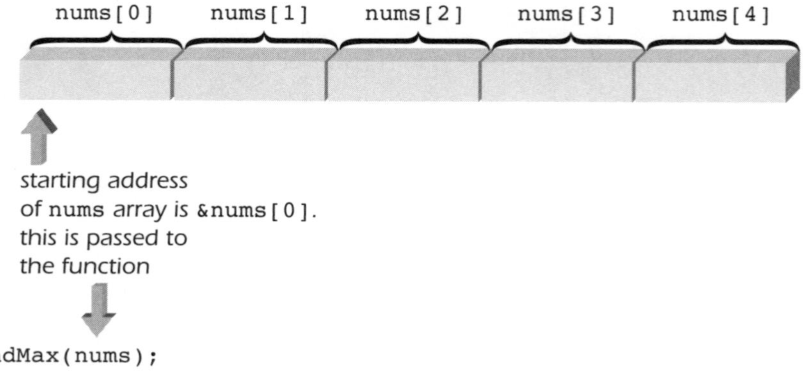
nums[0] nums[1] nums[2] nums[3] nums[4]
starting address
of nums array is &nums[0].
this is passed to
the function
findMax(nums);

Figure 11.12 *The starting address of the array is passed.*

Since only the starting address of `vals` is passed to `findMax`, the number of elements in the array need not be included in the declaration for `vals`.[5] In fact, it is generally advisable to omit the size of the array in the function header line. For example, consider the more general form of `findMax()`, which can be used to find the maximum value of an integer array of arbitrary size.

```
int findMax(int vals[], int numels)    // find the maximum value
{
  int i, max = vals[0];

  for (i = 1; i < numels; i++)
   if (max < vals[i])
     max = vals[i];

  return max;
}
```

The more general form of `findMax()` declares that the function returns an integer value. The function expects the starting address of an integer array and the number of elements in the array as arguments. Then, using the number of elements as the boundary for its search, the function's `for` loop causes each array element to be examined in sequential order to locate the maximum value. Program 11.9 illustrates the use of `findMax()` in a complete program.

The output displayed by both Programs 11.8 and 11.9 is

```
The maximum value is 27
```

Passing two-dimensional arrays into a function is a process identical to passing single-dimensional arrays. The called function receives access to the entire array. For example, assuming that `val` is a two-dimensional array, the function call `display(val);` makes the complete `val` array available to the function named `display()`. Thus, any changes made by `display()` will be made directly to the `val` array. As further examples, assume that the following two-dimensional arrays named `test`, `factors`, and `thrusts` are declared as:

```
int test[7][9];
float factors[26][10];
double thrusts[256][52];
```

then the following function calls are valid:

```
findMax(test);
obtain(factors);
average(thrusts);
```

[5] An important consequence of this is that `findMax()` has direct access to the passed array. This means that any change to an element of the `vals` array is a change to the `nums` array. This is significantly different than the situation with scalar variables, where the called function does not receive direct access to the passed variable.

Program 11.9

```
// this program displays a message
#include <iostream>
using namespace std;

int findMax(int [], int);    // function prototype

int main()
{
  const int MAXELS = 5;
  int nums[MAXELS] = {2, 18, 1, 27, 16};

  cout << "The maximum value is "
       << findMax(nums, MAXELS) << endl;

  return 0;
}

// find the maximum value
int findMax(int vals[], int numels)
{
  int i, max = vals[0];

  for (i = 1; i < numels; i++)
    if (max < vals[i]) max = vals[i];

  return max;
}
```

On the receiving side, the called function must be alerted that a two-dimensional array is being made available. For example, assuming that each of the previous functions returns an integer, suitable function header lines for these functions are:

```
int findMax(int nums[7][9])
int obtain(float values[26][10])
int average(double vals[256][52])
```

In each of these function header lines, the parameter names chosen will be used internal to the function's body. However, these parameter names still refer to the original array created outside the function. Program 11.10 illustrates passing a two-dimensional array into a function that displays the array's values.

Program 11.10

```
#include <iostream>
#include <iomanip>
using namespace std;

const int ROWS = 3;
const int COLS = 4;
void display(int [ROWS][COLS]);    // function prototype

int main()
{
  int val[ROWS][COLS] = {8,16,9,52,
                          3,15,27,6,
                         14,25,2,10};

  display(val);

  return 0;
}

void display(int nums[ROWS][COLS])
{
  int rownum, colnum;
  for (rownum = 0; rownum < ROWS; rownum++)
  {
    for(colnum = 0; colnum < COLS; colnum++)
      cout << setw(4) <<nums[rownum][colnum];
    cout << endl;
  }

  return;
}
```

Only one array is created in Program 11.10. This array is known as `val` in `main()` and as `nums` in `display()`. Thus, `val[0][2]` refers to the same element as `nums[0][2]`.

Notice the use of the nested `for` loop in Program 11.10 for cycling through each array element. In Program 11.10, the variable `rownum` controls the outer loop and the variable `colnum` controls the inner loop. For each pass through the outer loop, which corresponds to a single row, the inner loop makes one pass through the column elements. After a complete row is printed, a new line is started for the next row. The effect is a display of the array in a row-by-row fashion:

```
   8  16   9  52
   3  15  27   6
  14  25   2  10
```

The parameter declaration for `nums` in `display()` contains extra information that is not required by the function. The declaration for `nums` can omit the row size of the array. Thus, an alternative function prototype is

```
display(int nums[][4]);
```

The reason the column size must be included while the row size is optional becomes obvious when you consider how the array elements are stored in memory. Starting with element `val[0][0]`, each succeeding element is stored consecutively, row by row, as `val[0][0]`, `val[0][1]`, `val[0][2]`, `val[0][3]`, `val[1][0]`, `val[1][1]`, etc., as illustrated in Figure 11.13.

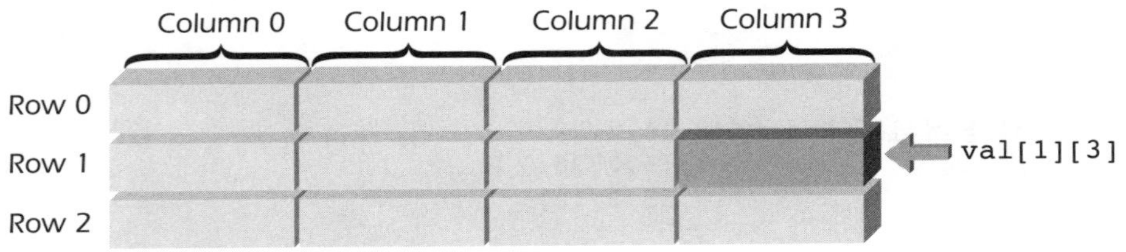

Figure 11.13 *Storage of the* `val` *array.*

As with all array accesses, an individual element of the `val` array is obtained by adding an offset to the starting location of the array. For example, element `val[1][3]` of the `val` array illustrated in Figure 11.13 is located at an offset of 14 bytes from the start of the array. Internally, the compiler uses the row index, column index, and column size to determine this offset using the following calculation (again, assuming four bytes for an `int`):

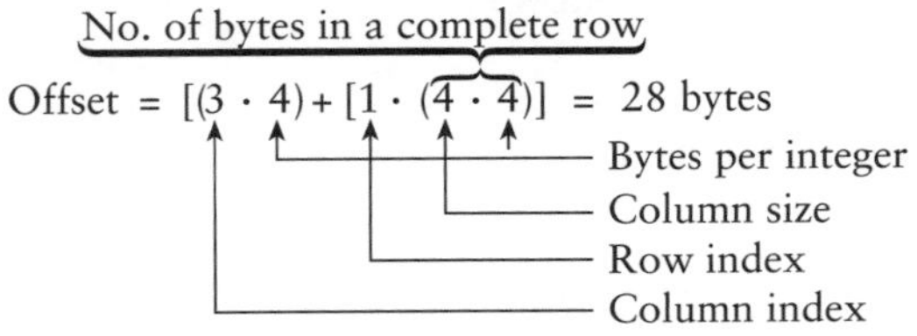

The column size is necessary in the offset calculation so that the compiler can determine the number of positions to skip over in order to get to the desired row.

Exercises 11.5

1. The following declaration was used to create the `volts` array:

```
int volts[500];
```

Write two different function header lines for a function named `sortArray()` that accepts the `volts` array as a parameter named `inArray`.

2. The following declaration was used to create the `factors` array:

```
double factors[256];
```

Write two different function header lines for a function named `findKey()` that accepts the `factors` array as a parameter named `select`.

3. The following declaration was used to create the `power` array:

```
double power[256];
```

Write two different function header lines for a function named `prime()` that accepts the `power` array as an argument named `rates`.

4. a. Modify the `findMax()` function in Program 11.8 to locate the minimum value of the passed array.
   b. Include the function written in Exercise 4a in a complete program and run the program on a computer.

5. Write a program that has a declaration in `main()` to store the following numbers into an array named `temps`: 6.5, 7.2, 7.5, 8.3, 8.6, 9.4, 9.6, 9.8, 10.0. There should be a function call to `show()` that accepts the `temps` array as a parameter named `temps` and then displays the numbers in the array.

6. Write a program that declares three single-dimensional arrays named `volts`, `current`, and `resistance`. Each array should be declared in `main()` and should be capable of holding ten double-precision numbers. The numbers that should be stored in `current` are 10.62, 14.89, 13.21, 16.55, 18.62, 9.47, 6.58, 18.32, 12.15, 3.98. The numbers that should be stored in `resistance` are 4, 8.5, 6, 7.35, 9, 15.3, 3, 5.4, 2.9, 4.8. Your program should pass these three arrays to a function named `calc_volts()`, which should calculate the elements in the `volts` array as the product of the corresponding elements in the `current` and `resistance` arrays (for example, `volts[1] = current[1] * resistance[1]`). After `calc_volts()` has put values into the `volts` array, the values in the array should be displayed from within `main()`.

7. Write a program that includes two functions named `calcavg()` and `variance()`. The `calcavg()` function should calculate and return the average of the values stored in an array named `testvals`. The array should be declared in `main()` and include the values 89, 95, 72, 83, 99, 54, 86, 75, 92, 73, 79, 75, 82, 73. The `variance()` function should calculate and return the variance of the data. The variance is obtained by subtracting the average from each value in `testvals`, squaring the values obtained, adding them, and dividing by the number of elements in `testvals`. The values returned from `calcavg()` and variance should be displayed using `cout` statements in `main()`.

11.6 THE STL VECTOR CLASS

Many programming applications require lists to be expanded and contracted as items are added to and removed from the list. Though expanding and contracting an array can be accomplished by creating, copying, and deleting arrays, this solution is costly in terms of initial programming, maintenance, and testing time. To meet the need of providing a tested and generic set of data structures that can be modified, expanded, and contracted, C++ provides a useful set of classes in its Standard Template Library (STL).

Each STL class is coded as a template (see Section 6.1) that permits the construction of a generic data structure, which is referred to as a **container**. The terms **list** and **collection** are synonyms for a container, with each term referring to a set of data items that form a natural unit or group. Using this definition, an array is a container; however, a container is provided as a built-in type as contrasted to the containers created using STL.

In this section, the STL vector container class is presented. A vector is similar to an array in that it stores elements that can be accessed using an integer index that starts at zero but is dissimilar in that a vector will automatically expand as needed and is provided by a number of useful class methods (functions) for operating on the vector. Table 11.1 lists these vector class methods, with highlighting used to identify the methods that we will use in our demonstration program

Table 11.1 Summary of Vector Class Methods (Functions) and Operations

Functions (Class Methods) and Operations	Description
vector<DataType> name	Creates an empty vector with compiler-dependent initial size
vector<DataType> name(source)	Creates a copy of the source vector
vector<DataType> name(*n*)	Creates a vector of size *n*
vector<DataType> name(*n*, elem)	Creates a vector of size *n* with each element initialized as elem
vector<DataType> name(src.beg, src.end)	Creates a vector initialized with elements from a source container beginning at src.beg and ending and src.end
~vector(DataType>()	Destroys the vector and all elements it contains
name[index]	Returns the element at the designated index, with no bounds checking
name.at(index)	Returns the element at the specified index argument, with bounds checking on the index value
name.front()	Returns the first element in the vector
name.back()	Returns the last element in the vector
dest = src	Assigns all elements of src vector to dest vector

Table 11.1 Summary of Vector Class Methods (Functions) and Operations (continued)

Functions (Class Methods) and Operations	Description
`name.assign(n, elem)`	Assigns *n* copies of `elem`
`name.assign(src.begin, src.end)`	Assigns the elements of the src container (need not be a vector) between the range `src.begin` and `src.end`, to the name vector
`insert(pos, elem)`	Insert elem at position pos
`name.insert(pos, n, elem)`	Insert *n* copies of `elem` starting at position *pos*
`name.insert(pos, src.begin, src.end)`	Insert
`name.push_back(elem)`	Append `elem` at the end of the vector
`name.erase(pos)`	Removes the element at the specified position
`name.erase(begin, end)`	Removes the elements within the specified range
`name.resize(value)`	Resizes the vector to a larger size, with new elements instantiated using the default constructor
`name.resize(value, elem)`	Resizes the vector to a larger size, with new elements instantiated as `elem`
`name.clear()`	Removes all elements from the vector
`name.swap(nameB)`	Swaps the elements of `nameA` and `nameB` vectors; can be performed using the `swap()` algorithm
`nameA == nameB`	Returns a Boolean `true` if `nameA` elements equal `nameB` elements; otherwise, returns `false`
`nameA != nameB`	Returns a Boolean `false` if `nameA` elements equal `nameB` elements; otherwise, returns `true`; same as !(nameA == nameB)
`nameA < nameB`	Returns a Boolean `true` if `nameA` is less than `nameB`; otherwise, returns `false`
`nameA > nameB`	Returns a Boolean `true` if `nameA` is greater than `nameB`; otherwise, returns `false`; same as `nameB < nameA`
`nameA <= nameB`	Returns a Boolean `true` if `nameA` is less than or equal to `nameB`
`nameA >= nameB`	Returns a Boolean `true` if `nameA` is greater than or equal to `nameB`
`name.size()`	Returns the size of the vector
`name.empty()`	Returns a Boolean `true` if vector is empty; otherwise, returns `false`
`name.max_size()`	Returns the maximum possible elements as an integer
`name.capacity()`	Returns the maximum possible elements, as an integer, without relocation of the vector

In addition to the specific vector class methods listed in Table 11.1, vectors have access to the complete set of generic STL functions, referred to in STL as algorithms. Table 11.2 summarizes the most commonly used of these algorithms.

Table 11.2 Commonly Used Standard Template Library (STL) Algorithms

Algorithm Name	Description
`accumulate`	Returns the sum of the numbers in a specified range
`binary_search`	Returns a Boolean value of `true` if the specified value exists within the specified range; otherwise, returns `false`. Can only be used on a sorted set of values.
`copy`	Copies elements from a source range to a destination range
`copy_backward`	Copies elements from a source range to a destination range in a reverse direction
`count`	Returns the number of elements in a specified range that match a specified value
`equal`	Compares the elements in one range of elements, element by element, to the elements in a second range
`fill`	Assigns every element in a specified range to a specified value
`find`	Returns the position of the first occurrence of an element in a specified range having a specified value if the value exists. Performs a linear search, starting with the first element in a specified range and proceeds one element at a time until the complete range has been searched or the specified element has been found.
`max_element`	Returns the maximum value of the elements in the specified range
`min_element`	Returns the minimum value of the elements in the specified range
`random_shuffle`	Randomly shuffles element values in a specified range
`remove`	Removes a specified value within a specified range without changing the order of the remaining elements
`replace`	Replaces each element in a specified range having a specified value with a newly specified value
`reverse`	Reverses elements in a specified range
`search`	Finds the first occurrence of a specified value or sequence of values within a specified range
`sort`	Sorts elements in a specified range into an ascending order
`swap`	Exchanges element values between two objects
`unique`	Removes duplicate adjacent elements within a specified range

Notice that there is both a swap algorithm (Table 11.2) and a swap vector class method (Table 11.1). Because a class method is targeted to work specifically with its container type and generally will execute faster whenever a container class provides a method with the same name as an algorithm, you should use the class method.

Finally, a number of additional items, referred to as iterators, are also provided by the STL. Iterators provide the means of specifying which elements in a container are to be operated on when an algorithm is called. Two of the most useful iterators are returned by the STL iterator functions named `begin()` and `end()`. These are general purpose functions that return the positions of the first and last elements in a container, respectively.

Point of Information

When to Use an Array or a Vector

An array is the data structure of first choice whenever you have a list of primitive data types or objects that do not have to be expanded or contracted.

A vector is the data structure of first choice whenever you have a list of primitive data types or objects that can be grouped as an array but must be expanded or contracted.

Whenever possible, always use STL's algorithms to operate on arrays (see Section 12.4) and vectors (described in this section). Both STL's classes and algorithms provide verified and reliable code that can shorten program development time.

To make this more tangible and provide a meaningful introduction to using an STL container class, we will use the vector container class to create a vector for holding a list of part numbers. As we shall see, a vector is similar to a C++ array, except that it can automatically expand as needed.

Program 11.11 constructs a vector and initializes it with integers stored in an integer array. Once it is initialized, various vector methods and STL algorithms are used to operate on the vector. Specifically, one method is used to change an existing value, a second is used to insert a value within the vector, and a third method is used to append a value to the end of the list. After each method and algorithm is applied, a `cout` object is employed to display the results.

Program 11.11

```
#include <iostream>
#include <string>
#include <vector>
#include <algorithm>
using namespace std;

int main()
{
  const int NUMELS = 4;
  int n[] ={136, 122, 109, 146};
  int i;

  // instantiate a vector of strings using the n[] array
  vector<int> partnums(n, n + NUMELS);
```

(Continued)

(Continued)

```
    cout << "\nThe vector initially has a size of "
         << int(partnums.size()) << ",\n and contains the elements:\n";
    for (i = 0; i < int(partnums.size()); i++)
      cout << partnums[i] << "   ";

    // modify the element at position 4 (i.e. index = 3) in the vector
    partnums[3] = 144;
    cout << "\n\nAfter replacing the fourth element, the vector has a size of "
         << int(partnums.size()) << ",\n and contains the elements:\n";
    for (i = 0; i < int(partnums.size()); i++)
      cout << partnums[i] << "  ";

    // insert an element into the vector at position 2 (i.e. index = 1)
    partnums.insert(partnums.begin()+1, 142);
    cout << "\n\nAfter inserting an element into the third position,"
         << "\n the vector has a size of " << int(partnums.size()) << ","
         << " and contains the elements:\n";
    for (i = 0; i < int(partnums.size()); i++)
      cout << partnums[i] << "  ";

    // add an element to the end of the vector
    partnums.push_back(157);
    cout << "\n\nAfter adding an element to the end of the list,"
         << "\n  the vector has a size of " << int(partnums.size()) << ","
         << " and contains the elements:\n";
    for (i = 0; i < int(partnums.size()); i++)
      cout << partnums[i] << "  ";

    // sort the vector
    sort(partnums.begin(), partnums.end());
    cout << "\n\nAfter sorting, the vector's elements are:\n";
    for (i = 0; i < int(partnums.size()); i++)
      cout << partnums[i] << "  ";

    cout << endl;

    return 0;
  }
```

In reviewing Program 11.11, the four header files `<iostream>`, `<string>`, `<vector>`, and `<algorithm>` and the `using namespace std;` statement have been included. The `<iostream>` header is needed to create and use the `cout` stream; the `<string>` header is required for constructing strings; the `<vector>` header to create one or move `vector` objects; and the `<algorithm>` header is required for the `sort` algorithm that is applied after we have completed adding and replacing `vector` elements.

The statement in Program 11.11 used to create and initialize the vector named `partnums` is the following:

```
vector<int> partnums(n, n + NUMELS);
```

Here, the vector `partnums` is declared as a vector of type `int` and is initialized with elements from the n array, starting with the first element of the array (element `n[0]`) and ending with the last array element, which is located at position `n + NUMELS`. Thus, the vector has a size sufficient for four integer values and has been initialized with the integers 136, 122, 109, and 146. The next set of statements in Program 11.11 display the initial values in the vector using standard subscripted vector notation that is identical to the notation used for accessing array elements. Displaying the vector values in this manner, however, requires knowing how many elements each vector contains. As we insert and remove elements, we would like the vector to track the first and last elements location. This capability is automatically provided by two methods furnished for each STL container: `begin()` and `end()`.

The next major set of statements consists of the following:

```
// modify the element at position 4 (i.e. index = 3) in the vector
  partnums[3] = 144;


  // insert an element into the vector at position 2 (i.e. index = 1)
  partnums.insert(partnums.begin()+1, 142);
```

These statements are used to modify an existing vector value and insert a new value into the vector. Specifically, the `partnums[3]` notation uses standard indexing, and the `insert()` method uses an argument referred to in STL as an iterator. Such arguments are constructed as offsets using the `begin()` or `end()` functions. Additionally, we have to specify the value to be inserted at the designated position. Thus, `names[3]` specifies the fourth element in the vector will be changed. (Vectors, like arrays, begin at index position 0.) The `insert()` method is used to insert the integer value 142 in the second position of the vector. Because the `begin()` method returns a value corresponding to the start of the vector, adding 1 to it designates the second position in the vector.[6] It is at this position the new value is inserted with all subsequent values moved up by one position in the vector and with the vector automatically expanding to accept the inserted value. At this point in the program, the vector `partnums` now contains the following elements:

```
136   142   122   109   144
```

This arrangement of values was obtained by replacing the original value 146 with 144 and inserting the 142 into the second position, which automatically moves all subsequent elements to move up by one position and increases the total vector size to five integers.

Next, the statement `partnums.push_back(157);` is used to append the integer 157 to the end of the vector, which results in the following elements:

```
136   142   122   109   144   157
```

[6]More precisely, this method requires an *iterator* argument, not an integer index argument. The `begin()` and `end()` algorithms return iterators, to which offsets can be applied. In this, they are similar to pointers (presented in the next chapter).

Finally, the last section of code used in Program 11.11 uses the `sort()` algorithm to sort the elements in the vector. After the algorithm is applied, the values in the vector are displayed again. Following is the complete output produced by Program 11.11:

```
The vector initially has a size of 4,
 and contains the elements:
136   122   109   146

After replacing the fourth element, the vector has a size of 4,
 and contains the elements:
136  122  109  144

After inserting an element into the second position,
 the vector has a size of 5, and contains the elements:
136  142  122  109  144

After adding an element to the end of the list,
  the vector has a size of 6, and contains the elements:
136  142  122  109  144  157

After sorting, the vector's elements are:
109  122  136  142  144  157
```

Exercises 11.6

1. Define the terms "container" and "Standard Template Library."
2. What `include` statements should be included with programs that use the Standard Template Library?
3. Enter and execute Program 11.11.
4. Modify Program 11.11 so the user inputs the initial set of numbers when the program executes. Have the program request the number of initial numbers to be entered.
5. Modify Program 11.11 to use and display the results reported by the vector class's `capacity()` and `max_size()` methods.
6. Modify Program 11.11 to use the `random_shuffle()` algorithm.
7. Modify Program 11.11 to use the `binary_search()` and `find()` algorithms. Have your program request the number to be found.
8. Using Program 11.11 as a starting point, create an equivalent program that uses a vector of strings. Initialize the vector using the array `string names[] = {"Donavan", "Michaels", "Smith", "Jones"};`.

9. Use the `max_element()` and `min_element()` algorithms to determine the maximum and minimum values, respectively, in the vector created for Exericise 8. (*Hint:* Use the expression `max_element(vectorName.begin(), vectorName.end())` to determine the maximum value stored in the vector. Then use the same arguments for the `min_element()` algorithm.)

10. Redo Application 2 in Section 11.4 using a vector rather than an array.

11.7 COMMON PROGRAMMING ERRORS

Four common errors are associated with using arrays.

1. Forgetting to declare the array. This error results in a compiler error message equivalent to "invalid indirection" each time a subscripted variable is encountered within a program. The exact meaning of this error message will become clear when the correspondence between arrays and pointers is established in Chapter 12.

2. Using a subscript that references a non-existent array element. For example, declaring the array to be of size 20 and using a subscript value of 25. This error is not detected by most C++ compilers. It will, however, result in a run-time error that results either in a program crash or a value that has no relation to the intended element being accessed from memory. In either case it is usually an extremely troublesome error to locate. The only solution to this problem is to make sure, either by specific programming statements or by careful coding, that each subscript references a valid array element.

3. Not using a large enough counter value in a `for` loop counter to cycle through all the array elements. This error usually occurs when an array is initially specified to be of size *n* and there is a `for` loop within the program of the form `for (i = 0; i < n; i++)`. The array size is then expanded, but the programmer forgets to change the interior `for` loop parameters. Declaring an array's size using a named constant and consistently using the named constant throughout the function in place of the variable *n* eliminates this problem.

4. Forgetting to initialize the array. Although many compilers automatically set all elements of integer and real valued arrays to zero, and all elements of character arrays to blanks, it is up to the programmer to ensure that each array is correctly initialized before processing of array elements begins.

11.8 CHAPTER SUMMARY

1. A single-dimensional array is a data structure that can be used to store a list of values of the same data type. Such arrays must be declared by giving the data type of the values that are stored in the array and the array size. For example, the declaration:

   ```
   int num[100];
   ```

   creates an array of 100 integers. A preferable approach is to first use a named constant to set the array size, and then use this constant in the definition of the array. For example,

   ```
   const int MAXSIZE = 100;
   ```

   and

   ```
   int num[MAXSIZE];
   ```

2. Array elements are stored in contiguous locations in memory and referenced using the array name and a subscript, for example, `num[22]`. Any non-negative integer value expression can be used as a subscript and the subscript 0 always refers to the first element in an array.

3. A two-dimensional array is declared by listing both a row and a column size with the data type and name of the array. For example, the declaration

   ```
   int mat[5][7];
   ```

   creates a two-dimensional array consisting of five rows and seven columns of integer values.

4. Arrays may be initialized when they are declared. For two-dimensional arrays this is accomplished by listing the initial values, in a row-by row manner, within braces and separating them with commas. For example, the declaration

   ```
   int vals[3][2] = { {1, 2},
                      {3, 4},
                      {5, 6} };
   ```

   produces the following 3-row-by-2-column array:

   ```
   1  2
   3  4
   5  6
   ```

   As C++ uses the convention that initialization proceeds in rowwise order, the inner braces can be omitted. Thus, an equivalent initialization is provided by the statement:

   ```
   int vals[3][2] = { 1, 2, 3, 4,  5, 6};
   ```

5. Arrays are passed to a function by passing the name of the array as an argument. The value actually passed is the address of the first array storage location. Thus, the called function receives direct access to the original array and not a copy of the array elements. Within the called function a formal argument must be declared to receive the passed array name. The declaration of the formal argument can omit the row size of the array.

11.9 Chapter Appendix: Searching and Sorting

Most programmers encounter the need to both sort and search a list of data items at some time in their programming careers. For example, experimental results might have to be arranged in either increasing (ascending) or decreasing (descending) order for statistical analysis, lists of names may have to be sorted in alphabetical order, or a list of dates may have to be rearranged in ascending date order. Similarly, a list of names may have to be searched to find a particular name in the list, or a list of dates may have to be searched to locate a particular date. In this section we introduce the fundamentals of both sorting and searching lists. Note that it is not necessary to sort a list before searching it, although, as we shall see, much faster searches are possible if the list is in sorted order.

Search Algorithms

A common requirement of many programs is to search a list for a given element. For example, in a list of names and telephone numbers, we might search for a specific name so that the corresponding telephone number can be printed, or we might wish to search the list simply to determine if a name is there. The two most common methods of performing such searches are the linear and binary search algorithms.

Linear Search

In a **linear search**, which is also known as a **sequential search**, each item in the list is examined in the order in which it occurs in the list until the desired item is found or the end of the list is reached. This is analogous to looking at every name in the phone directory, beginning with Aardvark, Aaron, until you find the one you want or until you reach Zzxgy, Zora. Obviously, this is not the most efficient way to search a long alphabetized list. However, a linear search has these advantages:

1. The algorithm is simple.
2. The list need not be in any particular order.

In a linear search the search begins at the first item in the list and continues sequentially, item by item, through the list. The pseudocode for a function performing a linear search is

For all the items in the list
    Compare the item with the desired item

If the item was found
Return the index value of the current item
Endif
EndFor
Return –1 if the item was not found

Notice that the function's `return` value indicates whether the item was found or not. If the `return` value is `-1`, the item was not in the list; otherwise, the `return` value within the `for` loop provides the index of where the item is located within the list.

The function `linearSearch()` illustrates this procedure as a C++ function:

```
// this function returns the location of key in the list
// a -1 is returned if the value is not found
int linearSearch(int list[], int size, int key)
{
  int i;

  for (i = 0; i < size; i++)
  {
    if (list[i] == key)
      return i;
  }

  return -1;
}
```

In reviewing `linearSearch()` notice that the `for` loop is simply used to access each element in the list, from first element to last, until a match is found with the desired item. If the desired item is located the index value of the current item is returned, which causes the loop to terminate; otherwise, the search continues until the end of the list is encountered.

To test this function we have written a `main()` driver function to call it and display the results returned by `linearSearch()`. The complete test program is illustrated in Program 11.12.

Sample runs of Program 11.12 follow:

```
Enter the item you are searching for: 101
The item was found at index location 9
```

and

```
Enter the item you are searching for: 65
The item was not found in the list
```

As has already been pointed out, an advantage of linear searches is that the list does not have to be in sorted order to perform the search. Another advantage is that if the desired item is toward the front of the list, only a small number of comparisons will be done. The worst case, of course, occurs when the desired item is at the end of the list. On average, however, and assuming that the desired item is equally likely to be anywhere within the list, the number of required comparisons will be $n/2$, where n is the list's size. Thus, for a 10-element list, the average number of comparisons needed for a linear search is 5, and for a 10,000 element list, the average number of comparisons needed is 5,000. As we show next, this number can be significantly reduced using a binary search algorithm.

Program 11.12

```
#include <iostream>
using namespace std;

int linearSearch(int [], int, int);

int main()
{
  const int NUMEL = 10;
  int nums[NUMEL] = {5,10,22,32,45,67,73,98,99,101};
  int item, location;


  cout << "Enter the item you are searching for: ";
  cin  >> item;

  location = linearSearch(nums, NUMEL, item);

  if (location > -1)
    cout << "The item was found at index location " << location
         << endl;
  else
    cout << "The item was not found in the list\n";

  return 0;
}

// this function returns the location of key in the list
// a -1 is returned if the value is not found
int linearSearch(int list[], int size, int key)
{
  int i;

  for (i = 0; i < size; i++)
  {
    if (list[i] == key)
      return i;
  }

  return -1;
}
```

Binary Search

In a **binary search** the list must be in sorted order. Starting with an ordered list, the desired item is first compared to the element in the middle of the list (for lists with an even number of elements, either of the two middle elements can be used). Three possibilities present themselves once the comparison is made: the desired item may be equal to the middle element, it may be greater than the middle element, or it may be less than the middle element.

In the first case the search has been successful, and no further searches are required. In the second case, since the desired item is greater than the middle element, if it is found at all it must be in the second half of the list. This means that the first part of the list consisting of all elements from the first to the midpoint element can be discarded from any further search. In the third case, since the desired item is less than the middle element, if it is found at all it must be found in the first part of the list. For this case the second half of the list containing all elements from the midpoint element to the last element can be discarded from any further search.

The algorithm for implementing this search strategy is illustrated in Figure 11.14 and defined by the following pseudocode:

```
Set the lower index to 0
Set the upper index to one less than the size of the list
Begin with the first item in the list
While the lower index is less than or equal to the upper index
  Set the midpoint index to the integer average of the lower and upper index values
  Compare the desired item to the midpoint element
    If the desired element equals the midpoint element
       Return the index value of the current item
   Else If the desired element is greater than the midpoint element
      Set the lower index value to the midpoint value plus 1
   Else if the desired element is less than the midpoint element
      Set the upper index value to the midpoint value less 1
   Endif
EndWhile
Return -1 if the item was not found
```

As illustrated by both the pseudocode and the flowchart of Figure 11.14, a `while` loop is used to control the search. The initial list is defined by setting the left index value to 0 and the right index value to one less than the number of elements in the list. The midpoint element is then taken as the integerized average of the left and right values. Once the comparison to the midpoint element is made, the search is subsequently restricted by moving either the left index to one integer value above the midpoint, or by moving the right index one integer value below the midpoint. This process is continued until the desired element is found or the left and right index values become equal. The function `binarySearch()` presents the C++ version of this algorithm.

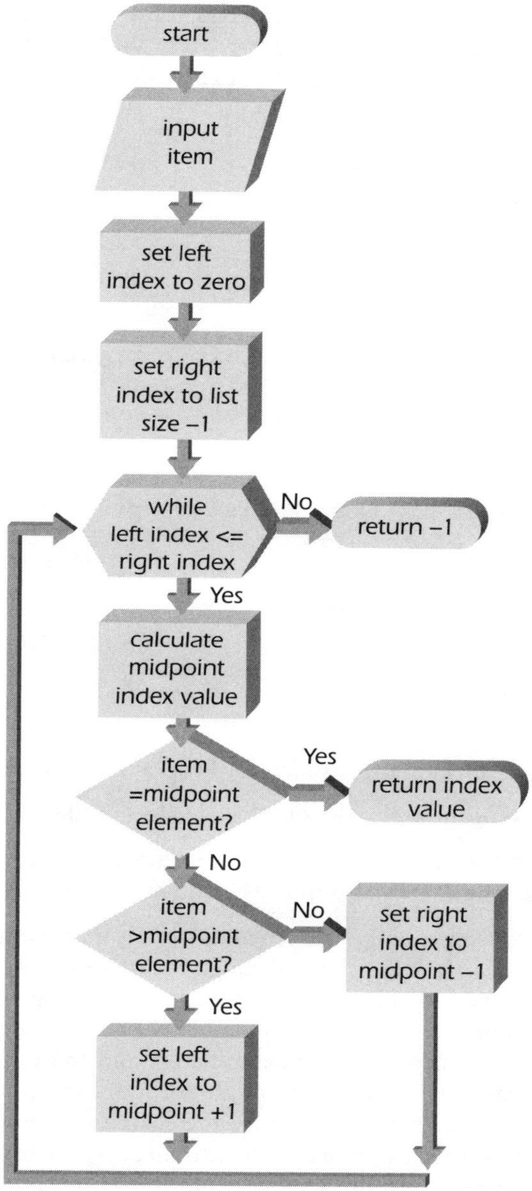

Figure 11.14 The binary search algorithm.

```
// this function returns the location of key in the list
// a -1 is returned if the value is not found
int binarySearch(int list[], int size, int key)
{
  int left, right, midpt;

  left = 0;
  right = size -1;

  while (left <= right)
  {
    midpt = (int) ((left + right) / 2);
    if (key == list[midpt])
    {
      return midpt;
    }
    else if (key > list[midpt])
      left = midpt + 1;
    else
      right = midpt - 1;
  }

  return -1;
}
```

For purposes of testing this function, Program 11.13 is used.

A sample run using Program 11.13 yielded the following:

```
Enter the item you are searching for: 101
The item was found at index location 9
```

The value of using a binary search algorithm is that the number of elements that must be searched is cut in half each time through the `while` loop. Thus, the first time through the loop n elements must be searched; the second time through the loop $n/2$ of the elements has been eliminated and only $n/2$ remain. The third time through the loop another half of the remaining elements has been eliminated, and so on.

In general, after p passes through the loop, the number of values remaining to be searched is $n/(2^p)$. In the worst case the search can continue until there is less than or equal to 1 element remaining to be searched. Mathematically, this can be expressed as $n/(2^p) \leq 1$. Alternatively, this may be rephrased as p is the smallest integer such that $2^p \geq n$. For example, for a 1000 element array, n is 1000 and the maximum number of passes, p, required for a binary search is 10. Table 11.3 compares the number of loop passes needed for a linear and binary search for various list sizes.

Program 11.13

```
#include <iostream>
using namespace std;

int binarySearch(int [], int, int);

int main()
{
  const int NUMEL = 10;
  int nums[NUMEL] = {5,10,22,32,45,67,73,98,99,101};
  int item, location;
  cout << "Enter the item you are searching for: ";
  cin  >> item;
  location = binarySearch(nums, NUMEL, item);
  if (location > -1)
    cout << "The item was found at index location "
         << location << endl;
  else
    cout << "The item was not found in the array\n";

  return 0;
}

// this function returns the location of key in the list
// a -1 is returned if the value is not found
int binarySearch(int list[], int size, int key)
{
  int left, right, midpt;

  left = 0;
  right = size -1;

  while (left <= right)
  {
    midpt = (int) ((left + right) / 2);
    if (key == list[midpt])
    {
      return midpt;
    }
    else if (key > list[midpt])
      left = midpt + 1;
    else
      right = midpt - 1;
  }

  return -1;
}
```

Table 11.3 A Comparison of `while` Loop Passes for Linear and Binary Searches

Array Size	10	50	500	5000	50,000	500,000	5,000,000	50,000,000
Average Linear Search Passes	5	25	250	2500	25,000	250,000	2,500,000	25,000,000
Maximum Linear Search Passes	10	50	500	5000	50,000	500,000	5,000,000	50,000,000
Maximum Binary Search Passes	4	6	9	13	16	19	23	26

As illustrated, the maximum number of loop passes for a 50-item list is almost 10 times more for a linear search than for binary search, and even more spectacular for larger lists. As a rule of thumb, 50 elements are usually taken as the switch/over point: For lists smaller than 50 elements linear searches are acceptable; for larger lists a binary search algorithm should be used.

Big O Notation

On average, over a large number of linear searches with n items in a list, we would expect to examine half ($n/2$) of the items before locating the desired item. In a binary search the maximum number of passes, p, occurs when $n/(2)^p = 1$. This relationship can be algebraically manipulated to $2^p = n$, which yields $p = \log_2 n$, which approximately equals $3.33 \log_{10} n$.

For example, finding a particular name in an alphabetical directory with $n = 1000$ names would require an average of 500 ($=n/2$) comparisons using a linear search. With a binary search, only about 10 ($\approx 3.33 * \log_{10} 1000$) comparisons would be required.

A common way to express the number of comparisons required in any search algorithm using a list of n items is to give the order of magnitude of the number of comparisons required, on average, to locate a desired item. Thus, the linear search is said to be of order n and the binary search of order $\log_2 n$. Notationally, this is expressed as $O(n)$ and $O(\log_2 n)$, where the O is read as "the order of."

Sort Algorithms

For sorting data, two major categories of sorting techniques exist, called internal and external sorts, respectively. **Internal sorts** are used when the data list is not too large and the complete list can be stored within the computer's memory, usually in an array. **External sorts** are used for much larger data sets that are stored in large external disk or tape files and cannot be accommodated within the computer's memory as a complete unit. Here we present two internal sort algorithms that can be effectively used when sorting lists with less than approximately 50 elements. For larger lists more sophisticated sorting algorithms are typically employed.

Selection Sort

One of the simplest sorting techniques is the selection sort. In a **selection sort** the smallest value is initially selected from the complete list of data and exchanged with the first element in the list. After this first selection and exchange, the next smallest element in the revised list is selected and exchanged with the second element in the list. Since the smallest element is already in the first position in the list, this second pass need only consider the second through last elements. For a list consisting of n elements, this process is repeated $n - 1$ times, with each pass through the list requiring one less comparison than the previous pass.

For example, consider the list of numbers illustrated in Figure 11.15. The first pass through the initial list results in the number 32 being selected and exchanged with the first element in the list. The second pass, made on the reordered list, results in the number 155 being selected from the second through fifth elements. This value is then exchanged with the second element in the list. The third pass selects the number 307 from the third through fifth elements in the list and exchanges this value with the third element. Finally, the fourth and last pass through the list selects the remaining minimum value and exchanges it with the fourth list element. Although each pass in this example resulted in an exchange, no exchange would have been made in a pass if the smallest value were already in the correct location.

initial list	pass 1	pass 2	pass 3	pass 4
690	32	32	32	32
307	307	155	144	144
32	690	690	307	307
155	155	307	690	426
426	426	426	426	690

Figure 11.15 A sample selection sort.

In pseudocode, the selection sort is described as

```
Set interchange count to zero (not required, but done just to keep track of the interchanges)
For each element in the list from first to next-to-last
  Find the smallest element from the current element being referenced to the last element by;
    Setting the minimum value equal to the current element
    Saving (storing) the index of the current element
    For each element in the list from the current element + 1 to the last element in the list
      If element[inner loop index] < minimum value
        Set the minimum value = element[inner loop index]
        Save the index the new found minimum value
      Endif
    EndFor
    Swap the current value with the new minimum value
    Increment the interchange count
EndFor
Return the interchange count
```

The function `selectionSort()` incorporates this procedure into a C++ function.

```
int selectionSort(int num[], int numel)
{
  int i, j, min, minidx, temp, moves = 0;

  for ( i = 0; i < (numel - 1); i++)
  {
    min = num[i];     // assume minimum is the first array element
    minidx = i;       // index of minimum element
    for(j = i + 1; j < numel; j++)
    {
      if (num[j] < min)    // if we've located a lower value
      {                    // capture it
      min = num[j];
      minidx = j;
      }
    }
    if (min < num[i])   // check if we have a new minimum
    {                   // and if we do, swap values
      temp = num[i];
      num[i] = min;
      num[minidx] = temp;
      moves++;
    }
  }

  return moves;
}
```

The `selectionSort()` function expects two arguments: the list to be sorted and the number of elements in the list. As specified by the pseudocode, a nested set of `for` loops performs the sort. The outer `for` loop causes one less pass through the list than the total number of data items in the list. For each pass, the variable `min` is initially assigned the value `num[i]`, where `i` is the outer `for` loop's counter variable. Since `i` begins at 0 and ends at one less than `numel`, each element in the list, except the last, is successively designated as the current element.

The inner loop cycles through the elements below the current element and is used to select the next smallest value. Thus, this loop begins at the index value `i + 1` and continues through the end of the list. When a new minimum is found, its value and position in the list are stored in the variables named `min` and `minidx`, respectively. Upon completion of the inner loop, an exchange is made only if a value less than that in the current position was found.

For purposes of testing `selectionSort()`, Program 11.14 was constructed. This program implements a selection sort for the same list of 10 numbers that was previously used to test our search algorithms. For later comparison to the other sorting algorithms that will be presented, the number of actual moves made by the program to get the data into sorted order is counted and displayed.

Program 11.14

```
#include <iostream>
using namespace std;

int selectionSort(int [], int);

int main()
{
  const int NUMEL = 10;
  int nums[NUMEL] = {22,5,67,98,45,32,101,99,73,10};
  int i, moves;

  moves = selectionSort(nums, NUMEL);

  cout << "The sorted list, in ascending order, is:\n";
  for (i = 0; i < NUMEL; i++)
    cout << "  " <<nums[i];

  cout << endl << moves << " moves were made to sort this list\n";

  return 0;
}

int selectionSort(int num[], int numel)
{
  int i, j, min, minidx, temp, moves = 0;

  for ( i = 0; i < (numel - 1); i++)
  {
    min = num[i];    // assume minimum is the first array element
    minidx = i;      // index of minimum element
    for(j = i + 1; j < numel; j++)
    {
      if (num[j] < min)    // if we've located a lower value
      {                    // capture it
      min = num[j];
      minidx = j;
      }
    }
    if (min < num[i])  // check if we have a new minimum
    {                  // and if we do, swap values
      temp = num[i];
      num[i] = min;
      num[minidx] = temp;
      moves++;
    }
  }

  return moves;
}
```

The output produced by Program 11.14 is as follows:

```
The sorted list, in ascending order, is:
  5  10  22  32  45  67  73  98  99  101
8 moves were made to sort this list
```

Clearly, the number of moves displayed depends on the initial order of the values in the list. An advantage of the selection sort is that the maximum number of moves that must be made is $n - 1$, where n is the number of items in the list. Further, each move is a final move that results in an element residing in its final location in the sorted list.

A disadvantage of the selection sort is that $n(n - 1)/2$ comparisons are always required, regardless of the initial arrangement of the data. This number of comparisons is obtained as follows: the last pass always requires one comparison, the next-to-last pass requires two comparisons, and so on, to the first pass, which requires $n - 1$ comparisons. Thus, the total number of comparisons is

$$1 + 2 + 3 + \cdots + n - 1 = n(n - 1)/2 = n^2/2 - n/2.$$

For large values of n the n^2 dominates, and the order of the selection sort is $O(n^2)$.

Exchange (Bubble) Sort

In an **exchange sort**, adjacent elements of the list are exchanged with one another in such a manner that the list becomes sorted. One example of such a sequence of exchanges is provided by the `bubble sort`, where successive values in the list are compared, beginning with the first two elements. If the list is to be sorted in ascending (from smallest to largest) order, the smaller value of the two being compared is always placed before the larger value. For lists sorted in descending (from largest to smallest) order, the smaller of the two values being compared is always placed after the larger value.

For example, assuming that a list of values is to be sorted in ascending order, if the first element in the list is larger than the second, the two elements are interchanged. Then the second and third elements are compared. Again, if the second element is larger than the third, these two elements are interchanged. This process continues until the last two elements have been compared and exchanged, if necessary. If no exchanges were made during this initial pass through the data, the data is in the correct order and the process is finished; otherwise, a second pass is made through the data, starting from the first element and stopping at the next-to-last element. The reason for stopping at the next-to-last element on the second pass is that the first pass always results in the most positive value "sinking" to the bottom of the list.

As a specific example of this process, consider the list of numbers illustrated in Figure 11.16. The first comparison results in the interchange of the first two element values, 690 and 307. The next comparison, between elements two and three in the revised list, results in the interchange of values between the second and third elements, 690 and 32. This comparison and possible switching of adjacent values is continued until the last two elements have been compared and possibly switched. This process completes the first pass through the data and results in the largest number moving to the bottom of the list. As the largest value sinks to its resting place at the bottom of the list, the smaller elements slowly rise, or "bubble," to the top of the list. This bubbling effect of the smaller elements is what gave rise to the name "bubble" sort for this sorting algorithm.

690	307	307	307	307
307	690	32	32	32
32	32	690	155	155
155	155	155	690	426
426	426	426	426	690

Figure 11.16 The first pass of an exchange sort.

Because the first pass through the list ensures that the largest value always moves to the bottom of the list, the second pass stops at the next-to-last element. This process continues with each pass stopping at one higher element than the previous pass, until either $n - 1$ passes through the list have been completed or no exchanges are necessary in any single pass. In both cases the resulting list is in sorted order. The pseudocode describing this sort is

```
Set interchange count to zero (not required, but done just to keep track of the interchanges)
For the first element in the list to one less than the last element (i index)
  For the second element in the list to the last element (j index)
    If num[j] < num[j - 1]
    {
      Swap num[j] with num[j - 1]
      Increment interchange count
    }
  EndFor
EndFor
Return interchange count
```

This sort algorithm is coded in C++ as the function `bubbleSort()`, which is included within Program 11.15 for testing purposes. This program tests `bubbleSort()` with the same list of 10 numbers used in Program 11.14 to test `selectionSort()`. For comparison to the earlier selection sort, the number of adjacent moves (exchanges) made by `bubbleSort()` is also counted and displayed.

Here is the output produced by Program 11.15.

```
The sorted list, in ascending order, is:
  5  10  22  32  45  67  73  98  99  101
18 moves were made to sort this list
```

As with the selection sort, the number of comparisons using a bubble sort is $O(n^2)$ and the number of required moves depends on the initial order of the values in the list. In the worst case, when the data is in reverse sorted order, the selection sort performs better than the bubble sort. Here both sorts require $n(n - 1)/2$ comparisons, but the selection sort needs only $n - 1$ moves while the bubble sort needs $n(n - 1)/2$ moves. The additional moves required by the bubble sort result from the intermediate exchanges between adjacent elements to "settle" each element into its final position. In this regard the selection sort is superior, because no intermediate moves are necessary. For random data, such as that used in Programs 11.14 and 11.15, the selection sort generally performs equal to or better than the bubble sort.

Program 11.15

```
#include <iostream>
using namespace std;

int bubbleSort(int [], int);

int main()
{
  const int NUMEL = 10;
  int nums[NUMEL] = {22,5,67,98,45,32,101,99,73,10};
  int i, moves;

  moves = bubbleSort(nums, NUMEL);

  cout << "The sorted list, in ascending order, is:\n";
  for (i = 0; i < NUMEL; ++i)
    cout << "  " <<nums[i];

  cout << endl << moves << " were made to sort this list\n";

  return 0;
}

int bubbleSort(int num[], int numel)
{
  int i, j, temp, moves = 0;

  for ( i = 0; i < (numel - 1); i++)
  {
    for(j = 1; j < numel; j++)
    {
      if (num[j] < num[j-1])
      {
        temp = num[j];
        num[j] = num[j-1];
        num[j-1] = temp;
        moves++;
      }
    }
  }

  return moves;
}
```

CHAPTER 12

Pointers

TOPICS

One of C++'s advantages is that it allows the programmer access to the addresses of variables used in a program. This permits programmers to directly enter into a computer's inner workings and access its basic storage structure. This gives the C++ programmer capabilities and programming power that is not available in other high-level languages. This is accomplished using a feature called pointers. Although other languages provide pointers, C++ extends this feature by providing pointer arithmetic; that is, pointer values can be added, subtracted, and compared.

Fundamentally, pointers are simply variables that are used to store memory addresses. This chapter presents the basics of declaring pointers, and then provides methods of applying pointer variables to access and use their stored addresses in meaningful ways.

12.1 ADDRESSES AND POINTERS

As we saw in Section 2.5, to display the address of a variable we can use C++'s address operator, `&`. To determine the address of `num`, we can use C++'s address operator, `&`, which means "the address of." When used in a nondeclarative statement, the address operator placed in front of a variable's name refers to the address of the variable.[1] For example, in a nondeclarative statement, `&num` means *the address of* `num`, `&miles` means *the address of* `miles`, and `&foo` means *the address of* `foo`. Program 12.1, which is a copy of Program 2.10, uses the address operator to display the address of the variable `num`.

Program 12.1

```
#include <iostream>
using namespace std;

int main()
{
  int num;

  num = 22;
  cout << "num = " << num << endl;
  cout << "The address of num = " << &num << endl;

  return 0;
}
```

The output of Program 12.1 is

```
num = 22
The address of num = 0012FED4
```

Figure 12.1 illustrates both the contents and address of the `num` variable provided by the output of Program 12.1.

[1] As we have seen in Chapter 6, when used in declaring reference arguments the ampersand refers to the data type *preceding* it. Thus, both the declarations `double& num` and `double #` are read as "`num` is the address of a `double`," or more commonly as "`num` is a reference to a `double`."

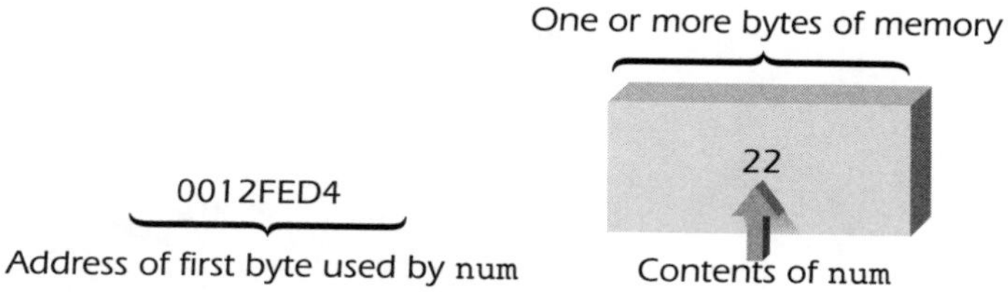

Figure 12.1 A more complete picture of the variable `num`.

As was mentioned in Section 2.5, address information will change depending on what computer is executing the program and how many other programs are currently loaded into memory.

Storing Addresses

Besides displaying the address of a variable, as was done in Program 12.1, we can also store addresses in suitably declared variables. For example, the statement

```
numAddr = &num;
```

stores the address corresponding to the variable `num` in the variable `numAddr`, as illustrated in Figure 12.2. Similarly, the statements

```
d = &m;
tabPoint = &list;
chrPoint = &ch;
```

store the addresses of the variables `m`, `list`, and `ch` in the variables `d`, `tabPoint`, and `chrPoint`, respectively, as illustrated in Figure 12.3.

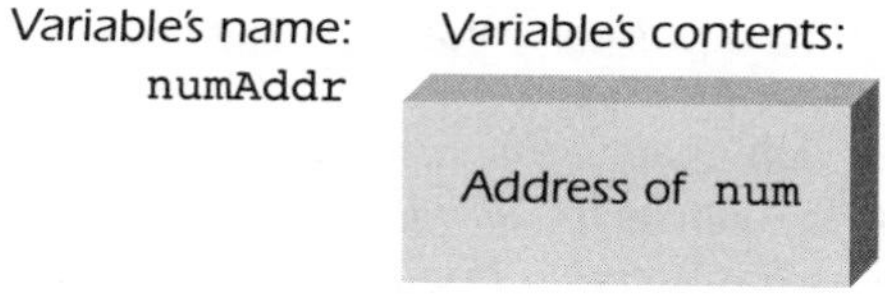

Figure 12.2 Storing `num`'s address into `numAddr`.

The variables `numAddr`, `d`, `tabPoint`, and `chrPoint` are formally called **pointer variables**, or **pointers** for short. **Pointers** are simply variables that are used to store the addresses of other variables.

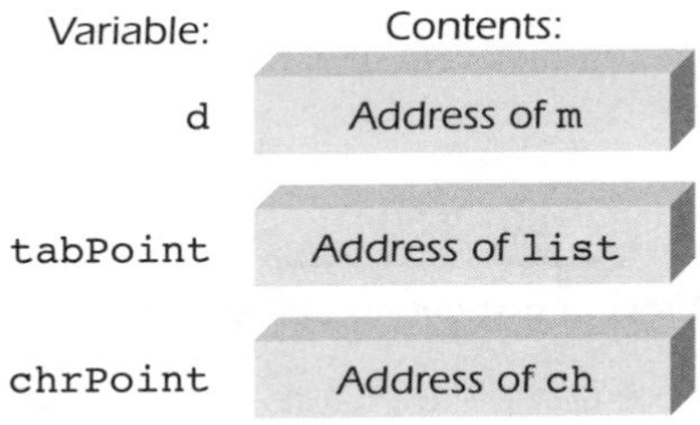

Figure 12.3 Storing more addresses.

Using Addresses

To use a stored address, C++ provides us with an **indirection operator**, `*`. The `*` symbol, when followed by a pointer (with a space permitted both before and after the `*`), means *the variable whose address is stored in*. Thus, if `numAddr` is a pointer (remember that a pointer is a variable that stores an address), `*numAddr` means *the variable whose address is stored in* `numAddr`. Similarly, `*tabPoint` means *the variable whose address is stored in* `tabPoint` and `*chrPoint` means *the variable whose address is stored in* `chrPoint`. Figure 12.4 shows the relationship between the address contained in a pointer variable and the variable ultimately addressed.

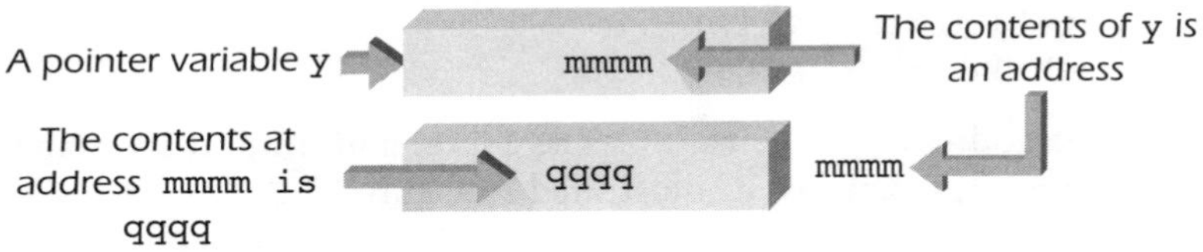

Figure 12.4 Using a pointer variable.

Although `*d` literally means *the variable whose address is stored in* `d`, this is commonly shortened to the statement *the variable pointed to by d*. Similarly, referring to Figure 12.4, `*y` can be read as *the variable pointed to by* `y`. The value ultimately obtained, as shown in Figure 12.4, is `qqqq`.

When using a pointer variable, the value that is finally obtained is always found by first going to the pointer variable (or pointer, for short) for an address. The address contained in the pointer is then used to get the desired contents. Certainly, this is a rather indirect way of getting to the final value and, not unexpectedly, the term indirect addressing is used to describe this procedure.

Because use of a pointer requires the computer to do a double lookup (first the address is retrieved, then the address is used to retrieve the actual data), a worthwhile question is, why would you want to store an address in the first place? The answer to this question rests on the intimate relationship between pointers and arrays and the ability of pointers to create and delete new variable storage locations dynamically, as a program is running. Both of these topics are presented later in this chapter. For now, however, given that each variable has a memory address associated with it, the idea of actually storing an address should not seem overly strange.

Declaring Pointers

Like all variables, pointers must be declared before they can be used to store an address. When we declare a pointer variable, C++ requires that we also specify the type of variable that is pointed to. For example, if the address in the pointer `numAddr` is the address of an integer, the correct declaration for the pointer is

```
int *numAddr;
```

This declaration is read as *the variable pointed to by* `numAddr` (from the `*numAddr` in the declaration) *is an integer.*[2]

Notice that the declaration `int *numAddr;` specifies two things: first that the variable pointed to by `numAddr` is an integer, and second that `numAddr` must be a pointer (because it is used with the indirection operator `*`). Similarly, if the pointer `tabPoint` points to (contains the address of) a double-precision number and `chrPoint` points to a character variable, the required declarations for these pointers are

```
double *tabPoint;
char *chrPoint;
```

These two declarations can be read, respectively, as *the variable pointed to by* `tabPoint` *is a* `double` and *the variable pointed to by* `chrPoint` *is a* `char`. Because all addresses appear the same, this additional information is needed by the compiler to know how many storage locations to access when it uses the address stored in the pointer. Other examples of pointer declarations are

```
char *inkey;
int *numPt;
double *nm1Ptr
```

To understand pointer declarations, it is helpful to read them "backward," starting with the indirection operator, the asterisk, `*`, and translating it either as *the variable whose address is stored in* or *the variable pointed to by*. Applying this to pointer declarations, the declaration `char *inkey;`, for example, can be read as either *the variable whose address is stored in* `inkey` *is a character* or *the variable pointed to by* `inkey` *is a character*. Both of these statements are frequently shortened to the simpler statement that `inkey` *points to a character*. Because all three interpretations of the declaration statement are correct, you can select and use whichever description makes more sense to you. We now put this together to construct a program using pointers. Consider Program 12.2.

---

[2]Pointer declarations may also be written in the form *dataType* pointerName;* where a space is placed between the indirection operator symbol and the pointer variable name. This form, however, becomes error prone when multiple pointer variables are declared in the same declaration statement and the asterisk symbol is inadvertently omitted after the first pointer name is declared. For example, the declaration `int* num1, num2;` declares `num1` as a pointer variable and `num2` as an integer variable. In order to more easily accomodate multiple pointers in the same declaration and clearly mark a variable as a pointer, we will adhere to the convention that places an asterisk directly in front of each pointer variable name. This possible error rarely occurs with reference declarations because references are almost exclusively used as formal parameters and single declarations of parameters is mandatory.

Program 12.2

```
#include <iostream>
using namespace std;

int main()
{
  int *numAddr;        // declare a pointer to an int
  int miles, dist;     // declare two integer variables

  dist = 158;          // store the number 158 into dist
  miles = 22;          // store the number 22 into miles
  numAddr = &miles;    // store the 'address of miles' in numAddr

  cout << "The address stored in numAddr is " << numAddr << endl;
  cout << "The value pointed to by numAddr is " << *numAddr << "\n\n";

  numAddr = &dist;  // now store the address of dist in numAddr
  cout << "The address now stored in numAddr is " << numAddr << endl;
  cout << "The value now pointed to by numAddr is " << *numAddr << endl;

  return 0;
}
```

The output of Program 12.2 is:

```
The address stored in numAddr is 0012FEC8
The value pointed to by numAddr is 22

The address now stored in numAddr is 0012FEBC
The value now pointed to by numAddr is 158
```

The only use for Program 12.2 is to help us understand "what gets stored where." Let's review the program to see how the output was produced.

The declaration statement `int *numAddr;` declares `numAddr` to be a pointer variable used to store the address of an integer variable. The statement `numAddr = &miles;` stores the address of the variable miles into the pointer `numAddr`. The first activation of `cout` causes this address to be displayed. The second activation of `cout` in Program 12.2 uses the indirection operator to retrieve and print out *the value pointed to by* `numAddr`, which is, of course, the value stored in `miles`.

Because `numAddr` has been declared as a pointer to an integer variable, we can use this pointer to store the address of any integer variable. The statement `numAddr = &dist` illustrates this by storing the address of the variable `dist` in `numAddr`. The last two `cout` statements verify the change in `numAddr`'s value and that the new stored address does point to the variable `dist`. As illustrated in Program 12.2, only addresses should be stored in pointers.

It certainly would have been much simpler if the pointer used in Program 12.2 could have been declared as `pointer numAddr;`. Such a declaration, however, conveys no information as to the storage used by the variable whose address is stored in `numAddr`. This information is essential when the pointer is used with the indirection operator, as it is in the second `cout` statement in Program 12.2. For example, if the address of an integer is stored in `numAddr`, then only four bytes of storage are typically retrieved when the address is used. If the address of a character is stored in `numAddr`, only 1 byte of storage would be retrieved, and a `double` typically requires the retrieval of eight bytes of storage. The declaration of a pointer must, therefore, include the type of variable being pointed to. Figure 12.5 illustrates this concept.

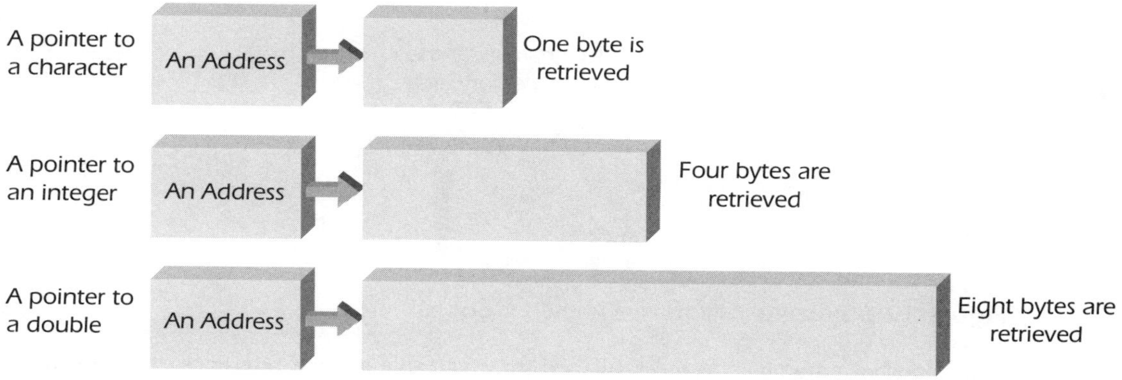

Figure 12.5 Addressing different data types using pointers.

References and Pointers

At this point you might be asking what the difference is between a pointer and a reference. Essentially, a reference is a named constant for an address; as such, the address named as a reference cannot be altered. Since a pointer is a variable, the address in the pointer can be changed. For most applications the use of references over pointers as arguments to functions is easier and clearly preferred. This is due to the simpler notation used in locating a reference parameter, which eliminates using the address operator, `&`, and the dereferencing operator, `*`, required for pointers. Technically, references are said to be **automatically dereferenced** or **implicitly dereferenced** (the two terms are used synonymously), while pointers must be explicitly dereferenced to locate the value being accessed.

For example, in passing a scalar variable's address as a function argument, references provide a simpler notational interface and are usually preferred. For other situations, such as dynamically allocating new sections of memory for additional variables as a program is running or using alternatives to array notation (both topics are presented in this chapter), pointers are required.

Reference Variables[3]

References are used almost exclusively as formal function parameters and return types. Nevertheless, reference variables are also available in C++. For completeness, we now show how such variables can be declared and used.

Once a variable has been declared it may be given additional names. This is accomplished using a reference declaration, which has the form

dataType& newName = existingName;

For example, the reference declaration

```
double& sum = total;
```

equates the name `sum` to the name `total`—both now refer to the same variable, as illustrated in Figure 12.6.

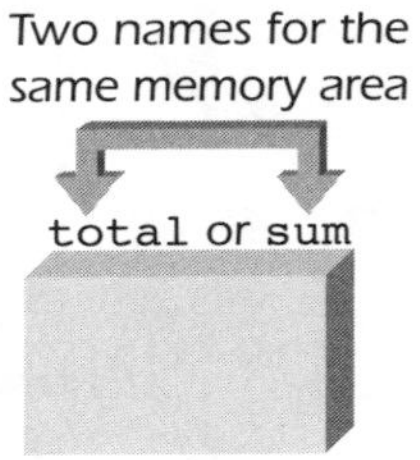

Figure 12.6 `sum` *is an alternative name for* `total`.

Once another name has been established for a variable using a reference declaration, the new name, which is referred to as an alias, can be used in place of the original name. For example, consider Program 12.3.

The following output is produced by Program 12.3:

```
sum = 20.5
total = 18.6
```

Since the variable `sum` is simply another reference to the variable `total`, it is the value stored in `total` that is obtained by the first `cout` object in Program 12.3. Changing the value in `sum` then changes the value in `total`, which is displayed by the second `cout` object in Program 12.3.

[3]This section may be omitted with no loss of subject continuity.

Program 12.3

```
#include <iostream>
using namespace std;

int main()
{
  double total = 20.5;      // declare and initialize total
  double& sum = total;      // declare another name for total

  cout << "sum = " << sum << endl;
  sum = 18.6;               // this changes the value in total
  cout << "total = " << total << endl;

  return 0;
}
```

In constructing references, two considerations must be kept in mind. First, the reference should be of the same data type as the variable it refers to. For example, the sequence of declarations

```
int num = 5;
double& numref = num;  // INVALID - CAUSES A COMPILER ERROR
```

does not equate `numref` to `num`; rather, it causes a compiler error because the two variables are of different data types. Secondly, a compiler error is produced when an attempt is made to equate a reference to a constant. For example, the following declaration is invalid:

```
int& val = 5;  // INVALID - CAUSES A COMPILER ERROR
```

Once a reference name has been correctly equated to one variable name, the reference cannot be changed to refer to another variable.

As with all declaration statements, multiple references may be declared in a single statement as long as each reference name is preceded by the ampersand symbol. Thus, the declaration

```
double& sum = total, & average;
```

creates two reference variables named sum and average.[4]

[4]Reference declarations may also be written in the form *dataType &newName=existingName;* where a space is placed between the ampersand symbol and the data-type. This form is not much used, however, probably to distinguish reference variable address notation from that used in assigning addresses to pointer variables.

Another way of looking at references is to consider them as pointers with restricted capabilities that implicitly hide a lot of dereferencing that is explicitly required with pointers.

For example, consider the statements

```
int b;       // b is an integer variable
int& a = b; // a is a reference variable that stores b's address
a = 10;      // this changes b's value to 10
```

Here, a is declared as a reference variable that is effectively a named constant for the address of the b variable. Since the compiler knows from the declaration that a is a reference variable, it automatically assigns the address of b (rather than the contents of b) to a in the declaration statement. Finally, in the statement `a = 10;` the compiler uses the address stored in a to change the value stored in b to 10. The advantage of using the reference is that it automatically performs an indirect access of b's value without the need for explicitly using the indirection symbol, *. As we have noted previously, this type of access is referred to as an **automatic dereference.**

Implementing this same correspondence between a and b using pointers is done by the following sequence of instructions:

```
int b;        // b is an integer variable
int *a = &b; // a is a pointer - store b's address in a
*a = 10;      // this changes b's value to 10 by explicit
              // dereference of the address in a
```

Here a is defined as a pointer that is initialized to store the address of b. Thus, *a, which can be read as either "the variable whose address is in a" or "the variable pointed to by a" is b, and the expression `*a = 10` changes b's value to 10. Notice that in the pointer case that the stored address can be altered to point to another variable; in the reference case the reference variable cannot be altered to refer to any variable except the one it is initialized to. Also notice that to dereference a, we must explicitly use the indirection operator, *. As you might expect, the * is also referred to as the dereferencing operator.

Exercises 12.1

1. If average is a variable, what does &average mean?
2. For the variables and addresses illustrated in Figure 12.7, determine &temp, &dist, &date, and &miles.

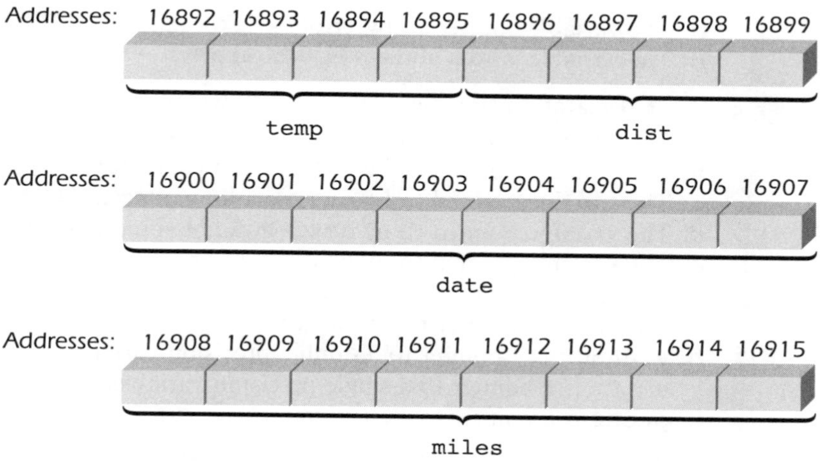

Figure 12.7 Memory bytes for Exercise 2.

3. a. Write a C++ program that includes the following declaration statements. Have the program use the address operator and the `cout` object to display the addresses corresponding to each variable.

```
int num, count;
long date;
float slope;
double power;
```

b. After running the program written for Exercise 3a, draw a diagram of how your computer has set aside storage for the variables in the program. On your diagram, fill in the addresses displayed by the program.

c. Modify the program written in Exercise 3a to display the amount of storage your computer reserves for each data type (use the `sizeof()` operator). With this information and the address information provided in Exercise 3b, determine if your computer set aside storage for the variables in the order in which they were declared.

4. If a variable is declared as a pointer, what must be stored in the variable?

5. Using the indirection operator, write expressions for the following.

a. The variable pointed to by `xAddr`
b. The variable whose address is in `yAddr`
c. The variable pointed to by `ptYld`
d. The variable pointed to by `ptMiles`
e. The variable pointed to by `mptr`
f. The variable whose address is in `pdate`
g. The variable pointed to by `distPtr`

h. The variable pointed to by `tabPt`
i. The variable whose address is in `hoursPt`

6. Write declaration statements for the following:
   a. The variable pointed to by `yAddr` is an integer.
   b. The variable pointed to by `chAddr` is a character.
   c. The variable pointed to by `ptYr` is a long integer.
   d. The variable pointed to by `amt` is a double-precision variable.
   e. The variable pointed to by `z` is an integer.
   f. The variable pointed to by `qp` is a single-precision variable.
   g. `datePt` is a pointer to an integer.
   h. `yldAddr` is a pointer to a double-precision variable.
   i. `amtPt` is a pointer to a single-precision variable.
   j. `ptChr` is a pointer to a character.

7. a. What are the variables `yAddr`, `chAddr`, `ptYr`, `amt`, `z`, `qp`, `datePt`, `yldAddr`, `amtPt`, and `ptChr` used in Exercise 6 called?
   b. Why are the variable names `amt`, `z`, and `qp` used in Exercise 6 not good choices for pointer variable names?

8. Write English sentences that describe what is contained in the following declared variables:
   a. `char *keyAddr;`
   b. `int *m;`
   c. `double *yldAddr;`
   d. `long *yPtr;`
   e. `double *pCou;`
   f. `int *ptDate;`

9. Which of the following are declarations for pointers?
   a. `long a;`
   b. `char b;`
   c. `char *c;`
   d. `int x;`
   e. `int *p;`
   f. `double w;`
   g. `float *k;`
   h. `float l;`
   i. `double *z;`

10. For the following declarations,

```
int *xPt, *yAddr;
long *dtAddr, *ptAddr;
double *ptZ;
int a;
long b;
double c;
```

determine which of the following statements is valid:

a. `yAddr = &a;` b. `yAddr = &b;` c. `yAddr = &c;`
d. `yAddr = a;` e. `yAddr = b;` f. `yAddr = c;`
g. `dtAddr = &a;` h. `dtAddr = &b;` i. `dtAddr = &c;`
j. `dtAddr = a;` k. `dtAddr = b;` l. `dtAddr = c;`
m. `ptZ = &a;` n. `ptAddr = &b;` o. `ptAddr = &c;`
p. `ptAddr = a;` q. `ptAddr = b;` r. `ptAddr = c;`
s. `yAddr = xPt;` t. `yAddr = dtAddr;` u. `yAddr = ptAddr;`

11. For the variables and addresses illustrated in Figure 12.8, fill in the appropriate data as determined by the following statements:

a. `ptNum = &m;`
b. `amtAddr = &amt;`
c. `*zAddr = 25;`
d. `k = *numAddr;`
e. `ptDay = zAddr;`
f. `*ptYr = 1987;`
g. `*amtAddr = *numAddr;`

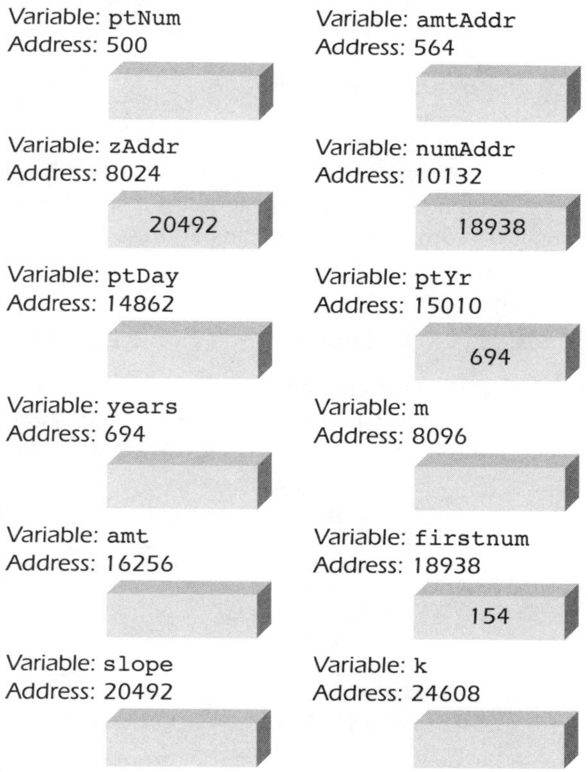

Figure 12.8 Memory locations for Exercise 11.

12. Using the `sizeof()` operator, determine the number of bytes used by your computer to store the address of an integer, character, and double-precision number. (*Hint:* `sizeof(*int)` can be used to determine the number of memory bytes used for a pointer to an integer.) Would you expect the size of each address to be the same? Why or why not?

12.2 ARRAY NAMES AS POINTERS

Although pointers are simply, by definition, variables used to store addresses, there is also a direct and intimate relationship between array names and pointers. In this section we describe this relationship in detail.

Figure 12.9 illustrates the storage of a single-dimensional array named `grade`, which contains five integers. Assume that each integer requires two bytes of storage.

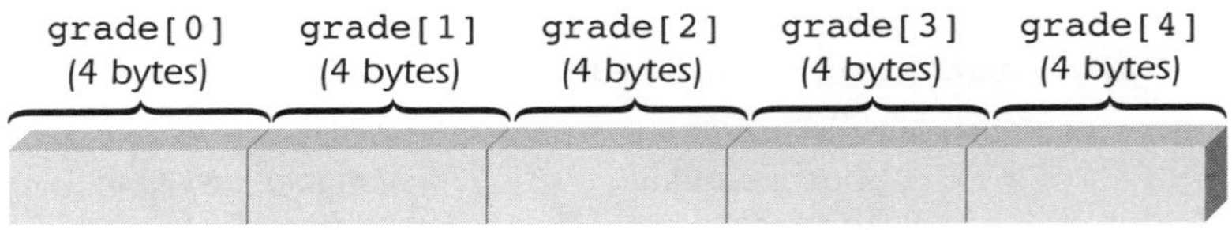

Figure 12.9 *The* `grade` *array in storage.*

Using subscripts, the fourth element in the `grade` array is referred to as `grade[3]`. The use of a subscript, however, conceals the extensive use of addresses by the computer. Internally, the computer immediately uses the subscript to calculate the address of the desired element based on both the starting address of the array and the amount of storage used by each element. Calling the fourth element `grade[3]` forces the compiler, internally, to make the address computation

```
&grade[3] = &grade[0] + (3 * sizeof(int))
```

Remembering that the address operator, `&`, means "the address of," this last statement is read "the address of `grade[3]` equals the address of `grade[0]` plus 12." Figure 12.10 illustrates the address computation used to locate `grade[3]`.

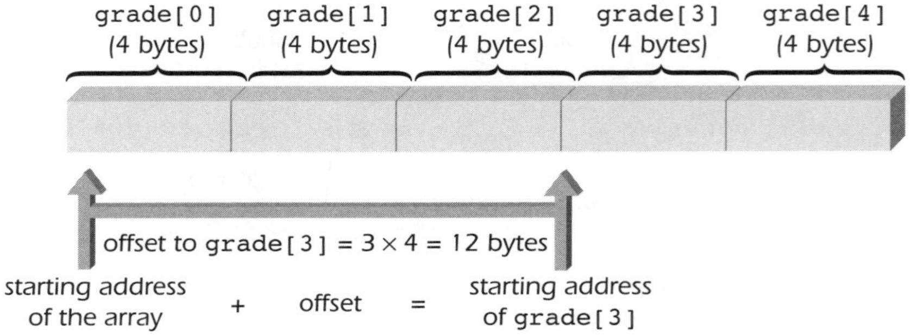

Figure 12.10 *Using a subscript to obtain an address.*

Recall that a pointer is a variable used to store an address. If we create a pointer to store the address of the first element in the **`grade`** array, we can mimic the operation used by the computer to access the array elements. Before we do this, let us first consider Program 12.4.

When Program 12.4 is run, the following display is obtained:

```
Element 0 is 98
Element 1 is 87
Element 2 is 92
Element 3 is 79
Element 4 is 85
```

Program 12.4

```
#include <iostream>
using namespace std;

int main()
{
  const int ARRAYSIZE = 5;

  int i, grade[ARRAYSIZE] = {98, 87, 92, 79, 85};

  for (i = 0; i < ARRAYSIZE; i++)
    cout << "\nElement " << i << " is " << grade[i];
  cout << endl;

  return 0;
}
```

Program 12.4 displays the values of the array grade using standard subscript notation. Now, let us store the address of array element 0 in a pointer. Then, using the indirection operator, `*`, we can use the address in the pointer to access each array element. For example, if we store the address of `grade[0]` into a pointer named `gPtr` (using the assignment statement `gPtr = &grade[0];`), then, as illustrated in Figure 12.11, the expression `*gPtr`, which means "the variable pointed to by `gPtr`," references `grade[0]`.

One unique feature of pointers is that offsets may be included in expressions using pointers. For example, the 1 in the expression `*(gPtr + 1)` is an **offset**. The complete expression references the integer that is one beyond the variable pointed to by `gPtr`. Similarly, as illustrated in Figure 12.12, the expression `*(gPtr + 3)` references the variable that is three integers beyond the variable pointed to by `gPtr`. This is the variable `grade[3]`.

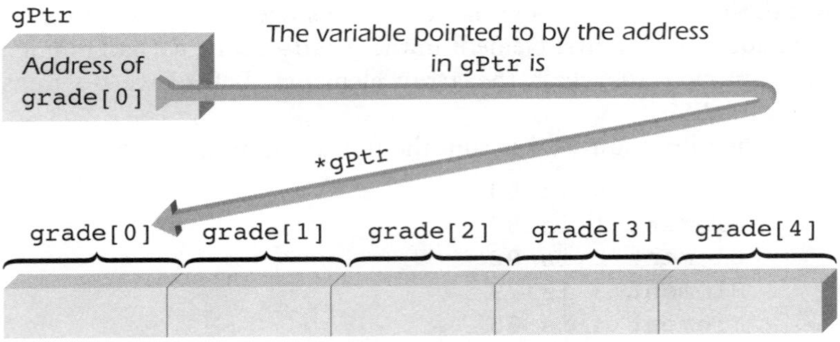

Figure 12.11 The variable pointed to by `*gPtr` is `grade[0]`.

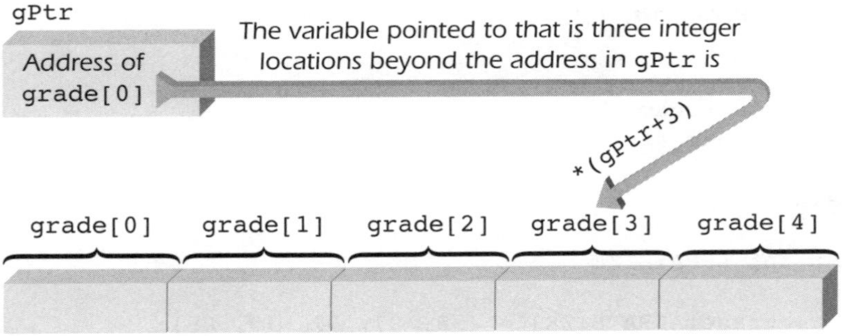

Figure 12.12 An offset of 3 from the address in `gPtr`.

Table 12.1 lists the complete correspondence between elements referenced by subscripts and by pointers and offsets. The relationships listed in Table 12.1 are illustrated in Figure 12.13.

Table 12.1 Array Elements May Be Referenced in Two Ways

Array Element	Subscript Notation	Pointer Notation
Element 0	`grade[0]`	`*gPtr` and `(gPtr + 0)`
Element 1	`grade[1]`	`*(gPtr + 1)`
Element 2	`grade[2]`	`*(gPtr + 2)`
Element 3	`grade[3]`	`*(gPtr + 3)`
Element 4	`grade[4]`	`*(gPtr + 4)`

Using the correspondence between pointers and subscripts illustrated in Figure 12.13, the array elements previously accessed in Program 12.4 using subscripts can now be accessed using pointers. This is done in Program 12.5.

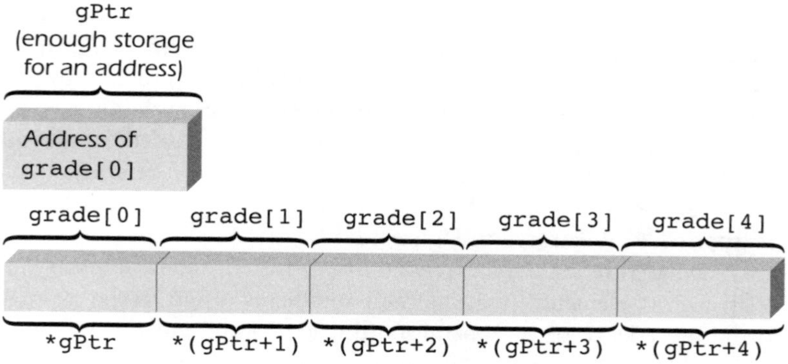

Figure 12.13 The relationship between array elements and pointers.

Program 12.5

```
#include <iostream>
using namespace std;

int main()
{

  const int ARRAYSIZE = 5;

  int *gPtr;             // declare a pointer to an int
  int i, grade[ARRAYSIZE] = {98, 87, 92, 79, 85};

  gPtr = &grade[0];      // store the starting array address
  for (i = 0; i < ARRAYSIZE; i++)
    cout << "\nElement " << i << " is " << *(gPtr + i);
  cout << endl;

  return 0;
}
```

The following display is obtained when Program 12.5 is run:

```
Element 0 is 98
Element 1 is 87
Element 2 is 92
Element 3 is 79
Element 4 is 85
```

Notice that this is the same display produced by Program 12.4.

The method used in Program 12.5 to access individual array elements simulates how the compiler internally references all array elements. Any subscript used by a programmer is automatically converted to an equivalent pointer expression by the compiler. In our case, since the declaration of `gPtr` included the information that integers are pointed to, any offset added to the address in `gPtr` is automatically scaled by the size of an integer. Thus, `*(gPtr + 3)`, for example, refers to the address of `grade[0]` plus an offset of twelve bytes `(3 * 4)`, where we have assumed that the `sizeof(int) = 4`. This is the address of `grade[3]` illustrated in Figure 12.13.

The parentheses in the expression `*(gPtr + 3)` are necessary to correctly reference the desired array element. Omitting the parentheses results in the expression `*gPtr + 3`. Due to the precedence of the operators, this expression adds 3 to "the variable pointed to by `gPtr`." Since `gPtr` points to `grade[0]`, this expression adds the value of `grade[0]` and `3` together. Note also that the expression `*(gPtr + 3)` does not change the address stored in `gPtr`. Once the computer uses the offset to locate the correct variable from the starting address in `gPtr`, the offset is discarded and the address in `gPtr` remains unchanged.

Although the pointer `gPtr` used in Program 12.4 was specifically created to store the starting address of the grade array, this was, in fact, unnecessary. When an array is created, the compiler automatically creates an internal pointer constant for it and stores the starting address of the array in this pointer. In almost all respects, a pointer constant is identical to a pointer variable created by a programmer; but, as we shall see, there are some differences.

For each array created, the name of the array becomes the name of the pointer constant created by the compiler for the array, and the starting address of the first location reserved for the array is stored in this pointer. Thus, declaring the `grade` array in Programs 12.4 and 12.5 actually reserved enough storage for five integers, created an internal pointer named `grade`, and stored the address of `grade[0]` in the pointer. This is illustrated in Figure 12.14.

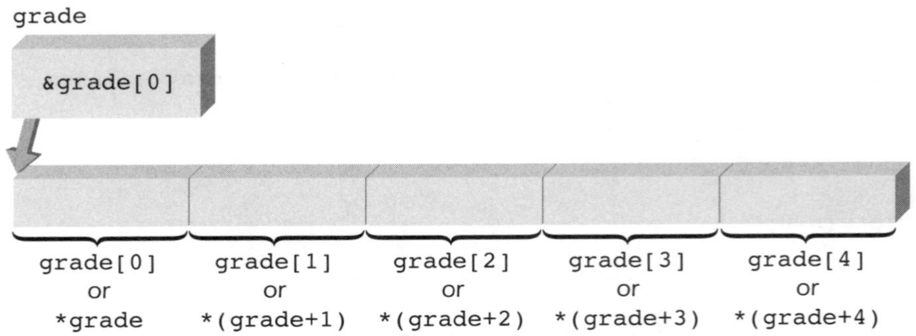

Figure 12.14 *Creating an array also creates a pointer.*

The implication is that every reference to `grade` using a subscript can be replaced by an equivalent reference using `grade` as a pointer. Thus, wherever the expression `grade[i]` is used, the expression `*(grade + i)` can also be used. This is illustrated in Program 12.6, where `grade` is used as a pointer to reference all of its elements.

Executing Program 12.6 produces the same output previously produced by Program 12.4 and Program 12.5. However, using `grade` as a pointer made it unnecessary to declare and initialize the pointer `gPtr` used in Program 12.5.

In most respects an array name and pointer can be used interchangeably. *A true pointer, however, is a variable and the address stored in it can be changed. An array name is a pointer constant and the address stored in the pointer cannot be changed by an assignment statement.* Thus, a statement such as `grade = &grade[2];` is invalid. This should come as no surprise. Since the whole purpose of an array name is to correctly locate the beginning of the array, allowing a programmer to change the address stored in the array name would defeat this purpose and lead to havoc whenever array elements were referenced. Also, expressions taking the address of an array name are invalid because the pointer created by the compiler is internal to the computer, not stored in memory, as are pointer variables. Thus, trying to store the address of `grade` using the expression `&grade` results in a compiler error.

Program 12.6

```
#include <iostream>
using namespace std;

int main()
{
  const int ARRAYSIZE = 5;

  int i, grade[ARRAYSIZE] = {98, 87, 92, 79, 85};

  for (i = 0; i < ARRAYSIZE; i++)
    cout << "\nElement " << i << " is " << *(grade + i);
  cout << endl;

  return 0;
}
```

An interesting sidelight to the observation that elements of an array can be referenced using pointers is that a pointer reference can always be replaced with a subscript reference. For example, if `numPtr` is declared as a pointer variable, the expression `*(numPtr + i)` can also be written as `numPtr[i]`. This is true even though `numPtr` is not created as an array. As before, when the compiler encounters the subscript notation, it replaces it internally with the pointer notation.

Dynamic Array Allocation[5]

As each variable is defined in a program, sufficient storage for it is assigned from a pool of computer memory locations made available to the compiler. Once specific memory locations have been reserved for a variable, these locations are fixed for the life of that variable, whether or not they are used. For example, if a function requests storage for an array of 500 integers, the storage for the array is allocated and fixed from the point of the array's definition. If the application requires fewer than 500 integers, the unused allocated storage is not released back to the system until the array goes out of existence. If, on the other hand, the application requires more than 500 integers, the size of the integer array must be increased and the function defining the array recompiled.

An alternative to this fixed or static allocation of memory storage locations is the dynamic allocation of memory. Under a **dynamic allocation** scheme, the amount of storage to be allocated is determined and adjusted as the program is run, rather than being fixed at compile time.

The dynamic allocation of memory is extremely useful when dealing with lists, because it allows the list to expand as new items are added and contract as items are deleted. For example, in constructing a list of grades, the exact number of grades ultimately needed may not be known. Rather than creating a fixed array to store the grades, it is extremely useful to have a mechanism whereby the array can be enlarged and shrunk as necessary. Two C++ operators, `new` and `delete`, that provide this capability are described in Table 12.2. (These operators require the `stdlib.h` header file.)

Table 12.2 The `new` and `delete` Operators (requires `new` header file)

Operator Name	Description
`new`	Reserves the number of bytes requested by the declaration. Returns the address of the first reserved location or `NULL` if sufficient memory is not available.
`delete`	Releases a block of bytes previously reserved. The address of the first reserved location must be passed as an argument to the operator.

Explicit dynamic storage requests for scalar variables or arrays are made either as part of a declaration or assignment statement.[6] For example, the declaration statement `int *num = new int;` reserves an area sufficient to hold one integer and places the address of this storage area into the pointer `num`. This same dynamic allocation can be made by first declaring the pointer using the declaration statement `int *num;` and then subsequently assigning the pointer an address with the assignment statement `num = new int;`. In either case the allocated storage area comes from the computer's free storage area.[7]

---

[5]This topic may be omitted on first reading with no loss of subject continuity.

[6]It should be noted that the compiler automatically provides this dynamic allocation and deallocation from the stack for all auto variables.

[7]The free storage area of a computer is formally referred to as the *heap*. The heap consists of unallocated memory that can be allocated to a program, as requested, while the program is running.

In a similar manner and of more usefulness is the dynamic allocation of arrays. For example, the declaration

```
int *grades = new int[200];
```

reserves an area sufficient to store 200 integers and places the address of the first integer into the pointer `grades`. Although we have used the constant 200 in this example declaration, a variable dimension can be used. For example, consider the sequence of instructions

```
cout << "Enter the number of grades to be processed: ";
cin  >> numgrades;
int *grades = new int[numgrades];
```

In this sequence the actual size of the array that is created depends on the number input by the user. Since pointer and array names are related, each value in the newly created storage area can be accessed using standard array notation, such as `grades[i]`, rather than the equivalent pointer notation `*(grades + i)`. Program 12.7 illustrates this sequence of code in the context of a complete program.

Program 12.7

```
#include <iostream>
#include <new>
using namespace std;

int main()
{
  int numgrades, i;

  cout << "Enter the number of grades to be processed: ";
  cin  >> numgrades;

  int *grades = new int[numgrades];  // create the array

  for(i = 0; i < numgrades; i++)
  {
    cout << "  Enter a grade: ";
    cin  >> grades[i];
  }
  cout << "\nAn array was created for " << numgrades << " integers\n";
  cout << " The values stored in the array are:";
  for (i = 0; i < numgrades; i++)
    cout << "\n   " << grades[i];
  cout << endl;

  delete[] grades;   // return the storage to the heap

  return 0;
}
```

Notice in Program 12.7 that the `delete` operator is used with braces whenever the `new` operator was previously used to create an array. The `delete[]` statement restores the allocated block of storage back to the operating system while the program is executing.[8] The only address required by `delete` is the starting address of the block of storage that was dynamically allocated. Thus, any address returned by `new` can subsequently be used by `delete` to restore the reserved memory back to the computer. The `delete` operator does not alter the address passed to it, but simply removes the storage that the address references. Following is a sample run using Program 12.7:

```
Enter the number of grades to be processed: 4
  Enter a grade: 85
  Enter a grade: 96
  Enter a grade: 77
  Enter a grade: 92

An array was created for 4 integers
 The values stored in the array are:
   85
   96
   77
   92
```

Exercises 12.2

1. Replace each of the following references to a subscripted variable with a pointer reference.

   a. `prices[5]` b. `grades[2]` c. `yield[10]`
   d. `dist[9]` e. `mile[0]` f. `temp[20]`
   g. `celsius[16]` h. `num[50]` i. `time[12]`

2. Replace each of the following references using a pointer with a subscript reference.

   a. `*(message + 6)` b. `*amount` c. `*(yrs + 10)`
   d. `*(stocks + 2)` e. `*(rates + 15)` f. `*(codes + 19)`

3. a. List the three things that the declaration statement `double slopes[5];` causes the compiler to do.
   b. If each double-precision number uses eight bytes of storage, how much storage is set aside for the `slopes` array?
   c. Draw a diagram similar to Figure 12.14 for the `slopes` array.
   d. Determine the byte offset relative to the start of the `slopes` array, corresponding to the offset in the expression `*(slopes + 3)`.

---

[8]The allocated storage should automatically be returned to the heap, by the operating system, when the program has completed execution. Since this is not always the case, however, it is extremely important to formally restore dynamically allocated memory to the heap when the storage is no longer needed. The term **memory leak** is used to describe the condition that occurs when dynamically allocated memory is not formally returned using the `delete` operator and the operating system does not reclaim the allocated memory area.

4. Write a declaration to store the following values into an array named `rates`: 12.9, 18.6, 11.4, 13.7, 9.5, 15.2, 17.6. Include the declaration in a program that displays the values in the array using pointer notation.

12.3 POINTER ARITHMETIC

Pointer variables, like all variables, contain values. The value stored in a pointer is, of course, an address. Thus, by adding and subtracting numbers to pointers we can obtain different addresses. Additionally, the addresses in pointers can be compared using any of the relational operators (==, !=, < , >, etc.) that are valid for comparing other variables. In performing arithmetic on pointers we must be careful to produce addresses that point to something meaningful. In comparing pointers we must also make comparisons that make sense. Consider the declarations:

```
int nums[100];
int *nPt;
```

To set the address of `nums[0]` into `nPt`, either of the following two assignment statements can be used:

```
nPt = &nums[0];
nPt = nums;
```

The two assignment statements produce the same result because `nums` is a pointer constant that contains the address of the first location in the array. This is, of course, the address of `nums[0]`. Figure 12.15 illustrates the allocation of memory resulting from the previous declaration and assignment statements, assuming that each integer requires four bytes of memory and that the location of the beginning of the `nums` array is at address 18934.

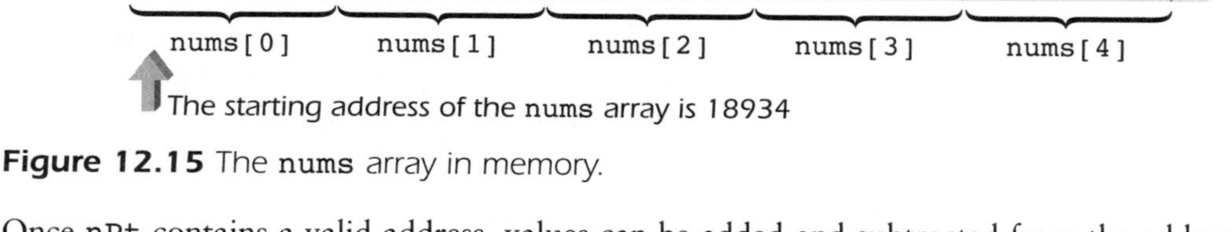

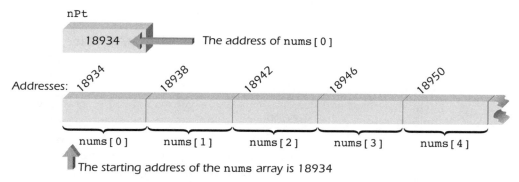

Figure 12.15 The `nums` array in memory.

Once `nPt` contains a valid address, values can be added and subtracted from the address to produce new addresses. When adding or subtracting numbers to pointers, the computer automatically adjusts the number to ensure that the result still "points to" a value of the correct type. For example, the statement `nPt = nPt + 4;` forces the computer to scale the 4 by the correct number to ensure that the resulting address is the address of an integer. Assuming that each integer requires four bytes of storage, as illustrated in Figure 12.15, the computer multiplies the 4 by 4 and adds 16 to the address in `nPt`. The resulting address is 18950, which is the correct address of `nums[4]`.

This automatic scaling by the computer ensures that the expression `nPt + i`, where `i` is any positive integer, correctly points to the `i`th element beyond the one currently being pointed to by `nPt`. Thus, if `nPt` initially contains the address of `nums[0]`, `nPt + 4` is the address of `nums[4]`, `nPt + 50` is the address of `nums[50]`, and `nPt + i` is the address of `nums[i]`. Although we have used actual addresses in Figure 12.15 to illustrate the scaling process, the programmer need never know or care about the actual addresses used by the computer. The manipulation of addresses using pointers generally does not require knowledge of the actual address.

Addresses can also be incremented or decremented using both prefix and postfix increment and decrement operators. Adding one to a pointer causes the pointer to point to the next element of the type being pointed to. Decrementing a pointer causes the pointer to point to the previous element. For example, if the pointer variable `p` is a pointer to an integer, the expression `p++` causes the address in the pointer to be incremented to point to the next integer. This is illustrated in Figure 12.16.

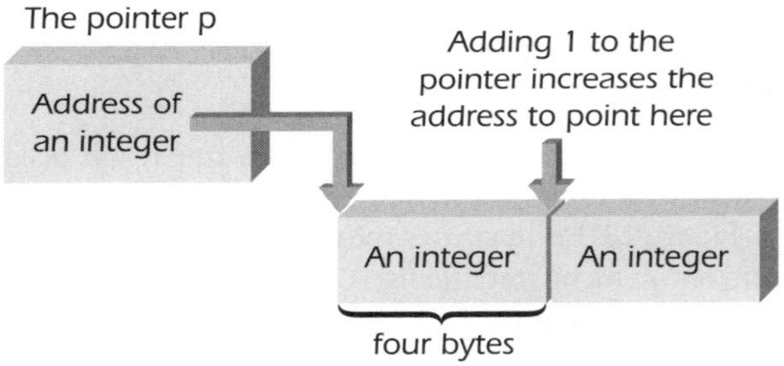

Figure 12.16 *Increments are scaled when used with pointers.*

In reviewing Figure 12.16, notice that the increment added to the pointer is correctly scaled to account for the fact that the pointer is used to point to integers. It is, of course, up to the programmer to ensure that the correct type of data is stored in the new address contained in the pointer.

The increment and decrement operators can be applied as both prefix and postfix pointer operators. All of the following combinations using pointers are valid:

```
*ptNum++     // use the pointer and then increment it
*++ptNum     // increment the pointer before using it
*ptNum--     // use the pointer and then decrement it
*--ptNum     // decrement the pointer before using it
```

Of the four possible forms, the most commonly used is the form `*ptNum++`. This is because such an expression allows each element in an array to be accessed as the address is "marched along" from the starting address of the array to the address of the last array element. The use of the increment operator is shown in Program 12.8. In this program each element in the `nums` array is retrieved by successively incrementing the address in `nPt`.

The output produced by Program 12.8 is:

```
The total of the array elements is 115
```

The expression `total = total + *nPt++` used in Program 12.8 accumulates the values "pointed to" by the `nPt` pointer variable. Within this expression, the term `*nPt++` first causes the computer to retrieve the integer pointed to by `nPt`. This is done by the `*nPt` part of the term. The postfix increment, `++`, then adds one to the address in `nPt` so that `nPt` now contains the address of the next array element. The increment is, of course, scaled by the computer so that the actual address in `nPt` is the correct address of the next element.

Program 12.8

```
#include <iostream>
using namespace std;

int main()
{
  const int NUMS = 5;

  int nums[NUMS] = {16, 54, 7, 43, -5};
  int i, total = 0, *nPt;

  nPt = nums;    // store address of nums[0] in nPt
  for (i = 0; i < NUMS; i++)
    total = total + *nPt++;
  cout << "The total of the array elements is " << total << endl;

  return 0;
}
```

Pointers may also be compared. This is particularly useful when dealing with pointers that point to elements in the same array. For example, rather than using a counter in a `for` loop to access each element in an array correctly, the address in a pointer can be compared to the starting and ending address of the array itself. The expression

```
nPt <= &nums[4]
```

is true (non-zero) as long as the address in `nPt` is less than or equal to the address of `nums[4]`. Since `nums` is a pointer constant that contains the address of `nums[0]`, the term `&nums[4]` can be replaced by the equivalent term `nums + 4`. Using either of these forms, Program 12.8 can be rewritten in Program 12.9 to continue adding array elements while the address in `nPt` is less than or equal to the address of the last array element.

In Program 12.9 the compact form of the accumulating expression, `total += *nPt++`, was used in place of the longer form, `total = total + *nPt++`. Also, the expression `nums + 4` does not change the address in `nums`. Since `nums` is an array name and not a pointer variable, its value cannot be changed. The expression `nums + 4` first retrieves the address in `nums`, adds 4 to this address (appropriately scaled) and uses the result for comparison purposes. Expressions such as `*nums++`, which attempt to change the address, are invalid. Expressions such as `*nums` or `*(nums + i)`, which use the address without attempting to alter it, are valid.

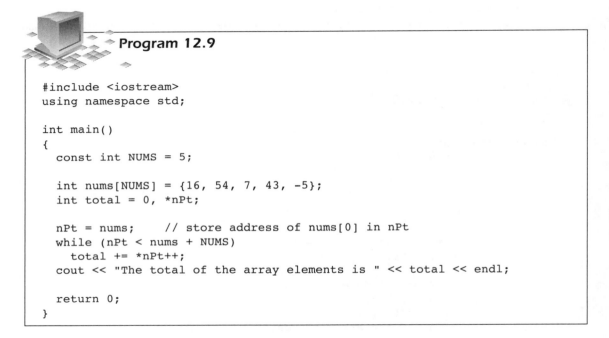

Program 12.9

```
#include <iostream>
using namespace std;

int main()
{
  const int NUMS = 5;

  int nums[NUMS] = {16, 54, 7, 43, -5};
  int total = 0, *nPt;

  nPt = nums;    // store address of nums[0] in nPt
  while (nPt < nums + NUMS)
    total += *nPt++;
  cout << "The total of the array elements is " << total << endl;

  return 0;
}
```

Pointer Initialization

Like all variables, pointers can be initialized when they are declared. When initializing pointers, however, you must be careful to set an address in the pointer. For example, an initialization such as

```
int *ptNum = &miles;
```

is only valid if `miles` itself is declared as an integer variable before `ptNum` is. Here, we are creating a pointer to an integer and setting the address in the pointer to the address of an integer variable. If the variable `miles` is declared after `ptNum` is declared, as follows,

```
int *ptNum = &miles;
int miles;
```

an error occurs. This is because the address of `miles` is used before `miles` has even been defined. Since the storage area reserved for `miles` has not been allocated when `ptNum` is declared, the address of `miles` does not yet exist.

Pointers to arrays can also be initialized within their declaration statements. For example, if `volts` has been declared an array of double-precision numbers, either of the following two declarations can be used to initialize the pointer named `zing` to the address of the first element in `volts`:

```
double *zing = &volts[0];
double *zing = volts;
```

The last initialization is correct because `volts` is itself a pointer constant containing an address of the proper type. (The variable name `zing` was selected in this example to reinforce the idea that any variable name can be selected for a pointer.)

Exercises 12.3

1. Replace the `while` statement in Program 12.9 with a `for` statement.
2. a. Write a program that stores the following numbers in the array named `rates`: 6.25, 6.50, 6.8, 7.2, 7.35, 7.5, 7.65, 7.8, 8.2, 8.4, 8.6, 8.8, 9.0. Display the values in the array by changing the address in a pointer called `dispPt`. Use a `for` statement in your program.
   b. Modify the program written in Exercise 2a to use a `while` statement.
3. Write a program that stores the following numbers in the array named `miles`: 15, 22, 16, 18, 27, 23, 20. Have your program copy the data stored in `miles` to another array named `dist` and then display the values in the `dist` array. Have your program use pointer rotation when copying and displaying array elements.
4. Write a program that declares three single-dimensional arrays named `miles`, `gallons`, and `mpg`. Each array should be capable of holding ten elements. In the `miles` array store the numbers 240.5, 300.0, 189.6, 310.6, 280.7, 216.9, 199.4, 160.3, 177.4, 192.3. In the `gallons` array store the numbers 10.3, 15.6, 8.7, 14, 16.3, 15.7, 14.9, 10.7, 8.3, 8.4. Each element of the `mpg` array should be calculated as the corresponding element of the `miles` array divided by the equivalent element of the `gallons` array: for example, `mpg[0] = miles[0] / gallons[0]`. Use pointers when calculating and displaying the elements of the `mpg` array.
5. Define an array of ten pointers to double-precision numbers. Then read ten numbers into the individual locations referenced by the pointers. Now add all of the numbers and store the result in a pointer-referenced location. Display the contents of all of the locations.

12.4 Passing Addresses

We have already seen one method of passing addresses to a function. This was accomplished using reference variables, as was described in Section 6.3. Although passing reference variables to a function provides the function with the address of the passed variables, it is an implied use of addresses because the function call does not reveal the fact that reference variables are being used. For example, the function call `swap(num1, num2);` does not reveal whether `num1` or `num2` is a reference variable. Only by looking at the declaration for these variables or by examining the function header line for `swap()` are the data types of `num1` and `num2` revealed.

In contrast to implicitly passing addresses using reference variables, addresses can be explicitly passed using pointer variables. Let us see how this is accomplished.

To explicitly pass an address to a function all that needs to be done is to place the address of operator, `&`, in front of the variable being passed. For example, the function call

```
swap(&firstnum, &secnum);
```

passes the addresses of the variables `firstnum` and `secnum` to `swap()`, as illustrated in Figure 12.17. Explicitly passing addresses using the address operator effectively is a *pass by reference* because the called function can reference, or access, variables in the calling function using the passed addresses. As we saw in Section 6.3, calls by reference are also accomplished using reference parameters. Here we will use the passed addresses and pointers to directly access the variables `firstnum` and `secnum` from within `swap()` and exchange their values—a procedure that was previously accomplished in Program 6.8 using reference parameters.

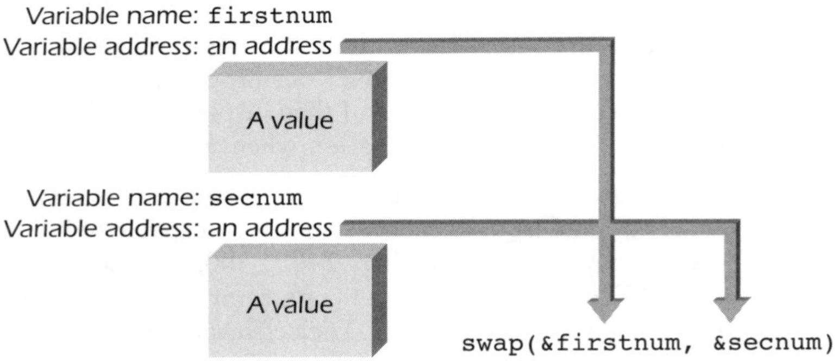

Figure 12.17 *Explicitly passing addresses to* `swap()`.

One of the first requirements in writing `swap()` is to construct a function header line that correctly receives and stores the passed values, which in this case are two addresses. As we saw in Section 12.1, addresses are stored in pointers, which means that the parameters of `swap()` must be declared as pointers.

Assuming that `firstnum` and `secnum` are double-precision variables, and that `swap()` returns no value, a suitable function header line for `swap` is

```
void swap(double *nm1Addr, double *nm2Addr);
```

The choice of the parameter names `nm1Addr` and `nm2Addr` is, as with all parameter names, up to the programmer. The declaration `double *nm1Addr`, however, declares that the parameter named `nm1Addr` will be used to store the address of a double-precision value. Similarly, the declaration `double  *nm2Addr` declares that `nm2Addr` will also store the address of a double-precision value.

Before writing the body of `swap()` to exchange the values in `firstnum` and `secnum`, let's first check that the values accessed using the addresses in `nm1Addr` and `nm2Addr` are correct. This is done in Program 12.10.

The output displayed when Program 12.10 is run is

```
The number whose address is in nm1Addr is 20.5
The number whose address is in nm2Addr is 6.25
```

Program 12.10

```
#include <iostream>
using namespace std;

void swap(double *, double *);      // function prototype

int main()
{
  double firstnum = 20.5, secnum = 6.25;

  swap(&firstnum, &secnum);            // call swap

  return 0;
}

// this function illustrates passing pointer arguments
void swap(double *nm1Addr, double *nm2Addr)
{

  cout << "The number whose address is in nm1Addr is "
       << *nm1Addr << endl;
  cout << "The number whose address is in nm2Addr is "
       << *nm2Addr << endl;

  return;
}
```

In reviewing Program 12.10, note two things. First, the function prototype for `swap()`

```
void swap(double *, double *)
```

declares that `swap()` returns no value directly and that its parameters are two pointers that "point to" double-precision values. As such, when the function is called it will require that two addresses be passed, and that each address is the address of a double-precision value.

The second item to notice is that within `swap()` the indirection operator is used to access the values stored in `firstnum` and `secnum`. The function `swap()` itself has no knowledge of these variable names, but it does have the address of `firstnum` stored in `nm1Addr` and the address of `secnum` stored in `nm2Addr`. The expression `*nm1Addr` used in the first `cout` statement means "the variable whose address is in `nm1Addr`." This is of course the variable `firstnum`. Similarly, the second `cout` statement obtains the value stored in `secnum` as "the variable whose address is in `nm2Addr`." Thus, we have successfully used pointers to allow `swap()` to access variables in `main()`. Figure 12.18 illustrates the concept of storing addresses in parameters.

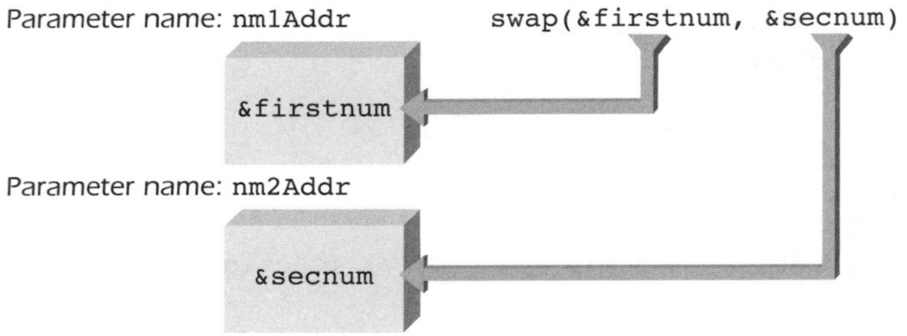

Figure 12.18 *Storing addresses in parameters.*

Having verified that `swap()` can access `main()`'s local variables `firstnum` and `secnum`, we can now expand `swap()` to exchange the values in these variables. The values in `main()`'s variables `firstnum` and `secnum` can be interchanged from within `swap()` using the three-step interchange algorithm previously described in Section 6.3, which for convenience is relisted below:

1. Store `firstnum`'s value in a temporary location.
2. Store `secnum`'s value in `firstnum`.
3. Store the temporary value in `secnum`.

Using pointers from within `swap()`, this takes the form:

1. Store the value of the variable pointed to by `nm1Addr` in a temporary location. The statement `temp = *nm1Addr;` does this (see Figure 12.19).
2. Store the value of the variable whose address is in `nm2Addr` in the variable whose address is in `nm1Addr`. The statement `*nm1Addr = *nm2Addr;` does this (see Figure 12.20).
3. Move the value in the temporary location into the variable whose address is in `nm2Addr`. The statement `*nm2Addr = temp;` does this (see Figure 12.21).

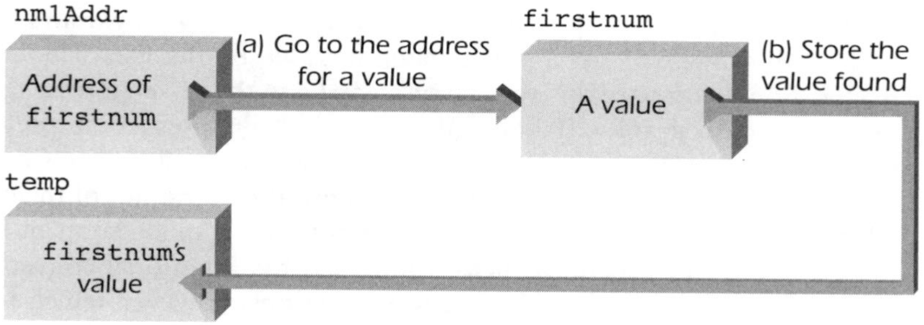

Figure 12.19 Indirectly storing `firstnum`'s value.

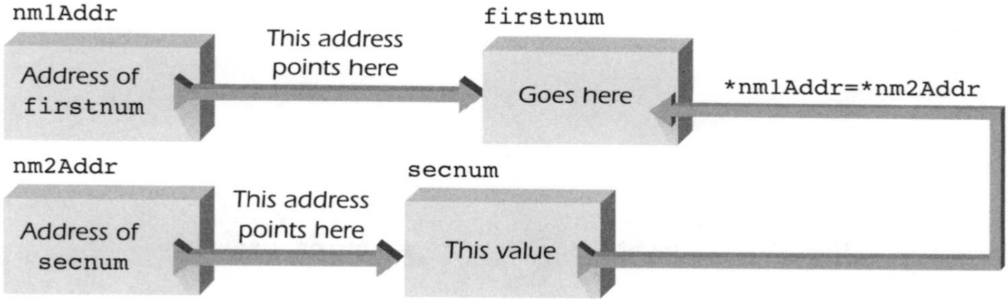

Figure 12.20 Indirectly changing `firstnum`'s value.

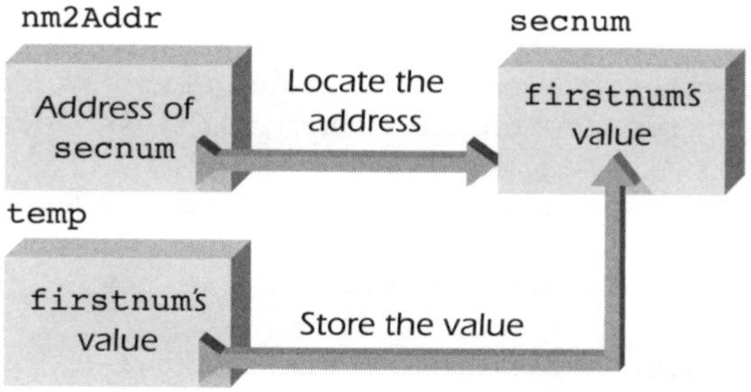

Figure 12.21 Indirectly changing `secnum`'s value.

Program 12.11 contains the final form of `swap()`, written according to our description.

The following sample run was obtained using Program 12.11:

```
The value stored in firstnum is: 20.5
The value stored in secnum is: 6.25

The value stored in firstnum is now: 6.25
The value stored in secnum is now: 20.5
```

As illustrated in this output, the values stored in `main()`'s variables have been modified from within `swap()`, which was made possible by the use of pointers. The interested reader should compare this version of `swap()` with the version using references that was presented in Program 6.10. The advantage of using pointers in preference to references is that the function call itself explicitly designates that addresses are being used, which is a direct alert that the function will most likely alter variables of the calling function. The advantages of using references is that the notation is much simpler.

Generally, for functions such as `swap()`, the notational convenience wins out, and references are used. In passing arrays to functions, however, which is our next topic, the compiler automatically passes an address. This dictates that pointer variables will be used to store the address.

Program 12.11

```
#include <iostream>
using namespace std;

void swap(double *, double *);     // function prototype

int main()
{
  double firstnum = 20.5, secnum = 6.25;


  cout << "The value stored in firstnum is: " << firstnum << endl;
  cout << "The value stored in secnum is: " << secnum << "\n\n";

  swap(&firstnum, &secnum);          // call swap

  cout << "The value stored in firstnum is now: "
       << firstnum <<  endl;
  cout << "The value stored in secnum is now: "
       << secnum << endl;

  return 0;
}

// this function swaps the values in its two arguments
void swap(double *nm1Addr, double *nm2Addr)
{
  double temp;
```

(Continued)

(Continued)

```
  temp = *nm1Addr;             // save firstnum's value
  *nm1Addr = *nm2Addr;         // move secnum's value in firstnum
  *nm2Addr = temp;             // change secnum's value

  return;
}
```

Passing Arrays

When an array is passed to a function, its address is the only item actually passed. By this we mean the address of the first location used to store the array, as illustrated in Figure 12.22. Since the first location reserved for an array corresponds to element 0 of the array, the "address of the array" is also the address of element 0.

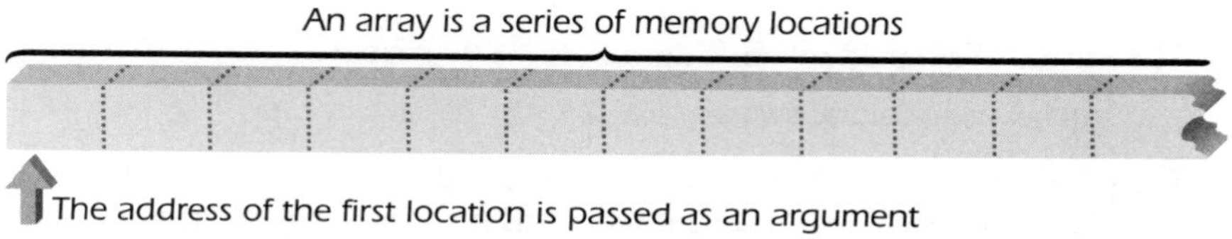
An array is a series of memory locations
The address of the first location is passed as an argument

Figure 12.22 The address of an array is the address of the first location reserved for the array.

For a specific example in which an array is passed to a function, consider Program 12.12. In this program, the nums array is passed to the `findMax()` function using conventional array notation.

Program 12.12

```
#include <iostream>
using namespace std;

int findMax(int [], int);    // function prototype

int main()
{
  const int NUMPTS = 5;

  int nums[NUMPTS] = {2, 18, 1, 27, 16};
```

(Continued)

(Continued)

```
  cout << "\nThe maximum value is "
       << findMax(nums,NUMPTS) << endl;
  return 0;
}
// this function returns the maximum value in an array of ints
int findMax(int vals[], int numels)
{
  int i, max = vals[0];

  for (i = 1; i < numels; i++)
   if (max < vals[i])
     max = vals[i];

  return max;
}
```

The output displayed when Program 12.12 is executed is

```
The maximum value is 27
```

The parameter named `vals` in the header line declaration for `findMax()` actually receives the address of the array nums. As such, `vals` is really a pointer, since pointers are variables (or parameters) used to store addresses. Since the address passed into `findMax()` is the address of an integer, another suitable header line for `findMax()` is

```
int findMax(int *vals, int numels) // here vals is declared as
                                   // a pointer to an integer
```

The declaration `int *vals` in the header line declares that `vals` is used to store an address of an integer. The address stored is, of course, the location of the beginning of an array. The following is a rewritten version of the `findMax()` function that uses the new pointer declaration for `vals`, but retains the use of subscripts to refer to individual array elements:

```
int findMax(int *vals, int numels)   // find the maximum value
{
  int i, max = vals[0];

  for (i = 1; i < numels; i++)
   if (max < vals[i])
     max = vals[i];

  return max;
}
```

Regardless of how `vals` is declared in the function header or how it is used within the function body, it is truly a pointer variable. Thus, the address in `vals` may be modified.

This is not true for the name nums. Since nums is the name of the originally created array, it is a pointer constant. As described in Section 12.2, this means that the address in nums cannot be changed and that the address of nums itself cannot be taken. No such restrictions, however, apply to the pointer variable named vals. All the address arithmetic that we learned in the previous section can be legitimately applied to vals.

We shall write two additional versions of `findMax()`, both using pointers instead of subscripts. In the first version we simply substitute pointer notation for subscript notation. In the second version we use address arithmetic to change the address in the pointer.

As previously stated, access to an array element using the subscript notation `arrayName[i]` can always be replaced by the pointer notation `*(arrayName + i)`. In our first modification to `findMax()`, we make use of this correspondence by simply replacing all references to `vals[i]` with the equivalent expression `*(vals + i)`.

```
int findMax(int *vals, int numels)   // find the maximum value
{
  int i, max = *vals;

  for (i = 1; i < numels; i++)
   if (max < *(vals + i) )
     max = *(vals + i);

  return max;
}
```

Our next version of `findMax()` makes use of the fact that the address stored in vals can be changed. After each array element is retrieved using the address in vals, the address itself is incremented by one in the altering list of the for statement. The expression `max = *vals` previously used to set max to the value of `vals[0]` is replaced by the expression `max = *vals++`, which adjusts the address in vals to point to the second element in the array. The element assigned to max by this expression is the array element pointed to by vals before vals is incremented. The postfix increment, ++, does not change the address in vals until after the address has been used to retrieve the first array element.

```
int findMax(int *vals, int numels)   // find the maximum value
{
  int i, max = *vals++;    // get the first element and increment
  for (i = 1; i < numels; i++, vals++)
  {
    if (max < *vals)
      max = *vals;
  }
  return max;
}
```

Let us review this version of `findMax()`. Initially the maximum value is set to "the thing pointed to by vals." Since vals initially contains the address of the first element in the array passed to findMax(), the value of this first element is stored in max. The address in vals is then incremented by one. The one that is added to vals is automatically scaled by the number of bytes used to store integers. Thus, after the increment, the address stored in vals is the address of the next array element. This is illustrated in Figure 12.23. The value of this next element is compared to the maximum and the address is again incremented, this time from within the altering list of the for statement. This process continues until all the array elements have been examined.

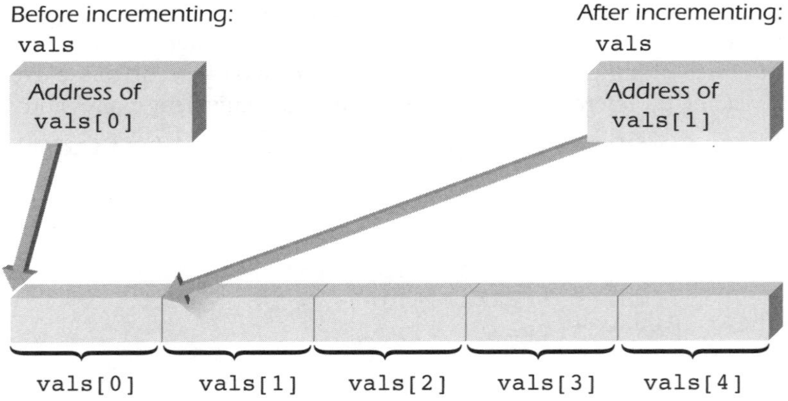

Figure 12.23 Pointing to different elements.

The version of findMax() that you should choose is a matter of personal style and taste. Generally, beginning programmers feel more at ease using subscripts rather than using pointers. Also, if the program uses an array as the natural storage structure for the application and data at hand, an array access using subscripts is more appropriate to clearly indicate the intent of the program. However, as we learn about data structures, the use of pointers becomes an increasingly useful and powerful tool in its own right. In these instances there is no simple or easy equivalence to the use of subscripts.

One further "neat trick" can be gleaned from our discussion. Since passing an array to a function really involves passing an address, we can just as well pass any valid address. For example, the function call findMax(&nums[2],3) passes the address of nums[2] to findMax(). Within findMax() the pointer vals stores the address and the function starts the search for a maximum at the element corresponding to this address. Thus, from findMax()'s perspective, it has received an address and proceeds appropriately.

Advanced Pointer Notation[9]

Access to multidimensional arrays can also be made using pointer notation, although the notation becomes more and more cryptic as the array dimensions increase. An extremely useful application of this notation occurs with two-dimensional character arrays. Here we

[9]This topic may be omitted without loss of subject continuity.

consider pointer notation for two-dimensional numeric arrays. For example, consider the declaration

```
int nums[2][3] = { {16,18,20},
                   {25,26,27} };
```

This declaration creates an array of elements and a set of pointer constants named **nums**, **nums[0]**, and **nums[1]**. The relationship between these pointer constants and the elements of the **nums** array are illustrated in Figure 12.24.

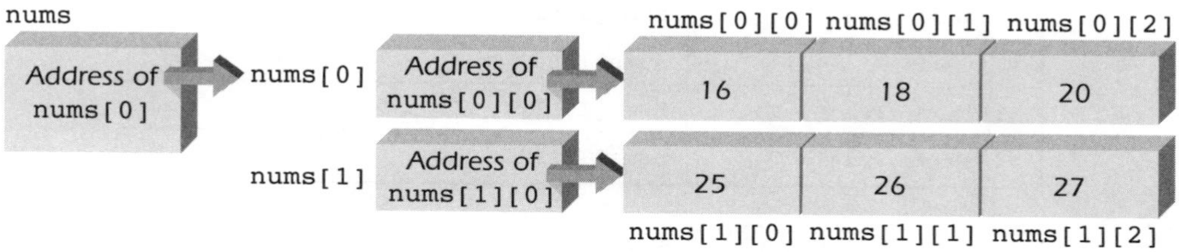

Figure 12.24 Storage of the **nums** array and associated pointer constants.

The availability of the pointer constants associated with a two-dimensional array allows us to access array elements in a variety of ways. One way is to consider the two-dimensional array as an array of rows, where each row is itself an array of three elements. Considered in this light, the address of the first element in the first row is provided by **nums[0]** and the address of the first element in the second row is provided by **nums[1]**. Thus, the variable pointed to by **nums[0]** is **nums[0][0]** and the variable pointed to by **nums[1]** is **nums[1][0]**. Once the nature of these constants is understood, each element in the array can be accessed by applying an appropriate offset to the appropriate pointer. Thus, the following notations are equivalent:

Pointer Notation	Subscript Notation	Value
`*nums[0]`	`nums[0][0]`	16
`*(nums[0] + 1)`	`nums[0][1]`	18
`*(nums[0] + 2)`	`nums[0][2]`	20
`*nums[1]`	`nums[1][0]`	25
`*(nums[1] + 1)`	`nums[1][1]`	26
`*(nums[1] + 2)`	`nums[1][2]`	27

We can now go even further and replace **nums[0]** and **nums[1]** with their respective pointer notations, using the address of **nums** itself. As illustrated in Figure 12.24, the variable pointed to by nums is nums[0]. That is, *nums is nums[0]. Similarly, *(nums + 1) is nums[1]. Using these relationships leads to the following equivalences:

Pointer Notation	Subscript Notation	Value
*(*nums)	nums[0][0]	16
*(*nums + 1)	nums[0][1]	18
*(*nums + 2)	nums[0][2]	20
((nums + 1))	nums[1][0]	25
((nums + 1) + 1)	nums[1][1]	26
((nums + 1) + 2)	nums[1][2]	27

The same notation applies when a two-dimensional array is passed to a function. For example, assume that the two-dimensional array nums is passed to the function calc() using the call calc(nums);. Here, as with all array passes, an address is passed. A suitable function header line for the function calc() is

```
calc(int pt[2][3])
```

As we have already seen, the parameter declaration for pt can also be

```
calc(int pt[][3])
```

Using pointer notation, another suitable declaration is

```
calc(int (*pt)[3])
```

In this last declaration the inner parentheses are required to create a single pointer to arrays of three integers. Each array is, of course, equivalent to a single row of the nums array. By suitably offsetting the pointer, each element in the array can be accessed. Notice that without the parentheses the declaration becomes

```
int *pt[3]
```

which creates an array of three pointers, each one pointing to a single integer.

Once the correct declaration for pt is made (any of the three valid declarations can be used), the following notations within the function calc() are all equivalent:

Pointer Notation	Subscript Notation	Value
*(*pt)	pt[0][0]	16
*(*pt+1)	pt[0][1]	18
*(*pt+2)	pt[0][2]	20
((pt+1))	pt[1][0]	25
((pt+1)+1)	pt[1][1]	26
((pt+1)+2)	pt[1][2]	27

The last two notations using pointers are encountered in more advanced C++ programs. The first of these occurs because functions can return any valid C++ scalar data type, including pointers to any of these data types. If a function returns a pointer, the data type being pointed to must be declared in the function's declaration. For example, the declaration

```
int *calc()
```

declares that `calc()` returns a pointer to an integer value. This means that an address of an integer variable is returned. Similarly, the declaration

```
double *taxes()
```

declares that `taxes()` returns a pointer to a double-precision value. This means that an address of a double-precision variable is returned.

In addition to declaring pointers to integers, double-precision numbers, and C++'s other data types, pointers can also be declared that point to (contain the address of) a function. Pointers to functions are possible because function names, like array names, are themselves pointer constants. For example, the declaration

```
int (*calc)()
```

declares `calc()` to be a pointer to a function that returns an integer. This means that `calc` will contain the address of a function, and the function whose address is in the variable `calc` returns an integer value. If, for example, the function `sum()` returns an integer, the assignment `calc = sum;` is valid.

Exercises 12.4

1. The following declaration was used to create the `prices` array:

   ```
   double prices[500];
   ```

   Write three different headers for a function named `sortArray()` that accepts the `prices` array as a parameter named `inArray` and returns no value.

2. The following declaration was used to create the `keys` array:

   ```
   char keys[256];
   ```

   Write three different headers for a function named `findKey()` that accepts the `keys` array as a parameter named select and returns no value.

3. The following declaration was used to create the `rates` array:

   ```
   double rates[256];
   ```

   Write three different headers for a function named `maximum()` that accepts the `rates` array as a parameter named `speed` and returns a double-precision value.

4. Modify the `findMax()` function to locate the minimum value of the passed array. Write the function using only pointers.

5. In the last version of findMax() presented, vals was incremented inside the altering list of the for statement. Instead, suppose that we do the incrementing within the condition expression of the if statement as follows:

```
int findMax(int *vals, int numels)    // incorrect version
{
  int i, max = *vals++;   // get the first element and increment

  for (i = 1; i < numels; i++)
    if (max < *vals++)
      max = *vals;
  return (max);
}
```

This version produces an incorrect result. Determine why.

6. a. Write a program that has a declaration in main to store the following numbers into an array named rates: 6.5, 7.2, 7.5, 8.3, 8.6, 9.4, 9.6, 9.8, 10.0. There should be a function call to show() that accepts rates in a parameter named rates and then displays the numbers using the pointer notation *(rates + i).

b. Modify the show() function written in Exercise 6a to alter the address in rates. Always use the expression *rates rather than *(rates + i) to retrieve the correct element.

7. a. Determine the output of the following program:

```
#include <iostream>
using namespace std;

const int ROWS = 2;
const int COLS = 3;

void arr(int [][COLS]);

int main()
{
  int nums[ROWS][COLS] = { {33,16,29},
                           {54,67,99}};
  arr(nums);

  return 0;
}
```

```
void arr(int (*val)[COLS])
{
  cout << '\n' << *(*val);
  cout << '\n' << *(*val + 1);
  cout << '\n' << *(*(val + 1) + 2);
  cout << '\n' << *(*val) + 1;

  return;
}
```

b. Given the declaration for `val` in the `arr()` function, would the notation `val[1][2]` be valid within the function?

12.5 COMMON PROGRAMMING ERRORS

In using the material presented in this chapter, be aware of the following possible errors.

1. Attempting to store an address in a variable that has not been declared as a pointer.
2. Using a pointer to access non-existent array elements. For example, if `nums` is an array of ten integers, the expression `*(nums + 15)` points to a location six integer locations beyond the last element of the array. Because C++ does not do any bounds checking on array accesses, this type of error is not caught by the compiler. This is the same error, disguised in pointer notation form, that occurs when using a subscript to access an out-of-bounds array element.
3. Forgetting to use the bracket set, `[]`, following the `delete` operator when dynamically deallocating memory that was previously allocated using the new `[]` operator.
4. Incorrectly applying the address and indirection operators. For example, if `pt` is a pointer variable, the expressions

   ```
   pt = &45
   pt = &(miles + 10)
   ```

   are both invalid because they attempt to take the address of a value. Notice that the expression `pt = &miles + 10`, however, is valid. Here, `10` is added to the address of `miles`. Again, it is the programmer's responsibility to ensure that the final address "points to" a valid data element.
5. Taking addresses of pointer constants. For example, given the declarations

   ```
   int nums[25];
   int *pt;
   ```

the assignment

```
pt = &nums;
```

is invalid. The constant `nums` is a pointer constant that is itself equivalent to an address. The correct assignment is `pt = nums`.

6. Taking addresses of a reference argument, reference variable, or register variable. The reason for this is that reference arguments and variables are essentially the same as pointer constants, in that they are named address values. Similarly, the address of a register variables cannot be taken. Thus, for the declarations

   ```
   register in total;
   int *ptTot;
   ```

   the assignment

   ```
   ptTot = &total;   // INVALID
   ```

   is invalid. The reason for this is that register variables are stored in a computer's internal registers, and these storage areas do not have standard memory addresses.

7. Initializing pointer variables incorrectly. For example, the initialization

   ```
   int *pt = 5;
   ```

   is invalid. Since `pt` is a pointer to an integer, it must be initialized with a valid address.

8. Becoming confused about whether a variable *contains* an address or *is* an address. Pointer variables and pointer arguments contain addresses. Although a pointer constant is synonymous with an address, it is useful to treat pointer constants as pointer variables with two restrictions:

   - The address of a pointer constant cannot be taken.
   - The address "contained in" the pointer constant cannot be altered.

   Except for these two restrictions, pointer constants and pointer variables can be used almost interchangeably. Therefore, when an address is required, any of the following can be used:

   - a pointer variable name
   - a pointer argument name
   - a pointer constant name
   - a non-pointer variable name preceded by the address operator (e.g., `&variable`)
   - a non-pointer argument name preceded by the address operator (e.g., `&argument`)

   Some of the confusion surrounding pointers is caused by the cavalier use of the word *pointer*. For example, the phrase "a function requires a pointer argument" is more clearly understood when it is realized that the phrase really means "a function requires an address as an argument." Similarly, the phrase "a function returns a pointer" really means "a function returns an address."

If you are ever in doubt as to what is really contained in a variable or how it should be treated, use the `cout` object to display the contents of the variable, the "thing pointed to," or "the address of the variable." Seeing what is displayed frequently helps sort out what is really in the variable.

12.6 Chapter Summary

1. Every variable has a data type, an address, and a value. In C++ the address of a variable can be obtained by using the address operator `&`.

2. A pointer is a variable that is used to store the address of another variable. Pointers, like all C++ variables, must be declared. The indirection operator, `*`, is used both to declare a pointer variable and to access the variable whose address is stored in a pointer.

3. An array name is a pointer constant. The value of the pointer constant is the address of the first element in the array. Thus, if `val` is the name of an array, `val` and `&val[0]` can be used interchangeably.

4. Any access to an array element using subscript notation can always be replaced using pointer notation. That is, the notation `a[i]` can always be replaced by the notation `*(a + i)`. This is true whether `a` was initially declared explicitly as an array or as a pointer.

5. Arrays can be dynamically created as a program is executing. For example, the sequence of statements

   ```
   cout  << "Enter the array size: ";
   cin   >> num;
   int  *grades = new int[num];
   ```

   creates an array named `grades` of size `num`. The area allocated for the array can be dynamically destroyed using the `delete[]` operator. For example, the statement `delete[] grades;` will return the allocated area for the `grades` array back to the computer.

6. Arrays are passed to functions as addresses. The called function always receives direct access to the originally declared array elements.

7. When a single-dimensional array is passed to a function, the parameter declaration for the function can be either an array declaration or a pointer declaration. Thus, the following parameter declarations are equivalent:

   ```
   double a[];
   double *a;
   ```

8. Pointers can be incremented, decremented, compared, and assigned. Numbers added to or subtracted from a pointer are automatically scaled. The scale factor used is the number of bytes required to store the data type originally pointed to.

Chapter 13

Structures

Topics

A structure is a historical holdover from C. From a programmer's perspective, a structure can be thought of as a class that has all public instance variables and no member methods. In commercial applications, a structure is referred to, and is the same thing as, a record. In C and C++, a structure provides a means of storing values that have different data types, such as an integer part number, a character part type, and a double-precision supply voltage.

For example, assume that an integrated circuit (IC) manufacturer maintains a summary of information for each of the circuits it fabricates. The data items kept for each circuit are illustrated in Figure 13.1.

Part Number:
Integrated Circuit Family:
Function Type:
Supply Voltage:
Units in Stock:

Figure 13.1 An inventory record.

Each of the individual data items listed in Figure 13.1 is an entity by itself that is referred to as a **data field**. *Taken together, all the data fields form a single unit that is referred to as a* **structure**.

Although the integrated circuit manufacturer could keep track of hundreds of components, the form of each character's structure is identical. In dealing with structures it is important to distinguish between a structure's form and its contents.

A structure's form consists of the symbolic names, data types, and arrangement of individual data fields in the structure. The structure's contents refers to the actual data stored in the symbolic names. Figure 13.2 shows acceptable contents for the structure form illustrated in Figure 13.1.

Part Number: 23421
Integrated Circuit Family: TTL
Function Type: AND
Supply Voltage: 6.0
Units in Stock: 345

Figure 13.2 The form and contents of a record.

In this chapter, we describe the C++ statements required to create, fill, use, and pass structures between functions.

13.1 SINGLE STRUCTURES

Creating and using a structure requires the same two steps needed for creating and using any variable. First the record structure must be declared. Then specific values can be assigned to the individual structure elements. Declaring a structure requires listing the data types, data names, and arrangement of data items. For example, the definition

```
struct
{
  int month;
  int day;
  int year;
} birth;
```

gives the form of a structure called `birth` and reserves storage for the individual data items listed in the structure. The `birth` structure consists of three data items or fields, which are called members of the structure.

Assigning actual data values to the data items of a structure is referred to as *populating the structure* and is a relatively straightforward procedure. Each member of a structure is accessed by giving both the structure name and individual data item name, separated by a period. Thus, `birth.month` refers to the first member of the `birth` structure, `birth.day` refers to the second member of the structure, and `birth.year` refers to the third member. Program 13.1 illustrates assigning values to the individual members of the birth structure.

Program 13.1

```
// a program that defines and populates a record
#include <iostream>
using namespace std;

int main()
{
  struct
  {
    int month;
    int day;
    int year;
  } birth;

  birth.month = 12;
  birth.day = 28;
  birth.year = 86;

  cout << "My birth date is "
       << birth.month << '/'
       << birth.day   << '/'
       << birth.year  << endl;

  return 0;
}
```

The output produced by Program 13.1 is

```
My birth date is 12/28/86
```

As in most C++ statements, the spacing of a structure definition is not rigid. For example, the birth structure could just as well have been defined

```
struct {int month; int day; int year;} birth;
```

Also, as with all C++ definition statements, multiple variables can be defined in the same statement. For example, the definition statement

```
struct
{
  int month;
  int day;
  int year;
} birth, current;
```

creates two structure variables having the same form. The members of the first structure are referenced by the individual names `birth.month`, `birth.day`, and `birth.year`, while the members of the second structure are referenced by the names `current.month`, `current.day`, and `current.year`. Notice that the form of this particular structure definition statement is identical to the form used in defining any program variable: the data type is followed by a list of variable names.

A helpful and commonly used modification for defining structure types is to list the form of the structure with no following variable names. In this case, however, the list of structure members must be preceded by a user-selected data type name. For example, in the declaration

```
struct Date
{
  int month;
  int day;
  int year;
};
```

the term `Date` is a structure type name: It defines a new data type that is a data structure of the declared form.[1] By convention the first letter of a user-selected data type name is uppercase, as in the name `Date`, which helps to identify it when it is used in subsequent definition statements. Here, the declaration for the `Date` structure creates a new data type without actually reserving any storage locations. As such it is not a definition statement. It simply declares a `Date` structure type and describes how individual data items are arranged within the structure. Actual storage for the members of the structure is reserved only when specific variable names are assigned. For example, the definition statement

```
Date birth, current;
```

reserves storage for two `Date` structure variables named `birth` and `current`, respectively. Each of these individual structures has the form previously declared for the `Date` structure.

The declaration of a structure data types, like all declarations, may be global or local. Program 13.2 illustrates the global declaration of a `Date` data type. Internal to `main()`, the variable `birth` is defined as a local variable of `Date` type.

The output produced by Program 13.2 is identical to the output produced by Program 13.1.

The initialization of structures follows the same rules as for the initialization of arrays: global and local structures may be initialized by following the definition with a list of initializers. For example, the definition statement

```
Date birth = {12, 28, 86};
```

can be used to replace the first four statements internal to `main()` in Program 13.2. Notice that the initializers are separated by commas, not semicolons.

[1]For completeness it should be mentioned that a C++ structure can also be declared as a class with no member functions and all public data members. Similarly, a C++ class can be declared as a struct having all private data members and all public member functions. Thus, C++ provides two syntaxes for both structs and classes. The convention, however, is not to mix notations and always use structures for creating record types and classes for providing true information and implementation hiding.

Program 13.2

```
#include <iostream>
using namespace std;

struct Date     // this is a global declaration
{
  int month;
  int day;
  int year;
};

int main()
{
  Date birth;

  birth.month = 12;
  birth.day = 28;
  birth.year = 86;

  cout << "My birth date is " << birth.month << '/'
       << birth.day   << '/'
       << birth.year  << endl;

  return 0;
}
```

The individual members of a structure are not restricted to integer data types, as illustrated by the `Date` structure. Any valid C++ data type can be used. For example, consider an employee record consisting of the following data items:

```
Name:
Identification Number:
Regular Pay Rate:
Overtime Pay Rate:
```

A suitable declaration for these data items is

```
struct PayRec
{
  string name;
  int idNum;
  double regRate;
  double otRate;
};
```

Once the `PayRec` data type is declared, a specific structure variable using this type can be defined and initialized. For example, the definition

```
PayRec employee = {"H. Price",12387,15.89,25.50};
```

creates a structure named `employee` of the `PayRec` data type. The individual members of `employee` are initialized with the respective data listed between braces in the definition statement.

Notice that a single structure is simply a convenient method for combining and storing related items under a common name. Although a single structure is useful in explicitly identifying the relationship among its members, the individual members could be defined as separate variables. One of the real advantages to using structures is only realized when the same data type is used in a list many times over. Creating lists with the same data type is the topic of the next section.

Before leaving single structures, it is worth noting that the individual members of a structure can be any valid C++ data type, including both arrays and structures. An array of characters was used as a member of the employee structure defined previously. Accessing an element of a member array requires giving the structure's name, followed by a period, followed by the array designation.

Including a structure within a structure follows the same rules for including any data type in a structure. For example, assume that a structure is to consist of a name and a date of birth, where a `Date` structure has been declared as

```
struct Date
{
  int month;
  int date;
  int year;
};
```

A suitable definition of a structure that includes a `name` and a `Date` structure is

```
struct
{
  string name;
  Date birth;
} person;
```

Notice that in declaring the `Date` structure, the term `Date` is a data type name; thus it appears before the braces in the declaration statement. In defining the person structure variable, `person` is a variable name; thus it is the name of a specific structure. The same is true of the variable named `birth`. This is the name of a specific `Date` structure. Individual members in the `person` structure are accessed by preceding the desired member with the structure name followed by a period. For example, `person.birth.month` refers to the `month` variable in the `birth` structure contained in the `person` structure.

Exercises 13.1

1. Declare a structure data type named `Stemp` for each of the following records:
   a. a student record consisting of a student identification number, number of credits completed, and cumulative grade point average
   b. a student record consisting of a student's name, date of birth, number of credits completed, and cumulative grade point average
   c. an inventory record consisting of the items previously illustrated in Figure 13.1
   d. a stock record consisting of the stock's name, the price of the stock, and the date of purchase
   e. an inventory record consisting of an integer part number, part description, number of parts in inventory, and an integer reorder number

2. For the individual data types declared in Exercise 1, define a suitable structure variable name, and initialize each structure with the appropriate following data:
   a. Identification Number: 4672
      Number of Credits Completed: 68
      Grade Point Average: 3.01
   b. Name: Rhona Karp
      Date of Birth: 8/4/60
      Number of Credits Completed: 96
      Grade Point Average: 3.89
   c. Part Number: 54002
      IC Family: ECL
      Function Type: NAND
      Supply Voltage: –5
      Units in Stock: 123
   d. Stock: IBM
      Price Purchased: 134.5
      Date Purchased: 10/1/86
   e. Part Number: 16879
      Description: Battery
      Number in Stock: 10
      Reorder Number: 3

3. a. Write a C++ program that prompts a user to input the current month, day, and year. Store the data entered in a suitably defined record and display the date in an appropriate manner.
   b. Modify the program written in Exercise 3a to use a record that accepts the current time in hours, minutes, and seconds.

Point of Information

Homogeneous and Heterogeneous Data Structures

Both arrays and structures are structured data types. The difference between these two data structures is the types of elements they contain. An array is a *homogeneous* data structure, which means that each of its components must be of the same data type. A structure is a *heterogeneous* data structure, which means that each of its components can be of different data types. Thus, an array of records would be a homogeneous data structure whose elements are of the same heterogenous type.

4. Write a C++ program that uses a structure for storing the name of a stock, its estimated earnings per share, and its estimated price-to-earnings ratio. Have the program prompt the user to enter these items for five different stocks, each time using the same structure to store the entered data. When the data has been entered for a particular stock, have the program compute and display the anticipated stock price based on the entered earnings and price-per-earnings values. For example, if a user entered the data XYZ 1.56 12, the anticipated price for a share of XYZ stock is (1.56)*(12) = $18.72.

5. Write a C++ program that accepts a user-entered time in hours and minutes. Have the program calculate and display the time one minute later.

6. a. Write a C++ program that accepts a user-entered date. Have the program calculate and display the date of the next day. For purposes of this exercise, assume that all months consist of 30 days.

   b. Modify the program written in Exercise 6a to account for the actual number of days in each month.

13.2 ARRAYS OF STRUCTURES

The real power of structures is realized when the same structure is used for lists of data. For example, assume that the data shown in Figure 13.3 must be processed. Clearly, the employee numbers can be stored together in an array of integers, the names in an array of strings, and the pay rates in an array of double-precision numbers. In organizing the data in this fashion, each column in Figure 13.3 is considered as a separate list, which is stored in its own array. The correspondence between items for each individual employee is maintained by storing an employee's data in the same array position in each array.

Employee Number	Employee Name	Employee Pay Rate
32479	Abrams, B.	6.72
33623	Bohm, P.	7.54
34145	Donaldson, S.	5.56
35987	Ernst, T.	5.43
36203	Gwodz, K.	8.72
36417	Hanson, H.	7.64
37634	Monroe, G.	5.29
38321	Price, S.	9.67
39435	Robbins, L.	8.50
39567	Williams, B.	7.20

Figure 13.3 *A list of employee data.*

The separation of the complete list into three individual arrays is unfortunate, because all of the items relating to a single employee constitute a natural organization of data into structures, as illustrated in Figure 13.4. Using a structure, the integrity of the data organization as a record can be maintained and reflected by the program. Under this approach, the list illustrated in Figure 13.4 can be processed as a single array of ten structures.

	Employee Number	Employee Name	Employee Pay Rate
1st structure →	32479	Abrams, B.	6.72
2nd structure →	33623	Bohm, P.	7.54
3rd structure →	34145	Donaldson, S.	5.56
4th structure →	35987	Ernst, T.	5.43
5th structure →	36203	Gwodz, K.	8.72
6th structure →	36417	Hanson, H.	7.64
7th structure →	37634	Monroe, G.	5.29
8th structure →	38321	Price, S.	9.67
9th structure →	39435	Robbins, L.	8.50
10th structure →	39567	Williams, B.	7.20

Figure 13.4 *A list of structures.*

Declaring an array of structures is the same as declaring an array of any other variable type. For example, if the data type `PayRec` is declared as

```
struct PayRec {int idnum; string name; double rate;};
```

then an array of ten such structures can be defined as

```
PayRec employee[10];
```

This definition statement constructs an array of ten elements, each of which is a structure of the data type `PayRec`. Notice that the creation of an array of ten structures has the same form as the creation of any other array. For example, creating an array of ten integers named employee requires the declaration

```
int employee[10];
```

In this declaration the data type is integer, while in the former declaration for `employee` the data type is `PayRec`.

Once an array of structures is declared, a particular data item is referenced by giving the position of the desired structure in the array followed by a period and the appropriate structure member. For example, the variable `employee[0].rate` references the `rate` member of the first `employee` structure in the `employee` array. Including structures as elements of an array permits a list of structures to be processed using standard array programming techniques. Program 13.3 displays the first five employee records illustrated in Figure 13.4.

Program 13.3

```
#include <iostream>
#include <iomanip>
#include <string>
using namespace std;

const int NUMRECS = 5;   // maximum number of records

struct PayRec   // this is a global declaration
{
  int id;
  string name;
  double rate;
};

int main()
{
  int i;
  PayRec employee[NUMRECS] = {
                              { 32479, "Abrams, B.", 6.72 },
                              { 33623, "Bohm, P.", 7.54},
                              { 34145, "Donaldson, S.",  5.56},
                              { 35987, "Ernst, T.", 5.43 },
                              { 36203, "Gwodz, K.", 8.72 }
                              };
```

(Continued)

(Continued)

```
  cout << endl;   // start on a new line
  cout << setiosflags(ios::left);  // left justify the output
  for ( i = 0; i < NUMRECS; i++)
    cout << setw(7)  << employee[i].id
         << setw(15) << employee[i].name
         << setw(6)  << employee[i].rate << endl;

  return 0;
}
```

The output displayed by Program 13.3 is:

```
32479  Abrams, B.      6.72
33623  Bohm, P.        7.54
34145  Donaldson, S.   5.56
35987  Ernst, T.       5.43
36203  Gwodz, K.       8.72
```

In reviewing Program 13.3, notice the initialization of the array of structures. Although the initializers for each structure have been enclosed in inner braces, these are not strictly necessary because all members have been initialized. As with all external and static variables, in the absence of explicit initializers, the numeric elements of both static and external arrays or structures are initialized to zero and their character elements are initialized to `NULL`s. The `setiosflags(ios::left)` manipulator included in the `cout` object stream forces each name to be displayed left justified in its designated field width.

Exercises 13.2

1. Define arrays of 100 structures for each of the data types described in Exercise 1 of the previous section.

2. a. Using the data type

```
struct MonthDays
{
  string name;
  int days;
};
```

   define an array of 12 structures of type `MonthDays`. Name the array `convert[ ]`, and initialize the array with the names of the 12 months in a year and the number of days in each month.

   b. Include the array created in Exercise 2a in a program that displays the names and number of days in each month.

3. Using the data type declared in Exercise 2a, write a C++ program that accepts a month from a user in numerical form and displays the name of the month and the number of days in the month. Thus, in response to an input of 3, the program would display `March has 31 days.`

4. a. Declare a single structure data type suitable for an employee structure of the type illustrated below:

Number	Name	Rate	Hours
3462	Jones	4.62	40
6793	Robbins	5.83	38
6985	Smith	5.22	45
7834	Swain	6.89	40
8867	Timmins	6.43	35
9002	Williams	4.75	42

b. Using the data type declared in Exercise 4a, write a C++ program that interactively accepts the above data into an array of six structures. Once the data have been entered, the program should create a payroll report listing each employee's name, number, and gross pay. Include the total gross pay of all employees at the end of the report.

5. a. Declare a single structure data type suitable for a car structure of the type illustrated:

Car Number	Miles Driven	Gallons Used
25	1450	62
36	3240	136
44	1792	76
52	2360	105
68	2114	67

b. Using the data type declared for Exercise 5a, write a C++ program that interactively accepts the above data into an array of five structures. Once the data have been entered, the program should create a report listing each car number and the miles per gallon achieved by the car. At the end of the report include the average miles per gallon achieved by the complete fleet of cars.

13.3 STRUCTURES AS FUNCTION ARGUMENTS

Individual structure members may be passed to a function in the same manner as any scalar variable. For example, given the structure definition

```
struct
{
  int idNum;
  double payRate;
  double hours;
} emp;
```

the statement

```
display(emp.idNum);
```

passes a copy of the structure member `emp.idNum` to a function named `display()`. Similarly, the statement

```
calcPay(emp.payRate,emp.hours);
```

passes copies of the values stored in structure members `emp.payRate` and `emp.hours` to the function `calcPay()`. Both functions, `display()` and `calcPay()`, must declare the correct data types for their respective arguments.

Complete copies of all members of a structure can also be passed to a function by including the name of the structure as an argument to the called function. For example, the function call

```
calcNet(emp);
```

passes a copy of the complete `emp` structure to `calcNet()`. Internal to `calcNet()`, an appropriate declaration must be made to receive the structure. Program 13.4 declares a global data type for an employee structure. This type is then used by both the `main()` and `calcNet()` functions to define specific structures with the names `emp` and `temp`, respectively.

The output produced by Program 13.4 is:

```
The net pay for employee 6782 is $361.66
```

In reviewing Program 13.4, observe that both `main()` and `calcNet()` use the same data type to define their individual structure variables. The structure variable defined in `main()` and the structure variable defined in `calcNet()` are two completely different structures. Any changes made to the local temp variable in `calcNet()` are not reflected in the `emp` variable of `main()`. In fact, since both structure variables are local to their respective functions, the same structure variable name could have been used in both functions with no ambiguity.

Program 13.4

```
#include <iostream>
#include <iomanip>
using namespace std;

struct Employee       // declare a global type
{
  int idNum;
  double payRate;
  double hours;
};

double calcNet(Employee);   // function prototype

int main()
{
  Employee emp = {6782, 8.93, 40.5};
  double netPay;

  netPay = calcNet(emp);       // pass copies of the values in emp
    // set output formats
  cout << setw(10)
       << setiosflags(ios::fixed)
       << setiosflags(ios::showpoint)
       << setprecision(2);

  cout << "The net pay for employee " << emp.idNum
       << " is $" << netPay << endl;

  return 0;
}

double calcNet(Employee temp) // temp is of data type Employee
{
  return temp.payRate * temp.hours;
}
```

When `calcNet()` is called by `main()`, copies of `emp`'s structure values are passed to the `temp` structure. `calcNet()` then uses two of the passed member values to calculate a number, which is returned to `main()`. Since `calcNet()` returns a non-integer number, the data type of the value returned must be included in all declarations for `calcNet()`.

An alternative to the pass-by-value function call illustrated in Program 13.4, in which the called function receives a copy of a structure, is a pass-by reference that passes a reference to a structure. Doing so permits the called function to directly access and alter values in the calling function's structure variable. For example, referring to Program 13.4, the prototype of `calcNet()` can be modified to

```
double calcNet(Employee &);
```

If this function prototype is used and the `calcNet()` function is rewritten to conform to it, the `main()` function in Program 13.4 may be used as is. Program 13.4a illustrates these changes within the context of a complete program.

Program 13.4a

```
#include <iostream>
#include <iomanip>
using namespace std;

struct Employee        // declare a global type
{
  int idNum;
  double payRate;
  double hours;
};

double calcNet(Employee&);    // function prototype

int main()
{
  Employee emp = {6782, 8.93, 40.5};
  double netPay;

  netPay = calcNet(emp);        // pass a reference

    // set output formats
  cout << setw(10)
       << setiosflags(ios::fixed)
       << setiosflags(ios::showpoint)
       << setprecision(2);

  cout << "The net pay for employee " << emp.idNum
       << " is $" <<  netPay << endl;

  return 0;
}

double calcNet(Employee& temp)    // temp is a reference variable
{
  return temp.payRate * temp.hours;
}
```

Program 13.4a produces the same output as Program 13.4, except that the `calcNet()` function in Program 13.4a receives direct access to the `emp` structure rather than a copy of it. This means that the variable name `temp` within `calcNet` is an alternate name for the variable `emp` in `main()`, and any changes to `temp` are direct changes to `emp`. Although the same function call, `calcNet(emp)` is made in both programs, the call in Program 13.4a passes a reference while the call in Program 13.4 passes values.

Passing a Pointer

In place of passing a reference, a pointer can be used. Using a pointer requires, in addition to modifying the function's prototype and header line, that the call to `calcNet()` in Program 13.4 be modified to

```
calcNet(&emp);
```

Here the function call clearly indicates that an address is being passed (which is not the case in Program 13.4a). The disadvantage, however, is in the dereferencing notation required internal to the function. However, as pointers are widely used in practice, it is worthwhile to become familiar with the notation used.

To correctly store the passed address, `calcNet()` must declare its parameter as a pointer. A suitable function definition for `calcNet()` is

```
calcNet(Employee *pt)
```

Here, the declaration for `pt` declares this parameter as a pointer to a structure of type `Employee`. The pointer `pt` receives the starting address of a structure whenever `calcNet()` is called. Within `calcNet()`, this pointer is used to directly reference any member in the structure. For example, `(*pt).idNum` refers to the `idNum` member of the structure, `(*pt).payRate` refers to the `payRate` member of the structure, and `(*pt).hours` refers to the `hours` member of the structure. These relationships are illustrated in Figure 13.5.

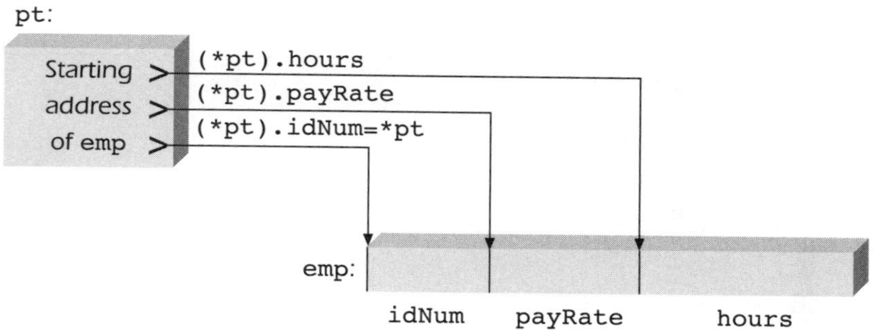

Figure 13.5 *A pointer can be used to access structure members.*

The parentheses around the expression `*pt` in Figure 13.5 are necessary to initially access "the structure whose address is in `pt`." This is followed by an identifier to access the desired member within the structure. In the absence of the parentheses, the structure member operator `.` takes precedence over the indirection operator. Thus, the expression `*pt.hours` is another way of writing `*(pt.hours)`, which would refer to "the variable whose address is in the `pt.hours` variable." This last expression clearly makes no sense because there is no structure named `pt` and `hours` does not contain an address.

As illustrated in Figure 13.5, the starting address of the `emp` structure is also the address of the first member of the structure.

The use of pointers in this manner is so common that a special notation exists for it. The general expression `(*pointer).member` can always be replaced with the notation `pointer->member`, where the `->` operator is constructed using a minus sign followed by a right-facing arrow (greater than symbol). Either expression can be used to locate the desired member. For example, the following expressions are equivalent:

`(*pt).idNum`	can be replaced by	`pt->idNum`
`(*pt).payRate`	can be replaced by	`pt->payRate`
`(*pt).hours`	can be replaced by	`pt->hours`

Program 13.5 illustrates passing a structure's address and using a pointer with the new notation to directly reference the structure.

The name of the pointer parameter declared in Program 13.5 is, of course, selected by the programmer. When `calcNet()` is called, `emp`'s starting address is passed to the function. Using this address as a starting point, individual members of the structure are accessed by including their names with the pointer.

Program 13.5

```
#include <iostream>
#include <iomanip>
using namespace std;

struct Employee   // declare a global type
{
  int idNum;
  double payRate;
  double hours;
};

double calcNet(Employee *);   //function prototype

int main()
{
  Employee emp = {6782, 8.93, 40.5};
  double netPay;
  netPay = calcNet(&emp);       // pass an address

    // set output formats
  cout << setw(10)
       << setiosflags(ios::fixed)
       << setiosflags(ios::showpoint)
       << setprecision(2);

  cout << "The net pay for employee " << emp.idNum
       << " is $" << netPay << endl;

  return 0;
}

double calcNet(Employee *pt)   // pt is a pointer to a
{                                // structure of Employee type
  return(pt->payRate * pt->hours);
}
```

As with all C++ expressions that access a variable, the increment and decrement operators can also be applied to them. For example, the expression

```
++pt->hours
```

adds one to the `hours` member of the `emp` structure. Since the `->` operator has a higher priority than the increment operator, the `hours` member is accessed first and then the increment is applied. Alternatively, the expression `(++pt)->hours` uses the prefix increment operator to increment the address in `pt` before the `hours` member is accessed.

Similarly, the expression `(pt++)->hours` uses the postfix increment operator to increment the address in `pt` after the hours member is accessed. In both of these cases, however, there must be sufficient defined structures to ensure that the incremented pointers actually point to legitimate structures.

As an example, Figure 13.6 illustrates an array of three structures of type `employee`. Assuming that the address of `emp[1]` is stored in the pointer variable `pt`, the expression `++pt` changes the address in `pt` to the starting address of `emp[2]`, while the expression `--pt` changes the address to point to `emp[0]`.

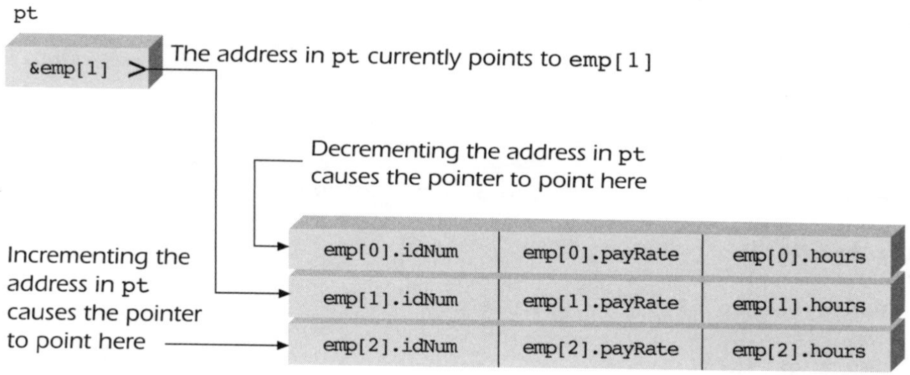

Figure 13.6 Changing pointer addresses.

Returning Structures

In practice, most structure handling functions receive direct access to a structure by receiving a structure reference or address. Then any changes to the structure can be made directly from within the function. If you want to have a function return a separate structure, however, you must follow the same procedures for returning complete data structures as for returning scalar values. These procedures include declaring the function appropriately and alerting any calling function to the type of data structure being returned. For example, the function `getVals()` in Program 13.6 returns a complete structure to `main()`.

Program 13.6

```
#include <iostream>
#include <iomanip>
using namespace std;

struct  Employee       // declare a global type
{
  int idNum;
  double payRate;
  double hours;
};

Employee getVals();   // function prototype

int main()
{
  Employee emp;

  emp = getVals();
  cout << "\nThe employee id number is " << emp.idNum
       << "\nThe employee pay rate is $" << emp.payRate
       << "\nThe employee hours are " << emp.hours << endl;

  return 0;
}

Employee getVals() // return an employee structure
{
  Employee next;

  next.idNum = 6789;
  next.payRate = 16.25;
  next.hours = 38.0;

  return next;
}
```

The following output is displayed when Program 13.6 is run:

```
The employee id number is 6789
The employee pay rate is $16.25
The employee hours are 38
```

Since the `getVals()` function returns a structure, the function header for `getVals()` must specify the type of structure being returned. Because `getVals()` does not receive any arguments, the function header has no parameter declarations and consists of the line

```
Employee getVals();
```

Within `getVals()`, the variable `next` is defined as a structure of the type to be returned. After values have been assigned to the `next` structure, the structure values are returned by including the structure name within the parentheses of the return statement.

On the receiving side, `main()` must be alerted that the function `getVals()` will be returning a structure. This is handled by including a function declaration for `getVals()` in `main()`. Notice that these steps for returning a structure from a function are identical to the normal procedures for returning scalar data types previously described in Chapter 6.

Exercises 13.3

1. Write a C++ function named `days()` that determines the number of days from the turn of the century for any date passed as a structure. Use the `Date` structure

```
struct Date
{
  int month;
  int day;
  int year;
};
```

In writing the `days()` function, use the convention that all years have 360 days and each month consists of 30 days. The function should return the number of days for any `Date` structure passed to it.

2. Write a C++ function named `difDays()` that calculates and returns the difference between two dates. Each date is passed to the function as a structure using the following global type:

```
struct Date
{
  int month;
  int day;
  int year;
};
```

The `difDays()` function should make two calls to the `days()` function written for Exercise 1.

3. a. Rewrite the `days()` function written for Exercise 1 to receive a reference to a `Date` structure, rather than a copy of the complete structure.

b. Redo Exercise 3a using a pointer rather than a reference.

4. a. Write a C++ function named `larger()` that returns the later date of any two dates passed to it. For example, if the dates 10/9/2005 and 11/3/2005 are passed to `larger()`, the second date would be returned.

b. Include the `larger()` function that was written for Exercise 4a in a complete program. Store the `Date` structure returned by `larger()` in a separate `Date` structure and display the member values of the returned `Date`.

5. a. In two dimensions a mathematical vector is a pair of numbers that represent directed arrows in a plane, as shown by the mathematical vectors v_1 and v_2 in Figure 13.7.

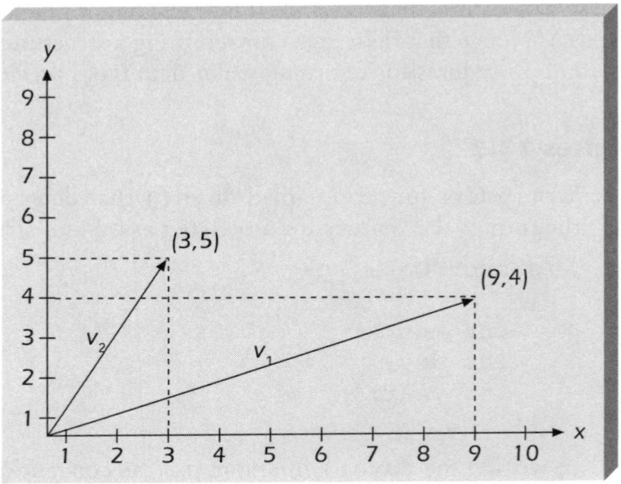

Figure 13.7 Graph for Exercise 5.

Two-dimensional mathematical vectors can be written in the form (a,b), where a and b are called the x and y components of the vector, respectively. For example, for the vectors illustrated in Figure 13.17, $v_1 = (9, 4)$ and $v_2 = (3, 5)$. For vectors, the following operations apply:

If $v_1 = (a,b)$ and $v_2 = (c,d)$
$v_1 + v_2 = (a,b) + (c,d) = (a + c, b + d)$
$v_1 - v_2 = (a,b) - (c,d) = (a - c, b - d)$

Using this information, write a C++ program that defines an array of two vector records, where each record consists of two double-precision components a and b. Your program should permit a user to enter two vectors, call two functions that return the sum and difference of the entered vectors, and display the results calculated by these functions.

b. In addition the operations defined in Exercise 5a, two additional vector operations are negation and absolute value. For a vector v_1 with components (a,b) these operations are defined as follows:

negation: $-v_1 = -(a,b) = (-a,-b)$
absolute value: $| v_1 | = \text{sqrt}\ (a * a + b * b)$

Using this information, modify the program that you wrote for Exercise 5a to display the negation and absolute values of both vectors input by a user as well as the negation and absolute value of the sum of the two input vectors.

13.4 LINKED LISTS

A classic data-handling problem is making additions or deletions to existing structures that are maintained in a specific order. This is best illustrated by considering the alphabetical telephone list shown in Figure 13.8. Starting with this initial set of names and telephone numbers, we desire to add new structures to the list in the proper alphabetical sequence, and to delete existing structures in such a way that the storage for deleted structures is eliminated.

Acme, Sam
(555) 898-2392
Dolan, Edith
(555) 682-3104
Lanfrank, John
(555) 718-4581
Mening, Stephen
(555) 382-7070
Zemann, Harold
(555) 219-9912

Figure 13.8 *A telephone list in alphabetical order.*

Although the insertion or deletion of ordered structures can be accomplished using an array of structures, these arrays are not efficient representations for adding or deleting structures internal to the array. Arrays are fixed and prespecified in size. Deleting a structure from an array creates an empty slot that requires either special marking or shifting up all elements below the deleted structure to close the empty slot. Similarly, adding a structure to the body of an array of structures requires that all elements below the addition be shifted down to make room for the new entry, or the new element could be added to the bottom of the existing array and the array then resorted to restore the proper order of the structures. Thus, either adding or deleting records to such a list generally requires restructuring and rewriting the list—a cumbersome, time-consuming, and inefficient practice.

A linked list provides a convenient method for maintaining a constantly changing list, without the need to continually reorder and restructure the complete list. A linked list is simply a set of structures in which each structure contains at least one member whose value is the address of the next logically ordered structure in the list. Rather than requiring each record to be physically stored in the proper order, each new structure is physically added wherever the computer has free space in its storage area. The records are "linked" together by including the address of the next record in the record immediately preceding it. From a programming standpoint, the current structure being processed contains the address of the next record, no matter where the next structure is actually stored.

The concept of a linked list is illustrated in Figure 13.9. Although the actual data for the `Lanfrank` structure illustrated in the figure may be physically stored anywhere in the computer, the additional member included at the end of the Dolan structure maintains the proper alphabetical order. This member provides the starting address of the location where the Lanfrank record is stored. As you might expect, this member is a pointer.

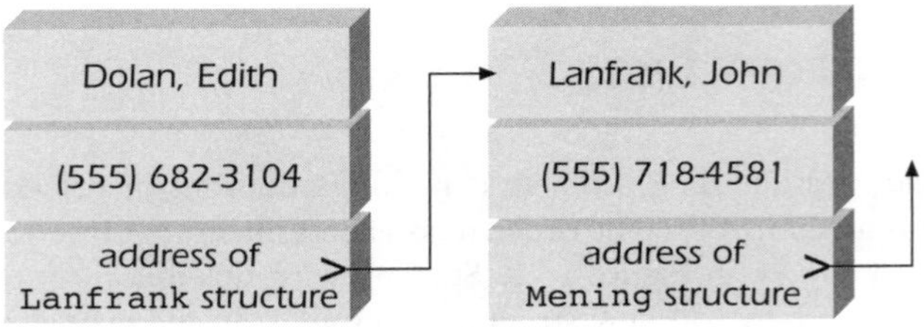

Figure 13.9 *Using pointers to link structures.*

To see the usefulness of the pointer in the Dolan structure, let us add a telephone number for June Hagar into the alphabetical list shown in Figure 13.8. The data for June Hagar is stored in a data structure using the same type as that used for the existing structures. To ensure that the telephone number for Hagar is correctly displayed after the Dolan telephone number, the address in the Dolan structure must be altered to point to the Hagar structure, and the address in the Hagar structure must be set to point to the Lanfrank structure. This is illustrated in Figure 13.10. Notice that the pointer in each structure simply points to the location of the next ordered structure, even if that structure is not physically located in the correct order.

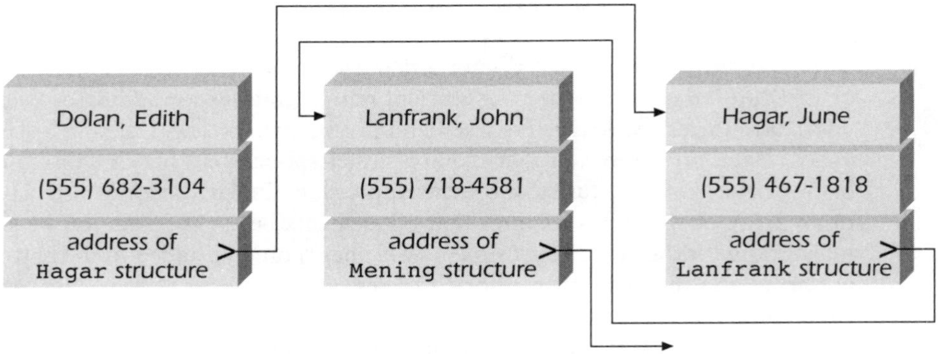

Figure 13.10 *Adjusting addresses to point to appropriate structures.*

Removal of a structure from the ordered list is the reverse process of adding a record. The actual record is logically removed from the list by simply changing the address in the structure preceding it to point to the structure immediately following the deleted record.

Each structure in a linked list has the same format; however, it is clear that the last record cannot have a valid pointer value that points to another record, because there is none. C++ provides a special pointer value called `NULL` that acts as a sentinel or flag to indicate when the last record has been processed. The `NULL` pointer value, like its end-of-string counterpart, has a numerical value of zero.

Besides an end-of-list sentinel value, a special pointer must also be provided for storing the address of the first structure in the list. Figure 13.11 illustrates the complete set of pointers and structures for a list consisting of three names.

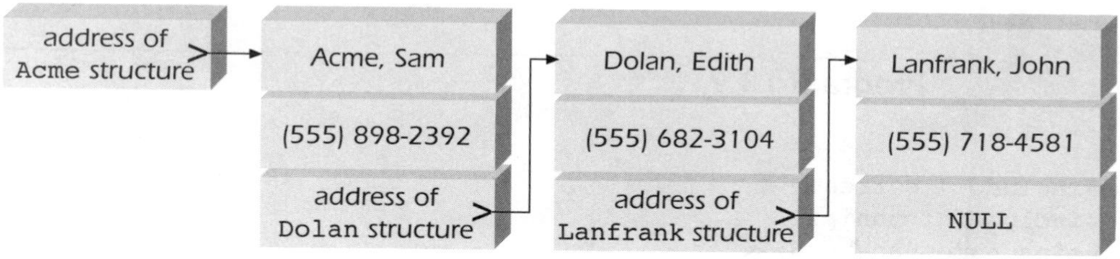

Figure 13.11 *Use of the initial and final pointer values.*

The inclusion of a pointer in a structure should not seem surprising. As we discovered in Section 13.1, a structure can contain any C++ data type. For example, the structure declaration

```
struct Test
{
  int idNum;
  double *ptPay
};
```

declares a structure type consisting of two members. The first member is an integer variable named `idNum`, and the second variable is a pointer named `ptPay`, which is a pointer to a double-precision number. Program 13.7 illustrates that the pointer member of a structure is used like any other pointer variable.

The output produced by executing Program 13.7 is

```
Employee number 12345 was paid $456.20
```

Figure 13.12 illustrates the relationship between the members of the `emp` structure defined in Program 13.7 and the variable named `pay`. The value assigned to `emp.idNum` is the number 12345 and the value assigned to `pay` is 456.20. The address of the `pay` variable is assigned to the structure member `emp.ptPay`. Since this member has been defined as a pointer to a double-precision number, placing the address of the double-precision variable `pay` in it is a correct use of this member. Finally, since the member operator `.` has a higher precedence than the indirection operator `*`, the expression used in the `cout` statement in Program 13.7 is correct. The expression `*emp.ptPay` is equivalent to the expression `*(emp.ptPay)`, which is translated as "the variable whose address is contained in the member `emp.ptPay`."

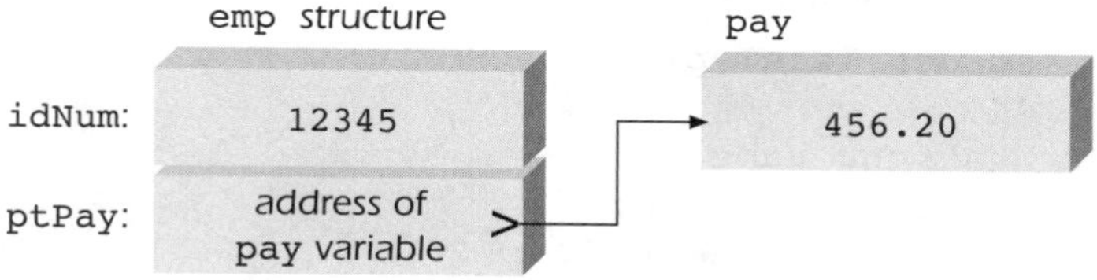

Figure 13.12 *Storing an address in a structure member.*

Program 13.7

```
#include <iostream>
#include <iomanip>
using namespace std;

struct Test
{
  int idNum;
  double *ptPay;
};

int main()
{
  Test emp;
  double pay = 456.20;

  emp.idNum = 12345;
  emp.ptPay = &pay;
    // set output formats
  cout << setw(6)
       << setiosflags(ios::fixed)
       << setiosflags(ios::showpoint)
       << setprecision(2);

  cout << "\nEmployee number " << emp.idNum << " was paid $"
       << *emp.ptPay << endl;

  return 0;
}
```

Although the pointer defined in Program 13.7 has been used in a rather trivial fashion, the program does illustrate the concept of including a pointer in a structure. This concept can be easily extended to create a linked list of structures suitable for storing the names and telephone numbers listed in Figure 13.8. The following declaration creates a type for such a structure:

```
struct TeleType
{
  string name;
  string phoneNo;
  TeleType *nextaddr;
};
```

The last member in this structure is a pointer suitable for storing the address of a structure of the `TeleType` type.

Program 13.8 illustrates the use of the `TeleType` type by specifically defining three structures having this form. The three structures are named `t1`, `t2`, and `t3`, respectively, and the name and telephone members of each of these structures are initialized when the structures are defined, using the data listed in Figure 13.8.

Program 13.8

```
#include <iostream>
#include <string>
using namespace std;

struct TeleType
{
  string name;
  string phoneNo;
  TeleType *nextaddr;
};

int main()
{
  TeleType t1 = {"Acme, Sam","(555) 898-2392"};
  TeleType t2 = {"Dolan, Edith","(555) 682-3104"};
  TeleType t3 = {"Lanfrank, John","(555) 718-4581"};
  TeleType *first;      // create a pointer to a structure

  first = &t1;          // store t1's address in first
  t1.nextaddr = &t2;    // store t2's address in t1.nextaddr
  t2.nextaddr = &t3;    // store t3's address in t2.nextaddr
  t3.nextaddr = NULL;   // store a NULL address in t3.nextaddr

  cout << endl << first->name
       << endl << t1.nextaddr->name
       << endl << t2.nextaddr->name
       << endl;

  return 0;
}
```

The output produced by executing Program 13.8 is

```
Acme, Sam
Dolan, Edith
Lanfrank, John
```

Program 13.8 demonstrates the use of pointers to access successive structure members. As illustrated in Figure 13.13, each structure contains the address of the next structure in the list.

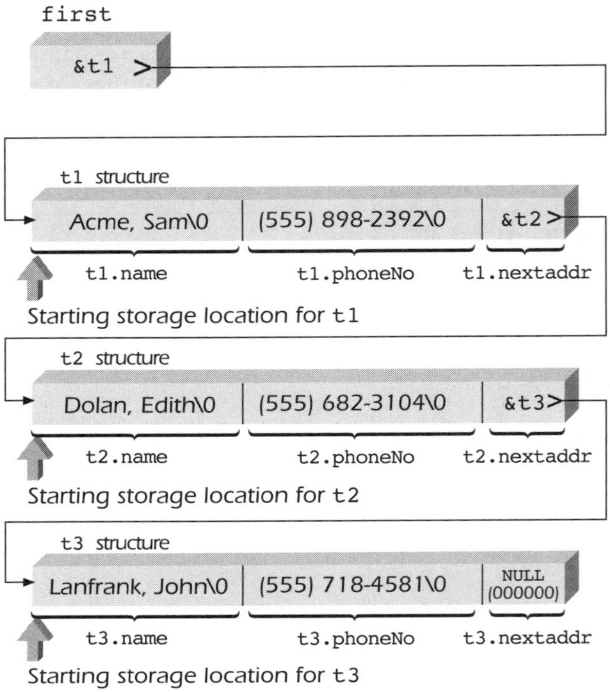

Figure 13.13 The relationship between structures in Program 13.8.

The initialization of the names and telephone numbers for each of the structures defined in Program 13.9 is straightforward. Although each structure consists of three members, only the first two members of each structure are initialized. As both of these members are arrays of characters, they can be initialized with strings. The remaining member of each structure is a pointer. To create a linked list, each structure pointer must be assigned the address of the next structure in the list.

The four assignment statements in Program 13.8 perform the correct assignments. The expression `first = &t1` stores the address of the first structure in the list in the pointer variable named `first`. The expression `t1.nextaddr = &t2` stores the starting address of the `t2` structure into the pointer member of the `t1` structure. Similarly, the expression `t2.nextaddr = &t3` stores the starting address of the `t3` structure into the pointer member of the `t2` structure. To end the list, the value of the `NULL` pointer, which is zero, is stored into the pointer member of the `t3` structure.

Once values have been assigned to each structure member and correct addresses have been stored in the appropriate pointers, the addresses in the pointers are used to access each structure's name member. For example, the expression `t1.nextaddr->name` refers to the `name` member of the structure whose address is in the `nextaddr` member of the `t1` structure. The precedence of the member operator `.` and the structure pointer operator `->` are equal and are evaluated from left to right. Thus, the expression `t1.nextaddr->name` is evaluated as `(t1.nextaddr)->name`. Since `t1.nextaddr` contains the address of the `t2` structure, the proper name is accessed.

The expression `t1.nextaddr->name` can, of course, be replaced by the equivalent expression `(*t1.nextaddr).name`, which uses the more conventional indirection operator. This expression also refers to "the name member of the variable whose address is in `t1.nextaddr`."

The addresses in a linked list of structures can be used to loop through the complete list. As each structure is accessed it can be either examined to select a specific value or used to print out a complete list. For example, the `display()` function in Program 13.9 illustrates the use of a `while` loop, which uses the address in each structure's pointer member to cycle through the list and successively display data stored in each structure.

The output produced by Program 13.9 is

```
Acme, Sam                   (555) 898-2392
Dolan, Edith                (555) 682-3104
Lanfrank, John              (555) 718-4581
```

The important concept illustrated by Program 13.9 is the use of the address in one structure to access members of the next structure in the list. When the `display()` function is called, it is passed the value stored in the variable named `first`. Since `first` is a pointer variable, the actual value passed is an address (the address of the `t1` structure).The function `display()` accepts the passed value in the argument named `contents`. To store the passed address correctly, `contents` is declared as a pointer to a structure of the `teleType` type. Within `display()`, a `while` loop is used to cycle through the linked structures, starting with the structure whose address is in `contents`. The condition tested in the `while` statement compares the value in `contents`, which is an address, to the `NULL` value. For each valid address the name and phone number members of the addressed structure are displayed. The address in `contents` is then updated with the address in the pointer member of the current structure. The address in `contents` is then retested, and the process continues while the address in contents is not equal to the `NULL` value.The function `display()` "knows" nothing about the names of the structures declared in `main()` or even how many structures exist. It simply cycles through the linked list, structure by structure, until it encounters the end-of-list `NULL` address. Since the value of `NULL` is zero, the tested condition can be replaced by the equivalent expression `contents`.

A disadvantage of Program 13.9 is that exactly three structures are defined in `main()` by name and storage for them is reserved at compile time. Should a fourth structure be required, the additional structure would have to be declared and the program recompiled. In the next section we show how to have the computer dynamically allocate and release storage for structures at run time, as storage is required. Only when a new structure is to be added to the list, and while the program is running, is storage for the new structure created. Similarly, when a structure is no longer needed and can be deleted from the list, the storage for the deleted record is relinquished and returned to the computer.

Program 13.9

```
#include <iostream>
#include <iomanip>
#include <string>
using namespace std;

struct TeleType
{
  string name;
  string phoneNo;
  TeleType *nextaddr;
};

void display(TeleType *);       // function prototype

int main()
{
  TeleType t1 = {"Acme, Sam","(555) 898-2392"};
  TeleType t2 = {"Dolan, Edith","(555) 682-3104"};
  TeleType t3 = {"Lanfrank, John","(555) 718-4581"};
  TeleType *first;    // create a pointer to a structure

  first = &t1;         // store t1's address in first
  t1.nextaddr = &t2;  // store t2's address in t1.nextaddr
  t2.nextaddr = &t3;  // store t3's address in t2.nextaddr
  t3.nextaddr = NULL; // store the NULL address in t3.nextaddr

  display(first);     // send the address of the first structure

  return 0;
}

void display(TeleType *contents) // contents is a pointer to a structure
{                                // of type TeleType
  while (contents != NULL)   // display till end of linked list
  {
    cout << endl << setiosflags(ios::left)
         << setw(30) << contents->name
         << setw(20) << contents->phoneNo ;
    contents = contents->nextaddr;     // get next address
  }
  cout << endl;

  return;
}
```

Exercises 13.4

1. Modify Program 13.9 to prompt the user for a name. Have the program search the existing list for the entered name. If the name is in the list, display the corresponding phone number; otherwise display this message:
   `The name is not in the current phone directory.`

2. Write a C++ program containing a linked list of ten integer numbers. Have the program display the numbers in the list.

3. Using the linked list of structures illustrated in Figure 13.13, write the sequence of steps necessary to delete the record for Edith Dolan from the list.

4. Generalize the description obtained in Exercise 3 to describe the sequence of steps necessary to remove the *n*th structure from a list of linked structures. The *n*th structure is preceded by the $(n - 1)$st structure and followed by the $(n + 1)$st structure. Make sure to store all pointer values correctly.

5. a. A doubly linked list is a list in which each structure contains a pointer to both the following and previous structures in the list. Define an appropriate type for a doubly linked list of names and telephone numbers.
   b. Using the type defined in Exercise 5a, modify Program 13.9 to list the names and phone numbers in reverse order.

13.5 Dynamic Data Structure Allocation

We have already encountered the concept of explicitly allocating and deallocating memory space using the new and delete operators (see Section 12.2). For convenience the description of these operators are repeated in Table 13.1.

Table 13.1

Operator Name	Description
`new`	Reserves the number of bytes required by the requested data type. Returns the address of the first reserved location or `NULL` if sufficient memory is not available.
`delete`	Releases a block of bytes previously reserved. The address of the first reserved location is passed as an argument to the operator.

This dynamic allocation of memory is especially useful when dealing with a list of structures because it permits the list to expand as new records are added and contract as records are deleted.

In requesting additional storage space, the user must provide the new function with an indication of the amount of storage needed. This is done by requesting enough space for a particular type of data. For example, the expression `new(int)` or `new int` (the two forms may be used interchangeably) requests enough storage to store an integer number. A request for enough storage for a data structure is made in the same fashion. For example, using the declaration

```
struct TeleType
{
  string name;
  string phoneNo;
};
```

both the expressions `new TeleType` and `new(TeleType)` reserve enough storage for one `TeleType` data structure.

In allocating storage dynamically, we have no advance indication as to where the computer system will physically reserve the requested number of bytes, and we have no explicit name to access the newly created storage locations. To provide access to these locations, `new` returns the address of the first location that has been reserved. This address must, of course, be assigned to a pointer. The return of a pointer by `new` is especially useful for creating a linked list of data structures. As each new structure is created, the pointer returned by `new` to the structure can be assigned to a member of the previous structure in the list.

Program 13.10 illustrates using `new` to create a structure dynamically in response to a user-input request.

Program 13.10

```
// a program illustrating dynamic structure allocation

#include <iostream>
#include <string>
using namespace std;

struct TeleType
{
  string name;
  string phoneNo;
};

void populate(TeleType *);  // function prototype needed by main()
void dispOne(TeleType *);   // function prototype needed by main()
```

(Continued)

(Continued)

```
int main()
{
  char key;
  TeleType *recPoint;     // recPoint is a pointer to a
                          // structure of type TeleType

  cout << "Do you wish to create a new record (respond with y or n): ";
  key = cin.get();
  if (key == 'y')
  {
    key = cin.get();       // get the Enter key in buffered input
    recPoint = new TeleType;
    populate(recPoint);
    dispOne(recPoint);

  }
  else
    cout << "\nNo record has been created.";

  return 0;
}

  // input a name and phone number
void populate(TeleType *record) // record is a pointer to a
  {                             // structure of type TeleType
    cout << "Enter a name: ";
    getline(cin,record->name);
    cout << "Enter the phone number: ";
    getline(cin,record->phoneNo);

    return;
  }
  // display the contents of one record
void dispOne(TeleType *contents)  // contents is a pointer to a
{                                 // structure of type TeleType
  cout << "\nThe contents of the record just created is:"
       << "\nName: " << contents->name
       << "\nPhone Number: " << contents->phoneNo << endl;

  return;
}
```

A sample session produced by Program 13.10 is

```
Do you wish to create a new record (respond with y or n): y
Enter a name: Monroe, James
Enter the phone number: (555) 617-1817

The contents of the record just created is:
Name: Monroe, James
Phone Number: (555) 617-1817
```

In reviewing Program 13.10, notice that only two variable declarations are made in `main()`. The variable `key` is declared as a character variable and the variable `recPoint` is declared as being a pointer to a structure of the `TeleType` type. Because the declaration for the type `TeleType` is global, `TeleType` can be used within `main()` to define `recPoint` as a pointer to a structure of the `TeleType` type.

If a user enters `y` in response to the first prompt in `main()`, a call to `new` is made for the required memory to store the designated structure. Once `recPoint` has been loaded with the proper address, this address can be used to access the newly created structure. The function `populate()` is used to prompt the user for data needed in filling the structure and to store the user-entered data in the correct members of the structure. The argument passed to `populate()` in `main()` is the pointer `recPoint`. Like all passed arguments, the value contained in `recPoint` is passed to the function. Since the value in `recPoint` is an address, `populate()` receives the address of the newly created structure and can directly access the structure members.

Within `populate()`, the value received by it is stored in the argument named `record`. Since the value to be stored in `record` is the address of a structure, `record` must be declared as a pointer to a structure. This declaration is provided by the statement `TeleType *record;`. The statements within `populate()` use the address in `record` to locate the respective members of the structure.

The `dispOne()` function in Program 13.10 is used to display the contents of the newly created and populated structure. The address passed to `dispOne()` is the same address that was passed to `populate()`. Because this passed value is the address of a structure, the argument name used to store the address is declared as a pointer to the correct structure type.

Once you understand the mechanism of calling `new`, you can use this function to construct a linked list of structures. As described in the previous section, the structures used in a linked list must contain at least one pointer member. The address in the pointer member is the starting address of the next structure in the list. Additionally, a pointer must be reserved for the address of the first structure, and the pointer member of the last structure in the list is given a `NULL` address to indicate that no more members are being pointed to. Program 13.11 illustrates the use of `new` to construct a linked list of names and phone numbers. The `populate()` function used in Program 13.11 is the same function used in Program 13.10, while the `display()` function is the same function used in Program 13.9.

Program 13.11

```
#include <iostream>
#include <iomanip>
#include <string>
using namespace std;

const int MAXRECS = 3;   // maximum no. of records

struct TeleType
{
  char name;
  char phoneNo;
  TeleType *nextaddr;
};

void populate(TeleType *);   // function prototype needed by main()
void display(TeleType *);    // function prototype needed by main()

int main()
{
  int i;
  TeleType *list, *current; // two pointers to structures of
                            // type TeleType

    // get a pointer to the first structure in the list
  list = new TeleType;
  current = list;

    // populate the current structure and create the remaining structures
  for(i = 0; i < MAXRECS - 1; i++)
  {
    populate(current);
    current->nextaddr = new TeleType;
    current = current->nextaddr;
  }

  populate(current);          // populate the last structure
  current->nextaddr = NULL;   // set the last address to a NULL address
  cout << "\nThe list consists of the following records:\n";
  display(list);   // display the structures

  return 0;
}
```

(Continued)

(Continued)

```
  // input a name and phone number
void populate(TeleType *record) // record is a pointer to a
{                               // structure of type TeleType

  cout << "Enter a name: ";
  getline(cin,record->name);
  cout << "Enter the phone number: ";
  getline(cin,record->phoneNo);

  return;
}

void display(TeleType *contents) // contents is a pointer to a
{                                      // structure of type TeleType
  while (contents != NULL)        // display till end of linked list
  {
    cout << endl << setiosflags(ios::left)
         << setw(30) << contents->name
         << setw(20) << contents->phoneNo;
    contents = contents->nextaddr;
  }
  cout << endl;

  return;
}
```

The first time new is called in Program 13.11 it is used to create the first structure in the linked list. As such, the address returned by new is stored in the pointer variable named `list`. The address in `list` is then assigned to the pointer named `current`. This pointer variable is always used by the program to point to the `current` structure. Because the `current` structure is the first structure created, the address in the pointer named `list` is assigned to the pointer named `current`.

Within `main()`'s `for` loop, the name and phone number members of the newly created structure are populated by calling `populate()` and passing the address of the current structure to the function. Upon return from `populate()`, the pointer member of the `current` structure is assigned an address. This address is the address of the next structure in the list, which is obtained from new. The call to new creates the next structure and returns its address into the pointer member of the `current` structure. This completes the population of the `current` member. The final statement in the `for` loop resets the address in the `current` pointer to the address of the next structure in the list.

After the last structure has been created, the final statements in `main()` populate this structure, assign a `NULL` address to the pointer member, and call `display()` to display all the structures in the list. A sample run of Program 13.11 is provided below:

```
Enter a name: Acme, Sam
Enter the phone number: (555) 898-2392
Enter a name: Dolan, Edith
Enter the phone number: (555) 682-3104
Enter a name: Lanfrank, John
Enter the phone number: (555) 718-4581

The list consists of the following records:

Acme, Sam                     (555) 898-2392
Dolan, Edith                  (555) 682-3104
Lanfrank, John                (555) 718-4581
```

Just as `new` dynamically creates storage while a program is executing, the `delete` function restores a block of storage back to the computer while the programming is executing. The only argument required by `delete` is the starting address of a block of storage that was dynamically allocated. Thus, any address returned by `new` can subsequently be passed to `delete` to restore the reserved memory back to the computer. The `delete` function does not alter the address passed to it, but simply removes the storage that the address references.

Exercises 13.5

1. As described in Table 13.1, the `new` operator returns either the address of the first new storage area allocated or `NULL` if insufficient storage is available. Modify Program 13.11 to check that a valid address has been returned before a call to `populate()` is made. Display an appropriate message if sufficient storage is not available.

2. Write a C++ function named `remove()` that removes an existing structure from the linked list of structures created by Program 13.11. The algorithm for removing a linked structure should follow the sequence developed for removing a structure developed in Exercise 4 in Section 13.4. The argument passed to `remove()` should be the address of the structure preceding the record to be removed. In the removal function, make sure that the value of the pointer in the removed structure replaces the value of the pointer member of the preceding structure before the structure is removed.

3. Write a function named `insert()` that inserts a structure into the linked list of structures created in Program 13.11. The algorithm for inserting a structure in a linked list should follow the sequence for inserting a record previously illustrated in Figure 13.10. The argument passed to `insert()` should be the address of the structure preceding the structure to be inserted. The inserted structure should follow this current structure. The `insert()` function should create a new structure dynamically, call the `populate` function used in Program 13.11, and adjust all pointer values appropriately.

4. We desire to insert a new structure into the linked list of structures created by Program 13.11. The function developed to do this in Exercise 3 assumed that the address of the preceding structure is known. Write a function called `findRec()` that returns the address of the structure immediately preceding the point at which the new structure is to be inserted. (*Hint*: `findRec()` must request the new name as input and compare the entered name to existing names to determine where to place the new name.)

5. Write a C++ function named `modify()` that can be used to modify the name and phone number members of a structure of the type created in Program 13.11. The argument passed to `modify()` should be the address of the structure to be modified. The `modify()` function should first display the existing name and phone number in the selected structure and then request new data for these members.

6. a. Write a C++ program that initially presents a menu of choices for the user. The menu should consist of the following choices:

    Create an initial linked list of names and phone numbers
    Insert a new structure into the linked list
    Modify an existing structure in the linked list
    Delete an existing structure from the list
    Exit from the program

   Upon the user's selection, the program should execute the appropriate functions to satisfy the request.

   b. Why is the original creation of a linked list usually done by one program, and the options to add, modify, or delete a structure in the list provided by a different program?

13.6 UNIONS[2]

A union is a data type that reserves the same area in memory for two or more variables, each of which can be a different data type. A variable that is declared as a union data type can be used to hold a character variable, an integer variable, a double-precision variable, or any other valid C++ data type. Each of these types, but only one at a time, can actually be assigned to the union variable.

The definition of a union has the same form as a structure definition, with the keyword `union` used in place of the keyword `struct`. For example, the declaration

```
union
{
  char key;
  int num;
  double volts;
} val;
```

[2]This topic may be omitted on first reading with no loss of subject continuity.

creates a union variable named `val`. If `val` were a structure it would consist of three individual members. As a union, however, `val` contains a single member that can be either a character variable named `key`, an integer variable named `num`, or a double-precision variable named `volts`. In effect, a union reserves sufficient memory locations to accommodate its largest member's data type. This same set of locations is then referenced by different variable names depending on the data type of the value currently residing in the reserved locations. Each value stored overwrites the previous value, using as many bytes of the reserved memory area as necessary.

Individual union members are referenced using the same notation as structure members. For example, if the `val union` is currently being used to store a character, the correct variable name to access the stored character is `val.key`. Similarly, if the union is used to store an integer, the value is accessed by the name `val.num`, and a double-precision value is accessed by the name `val.volts`. In using union members, it is the programmer's responsibility to ensure that the correct member name is used for the data type currently residing in the union.

Typically a second variable is used to keep track of the current data type stored in the union. For example, the following code could be used to select the appropriate member of `val` for display. Here the value in the variable `uType` determines the currently stored data type in the `val union`.

```
switch(uType)
{
  case 'c': cout << val.key;
            break;
  case 'i': cout << val.num;
            break;
  case 'd': cout << val.volts;
            break;
  default : cout << "Invalid type in uType : " << uType;
}
```

As they are in structures, a data type can be associated with a union. For example, the declaration

```
union DateTime
{
  int days;
  double time;

};
```

provides union data type without actually reserving any storage locations. This data type can then be used to define any number of variables. For example, the definition

```
DateTime first, second, *pt;
```

creates a union variable named `first`, a union variable named `second`, and a pointer that can be used to store the address of any union having the form of `DateTime`. Once a pointer to a union has been declared, the same notation used to access structure members can be used to access union members. For example, if the assignment `pt = &first;` is made, then `pt->date` references the `date` member of the union named `first`.

Unions may themselves be members of structures or arrays. Structures, arrays, and pointers may also be members of unions. In each case, the notation used to access a member must be consistent with the nesting employed. For example, in the structure defined by

```
struct
{
  char uType;
  union
  {
    char *text;
    float rate;
  } uTax;
}  flag;
```

the variable `rate` is referenced as

```
flag.uTax.rate
```

Similarly, the first character of the string whose address is stored in the pointer `text` is referenced as

```
*flag.uTax.text
```

Exercises 13.6

1. Assume that the following definition has been made

```
union
{
  double rate;
  double taxes;
  int num;
} flag;
```

For this union write appropriate `cout` stream activations to display the various members of the union.

2. Define a union variable named `car` that contains an integer named `year`, an array of 10 characters named `name`, and an array of 10 characters named `model`.

3. Define a union variable named `lang` that would allow a double-precision number to be referenced by both the variable names `volts` and `emf`.

4. Declare a union data type named `Amt` that contains an integer variable named `intAmt`, a double-precision variable named `dblAmt`, and a pointer to a character named `ptKey`.

5. a. What do you think will be displayed by the following section of code?

```
union
{
  char ch;
  double btype;
} alt;
alt.ch = 'y';
cout << alt.btype;
```

b. Include the code presented in Exercise 5a in a program and run the program to verify your answer to Exercise 5a.

13.7 Common Programming Errors

Three common errors are often made when using structures or unions. The first error occurs because structures and unions, as complete entities, cannot be used in relational expressions. For example, even if `TeleType` and `PhonType` are two structures of the same type, the expression `TeleType == PhonType` is invalid. Individual members of a structure or union can, of course, be compared if they are of the same data type, using any of C++'s relational operators.

The second common error is really an extension of a pointer error as it relates to structures and unions. Whenever a pointer is used to "point to" either of these data types, or whenever a pointer is itself a member of a structure or a union, take care to use the address in the pointer to access the appropriate data type. Should you be confused about just what is being pointed to, remember, "If in doubt, print it out."

The final error relates specifically to unions. Since a union can store only one of its members at a time, you must be careful to keep track of the currently stored variable. Storing one data type in a union and accessing it by the wrong variable name can result in an error that is particularly troublesome to locate.

13.8 CHAPTER SUMMARY

1. A structure allows individual variables to be grouped under a common variable name. Each variable in a structure is accessed by its structure variable name, followed by a period, followed by its individual variable name. Another term for a data structure is a record. One form for declaring a structure is:

```
struct
{
  individual member declarations;
} structureName;
```

2. A data type can be created from a structure using the declaration form

```
struct DataType
{
  individual member declarations;
};
```

   Individual structure variables may then be defined as this `DataType`. By convention, the first letter of the `DataType` name is always capitalized.

3. Structures are particularly useful as elements of arrays. Used in this manner, each structure becomes one record in a list of records.

4. Complete structures can be used as function arguments, in which case the called function receives a copy of each element in the structure. The address of a structure may also be passed, either as a reference or a pointer, which provides the called function with direct access to the structure.

5. Structure members can be any valid C++ data type, including other structures, unions, arrays, and pointers. When a pointer is included as a structure member, a linked list can be created. Such a list uses the pointer in one structure to "point to" (contain the address of) the next logical structure in the list.

6. Unions are declared in the same manner as structures. The definition of a union creates a memory overlay area, with each union member using the same memory storage locations. Thus, only one member of a union may be active at a time.

Part Four
Additional Topics

CHAPTERS

Chapter 14
Numerical Methods

Topics

One of the most common tasks in science and engineering is finding the roots of equations; that is, given a function f(x)*, finding values of* x *such that* f(x) = 0.0*. This type of problem also includes determining the points of intersection of two curves. If the curves are represented by functions* f(x) *and* g(x)*, respectively, the intersection points correspond to the roots of the function* F(x) = f(x) – g(x).

A second important task is numerical integration—where approximation methods are used to determine the integral's value when exact solutions do not exist. In this chapter we first present and apply several programming techniques for finding the roots of equations. This is followed by techniques commonly employed in numerical integration.

14.1 INTRODUCTION TO ROOT FINDING

Root-finding techniques are important for a number of reasons. They are useful, easy to understand, and usually easy to carry out. Thus, with a minimum of instruction you are able to solve genuine problems in engineering. Vital elements in numerical analysis are appreciating what can or cannot be solved and clearly understanding the accuracy of the answers obtained. Since this appreciation and understanding come mostly from experience, you need to begin solving numerical problems immediately. Besides, you will find that root-solving problems are fun.

Some examples of the types of functions that are encountered in root-solving problems are

$$ax^2 + bx + c = 0 \tag{14.1}$$

$$2x^4 - 7x^3 + 4x^2 + 7x - 6 = (x - 2)(x - 1)(x + 1)(2x - 3) = 0 \tag{14.2}$$

$$x^5 - 2x^3 - 5x^2 + 2 = 0 \tag{14.3}$$

$$\sin^5(x) + \sin^3(x) + 5\cos(x) - 7 = 0 \tag{14.4}$$

$$100e - x - \sin(2\pi x) = 0 \tag{14.5}$$

The general quadratic equation, Equation 14.1, can be solved easily and exactly by using the quadratic formula

$$r = \frac{-b \pm \sqrt{(b^2 - 4ac)}}{2a}$$

Equation 14.2 can be solved for x exactly by factoring the polynomial. The roots are then clearly 1, –1, 2, 3/2. However, most polynomials cannot be factored so easily, and other more general techniques are required. There are formulas for the exact solution of general cubic or quartric equations, but they are cumbersome and thus seldom used. No exact formula is possible for a polynomial like Equation 14.3, in which the highest power of x is greater than 4. For these polynomials numerical means must generally be used to determine the roots.

You will recall from high school algebra that a polynomial of degree n (i.e., the highest power of x^n) has precisely n roots, of which some may be complex numbers and others may be multiple roots. Thus Equation 14.3 has three real roots,

$$r_1 = -0.712780744625\ldots$$

$$r_2 = 0.57909844162\ldots$$

$$r_3 = 2.0508836199\ldots$$

and two complex roots,

$$r_4 = 0.757225433526 + i(0.57803468208)$$

$$r_5 = 0.757225433526 - i(0.57803468208)$$

The equation

$$x^2 - 2x + 1 = 0$$

can be factored as

$$(x - 1)^2 = 0$$

and has two real roots, both of which happen to be the same. In this case the root is said to be a multiple root with multiplicity 2.

Equations 14.4 and 14.5 are called **transcendental equations** and represent an entirely different class of functions. Transcendental equations typically involve trigonometric, exponential, or logarithmic functions and cannot be reduced to any polynomial equation in x. The real roots of polynomials are usually classified as being either rational numbers (that is, a simple fraction) or irrational, for example, $\sqrt{2}$). The roots of transcendental equations are often transcendental numbers like π or e. Irrational numbers and transcendental numbers are represented by nonrepeating decimal fractions and cannot be expressed as simple fractions. These numbers are important to mathematics since they are responsible for the real number system being dense or continuous. Thus, the classification of equations as polynomials or transcendental and the roots of these equations as rational or irrational is vital to traditional mathematics; however, the distinction is of less consequence to the computer. In fact, not only is the number system available to the computer not continuous, it is a finite set.

At any rate, when finding the roots of equations, the distinction between polynomials and transcendental equations is unnecessary and the same numerical procedures are applied to both. The distinction between the two types of functions is, however, important in other regards. Many of the theorems you learned concerning roots of polynomials do not apply to transcendental equations. For instance both equations 14.4 and 14.5 have an infinite number of real roots.

All of the root-solving techniques discussed in this chapter are interactive; that is, you specify an interval that is known to contain a root or simply an initial guess for the root and the various routines will return a more limited interval or a better guess. Some of the schemes we will discuss will be guaranteed to find a root eventually but may take considerable computer time to arrive at the answer. Others may converge to a root much faster but are more susceptible to problems of divergence; that is, they come with no guarantees.

The common ingredient in all root-solving recipes is that potential computational difficulties of any nature are best avoided by mastering as much intelligence as possible in the initial choice of the method used and the accompanying initial guess. This part of the problem is often the most difficult and time consuming. The art involved in numerical analysis consists in balancing time spent optimizing the solution of the problem before computation against time spent correcting unforeseen errors during computation. If at all possible, the function should be roughly sketched before root solving is attempted, either by using graphing routines or by generating a table of function values that are then graphed by hand. These graphs are extremely useful to the programmer not only in estimating the first guess for the root, but also in anticipating potential difficulties. If a sketch is not feasible, some method of monitoring the function must be utilized to arrive at some understanding of what the function is doing before the actual computation is initiated. As an example of the general procedure we will follow, consider the transcendental function

$$f(x) = e^{-x} - \sin(\tfrac{1}{2}\pi x)$$

This equation, as we will shortly see, has an infinite number of positive roots. For the moment, we will concentrate on obtaining an initial guess for the first root, and then use this initial guess to find a more precise root value.

We begin by gathering as much information as possible before trying to construct a C++ program. This step almost always involves making a rough sketch of the function being considered. The previous equation can be written as

$$e^{-x} = \sin(\tfrac{1}{2}\pi x)$$

A root of this equation then corresponds to any value of x such that the left side and right side are equal. If the left and right sides are plotted independently, the roots of the original equation are then given by the points of intersection of the two curves (see Figure 14.1). From the sketch we see that the roots are

Roots ≈ 0.4, 1.9, 4.0, . . .

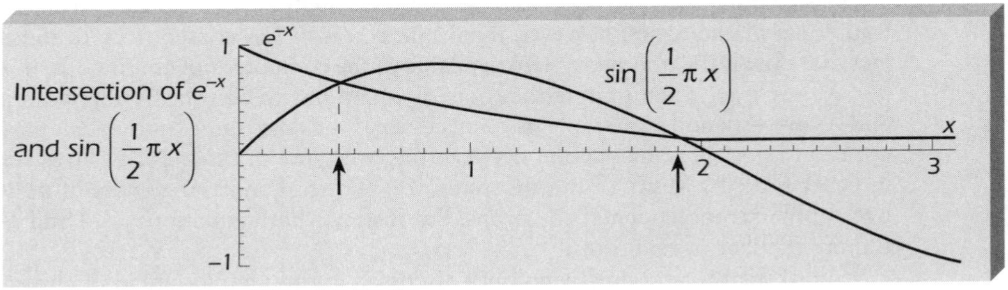

Figure 14.1 Graph of e^{-x} and $\sin(\tfrac{1}{2}\pi x)$ for locating the intersection points.

Since the sine oscillates, there will be an infinite number of positive roots. We will concentrate first on improving the estimate of the first root near 0.4. We begin by establishing a procedure, or algorithm, that is based on the most obvious method of attack when using a pocket calculator; that is, we begin at some value of x just before the root (say 0.3) and step along the x axis, carefully watching the magnitude and particularly the sign of the function.

Step	x	e^{-x}	$\sin(\frac{1}{2}\pi x)$	$f(x) = e^{-x} - \sin(\frac{1}{2}\pi x)$
0	0.3	0.741	0.454	0.297
1	0.4	0.670	0.588	0.082
2	0.5	0.606	0.707	−0.101

Notice that the function has changed sign between 0.4 and 0.5, indicating a root between these two x values. Thus, for the next approximation we will use the midpoint value, $x = 0.45$ for our next step:

Step	x	e^{-x}	$\sin(\frac{1}{2}\pi x)$	$f(x) = e^{-x} - \sin(\frac{1}{2}\pi x)$
3	0.45	0.638	0.649	−0.012

The function is again negative at 0.45, indicating that the root is between 0.4 and 0.45. The next approximation will, therefore, be the midpoint of this interval, 0.425. In this way we can proceed systematically to a computation of the root to any desired degree of accuracy.

Step	x	e^{-x}	$\sin(\frac{1}{2}\pi x)$	$f(x) = e^{-x} - \sin(\frac{1}{2}\pi x)$
4	0.425	0.654	0.619	0.0347
5	0.4375	0.6456	0.6344	0.01126
6	0.44365	0.6417	0.6418	−0.00014

The key element in the procedure is the monitoring of the sign of the function. When the sign changes, specific action is taken to refine the estimate of the root. This change in sign of the function, indicating the vicinity of a root has been located, forms the key element in the computer code for locating roots. In the next three sections we consider a number of root finding methods that use this procedure as their basis.

Exercises 14.1

1. Use the iterative technique presented in this section to find a root of the equation

$$f(x) = \sin x - x/3 = 0 \quad (x \text{ is in radians})$$

To do this, first rewrite the equation as

$$\sin x = x/3$$

and plot the left and right sides independently on the same graph.

14.2 The Bisection Method

The root-solving procedure illustrated in the preceding section is suitable for hand calculations; however, a slight modification will make it more "systematic" and easier to adapt to computer coding.

Suppose we already know that there is a root between $x = a$ and $x = b$; that is, the function changes sign in this interval. For simplicity we will assume that there is only one root between $x = a$ and $x = b$ and that the function is continuous in this interval.

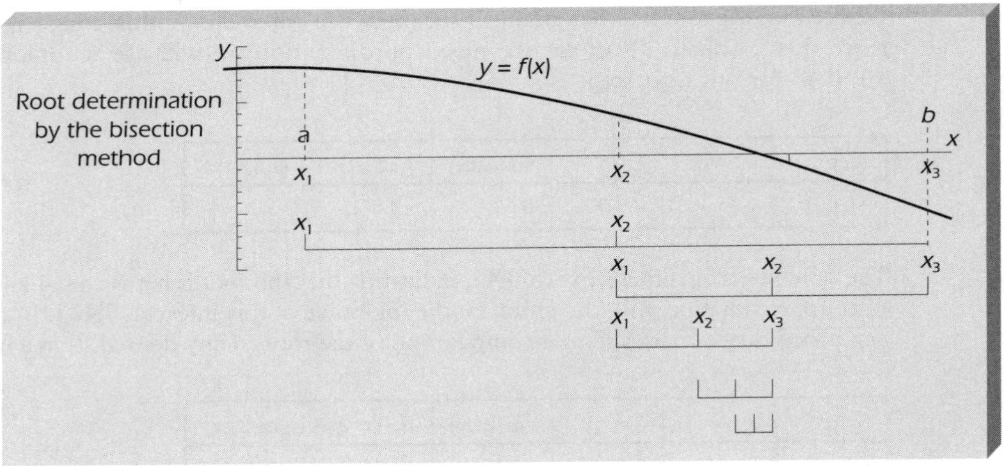

Figure 14.2 *A sketch of a function with one root between a and b.*

The function might then resemble the sketch in Figure 14.2. If we next define $x_1 = a$ and $x_3 = b$ as the left and right ends of the interval, respectively, and $x_2 = \frac{1}{2}(x_1 + x_3)$ as the midpoint, in which half-interval does the function crosses the x-axis? In the figure, the crossing is on the right, so we replace the full interval by the right half-interval. Thus,

x_2 now becomes x_1

x_3 remains as it is

x_2 is recalculated as the value $\frac{1}{2}(x_1 + x_3)$

and the question is again posed as "In which half-interval does the function cross the x axis?" After determining a second time whether the left half or the right half contains the root, the interval is once more replaced by either the left or right half-interval. This process is continued until we narrow in on the root to within some previously assigned accuracy. Each step halves the interval, and so after n iterations, the size of the interval containing the root will be $(b - a)/2^n$. If we are required to find a root to within a tolerance δ, that is, $|x - \text{root}| < \delta$, the number of iterations n required can be determined from

$$\frac{b-a}{2^n} < \delta$$

For example, the initial search interval in the example presented in the previous section was $(b - a) = 0.1$. If the root was required to an accuracy of $\delta = 10^{-5}$, then

$$\frac{0.1}{2^n} < 10^{-5}$$

or

$$2^n > 10^4$$

This can be solved for n as follows:

$$n > \frac{\log(10^4)}{\log(2)} > 13$$

Thus, the calculation reveals that the desired degree of accuracy is achieved after the 13th application of the interval halving procedure. The only element of the method that has been omitted is how the computer is to determine which half of the interval contains the axis crossing. To that end, consider the product of the function evaluated at the left, $f_1 = f(x_1)$, and the function evaluated at the midpoint, $f_2 = f(x_2)$.

If	Then
$f_1 f_2 > 0.0$	f_1 and f_2 are both positive or both negative. In either case, there is no crossing between x_1 and x_2, and no root lies within the interval.
$f_1 f_2 < 0.0$	$f(x)$ has changed sign between x_1 and x_2. In this case, there is a root within the interval bounded by x_1 and x_2.

A program to compute the roots of an equation using this procedure is illustrated by Program 14.1. In reviewing this program, the following features should be especially noted:

- In each iteration after the first, there is only one function evaluation. It would be highly inefficient to reevaluate $f(x_1)$, $f(x_2)$ and $f(x_3)$ for each iteration since two of them are already known. If the function were extremely complicated, redundant computations like this would be a serious problem. A great deal of computer time can be wasted by unnecessary function evaluations.
- The program contains several checks for potential problems along with diagnostic messages (e.g., excessive iteration, no roots in interval, etc.), even though the programmer may think these possibilities are remote. Generally, the more of these checks a program contains, the better. They take only a few minutes to code and can save hours of debugging.
- The criterion for success is based on the size of the interval. Thus, even if the function were not close to zero at a point, x is changing very little, and continuing would not substantially improve the accuracy of the root.

Program 14.1

```
#include <iostream>
#include <cmath>
using namespace std;

void bisection(double, double, double, int); // function prototype
double f(double); // function prototype
using namespace std;

int main()
{
  int imax;           // maximum number of iterations
  double a, b;        // left and right ends of the original interval
  double epsilon;     // convergence criterion

  // obtain the input data
  cout << "Enter the limits of the original search interval, a and b: ";
  cin  >> a >> b;
  cout << "Enter the convergence criteria: ";
  cin  >> epsilon;
  cout << "Enter the maximum number of iterations allowed: ";
  cin  >> imax;

  bisection(a, b, epsilon, imax);

  return 0;
}

// A bisection function that finds roots of a function
// The interval a < x < b is known to contain a root of f(x). The estimate
// of the root is successively improved by finding in which half of the interval
// the root lies and then replacing the original interval by that half-interval.
//
void bisection(double a, double b, double epsilon, int imax)
{
  int i;              // current iteration counter
  double x1, x2, x3; // left, right, and midpoint of current interval
  double f1, f2, f3; // function evaluated at these points
  double width;       // width of original interval = (b - a)
  double curwidth;    // width of current interval = (x3 - x1)

  // echo back the passed input data
  cout << "\nThe original search interval is from " << a << " to " << b << endl;
  cout << "The convergence criterion is: interval < " << epsilon << endl;
  cout << "The maximum number of iterations allowed is " << imax << endl;

  // calculate the root
```

(Continued)

(Continued)

```
    x1 = a;
    x3 = b;
    f1 = f(x1);
    f3 = f(x3);
    width = (b - a);

    // verify there is a root in the interval
    if (f1 * f3 > 0.0)
      cout << "\nNo root in the original interval exists" << endl;
    else
    {
      for (i = 1; i <= imax; i++)
      {
        // find which half of the interval contains the root
        x2 = (x1 + x3) / 2.0;
        f2 = f(x2);
        if (f1 * f2 <= 0.0) // root is in left half interval
        {
          curwidth = (x2 - x1) / 2.0;
          f3 = f2;
          x3 = x2;
        }
        else // root is in right half interval
        {
          curwidth = (x3 - x2) / 2.0;
          f1 = f2;
          x1 = x2;
        }
        if (curwidth < epsilon)
        {
          cout << "\nA root at x = " << x2 << " was found "
               << "in " << i << " iterations" << endl;
          cout << "The value of the function is " << f2 << endl;
          return;
        }
      }
    }
    cout << "\nAfter " << imax << " iterations, no root was found "
         << "within the convergence criterion" << endl;

    return;
  }

  // function to evaluate f(x)
  double f(double x)
  {
    const double PI = 2*asin(1.0); // value of pi

    return (exp(-x) - sin(0.5 * PI * x));
  }
```

A sample run using Program 14.1 produced the following:

```
Enter the limits of the original search interval, a and b: .4 .5
Enter the convergence criteria: .00001
Enter the maximum number of iterations allowed: 25

The original search interval is from 0.4 to 0.5
The convergence criterion is: interval < 1e-005
The maximum number of iterations allowed is 25

A root at x = 0.443567 was found in 13 iterations
The value of the function is 1.22595e-005
```

Although Program 14.1 is used to evaluate the roots of the equation $f(x) = e^x - \sin(\pi x/2)$, by changing the calculation in the return statement in the last function, `f()`, listed in the program, this program can be used for any function.

One final comment: the bisection method used in Program 14.1 is an example of a so-called brute-force method; that is, it possesses a minimum of finesse. Although it illustrates fundamental C++ techniques, much more powerful and clever numerical procedures are available. These techniques are presented in the next section.

Exercises 14.2

1. Use the bisection procedure for finding the roots of an equation. First construct a table of the following form:

Step	x_1	x_2	x_3	$f(x_1)$	$f(x_2)$	$f(x_3)$	Crossing	
							Left	Right
0	a	$\frac{1}{2}(a+b)$	b					
1								
.	.	.	.	.	.	.	.	.
.	.	.	.	.	.	.	.	.
.	.	.	.	.	.	.	.	.

Next, use the bisection procedure and a pocket calculator to obtain the roots of the following functions to an accuracy of five significant figures.

a. $f(x) = x^2 + 2x - 15$ (Use $a = 2.8$, $b = 3.1$. The exact answer = 3.0)

b. $g(x) = \frac{1}{2}\sin(x)(e^x - e^{-x})$ (This is the elliptic gear equation, with x in radians. Use $a = 1$, $b = 4$)

c. $E(x) = \sqrt{(R^2 - x^2)} - x\tan(x)$ (This is the equation for quantum energies of a particle in a box. Use $R = 10$, $a = 4.0$, $b = 4.7$)

d. Predict the number of steps needed to obtain the answer to the specified accuracy of five significant figures in parts a through c.

2. a. Modify Program 14.1 to solve for the indicated roots of each of the functions of Exercise 1.
   b. Modify Program 14.1 to produce a table similar to the one required in Exercise 1 for each of the functions listed in Exercise 1.

3. Write a C++ program to find the maximum of a function $f(x)$ over an interval $a \leq x \leq b$ by starting at $x = a$ with a step size Δx. Evaluate $f_1 = f(x)$ and $f_2 = f(x + \Delta x)$. If $f_1 < f_2$, replace x with $x + \Delta x$ and continue; otherwise, reduce the step size by half and repeat the comparison. The program should terminate successfully when $\Delta < 10^{-6}$.

14.3 REFINEMENTS TO THE BISECTION METHOD

The bisection method described in the previous section presents the basics upon which most root-finding methods are constructed. It is a so-called brute-force method that is rarely used in practice, since for almost any problem an alternative method that is faster, more accurate, and only slightly more complex is available. All of the refinements of the bisection method that might be devised are based on attempts to use as much information as is available about the behavior or the function at each iteration. In the ordinary bisection method, the only feature of the function that is monitored is its sign. Thus, if we were searching for roots of the function

$$f(x) = e^{-x} - \sin(\tfrac{1}{2}\pi x)$$

we would begin the search, as described in Section 14.1, by stepping along the x axis and watching for a change in sign of the function, as follows:

i	x_i	$f(x_i)$
0	0.0	2.0
1	0.1	1.33
2	0.2	0.75
3	0.3	0.29
4	0.4	–.05

The next step in the bisection procedure is to reduce the step size by half; that is, try, $x_5 = 0.35$. However, from the magnitude of the numbers above we would expect the root to be closer to 0.4 than to 0.3. Thus, by using information about the size of the functional value in addition to its sign, we may be able to speed up the convergence. In the present case we might interpolate the root to be approximately

$$\frac{0.29 - 0.0}{0.29 - (-0.05)} = \frac{f_3 - 0}{f_3 - f_4} = 0.853$$

of the distance from $x_3 = 0.3$ to $x_4 = 0.4$, or $x_5 = 0.3853$. Continuing in this manner and interpolating at each step, we would obtain the following results:

i	x_i	$f(x_i)$
3	0.30	0.29
4	0.40	−0.05
5	0.385	−0.0083
6	0.3823	−0.0013
7	0.3819	−0.00019
8	0.38185	−0.000028
9	0.38184	−0.000004

Comparing these results with the bisection method applied to a similar function in the previous section, we see that the convergence rate for the present method is significantly faster. The next task is to formalize this procedure into a method suitable for a general function.

Regula Falsi Method

The basic idea in the first refinement of the bisection algorithm is that the new method will be essentially the same as bisection except that in place of using the midpoint of the interval at each step of the calculation, an interpolated value for the root is used. The method is illustrated in Figure 14.3. In the figure a root is known to exist in the interval $(x_1 \leftrightarrow x_3)$, and in the drawing f_1 is negative, whereas f_3 is positive. The interpolated position of the root is x_2. Since the two triangles ABC and CDE are similar, the lengths of the sides are related by

$$\frac{\text{DE}}{\text{AB}} = \frac{\text{CD}}{\text{BC}}$$

or

$$\frac{0.0 - f_1}{f_3 - f_1} = \frac{x_2 - x_1}{x_3 - x_1}$$

which may be solved for the unknown position x_2 to yield

$$x_2 = x_1 - (x_3 - x_1)\frac{f_1}{f_3 - f_1}$$

This value of x_2 then replaces the midpoint used in the bisection algorithm, and the rest of the procedure remains exactly the same. Thus, the next step would be to determine whether the actual root is to the left or to the right of x_2. As before,

If $f_1 \times f_2 < 0$ then the root is on the left

If $f_2 \times f_3 < 0$ then the root is on the right

In the figure the root is to the left of x_2, so the interval used for the next iteration would be

$$x_3 = x_2$$

$$f_3 = f_2$$

$$x_2 = x_1 - (x_3 - x_1)\frac{f_1}{f_3 - f_1}$$

$$f_2 = f(x_2)$$

In other words, to employ this slightly faster algorithm, the only change that has to be made to the previous bisection code is to replace statements of the form

$$x_2 = (\ x_1 + x_3)\ /\ 2.$$

by a statement of the form

$$x_2 = x_1 - (x_3 - x_1)\frac{f_1}{f_3 - f_1}$$

This method is still guaranteed to obtain a root eventually and will almost always converge faster than the conventional bisection algorithm. We do, however, pay a small price. The values of f_1 and f_3 used in solving for x_2 may be very nearly equal, and we could be plagued by round-off errors in their difference. Also, in the bisection algorithm we could predict with some precision the number of iterations required to obtain the root to a desired accuracy (see Section 14.1). This prediction is no longer possible if we use the interpolated values, and the code must now include a check for excessive iterations.

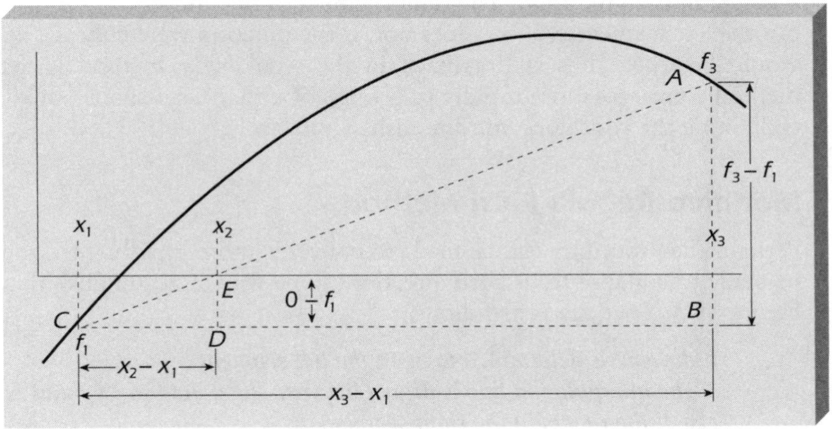

Figure 14.3 Estimating the root by interpolation.

This method illustrates that an almost trivial change in the algorithm, which is based on more intelligent monitoring of the function, can reap considerable rewards in more rapid convergence. The formal name of the method just described is the **regula falsi method** (the method of false position).

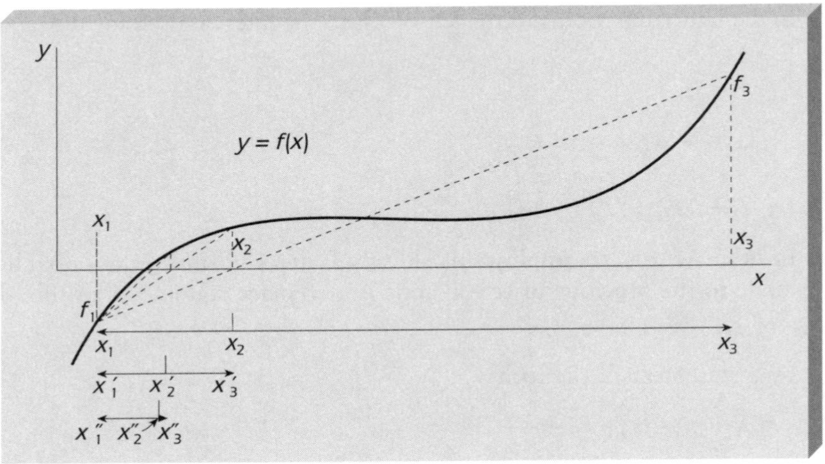

Figure 14.4 Graphical illustration of several iterations of the regula falsi algorithm.

Are there any additional improvements in the basic bisection algorithm that can be easily implemented? To answer this question we must examine in more detail the manner in which the regula falsi method arrives at a solution. This is best done graphically. The calculation begun in Figure 14.3 is continued in Figure 14.4. Notice that in this example, in which the function is concave downward near the root, the value of the left limit of the search interval near the root, x_1, never changes. The actual root always remains in the left segment in each iteration. The right segment of the interval, $x_3 - x_2$, shrinks quite rapidly; but the left segment, $x_2 - x_1$, does not. If the function were concave upward, the converse would be true. Thus, a drawback in the regula falsi method is that even though the method converges more rapidly to a value of x that results in a "small" $|f(x)|$, the interval containing the root does *not* diminish significantly.

Modified Regula Falsi Method

Perhaps the procedure can be made to converge more rapidly if the interval can somehow be made to collapse from both directions. One way to accomplish this is demonstrated in Figure 14.5. The idea is as follows:

> ***If the root is determined to lie in the left segment*** $(x_2 - x_1)$
> ***The interpolation line is drawn between the points*** $(x_1, \frac{1}{2}f_1)$ ***and*** (x_3, f_3)
> ***Else If the root is in the right segment***
> ***The interpolation line is drawn between the points*** (x_1, f_1)***and*** $(x_3, \frac{1}{2}f_3)$
> ***Endif***

Using this algorithm, the slope of the line is *artificially* reduced. The effect of this reduction is that if the root is in the left of the original interval, it will eventually turn up in the right segment of a later interval and subsequently will alternate between left and right. The last modification to the bisection method in combination with the regula falsi method is known as the *modified regula falsi method*, a very powerful and popular procedure for finding roots of equations. The alternatives to the original bisection code presented in Program 14.1 are quite trivial and are incorporated within Program 14.2.

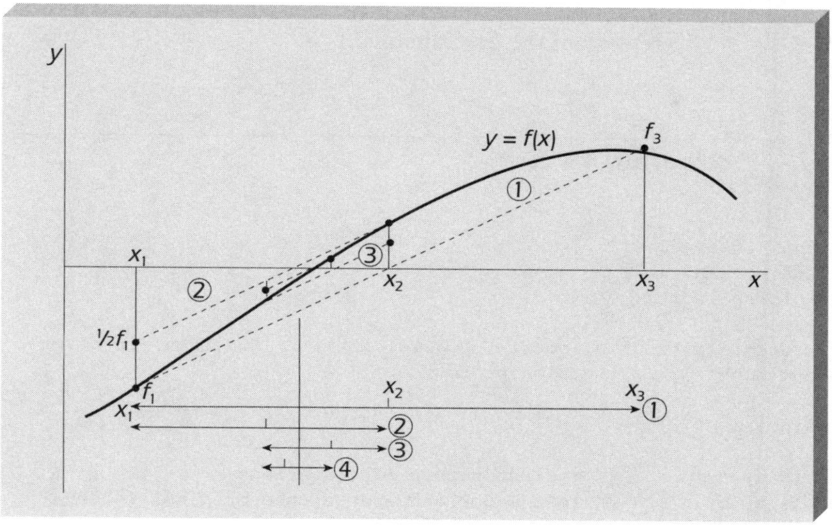

Figure 14.5 Graphical illustration of the modified regula falsi method.

The C++ code in Program 14.2 requires some explanation:

1. The function $f(x)$ is evaluated only once per cycle. If the function is complicated and therefore costly to compute, this measure of efficiency can be attractive, even decisive, in choosing the appropriate method of solution.
2. The code can terminate in only three ways.
   a. One success path: If the current fractional size of the search interval [i.e., (current interval)/(original interval)] is less than the user-supplied convergence criterion. If so, the original aim of the program to narrowly bracket a root has been achieved. There is no guarantee that this criterion will result in a value of $f(x)$ that is "small." The point is, however, that successive iterations have resulted in only small changes in the interval containing the root and so continuing the process is not necessary or productive.
   b. There are two failure paths: (1) If the number of iterations is greater than I_{max}, the maximum number of iterations set by the programmer, then the process is stopped. This test allows the programmer to specify the maximum cost that will be accepted for an attempted solution. Since in the regula falsi and modified regula falsi methods the number of iterations is not predictable, this form of safeguard is essential. It is also a prudent precaution against unforeseen errors in the construction of the problem that could cause the program to cycle forever and not obtain a solution. Statements of this type are required in any program in which there is a danger of infinite looping.

(2) If the function does not change sign ($f_1 \times f_3 > 0$), then the process is stopped. Since the original interval was known to contain a root, the only way this condition can arise is by error. Usually the error is in the code for the function $f(x)$; that is, you are attempting to find a root of a function different from the one intended.

Program 14.2

```
#include <iostream>
#include <cmath>
using namespace std;

void modregfalsi(double, double, double, int); // function prototype
double f(double); // function prototype

int main()
{
  int imax;          // maximum number of iterations
  double a, b;       // left and right ends of the original interval
  double epsilon;    // convergence criterion

  // obtain the input data
  cout << "Enter the limits of the original search interval, a and b: ";
  cin  >> a >> b;
  cout << "Enter the convergence criteria: ";
  cin  >> epsilon;
  cout << "Enter the maximum number of iterations allowed: ";
  cin  >> imax;

  modregfalsi(a, b, epsilon, imax);

  return 0;
}

// A modified regula falsi function that finds roots of a function
// The maximum number of iterations permitted is imax. The convergence
// criterion is the fractional size of the search interval (x3 - x1) / (b - a)
// is less than epsilon. A relaxation factor RELAX is used
void modregfalsi(double a, double b, double epsilon, int imax)
{
  const double RELAX = 0.9; // the relaxation factor

  int i;             // current iteration counter
  double x1, x2, x3; // left, right, and midpoint of current interval
  double f1, f2, f3; // function evaluated at these points
  double width;      // width of original interval = (b - a)
  double curwidth;   // width of current interval = (x3 - x1)
```

(Continued)

(Continued)

```
// echo back the passed input data
cout << "\nThe original search interval is from " << a << " to " << b
     << "\nThe convergence criterion is: interval < " << epsilon
     << "\nThe maximum number of iterations allowed is " << imax << endl;

// calculate the root
x1 = a;
x3 = b;
f1 = f(x1);
f3 = f(x3);
width = abs(b - a);

// iterations
for (i = 1; i <= imax; i++)
{
  curwidth = (x3 - x1) / width;
  x2 = x1 - width * curwidth * f1 / (f3 - f1);
  f2 = f(x2);
  if (abs(curwidth) < epsilon) // root is found
  {
    cout << "\nA root at x = " << x2 << " was found "
         << "in " << i << " iterations" << endl;
    cout << "The value of the function is " << f2 << endl;
    return;
  }
  else // check for left and right crossing
  {
    if(f1 * f2 < 0.0) // check for crossing on the left
    {
      x3 = x2;
      f3 = f2;
      f1 = RELAX * f1;
    }
    else if (f2 * f3 < 0.0) // check for crossing on the right
    {
      x1 = x2;
      f1 = f2;
      f3 = RELAX * f3;
    }
    else // no crossing in the interval
    {
      cout << "The search for a root has failed due to no root in the interval\n"
           << "In step " << i << " of the iteration the function does not change sign"
         << endl;
    }
  }
}
cout << "\nAfter " << imax << " iterations, no root was found "
     << "within the convergence criterion\n"
     << "The search for a root has failed due to excessive iterations\n"
     << "after the maximum number of " << imax << " iterations" << endl;
```

(Continued)

(Continued)

```
    return;
  }
  // function to evaluate f(x)
  double f(double x)
  {
    const double PI = 2*asin(1.0); // value of pi

    return (exp(-x) - sin(0.5 * PI * x));
  }
```

A sample run using Program 14.2 produced the following:

```
Enter the limits of the original search interval, a and b: .4 .5
Enter the convergence criteria: .00001
Enter the maximum number of iterations allowed: 25

The original search interval is from 0.4 to 0.5
The convergence criterion is: interval < 1e-005
The maximum number of iterations allowed is 25

A root at x = 0.443574 was found in 7 iterations
The value of the function is -2.25374e-009
```

In comparing the results from the sample run of Program 14.2 to those of Program 14.1, notice that a more exact root was located by the modified regula falsi function in six fewer iterations (7 as opposed to 13). The exactness of the root is indicated by the functional value at the root, which is closer to 0.0 in the output produced by Program 14.2. A more complete comparison of the rate of convergence for all three root-finding methods presented so far, as these methods applied to the function

$$f(x) = 2e^{-2x} - \sin(\pi x)$$

is presented in Table 14.1.

A slope-reduction factor of one-half was used in constructing the drawing in Figure 14.5 and is an example of what is called a **relaxation factor**, a number used to alter the results of one iteration before inserting them into the next. Determining the optimum relaxation factor is almost always an extremely complex problem in any calculation and is well beyond the scope of this text. However, in this instance a little trial and error shows that a less drastic decrease in the slope will result in improved convergence. Using a relaxation factor of 0.9 should be adequate for most problems; this factor was used to generate the values in Table 14.1.

Table 14.1 Comparison of Root-Finding Methods Using the Function $f(x) = 2e^{-2x} - \sin(\pi x)$

i	Bisection x_2	Regula Bisection x_2	Modified Regula Bisection x_2
1	0.35	0.385	0.385
2	0.375	0.3823	0.3820
3	0.3875	0.3819	0.38183
4	0.38125	0.38185	0.381843
5	0.38438	0.381844	0.38184267
6	0.38281	0.381843	0.38184276
7	0.38203	0.3818428	0.38184275
8	0.38164	0.38184275	0.38184275

Summary of the Algorithms Based on Bisection

The characteristic features of the three methods discussed in this and the previous section are listed below:

Bisection	Success based on size of interval Slow convergence Predictable number of iterations Interval halved in each iteration Guaranteed to bracket a root
Regula falsi	Success based on size of function Faster convergence Unpredictable number of iterations Interval containing root is not small Monitors size of function as well as its sign
Modified regula falsi	Success based on size of interval Faster convergence Unpredictable number of iterations

Of the three methods, the modified regula falsi is probably the most efficient for common problems and is the recommended algorithm whenever the only information available is that the function changes sign between x_1 and x_3.

The requirement that the initial search interval be one in which the function changes sign (only once) can occasionally be troublesome. For example, the problem of finding the root of the function

$$f(x) = x^2 - 2x + 1 = (x - 1)^2$$

is not suited to any of the algorithms based on bisection since the function never changes sign. This difficulty occurs whenever the root of the function is a multiple root of even multiplicity. A method that overcomes this limitation is the secant method, which is the topic of the next section.

Exercises 14.3

1. Roughly reproduce the sketch in Figure 14.6 and then graphically apply the regula falsi method for three iterations.

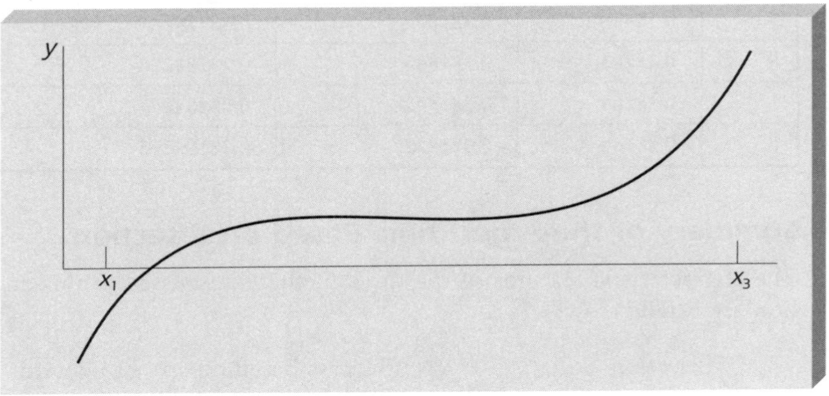

Figure 14.6 Function for Exercise 1.

2. Using a pocket calculator, apply the regula falsi procedure for three iterations to the following functions:

- **a.** $f(x) = xe^{-x^2} - \cos(x)$; $a = 0$, $b = 2$; exact root = 1.351491185. . .
- **b.** $g(x) = x^2 - 2x - 3$; $a = 0$, $b = 4$; exact root = 3.0
- **c.** $h(x) = e^x - (1 + x + x^2/2)$; $a = -1$, $b = 1$; exact root = 0.0
- **d.** $F(x) = x^3 - 2x - 5$; $a = 1$, $b = 3$; exact root = 2.0945514815. . .
- **e.** $G(x) = 10 \ln(x) - x$; $a = 1$, $b = 2$; exact root = 1.1183255916. . .

3. Roughly reproduce Figure 14.6 and then graphically apply the modified regula falsi method for three iterations.

4. **a.** Execute Program 14.2.

- **b.** Use Program 14.2 to find the root of one of the functions in Exercise 2 to an accuracy of 10^{-5}.
- **c.** Change the relaxation factor from 0.9 to 0.75 and rerun the program. Comment on the difference between the two calculations.

14.4 The Secant Method

The secant method is identical to the method of false position (regula falsi method) except that the sign of $f(x)$ need not be checked at each iteration. As in the regula falsi method, the values of x_0 and x_1 are required to start the procedure but then the following algorithm is employed to obtain an improvement for the next value of x:

Start with the interval defined by (x_0, x_1)
Compute the next value of x as

$$x_2 = \frac{f(x_0)}{f(x_0) - f(x_1)}(x_1 - x_0)$$

Replace the pair of values (x_0, x_1) by the pair (x_1, x_2)
Repeat steps 2 and 3 until the value of $f(x)$ is within an acceptable limit of zero

The secant method can be shown (see Exercise 2) to be equivalent to repeatedly replacing the function by straight lines drawn through the points $[x_0, f(x_0)]$ and $[x_1, f(x_1)]$—that is, secant lines. The C++ code for a function implementing the secant method is included in Program 14.3.

A sample run using Program 14.3 produced the following:

```
Enter the limits of the original search interval, a and b: .4 .5
Enter the convergence criteria: .00001
Enter the maximum number of iterations allowed: 25

The original search interval is from 0.4 to 0.5
The convergence criterion is: interval < 1e-005
The maximum number of iterations allowed is 25

A root at x = 0.443567 was found in 4 iterations
The value of the function is -9.014174e-008
```

Although the secant method is probably the most popular method used to find the root of a function, it does pose divergence problems. As such, a check should be built into the C++ code for this method that detects when successive intervals start to become larger rather than smaller.

Program 14.3

```
#include <iostream>
#include <cmath>
using namespace std;

void secant(double, double, double, int); // function prototype
double f(double); // function prototype

int main()
{
  int imax;           // maximum number of iterations
  double a, b;        // left and right ends of the original interval
  double epsilon;     // convergence criterion

  // obtain the input data
  cout << "Enter the limits of the original search interval, a and b: ";
  cin  >> a >> b;
  cout << "Enter the convergence criteria: ";
  cin  >> epsilon;
  cout << "Enter the maximum number of iterations allowed: ";
  cin  >> imax;

  secant(a, b, epsilon, imax);

  return 0;
}

// This function implements the secant method for finding
// a root of a function
void secant(double a, double b, double epsilon, int imax)
{

  int i;              // current iteration counter
  double x0, x1;      // left and right x values of current interval
  double f0, f1;      // function evaluated at these points
  double dx0;         // delta x0
  double dx1;         // delta x1

  // echo back the passed input data
  cout << "\nThe original search interval is from " << a << " to " << b
       << "\nThe convergence criterion is: interval < " << epsilon
       << "\nThe maximum number of iterations allowed is " << imax << endl;
```

(Continued)

(Continued)

```
  // determine the root
  x0 = a;
  f0 = f(x0);
  dx0 = abs(b - a);

  // iterations
  for (i = 1; i <= imax; i++)
  {
    x1 = x0 + dx0;
    f1 = f(x1);
    if (abs(f1) < epsilon) // root is found
    {
      cout << "\nA root at x = " << x1 + dx1 << " was found "
           << "in " << i << " iterations" << endl;
      cout << "The value of the function is " << f1 << endl;
      return;
    }
    else // do next iteration
    {
      dx1 = ( f1/(f0 - f1) ) * dx0;
      x0 = x1;
      dx0 = dx1;
      f0 = f1;
    }
  }
  cout << "\nAfter " << imax << " iterations, no root was found "
       << "within the convergence criterion\n"
       << "The search for a root has failed due to excessive iterations\n"
       << "after the maximum number of " << imax << " iterations" << endl;

  return;
}

// function to evaluate f(x)
double f(double x)
{
  const double PI = 2*asin(1.0); // value of pi

  return (exp(-x) - sin(0.5 * PI * x));
}
```

Exercises 14.4

1. a. Execute Program 14.3 on your computer.
   b. Use Program 14.3 to find the root of the function $f(x) = x^2 - 2x + 0.9$ starting with an initial guess of $x_0 = 0.6$ and $x_1 = 0.9$.
2. The function `secant` of Program 14.3 was used to find a root of the function $f(x) = x^2 - 2x + 0.9$ starting with an initial guess of $x_0 = 0.6$, $x_1 = 0.9$ and the values of x_0 and $x_1 - x_0$ were printed for each iteration. The results are

Step	x_0	$x_1 - x_0$
0	0.600	0.300
1	0.900	−0.180
2	0.720	−0.057
3	0.663	0.022
4	0.685	−0.001

   Carefully graph the function for $0.5 \le x \le 1.0$ and use the above numbers to graphically demonstrate how the secant method arrives at a root of the function.
3. Use Program 14.3 to find a root of the function $f(x) = x^2 - 2x - 3$.

14.5 INTRODUCTION TO NUMERICAL INTEGRATION

The integration of a function of a single variable can be thought of as either the opposite of differentiation—that is, the antiderivative—or as the area under a curve. Antiderivatives are ordinarily discussed in depth in a calculus course. Here we will concentrate instead on the less analytic, more visual approach of interpreting a definite integral as an area. That is, the integral of the function $f(x)$ from $x = a$ to $x = b$, designated as

$$I = \int_a^b f(x)\,dx$$

will be evaluated by devising schemes for measuring the area under the graph of the function over this interval (see Figure 14.7). This method of evaluating an integral lends itself so naturally to numerical computation that the most effective way to understand the process of integration is to learn the numerical approach first and later have these ideas reinforced by the more formal concepts of the antiderivative.

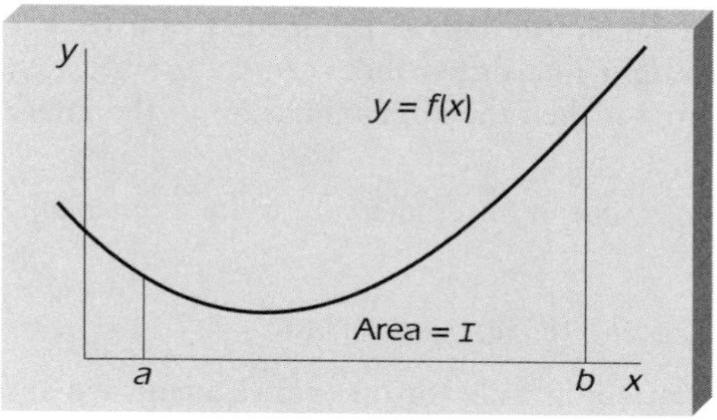

Figure 14.7 An integral as an area under a curve.

Another reason for studying numerical integration at this stage is that it is a so-called stable process; it almost always works. This is because numerical integration consists of expressing the area as the sum of areas of smaller segments, a procedure that is relatively safe from problems such as division by zero or round-off error caused by subtracting numbers of approximately the same magnitude.

Finally, it is unfortunately true that many, perhaps most, of the integrals that occur in actual engineering or science problems cannot be expressed in any closed form.

To formally integrate a function—that is, to obtain a closed expression for the answer—often takes considerable training and experience. Dozens of "tricks" must be learned and understood. On the other hand, the procedures of numerical integration are few in number, all quite easy to understand and remember. As in many earlier numerical procedures, we begin by replacing the function over a limited range by straight-line segments. The interval $x = a$ to $x = b$ is divided into subintervals or panels of size Δx, the function is replaced by line segments over each subinterval, and the area under the function is then approximated by the area under the line segments. This is the trapezoidal rule approximation for an integral and is described in the next section. The next order approximation is to replace the function by parabolic segments and is known as Simpson's rule, which is presented in Section 14.7.

14.6 THE TRAPEZOIDAL RULE

An approximation to the area under a complicated curve is obtained by assuming that the function can be replaced by simpler functions over a limited range. A straight line, the simplest approximation to a function, is the first to be considered and leads to what is called the **trapezoidal rule**.

The area under the curve $f(x)$ from $x = a$ to $x = b$ is approximated by the area beneath a straight line drawn between the points $x_a, f(a)$ and $x_b, f(b)$ (see Figure 14.8). The lighter area is then the approximation to the integral and is the area of a trapezoid, which is

$$I \simeq (\text{average value of } f \text{ over interval})\ (\text{width of interval})$$

or

$$I \simeq \tfrac{1}{2}\,[f(a) + f(b)]\,(b - a) = T_0 \qquad (14.6)$$

This is the trapezoidal rule for one panel, identified as T_0.

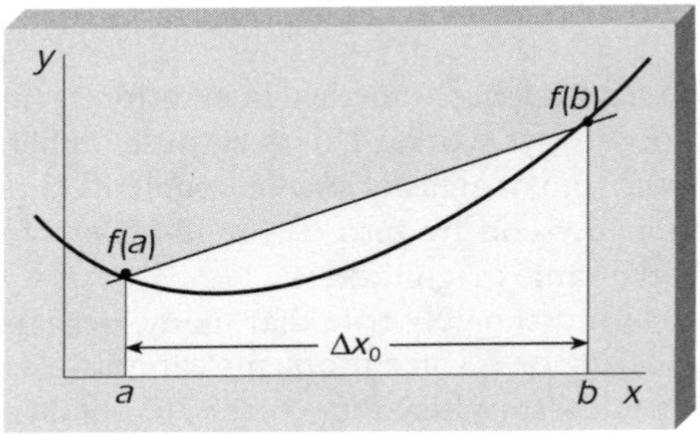

Figure 14.8 Approximating the area under a curve by a single trapezoid.

To improve the accuracy of the approximation to the area under a curve, the interval is next divided in half and the function approximated by straight-line segments over each half. The area in this case is approximated by the area of two trapezoids, as illustrated in Figure 14.9.

$$I \approx T_1 = \left[\tfrac{1}{2}\left(f(a) + f_1\right)\Delta x_L\right] + \left[\tfrac{1}{2}\left(f_1 + f(b)\right)\Delta x_L\right]$$

or

$$T_1 = \frac{\Delta x_L}{2}\left[f(a) + 2f_1 + f(b)\right] \qquad \mathbf{(14.7)}$$

where

$$\Delta x_L = \frac{(b - a)}{2}$$

$$f_1 = f(x = a + \Delta x_L)$$

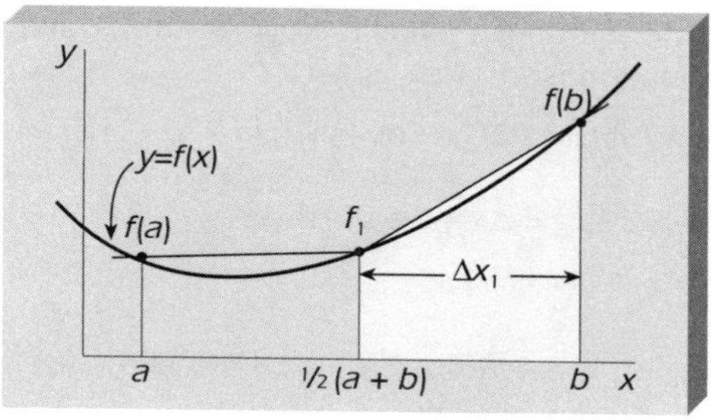

Figure 14.9 Two-panel approximation to the area.

Notice that when adding the areas of the trapezoids, the sides at $f(a)$ and $f(b)$ are sides of only the first and last trapezoid, whereas the side at f_1 is a side of two trapezoids and thus "counts twice," explaining the factor of 2 in Equation 14.7.

Furthermore, the two-panel approximation, T_1, can be related to the one-panel results, T_0, as

$$T_1 = \frac{T_0}{2} + \Delta x_1 f_1 \quad (14.8)$$

To increase the accuracy further, the interval is simply subdivided into a large number of panels. The result for n panels is clearly

$$I \approx T_n = \tfrac{1}{2}\Delta x_n \left[f(a) + 2\sum_{i=1}^{n-1} f_i + f(b) \right] \quad (14.9)$$

where $\Delta x_n = (b - a)/n$ and f_i is the function evaluated at each of the interior points,

$$f_i = f(x = a + i\,\Delta x_n)$$

The reason for the extra factor of 2 in Equation 14.9 is the same as in the two-panel example. Equation 14.9 is known as the **trapezoidal rule.**

Computational Form of the Trapezoidal Rule Equation

Equation 14.9 was derived assuming that the widths of all the panels are the same and equal to Δx_n. However, equal panel widths are not required in the derivation, and the equation can easily be generalized to a partition of the interval into unequal panels of width Δx_i, $i = 1, \ldots, n - 1$. However, for reasons to be explained a bit later, we will not only restrict the panel widths to be equal but the number of panels to be a power of 2—that is,

$$n = 2^k$$

The number of panels is n, the order of the calculation will be called k, and the corresponding trapezoidal rule approximation will be labeled as T_k. Thus, T_0 is the result for $n = 2^0 = 1$ panel. The situation for $k = 2$ or $2^2 = 4$ panels is illustrated in Figure 14.10.

In the figure the width of a panel is $\Delta x_2 = (b - a)/2^2$, and the value of the $k = 2$ trapezoidal rule approximation is

$$T_2 = (\Delta x_2/2)\left[f(a) + 2f(a + \Delta x_2) + 2f(a + \Delta x_2) + 2f(a + 3\Delta x_2) + f(b)\right] \quad \textbf{(14.10)}$$

However, since $2\Delta x_2 = \Delta x_1$, we see that

$$f(a + 2\Delta x_2) = f(a + x_1)$$

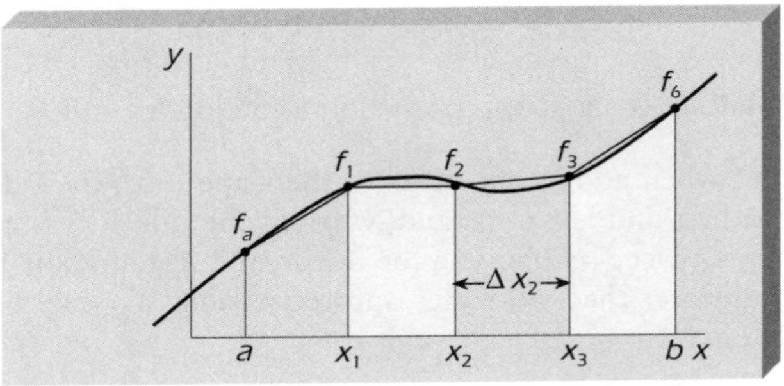

Figure 14.10 Four-panel trapezoidal approximation, T_2.

and $f(a + \Delta x_1)$ was already determined in the previous calculation of T_1 (Equation 14.8). The point is that by successively doubling the number of panels in each stage, the only new information we require to proceed to the next order trapezoidal rule approximation is the evaluation of the function at the midpoints of the current intervals.

To exploit this fact further, Equations 14.7 and 14.8 can be used to rewrite Equation 14.10 in the form

$$T_2 = (\Delta x_1/4)\left[f(a) + 2f(a + \Delta x_1) + f(b)\right] + \Delta x_2\left[f(a + \Delta x_2) + f(a + 3\Delta x_2)\right]$$
$$= T_1/2 + \Delta x_2\left[f(a + \Delta x_2) + f(a + 3\Delta x_2)\right]$$

This equation can easily be generalized to yield

$$T_k = \tfrac{1}{2}\, T_{k-1} + \Delta x_k \sum_{\substack{i=1 \\ \text{odd only}}}^{n-1} f(a + i\,\Delta x_k) \quad \textbf{(14.11)}$$

where

$$\Delta x_k = \frac{b-a}{2^k}$$

The procedure for using Equation 14.11 to approximate an integral by the trapezoidal rule is then:

1. Compute T_0 by using Equation 14.6.
2. Repeatedly apply Equation 14.11 for k = 1,2, ... until sufficient accuracy is obtained.

Example of a Trapezoidal Rule Calculation

To illustrate the ideas of this section, we use the integral

$$I = \int_1^2 (1/x)\,dx$$

The function $f(x) = 1/x$ can of course be integrated analytically to give $\ln(x)$, and since $\ln(1) = 0$, the value of the integral is $\ln(2) = 0.69314718$. The trapezoidal rule approximation to the integral with $a = 1$ and $b = 2$ begins with Equation 14.6 to obtain T_0.

$$T_0 = \frac{1}{2}\left(\frac{1}{1} + \frac{1}{2}\right)(2 - 1) = 0.75$$

Repeated use of Equation 14.11 then yields

$k = 1$ $\quad \Delta x_1 = ½$

$$T_1 = T_0/2 + ½\left[f\left(1 + ½\right)\right] = 0.75/2 + ½\ (1/1.5)$$

$$= 0.708333$$

$k = 2$ $\quad \Delta x_2 = ¼$

$$T_2 = T_1/2 + ¼\ (1/1.25 + 1/1.75)$$

$$= 0.6970238$$

$k = 3$ $\quad \Delta x_3 = ⅛$

$$T_3 = T_2/2 + ⅛\ (1/1.25 + 1/1.375 + 1/1.625 + 1/1.875)$$

$$= 0.69412185$$

Continuing the calculation through $k = 5$ yields

k	T_k
0	0.75
1	0.70833
2	0.69702
3	0.69412
4	0.69339
5	0.693208
.	.
.	.
.	.
Exact	0.693147. . .

The convergence of the computed values of the trapezoidal rule is not particularly fast, but the method is quite simple.

Exercises 14.6

1. Evaluate the integrals below by using the trapezoidal rule.
   a. Evaluate T_0 for one panel by using Equation 14.6.
   b. ComputeT_1 using the value of T_0 and Equation 14.11.
   c. Continue the calculation through T_4.

   Collect your results in the form of a table. (Be careful: errors in one step will carry over into the next.)

		Exact Result
a.	$\int_0^8 x^2 dx$	170⅔
b.	$\int_0^8 x^4 dx$	6553.6
c.	$\int_0^1 xe^{-x} dx$	1 – 2/e = 0.2642411175. . .
d.	$\int_0^{\pi/2} x \sin(x) dx$	1.0
e.	$\int_0^1 \left(1+x^2\right)^{3/2} dx$	1.567951963. . .
f.	$\int_0^1 e^{-x^2} dx$	0.74682404. . .

14.7 SIMPSON'S RULE

The trapezoidal rule is based on approximating the function by straight-line segments. To improve the accuracy and the convergence rate of the method, an obvious direction to take would be to approximate the function by parabolic segments in place of straight lines. This idea results in an approximation for the integral known as **Simpson's rule**, the simplest example of which is illustrated in Figure 14.11. To uniquely specify a parabola requires three points, and so the lowest-order Simpson's rule has two panels.

To proceed, we need to know the area under a parabola drawn through three points. Note that the corresponding step in the derivation of the trapezoidal rule was trivial: the area under a line through two points is simply $\Delta x[f(a) + f(b)]/2$.

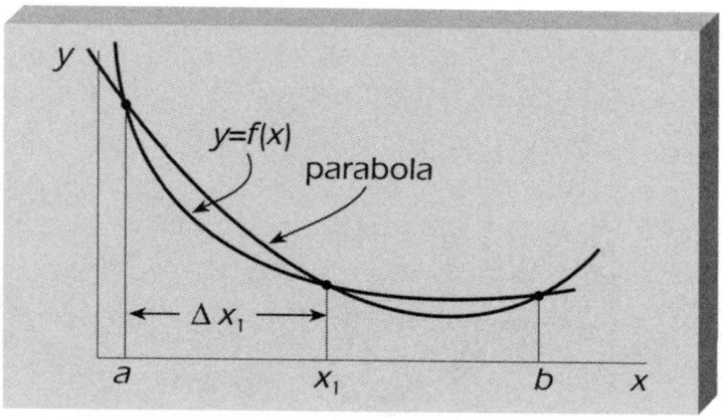

Figure 14.11 Area under a parabola drawn through three points.

If the curve $f(x)$ drawn in Figure 14.11 is approximated by a parabola drawn through the three points $f(a)$, $f(b)$, and the value of $f(x)$ at the midpoint of the interval f_{mid}, it can be shown using calculus that the area under this parabola, denoted as S_1, is

$$S_1 = \tfrac{1}{3}\Delta x_1\left[f(a) + 4f(a + \Delta x_1) + f(b)\right]$$

where

$$\Delta x_1 = \frac{b-a}{2}$$

This is the first-order Simpson's rule approximation where $k = 1$ and $n = 2^1$ panels. The next level of approximation is to halve the interval width and partition the interval into four panels, as shown in Figure 14.12. The area under the function $f(x)$ is then approximated as the area under the two parabolas shown in the figure. Again, using calculus, it can be shown that the area under the two parabolas is

$$\begin{aligned} S_2 &= \tfrac{1}{3}\Delta x_2\left\{\left[f(a) + 4f(x_1) + f(x_2)\right] + \left[f(x_2) + 4f(x_3) + f(b)\right]\right\} \\ &= \tfrac{1}{3}\Delta x_2\left\{f(a) + 4\left[f(x_1) + f(x_3)\right] + 2f(x_2) + f(b)\right\} \qquad \textbf{(14.12)} \end{aligned}$$

where

$$\Delta x_2 = \frac{b-a}{2^2}$$

and

$$f_i = f(x = a + i\Delta x_2)$$

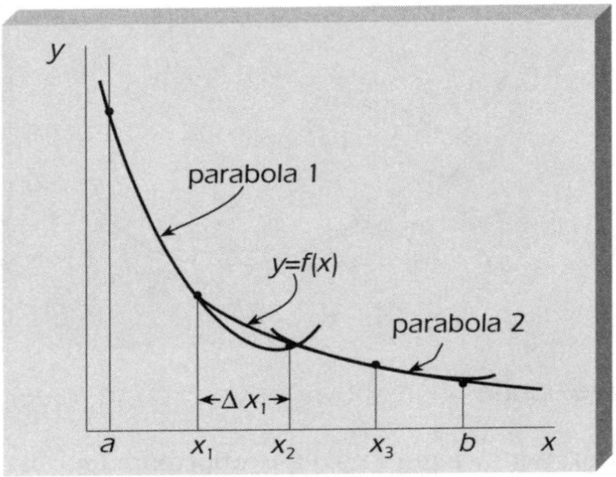

Figure 14.12 Second-order Simpson's rule approximation is the area under two parabolas.

This procedure can be extended to 8,16, 32, and so on panels. The result is a rather simple generalization of Equation 14.12 and for $n = 2^k$ panels is

$$S_k = \tfrac{1}{3}\Delta x_k \left[f(a) + 4\sum_{\substack{i=1 \\ \text{odd only}}}^{n-1} f(a + i\,\Delta x_k) + 2\sum_{\substack{i=2 \\ \text{even only}}}^{n-2} f(a + i\,\Delta x_k) + f(b) \right] \quad \textbf{(14.13)}$$

Equation 14.13, which is known as **Simpson's rule**, is an extremely popular method of evaluating integrals of functions that are smooth, and rightly so. As we shall see later in the chapter, Simpson's rule converges nicely in most instances and it is relatively easy to use. Also, Equation 14.13 can easily be adapted to handle an odd number of unevenly spaced points and is the most common method for estimating the integral of experimentally obtained data.

Example of Simpson's Rule as an Approximation to an Integral

Again consider the integral

$$I = \int_1^2 (1/x)\, dx$$

Using Equation 14.13 first for $k = 1$ yields

$$k = 1$$
$$n = 2^1 = 2$$
$$\Delta x_1 = \frac{\text{b} - \text{a}}{2^2} = \frac{1}{2}$$
$$S_1 = \tfrac{1}{3}(\tfrac{1}{2})[1 + 4(1/1.5) + \tfrac{1}{2}] = 0.6944444$$

Repeating for $k = 2$

$k = 2$

$n = 2^2 = 4$

$\Delta x_2 = 1/4$

$S_2 = \frac{1}{3}(\frac{1}{4})[1 + 4(1/1.25 + 1/1.75) + 2(1/1.5) + \frac{1}{2}] = 0.69325397$

Continuing the calculation, we obtain the values listed in Table 14.2. For comparison, results are also included for the same integral obtained in the previous section using the trapezoidal rule. Clearly, Simpson's rule converges much faster that the trapezoidal rule, at least for this example.

Table 14.2 Trapezoidal and Simpson's Rule Results for the Integral $\int_1^2 (1/x)\,dx$

Order k	Number of Panels n	T_k	S_k
0	1	0.75	–
1	2	0.7083	0.6944
2	4	0.69702	0.69325
3	8	0.69412	0.69315
4	16	0.69339	0.6931466
5	32	0.693208	0.6931473
6	64	0.693162	0.6931472

Exercises 14.7

1. Using Equation 14.13, calculate the two-panel and the four-panel Simpson's rule results, S_1 and S_2 for the following integrals.

		Exact Result
a.	$\int_0^8 x^2 dx$	$170\frac{2}{3}$
b.	$\int_0^8 x^4 dx$	6553.6
c.	$\int_0^1 xe^{-x} dx$	1 – 2/e = 0.2642411175. . .
d.	$\int_0^{\pi/2} x \sin(x)\, dx$	1.0

e. $\int_0^1 \left(1 + x^2\right)^{3/2} dx$ 1.567951962. . .

f. $\int_0^1 e^{-x^2} dx$ 0.74682404. . .

2. Using Equation 14.13, calculate S_1 through S_4 for the integrals listed in Exercise 1.

14.8 COMMON PROGRAMMING ERRORS

In using the modified bisection root-finding method, two problems can occur.

The first problem is round-off error, which can occur whenever the values of $f(x_1)$ and $f(x_3)$ used in the computation are very nearly equal. The second problem occurs because a prediction of the exact number of iterations required to achieve a desired accuracy is not available. To successfully counter these two problems, the code used in these two methods must detect their occurrence to prevent excessive and possibly infinite iterations.

With respect to numerical integration, excessive computation times can also be a problem. This typically occurs whenever the number of iterations exceeds fifty. Frequently, it is possible to significantly reduce run time by carefully inspecting each program loop to ensure that only those calculations that must be iteratively computed are included within the loop, and moving all other calculations to be computed either before or after the loop is completed.

14.9 CHAPTER SUMMARY

All of the root-solving methods described in this chapter are of an iterative nature and can be categorized within two classes of root-finding algorithms, depending on whether you are starting with an interval containing a root or with an initial estimate of the root. The bisection-based procedures begin with an interval that is known to contain a root and are guaranteed to converge to within a prescribed tolerance bracketing the root. Of the bisection methods, the modified regula falsi is the fastest converging and is recommended.

In algorithms based on the bisection method, the initial interval is refined by repeatedly evaluating the function at points within the interval and then, by monitoring the sign of the function, and determining in which subinterval the root lies. If the left and right ends of the current interval are x_1 and x_3, respectively, the standard bisection method uses the function evaluated at the midpoint, $x_2 = ½(x_1 + x_3)$. The sign of the function at x_2 is compared with that at either end of the interval to determine which half of the interval contains the root. The full interval is then replaced by this half and the process repeated. After n iterations, the root will be contained in an interval of size $(x_3 - x_1)/2n$.

In the regula falsi method, the conditions are the same as for the bisection method. But instead of using the midpoint of the interval, a straight line connecting the points at the ends of the interval is used to interpolate the position of the root. The intersection of this line with the x axis determines the value of x_2 to be used in the next step. This value of x_2 is given by the equation

$$x_2 = x_1 - (x_3 - x_1)\frac{f(x_1)}{f(x_3) - f(x_1)}$$

in place of the equation for the midpoint. Convergence is faster than with the bisection method. However, it is likely that the interval will converge to the root from one side only.

The modified regula falsi method is the same as the regula falsi method except for the following change: in each iteration, when the full interval is replaced by the subinterval containing the root, a relaxation factor is used to first modify the value of the function at the fixed end of the subinterval. A relaxation factor of approximately 0.9 is suggested. This additional feature will cause the interval to converge from both ends, and convergence is then based on interval size. This method is the preferred procedure for finding a root of a function that is not too expensive to evaluate and that is known to have a root in a specified interval.

The secant method replaces the function by a secant line through two points and then finds the point of intersection of the line with the x axis. The algorithm requires two input numbers, x_0 and Δx_0, corresponding to initial guesses for the root and for an interval containing the root. This pair of values is then replaced by the pair $(x_1, \Delta x_1)$ where

$$x_1 = x_0 + \Delta x_0$$

and

$$\Delta x_1 = \frac{f(x_1)}{f(x_0) - f(x_1)} \Delta x_0$$

and the process is continued until the new interval Δx is sufficiently small.

Root-solving methods are amenable to C++ coding. However, the success of a program to find the root of a function usually depends on the quality of the information supplied by the user; that is, how accurate is the initial guess or search interval and how well does the method chosen match the circumstances of the problem. Execution-time problems are most frequently traceable to errors in coding the function or to inadequate user-supplied diagnostics for potential problems.

The integral of $f(x)$ from $x = a$ to $x = b$, written as

$$I = \int_a^b f(x)\,dx$$

is evaluated numerically by computing the area under the curve $f(x)$ over the specified range of x. The procedures for estimating this area consist of partitioning the interval $a \le x \le b$ into n panels of width $\Delta x_i (i = 1,n)$, and approximating the function $f(x)$ over each panel by a simpler function.

The trapezoidal rule results from replacing the function $f(x)$ by straight-line segments over the panels Δx_i. The approximate value for the integral is then given by the following formula, which is known as the trapezoidal rule:

$$\int_a^b f(x)\,dx \approx \tfrac{1}{2}\,\Delta x_n\left(f(a) + 2\sum_{i-1}^{n-1} f_i + f(b)\right)$$

If the panels are of equal size *and* the number of panels is $n = 2^k$, where k is a positive integer, the trapezoidal rule approximation is then labeled as T_k and satisfies the equation

$$T_k = \tfrac{1}{2}\,T_{k-1} + \Delta x_k \sum_{\substack{i=1 \\ \text{odd only}}}^{n-1} f\left(a + i\Delta x_k\right)$$

where

$$\Delta x_k = \frac{b-a}{2^k}$$

In the next level of approximation the function $f(x)$ is replace by $n/2$ parabolic segments over pairs of equal-size panels, $\Delta x = (b - a)/n$ and results in the formula for the area known as Simpson's rule:

$$\int_a^b f(x)\,dx \approx \tfrac{1}{3}\Delta x_k\left[f(a) + 4\sum_{\substack{i=1 \\ \text{odd only}}}^{n-1} f\left(a + i\Delta x_k\right) + 2\sum_{\substack{i=2 \\ \text{even only}}}^{n-2} f\left(a + i\Delta x_k\right) + f(b)\right]$$

CHAPTER 15

Bit Operations

TOPICS

C++ operates with data entities that are stored as one or more bytes, such as character, integer, and double-precision constants and variables. In addition, C++ provides for the manipulation of individual bits of character and integer values and variables. The operators that are used to perform bit manipulations are called bit operators and are listed in Table 15.1.

All the operators listed in Table 15.1, except ~, are binary operators, requiring two operands. Each operand is treated as a binary number consisting of a series of individual 1s and 0s. The respective bits in each operand are then compared on a bit-by-bit basis and the result is determined based on the selected operation.

Table 15.1 Bit Operators

Operator	Description
&	Bit-by-bit AND
|	Bit-by-bit Inclusive OR
^	Bit-by-bit Exclusive OR
~	Bit-by-bit one's complement
<<	Left shift
>>	Right shift

15.1 THE AND OPERATOR

The AND operator causes a bit-by-bit AND comparison between its two operands. *The result of each bit-by-bit comparison is a 1 only when both bits being compared are 1s; otherwise, the result of the AND operation is a 0.* For example, assume that the following two eight-bit numbers are to be ANDed:

```
1 0 1 1 0 0 1 1
1 1 0 1 0 1 0 1
- - - - - - - -
```

To perform an AND operation, each bit in one operand is compared to the bit occupying the same position in the other operand. Figure 15.1 illustrates the correspondence between bits for these two operands. As shown in the figure, when both bits being compared are 1s, the result is a 1, otherwise the result is a 0. The result of each comparison is, of course, independent of any other bit comparison.

```
  1 0 1 1 0 0 1 1
& 1 1 0 1 0 1 0 1
  - - - - - - - -
  1 0 0 1 0 0 0 1
```

Figure 15.1 A sample AND operation.

Program 15.1 illustrates the use of an AND operation. In this program, the variable `op1` is initialized to the octal value 325, which is the octal equivalent of the binary number 1 1 0 1 0 1 0 1, and the variable `op2` is initialized to the octal value 263, which is the octal representation of the binary number 1 0 1 1 0 0 1 1. These are the same two binary numbers illustrated in Figure 15.1.

Program 15.1

```
#include <iostream>
using namespace std;

int main()
{
  int op1 = 0325, op2 = 0263;

  int op3 = op1 & op2;
  cout << oct << op1 << " ANDed with "<< op2 << " is " << op3 << endl;

  return 0;
}
```

Program 15.1 produces the following output:

```
325 ANDed with 263 is 221
```

The result of ANDing the octal numbers 325 and 263 is the octal number 221. The binary equivalent of 221 is the binary number 1 0 0 1 0 0 0 1, which is the result of the AND operation illustrated in Figure 15.1.

AND operations are extremely useful in masking, or eliminating, selected bits from an operand. This is a direct result of the fact that ANDing any bit (1 or 0) with a 0 forces the resulting bit to be a 0, while ANDing any bit (1 or 0) with a 1 leaves the original bit unchanged. For example, assume that the variable `op1` has the arbitrary bit pattern x x x x x x x x, where each x can be either 1 or 0, independent of any other x in the number. The result of ANDing this binary number with the binary number 0 0 0 0 1 1 1 1 is:

```
     op1 =   x x x x x x x x
     op2 =   0 0 0 0 1 1 1 1
             - - - - - - - -
  Result =   0 0 0 0 x x x x
```

As can be seen from this example, the zeros in `op2` effectively mask, or eliminate, the respective bits in `op1`, while the ones in `op2` filter, or pass, the respective bits in `op1` through with no change in their values. In this example, the variable `op2` is called a **mask**. By choosing the mask appropriately, any individual bit in an operand can be selected, or filtered, out of an operand for inspection. For example, ANDing the variable `op1` with the mask 0 0 0 0 0 1 0 0 forces all the bits of the result to be 0, except for the third bit. The third bit of the result will be a copy of the third bit of `op1`. Thus, if the result of the AND is 0, the third bit of `op1` must have been 0, and if the result of the AND is a nonzero number, the third bit must have been a 1.

Program 15.2 uses this masking property to convert lowercase letters into their uppercase form, assuming the letters are stored using the ASCII code. The algorithm for converting letters is based on the fact that the binary codes for lowercase and uppercase letters in ASCII are the same except for bit five, which is a 1 for lowercase letters and

0 for uppercase letters.[1] For example the binary code for the letter a is 01100001 (hex 61), while the binary code for the letter A is 01000001 (hex 41). Similarly, the binary code for the letter z is 01111010 (hex 7A), while the binary code for the letter Z is 01011010 (hex 5A). (See Appendix B for the hexadecimal values of the upper- and lowercase letters.) Thus, given a lowercase letter, it can be converted into its uppercase form by forcing the fifth bit to 0. This is accomplished in Program 15.2 by masking the letter's code with the binary value 11011111, which has the hexadecimal value DF.

Program 15.2

```
#include <iostream>
using namespace std;

const int TOUPPER = 0xDF;
void upper(char *);  // function prototype

int main()
{
  char word[81];       // enough storage for a complete line

  cout << "Enter a string of both upper and lowercase letters:\n";
  cin.getline(word,80,'\n');
  cout << "\nThe string of letters just entered is:\n"
       << word << endl;
  upper(word);
  cout << "\nThis string, in uppercase letters is:\n"
       << word << endl;
}
void upper(char *word)
{
  while (*word != '\0')
    *word++ &= TOUPPER;
}
```

A sample run using Program 15.2 follows:

```
Enter a string of both upper and lowercase letters:
abcdefgHIJKLMNOPqrstuvwxyz

The string of letters just entered is:
abcdefgHIJKLMNOPqrstuvwxyz

This string, in uppercase letters is:
ABCDEFGHIJKLMNOPQRSTUVWXYZ
```

[1]This assumes the conventional numbering scheme starting with bit 0 as the rightmost bit. Using this convention the rightmost bit (or bit 0) is referred to as the least significant bit (LSB) and the leftmost bit is referred to as the most significant bit (MSB). Here the MSB is bit 7.

In reviewing Program 15.2, first notice that the input string has been stored and passed to `upper()` as a C-string, which is an array of characters. Doing so permits the function to receive and operate on the original character values rather than receiving a copy of these values. Second, notice that the lowercase letters are converted to uppercase form, while uppercase letters are unaltered. This is because bit five of all uppercase letters is 0 to begin with, so that forcing this bit to 0 using the mask has no effect. Only when bit five is a 1, as it is for lowercase letters, is the input character altered.

15.2 The Inclusive OR Operator

The inclusive OR operator, |, performs a bit-by-bit comparison of its two operands in a similar fashion to the bit-by-bit AND. The result of the OR comparison, however, is determined by the following rule:

The result of the comparison is 1 if either bit being compared is a 1, otherwise the result is a 0.

Figure 15.2 illustrates an OR operation. As shown in the figure, when either of the two bits being compared is a 1, the result is a 1; otherwise the result is a 0. As with all bit operations, the result of each comparison is, of course, independent of any other comparison.

```
   1 0 1 1 0 0 1 1
 | 1 1 0 1 0 1 0 1
   ---------------
   1 1 1 1 0 1 1 1
```

Figure 15.2 A sample OR operation.

Program 15.3 illustrates an OR operation, using the octal values of the operands illustrated in Figure 15.2.

Program 15.3

```cpp
#include <iostream>
using namespace std;

int main()
{
  int op1 = 0325, op2 = 0263;

  int op3 = op1 | op2;
  cout << oct << op1 << " ORed with " << op2 << " is " << op3 << endl;
}
```

Program 15.3 produces the following output:

```
325 ORed with 263 is 367
```

The result of ORing the octal numbers 325 and 263 is the octal number 367. The binary equivalent of 367 is 1 1 1 1 0 1 1 1, which is the result of the OR operation illustrated in Figure 15.2.

Inclusive OR operations are extremely useful in forcing selected bits to take on a 1 value or for passing through other bit values unchanged. This is a direct result of the fact that ORing any bit (1 or 0) with a 1 forces the resulting bit to be a 1, while ORing any bit (1 or 0) with a 0 leaves the original bit unchanged. For example, assume that the variable `op1` has the arbitrary bit pattern x x x x x x x x, where each x can be either 1 or 0, independent of any other x in the number. The result of ORing this binary number with the binary number 1 1 1 1 0 0 0 0 is

```
    op1 =   x x x x x x x x
    op2 =   1 1 1 1 0 0 0 0
            _ _ _ _ _ _ _ -
 Result =   1 1 1 1 x x x x
```

As can be seen from this example, the ones in `op2` force the resulting bits to 1, while the zeros in `op2` filter, or pass, the respective bits in `op1` through with no change in their values. Thus, using an OR operation a similar masking operation can be produced, as with an AND operation, except the masking bits are set to 1s rather than to 0s. Another way of looking at this is to say that ORing with a 0 has the same effect as ANDing with a 1.

Program 15.4 uses this masking property to convert uppercase letters in a word into their respective lowercase form, assuming the letters are stored using the ASCII code. The algorithm for converting letters is similar to that used in Program 15.2, and converts uppercase letters into their lowercase form by forcing the fifth bit in each letter to a 1. This is accomplished in Program 15.4 by masking the letter's code with the binary value 00100000, which has the hexadecimal value 20.

A sample run using Program 15.4 follows:

```
Enter a string of both upper and lowercase letters:
abcdefgHIJKLMNOPqrstuvwxyz

The string of letters just entered is:
abcdefgHIJKLMNOPqrstuvwxyz

This string, in lowercase letters is:
abcdefghijklmnopqrstuvwxyz
```

In reviewing Program 15.4, first notice that the input string has been stored and passed to `lower()` as a C-string, which is an array of characters. This permits the called function to receive and process the original character values rather than a copy of the values. Secondly, notice that the uppercase letters are converted to lowercase form, while uppercase letters are unaltered. This is because bit five of all lowercase letters is 1 to begin with, so that forcing this bit to one using the mask has no effect. Only when bit five is a 0, as it is for uppercase letters, is the input character altered.

Program 15.4

```
#include <iostream>
using namespace std;

const int TOLOWER = 0x20;
void lower (char *);  // function prototype

int main()
{
  char word[81];         // enough storage for a complete line

  cout << "Enter a string of both upper and lowercase letters:\n";
  cin.getline(word,80,'\n');
  cout << "\nThe string of letters just entered is:\n"
       << word << endl;
  lower(word);
  cout << "\nThis string, in lowercase letters is:\n"
       << word << endl;
}
void lower(char *word)
{
  while (*word != '\0')
    *word++ |= TOLOWER;
}
```

15.3 THE EXCLUSIVE OR OPERATOR

The exclusive OR operator, ^, performs a bit-by-bit comparison of its two operands. The result of the comparison is determined by the following rule:

The result of the comparison is 1 if one and only one of the bits being compared is a 1, otherwise the result is 0.

Figure 15.3 illustrates an exclusive OR operation. As shown in the figure, when both bits being compared are the same value (both 1 or both 0), the result is a 0. Only when both bits have different values (one bit a 1 and the other a 0) is the result a 1. Again, each pair or bit comparison is independent of any other bit comparison.

```
  1 0 1 1 0 0 1 1
^ 1 1 0 1 0 1 0 1
  _ _ _ _ _ _ _ _
  0 1 1 0 0 1 1 0
```

Figure 15.3 A sample exclusive OR operation.

An exclusive OR operation can be used to create the opposite value, or complement, of any individual bit in a variable. This is a direct result of the fact that exclusive ORing any bit (1 or 0) with a 1 forces the resulting bit to be of the opposite value of its original state, while exclusive ORing any bit (1 or 0) with a 0 leaves the original bit unchanged. For example, assume that the variable `op1` has the arbitrary bit pattern x x x x x x x x, where each x can be either 1 or 0, independent of any other x in the number. Using the notation that $\bar{x}$ is the complement (opposite) value of x, the result of exclusive ORing this binary number with the binary number 0 1 0 1 0 1 0 1 is:

```
           op1 =    x x x x x x x x
           op2 =    0 1 0 1 0 1 0 1
                    - - - - - - - -
                    _   _   _   _
        Result =    x x x x x x x x
```

As can be seen from this example, the ones in `op2` force the resulting bits to be the complement of their original bit values, while the zeros in `op2` filter, or pass, the respective bits in `op1` through with no change in their values.

Many encryption methods use the exclusive OR operation to code data by exclusive ORing each character in the string with a mask value. The choice of the mask value, which is referred to as the encryption key, is arbitrary, and any key value can be used.

Program 15.5 uses an encryption key of 52 to code a user-entered message.

Following is a sample run using Program 15.5.

```
Enter a sentence:
Good morning

The sentence just entered is:
Good morning

The encrypted version of this sentence is:
s[[P¶Y[FZ]ZS
```

Decoding an encrypted message requires exclusive ORing the coded message using the original encryption key, which is left as a homework exercise.

Program 15.5

```
#include <iostream>
using namespace std;

void encrypt(char *); // function prototype

int main()
{
  char message[81];     // enough storage for a complete line

  cout << "\nEnter a sentence:\n";
  cin.getline(message,80,'\n');
  cout << "\nThe sentence just entered is:\n"
       << message << endl;
  encrypt(message);
  cout << "\nThe encrypted version of this sentence is:\n"
       << message << endl;
}

void encrypt(char *message)
{
  while (*message != '\0')
    *message++ ^= 52;
}
```

15.4 THE COMPLEMENT OPERATOR

The complement operator, ~, is a unary operator that changes each 1 bit in its operand to 0 and each 0 bit to 1. For example, if the variable `op1` contains the binary number 11001010, ~`op1` replaces this binary number with the number 00110101. The complement operator is used to force any bit in an operand to 0, independent of the actual number of bits used to store the number. For example, the statement

```
op1 = op1 & ~07;    // 07 is an octal number
```

or its shorter form,

```
op1 &= ~07;     // 07 is an octal number
```

both set the last three bits of `op1` to zero, regardless of how `op1` is stored within the computer. Either of these two statements can, of course, be replaced by ANDing the last three bits of op1 with zeros, if the number of bits used to store op1 is known. In a computer that uses 16 bits to store integers, the appropriate AND operation is

```
op1 = op1 & 0177770;    // in octal
```

or

```
op1 = op1 & 0xFFF8;    // in hexadecimal
```

For a computer that uses 32 bits to store integers, the above AND sets the leftmost or higher order 16 bits to zero also, which is an unintended result. The correct statement for 32 bits is:

```
op1 = op1 & 027777777770;    // in octal
```

or

```
op1 = op1 & 0xFFFFFFF8;    // in hexadecimal
```

Using the complement operator in this situation frees the programmer from having to determine the storage size of the operand and, more importantly, makes the program portable between machines using different integer storage sizes.

15.5 DIFFERENT-SIZE DATA ITEMS

When the bit operators &, |, and ^ are used with operands of different sizes, the shorter operand is always increased in bit size to match the size of the larger operand. Figure 15.4 illustrates the extension of a 16-bit unsigned integer into a 32-bit number.

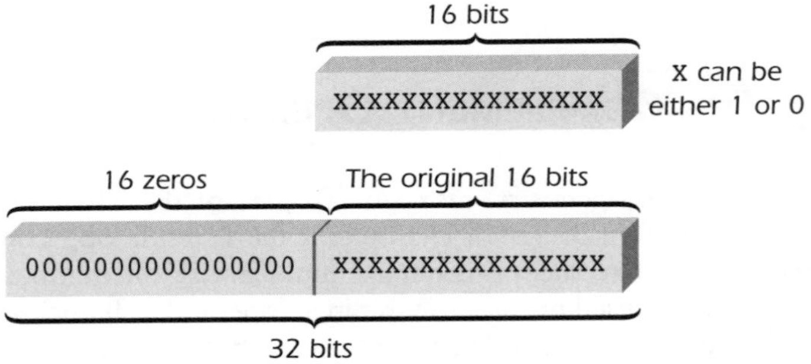

Figure 15.4 Extending 16-bit unsigned data to 32 bits.

As the figure shows, the additional bits are added to the left of the original number and filled with zeros. This is the equivalent of adding leading zeros to the number, which has no effect on the number's value.

When extending signed numbers, the original leftmost bit is reproduced in the additional bits that are added to the number. As illustrated in Figure 15.5, if the original leftmost bit is 0, corresponding to a positive number, 0 is placed in each of the additional bit positions. If the leftmost bit is 1, which corresponds to a negative number, 1 is placed in the additional bit positions. In either case, the resulting binary number has the same sign and magnitude of the original number.

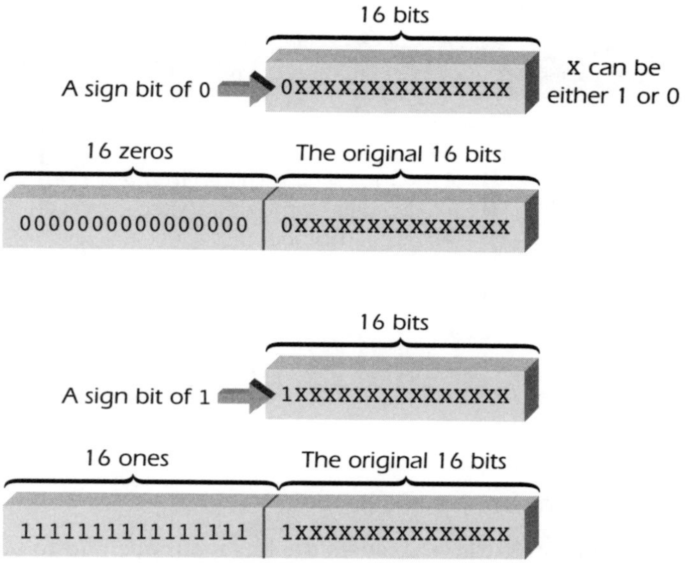

Figure 15.5 Extending 16-bit signed data to 32 bits.

15.6 THE SHIFT OPERATORS

The left shift operator, <<, causes the bits in an operand to be shifted to the left by a given amount. For example, the statement

```
op1 = op1 << 4;
```

causes the bits in `op1` to be shifted four bits to the left, filling any vacated bits with a zero. Figure 15.6 illustrates the effect of shifting the binary number 1111100010101011 to the left by four bit positions.

For unsigned integers, each left shift corresponds to multiplication by two. This is also true for signed numbers using two's complement representation, as long as the leftmost bit does not switch values. Since a change in the leftmost bit of a two's complement number represents a change in both the sign and magnitude represented by the bit, such a shift does not represent a simple multiplication by two.

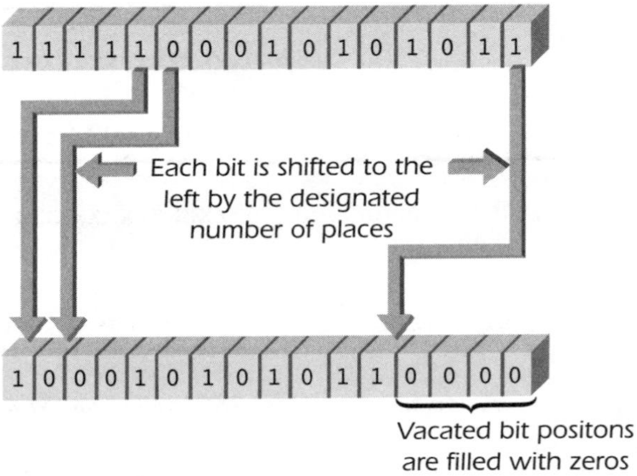
1 1 1 1 1 0 0 0 1 0 1 0 1 0 1 1
Each bit is shifted to the left by the designated number of places
1 0 0 0 1 0 1 0 1 0 1 1 0 0 0 0
Vacated bit positons are filled with zeros

Figure 15.6 *An example of a left shift.*

The right shift operator, >>, causes the bits in an operand to be shifted to the right by a given amount. For example, the statement

```
op2 = op1 >> 3;
```

causes the bits in `op1` to be shifted to the right by three bit positions. Figure 15.7a illustrates the right shift of the unsigned binary number 1111100010101011 by three bit positions. As illustrated, the three rightmost bits are shifted "off the end" and are lost.

For unsigned numbers, the leftmost bit is not used as a sign bit. For this type of number, the vacated leftmost bits are always filled with zeros. This is the case that is illustrated in Figure 15.7a.

For signed numbers, what is filled in the vacated bits depends on the computer. Most computers reproduce the original sign bit of the number. Figure 15.7b illustrates the right shift of a negative binary number by four bit positions, where the sign bit is reproduced in the vacated bits. Figure 15.7c illustrates the equivalent right shift of a positive signed binary number.

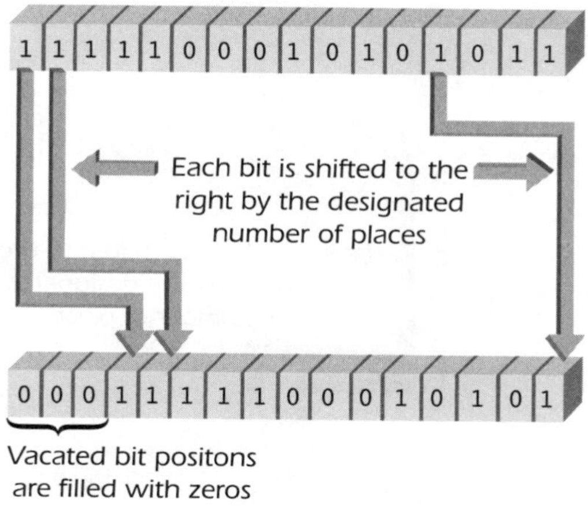
1 1 1 1 1 0 0 0 1 0 1 0 1 0 1 1
Each bit is shifted to the right by the designated number of places
0 0 0 1 1 1 1 1 0 0 0 1 0 1 0 1
Vacated bit positons are filled with zeros

Figure 15.7a An unsigned arithmetic right shift.

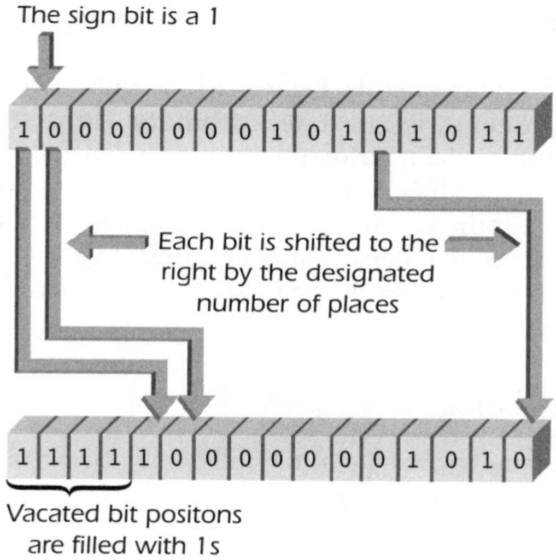
The sign bit is a 1
1 0 0 0 0 0 0 0 1 0 1 0 1 0 1 1
Each bit is shifted to the right by the designated number of places
1 1 1 1 1 0 0 0 0 0 0 0 1 0 1 0
Vacated bit positons are filled with 1s

Figure 15.7b The right shift of a negative binary number.

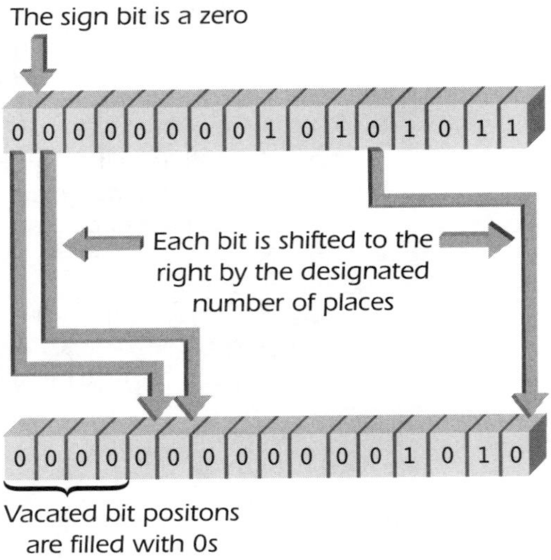
The sign bit is a zero
0 0 0 0 0 0 0 0 1 0 1 0 1 0 1 1
Each bit is shifted to the right by the designated number of places
0 0 0 0 0 0 0 0 0 0 0 1 0 1 0
Vacated bit positons are filled with 0s

Figure 15.7c *The right shift of a positive binary number.*

The type of fill illustrated in Figures 15.7b and c, where the sign bit is reproduced in vacated bit positions, is called an **arithmetic right shift**. In an arithmetic right shift, each single shift to the right corresponds to a division by two.

Instead of reproducing the sign bit in right-shifted signed numbers, some computers automatically fill the vacated bits with zeros. This type of shift is called a **logical shift**. For positive signed numbers, where the leftmost bit is 0, both arithmetic and logical right shifts produce the same result. The results of these two shifts are only different when negative numbers are involved.

Exercises for Chapter 15

1. Determine the results of the following operations:

```
a.   11001010    b.   11001010    c.   11001010
   & 10100101       | 10100101       ^ 10100101
     --------         --------         --------
```

2. Write the octal representations of the binary numbers given in Exercise 1.

3. Determine the octal results of the following operations, assuming unsigned numbers:

a. the octal number 0157 shifted left by one bit position
b. the octal number 0701 shifted left by two bit positions
c. the octal number 0673 shifted right by two bit positions
d. the octal number 067 shifted right by three bit positions

4. Repeat Exercise 3 assuming that the numbers are treated as signed values.

5. **a.** Assume that the arbitrary bit pattern xxxxxxxx, where each x can represent either 1 or 0, is stored in the integer variable named `flag`. Determine the octal value of a mask that can be ANDed with the bit pattern to reproduce the third and fourth bits of `flag` and set all other bits to zero. The rightmost bit in `flag` is considered bit 0.

b. Determine the octal value of a mask that can be inclusively ORed with the bit pattern in `flag` to reproduce the third and fourth bits of `flag` and set all other bits to 1. Again, consider the rightmost bit in `flag` to be bit 0.

c. Determine the octal value of a mask that can be used to complement the values of the third and fourth bits of `flag` and leave all other bits unchanged. Determine the bit operation that should be used with the mask value to produce the desired result.

6. a. Write the two's complement form of the decimal number –1, using eight bits. (*Hint:* Refer to Section 1.6 for a review of two's complement numbers.)

b. Repeat Exercise 6a using 16 bits to represent the decimal number –1 and compare your answer to your previous answer. Could the 16-bit version have been obtained by sign-extending the 8-bit version?

7. As was noted in the text, Program 15.2 has no effect on uppercase letters. Using the ASCII codes listed in Appendix B, determine what other characters would be unaffected by Program 15.2.

8. Modify Program 15.2 so that a complete sentence can be read in and converted to lowercase values. (*Hint:* When a space is masked by Program 15.2, the resulting character is `\0`, which terminates the output.)

9. Modify Program 15.4 to allow a complete sentence to be input and converted to uppercase letters. Make sure that your program does not alter any other characters or symbols entered.

10. Modify Program 15.5 to permit the encryption key to be a user-entered input value.

11. Modify Program 15.5 to have its output written to a file named `coded.dat`.

12. Write a C++ program that reads the encrypted sentence produced by the program written for Exercise 10, decodes the sentence, and prints the decoded values on your system's standard output device.

13. Write a C++ program that displays the first eight bits of each character value input into a variable named `ch`. (*Hint:* Assuming each character is stored using eight bits, start by using the hexadecimal mask 80, which corresponds to the binary number 10000000. If the result of the masking operation is a 0, display a 0; else display a 1. Then shift the mask one place to the right to examine the next bit, and so on until all bits in the variable `ch` have been processed.)

14. Write a C++ program that reverses the bits in an integer variable named `okay` and stores the reversed bits in the variable named `revokay`. For example, if the bit pattern 11100101, corresponding to the octal number 0345, is assigned to `okay`, the bit pattern 10100111, corresponding to the octal number 0247, should be produced and stored in `revokay`.

15.7 CHAPTER SUMMARY

1. Individual bits of character and integer variables and constants can be manipulated using C++'s bit operators. These are the AND, inclusive OR, exclusive OR, one's complement, left shift, and right shift operators.
2. The AND and inclusive OR operators are useful in creating masks. These masks can be used to pass or eliminate individual bits from the selected operand. The exclusive OR operator is useful in complementing an operand's bits.
3. When the AND and OR operators are used with operands of different sizes, the shorter operand is always increased in bit size to match the size of the larger operand.
4. The shift operators produce different results depending on whether the operand is a signed or an unsigned value.

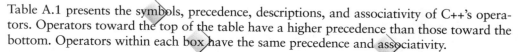

Appendix A
Operator Precedence Table

Table A.1 presents the symbols, precedence, descriptions, and associativity of C++'s operators. Operators toward the top of the table have a higher precedence than those toward the bottom. Operators within each box have the same precedence and associativity.

Table A.1 Summary of C++ Operators

Operator	Description	Associativity

`()`
`[]`
`->`
`.`
	Function call
	Array element
	Structure member pointer reference
	Structure member reference
		Left to right

`++`
`--`
`-`
`!`
`~`
`(type)`
`sizeof`
`&`
`*`
	Increment
	Decrement
	Unary minus
	Logical negation
	One's complement
	Type conversion (cast)
	Storage size
	Address of
	Indirection
		Right to left

`*`
`/`
`%`
	Multiplication
	Division
	Modulus (remainder)
		Left to right

`+` `-`	Addition Subtraction	Left to right
`<<` `>>`	Left shift Right shift	Left to right

`<`
`<=`
`>`
`>=`
	Less than
	Less than or equal to
	Greater than
	Greater than or equal to
		Left to right

Table A.1 Summary of C++ Operators (continued)

<table>
<tr><th>Operator</th><th>Description</th><th>Associativity</th></tr>
<tr><td>==
!=</td><td>Equal to
Not equal to</td><td>Left to right</td></tr>
<tr><td>&</td><td>Bitwise AND</td><td>Left to right</td></tr>
<tr><td>^</td><td>Bitwise exclusive OR</td><td>Left to right</td></tr>
<tr><td>|</td><td>Bitwise inclusive OR</td><td>Left to right</td></tr>
<tr><td>&&</td><td>Logical AND</td><td>Left to right</td></tr>
<tr><td>||</td><td>Logical OR</td><td>Left to right</td></tr>
<tr><td>?:</td><td>Conditional expression</td><td>Right to left</td></tr>
<tr><td>=
+= -= *=
/= %= &=
^= |=
<<= >>=</td><td>Assignment
Assignment
Assignment
Assignment
Assignment</td><td>Right to left</td></tr>
<tr><td>,</td><td>Comma</td><td>Left to right</td></tr>
</table>

Appendix B

ASCII Character Codes

Key(s)	Dec	Oct	Hex	Key(s)	Dec	Oct	Hex	Key(s)	Dec	Oct	Hex
Ctrl 1	0	0	0	Esc	27	33	1B	6	54	66	36
Ctrl A	1	1	1	Ctrl <	28	34	1C	7	55	67	37
Ctrl B	2	2	2	Ctrl /	29	35	1D	8	56	70	38
Ctrl C	3	3	3	Ctrl =	30	36	1E	9	57	71	39
Ctrl D	4	4	4	Ctrl –	31	37	1F	:	58	72	3A
Ctrl E	5	5	5	Space	32	40	20	;	59	73	3B
Ctrl F	6	6	6	!	33	41	21	<	60	74	3C
Ctrl G	7	7	7	"	34	42	22	=	61	75	3D
Ctrl H	8	10	8	#	35	43	23	>	62	76	3E
Ctrl I	9	11	9	$	36	44	24	?	63	77	3F
Ctrl J (lf)	10	12	A	%	37	45	25	@	64	100	40
Ctrl K	11	13	B	&	38	46	26	A	65	101	41
Ctrl L	12	14	C	'	39	47	27	B	66	102	42
Ctrl M (Ret)	13	15	D	(	40	50	28	C	67	103	43
Ctrl N	14	16	E	)	41	51	29	D	68	104	44
Ctrl O	15	17	F	*	42	52	2A	E	69	105	45
Ctrl P	16	20	10	+	43	53	2B	F	70	106	46
Ctrl Q	17	21	11	,	44	54	2C	G	71	107	47
Ctrl R	18	22	12	–	45	55	2D	H	72	110	48
Ctrl S	19	23	13	.	46	56	2E	I	73	111	49
Ctrl T	20	24	14	/	47	57	2F	J	74	112	4A
Ctrl U	21	25	15	0	48	60	30	K	75	113	4B
Ctrl V	22	26	16	1	49	61	31	L	76	114	4C
Ctrl W	23	27	17	2	50	62	32	M	77	115	4D
Ctrl X	24	30	18	3	51	63	33	N	78	116	4E
Ctrl Y	25	31	19	4	52	64	34	O	79	117	4F
Ctrl Z	26	32	1A	5	53	65	35	P	80	120	50

(continued)

Key(s)	Dec	Oct	Hex	Key(s)	Dec	Oct	Hex	Key(s)	Dec	Oct	Hex
Q	81	121	51	a	97	141	61	q	113	161	71
R	82	122	52	b	98	142	62	r	114	162	72
S	83	123	53	c	99	143	63	s	115	163	73
T	84	124	54	d	100	144	64	t	116	164	74
U	85	125	55	e	101	145	65	u	117	165	75
V	86	126	56	f	102	146	66	v	118	166	76
W	87	127	57	g	103	147	67	w	119	167	77
X	88	130	58	h	104	150	68	x	120	170	78
Y	89	131	59	i	105	151	69	y	121	171	79
Z	90	132	5A	j	106	152	6A	z	122	172	7A
[	91	133	5B	k	107	153	6B	{	123	173	7B
\	92	134	5C	l	108	154	6C	|	124	174	7C
]	93	135	5D	m	109	155	6D	}	125	175	7D
^	94	136	5E	n	110	156	6E	~	126	176	7E
_	95	137	5F	o	111	157	6F	del	127	177	7F
'	96	140	60	p	112	160	70				

APPENDIX C
Floating-Point Number Storage

The two's complement binary code used to store integer values was presented in Section 1.6. In this appendix we present the binary storage format typically used in C++ to store single-precision and double-precision numbers, which are stored as floats and doubles, respectively. Collectively, both single- and double-precision values are commonly referred to as floating-point values.

Like their decimal number counterparts that use a decimal point to separate the integer and fractional parts of a number, floating-point numbers are represented in a conventional binary format with a binary point. For example, consider the binary number 1011.11. The digits to the left of the binary point (1011) represent the integer part of the number and the digits to the right of the binary point (11) represent the fractional part.

To store a floating-point binary number a code similar to decimal scientific notation is used. To obtain this code the conventional binary number format is separated into a mantissa and an exponent. The following examples illustrate floating-point numbers expressed in this scientific notation.

Conventional Binary Notation	Binary Scientific Notation
1010.0	1.01 exp 011
-10001.0	-1.0001 exp 100
0.001101	1.101 exp -011
-0.000101	-1.01 exp -100

In binary scientific notation, the term exp stands for exponent. The binary number in front of the exp term is the mantissa and the binary number following the exp term is the exponent value. Except for the number zero, the mantissa always has a single leading 1 followed immediately by a binary point. The exponent represents a power of 2 and indicates the number of places the binary point should be moved in the mantissa to obtain the conventional binary notation. If the exponent is positive, the binary point is moved to the right. If the exponent is negative, the binary point is moved to the left. For example, the exponent 011 in the number

```
1.01 exp 011
```

means move the binary point three places to the right, so that the number becomes 1010. The –011 exponent in the number

```
1.101 exp -011
```

means move the binary point three places to the left, so that the number becomes

```
.001101
```

In storing floating-point numbers, the sign, mantissa, and exponent are stored individually within separate fields. The number of bits used for each field determines the precision of the number. Single-precision (32-bit), double-precision (64-bit), and extended-precision (80-bit) floating-point data formats are defined by the Institute of Electrical and Electronics Engineers (IEEE) Standard 754-1985 to have the characteristics given in Table C.1. The format for a single-precision floating-point number is illustrated in Figure C.1.

Table C.1 IEEE Standard 754-1985 Floating-Point Specification

Data Format	Sign Bits	Mantissa Bits	Exponent Bits
Single-precision	1	23	8
Double-precision	1	52	11
Extended-precision	1	64	15

The sign bit shown in Figure C.1 refers to the sign of the mantissa. A sign bit of 1 represents a negative number and a 0 sign bit represents a positive value. Since all mantissas, except for the number 0, have a leading 1 followed by their binary points, these two items are never stored explicitly. The binary point implicitly resides immediately to the left of mantissa bit 22, and a leading 1 is always assumed. The binary number 0 is specified by setting all mantissa and exponent bits to 0. For this case only, the implied leading mantissa bit is also 0.

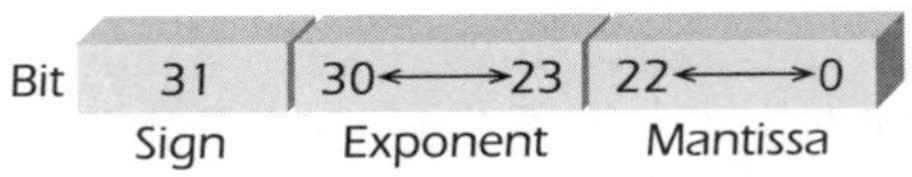

Figure C.1 Single-precision floating-point number storage format.

The exponent field contains an exponent that is biased by 127. For example, an exponent of 5 would be stored using the binary equivalent of the number 132 (127 + 5). Using eight exponent bits, this is coded as 100000100. The addition of 127 to each exponent allows negative exponents to be coded within the exponent field without the need for an explicit sign bit. For example, the exponent –011, which corresponds to –3, would be stored using the binary equivalent of +124 (127 – 3).

Figure C.2 The encoding and storage of the decimal number 59.75.

Figure C.2 illustrates the encoding and storage of the decimal number 59.75 as a 64-bit single-precision binary number. The sign, exponent, and mantissa are determined as follows. The conventional binary equivalent of

```
-59.75
```

is

```
-111011.11
```

Expressed in binary scientific notation this becomes

```
-1.1101111 exp 101
```

The minus sign is signified by setting the sign bit to 1. The mantissa's leading 1 and binary point are omitted and the 23-bit mantissa field is encoded as

```
11011110000000000000000
```

The exponent field encoding is obtained by adding the exponent value of 101 to 1111111, which is the binary equivalent of the 127_{10} bias value:

$$\begin{array}{r l}
1\ 1\ 1\ 1\ 1\ 1\ 1 & = 127_{10} \\
+\ 1\ 0\ 1 & = 5_{10} \\
\hline
1\ 0\ 0\ 0\ 0\ 1\ 0\ 0 & = 132_{10}
\end{array}$$

APPENDIX D

Command Line Arguments

Arguments can be passed to any function in a program, including the `main()` function. In this section we describe the procedures for passing arguments to `main()` when a program is initially invoked and having `main()` correctly receive and store the arguments passed to it. Both the sending and receiving sides of the transaction must be considered. Fortunately, the interface for transmitting arguments to a `main()` function has been standardized in C++, so both sending and receiving arguments can be done almost mechanically.

All the programs that have been run so far have been invoked by typing the name of the executable version of the program after the operating system prompt is displayed. The command line for these programs consists of a single word, which is the name of the program. For computers that use the UNIX operating system, the prompt is usually the `$` symbol and the executable name of the program is `a.out`. For these systems, the simple command line

```
$a.out
```

begins program execution of the last compiled source program currently residing in `a.out`.

If you are using a C++ compiler on an IBM PC, the equivalent operating system prompt is typically `C:\>`, and the name of the executable program is typically the same name as the source program with an `.exe` extension rather than a `.cpp` extension. Assuming that you are using an IBM PC with the `C:\>` operating system prompt, the complete command line for running an executable program named `pgmD-1.exe` is `C:\> pgmD-1`. As illustrated in Figure D.1, this command line causes the `pgmD-1` program to begin execution with its `main()` function, but no additional arguments are passed to `main()`.

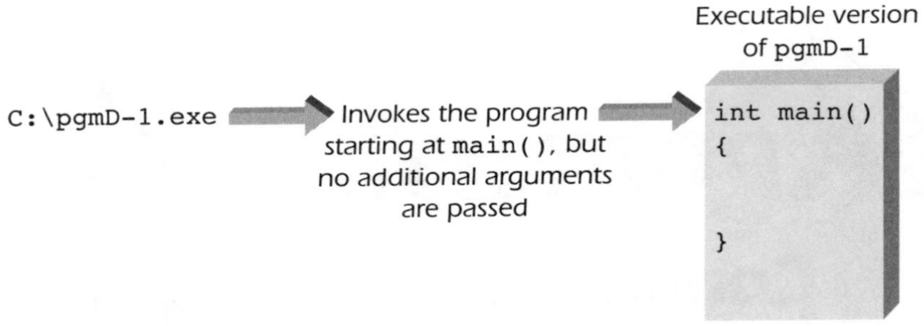

Figure D.1 Invoking program `pgmD-1.exe`.

Now assume that we want to pass the three separate string arguments `three blind mice` directly into `pgmD-1`'s main function. Sending arguments into a `main()` function is extremely easy. It is accomplished by including the arguments on the command line used to begin program execution. Because the arguments are typed on the command line, they are, naturally, called command line arguments. To pass the arguments `three blind mice` directly into the `main()` function of the `pgmD-1` program, we only need to add the desired words after the program name on the command line:

```
C:\>pgmD-1 three blind mice
```

Upon encountering this command line, the operating system stores the strings after the prompt (some systems also store the prompt as part of the first string) as a sequence of four strings. Figure D.2 illustrates the storage of these, assuming that each character uses one byte of storage. As shown in the figure, each string terminates with the standard C++ `null` character `\0`.

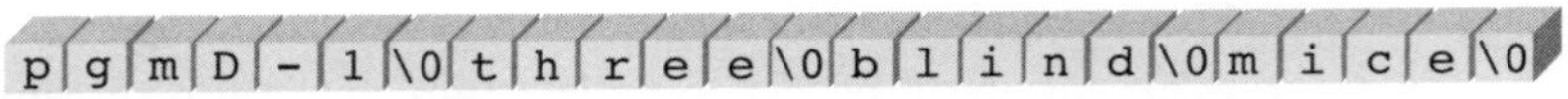

Figure D.2 The command line arguments stored in memory.

Sending command-line arguments to `main()` is always this simple. The arguments are typed on the command line and the operating system nicely stores them as a sequence of separate strings. We must now handle the receiving side of the transaction and let `main()` know that arguments are being passed to it.

Arguments passed to `main()`, like all function arguments, must be declared as part of the function's definition. To standardize argument-passing to a `main()` function, only two items are allowed: a number and an array. The number is an integer variable, which conventionally is named `argc` (short for argument counter), and the array is a one-dimensional list, which is conventionally named `argv` (short for argument values). Figure D.3 illustrates these two arguments. The integer passed to `main()` is the total number of items on the command line. In our example, the value of `argc` passed to `main()` is 4, which includes the name of the program plus the three command line arguments. The one-dimensional list passed to `main()` is a list of pointers containing the starting storage address of each string typed on the command line, as illustrated in Figure D.4.

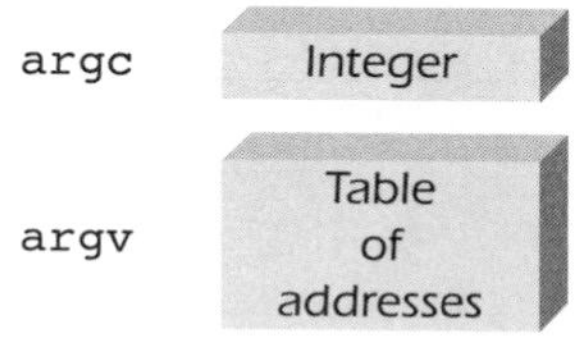

Figure D.3 *An integer and an array are passed to* `main()`.

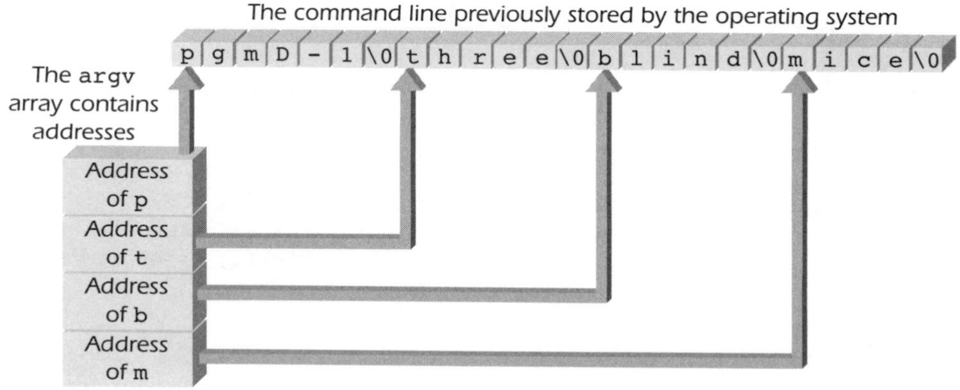

Figure D.4 *Addresses are stored in the* `argv` *array.*

We can now write the complete function definition for `main()` to receive arguments by declaring their names and data types. For `main`'s two arguments the names conventionally used are `argv` and `argc`, respectively.[1] Because `argc` will store an integer value, its declaration will be `int argc`. Because `argv` is the name of an array whose elements are addresses that point to where the actual command-line arguments are stored, its proper declaration is `char *argv[]`. This is nothing more than the declaration of an array of pointers. It is read "`argv` is an array whose elements are pointers to characters." Putting all this together, the full function header for a `main()` function that will receive command-line arguments is:

```
int main(int argc, char *argv[])
```

No matter how many arguments are typed on the command line, `main()` only needs the two standard pieces of information provided by `argc` and `argv`: the number of items on the command line and the list of starting addresses indicating where each argument is actually stored.

Program D.1 verifies our description by printing the data actually passed to `main()`. The variable `argv[i]` used in Program D.1 contains an address. It is this address that is displayed by the first `cout` statement within the `for` loop. For ease of reading the output, this address is cast into an integer value. The string notation `*argv[i]` in the second `cout` stream refers to "the character pointed to" by the address in `argv[i]`.

---

[1]These names are not required, and any valid C++ identifier can be used in their place.

Program D.1

```
#include <iostream>
using namespace std;

int main(int argc, char *argv[])
{
  int i;

  cout << "\nThe number of items on the command line is "
       << argc << endl << endl;
  for(i = 0; i < argc; i++)
  {
    cout << "The address stored in argv[" << i <<"] is "
         << int(argv[i]) << endl;   // display the address as an integer number
    cout << "The character pointed to is " << *argv[i] << endl;
  }

  return 0;
}
```

Assuming that the executable version of Program D.1 is named `pgmD-1.exe`, a sample output for the command line `C:\>pgmD-1` is:

```
The number of items on the command line is 4

The address stored in argv[0] is 3280388
The character pointed to is p
The address stored in argv[1] is 3280395
The character pointed to is t
The address stored in argv[2] is 3280401
The character pointed to is b
The address stored in argv[3] is 3280407
The character pointed to is m
```

The addresses displayed by Program D.1 clearly depends on the machine used to run the program. Figure D.5 illustrates the storage of the command line as displayed by the sample output. As anticipated, the addresses in the `argv` array "point" to the starting characters of each string typed on the command line.

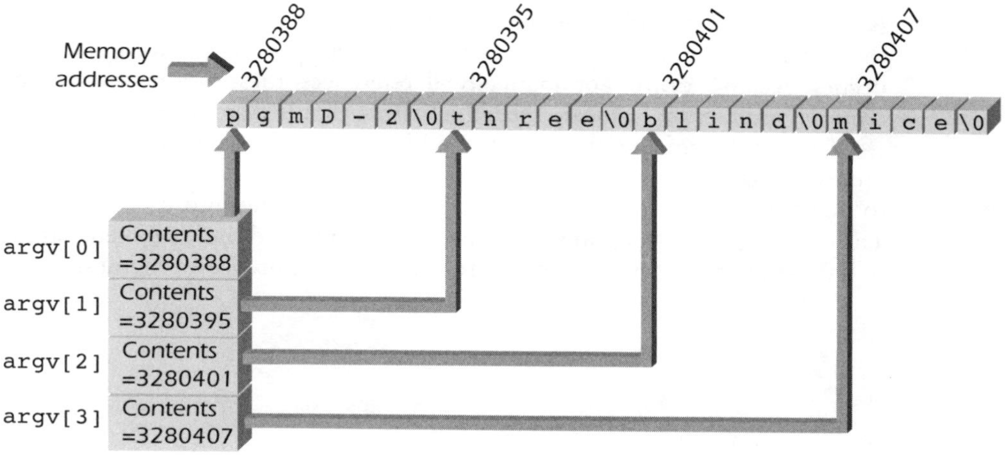

Figure D.5 The command line stored in memory.

Once command-line arguments are passed to a C++ program, they can be used like any other C-strings. Program D.2 causes its command-line arguments to be displayed from within `main()`.

Program D.2

```
// A program that displays its command line arguments
#include <iostream>
using namespace std;

int main(int argc, char *argv[])
{
  int i;

  cout << "\nThe following arguments were passed to main(): ";
  for (i = 0; i < argc; i++)
    cout << argv[i] << " ";
  cout << endl;

  return 0;
}
```

Assuming that the name of the executable version of Program D.2 is `pgmD-2.exe`, the output of this program for the command line `C:\>pgmD-2 three blind mice` is:

```
The following arguments were passed to main(): pgmD-2 three blind mice.
```

Notice that when the addresses in `argv[ ]` are inserted into the `cout` stream in Program D.2, the C-strings pointed to by these addresses are displayed. As was mentioned previously, this occurs because `cout` automatically dereferences these addresses and performs the required indirection to locate the actual string that is displayed.

One final comment about command-line arguments is in order. Any argument typed on a command line is considered to be a C-string. If you want numerical data passed to `main()`, it is up to you to convert the passed string into its numerical counterpart. This is seldom an issue, however, since most command-line arguments are used as flags to pass appropriate processing control signals to an invoked program.

INDEX